THIRD EDITION

LITERACY assessment & intervention for classroom teachers

Beverly A. DeVries
SOUTHERN NAZARENE UNIVERSITY

Holcomb Hathaway, Publishers
Scottsdale, Arizona

Library of Congress Cataloging-in-Publication Data

DeVries, Beverly A.
Literacy assessment & intervention for classroom teachers / Beverly A. DeVries. — 3rd ed.
p. cm.
Rev. ed. of: Literacy assessment and intervention for K-6 classrooms, 2008.
Includes bibliographical references and index.
ISBN 978-1-934432-15-0
1. Reading (Elementary) 2. Reading (Elementary)—Ability testing. 3. Literacy. I. DeVries, Beverly A.- Literacy assessment and intervention for K-6 classrooms. II. Title. III. Title: Literacy assessment and intervention for classroom teachers.

LB1573.D445 2011
372.4'8—dc22

2011014042

I dedicate this book to my husband, Merlyn, who is my cheerleader when the going gets tough.

Poetry Credits/Acknowledgments. The following materials may not be reproduced in any form or by any means without the prior written permission of the cited publisher: **Pg. 85:** Excerpt from "My Tooth Ith Loothe," copyright © 1995 by George Ulrich. Reprinted with permission. **Pg. 86:** Excerpt from "My Family of Dinosaurs," copyright © 1998 by Helen Ksypka. Reprinted from *Miles of Smiles* with permission from Meadowbrook Press. • Excerpt from "Kangaroos," copyright © 1998 by Kenn Nesbitt. Reprinted from *Miles of Smiles* with permission of Meadowbrook Press. • Excerpt from "Mr. Backward" in *BING BANG BOING,* copyright © 1994 by Douglas Florian, reprinted by permission of Houghton Mifflin Harcourt Publishing Company. • Excerpt from "Dainty Dottie Dee," text copyright © 1984 by Jack Prelutsky. Used by permission of HarperCollins Publishers. **Pg. 87:** Text copyright © 1989 by Joanna Cole. Used by permission of HarperCollins Publishers. • Excerpt from *Green Eggs and Ham* by Dr. Seuss, TM and copyright © by Dr. Seuss Enterprises, L.P., 1960, copyright renewed 1980. Used by permission of Random House Children's Books, a division of Random House, Inc. **Pg. 88:** From *The Roly-Poly Spider* by Jill Sardegna. Copyright © 1994 by Jill Sardegna. Reprinted by permission of Scholastic, Inc. • From *Miss Spider's New Car* © David Kirk and Calloway Arts and Entertainment. All rights reserved. • Excerpt from *In the Haunted House* by Eve Bunting, illustrated by Susan Meddaugh. Text copyright © 1990 by Eve Bunting. Reprinted by permission of Clarion Books, an imprint of Houghton Mifflin Company. All rights reserved. **Pg. 228:** Excerpt from Jacobs, F. (1979). *Sam the Sea Cow*. New York: Walker & Co. Printed by arrangement with Walker & Co. **Pg. 263:** Excerpt from *I Can Read With My Eyes Shut* by Dr. Seuss, TM and copyright © 1978 by Dr. Seuss Enterprises, L.P. and excerpt from *Oh, the Thinks You Can Think!* by Dr. Seuss, TM and © by Dr. Seuss Enterprises, L.P., 1975, copyright renewed 2003. Both excerpts used by permission of Random House Children's Books, a division of Random House, Inc. **Pg. 270:** From *Come On, Rain* by Karen Hesse. Scholastic Inc./Scholastic Press. Copyright ©1999 by Karen Hesse. Reprinted by permission.

Please note: The author and publisher have made every effort to provide current website addresses in this book. However, it is inevitable that some of the URLs listed here will change following publication of this book.

Holcomb Hathaway, Publishers, Inc.
8700 E. Via de Ventura Blvd., Suite 265
Scottsdale, Arizona 85258
480-991-7881
www.hh-pub.com

10 9 8 7 6 5 4 3

Print ISBN 978-1-934432-15-0
Ebook ISBN 978-1-934432-25-9

Printed in the United States of America.

Photo credits: *front cover,* mch67/123 RF *(top)*, Cathy Yeulet/123 RF *(bottom)*; *back cover,* Cathy Yeulet/123 RF *(top)*, Morozova Tatiana/123 RF *(bottom)*; *page iii,* Dmitriy Shironosov/123 RF; *page xiii,* iofoto/123 RF; *page xvi,* Petro Feketa/123 RF; *page xvii,* Benis Arapovic/123 RF; *page 1,* Cathy Yeulet/123 RF; *page 21,* Dmitriy Shironosov/123 RF; *page 41,* iofoto/123 RF; *page 75,* Cathy Yeulet/123 RF; *page 101,* JY Lee/123 RF; *page 125,* BananaStock Ltd; *page 151,* Flashon Studio/123 RF; *page 177,* forster forest/123 RF; *page 215,* Michal Bednarek/123 RF; *page 257,* forsterforest/123 RF; *page 281,* Cathy Yeulet/123 RF; *page 321,* nyul/123 RF; *page 341,* Graham Oliver/123 RF; *page 357,* Pavel Losevsky/123 RF; *page 358,* Sandra Van Der Steen/Dreamstime.com; *page 373,* Dmitriy Shironosov/123 RF; *page 387,* BananaStock Ltd; *page 411,* nyul/123 RF; *page 489,* Cathy Yeulet/123RF; *page 587,* Yuri Arcurs/123 RF; *page 611,* Ariadna De Raadt/123 RF; *page 615,* Wanda Anthony/123 RF

CONTENTS

Intervention Strategies & Activities *x*
Preface *xiii*
Acknowledgments *xvi*
About the Author *xvii*

1 FORMING A PERSONAL PHILOSOPHY ABOUT LITERACY ASSESSMENT AND INTERVENTION 1

INTRODUCTION 2
The Importance of Literacy 2
Theories Related to Literacy 3
Constructivist Theory 3
Zone of Proximal Development 3
Hierarchy of Human Needs 4
Critical Literacy Theory 4
Reading Models 5
Part-to-Whole Model 6
Whole-Part-Whole Model 7
Comprehensive Approach 7
Which Method Is the Most Effective? 8
English Learners 10
English Language Development 10
Effective Practices for English Learners 10
Forming Your Teaching Philosophy 13
Reflection on Assessing Reading Problems 13
Personal Philosophy of Intervention and Instruction for Struggling Readers 13
Historical Overview of Reading Reforms 13
Elementary and Secondary Education Act of 1966 15
The America Reads Challenge Act 15
The National Reading Panel Report 15
No Child Left Behind Act 15
Continuing Emphasis on Scientifically Based Research 15
Response to Intervention 16
Multimodal Literacy 19
CONCLUDING THOUGHTS 20
Reflective Learning: DIVERSE LEARNERS 20

2 THE LITERACY EVENT 21

INTRODUCTION 23
Teachers 23
Differentiating Instruction 24
Motivation 26
Students 28
Knowledge of General Information 29
Literacy Knowledge 29
Language Systems Readers Use 30
Learning Styles 31
Multiple Intelligences 31
Text 32
Levels of Readability 32
Selecting Appropriate Texts 33
Context 38
Task 38

CONCLUDING THOUGHTS 39
Reflective Learning: AT-RISK STUDENTS 39

3 ASSESSMENT 41

INTRODUCTION 43
Defining Assessment 43
Standards for Assessment 43
Formal/Standardized Assessment Instruments 44
Individual and Group Intelligence Tests 45
Achievement Tests 45
Diagnostic Tests 48
Informal Assessment Instruments 49
Emergent Reading and Writing Instruments 50
Informal Reading Inventories 51
Miscue Analysis 52
Retrospective Miscue Analysis 55
Running Records 55
Cloze Test 58
Anecdotal Records 60
Checklists 61
Rubrics 64
Portfolios 64
Informal Assessment for English Learners 66
Personal Interest Surveys 68
Attitude Surveys 69
Literacy Self-Perception Scales 69
Student Self-Assessment 69
Book Logs 69
Skill Logs 71
Reflection Logs 71
Accomplishment and Goal-Setting Logs 73
Technology and Assessment 73
CONCLUDING THOUGHTS 73
Reflective Learning: TESTING 73

4 PHONEMIC AWARENESS 75

INTRODUCTION 77
Definition 77
Dimensions of Phonemic Awareness 77
Phonemic Awareness and English Learners 79
What Teachers Should Know About Phonemic Awareness 81
Is Phonemic Awareness Necessary for Students to Become Proficient Readers? 81
Do Children Benefit From Intense, Explicit Phonemic Awareness Instruction? 82
If Not Through Intense, Explicit Instruction, How Do Children Become Aware of Phonemes Within Words? 82
Assessment 82
Assessing a Child's Level of Phonemic Awareness 82
Assessing a Child's Growth in Phonemic Awareness 84
Introducing Children to the Wonderful Sounds of Our Language 84
Songs 84
Nursery Rhymes and Poems 84
Jump Rope Jingles 86
Tongue Twisters 87
Children's Literature 87
INTERVENTION: *Strategies & Activities* 89
Activities Emphasizing Syllables 89
Activities Emphasizing Initial Sounds 90
Activities Emphasizing Rhymes 93
Activity Emphasizing Oddity 95
Activities Emphasizing Blending 95
Activity Emphasizing Segmenting 96
Activities Emphasizing Deleting 97
Activities Emphasizing Manipulating 98
Phonemic Awareness & Technology 99
CONCLUDING THOUGHTS 99
Reflective Learning: PHONEMIC AWARENESS 99

5 PHONICS 101

INTRODUCTION 102
Definitions 103
What Teachers Should Know 104
How Students Learn Phonics 105
English Spelling Patterns 105
English Learners and the Graphophonic System 108
Principles of Phonics Instruction 109

Principle One: Base Instruction on What Students Know 109
Principle Two: Provide Systematic Phonics Instruction 109
Principle Three: Use Appropriate Texts 109
Principle Four: Embed Instruction in Meaningful Contexts 111
Assessment 111
Informal Assessment 111
Formal Assessment 113
INTERVENTION: *Strategies & Activities* **113**
Activities Emphasizing Initial Consonant Sounds 114
Activities Emphasizing Onset and Rime 116
Activities Emphasizing Rhyme 117
Activities Emphasizing Word Patterns 118
Activities Emphasizing Sounds Within Words 120
Activity Emphasizing Words Within Words 122
Phonics and Technology 122
CONCLUDING THOUGHTS 122
Reflective Learning: ENGLISH LEARNERS 123

6 WORD IDENTIFICATION 125

INTRODUCTION 126
What Teachers Should Know 127
The Four Cueing Systems 127
Components of Word Identification 128
Sequence of Word Study for English Learners 132
Assessment 132
Informal Assessment 133
Formal Assessment 136
INTERVENTION: *Strategies & Activities* **137**
Small Group Activity for Teaching Word Identification Skills 137
Activities Emphasizing Receptive and Expressive Vocabularies 139
Activities Emphasizing Sight Words 140
Activities Emphasizing Sight Vocabulary 141
Activity Emphasizing Context Clues 144
Activities Emphasizing Visual Analysis of Monosyllabic Words 144
Activities Emphasizing Blending Polysyllabic Words and Structural Analysis 144
Word Identification and Technology 147
CONCLUDING THOUGHTS 149
Reflective Learning: ENGLISH LEARNERS 149

7 VOCABULARY BUILDING 151

INTRODUCTION 153
General Background 153
Increasing Students' Vocabulary 154
Ways of Increasing Vocabulary 154
Meeting the Vocabulary Needs of Struggling Readers 158
Meeting the Vocabulary Needs of English Learners 160
Accepting Students and Their Limited Vocabulary 161
Assessment 161
Informal Assessment 161
Formal Assessment 162
INTERVENTION: *Strategies & Activities* **163**
Vocabulary Building and Technology 174
CONCLUDING THOUGHTS 175
Reflective Learning: VOCABULARY BUILDING 175

8 COMPREHENSION OF NARRATIVE TEXT 177

INTRODUCTION 179
Reading Skills 180
Decoding 180
Fluency 180
Vocabulary 181
Reading Comprehension Strategies 181
Before Reading Strategies 181
During Reading Strategies 183
After Reading Strategies 187
Comprehension and Critical Literacy 188
Critical Literacy Themes and Topics 188
Questions to Encourage a Critical Stance 188
Skilled Versus Unskilled Comprehenders 188

Assessment **190**
Informal Assessment 190
Formal Assessment 193
English Learners and Narrative Texts **193**
Instructional Recommendations 193
Selecting Narrative Texts 193
Teaching Comprehension Strategies **194**
INTERVENTION: *Strategies & Activities* **195**
Strategies and Activities to Use Before, During, and After Reading **195**
Strategies and Activities to Use Before Reading **201**
Strategies and Activities to Use During Reading **202**
Strategies and Activities to Use After Reading **207**
Comprehension of Narrative Text and Technology **213**
CONCLUDING THOUGHTS **214**
Reflective Learning: **CRITICAL LITERACY** **214**

9 COMPREHENSION OF INFORMATIONAL TEXT 215

INTRODUCTION **216**
Factors Affecting the Comprehension Process **217**
Factors Within the Reader 217
Factors Within the Reader's Environment 218
Factors Within the Text 220
Organizational Structure of Expository Text **220**
Chronology or Sequence 221
Description or Enumeration 221
Listing 222
Classification or Hierarchy 222
Comparison/Contrast 222
Cause/Effect 223
Problem/Solution 223
Persuasion 223
Sequence for Teaching Expository Text Organizational Patterns 224
Analysis of Informational Texts **224**
Eye Appeal 224
Traditional Book Features 224
Electronic Text Features 226
Writing Style 227
Use of Technical Vocabulary 228
Author's Assumption of Readers' Background Knowledge 228
Readability 229
English Learners and Expository Text **230**
Instructional Recommendations 230
Selecting Informational Text 232
Developing Critical Literacy with Expository Texts **232**
Assessment **234**
Informal Assessment 234
Formal Assessment 236
Critical Literacy Assessment **237**
INTERVENTION: *Strategies & Activities* **237**
Strategies and Activities to Use Before, During, and After Reading **238**
Strategies and Activities to Use Before Reading **249**
Strategies and Activities to Use During Reading **250**
Strategies and Activities to Use After Reading **252**
Comprehension of Expository Text and Technology **255**
CONCLUDING THOUGHTS **256**
Reflective Learning: **ENGLISH LEARNERS** **256**

10 FLUENCY 257

INTRODUCTION **258**
What Is Fluency? **259**
Components of Fluency **259**
Rate 260
Automaticity/Accuracy 260
Phrasing or Prosody 262
Comprehension 265
Fluency Instruction **266**
Research-Based Guidelines for Fluency Instruction 266
Fluency Instruction for English Learners 268
Assessment **268**
Informal Assessment 268

Formal Assessment 269
INTERVENTION: *Strategies & Activities* 270
Strategies for Tutoring Settings 270
Strategies to Use with Small Groups 273
Fluency and Technology 279
CONCLUDING THOUGHTS 280
Reflective Learning: READING SPEED AND COMPREHENSION 280

11 WRITING 281
INTRODUCTION 283
The Reading–Writing Connection 283
Similarities in Reading and Writing Cognitive Processes 283
Similarities in the Goals of Reading and Writing 283
Differences Between Reading and Writing 284
Writing Instruction 284
Components of Writing 284
Stages of Emergent Writing 285
Writing Styles of Bilingual Spanish–English Writers 289
Skilled Versus Unskilled Writers 290
The Writing Process and Writing Workshop 290
Evaluating Writing Instruction 295
6 + 1 Trait Writing® Assessment and Instruction Model 297
The Traits 297
Teaching the 6 + 1 Traits 299
Assessing Writing with the 6 + 1 Traits 299
Assessment 299
Informal Assessment 299
Portfolios 299
Formal Assessment 302
INTERVENTION: *Strategies & Activities* 302
Writing and Technology 318
ReadWriteThink 319
Websites as Tools to Develop Writing Skills 319
CONCLUDING THOUGHTS 320
Reflective Learning: RELUCTANT WRITERS 320

12 SPELLING 321
INTRODUCTION 323
Spelling Instruction 323
Developmental Stages of Spelling 324
Instructional Practices for Each Spelling Stage 324
Instructional Practices for English Learners' Stages of Spelling Development 327
Patterns of English Spelling 329
Orthographic Patterns of Words 329
Complex Patterns of English Spelling 329
Comparisons Between English and Spanish Spelling Patterns 330
Good Versus Poor Spellers 330
Assessment 330
Informal Assessment 330
Formal Assessment 334
INTERVENTION: *Strategies & Activities* 334
Spelling and Technology 338
Spell Checking 338
The Internet 338
CONCLUDING THOUGHTS 339
Reflective Learning: IMPROVING SPELLING 339

13 TUTORING 341
INTRODUCTION 343
Benefits of Tutoring 343
Types of Tutors 343
Reading Specialists 343
Certified Teachers 344
Paraprofessionals 344
Computer-Assisted Tutoring 345
Web-Based Tutoring 347
Successful Tutoring Programs 347
Reading Recovery 347
Planning and Conducting the Tutoring Session 348
Lesson Plans for Tutoring Sessions 348
Getting Started 350
Tutoring Sessions for English Learners 351

Intervening with the Tutee During Reading 354
Tutoring and Technology 354
CONCLUDING THOUGHTS 356
Reflective Learning: **ENGLISH LEARNERS 356**

14 TEACHERS, CAREGIVERS, AND THE COMMUNITY WORKING IN COLLABORATION 357

INTRODUCTION 359
The Importance of Teachers Understanding Their Students' Home Lives 360
Benefits of Parental Involvement 361
Engaged Parents 361
Ways to Communicate with Parents 362
Introductory Letters 362
Introductory Parent–Teacher Conference 362
Newsletters 362
Bulletin Boards 363
Parents' Nook 364
Telephone Calls or E-mails 364
Happy Grams 364
Portfolios with Personal Notes 364
Daily Welcome 364
Family–Teacher Conference 365
Parental Involvement That Makes a Difference 366
General Suggestions to Share with Parents 366
Suggestions for Establishing a Home–School Literacy Connection 367
Working with Difficult Parents 369
Parents Who Do Not Seem to Value Education 369
Parents Who Seem Highly Critical 369
Parents Who Seem Not to Accept Their Child's Academic Difficulties 370
Community Volunteers 370
Caregiver Involvement and Technology 371
Technology Nights 371
Technology Classes for Parents 371
Technology in the Home 371
CONCLUDING THOUGHTS 372
Reflective Learning: **PARENT VOLUNTEERS 372**

Appendices

A RESOURCES 373

A.1 NCTE/IRA Standards for Assessment of Reading and Writing 374
A.2 Commercial Informal Reading Inventories 377
A.3 Alphabet Books 377
A.4 Poetry Collections and Mother Goose Books 378
A.5 Wordless Books 379
A.6 Wordless (or Almost Wordless) Picture Books for Content Area Learning 379
A.7 Books with Rhyme, Phonograms, Alliteration, and Other Language Play 380
A.8 Suggested Bilingual English–Spanish Concept Books 381
A.9 Suggested Bilingual English–Spanish Narrative Picture Books 382
A.10 Suggested Multicultural Picture Books 382
A.11 Computer Programs for Developing Various Skills 383
A.12 E-Storybooks 384
A.13 Audio Chapter Books 385
A.14 Computer Programs That Promote Comprehension and Problem Solving 385

B LISTS AND GUIDES 387

B.1 Most Common Word Families 388
B.2 Vowel Diphthongs, Digraphs, and Variants with Examples and Utility of Each 391
B.3 Consonant Pronunciation Guide 392

B.4 High-Frequency Word List 394
B.5 Dolch Word Lists 395
B.6 The Fry Phrase Lists 396
B.7 Frequently Used Suffixes and Prefixes 399
B.8 Greek and Latin Word Roots with Definitions and Examples 400
B.9 Generalizations About Word Spellings 409
B.10 Complex Patterns of English Spelling 410

C ASSESSMENT DEVICES 411

C.1 Checklist for Assessing Students' Multiple Intelligences 412
C.2 Concepts of Print Checklist 415
C.3 Concepts of Writing Checklist 416
C.4 Miscue Analysis Grid 417
C.5 Running Record Form 418
C.6 Sample Literacy Checklist 419
C.7 Checklist for Observations of Progress Toward Standards 420
C.8 Observational Checklist of Literacy Habits: Early Emergent Literacy Stage 422
C.9 Observational Checklist of Literacy Habits: Emergent Literacy Stage 423
C.10 Observational Checklist of Literacy Habits: Beginning Reading and Writing Stage 424
C.11 Observational Checklist of Literacy Habits: Nearly Fluent Stage 425
C.12 Observational Checklist of Literacy Habits: Fluent Reading and Writing Stage 426
C.13 Personal Interest Survey 427
C.14 Reading Attitude Survey for Primary Students 428
C.15 Writing Attitude Survey for Primary Students 430
C.16 Scoring Sheet for Attitude Surveys 432
C.17 Reading Attitude Survey for Older Students 433
C.18 Writing Attitude Survey for Older Students 434
C.19 Reader Self-Perception Scale 435
C.20 Writer Self-Perception Scale 437
C.21 Reading Log for Primary Students 440
C.22 Reading Log for Intermediate Students 441
C.23 Reading Reflection Log 442
C.24 Quick Phonemic Awareness Assessment Device 443
C.25 Pre-Assessment for Phonemic Awareness 444
C.26 Post-Assessment for Phonemic Awareness 448
C.27 Checklist for Phonemic Awareness for Primary Grades 452
C.28 Checklist of Known Letter Names and Sounds 453
C.29 Checklist for Letter–Sound Relationships, First Grade 455
C.30 Phonics Mastery Survey 456
C.31 Decoding and Word Recognition Checklist 459
C.32 Scoring Sheet for Word or Phrase List 460
C.33 Vocabulary Growth Checklist 461
C.34 Rubric for Narrative Reading Comprehension 462
C.35 Narrative Reading Rubric 463
C.36 General Reading Rubric 464
C.37 Interest Inventory for Informational Texts 465
C.38 Observation Checklist of Student's Expository Reading 466
C.39 Expository Reading Rubric 467
C.40 Checklist of Basic Internet Skills 468
C.41 Fluency Checklist 469
C.42 Fluency Checklist for Narrative Text 470
C.43 Oral Reading Fluency Rubric 471
C.44 Fluency Questions for Self-Evaluation 472
C.45 6 + 1 Traits® of Writing Assessment 473
C.46 Rubric for Assessing the Writing Process of Writers in Primary Grades 475
C.47 Rubric for Assessing the Writing Process of Third Graders 477
C.48 Rubric for Writing Stories 479
C.49 Rubric for Research Paper 480
C.50 Rubric for Story Writing 481
C.51 Research Report Rubric 482
C.52 Multimedia Group Project Rubric 483
C.53 Writing and Spelling Self-Assessment 484
C.54 Bear, Invernizzi, Templeton, & Johnston Qualitative Spelling Inventory 485
C.55 Recording and Analyzing Spelling 486
C.56 Checklist for Spelling, Fifth Grade 487

D INSTRUCTIONAL MATERIALS 489

D.1 Lesson Plan for English Learners 490
D.2 Directions for Creating Game Boards and Picture/Word Cards 491
D.3 How Many Syllables in the Zoo? Game Board and Picture Cards 492
D.4 Remember the Beginning Sound Picture Cards 495
D.5 Initial Sound Picture Bingo Cards 508
D.6 Toss the Cube Art 518
D.7 Go Fish Picture Cards 527
D.8 Humpty Dumpty Game Board and Picture Cards 534
D.9 Listen for the Initial Consonant Blend Sound Game Board and Picture Cards 539
D.10 Word Dominos 545
D.11 Concentration Word Cards 549
D.12 Listen to the Vowel Sound Game Board and Game Pieces 553
D.13 Dolch List Bingo Word Cards 559
D.14 Onset and Rime Cards 565
D.15 Templates for Morphology Rummy Cards 567
D.16 Vocabulary Bookmark Template 569
D.17 Cognate Sort 570
D.18 Multiple Meaning Racetrack Board 571
D.19 Text Mapping Form 572
D.20 Narrative E-Book Evaluation Form 573
D.21 Informational E-Text Evaluation Form 574
D.22 Textbook and Trade Book Evaluation Checklist 575
D.23 Informational DVD/CD Evaluation Form 577
D.24 Record, Check, Chart 578
D.25 Record, Time, Chart 579
D.26 Fluency Log 580
D.27 Template for a Story Board 581
D.28 Mt. Plot 582
D.29 Lesson Plan for Tutors 583
D.30 Log Sheet of Strategies 584
D.31 Log Sheet of Books Read 585
D.32 Postcard for Children Reading Books with Oral Reading and Comprehension Scaffolding 586

References 587
Author Index 611
Subject Index 615

Intervention Strategies & Activities BY CHAPTER

CHAPTER 4 PHONEMIC AWARENESS

Clapping Syllables to Familiar Songs and Rhymes 89
Clapping Syllables to Multisyllable Words 90
Let's Make Music 90
How Many Syllables in the Zoo? 90
Sound Boxes 90
Alphabet Booklets 91
Spanish/English Concept Books 92
Remember the Beginning Sound! 92
Initial Sound Bingo 92
Toss the Cube 92
Go Fish 93
Tongue Twisters 93
Identifying Rhyming Words in Poetry 93
Humpty Dumpty Board Game 94
Clowning Around with Rhyming Words 94
Odd-Card Out! 95
Children Are Sounds 95
Blending with Puppets 95
Onset and Rime Blending Card Game 96
Blending Individual Sounds Card Game 96
Segmenting Individual Sounds (Card Game) 97
Pop Off The Beads! 97
Children and Sounds 98
Moving the Tiles 98

CHAPTER 5 PHONICS

Word Sorting with Pictures 114
Word Sorting with Pictures for English Learners 114
Listen for the Initial Consonant Blends 114
Word Walls 115

Personalized Word Family Dictionary 115
Alphabiography 115
Alliteration 115
Dominoes 116
Word Family Word Walls 116
Find the Mystery Word 116
Flip Books 117
Word Family Concentration 117
Rhyming Word Concentration 118
Predictable Rhyming Texts 118
Yankee Doodle Poetry 118
Short Vowel Bingo 119
The Magical E! 119
Listen to the Vowel Sounds 120
Collecting Vowel Sounds Made with Different Spellings 120
Word Sorting with Words 121
Change Hen to Fox 121
Word Ladders 121
Secret Words 122

CHAPTER 6 WORD IDENTIFICATION

Guided Reading 138
Wordless Books 139
Picture Books 139
Using Pictures to Enhance the Expressive Vocabulary of Middle School Students 140
Match the Word 140
Dolch List Bingo 141
Unscramble the Sentence 141
Personalized Flash Cards 141
Personal Word Walls 142
Unscramble the Word 142
Technical Terms 142
Cloze Passages 144
Toss the Cube 144
Compound Words 144
Affixes Word Study 145
Personalized Word-Part Dictionaries: Affixes and Roots 146
Morphology Rummy 146

CHAPTER 7 VOCABULARY BUILDING

Vocabulary Bookmarks 163
Predict-O-Gram 163
Figurative Speech 163
Language Experience Approach (LEA) 164
Wordless Books 164
Science Experiment 164
Listening Walk 165
Schoolyard Safari 165
Total Physical Response 165
Categorizing 166
Possible Sentences 167
Analogies 167
Origin of Words 168
Crossword Puzzle 168
Synonym/Definition Concentration 169
Cognate Picture Cards 170
Multiple Meaning Racetrack 171
Hink Pinks 171
Lexical and Structure Riddles 172
Word Expert Cards 172
Collaborative Activities 173
Music Puzzlers 173
Matching Game 173
Two Cube Game 174
Pictionades 174
Action Jeopardy 174

CHAPTER 8 COMPREHENSION OF NARRATIVE TEXT

Pairing Nonfiction and Fiction Texts 195
The Memphis Comprehension Framework 196
Repeated Interactive Read-Aloud 199
Story Lines 200
Alternate Writing 201
Directed Listening–Thinking Activity (DL–TA) 201
Directed Reading–Thinking Activity (DR–TA) 202
Text Mapping 202
Reciprocal Questioning 203
Think-Aloud for Narrative Text 203
Think-Aloud Mystery 204
"And This Is the Rest of the Story" 205
Teacher-Made Audiobooks 205
Text-Talk 206
Wordless Books for Developing Inferential Reading 206
Repeated Readings 207
Different Perspectives: Diary Entries 207
Painting Mental Pictures 208
Spin the Discussion 209

Graphic Organizers for Narrative Text 209
Retelling with Puppets 210
Question Connect Transform (QCT) 211
Character Perspective Chart 211
Venn Diagrams for Narrative Text 212
Character Sketch 213

CHAPTER 9
COMPREHENSION OF INFORMATIONAL TEXT

Textmasters 238
Science Experiments, Crafts, and Math Games 239
Read-Alouds 240
Partner Reading and Content Too (PRC2) 241
Graphic Organizers for Expository Text 242
Lesson Cycle 246
K-W-L 246
Guided Reading Strategy 247
Inference Training 248
Question-Answer-Relationships (QARs) 249
Survey of Text Features 249
Pre-Reading Plan (PReP) 250
Think-Aloud for Expository Text 250
Checklist 251
Request 252
Scanning 252
Learning Logs 252
Collaborative Approach 254
Question Connect Transform (QCT) for Expository Text 254

CHAPTER 10 FLUENCY

Echo Reading 270
Preview-Pause-Prompt-Praise (PPPP) Strategy 271
Oral Recitation Lesson (ORL) 271
Carbo Recorded-Book Method 272
Record, Check, Chart 272
Flash Cards 273
Fluency Development Lesson (FDL) 273
Speech Reading 274
Telling Jokes 274
Supported-Reading Strategy 275
Dyad Reading 275
Repeated Readings 275
Poetry Party 276
Readers Theater 276
Choral Reading 277
Rhythm Walks 279

CHAPTER 11 WRITING

Interactive Writing ("Sharing the Pen") 302
Quick Writes (Writing on Demand) 303
POW 303
TREE 303
Activities for 6 + 1 Traits of Writing 303
Using Concrete Examples of Authors' Writing 306
Guided Writing 306
Mt. Plot 307
Expository Frames 308
Parodies 309
Sequels 310
Acrostic Poems 310
Cinquain Poems 311
Diamante 311
Biopoems 312
Fibbin Poems 312
Friendly Letters 313
Wordless Books 314
Noun Stories 314
Classroom Alphabet Books 314
Creating Brochures 314
Sentence Combining 315
Using Computers for Authentic Writing Tasks 315
Blog 315
Wikis 316
International Pen Pals 316
Connecting With Authors 316
Digital Storytelling 317
Publishing on the Web 318
Webquest 318

CHAPTER 12 SPELLING

Magnetic Letters 335
Foam Board Letters 335
Word Searches 336
Anagrams 337
Variation: Anagrams with Alphabet Cereal 337
Wheel-of-Fortune 337
Mnemonics, Memory Aids 337
Spelling In Parts (SIP) 338

PREFACE

The importance of literacy in today's world cannot be over emphasized. Students who struggle with reading and writing and other aspects of literacy require and deserve more instructional time than other students. This text will help future and in-service classroom teachers recognize and assess particular problems and provide effective interventions to help struggling students. It is intended for use by undergraduates majoring in elementary or middle school education, for graduate students as they tutor, and for classroom teachers as they work with struggling readers and writers; it may also be used by reading specialists who provide staff development for their districts and by coordinators of volunteer community tutoring programs.

The many aspects of literacy are interconnected—writing supports the growth of reading ability and reading supports writing ability, and both of these are intricately linked with success in the other language arts, that is, speaking, listening, viewing, and visually representing. Teachers encounter many types of literacy problems. Some students may struggle with word identification, comprehension, or fluency while others may need help understanding letter–sound relationships, writing or reading informational text, or spelling. This book focuses on the major areas of literacy, including phonemic awareness, phonics, word identification, comprehension (of both narrative and expository text), vocabulary, fluency, writing, and spelling.

The book is organized as follows. Chapters 1 and 2 help literacy educators understand the qualities of effective teachers, the traits of skilled and unskilled readers and writers, and the teacher's role in motivating students. These chapters also give readers (whether education majors or practicing educators) an opportunity to reflect on personal experiences and opinions that may affect their interaction with students and then use this reflection to formulate a teaching philosophy. I believe formulating such a philosophy helps each of us to become a more effective teacher.

Chapter 3 discusses formal and informal assessment, providing a variety of clear, concrete examples. It reviews the various types of standardized tests and explains how to administer informal literacy assessments such as informal reading inventories, miscue analyses, running records, cloze/maze tests, and checklists and rubrics that are based on state standards. Because the goal of this book is intervention based on informed assessment, Chapter 3 acts as an important foundation for the book.

The next nine chapters of this text (Chapters 4–12) are devoted to the major areas of literacy mentioned earlier. I believe that comprehension is the primary purpose of reading and that the other areas aid comprehension; therefore, two chapters of this book are devoted to comprehension—one focuses on comprehension of narrative texts and the other on comprehension of informational texts. These chapters are separate because readers must use different approaches to comprehend, analyze, and evaluate these distinct types of texts.

Chapter 13 provides evidence of the benefits of tutoring and describes a tutoring program that has proven to be successful. Many struggling readers and English learners benefit from the one-on-one instruction provided by tutoring; therefore, a sample tutoring session with adaptations for English learners, and based on the successful tutoring program described, is included.

Throughout the text, I emphasize the importance of teachers partnering with students' parents and caregivers. In Chapter 14, I discuss types and levels of parental involvement and how teachers can work effectively with all parents.

Chapters in this text offer a four-part approach to their topics:

- **Scenario:** Previewing the chapter topic, each chapter opens with a scenario in which an elementary or a middle school teacher encounters a real life literacy challenge in the classroom. The vignettes are followed by guiding questions to tie the scenarios to chapter content and provide a purpose for reading.
- **Research:** Each chapter discusses research studies and theories relevant to the particular topic highlighted in the chapter to help readers understand when and why particular assessments and interventions are effective.
- **Technology:** Each chapter includes a section on using technology to increase students' skills in the particular areas being discussed. Where relevant, technology is also incorporated in selected intervention strategies and activities, allowing readers to see its use in context.
- **Ending Scenario:** Finally, chapters close with another classroom scenario accompanied by questions for readers to answer and discuss with others as they review what they learned while reading.

In addition, the nine chapters covering the major areas of literacy include the following two sections:

- **Diagnosis and Assessment:** I discuss possible assessment instruments for diagnosing and assessing problems and growth in the literacy area being discussed.
- **Intervention:** I explore a wide variety of intervention strategies and activities in detail, recognizing that different students benefit from different strategies. In this edition I have added new interventions suitable for use with middle school students. The activities in these intervention sections call for students to read a great variety of materials, including fiction and nonfiction books and ebooks as well as online material that interests them.

Finally, teachers of every experience level will benefit from the multitude of resources, assessment devices, and instructional materials included in Appendices A through D of this book. The book's table of contents gives a complete list of these resources and tools.

NEW TO THIS EDITION

This edition has been substantively revised and updated. Here are some of the changes:

- This edition now offers assessment and intervention material suitable for use with older students because literacy problems do not stop when students finish elementary school. Many middle school students continue to struggle with literacy as they grapple with content area subjects dense with new vocabulary and concepts.

- The makeup of classrooms across the United States continues to change. Throughout this edition, I address the need for teachers to (1) understand the development stages of English learners and (2) learn how to scaffold these students as they become literate in English.
- This edition reflects the importance of using technology and online resources to aid students as they work with word identification, phonics, phonemic awareness, vocabulary, and all components of literacy. In each chapter I share student-friendly websites to help motivate students as they engage in the literacy activity being discussed.

ABOUT THE E-BOOK

This book is also available as an e-book. When adopting this book for use in your class, you may inform your students that the e-book version can be purchased on our website, www.hh-pub.com.

The electronic version of the book offers the same colorful layout and matches the print book page for page; this ensures ease of teaching if some of your students use the print book and some use the e-book. In addition, those reading the e-book will find the following interactive features:

- Active web links for all URLs cited in the text.
- Instant access to cross-reference links between chapters; for example, readers can link directly to (and from) tools and resources in the appendices as they are discussed.
- Active links to literature being discussed, allowing readers to learn more about the books and see what others have to say.
- Opportunity to respond to chapter opening and chapter closing questions using digital note-taking and unlimited bookmarking.
- When possible, video links that put the practices being discussed into action.

ACKNOWLEDGMENTS

As before, I wish to express special thanks to my friends and colleagues David Yellin, Jo Dorhout, and Betty Lou Thompson. Their help and encouragement allowed me to finish this text and make it far better than it would have been otherwise. I also want to thank my past and present students, who continue to find and share new websites with me.

It is my pleasure to thank the many individuals who have reviewed this book in manuscript stage, for this and previous editions. I appreciate their constructive comments, which have helped me to improve the text. For this edition, those individuals are: Julie Ankrum, University of Pittsburgh at Johnstown; Lijun Jin, Towson University; Michelle J. Kelley, University of Central Florida; Dixie Keyes, Arkansas State University; Rebecca A. Maloy, Towson University; Susan McGowan, Longwood University; Adriana Medina, University of North Carolina at Charlotte; Jerilou J. Moore, University of Mississippi; Jacqueline K. Peck, University of Akron; Jennifer Rasmussen, Mount Mercy College; Rebecca Short, Georgia Southwestern State University; Maureen V. Spelman, Saint Xavier University; Christina Walton, Ashland University; and Min Zou, Southeast Missouri State University. For earlier editions: Diane Allen, Suzanne Bell, Leonard Breen, Carol Bunch, William Edwards, Donna Harkins, Ginny Helwick-Jackson, Charlene Hildebrand, Peter B. Hilton, G. Peter Ienatsch, Jennifer Kagan, Michelle Kelley, Kouider Mokhtari, Kathleen A. J. Mohr, Jerilou Moore, Timothy Rasinski, Monica Riley, Elizabeth Rowell, Patsy Self, Martha Sheppard-Mahaffey, Janell Uffelman, Beth Walizer, and Vassiliki Zygouris-Coe.

My sincere thanks to my editor and the staff at Holcomb Hathaway, Publishers, who encourage me and design and enhance the text for users.

ABOUT THE AUTHOR

Beverly DeVries, Ed.D., has been teaching at Southern Nazarene University in Oklahoma since 1993. She teaches reading diagnosis and remediation and primary and elementary literature/language arts. In all of her courses, she demonstrates how teachers can use authentic assessment and instruction, using quality children's literature. When mentoring her students as they work with struggling readers, she finds that no two students approach reading in exactly the same manner, each reader responding uniquely to any specific strategy. This observation has helped DeVries formulate her teaching and intervention strategies and is a vital part of this book.

DeVries is presently on the Standards and Ethics Committee of the International Reading Association (IRA) and is the reading specialist on the Oklahoma Commission Program Advisory Board. She presents workshops on Writing Successful Reading Program Reports at the state and national levels. She also conducts workshops on various components of reading to classroom teachers.

DeVries received her doctorate in education from Oklahoma State University. Before beginning her college teaching career, she spent most of her years in the middle school, teaching composition and reading. It was during those years that she recognized the importance of early literacy intervention, and realized that struggling primary and middle school students benefit from one-on-one instruction.

CHAPTER ONE

FORMING A PERSONAL PHILOSOPHY ABOUT LITERACY ASSESSMENT AND INTERVENTION

Learning is not attained by chance,
it must be sought for with ardor and attended to with diligence.

ABIGAIL ADAMS

scenario

Ms. Gaytan and Ms. Greenberg are friends who are returning to teaching after staying home for ten years with their children. Ms. Gaytan has been appointed a first-grade position, and Ms. Greenberg will teach a seventh-grade language arts class. Both are thrilled with their positions because they are the same ones they had when they left teaching. They are quite confident in their abilities.

After the first in-service day, however, both are overwhelmed at the new jargon they have encountered. New terms include *tiers, RTI,* and *AYP.* Both left teaching just as the No Child Left Behind Act was being implemented, and they do not remember encountering any of these acronyms or terms. They also left teaching before an increasing number of students who are English learners moved to their rural community and before new literacies emerged from technology's impact on communication. As a result, they are also unfamiliar with jargon such as *TPR, SI,* and *critical* and *multimodal literacies.*

In a few days Ms. Gaytan and Ms. Greenberg will meet with their respective teams of teachers, and they want to understand these new terms ahead of time. At the meetings they will also be expected to share their personal philosophies of teaching, so each wants to prepare a summary.

guiding questions

As you read this chapter, consider the following questions:

1. How would you explain the terms *tiers, RTI, AYP, TPR, SI,* and *critical* and *multimodal literacy* to Ms. Gaytan and Ms. Greenberg?
2. If you were helping them prepare for their team meetings, what sources would you recommend for learning more about each term?
3. In preparing their personal philosophy of teaching summaries, which elements of teaching and literacy should they highlight?

INTRODUCTION

Education is always changing and evolving. Research findings and new local, state, and federal mandates result in continual changes in schools and classrooms. Like Ms. Gaytan and Ms. Greenberg, all teachers need to read professional journals and attend professional development courses and conferences in order to stay current with new teaching approaches, learning theories, research-based practices, and mandates. This chapter will introduce you to learning theories and reading models as aids in developing your literacy philosophy; explore issues surrounding the literacy development of English learners; illustrate the importance of differentiating instruction; encourage you to reflect on personal literacy experiences and views of reading instruction that may influence your philosophy; provide a familiarity with recent reading initiatives; and finally, discuss new technologies available to build and assess students' literacy.

THE IMPORTANCE OF LITERACY

For many of us, reading is enjoyable and effortless. Realistic fiction makes us laugh, cry, and empathize with the protagonist. Mysteries make us bite our nails or draw the blinds. Novels about other parts of the world help us appreciate other cultures. Historical fiction and nonfiction about the plights of nondominant cultures prompt us to take action. In addition to providing relaxation and pleasure, reading is a necessary skill for productive citizens in today's global society. Each day we are bombarded with text, both printed and electronic, that we must read in order to function: warning signs on medication and household cleaning products, disclaimers on television commercials, information on computer screens, directions on microwave dinners, nutritional information on packaged foods, road signs, application forms, instructional manuals, and the list goes on. The more advanced our society becomes, the higher the reading level we need to complete everyday reading activities. Figure 1.1 lists the reading grade levels required for various tasks. This information makes it obvious that children must become proficient readers in order to perform daily tasks. Classroom teachers must be prepared to teach reading and detect students who struggle to make sense of text.

Readers not only need to read at an advanced level for everyday tasks, they also must be able to read with discernment. The Internet holds a wide array of information. Responsible readers must analyze the source and synthesize the text, relying on their existing knowledge base in order to accurately evaluate the "information" presented.

Writing is also a necessary skill in today's society. Children must become fluent in expressing their ideas and feelings. From a very young age, children need to understand that writing is a key means of communication and that its most important aspect is the message. They need to value using standard spelling and grammar so readers will understand their intended message. Children also need to learn how to write for different audiences and purposes. All skills associated with writing must begin to be developed in the early grades.

Elementary and middle school teachers face great challenges and are frequently pressured by principals and school districts to achieve higher student performance. They cannot merely try a number of instructional strategies, hoping one will do the trick. Instead, they need to help every student become a proficient reader and writer. To do this, teachers must know how to assess literacy problems, match interventions to particular problems, teach students to use reading strategies effectively, and reflect on the effectiveness of their own pedagogic practices.

figure **1.1**

Reading levels of daily reading materials.

Help-wanted ads	6th–7th grade
Front-page newspaper stories	9th–12th grade
Information on medication	10th grade
Directions on frozen dinners	8th grade
Directions on 1040 income tax forms	9th–10th grade
Articles in romance, TV, and movie magazines	8th grade
Life insurance policies	12th grade

Source: McCormick, S. (2010). *Instructing Students Who Have Literacy Problems (6th ed.).* Upper Saddle River, NJ: Prentice Hall.

THEORIES RELATED TO LITERACY

Before developing your philosophy about how children learn to read and write, consider the learning theories you have studied in your other education courses and how they relate to literacy assessment and instruction. The following are some of the most important, relevant learning theories.

Constructivist Theory

All students make sense of new learning situations by linking what they know with what they are being taught. Through accommodation and assimilation, they build on their prior knowledge (Piaget & Inhelder, 1969). They categorize information by hypothesizing how it differs from and is similar to their existing knowledge (Bruner, 1960). Teachers provide authentic learning experiences for students, help them build connections, and provide background knowledge for students who have not yet acquired it. As proficient readers construct meaning, they activate prior knowledge and select the strategies necessary to complete the task. For struggling readers, teachers must build their background knowledge and explicitly teach strategies until the students become proficient readers. For example, if a story's setting is unfamiliar, teachers will explain its time and place so students can follow the plot.

Zone of Proximal Development

Students construct meaning and validate new information and processes by interacting with someone who already knows the information and processes (Vygotsky, 1962). Vygotsky uses the phrase *zone of proximal development* to describe "the distance between the [child's] actual development as determined by independent problem solving and the level of potential development as determined through problem solving under adult guidance or in collaboration with more capable peers" (1978, p. 86). Further, he argues that "what the child can do in cooperation today he can do alone tomorrow" (1962, p. 104). His ideas suggest that teachers can play a key role in students' learning by providing the necessary scaffolding (i.e., the support students need until they are able to work independently). This is why teachers demonstrate the skill or reading strategy, provide guided practice, maximize opportunities for peer modeling, and schedule time for independent practice.

Hierarchy of Human Needs

Psychologists suggest that all humans have a wide variety of needs, some of which are essential for survival and others that are necessary for psychological well-being. Maslow (1987) proposes that humans have the following basic needs:

1. physiological: oxygen, water, food, shelter, and so on
2. safety: security in one's present environment
3. love and belonging: acceptance by others
4. esteem: feeling good about oneself and having the respect of others
5. self-actualization: knowledge that one has fulfilled one's potential

Maslow contends that the most basic needs (food and shelter) must be satisfied before needs further up on the hierarchy can be considered or addressed. Therefore, most schools now provide free or reduced-cost breakfasts and lunches because children cannot concentrate if they are hungry. State departments of education are likewise concerned about students feeling safe at school. Most states now have laws requiring all visitors to sign in and wear badges so they are readily identifiable to administrators. Schools are also likely to have on file a list of individuals authorized to sign each student out of the building and with whom the student may leave after dismissal. Teachers may help each child experience a sense of belonging in the "classroom family" by forming students into small groups and having a teacher's helper for the day or a featured "star" for the week. Effective teachers also seek ways to build self-esteem by ensuring that all students experience some measure of success. For example, they involve students in readers theater so everyone gets to practice their lines before a performance. They know each student has different abilities, strengths, and weaknesses and provide specialized instruction accordingly.

Critical Literacy Theory

Critical literacy is not a distinctive instructional methodology, but rather a literacy theory with implications for action (Behrman, 2006). Teachers who embrace this theory view literacy as more than being able to accurately and fluently read a text in order to answer literal and inferential questions. Teachers of critical literacy understand that literacy involves many forms—print books, ebooks, text messages, websites, wikis, blogs, movies, advertisements, billboards, visual arts, songs, drama, and various multimedia forms. Critical literacy advocates focus on sociopolitical issues as expressed in these many forms. Their goal is for students to develop literacy skills that will enable them to actively engage with text in order to understand the potential for abuse of power and other forms of inequality and injustice among races, cultures, genders, sexual orientations, and social systems and then to engage students in appropriate social action (Beck, 2005; Cervetti, Pardales, & Damico, 2001; Lewison, Flint, & Van Sluys, 2002; Coffey, 2010; Behrman, 2006).

Teachers of critical literacy do not neglect helping their students develop proficient literacy skills. But their ultimate goal is helping students find their voice and take action against the social injustice in our society (Beck, 2005).

History

The term *critical literacy* was developed by social critical theorists who were concerned with social injustice in our world. They applied the tenets of critical social theory by helping students examine the text, multimedia, music, and visual images that surround them each day in order for them to develop "the ability to read texts in an active, reflective manner in order to better understand power, inequality, and injustice in human relationships" (Coffey, 2010, p. 1).

Paulo Freire (1970), an adult educator in Brazil in the 1970s, believed that in traditional classrooms teachers are the transmitters of knowledge that is poured into empty vessels—the students. In this type of classroom, students are not encouraged to read critically and challenge information being passed along to them. In contrast, Freire encouraged his students to think authentically and to discuss social conditions that were significant in their lives and to take appropriate action.

In today's classrooms, some teachers still play the role of transmitters of knowledge. However, others are interested in critical literacy and learning environments that teach students to become aware of social issues by guiding them through texts, media, and other forms of communication. They want their students to discover how the voice of the dominant may be heard at the expense of the voice of the minority (Beck, 2005).

Critical literacy classrooms

Teachers who promote critical literacy engage students in critical reading. However, there is a difference between critical reading and critical literacy. Critical reading encourages students "to use elements of logical analysis—that is, they examine claims of validity and reliability to better understand how these texts function in society" (Cervetti, Pardales, & Damico, 2001, p. 3). To test validity and reliability, teachers facilitate students as they examine authors' credentials, intentions, political interests, and their powerful ways of manipulating language in all forms of writing. Teachers encourage students to understand both the author's perspective and the perspective of those highlighted in the passage (Morgan & York, 2009). For example, students reading a story about Ruby Bridges, the first African-American child to attend an all-white elementary school in the South, question the author's credentials: Is the author knowledgeable? Does the author live in the same town? Is the author attempting to paint an honest picture, or color the text to reflect his or her ideals? Although students realize that only Ruby Bridges can explain what her experience was really like, they can attempt to walk in Ruby's shoes and reflect on how they would feel if they attended a school where they were the only student of their race: Would they be afraid? Do they think Ruby was afraid? Would they wish to be in a school with their neighborhood friends? Did Ruby? These are examples of the types of questions teachers use to help students read critically.

Critical literacy, however, is more than critical reading; it requires students to act on what they have read and analyzed. Classrooms in which critical literacy is taught are "places in which students should come to understand how and why knowledge and power are constructed" (Lloyd, 2003, p. 1). Teachers using critical literacy facilitate students as they begin to understand the historical, political, cultural, and economic context of their world (Cadiero-Kaplein, 2002). These teachers are not knowledge transmitters, but the activist component that encourages students to think critically about issues and become agents of social change (Coffey, 2010). Critical literacy focuses on getting students to understand that "language is never a neutral account of the world" (Beck, 2005, p. 393), and that it can contain the social, cultural, and ideological viewpoints of the dominant society. Critical literacy does more than make students aware of the biases in language; it also uses literacy for "the potential to transform and assist in preparing students for participation in a democratic society" (Lloyd, 2003, p. 1).

Critical literacy lessons

Critical literacy lessons are student-centered in that students dialogue with peers and state their viewpoints and concerns openly without teacher interference. Cervetti, Pardales, and Damico (2001, p. 8) suggest that teachers have students consider the following questions as they read and view various text and multimedia forms:

- How are the meanings assigned to a certain figure or events in a text?
- How does the text attempt to get readers to accept its constructs?
- What is the purpose of the text?
- Whose interests are served by the dissemination of this text? Whose interests are not served?
- What view of the world is put forth by the ideas in this text? What views are not?
- What are other possible constructions of the world?

Cervetti, Pardales, and Damico (2001) give the following example of a teacher engaging first-graders in critical literacy. The class studied how mothers were portrayed in catalogs advertising Mother's Day gifts. The teacher asked the students if their mothers resembled the mothers in the catalogs. Then she asked who bought gifts from the catalogs and where those children got the money to buy the gifts. The teacher then explained how the catalogs were produced and distributed by companies that wanted people to buy the items. After much discussion, the students realized the mothers in the catalogs didn't look like mothers who had been working all day and did not seem to represent their culture or social class. To take action, the students agreed it was more important to share the day with their mothers than to buy them things. They brainstormed ideas about what they could do on Mother's Day that would be more meaningful to their mothers than a gift from a catalog.

In today's schools test scores are emphasized, and some teachers understandably emphasize the separate skills of literacy so students can do well on the state-mandated tests. In classrooms where these skills are the focus, however, many students are often disengaged. Teachers must find ways to interrupt this disengagement. One way is to interest the class in a text that leads to a discussion of the types of questions that Cervetti, Pardales, and Damico (2001) pose. It is important to note, however, that not every lesson needs to include a critical literacy component nor every text be read from a critical literacy perspective. Critical literacy strategies will also be discussed in Chapters 8, 9, and 11.

Successful teachers help students recognize their abilities and provide appropriate praise when they fulfill their potential. They also understand reading theories that will aid them in reading instruction. The following section reviews three important reading models.

READING MODELS

There are many points of view on how children learn to read. These perspectives can be grouped into three major reading models: (1) the part-to-whole approach, often called the skills or phonics approach, (2) the whole-part-whole approach, often referred to as the socio-psycholinguistic approach (Weaver, 2002), and (3) the comprehensive approach, which integrates skill instruction with literature-based reading and process writing (Kaufman, 2002; Reutzel & Cooter, 2003; Routman, 2002). A teacher's philosophy about how children learn to read usually reflects one of these approaches, and it shapes the way he or she assesses and assists struggling readers. Figure 1.2 compares the three models.

Part-to-Whole Model

The **part-to-whole model** emphasizes the importance of students first learning letter names and sounds, followed by simple words that are easily decoded, and then reading stories that consist of these easily decoded words (Adams, 1990; Chall, 1983; Stanovich, 1991; Vellutino, 1991). Phonics concepts are taught in isolation. The part-to-whole model represents three approaches to teaching reading—phonics approach, linguistic approach, and sight word approach.

Phonics approach

The **phonics approach** emphasizes learning the names of each letter of the alphabet and the various sounds associated with the letters (e.g., the short and long vowel sounds, the two sounds of *c* and *g*). Blends (*cl, br, gr*, etc.), vowel digraphs (*oa* as in *road* and *ea* as in *sea*), consonant digraphs (*ck* as in *back* and *ch* as in *cheese*), and diphthongs (*oi* as in *oil, oy* as in *toy*, and *au* as in *caught*) are also studied out of their linguistic context. In phonics programs, students learn phonic rules along with the exceptions to these rules.

Commercial phonics programs differ; in general, however, phonics lessons are systematic and explicitly taught. Manuals for these programs are usually scripted; they indicate exactly what teachers are to say and which student responses are correct. Students are instructed in one concept at a time and complete worksheets based on that concept. Mastery in one concept is expected before students proceed to the next concept. Skills are often taught in isolation and teachers frequently do not integrate them with the texts used during shared reading.

Often, readers who are struggling receive a heavy dose of phonics and/or instruction in word identification (Weaver, 2002). Phonics-oriented teachers believe that struggling readers need to understand the simplest linguistic units (the sound of letters) before they can progress to single words and later to sentences composed of easily decoded words. These students often spend their reading time doing worksheets instead of actually reading.

Linguistic approach

In the **linguistic approach**, another part-to-whole approach, the emphasis is on identifying patterns in words. Proponents of this approach believe it is easier for children to learn words when they focus on two distinctive parts of each word (the onset and rime) instead of on individual letter sounds. **Onset** is "the part of the syllable that precedes the vowel." **Rime** is "the vowel and any consonants that follow it in a syllable" (Savage, 2001, p. 21). For example, in the word

figure **1.2** A Venn diagram comparing three reading models.

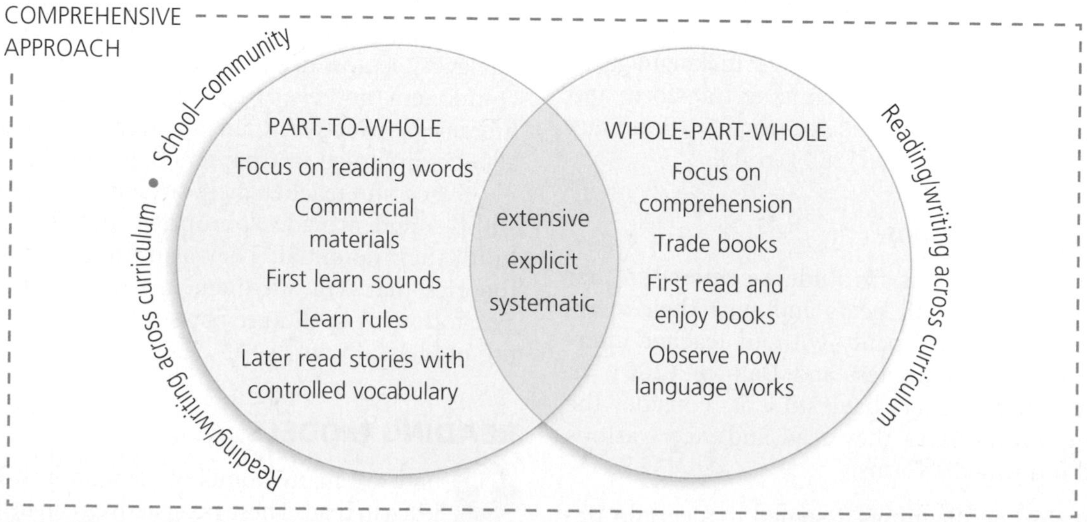

three, the *ee* is the rime and the *thr* is the onset. Onset and rime are also called **phonograms, word patterns,** or **word families** (Savage, 2001). The rime is taught first and then children add onsets to create different words. For example, students learn the rime *at,* and then add the /s/ to create *sat,* /h/ to create *hat,* and so on, until they know *fat, bat, cat, mat, pat, Nat,* and *rat.* Simple stories are then created from each word family. An example of a linguistic story might be: "Pat sat on a flat hat. Cat sat on a flat hat." The Bob series is an example of the linguistic approach. Many trade books also use word families. For example, Dr. Seuss's *Green Eggs and Ham* (1960) uses many words from the *am* family, and *The Cat in the Hat* (1957) uses words from the *at* family.

Sight word approach

In the **sight word approach,** children are first taught the words that will appear in a story they are about to read. The once-popular *Dick and Jane* series is an example of the sight word approach, in which students use flash cards to memorize lists of words. The goal is for children to automatically recognize large sets of words. With the sight word approach, struggling readers spend much of their reading time memorizing flash cards.

Whole-Part-Whole Model

The second major model is the **whole-part-whole model.** Some of the proponents of this model are Kenneth Goodman (1996), Yetta Goodman (1996), and Constance Weaver (2002). Teachers who use this model begin reading instruction with a reading activity known as shared reading or a shared book experience (Holdaway, 1986). Shared reading begins with teachers reading a story with the children. With young children, teachers often use a big book so the students can follow along as teachers read and point to the words. The initial emphasis is on enjoying the plot, characters, and language of the story, and relating the story to their lives. During repeated readings, children begin to chime in on the parts of the story they know, such as the repeated phrases. Later, the teacher and students discover and discuss rhyming words, word endings, new vocabulary, and mechanics such as punctuation. For example, after multiple readings of Lorinda Bryan Cauley's (1992) *Clap Your Hands,* a book with many rhyming words, students are guided to discover words that rhyme because they end in the same letters, such as *sand* and *land.* After they find *down, clown,* and *frown,* they discover with the teacher that these words end in *own.* Later, they find other rhyming words such as *toes* and *nose* and discover that they rhyme even though they do not end with the same letters. Children become aware of letter sounds as they talk about words in these stories. The teacher then returns to a discussion about the characters, plot and/or theme, or concepts in an informational book.

Teachers using the whole-part-whole method often appreciate the importance of phonics instruction and plan stories around a specific letter sound or word family. The phonics instruction in the whole-part-whole model is also explicit, systematic, and extensive; however, these teachers tend to avoid commercial phonics programs. Instead, they teach phonics concepts their students require, using texts they enjoy (Cunningham, 2004).

Struggling readers in the whole-part-whole programs receive the same type of instruction through individual tutoring. Teachers spend their tutoring time reading authentic texts, working on the parts students need help with, and finally discussing the elements of the story or concepts from the informational text. As teachers work with struggling readers, they carefully plan the instruction, building on concepts students already know and helping them discover new language patterns and strategies to aid comprehension (Cunningham, 2004).

Comprehensive Approach

Debate continues over the merits of skills-based versus holistic instruction. Given recent research findings and federal mandates, teachers are recognizing that a comprehensive approach to reading is needed. The **comprehensive approach** (Routman, 2002) integrates skills with literature-based reading and process-writing instruction. Teachers show students how language works by utilizing authentic texts and authentic writing tasks. They instruct students to identify small chunks within words as they attempt to pronounce unknown words. Teachers show students how to use the prefix, suffix, and root part of a word to understand the meaning of unfamiliar words. They teach fluency strategies when reading from trade books and how to organize new information obtained from multiple sources. Teachers impart these strategies while students are enjoying narrative texts, but also during science and social studies lessons. A comprehensive approach focuses on reading and writing for meaning, while recognizing that systematic instruction is essential to meet the needs of individual learners.

The comprehensive approach is "a complex and unified system" (Rasinski & Padak, 2004) in which all parts of the curriculum are interrelated. Reading and writing are important aspects of social studies, science, health, art, and music.

During literacy instruction, teachers using the comprehensive approach consider (1) the amount of time for various tasks, (2) the instructional grouping, (3) the types of text, (4) the cognitive and affective components of learning, (5) the importance of reading to writing and writing to reading, and (6) the relationship between school and home.

The comprehensive approach requires more than giving equal amounts of instructional time to learning literacy skills and reading authentic texts. Teachers need to understand students' individual needs and engage them in tasks that will develop their literacy skills. Students do not need the same amount of time to understand certain skills. It is meaningless for students who recognize all of the words on the Dolch word list (see Appendix B.5) to sit through 10 minutes of flash cards. For other students, 10 minutes may not be enough time to master these words. Teachers using the comprehensive approach should plan the literacy time so every student engages in tasks that will help him or her grow as a reader.

In the comprehensive approach, students are grouped differently for various tasks. Teachers recognize that whole-group instruction is not the most effective form of reading instruction. If struggling readers are always grouped together, they never hear fluent readers and begin to see themselves as poor readers. When students of mixed abilities read in unison, the struggling reader has an opportunity to be successful. Other times, students of varying reading abilities can practice a readers theater selection and perform it for the rest of the class. Teachers can also form groups with similar skills to provide direct instruction so all students will develop a needed skill. Instructional groups are flexible.

With the comprehensive approach, students read all types of materials. They are exposed to stories, informational texts, biographies and autobiographies, magazines, poetry, newspapers, and e-texts. These materials are either at the individual's instructional level in small group instruction or at her easy reading level during independent reading time when she is reading something of her choice.

Teachers using the comprehensive approach understand that students' affective learning domain is interrelated with their cognitive learning domain (Rasinski & Padak, 2004). They know that students who enjoy reading will read more; and the more students read, the better they will read. They assist students in selecting materials that suit their interests and reading level. If texts are too difficult, students, like adults, will feel defeated and quit reading. Successful teachers know the importance of choosing materials that interest students and creating a classroom library that has a wide choice of texts in all formats encompassing many different topics and reading levels. New texts are continually added to the collection via the Internet, the school library, and the public library. The teacher's goal is to have all her students become lifelong readers.

Reading and writing carry equal weight in the comprehensive approach (Rasinski & Padak, 2004) and should be integrated. Students should respond to their readings in journals, logs, poems, and in other written forms. They should be challenged to read to get ideas for their compositions. Students become better writers through reading, and they become better readers through writing.

Teachers using the comprehensive approach understand that students spend the majority of their time away from school, so they make sure students take texts home to share with their parents and caregivers. Even if the caregivers are not literate, teachers encourage them to provide quiet time at home and listen to their children read. Good teachers will let students know about literacy events at the local library and will see that children who cannot get to the library are exposed to more texts.

Teachers also model reading and writing. During DEAR (Drop Everything and Read) time, for example, teachers drop everything and pick up a book or magazine that interests them. They also share with students their stories, poems, and other compositions.

Figure 1.3 is a list of strategies found in classrooms that embrace the comprehensive approach.

Which Method Is the Most Effective?

As a preservice teacher, you may wonder which method is best for a classroom of students with diverse abilities and cultural backgrounds. How will you teach reading and writing to students who do not speak English? How will you teach reading and writing to an autistic child? How will you challenge a student who has been identified as gifted but struggles with reading and writing? How will you work with students who have learning disabilities? Finally, how will you work with students who lack motivation?

Those who study literacy practices and their impact on diverse populations often disagree about the most effective way to ensure that all students learn to read. Remember that no one method suits everyone. As you form your philosophy of reading instruction, understand that teachers teach children; they do not teach methods or materials (Allington, 2006). Always consider the strengths and needs of the individual student. Some children need to isolate small "parts" in order to understand the "whole," while other children are confused by many small parts and must first understand the whole (Carbo, 2007). There

figure 1.3 Classroom strategies used in the comprehensive approach.

BUDDY READING
- Older students share love of books with younger students.

COLLABORATIVE PROJECTS
- Students do authentic research and writing with other students in the classroom, the United States, and the world.

DROP EVERYTHING AND READ (DEAR) OR SUSTAINED SILENT READING (SSR)
- All students in school read books of their choice for 15 to 30 minutes.

E-PALS
- Students do authentic writing to form new friends around the world.

ELECTRONIC BOOKS
- Students follow along as computer reads books.
- Students hear fluent reading.
- Students are introduced to new vocabulary words.

ELECTRONIC RESEARCH PROJECT
- Students share research projects with other students around the world.

GUIDED READING
- Teachers work with homogeneous groups to teach reading skills.
- Teachers teach phonics, word analysis, vocabulary, etc.
- Students read under teacher's supervision.
- Students read graded books on their instructional level.

GUIDED WRITING
- Teachers work with homogeneous groups to teach writing skills.
- Teachers teach phonics, word analysis, vocabulary, etc.
- Students practice skills under teacher's supervision.

INTERACTIVE WRITING (e.g., MORNING MESSAGE)
- Teachers do majority of writing, and students "share the pen" when they know letters/words.
- Teachers explicitly teach phonics, word patterns, and other spelling skills.

JOURNAL WRITING
- Students express themselves personally.
- Students write for authentic purposes.

LANGUAGE EXPERIENCE APPROACH (LEA)
- Students express themselves while teacher acts as scribe.
- Students recognize words in print they use in their speech.

LITERACY CLUB
- Students who share interest in same book/author read and discuss books.

PUPPET SHOW
- Students work in small groups.
- Students improve expression and fluency.
- Students perform for audience.

READERS THEATRE
- Students work in small groups.
- Students improve expression and fluency.
- Students perform for audience.

READING WORKSHOP
- Students choose genre and topics.
- Students share favorite books with peers.

Mini-lessons
- Teachers share with class information about authors and genres.
- Teachers instruct class on reading skills.

Conferences
- Peers read to each other.
- Teachers give explicit instruction on skills to individuals.

Share time
- Students share favorite sections or passages.
- Students share new vocabulary words.

SHARED READING
- Teachers share good literature that is at higher reading level.
- Students hear advanced vocabulary.
- Teachers and students discuss elements of stories.
- Teachers and students discuss information given in passage.

THINK-ALOUDS
- Teachers model reading strategies.
- Teachers teach metacognition skills.

WORD WALLS
- Teachers display words in categories to help students automatically recognize words.
- Students learn patterns within words.
- Students increase their vocabulary.

WRITING WORKSHOP
- Students choose genre and topics.
- Students share writing with peers.

Mini-lessons
- Teachers give explicit instruction on writing skills to class.
- Teachers share types of writing with class.

Conferences
- Peers help with revising and editing.
- Teachers give explicit instruction on writing skills to individuals.

Share time
- Students share finished product with class.

Source: Yellin, D., Blake, M., & DeVries, B., *Integrating the Language Arts* (4th ed.). Copyright © 2008 by Holcomb Hathaway, Scottsdale, AZ. Used with permission.

is no perfect method to use for all students; effective teachers "understand the physical, psychosocial, and cognitive characteristics of their students" (Manning, 2002) so they can choose a method that fits the students' strengths and needs.

ENGLISH LEARNERS

Between 1994 and 2004, the number of English learners in schools increased by 72 percent. In 2004, 20 percent of U.S. students lived in homes where English was not the native language, and in 2007, 5 percent of K–12 students were English learners (Center for Public Education, 2010a). By 2050, this percentage is expected to increase to 40 percent (International Reading Association, 2001). Spanish speakers are the fastest growing group of English learners. In 2007, the Hispanic population of the United States (21.1 percent) was larger than the African-American population (16.6 percent) (Center for Public Education, 2010b). Despite these numbers, only 13 percent of the schools with English learners have either an ESL or bilingual program (International Reading Association, 2004).

Some researchers argue that English learners must first learn to read in their native language before they learn to read in English (Krashen, 2004/2005; Weber, 1991). Others believe this is not necessary and merely delays the English learners' academic progress (Fitzgerald & Noblit, 1999; Rossell, 2004/2005).

Regardless of your position on this argument, you must remember that English learners have different educational backgrounds, and thus, different needs. Some English learners have had strong academic schooling in their native country and are literate in their native language and perhaps a number of other languages. Others have had limited formal schooling and are not literate in their native language. Some English learners have parents who are university students or graduates and can read and speak English fluently, while other students' parents are illiterate in their native language and cannot speak English either (Short & Echevarria, 2004/2005).

Cummins (1979) distinguishes between English learners' basic interpersonal communicative skills (BICS) and their cognitive academic language proficiency (CALP). BICS refers to English learners' ability to be fluent in personal conversation, while CALP refers to their ability to read and write at the academic level of their peers. Most English learners achieve conversational English skills in about two years; however, they may not have the literacy skills for academic studies for five to seven years (Cummins, 1979; Otaiba & Pappamihiel, 2005). Yet in the classroom these students are expected to grasp the language well enough to understand new concepts.

Complicating the academic progress of English learners is the fact that many do not come to the United States during kindergarten or first grade. Some find themselves in upper-elementary or high-school classes where they do not understand the language and yet are expected to learn new, advanced concepts presented in English. For this reason, all teachers must have some background knowledge on English learners' literacy development and must choose effective strategies to make these students feel welcome in the classroom community and enable them to work toward academic success.

English Language Development

Otaiba and Pappamihiel (2005) classify the stages of English language development as (1) the silent stage, (2) the early production stage, (3) the productive language stage, and (4) the intermediate fluency language stage. They identify some observable characteristics of each stage, and provide appropriate instructional strategies for each (see Figure 1.4). Teachers must remember that some English learners in the silent stage may be in upper elementary or even middle school. However, the older silent stage learners may stay in the silent stage for a shorter period of time than the younger silent stage learners.

Effective Practices for English Learners

To be effective with English learners, teachers must strive to do the following (Bouchereau-Bauer & Manyak, 2008; Yaden et al., 2000):

1. Understand the families and culture of English learners.
2. Base lessons on students' interests.
3. Use collaborative learning groups as much as possible.
4. Provide tutoring by well-qualified tutors.
5. Connect tutoring lessons to classroom instruction.
6. Provide meaningful, challenging learning tasks.
7. Respect students' cultures and intellectual abilities.
8. Teach in both the native language and English when possible.
9. Be flexible in permitting students to use their native language.
10. Give English learners opportunities to talk and ask questions in a risk-free environment.
11. Display cognates on the word wall so English learners can see the comparison. This also aids native speakers in learning a second language.

figure 1.4 Progressive stages of English language development.

SILENT STAGE (ALSO KNOWN AS PREPRODUCTION)

Characteristics	*Appropriate Instructional Strategies*
Key characteristic: Communication with peers is very limited, which in turn hampers development of social language proficiency.	**Particular instructional focus:** Help children adapt to the classroom culture and establish instructional routines.
Student may continue speaking in his or her first language (L1).	Tutors are responsible for up to 90% of conversational burden.
Student is processing language, but oral communication is limited or nonexistent.	Use pictures, props, manipulatives, and other hands-on materials to ensure active student involvement.
This period may last longer in very young students than students in later elementary.	Use simplified language that focuses on key concepts and the repetition of essential vocabulary.
	Use total physical response (TPR).

THE EARLY PRODUCTION STAGE

Characteristics	*Appropriate Instructional Strategies*
Key characteristic: Students tend to use imitation and repetition (formulate phrases or speech patterns such as I goed to lunch) to become part of the social fabric of the class.	**Particular instructional focus:** Provide basic tools for immediate use including explicit instruction in vocabulary and social communication.
Student begins to develop aspects of social English that will become building blocks of English proficiency.	Tutors are responsible for up to 50%–60% of conversational burden.
Students' social skills in English are based on highly contextualized language.	Ask *who, what, where,* and *either/or* questions, labeling activities, questions that can be answered formulaically.
The student may decode print, but struggles to comprehend.	Use TPR with responses—verbal and nonverbal, role-playing activities.

THE PRODUCTIVE LANGUAGE STAGE

Characteristics	*Appropriate Instructional Strategies*
Key characteristic: Students begin to manipulate language on their own, rather than relying on formulaic phrases (e.g., I goed to lunch).	**Particular instructional focus:** Modeling, scaffolding, providing guided instruction with academic language. Increased support for reading to learn versus learning to read and for building content-area knowledge.
Students may begin to overgeneralize language rules and may appear to regress.	Tutors are responsible for up to 40% of conversational burden.
Students begin to develop academic skills in English.	Use language experience approach, ask *how* and *why* questions, and increase social interaction.
Students may appear to have fairly complete fluency because they can handle most social situations, but academic English development is still critical.	Emphasize increased problem solving, predicting, comparing, describing, labeling, listing.
	Provide graphic organizers that include more text.

THE INTERMEDIATE FLUENCY LANGUAGE STAGE

Characteristics	*Appropriate Instructional Strategies*
Key characteristic: Students struggle with reading comprehension and other advanced literacy skills although overall English skills appear fluent.	**Particular instructional focus:** Teachers should continue scaffolding academic skills and advanced critical thinking skills, providing motivation for wide reading.
Social English is well established and the student appears fully proficient in English to an outside observer. However, student will continue to struggle/develop higher level academic English.	Tutors are responsible for up to 10% of conversational burden.
Students may become frustrated with what they perceive to be their own language limitations.	Use scaffolded writing process activities that use graphic organizers, analyzing charts and graphs, more complex problem solving and evaluating, research and support questions, literary analysis.

Note that at all stages, tutors should support native language retention.

From Guidelines for Using Volunteer Literacy Tutors to Support Reading Instruction for English Language Learners by S. Otaiba, & N. E. Pappamihiel. *Teaching Exceptional Children* (2005 July/August), pp. 6–11. Copyright © 2005 by the Council for Exceptional Children. Reprinted with permission.

12. Provide social settings so English learners can learn from authentic communication with peers, just as they did when learning their native language.

Vaughn, Mathes, Linan-Thompson, and Francis (2005) found a number of additional practices in effective English-learner programs. Teachers use repetitive routines so students can readily become members of the class. They also use language that is slightly above the students' current level. Krashen (1981) calls this the I + 1 Theory, which states that English learners acquire language when they interact with language that is one level above their current stage of competency. They can comprehend new information when they receive only one or two new vocabulary words or concepts at any given time. English learners can make sense of the input because they comprehend most of the information given.

Visual scaffolding—showing an image of what is being explained—is particularly beneficial to English learners. For example, when a teacher refers to vowels and points to a list of vowels, an English learner quickly associates the word *vowel* with the letters.

The total physical response (TPR) approach is another effective practice. In TPR, students recite key vocabulary words, spell them, and act out their meaning so that they comprehend the difference between similar sounding words such as *ship* and *skip* (see Chapter 7). Effective teachers model new information, rather than merely explaining it. They use paralinguistic communication (hand gestures, body movements, facial expressions) as much as possible to help students understand routines and new concepts and encourage students to dialogue with them as well as with peers.

The sheltered instruction (SI) model is another practice that, according to Echevarria and Short (2007), helps English learners achieve significantly. The SI model is "an approach to teaching content in a strategic manner so that concepts are comprehensible and ELLs will develop English skills" (Echevarria & Short, 2007, p. 2). SI is a way of scaffolding English learners as they learn the social skills of the classroom, such as taking turns, waiting for one's turn, sharing classroom equipment, and not "sharing" answers (cheating).

In SI, teachers may do the following:

1. Adjust their speech by paraphrasing, giving examples, using hand gestures and facial expressions, elaborating on students' responses, and speaking more slowly.
2. Pre-teach new vocabulary words by acting them out.
3. Use visual aids such as demonstration graphic organizers to show relationships.
4. Use small groups and tutoring.
5. Use the native language, if possible, to explain content.
6. Provide a risk-free environment and encourage English learners to talk.
7. Connect concepts to students' life experiences.
8. Engage students at all times; no one sits passively.
9. Support students while they work.
10. Provide supplementary materials such as computer-based resources and trade books that are on the topic, but written at a lower grade level.

Several other specific instructional strategies are effective. Choral reading, interactive writing, language experience approach (LEA), audiobooks, and shared reading are all strategies that work with English learners (Drucker, 2003).

- In choral reading, the students and teacher read the text together so that English learners can hear the pronunciation and be actively involved in the reading process (see Chapter 10).
- In interactive writing, the teacher and students share the pen. Teachers do most of the writing; however, when they recognize that a student knows the initial letter or the spelling of the entire word, the student gets to write the letter or word (see Chapter 11).
- In the language experience approach (LEA), the student dictates to the teacher. The teacher is the scribe, writing down the exact words the child says. The student reads it back to the teacher so he can identify text that does not make sense or realize words are missing. LEA uses either short captions under pictures that the student draws or longer texts such as stories (see Chapter 7).
- During shared reading in the elementary grades, the teacher uses large books as much as possible and discusses a story with a small group. Instead of quizzing the students at the end of the story, students are encouraged to ask questions during and after the reading. Through the discussion, teachers can explain the setting, the background, and key words that will help the students as they listen to the story. Reading stories or folktales that relate to the students' cultures is advantageous (Alyousef, 2005; Drucker, 2003). Of course, teachers must ensure that such books do not reinforce stereotypes.
- Many audiobooks are available through publishers such as Scholastic and Libraries for the Blind. However, some of the best audiobooks

are those created by the teacher or other fluent readers who read a little slower than normal so English learners can follow along better (see Chapter 10).

- Also helpful are ebooks with highlighted text. English learners can easily follow along and click on unknown words for the correct pronunciation and definition (see Chapter 7 and Appendix A.12).

Additional strategies for use with English learners will be described throughout this book.

FORMING YOUR TEACHING PHILOSOPHY

Your personal teaching philosophy is important. You must understand how children learn and which factors affect student learning. Elementary and middle school teachers should also have a specific literacy philosophy. They must understand the processes of reading and writing, types of problems, methods of assessment, and strategies of instruction that will strengthen their students' literacy. For example, Ms. Rea's philosophy of reading instruction is that reading is learning to read words correctly. She believes the root of all reading problems is the failure to pronounce words correctly and automatically. She assesses her students by having them read word lists, and she spends many hours each week teaching them phonics rules. Mr. Garcia has a contrasting philosophy. He believes that reading involves bringing one's background knowledge to the reading event in order to comprehend the passage. He also knows that the students' personal vocabulary, both receptive and expressive, affects their ability to read text. He assesses what readers do while reading a passage that is at their instructional level. Mr. Garcia uses a variety of word walls (science words, social studies words, puns, "found an interesting word," and others) and draws from an array of instructional strategies to help readers become proficient. Both teachers have a philosophy of reading instruction, and both assess students and provide strategies based on their philosophies. Your philosophy may be completely different from both Ms. Rea's and Mr. Garcia's.

Reflection on Assessing Reading Problems

As you formulate your philosophy of reading instruction, consider your interpretation of reading errors. Ask yourself: "Do all of the reading errors I make while reading orally or silently disrupt comprehension?"

Proficient and struggling readers constantly make reading miscues (errors). Not all miscues, however, are bad (Goodman, Watson, & Burke, 1996) if they do not hinder comprehension. Some miscues indicate that the reader is reading for meaning instead of merely pronouncing words correctly. When assessing children's reading, teachers should be able to discern which miscues hinder comprehension and which do not.

Personal Philosophy of Intervention and Instruction for Struggling Readers

The DeFord Theoretical Orientation to Reading Profile (TORP) is designed for teachers to reflect on their personal views of reading and reading instruction. Complete the DeFord TORP found in Figure 1.5. The abbreviation SA means "strongly agree"; SD means "strongly disagree." There are no right or wrong answers. After completing the inventory, discuss your responses with your peers. When disagreement arises, explain the reason behind your response. You can also share the TORP with a practicing teacher who you consider to be an effective reading teacher. After each of you completes the inventory, discuss your responses.

To score the inventory, first add your responses from numbers 1, 2, 3, 6, 8, 9, 10, 12, 13, 14, 16, 19, 20, 21, 22, 24, 25, and 28. If the sum of these responses is low (18–45), it indicates that you view reading as a set of skills. You probably also believe that students must be taught phonics and other skills in order to read complete passages. Next, add your responses from numbers 4, 5, 7, 11, 15, 17, 18, 23, 26, and 27. If the sum of these responses is low (10–25), it indicates that you view reading as a holistic event. You would likely teach skills using stories that students have read and enjoyed. If your scores were neither low nor high on these sets, you probably have not given much thought to how you would teach and assess reading.

The DeFord inventory presents opposing points of view. For example, statement 5 is in direct contrast to statement 20, and statement 6 is in direct contrast to statement 15. If you strongly agree that early reading materials should be written in natural language (statement 5), you will strongly disagree that early reading materials should have controlled vocabulary (statement 20).

HISTORICAL OVERVIEW OF READING REFORMS

Teachers must be aware of the political issues surrounding the teaching of reading. Current federal mandates require teachers to provide quality

figure 1.5 DeFord Theoretical Orientation to Reading Profile.

SA = strongly agree, SD = strongly disagree.

	SA . . . SD
1. A child needs to be able to verbalize the rules of phonics in order to ensure proficiency in processing new words.	1 2 3 4 5
2. An increase in reading errors is usually related to a decrease in comprehension.	1 2 3 4 5
3. Dividing words into syllables according to rules is a helpful instructional practice for reading new words.	1 2 3 4 5
4. Fluency and expression are necessary components of reading that indicate good comprehension.	1 2 3 4 5
5. Materials for early reading should be written in natural language without concern for short, simple words and sentences.	1 2 3 4 5
6. When children do not know a word, they should be instructed to sound out its parts.	1 2 3 4 5
7. It is good practice to allow children to edit a text into their own dialect when they are learning to read.	1 2 3 4 5
8. The use of a glossary or dictionary is necessary for determining the meaning and pronunciation of new words.	1 2 3 4 5
9. Reversals (e.g., saying "saw" for "was") are significant problems in the teaching of reading.	1 2 3 4 5
10. It is good practice to correct a child as soon as she makes an oral reading mistake.	1 2 3 4 5
11. It is important for a word to be repeated a number of times after it has been introduced to ensure that it will become a part of sight vocabulary.	1 2 3 4 5
12. Paying close attention to punctuation marks is necessary to understanding story content.	1 2 3 4 5
13. The repetition of words and phrases is a sign of an ineffective reader.	1 2 3 4 5
14. Being able to label words according to grammatical function (nouns, verbs, etc.) is useful in proficient reading.	1 2 3 4 5

	SA . . . SD
15. When encountering an unknown word, the reader should be encouraged to guess about its meaning and go on.	1 2 3 4 5
16. Young readers need to be introduced to the root forms of words *(run, long)* before they are asked to read inflected forms *(running, longest)*.	1 2 3 4 5
17. It is necessary for a child to know the letters of the alphabet in order to learn to read.	1 2 3 4 5
18. Flash card drills with sight words is an unnecessary form of practice in reading instruction.	1 2 3 4 5
19. The ability to use accent patterns in multisyllable words *(pho' to graph, pho to' gra phy,* and *pho to gra' phic)* should be developed as part of reading instruction.	1 2 3 4 5
20. Controlling text through consistent spelling patterns ("The fat cat ran back. The fat cat sat on a hat.") is an effective means of learning to read.	1 2 3 4 5
21. Formal instruction in reading is necessary to ensure the adequate development of all the skills used in reading.	1 2 3 4 5
22. Phonics analysis is the most important form of analysis used when encountering new words.	1 2 3 4 5
23. Children's initial experiences with print should focus on meaning more than precise graphic representation.	1 2 3 4 5
24. Word shapes (word configuration) should be taught to aid in word recognition.	1 2 3 4 5
25. It is important to teach skills in relation to other skills.	1 2 3 4 5
26. If a child says "house" for the written word *home,* this response should be left uncorrected.	1 2 3 4 5
27. It is not necessary to introduce new words before they appear in the reading text.	1 2 3 4 5
28. Some problems in reading are caused by readers dropping the inflectional endings from words (e.g., jumps, jumped).	1 2 3 4 5

Source: DeFord, D. (1985, Spring). Validating the Construct of Theoretical Orientation in Reading Instruction. *Reading Research Quarterly, 20* (3), 351–367.

instruction that ensures that all children, regardless of race, gender, or ability, will reach their potential. This section reviews recent legislation that greatly impacts elementary classroom teachers.

Each state is responsible for providing a free education to all of its young people. However, in the last few decades federal government officials have become concerned with how U.S. students rank among their peers in other countries. These concerns persist despite the fact that in 2009 the National Center for Education Statistics (NCES) found fourth-grade reading scores the highest since testing began in the 1970s, eighth-grade reading scores slightly improved, and high school reading scores remaining the same (National Center for Education Statistics, 2010). The federal government is also concerned with the continued lag among minorities and lower socioeconomic groups. The NCES reported that in 2009 students who were enrolled in a school in which 75 percent of the students received free lunches scored lower in reading than students enrolled in schools in which 25 percent of the students received free lunches (National Center for Education Statistics, 2010). For example, the reading gap between white and Hispanic fourth- and eighth-grade students was 26 points, and the reading gap between white and African-American fourth- and eighth-grade students was 27 points. However, the reading gap between those eligible and those not eligible for free lunches was 35 points (U.S. Department of Education, 2010). These gaps are significant but they are not new; they have been recorded for several decades. To address these issues, legislators have passed laws with specific mandates.

Elementary and Secondary Education Act of 1966

In 1965 Congress passed the Elementary and Secondary Education Act of 1966 (ESEA) to establish Title I monies that funded supplementary reading instruction for students in high-poverty schools. Monies were used to purchase materials and tests and to pay certified reading specialists who provided extra instruction outside the regular classroom. The instruction, however, was seldom related to the reading tasks that students were asked to perform in the regular classroom. Schools submitted comprehensive plans for the use of these federal monies and then documented how the funds were used and the tests administered to gauge growth. Title I monies could only be used to provide reading instruction in high-poverty schools. Some of you may have heard about or attended one of these Title I schools.

The America Reads Challenge Act

In 1997 President Bill Clinton signed into law another act that influenced reading instruction: the America Reads Challenge Act. It mandated that all students would read at grade level by the end of the third grade and inaugurated many new community-based tutorial programs. These programs provided all struggling students in kindergarten through third grade with extra help in reading to ensure that they could read at the third-grade level before they entered fourth grade.

The National Reading Panel Report

Also in 1997 Congress commissioned the director of the National Institute of Child Health and Human Development and the U.S. Secretary of Education to form the National Reading Panel (NRP). The panel released a two-volume report titled *Teaching Children to Read: An Evidence-Based Assessment of the Scientific Research Literature on Reading and Its Implications for Reading Instruction.* The panel concluded that effective reading instruction included systematic, explicit instruction in five essential components of reading: phonemic awareness, phonics, vocabulary, comprehension, and fluency. Most teachers would agree with these five essential components of reading; however, some researchers (Allington, 2006; Cunningham, 2002; Garan, 2002) argue that there are additional components. See the box on the next page, which presents an alternative perspective from Richard Allington.

No Child Left Behind Act

Based on the NRP's report, President George W. Bush signed into law the No Child Left Behind Act of 2001 (NCLB). This act mandated that all students must show adequate yearly progress (AYP) in the five areas of reading identified by the NRP: phonemic awareness, phonics, vocabulary, comprehension, and fluency. It also outlined specific, detailed requirements with which schools must comply and sanctions for failing to do so and required that all materials purchased with federal funds be backed by scientific research.

Continuing Emphasis on Scientifically Based Research

In the years since passage of NCLB, the emphasis on scientifically based research has remained steadfast. What does the term *scientifically based research* mean? According to the National Institute for Literacy (2006), such research must:

- employ systematic, empirical methods that draw on observation or experiment;
- involve rigorous data analyses that are adequate to test the stated hypotheses and justify the general conclusions;
- rely on measurements or observational methods that provide valid data across evaluators and observers, and across multiple measurements and observation; and
- be accepted by a peer-reviewed journal or approved by a panel of independent experts through a comparatively rigorous, objective, and scientific review. (p. 1)

Given this emphasis, today's reading materials often are promoted as being "scientifically researched based." Teachers are advised to question who conducted the research, and if the publisher conducted its own research, teachers should be wary of a possible bias.

Response to Intervention

In addition to emphasizing scientifically based research, legislation has also specified how to identify students who need special services. The Individuals with Disabilities Education Act 2004 (IDEA 2004) requires districts to use a Response to Intervention (RTI) method for this identification. RTI is a framework for identifying students with learning disabilities and for providing instructional services. It has become the "process that incorporates both assess-

An Alternate View to the National Reading Panel's Findings

Richard Allington, one of the preeminent literacy researchers in the United States, agrees that the five components named by the NRP are essential elements of reading instruction; however, he also believes in five additional essential elements (Allington, 2006). He bases his premise on powerful scientific evidence and calls the additional essential elements the "Five Missing Pillars of Scientific Reading Instruction." They are:

1. Access to and a choice of a wide variety of interesting narrative and informational texts on students' reading levels. [Guthrie, J. T., & Humenick, N. M. (2004). Motivating students to read: Evidence for classroom practices that increase motivation and achievement. In P. McCardle & V. Chhabra (Eds.), *The Voice of Evidence in Reading Research,* pp. 329–354. Baltimore: Paul Brookes.]
2. All students need to be given text that they can read. [International Reading Association. (2006). Making it different makes the difference. Retrieved March 11, 2006, from www.reading.org; O'Connor, R. E., & Bell, K. M. (2002). Teaching reading to poor readers in intermediate grades: A comparison of text difficulty. *Journal of Educational Psychology, 94*(3), 474–485.]
3. Writing and reading are reciprocal. Programs that integrate reading, writing, composing, comprehension, decoding skills, and spelling have more positive effects on students' learning than do programs that emphasize reading, writing, spelling, and phonics as separate programs, showing no relationship to one another. [Tierney, R. J., & Shanahan, T. (1991). Research on reading–writing relationships: Interaction, transactions and outcomes. In R. Barr, M. Kamil, P. Mosenthal, & P. D. Pearson (Eds.), *Handbook of Reading Research,* pp. 246–280. New York: Longman.]
4. Students do not learn as well in whole class settings as they do in small groups or tutoring settings, and they vary greatly in their reading abilities at every grade level and require different instruction. [Taylor, B. M., Pearson, P. D., et al. (2000). Effective schools and accomplished teachers: Lessons about primary grade reading instruction in low income schools. *Elementary School Journal, 101,* 121–165; Allington, R. L., & Johnston, P. H. (Eds.). (2002). *Reading to Learn: Lessons from Exemplary 4th Grade Classrooms.* New York: Guilford.]
5. Many students need tutoring from an expert if they are to accelerate their reading development. Groups larger than three are rarely effective, and tutoring is the most effective way to aid struggling readers. [D'Agostino, J. V., & Murphy, J. A. (2004). A meta-analysis of Reading Recovery in the United States schools. *Educational Evaluation and Policy Analysis, 26*(1), 23–38; Allington, R. L. (2004). Setting the record straight. *Educational Leadership, 61*(6), 22–25.]

ment and intervention so that immediate benefits come to the student" (Mesmer & Mesmer, 2009, p. 287). Prior to IDEA, however, other laws attempted to identify students with learning disabilities and determine appropriate interventions for them. Some of these contributed to the development of RTI.

Relevant laws leading to RTI

In 1975 after Congress passed the Education for All Handicapped Children Act, all children with learning disabilities became eligible for special education. A child with a learning disability was defined as anyone with a "severe discrepancy between achievement and intellectual ability" (U.S. Department of Education, 1977, p. G1082). When IDEA was signed into law in 1997, it was intended to close the gap between the achievements of students with disabilities and what was required of them.

For both acts the most widely used method of identifying students with disabilities was the IQ–achievement discrepancy method, which is the difference between a student's IQ and his or her achievement. However, this resulted in over-identification and disproportionate representation of minority children. The number of students who were labeled as having a learning disability skyrocketed.

In 2004, the Individuals with Disabilities Education Act was signed into law. It stated that "a learning disability may be present when a student's performance is not adequate to meet grade-level standards when provided with appropriate instruction and research-based interventions" (Mesmer & Mesmer, 2009, p. 281). IDEA 2004 means that schools no longer need to consider the discrepancy between a student's achievement and IQ when attempting to determine if a student is eligible for special services. Instead schools can use the RTI approach, which identifies learning disabilities by observing how a student responds to research-based intervention. This method abandons the sole use of standardized tests and endorses the use of measuring how a student responds to scientifically based intervention. The advantage of the RTI method over the discrepancy method is that students struggling with literacy skills receive help immediately instead of waiting until they have taken a battery of tests, during which they would receive no intervention and fall further behind.

IDEA 2004 identified eight areas as the basis for learning disabilities. Six of the areas deal with language arts: oral expression, listening comprehension, written expression, basic reading skills, fluency, and reading comprehension.

IDEA 2004 did not provide states and districts with a prescribed method of implementing RTI. Although the specific approaches vary, the method should involve a cyclical process that begins with assessment, followed by intervention, more assessment, and more intense intervention until students are either reading and writing at grade level or receiving special services for a specific learning disability. Some states and districts have implemented a three-tier plan, while others use a five- or six-tier plan. However, "RTI is not a model to be imposed on schools, but rather a framework to help schools identify and support students before the difficulties they encounter with language and literacy become more serious" (International Reading Association, 2009, p. 2).

Guiding principles

The International Reading Association (IRA) commission on RTI has drafted guiding principles for teachers regarding implementation of RTI.

Principle 1, Instruction. Both classroom teachers and interventionists must provide high-quality instruction backed by research-based practices. This requires all classroom teachers, from first-year to seasoned, to be highly qualified literacy teachers capable of using strategies that have been proven to increase students' literacy skills.

Principle 2, Responsive teaching and differentiation. "Instruction and materials selection must derive from specific student-teacher interactions" (International Reading Association, 2009, p. 2). Teachers must be able to determine if students are responding to intervention. This requires individualized kid watching; that is, teachers watching students as they use various strategies.

Principle 3, Assessment. All teachers need to know how to assess students' literacy skills as they engage in authentic language activities.

Principle 4, Collaboration. Effective RTI requires classroom teachers to collaborate with reading specialists, speech pathologists, school psychologists, and other special education teachers. It must also involve parents so skills can be reinforced in the home.

Principle 5, Systemic and comprehensive. The school district must consider the culture of the community as administrators plan for a systemic and comprehensive RTI. The planning should include all levels of classroom teachers from pre-K through twelfth grade, reading specialists, and all other special education teachers so the students receive interventions that build from one grade level to another. Records should be comprehensive so teachers can build on interventions a student received the previous year. Accurate records eliminate time spent on reevaluating a student or offering interventions that did not prove to be useful.

Principle 6, Expertise. As stated earlier, all students deserve highly qualified teachers conversant in the latest materials and intervention practices. According to the International Reading Association, "important dimensions of teachers' expertise include their knowledge and understanding of language and literacy development, their ability to use powerful assessment tools and techniques, and their ability to translate information about student performance into instructionally relevant instructional techniques" (2009, p. 4).

The RTI process

As you can see, RTI requires all classroom teachers to be highly qualified to teach reading and to assess reading problems so they can closely monitor how students respond to intervention. They must know which assessments to use to determine a student's ability and which interventions to use; then they must determine if that student is responding to the intervention. The following is a sample five-step RTI process:

Step 1. Establish benchmarks. Early in the year literacy screening assessments such as Dynamic Indicators of Basic Early Literacy Skills (DIBELS), Phonological Awareness Literacy Screening (PALS), or Basic Early Assessment of Reading Scope and Sequence (BEARS) measure students' basic early literacy skills, such as phonemic awareness, phonics, vocabulary, fluency, and comprehension. When students are in middle school, they need more than basic literacy skills assessment. They need to be able to summarize, analyze, synthesize, and evaluate using multiple sources. These skills will be weak if students cannot comprehend a text. Therefore, teachers should use any assessment, such as an informal reading inventory, that measures students' reading levels and comprehension. Middle school subject area teachers are usually the ones to detect students' inabilities, even if they do not consider themselves reading teachers (Brozo, 2010). It is imperative that middle school teachers be trained to assess students' skills in these areas so they can calculate each student's benchmark score.

After teachers have assessed their students, they determine which skills the student has mastered and which require more practice. If the student falls below the expected mastery for his or her grade, he or she receives intervention.

Step 2. Based on the assessment scores determined in Step 1, the student receives intervention in her areas of greatest need. Often this first round takes place in a small group of students who are weak in the same areas. To be cost effective, early grade teachers often use the guided reading strategy in which the students are grouped so that reading materials are at their instructional level and not their frustration level. Middle school teachers should differentiate their instruction in order to provide appropriate intervention (Brozo, 2010). RTI requires materials and intervention strategies to be scientifically valid and given systematically so the student has every opportunity to improve. The emphasis of RTI is to see how a student responds to intervention. This intervention does not replace the regular classroom instruction; it is an additive.

Step 3. Student progress is constantly monitored and recorded. The teacher assesses the student's progress at least weekly. The instruments used for this assessment may be running records, miscue analyses, or subtests of one of the tests, such as DIBELS or PALS, given at the beginning of the year. For example, if DIBELS or PALS has been given as a benchmark assessment, it would be administered again to determine if the student is responding to the intervention. Middle school subject area teachers will collaborate with the reading specialist to determine which assessment was used for the student's benchmark score so the same test can be administered again. Because middle school teachers meet with large groups of students for a short period of time each day, the reading specialist is usually the one to administer the assessments. If the student shows that she is at grade level after this assessment, she is dropped from the small group intervention. If the assessment indicates that she is not progressing and is falling further behind her classmates, she is recommended for more intense intervention.

Step 4. More intense intervention is usually individualized or takes place in very small groups over longer periods of time. This intervention is also an additive; it does not replace general classroom instruction. The individualized attention is often from a reading interventionist. Again, the teacher constantly monitors the student and adjusts strategies according to need.

Step 5. After a long period of time—often a year—the student's response to the intervention is assessed again. If the student is falling further below his grade level, he is considered to have a learning disability. If the student is responding, he does not have a disability and simply needs more intense intervention.

During this intense intervention, a reading specialist, special education teacher, speech pathologist, and other specialists work together to give the student one-on-one instruction according to his needs. It is important that this intense instruction takes place in the setting that is most beneficial for the child. Sometimes this will be a room separate from the regular classroom; other times the reading specialist or special education teacher will work side-by-side with the student in the classroom so he receives the same curriculum as the other students. Then during individual practice time the student receives extra guidance from the specialized teacher.

The intense intervention usually includes 30- to 40-minute tutoring sessions by the specialist on the skill(s) that the student needs in order to progress. Even in the intermediate elementary grades or middle school, the reading specialist may need to work on such basic skills as letter–sound relationships or helping the student automatically recognize commonly used words such as those found in the Dolch list. In these cases, the reading specialist may spend time with flash cards and word phrases. As another example, a middle school student struggling to comprehend informational text in a social studies book may be taught how to complete simple graphic organizers so the information is easier to summarize.

MULTIMODAL LITERACY

A personal philosophy for teaching literacy should take into account not only learning theories, reading models, teaching English learners, and governmental mandates, but also the technology and multiple modes of communication that have emerged in recent years. Multimodal literacy is a fact of students' daily lives, so consider how you will help students develop these skills. Multimodal communication includes the ability to read and produce print, graphs, images, music, and videos. In today's classroom one can see students read and respond to all types of communication. "A transition from print-based education to multimodal education indicates a profound shift in the notion of reading as a whole" (Hassett & Curwood, 2009, p. 270).

Multimodal literacy is composed of four basic literacies: technological literacy, visual literacy, media literacy, and informational literacy (Sylvester & Greenidge, 2009). Technological literacy is the ability to read and manipulate all types of digital resources, such as computers, interactive whiteboards, tablets, e-readers, printers, scanners, MP3 players, video cameras, and other electronic devices. Visual literacy includes the ability to read and interpret images and icons on tool bars, videos, photographs, graphs, charts, and maps. Media literacy requires students to read, create, manipulate, analyze, and evaluate messages conveyed through images, narration, text, and music in a variety of media modes. Informational literacy refers to the ability to find, evaluate, analyze, and synthesize information from multiple sources, including the Internet. Besides developing these literacies, students must learn about copyright laws and how to give credit for any copyrighted materials they use (Sylvester & Greenidge, 2009).

Mouza (2005) found that students are motivated to develop multiliteracy skills because technology fosters interaction among peers. Traditional print sources often leave students isolated at a desk reading from stationary pages with static pictures. Multimodal communication frequently involves them interacting and collaborating with a small group of peers on tasks they find interesting. Learning becomes social, which is the way humans learn (Vygotsky, 1978). Mouza also found that collaborative and interactive programs, such as the MadLibs page on the Fun Brain website, work well because they encourage students "to wonder, explore, create, hypothesize, problem-solve, and interact with other children" (Mouza, 2005, p. 515). Social networking tools (e.g., blogs, wikis, Facebook) that students may use out of school can become tools for collaborative learning in schools.

Spence (2009) found English learners became motivated by partnering with peers to create a website based on their family's heritage. Students interviewed family members and then worked with peers to create pages about foods, stories, and jokes shared by the family. The pages also featured the Spanish alphabet, Spanish phrases, and the family's favorite places to visit in Mexico. As peers worked together they developed literacy, drawing, and technology skills, as well as creative, abstract, and complex thinking skills. Spence reported the project's greatest benefit was in building school–family relationships with parents who had not felt they were an integral part of the school. Parents were naturally drawn into the students' schooling as they shared family stories and jokes for the project, and they were proud when they viewed the websites their child had created. This activity built a family–school relationship that lasted throughout the year.

In another example, Sox and Rubinstein-Avila (2009) used WebQuest, an interdisciplinary learning unit they posted online. As middle school English learners worked with WebQuest, they developed reading skills by analyzing and synthesizing information from various websites. They developed writing skills by responding to tasks and problem-solving skills instead of memorization skills as they learned content material. They developed higher-order thinking skills as they persuaded peers to adopt their point of view when a group consensus was required. They developed technology skills as they produced a multimodal product. WebQuest projects also helped these middle-school English learners to develop oral skills during the collaboration process. WebQuest provided that zone of proximal development necessary for optimal learning conditions (Vygotsky, 1978).

Chandler-Olcott (2009) found that when middle school students edited Wikipedia articles, not only did their editing skills become more sophisticated, but they also became motivated by the social process. When state exams require students to edit, the questions usually pertain to mechanical errors, not misinformation. However, students editing Wikipedia focused not on mechanical errors, but on factual information. Correcting factual errors encouraged students to check different sources and use key social skills so that other readers accepted their changes.

Not only does multimodal literacy develop a wide array of literacy skills in elementary and middle school students, it also helps them become active learners as they work collaboratively with peers. Throughout this text, you will learn how to use websites to develop a variety of literacy skills, including phonics, phonemic awareness, vocabulary, comprehension, fluency, writing, and spelling.

CONCLUDING THOUGHTS

This chapter has given you an opportunity to reflect on reading models; reading practices; federal, state, and local mandates; and multimodal literacies. Effective teachers constantly examine how they impact student learning, and they continuously study the effective use of technology to enhance literacy skills. Teachers must formulate and revise their own opinions regarding reading instruction, assessment, and remediation through research and working with children.

So what should you, as a teacher, do with this information? First, you must understand the era in which you are entering the teaching profession. Second, you must strive to help all students to grow in their reading ability. For example, teachers must understand how English learners acquire English in order to help them. Third, you must develop your own philosophy of teaching through study, observation, and practice. Fourth, you must be knowledgeable about learning theories and reading models so you know how to assess reading problems, match interventions to particular problems, teach all students to use reading strategies effectively, and reflect on the effectiveness of your own pedagogic practices.

Reflective Learning — DIVERSE LEARNERS

At the end of each chapter, I will present a scenario that describes a dilemma or challenge that you may encounter as a teacher. Read each scenario and answer the questions that follow it. Then, discuss the scenario and questions with classmates.

Scenario. Unlike Ms. Gaytan and Ms. Greenberg from the opening scenario, Mr. Opp is a first-year seventh-grade language arts teacher in a large urban school. He is responsible for teaching all components of language arts: reading, writing, speaking, listening, viewing, and visual representing. His class is very diverse and he is amazed at his students' wide range of reading ability: Three of his students qualify for the gifted and talented program; four students have a learning disability; one student is from Kenya and speaks Swahili; one is from Ethiopia and speaks Arabic; and three are from Mexico and speak Spanish. Mr. Opp is fluent in Spanish and is not concerned about helping those students. But how can he help the other English learners, the gifted students, and the students with learning disabilities?

QUESTIONS

1. How do you think Mr. Opp should organize his class time to provide optimal learning for all students? Why?
2. Are there any federal mandates that Mr. Opp must consider? If so, which ones?
3. Building on all you have learned in your other professional education classes, write three suggestions you could give Mr. Opp to help him organize his class time.
4. Using an academic database, find three peer-reviewed articles about teaching English learners and summarize their findings so Mr. Opp would benefit from your information.

CHAPTER TWO

THE LITERACY EVENT

The great aim of education is not knowledge but action.

HERBERT SPENCER

Scenario

Ms. Young is the principal at Rockwell Elementary, a large school with eight fourth-grade classrooms. She is pleased with all her teachers, but every time she walks past Miss Brooke's fourth-grade room, she notices a hum of student activity; neither Miss Brooke nor the students are ever sitting still. Students are reading together, designing graphic organizers together, or searching for information on the Internet together. Throughout the school year, Ms. Young becomes familiar with Miss Brooke's idea of active learning.

One day in early fall, Ms. Young notices that a number of Miss Brooke's parents have checked into the school. She finds them in the school pit, a small amphitheatre, where they are watching the students perform fairy tales with unique twists. The skits are hilarious, and the children are wearing paper plate masks. The students later tell Ms. Young that after reading *The True Story of the Three Little Pigs,* Miss Brooke invited them to write their own modern fairy tales. The students were so pleased with their fairy tales they asked Miss Brooke if they could turn them into scripts and then perform them for the parents. Miss Brooke tells Ms. Young that she had used the humorous story to engage her students in a critical literacy activity. It would be perfect, she believed, to illustrate how most stories can be told from a different perspective.

Just before Thanksgiving break, Ms. Young witnesses Miss Brooke and her students visiting Ms. Hackler's first-grade classroom. Miss Brooke says to the first graders, "Each of my students has recorded a book that they think you will enjoy, and we're here to give you the recording and a copy of each book. You may keep these books, which we found at garage sales. My students worked hard to read the books with expression and they added background music to fit the story. Each student will read the name of his or her book and place it in your listening center."

As the fourth graders introduce their books, their pride is obvious.

In January Ms. Brooke's class invites the second graders to the school pit and performs their own versions of familiar songs. They have written funny rhyming lyrics to such tunes as "London Bridge" and "On Top of Old Smokey." They teach the second graders some of the words and have them sing along.

A few weeks later Ms. Young walks past Miss Brooke's room and sees students in pairs around the computers, scanning in photos, writing poetry, recording audio, and creating slideshow presentations. Ms. Young asks a student what they are doing and he explains, "We took pictures around our neighborhoods and wrote poems and essays about them. Now we're putting them into a slideshow with sound and we're going to critique them, revise them, and share them with our pen pals in Florida. They don't know what the desert looks like." Ms. Young asks them to invite her to see the slideshow presentations.

Yet another time Ms. Young observes groups of Miss Brooke's students browsing through newspaper advertisements. Each group is planning a party and trying to find the cheapest food and party favors from the ads, add up the cost, and see which group can give the grandest party for the least amount of money. Miss Brooke will use the winning group's list to buy items for the party, which is to reward the class for reading 2,000 pages during independent reading time, both in and out of school. Miss Brooke has documented the titles of the books and the number of pages read by each student.

When Ms. Young walks past the room in the spring, she notices another buzz of excitement. All the students are dressed in white tee-shirts that look like lab coats and the room is set up like a science fair. At each desk, or "station," are materials necessary for an experiment and colorful brochures illustrating how to perform it. The students have searched the Internet and Miss Brooke's science experiment books and each has selected an experiment to be performed at his or her station. They have each designed and printed a brochure so the other visiting fourth graders can do the experiment at home. For the afternoon, Miss Brooke's students are scientists performing experiments for their visitors.

In addition to all these activities, several times throughout the year Ms. Young observes Miss Brooke's class headed to the kindergarten and first-grade classrooms—books in hand—to read to their buddies. They are always greeted with a flutter of excitement. When the state reading and writing test scores are announced at the end of the year, it is no surprise to Ms. Young that Miss Brooke's class has outscored all the other fourth grades in the district.

guiding questions

As you read this chapter, consider the following questions:

1. What practices does Miss Brooke use to motivate her students to read and write?
2. What other recommendations do you have to ensure that her students remain engaged in various activities?
3. In your opinion, what are the primary reasons Miss Brooke's students' scores were high?
4. What qualities and teaching practices make Miss Brooke an effective teacher?

INTRODUCTION

Miss Brooke is an effective teacher. She creates a learning environment that engages students in challenging activities. She welcomes their ideas and is willing to try them. She understands that learning is social and that students learn from and encourage one another; thus, she chooses projects that involve cooperation and interaction, such as the skits. She is interested in what books her students enjoy reading and is willing to read them herself. Unlike many fourth graders, her students do not experience the fourth-grade slump. They remain excited about the variety of reading and writing activities she introduces them to. They strive to be fluent readers so their reading buddies will enjoy story time each week. They know that reading involves more than trade books and textbooks; they read from many different sources—the Internet, magazines, newspapers, and song lyrics. They understand the importance of editing their writing because an audience—pen pals or other fourth graders—will be reading their projects. Reading and writing always have a purpose in Miss Brooke's classroom.

Teachers such as Miss Brooke understand how five essential components—teacher, student, text, context, and task—come together to create a meaningful learning experience. This chapter examines the role of these five components in the reading event.

TEACHERS

We all remember good and bad teachers, and most of us can list a number of qualities our good teachers possessed. The list may include descriptions such as fair, consistent, sense of humor, made learning fun, organized, knowledgeable, caring, did not waste time, and even-tempered.

Just as much has been written about effective teachers in general, much has also been written about effective literacy teachers in particular. The International Reading Association (IRA; 2000) compiled a list of six critical qualities of knowledge and practice that excellent literacy teachers possess:

1. "They understand reading and writing development, and believe all children can learn to read and write.

2. They continually assess children's individual progress and relate reading instruction to children's previous experiences.
3. They know a variety of ways to teach reading, when to use each method, and how to combine the methods into an effective instructional program.
4. They offer a variety of materials and texts for children to read.
5. They use flexible grouping strategies to tailor instruction to individual students.
6. They are good reading 'coaches' (that is, they provide help strategically)." (p. 1)

Effective literacy teachers also continuously assess students' abilities and adjust their instruction accordingly (IRA, 2000).

Allington (2002) contends that teachers are more influential in the literacy learning process than in any other curriculum or strategy. After a decade of observing exemplary elementary classroom teachers, Allington (2002) concluded that "enhanced reading proficiency rests largely on the capacity of classroom teachers to provide expert, exemplary reading instruction—instruction that cannot be packaged or regurgitated from a common script because it is responsive to children's needs" (p. 740). He reported that all effective literacy teachers exhibit similar characteristics:

1. *Time:* Students are engaged in reading or writing authentic passages; they do not spend time filling out worksheets.
2. *Text:* Students read texts they find interesting and can read successfully.
3. *Teaching:* Teachers do more than assign and assess; they spend time demonstrating and modeling strategies that will make students successful readers and writers.
4. *Talk:* Teachers foster communication skills by posing higher-level thinking questions; they encourage students to ask questions and to discuss ideas with their peers.
5. *Tasks:* Students have a choice of tasks that require them to integrate reading, writing, thinking, speaking, and listening.
6. *Testing:* Teachers grade process as well as product through the use of rubrics.

Figure 2.1 lists other common traits and activities of effective literacy teachers.

Differentiating Instruction

"Good teaching is inevitably the fine art of connecting content and kids—of doing what it takes to adapt *how* we teach so *what* we teach takes hold in the lives and minds of students" (Tomlinson & Jarvis, 2006). This type of teaching is called *differentiating instruction.*

As discussed in Chapter 1, today's classrooms are diverse; not only do teachers have English learners, but they also have students with a wide range of learning abilities and special needs (e.g., hearing impaired, emotional problems, attention deficit disorder, and gifted). Once students' learning needs have been identified through testing done by the special education teacher, effective classroom teachers prepare instruction to reach all students by modifying lessons according to individual needs. For example, for students unable to form all the letters of the alphabet, the teacher adjusts their writing center tasks by having them create one page instead of six. For students who are academically gifted, the teacher can provide a blank "I Like . . ." booklet and invite them to write as much as they want. For a student who is hearing impaired, the teacher can have him sit as close as possible during read-alouds and can stand in close proximity to the child when giving lectures and instructions.

Diverse learners prevent one lesson plan from fitting all a class's needs; thus teachers are responsible for modifying each lesson to fit a range of individual needs. Work should always be worthy of the student's effort (Darling-Hammond, 2006). Tasks should be manageable; for example, students with learning disabilities may receive shorter assignments so they can finish in the same amount of time as average students. These students also need clear directions. Because many students with learning disabilities can only process one directive at a time, teachers should break assignments into small tasks. After one task is completed, the teacher can give the second directive. By breaking up assignments, students "taste" success and become motivated to continue. Some students may need their "own" space to function optimally, and the teacher will respond by setting their desks apart from the others.

Brain research indicates that all students need "emotional safety, appropriate challenges" (Theroux, 2004, p. 1), and environments in which they can construct meaning based on their previous knowledge. Teachers who provide emotional safety teach to their students' strengths and foster positive feelings in themselves. Because no two students have exactly the same strengths and background knowledge and no two students construct meaning in the same way, teachers need to differentiate instruction. Theroux (2004) identified four ways to differentiate instruction:

1. *Content:* Through pretesting, teachers determine which students know major concepts and which do not.

figure **2.1** Traits and activities of effective literacy teachers.

EFFECTIVE TEACHERS . . .

1. Teach letter sounds using big books.
2. Model sound activities.
3. Stress the importance of writing for an audience beyond the teacher.
4. Engage in interactive writing with students.
5. Avoid published materials for handwriting practice; instead, have students copy favorite poems.
6. Use whole texts for teaching concepts, instead of worksheets.
7. Teach the parts of speech through poetry study and composition.
8. Teach specific language features in the wider context of writing activities.
9. Teach fast-paced lessons.
10. Use large blocks of time (as much as 90 minutes) for literacy activities.
11. Set time limits for tasks.
12. Model writing extensively through the use of flip charts, posters, and chalkboards.
13. Demonstrate and explain the thought process behind reading or writing.
14. Model how to write dialogue.
15. Teach students how and when to skim and scan.
16. Model expressive reading.
17. Emphasize rhyme and word patterns through the study of poems.
18. Emphasize good diction by studying authors' word choices.
19. Use a wide range of higher-level thinking questions and ask students to provide reasons for their answers.
20. Hold students responsible by requiring them to submit a report of the work they accomplish in each literacy time block.
21. Teach metacognitive strategies.
22. Understand that no single strategy works best for all students.
23. Demonstrate to students when and where to use a particular strategy.
24. Instruct students to monitor their own performance.
25. Engage and challenge all students in constructing new knowledge.
26. Make modifications in instruction and materials as needed.
27. Provide explicit instructions for use with authentic reading and writing activities.
28. Understand the uniqueness of each student.
29. Respond to and provide feedback on students' assignments while they work.

Sources: Wray, D., Medwell, J., Fox, R., & Poulson, L. (2000). The Teaching Practices of Effective Teachers of Literacy. *Educational Review 52*(1), 75–85. Schmidt, R., Rozendal, M., & Greenman, G. (2002). Reading Instruction in the Inclusion Classroom. *Remedial and Special Education 23*(3), 130–141. Rankin-Erickson, J., & Pressley, M. (2000). A Survey of Instructional Practices of Special Educational Teachers Nominated as Effective Teachers of Literacy. *Learning Disabilities Research and Practice 15*(4), 206–226.

2. *Process/activities:* Teachers vary strategies and activities based on students' varying knowledge and abilities.
3. *Product:* Because teachers provide different activities, students produce different products.
4. *Learning styles:* At the beginning of the year, teachers assess students' interests and learning styles so they can better understand the whole child and adapt the learning environment to accommodate individual needs.

As you can tell, the emphasis is never on teaching a set curriculum, but rather on providing an enriched environment that enables all students to build on their existing knowledge. In enriched environments, teachers (1) provide positive support, (2) encourage risk taking without fear of ridicule, (3) allow social interaction, (4) provide challenging but attainable tasks, (5) foster an atmosphere of experimentation and discovery, (6) give students choices, and (7) expect students to become active rather than passive learners (Theroux, 2004).

Motivation

Before reading this section, discuss the following two quotes with classmates, colleagues, and/or effective teachers: "Motivation frequently makes the difference between learning that is temporary and superficial and learning that is permanent and internalized" (Edmunds & Bauserman, 2006, p. 414); and "The failure to align school curricula with students' interests and outside-of-school competencies is thought to be behind the general erosion of engagement in reading and learning" (Brozo, 2010, p. 279). How do these statements relate to your own life? What concepts or skills have you learned that will stay with you forever? Why will you remember these concepts and skills? Conversely, what have you read recently that was difficult to comprehend? What kept you plugging away until you succeeded?

If we have a personal goal or a difficult task to accomplish, we will invest much time and energy on it because we are highly motivated. So it is with children learning to read.

Effective teachers know that students will accomplish a particular reading task if they have reason to do so or believe that they can. Children enter kindergarten and first grade eager to learn to read. Somewhere between the first and fourth grades, however, their motivation to read declines. The decreased motivation results in students reading less, and by the time students reach middle school, motivation to read independently is very low. Why do students who enter school so eager to learn lose that desire only three or four years later?

Reasons for the decline in the motivation to read

Edmunds and Bauserman's (2006) study of 831 students in grades pre-K through fifth found that the greatest decline in motivation to read comes between the first and fourth grades. They suggest three reasons for the decline:

1. *Self-consciousness about reading proficiency.* Early in first grade, some students become aware that their peers can read better than they can. They hear themselves reading slowly, stumbling over many words, and are unable to discuss what they have read. These less proficient readers hear many of their peers read fluently, discuss what they have read, and even question some of the things they have read.
2. *Emphasis on competition.* Some students lose their motivation to read because instruction emphasizes competition. Teachers may give out rewards such as paper ice cream dips on a paper ice cream cone or paper gumballs from paper gumball machines. They applaud the students with many dips of ice cream and gumballs, but provide little encouragement to those who collect fewer rewards.
3. *Lack of interest in assigned reading.* Assigned reading may not appeal to students' interests. Some students enjoy learning about snakes, volcanoes, insects, sports heroes, or fishing, and do not care for stories in which dogs, cats, and teddy bears talk.

All of these reasons result in some students not reading as much as their peers, which leads to even poorer reading skills. The following sections discuss how teachers can counteract the decline in motivation and engagement.

Self-consciousness about reading proficiency. Students are aware when they lack skills their classmates possess. In sports, if children lack hand–eye coordination and struggle to hit a baseball, they will find reasons not to play with their peers. So it is with reading. Those who know their reading is not fluent or who pronounce words incorrectly will become self-conscious and shy away from reading in front of peers. Eventually, the reading experience will no longer be enjoyable and they will lose their motivation. To prevent this dilemma, make sure all students are reading texts that are not too difficult for them, especially when reading in front of others. Additionally, avoid having children read in front of the whole class too frequently. Divide students into groups of two or three, and tailor your teaching strategy to the needs of the group in order to increase their reading proficiency.

To build confidence in students' reading ability, initiate choral reading in somewhat larger groups (five to six students) so struggling readers become part of a successful reading experience. Readers theater, in which the struggling reader practices his line repeatedly before performing in front of classmates, is another technique. See Chapter 10 for more information on both activities.

A third way to build reading confidence is through buddy reading. For example, an eighth-grade teacher can partner with a fourth-grade teacher, having the older students buddy read with younger students. In buddy reading, the older student selects a book on the younger student's reading level and practices it so he can read it fluently to his buddy. The older student has a reason to practice an easy book, and this builds self-esteem. Chapter 13 includes more details about setting up a successful book buddies reading program.

Emphasis on competition. Competition is the second reason for declining motivation to read. Instead of extrinsic rewards that emphasize competition in the elementary classrooms, teachers might consider creating one large paper ice cream cone or one huge paper gumball machine on the bulletin board for the entire class. Any student who completes a book and has shared it with a classmate can add a dip of ice cream or a gumball to the chart. There is still a reward, but the whole class benefits.

Lack of interest in assigned reading. Lack of interest in required texts is the third reason for declining motivation to read. If students are given more choice of texts early in their reading experiences, will they stay interested in books? Yes, say those experienced with struggling readers. If students are given texts that expand their knowledge on topics that interest them, they will enjoy reading even if the text is somewhat difficult (Allington, 2006). A student interested in snakes, for example, who is provided with a text on her reading level about different types of snakes, their habitats, and eating habits and then encouraged to share her newfound knowledge with classmates may desire to read more books about snakes. A student who loves humorous stories or scary stories can select texts on his reading level from those genres, and will likely stick with reading longer than if he is required to read stories that are neither humorous nor scary. If students find stories interesting, they will want to share them with classmates. All children feel good when they can enlighten or entertain their classmates.

Edmunds and Bauserman (2006) found that fourth graders are interested in reading narrative text if stories relate to their interests; if the book's cover is exciting or enticing; if they like the story's genre, such as humor or adventure; and if they can select the book. The study also revealed that students become interested in expository text if they learn information they can share with others, if they choose the book, and if they are interested in the topic.

The researchers asked students who were motivated to read how they find good books. Most say they find them in the school library, their teacher recommends them, they find them in the classroom library, or their parents or peers recommend or give them the titles (Edmunds & Bauserman, 2006).

Teaching recommendations to increase motivation

Research shows that students become engaged when they are interested in a concept or activity and that engaged students perform better academically (Guthrie & Humenick, 2004; Brozo & Flynt, 2008; Partin & Hendricks, 2002; Patterson, Schaller, & Clemens, 2008). Disengagement, on the other hand, is the root of many students' learning problems (Edmunds & Bauserman, 2006). Disengaged readers are easily distracted and often unaware of what is going on. Teachers will often find disengaged students fake reading, getting out of their seats, daydreaming, flipping pages without reading, distracting others, wasting time finding a book, or constantly switching books (Kelley & Clausen-Grace, 2009). To prevent disengagement, Brozo and Flynt (2008) propose six evidence-based principles that motivate students to read in the classroom.

1. Inspiring academic self-efficacy: Students are confident they can complete a task that is meaningful to them; thus they produce acceptable projects they are excited to share with peers.
2. Engendering interest in new learning: Students' interest is aroused about the new topic by using multiple forms and sources of literacy (e.g., printed text, Internet, videos, film).
3. Connecting outside with inside school literacies: Teachers connect school literacy activities to students' everyday lives.
4. Providing an abundance of interesting texts: Teachers use materials from students' everyday lives (e.g., newspapers, magazines, brochures, advertisement flyers) and provide a wide range of books.
5. Expanding choices and options: Teachers permit students to produce projects that are more than written text (e.g., videos, drawing, oral presentations, monologues).
6. Structuring collaboration for motivation: Students, peers, and the teacher have plenty of opportunities to collaborate.

Edmunds and Bauserman (2006) offer the additional recommendations listed in Figure 2.2, which can be implemented in all elementary and middle school classrooms.

figure 2.2 Recommendations to motivate student reading.

1. Let students select their books from a large collection of books that are on their reading level.
2. Give all students ample time for silent independent reading, even struggling students.
3. Create a three-piece kit for each student, stored in a large, resealable plastic bag. Each kit should contain an expository text, a narrative text, and a poem on a topic that interests the student.
4. Suggest particular texts, both narrative and expository, that interest the student.
5. Permit students to visit the school library after completing their work. Let the librarian know that when your student is wearing a tag that says "I completed my work and I am here to find another GREAT book!" he will know you expect the student to quietly and independently find a text and check it out.
6. With the librarian's permission, provide one afternoon a month for parents and students to use the library to browse and read.
7. Read aloud every day to students. Make sure your selections include expository text on topics that will interest students and narrative books of various genres. Read both humorous and serious poems.
8. Have a large selection of texts, both expository and narrative, on a wide range of topics and reading levels in the classroom library. Consistently refresh the collection with titles from the public library.
9. Construct a bulletin board display titled "Books We Recommend as an Excellent Read!" near the classroom library where students can post the name of the book, the author's name, and one or two brief comments about the book's content. For example, one student may write, "This books gives details about the differences between poisonous and non-poisonous snakes." Another may write, "This book is a funny story about some rabbits that outwitted a lazy bear."

Guthrie and Davis (2003) offer additional ideas that work particularly well in motivating middle school students. Figure 2.3 lists these characteristics; notice that some are identical to the motivators of elementary students.

Research shows that (1) students who are motivated to read will read more (Wigfield & Guthrie, 1997); (2) when students spend more time reading, their reading ability increases (Mazzoni, Gambrell, & Korkeamaki, 1999); and (3) good readers become lifelong readers (Wang & Guthrie, 2004).

Those who work with children know that motivation and self-interest make any task easier and more enjoyable. So it is with reading. Students with a reason for reading a text and who have a choice in what they read are more apt to read. Ultimately, the more they read, the better readers they become.

STUDENTS

Figure 2.1 listed "Understand the uniqueness of each student" as the final trait. Uniqueness is what makes teaching so enjoyable and challenging. As stated earlier, the National Center for Education Statistics (2010) reported that the average national reading score for fourth graders was higher in 2009 than in 2007. While 33 percent scored below the basic reading level, 67 percent were at or above basic

figure 2.3 Motivators for middle school students.

1. Students pose their own questions on a topic and read to answer those questions. In science, this may involve reading about how to set up an experiment and then performing it with others or in front of their peers. In social studies, it may include reading about a particular time period or person in history and reenacting the era or presenting a monologue of the character.
2. Teachers provide many trade books about the topic being studied in any subject, and the trade books cover a wide range of reading levels.
3. Students choose the text they want to use and how they will present what they learn. They even get to construct the rubric used to grade their work.
4. Teachers introduce strategies for comprehending certain texts and then model how to use those strategies. Next, students practice the strategy while the teacher supervises.
5. Students form groups to work on a project. Each member selects an aspect of the project to complete. Students are free to help each other so the project is exemplary. All students receive credit for the final project.

level, and 33 percent were at or above the proficient level. Likewise, the national average reading score for eighth graders was higher in 2009 than in 2007; although 25 percent were at or below basic level, 75 percent were at or above basic level, and only 32 percent were at or above proficient level. At both grade levels, the African-American and Hispanic populations trailed behind the white population.

Despite the variation indicated in these scores, the Individuals with Disabilities Education Act (IDEA) states that regular classrooms are the most appropriate placement for all students, even those with disabilities. Thus, each classroom is home to students with a wide range of differences, and prudent teachers learn as much as possible about all of them. Students differ in (1) their background knowledge of subjects and in how they integrate new information; (2) their literacy knowledge; (3) the language systems they use; (4) their learning styles; and (5) their types of intelligences.

Knowledge of General Information

Some students enter school with a wide array of experiences beyond their families and communities. They may have visited zoos, museums, fire stations, mountains, oceans, rural areas, or cities and discussed these experiences with their parents and other adults. These students have a rich aural and oral vocabulary, which enhances their literacy skills. Research demonstrates that all students, both native language learners and English learners, have prior knowledge that aids them as they construct meaning through literacy activities (Carrell, 2010; Shaughnessy, 2010). Other students lack a variety of experiences and, as a result, have limited vocabulary and background knowledge related to many topics studied in school. Effective teachers will either activate or provide background knowledge, depending on the needs of individual students. They also understand that some students may rely too much on background knowledge when they read. Teachers need to help all students learn how to synthesize new information with prior knowledge.

Literacy Knowledge

This section requires an understanding of three terms—skills, strategies, and metacognition. **Skills** refer to one's ability to perform a task. **Strategies** are the plans or methods used to accomplish a task. **Metacognition** is the ability to explain what and how one knows. For example, professional golfers have the skills to drive a ball straight down the fairway, chip a ball onto the green, and putt a ball into the cup. In addition, they have strategies for performing each step—a specific stance depending on the position of the hole; a type of swing based on the number of yards to the pin; and a particular chip depending on the slope and conditions of the green. Despite how golfers were taught these strategies, they practiced different methods to decide which ones worked for them. Metacognition refers to the thought process a golfer uses as he decides which swing, chip, and putt to use and his explanation for why he chose them. The same three capacities apply to readers.

Literacy skills

Students' background with text greatly affects their literacy development. Some students enter kindergarten with rich language backgrounds and advanced literacy skills because their parents or others have read and discussed stories and informational texts with them. These children understand the conceptual organization of written material in English. They know that text is read from top to bottom and left to right. They know where a book begins and ends and the difference between letters and words. They know that some books convey good stories and other texts provide information about the world. Many of these students enter kindergarten knowing letter names and how to form them.

Other students may not have these skills because they have had limited reading experiences with adults. They do not understand narrative forms or that one reads top to bottom and left to right. They have little knowledge of letters and words, and they have a limited vocabulary. Students with these different skill levels are a challenge to teachers when they are in the same class. Those with limited literacy experience need guidance to become skilled readers. The teacher's responsibility is to understand the strengths and weaknesses of each reader's literacy skills.

Reading strategies

Teaching reading strategies explicitly helps students become more proficient when they read by themselves. The three types of reading strategies are (1) strategies to use *before* reading, which activate their prior knowledge; (2) strategies to use *while* reading, which improve their comprehension and skills; and (3) strategies to use *after* reading, which help them analyze and remember what they read (Walker, 2004). Effective teachers equip students with strategies for all three parts of a reading event. These strategies will be discussed in Chapters 8 and 9.

When teaching a strategy, be explicit in explaining its process, model it, and then supervise while the students practice it. For example, students need to know what to do when they encounter an unfamiliar word. You might instruct them to do the following:

1. Skip the word and read to the end of the sentence.
2. Look at the picture for clues.
3. Think of a word that would make sense in context.
4. Check to see if the letters of that word correspond to those of the word in the passage.
5. If the letters do not correspond, think of a different word that fits the context.

For example, in the book *The Wobbly Tooth* from the Oxford Reading Tree series, the teacher comes to the word *humungous*. She models the strategy above by first skipping over the word and reading to the end of the sentence. Then she says, "The picture looks like the girl has a *big* smile," and asks, "Would *big* make sense here?" As she reads the sentence with the word *big*, she agrees with the students that big makes sense; however, big begins with a *b* and the word in the book begins with an *h*. She asks, "What word means big, but begins with an *h*? Do any of you know of a word?" One student exclaims, "Humungous! My brother always says he wants a humungous hamburger!" The teacher then checks to see if the letter and sounds correspond by spelling out *humungous* on the whiteboard and comparing it to the word in the text. "Yes," she says, "the word is *humungous*." She then continues reading.

The teacher guides them as they practice this strategy the next few times they encounter an unfamiliar word. The goal is for the students to use the strategy automatically when they read by themselves.

Teaching appropriate strategies is demanding for teachers because they must constantly assess students as they read, demonstrate the appropriate steps, and teach students how and when to use them. They can teach reading strategies to large groups, small groups, or to individuals. Effective teachers teach reading strategies when the students need them, in the context of authentic reading or writing activities (Allington, 2002; Fountas & Pinnell, 2006b; Rankin-Erickson & Pressley, 2000; Schmidt, Rozendal, & Greenman, 2002; Stahl & Kuhn, 1995; Weaver, 1994).

Metacognition

Poor readers lack metacognitive strategies. Metacognition involves a person's awareness of his or her own thinking and the conscious effort to monitor this awareness. Effective teachers not only teach appropriate reading strategies, but also teach metacognitive techniques that help students decide how and when to employ such strategies (Schmidt et al., 2002).

One way to enhance students' metacognition is for a teacher to use a "think-aloud" to demonstrate her metacognitive process as she monitors her own reading. For example, when reading a passage on Abraham Lincoln, she might comment, "It says here that Abe Lincoln had very little schooling by the time he was 16. That doesn't seem right. It seems like he should have had more by that age in order to be president. I need to reread to see how old Lincoln was when he began school in order to confirm this fact." The teacher then invites the students to read with similar awareness; when they encounter a puzzling fact, she asks them questions to guide them through the process. Eventually, students will use metacognitive strategies independently to monitor their reading processes and comprehension.

Language Systems Readers Use

Readers use four cueing systems—syntactic, semantic, graphophonic, and pragmatic—as they make sense of written text. **Syntax** refers to the grammar of sentences: Does it sound right? In English most words in sentences must appear in a particular order. "Mary had a little lamb" is acceptable, but "Had little a lamb Mary" is not. Very young children learn the accepted syntax when they begin to talk. **Semantic** refers to the meaning of words and sentences: Does it make sense? For example, a writer conveys two very different ideas with the following two sentences: "I went to visit England" and "I went to conquer England." A change of one word results in two drastically different sentences. The third cueing system, **graphophonic**, refers to letter–sound relationships: Does it look right? When students do not produce the correct vowel sounds, they can easily mix up words (e.g., *dig* becomes *dog*, *cut* becomes *cat*, and *bag* becomes *big*). Obviously, students who misread *dog* for *dig* will misunderstand the meaning of the sentence. The fourth cueing system, **pragmatic**, refers to the situational context of the passage; it reflects the social and cultural aspects of language. Teachers support the use of this cueing system by showing how different forms of language are appropriate in different situations. Some texts, such as e-mails to friends, are less formal than business letters, for example, and different forms of language are appropriate for each.

Understand which language systems your students use when they read (Clay, 1993c; Fountas & Pinnell, 2006b; Walker, 2004). Some students use syntax clues to figure out unknown words. Syntax involves the study of grammar—the rules by which sentences are formed and ordered. Students who use syntactic clues recognize when a sentence does not "sound" right based on their knowledge of the common sentence patterns in English. Other readers use context clues; they recognize from the surrounding words, phrases, sentences, or paragraphs that a sentence does not make sense. Still other students use visual clues; they recognize the difference between *frog* and *toad* because frog begins with an /f/ sound, while toad begins with a /t/ sound. Once teachers understand which clues students use, they can demonstrate how to use the other clues. Proficient readers can explain what language systems and strategies they use when the reading process breaks down.

Learning Styles

Effective teachers determine all they can about students' learning preferences, not so they can label them, but so they can provide the environment most conducive to their learning style (Hall, 2006).

Two opposing learning styles that frequently affect reading instruction are the *analytical* and the *global* style of learning (Carbo, 1996b). Analytical readers are auditory learners and process information in logical, sequential steps. Because phonics programs are logical and sequential, analytical readers often learn to read best when first presented with phonics and then proceed to whole text with decodable words. Global processing is accomplished when students are first presented with an overview of the information and then taught to analyze the parts. Global readers tend to learn best if they first read the text and then learn skills in the context of the passage (Carbo, 1996c). Poor readers usually have an approach that is more global than analytical (Carbo, 1996b). Remember that both analytical and global readers need to read whole text and require explicit phonics and word study (Stahl & Kuhn, 1995). They just need them presented in a different order. For this reason, homogeneous groupings of students with similar learning styles may enhance instruction.

Multiple Intelligences

Howard Gardner's theory of multiple intelligences (1983, 1993) is relevant to teaching literacy skills. Gardner's multiple intelligences theory states that all humans possess nine different intelligences; however, one (or more) tends to be dominant in each person. Figure 2.4 lists the nine intelligences with a brief description of each.

For example, Joey, a third grader with musical ability, stays on task when background music is played. When he is asked to retell a story, he likes to make up a jingle about the plot. Juan, another boy in the same class, learns best when manipulating objects and has the ability to create intricate models. When Juan is asked to retell a story, he likes to retell it by creating a diorama. The more teachers know about their students' unique intelligences, talents, abilities, and learning styles, the better they can cater lessons and learning environments to fit the students' needs.

figure 2.4

Howard Gardner's multiple intelligences.

1. Linguistic: Ability to use and manipulate languages.
2. Logical–Mathematical: Ability to understand causes and effects, to calculate easily, and to think abstractly.
3. Spatial: Ability to represent the spatial world in one's mind.
4. Kinesthetic: Ability to use one's body.
5. Musical: Ability to hear rhythms and melodies.
6. Intrapersonal: Ability to understand oneself.
7. Interpersonal: Ability to interact with and understand others.
8. Naturalistic: Ability to discriminate among the parts of nature.
9. Existential: Ability to understand philosophies and theories.

Gardner did not initially develop the multiple intelligences theory for education, but many educators have written curricula based on the theory. Keep in mind, however, that teachers teach children, not curricula. Therefore, the theory of multiple intelligences is helpful inasmuch as it assists teachers in understanding the differences among learners. For example, students with a dominant musical intelligence, such as Joey, may be able to clap syllables while singing a song. Students with a dominant spatial intelligence may be able to relate concepts from informational text by creating drawings and graphs. Students with a dominant interpersonal intelligence may be able to provide effective organization for group activities, such as skits and readers theater, because they know how to motivate others to work as a group.

Figure 2.5 illustrates Armstrong's (2000) concise overview of eight of the nine intelligences to indicate how students with each dominant intelligence think, what they like to do, and what they need. Remember that Gardner believes that *all* intelligences must be developed; therefore, begin with the student's natural strength and gradually encourage him or her to develop other areas.

To determine your own dominant intelligence, take the multiple intelligences inventory online (www.ldrc.ca/projects/miinventory/mitest.html).

figure **2.5** Summary of the eight ways of teaching.

INTELLIGENCE	TEACHING ACTIVITIES (EXAMPLES)	TEACHING MATERIALS (EXAMPLES)	INSTRUCTIONAL STRATEGIES
Linguistic	lectures, discussions, word games, storytelling, choral reading, journal writing	books, audio recorders, stamp sets, audio books	read about it, write about it, talk about it, listen to it
Logical–Mathematical	brain teasers, problem solving, science experiments, mental calculation, number games, critical thinking	calculators, math manipulatives, science equipment, math games	quantify it, think critically about it, put it in a logical framework, experiment with it
Spatial	visual presentations, art activities, imagination games, mind-mapping, metaphor, visualization	graphs, maps, video, LEGO sets, art materials, optical illusions, cameras, picture library	see it, draw it, visualize it, color it, mind-map it
Bodily–Kinesthetic	hands-on learning, drama, dance, sports that teach, tactile activities, relaxation exercises	building tools, clay, sports equipment, manipulatives, tactile learning resources	build it, act it out, touch it, get a "gut feeling" of it, dance it
Musical	rhythmic learnings, rapping, using songs that teach	audio recorder, audio collection, musical instruments	sing it, rap it, listen to it
Interpersonal	cooperative learning, peer tutoring, community involvement, social gatherings, simulations	board games, party supplies, props for role plays	teach it, collaborate on it, interact with respect to it
Intrapersonal	individualized instruction, independent study, options in course of study, self-esteem building	self-checking materials, journals, materials for projects	connect it to your personal life, make choices with regard to it, reflect on it
Naturalistic	nature study, ecological awareness, care of animals	plants, animals, naturalists' tools (e.g., binoculars), gardening tools	connect it to living things and natural phenomena

Source: *Multiple Intelligences in the Classroom*, 2nd ed. (pp. 4–6), by Thomas Armstrong, Alexandria, VA: ASCD. ©2000 by ASCD. Reprinted with permission. Learn more about ASCD at www.ascd.org.

Your dominant intelligence is the one or two in which you placed the most checks.

Armstrong (2000) created a checklist for teachers to use to assess their students' multiple intelligences. Use this checklist as you observe the student in the classroom as he interacts in big group, in small group, and in independent work. See Appendix C.1.

TEXT

The third element of the reading event is the text. Effective teachers know that giving students texts that are too difficult or too easy causes frustration for all types of readers. Teachers need to find texts that are suitable for students to read by themselves and some challenge texts that they can read with the help of the teacher's instruction. This next section discusses the three different reading levels and how texts are leveled so teachers can aid students as they choose books.

Levels of Readability

Readability levels are based on the percentage of words students read correctly. Educators consider three different levels: independent, instructional, and frustration.

- *Independent reading level.* When reading independently, a student reads this passage with 95 to 100 percent accuracy. This means that in a passage of 100 words, the reader makes 5 or fewer errors and has a comprehension level of

90 percent or better. The student can read these passages at an appropriate rate, with correct phrasing and expression that conveys the meaning of the passage.

- *Instructional reading level.* When reading at an instructional level, a student reads this passage with 90 to 94 percent accuracy and with a comprehension level of 60 percent or better. Thus, in a 100-word passage the reader makes no more than 10 errors. At the instructional level, the reader can comprehend most of the unknown words quickly and accurately.
- *Frustration reading level.* At this level, a student reads the passage with less than 90 percent accuracy and a comprehension level of 50 percent or less. This means that in a 100-word passage, he makes more than 10 errors. If the passage is at his frustration level, he cannot comprehend unknown words quickly. His pace is slow and he reads words instead of phrases.

Selecting Appropriate Texts

When reading independently, students should work with texts they can read easily and successfully. To become proficient independent readers, they must spend substantial time reading books successfully. Children become motivated to read when they read easy material that interests them (Allington, 2006; Carbo, 1997; Clay, 1993c; Fountas & Pinnell, 2006b). When working with a teacher or other adult, however, students need to be challenged with a text at their instructional reading level, which means that the text offers a minimum of new words and concepts (Fountas & Pinnell, 2006b). Frustration-level texts are discouraging to children as well as adults.

Effective teachers give students a wide variety of reading materials. They expose students to historical fiction, biography, mysteries, folklore, science fiction, and poetry. They also use materials other than books, such as magazines and the Internet. All of these materials need to be at the student's easy reading level for independent reading and at instructional level when students are working with teachers or paraprofessionals (Allington, Johnston, & Day, 2002).

Follow these criteria for selecting both easy and instructional reading texts for your students:

1. Select texts that bring students enjoyment and meaning.
2. Choose those that are interesting for the particular readers.
3. Be certain they present accurate information.
4. Choose texts with accurate and diverse multicultural representations.
5. Use texts from a range of genres (e.g., poetry, stories, drama, and nonfiction exposition).
6. Use many texts at each reading level.
7. Choose texts with high-quality illustrations.
8. Choose texts with complementary texts and illustrations.
9. Select texts of a length appropriate for the desired reading level.
10. Use instructional reading–level texts that are challenging, but not discouraging.
11. Include easy reading–level books to build fluency.
12. Use easy reading–level texts to allow readers to build comprehension rather than focusing on deciphering words.

Leveled books

Over the last two decades, a number of different techniques to level books have emerged. These may be confusing to caregivers and teachers who are unfamiliar with the system assigned to a given book.

Age leveling. The publisher assigns an intended age for which the book was written and lists it on the cover. The age levels often refer to the interest level of the story or the amount and depth of information given. Many books for infants and toddlers have designated age levels.

Grade leveling. Another way publishers level books is according to grade. The formulas used to calculate grade levels are based on sentence length and the number of syllables in a sentence.

The Accelerated Reader program, used in many schools in the United States, classifies books according to grade level. Renaissance Learning, which levels books and quizzes for the Accelerated Reader program, assigns levels to thousands of books. Teachers can readily find a book's grade level by visiting their website (www.renlearn.com). Once at the website, click on "Order Quizzes" and then "Reading." Type in the book's title, and the grade level will appear. Titles used by more than one author (e.g., *The Mitten*) will give the reading level for each. Figure 2.6 lists websites for locating books for particular grade levels.

Two problems exist with this type of leveling. First, sentences can be short with single-syllable words, but the syntax may be awkward and difficult for students to comprehend. For example: "With his hat, map, pen, and pouch in hand, leaped the man."

Second, not all children read at grade level; therefore, teachers cannot assume students in the first grade will be able to read and comprehend first-grade books.

figure 2.6 Websites for locating books for given grade levels.

1. Questar Assessment (www.questari.com) offers computer software for over 12,500 textbooks and trade books, rated by difficulty.
2. Scholastic Reading Counts (www.readingcounts.com) offers access to 25,000 titles, rated by difficulty.
3. Advantage Learning Systems (www.renlearn.com) offers access to 22,000 trade book titles. This is the Accelerated Reader website. Accelerated Reader is a program that levels books by grade level and provides quizzes for students to take on the computer. The computer program administers the grades and quizzes and determines the "points" students earn. Points are based on students' grade level, the number of correct answers on the quiz, and the level of the book.

Lexile leveling. The Lexile scale, which ranges from 200L to 1700L, became popular in the 1990s. This leveling system does not consider the subject matter or content of the text; it is based solely on word frequency and sentence length. Because of this, teachers need to be aware that some books and magazines at students' Lexile level may not be appropriate subject material.

The purpose of the Lexile framework is to measure students' reading (Lexile) level and then match them to appropriate reading materials. Lexile level is determined through the Scholastic Reading Inventory (SRI). Other tests (Iowa Tests of Basic Skills, SAT-10, SAT-9, SDRT-4) and some norm-referenced tests (North California End-of-Grade Tests and Texas Assessment of Knowledge and Skills) also provide the Lexile level. Teachers can readily find the Lexile level of a book by entering the title at www.lexile.com.

Gradient leveling. A fourth way books are leveled is called gradient leveling. Some publishers (The Wright Group, Rigby, and Sundance) publish books with fine gradient texts for teachers to use for instruction purposes. Gradient-leveled books differ from grade-leveled books in that gradient-leveled books have a minute shift in difficulty between the levels. The following criteria determine the level:

1. Length and number of words in the book.
2. Size and layout of the print. First levels have a larger print size with the text on the same part of each page.
3. Vocabulary and concepts. First levels begin with vocabulary and concepts found in children's oral language.
4. Language structure. First levels can begin with a single word or simple phrases and continue to simple sentences.
5. Text structure and genre. First levels have a single incident or concept.
6. Predictability and pattern of language. First levels follow a single linguistic pattern.
7. Illustration support. The illustrations in the first levels thoroughly support the text.

Reading Recovery (see Chapter 13), a tutoring intervention program for first graders used in more than 6,000 U.S. school districts, and guided reading, a small group classroom based instructional strategy (see Chapter 6), use gradient or "leveled" books.

Reading Recovery books have a finer gradient than the books used for guided reading. Reading Recovery uses numbers and guided reading, based on Fountas and Pinnell's (2006a) scale, and uses the alphabet for leveling purposes. Figure 2.7 com-

figure 2.7

Comparison of three book-leveling systems.

GRADE LEVEL	LEXILE	READING RECOVERY	FOUNTAS & PINNELL
K	N/A	1,2	A,B
Preprimer	N/A	3–8	C–E
Primer	N/A	9,10	E
Primer	200–299	11,12	F
First	200–299	13,16	G–I
Second	300–399	17–20	H–K
Second	400–499	24–28	K–M
Third	500–599	29–30	K–N
Third	600–699	30–38	L–P
Fourth	700–799	40	Q–T
Fifth	800–899	44	R–W
Sixth	900–999	X	S–X
Seventh/Eighth	1000–1100	X	T–Z

Sources: Fountas, I. C., & Pinnell, G. S. (2006). *Leveled Books K–8: Matching Texts to Readers for Effective Teaching.* Portsmouth, NH: Heinemann; Thomas Jefferson Elementary. (2004). *About Reading Levels.* Falls Church, VA.

pares the Lexile, Reading Recovery, and Fountas and Pinnell's leveling systems. This chart allows teachers who use Lexile, Reading Recovery, or Fountas and Pinnell's scales to see how they relate to grade levels.

Fountas and Pinnell's (2006a) guided reading books are leveled from A to Z. The following discussion gives brief examples of several levels, but more in-depth descriptions can be found in the Fountas and Pinnell text *Guided Reading: Good First Teaching for All Children* (2006b).

Level A books are short and simple and demonstrate a "direct correspondence between the text and the pictures" (p. 117). Pages contain one to four lines of text on a page, and the words are spaced far enough apart so students can point to them as they read. Level F books feature varied placement of the text; proportionately smaller text; and the stories have plots with a beginning, a middle, and an end. Level J signifies short chapter books that still include pictures but offer a wider range of literacy language. Level L books represent a significant shift in reading material, including chapter books with few illustrations, more complex characterization, and more involved plots. Word spacing is narrower in Level L books, which presents a challenge to many students. Fountas and Pinnell name *Cam Jansen and the Mystery of the Monster Movie* by David Adler as a Level L book. Level P books, such as Jean Fritz's *George Washington's Breakfast* and Eloise Greenfield's *Rosa Parks,* are longer chapter books that take more than one sitting to complete, requiring readers to recall information from the previous sitting. Levels Q through Z offer challenging vocabulary and still more complex plots and characterization. Readers need to use many strategies to comprehend the text. As an example of a Level Q book, Fountas and Pinnell (2006a) cite Dick King-Smith's *Babe the Gallant Pig,* and as a Level Z book, *The Hobbit* by J.R.R. Tolkien.

Each of the following publications includes an extended list of books from many publishers:

- Fountas, I. C., & Pinnell, G. S. (2000). *Guided Reading: Good first teaching for all children.* Portsmouth, NH: Heinemann.
- Fountas, I. C., & Pinnell, G. S. (2009). *The Fountas and Pinnell leveled book list, K–8+* (2010–2012 ed.). Portsmouth, NH: Heinemann.
- Schulman, M. B., & Payne, C. D. (2000). *Guided Reading: Making it work.* New York: Scholastic.

All books are categorized according to guided reading levels. Figure 2.8 lists publishers of leveled books used in reading recovery and guided reading.

figure **2.8**

Publishers of leveled books.

Celebration Press, www.celebrationpress.com

Creative Teaching Press, www.creativeteaching.com

Houghton Mifflin, www.eduplace.com

Newbridge Educational Publishing, www.newbridgeonline.com

Rigby, www.rigby.com

Sadlier-Oxford, www.sadlier-oxford.com

Scott Foresman, http://books.atozteacherstuff.com/leveled-books

Sundance, www.sundancepub.com

McGraw-Hill, www.mheonline.com

Readability tests

Occasionally you may not have the reading level information for a book. In such cases, readability formulas (e.g., Dale-Chall, Flesch, Spache, and Fry) can be used to determine the grade level of a trade or textbook. The extended readability graph developed by Edward Fry (2002) is easy to use on texts over 100 words and is intended for grades 1 to 17.

The Fry Readability formula gives teachers an estimate (plus or minus one year) of the readability of the text. All readability formulas yield a mere approximation of the book's grade level, but this is better than no information (Allington, 2006). Many textbooks intended for a particular grade are often written at a higher grade level, and it is helpful for teachers to recognize when a textbook is too difficult for most students to read independently. Figure 2.9 includes a sample passage, the Fry Readability graph, and directions for estimating the reading level of a text. The best way to understand how the formula works is to choose an elementary science or social studies textbook and a trade book with narrative text, and then calculate the reading level of each using the Fry Readability formula.

Readability software programs are also available. Reading Calculations, available for both PC and Mac computers, includes nine readability formulas, including Fry. With this program, teachers can type the passage into a text file or merely cut-and-paste it. The computer then calculates the reading level of the passage.

figure 2.9 Applying the Fry Readability formula.

DIRECTIONS

1. Randomly select three 100-word passages from a book or an article. The three passages should be from the beginning, middle, and end of the book.
2. Count the number of syllables in each passage and find the average number of syllables of the three passages. For example, the sample passage below has 145 syllables.
3. Count the number of sentences, estimating length of the fraction of the last sentence to the nearest one-tenth. For example, the sample passage has eight complete sentences. The 100th word of the passage is the 6th word of the 9th sentence, which is not the end of the sentence. To find the fraction of the last sentence in the passage, divide the number of words in the 9th sentence through the 100th word (6) by the number of words in the entire sentence (16) and round to the nearest tenth (6/16 = .375 or .4). The total number of sentences for this passage would be 8.4 sentences.

   After finding the number of sentences in each 100-word passage, find the average number for the three passages.
4. On the Fry Readability Graph, plot the average number of syllables and the average number of sentences for the three passages to get the estimated reading level of the book.

SAMPLE PASSAGE

(Sample Passage from Boyle, D. [1998]. *Coral reef hideaway: The story of a clown anemonefish.* New York: Scholastic.)

3 1 1 1 1 1 1 1 1 1 1 2 1 1 1

Percula's mate cleans the rock. If they get the chance, some wrasses will eat the

5 1 1 1 1 1 2 2 1 1 1 1 3

anemonefish eggs when they are laid. Before twilight the rock is clean. Percula's

1 1 1 1 4 1 1 2 1 1 1 1 1

mate rests near the anemone mouth as darkness falls. Now sharks, jacks and

4 1 2 1 3 1 2 1 1 1 1 3

barracudas swarm around the shadowy reef, snapping up blue tangs and parrotfish

1 1 1 1 1 1 1 2 2 3 1 1 1 1 1

that have stayed too long in their daytime waters. Percula and her mate are safe

1 1 4 1 1 2 1 1 2 2 1 2 1 1 1

in the anemone. As the nearly full moon rises over the lagoon, the reef's night

2 1 1 2 1 3 1 1 2 2 1

creatures emerge. Like thousands of miniature stars, the coral itself blooms.

3 1 3 1 1 2

Squirrelfish and soldierfish leave the sheltered (100th word) crevices and hunt

along the bottom for worms and crabs.

NOTE:

1. Scores falling in the gray areas of the graph are invalid. If this occurs, another sample must be taken.
2. A word is defined as a group of symbols with a space on either side. Acronyms (IRA), dates (2004), initials (J.), titles (Jr.), and symbols (&) each count as one word.
3. With numerals, acronyms, initials, titles, and symbols, each symbol within them is one syllable. For example, 2004 = 4 syllables; IRA = 3 syllables; J. = 1 syllable.

figure **2.9** Continued.

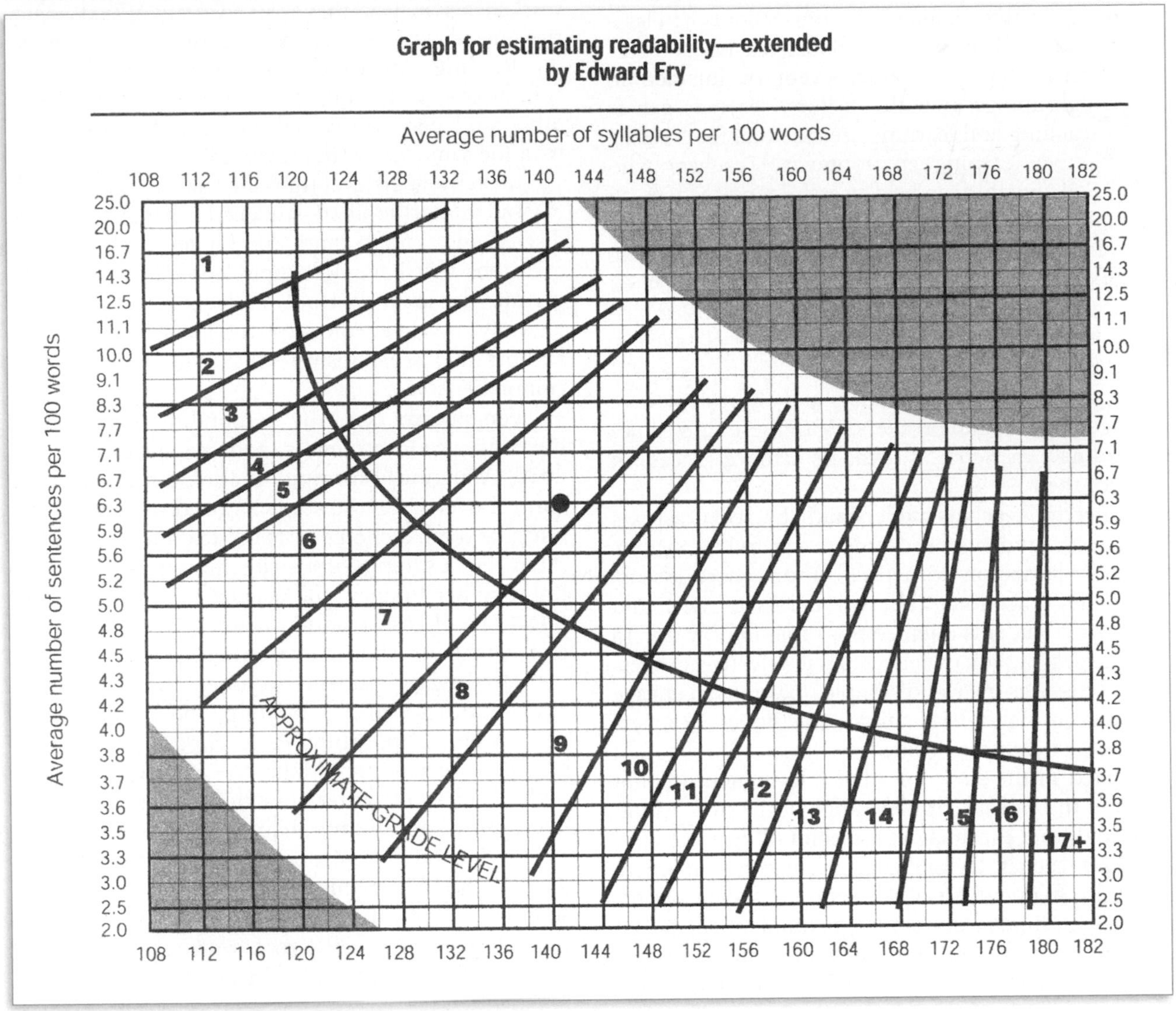

EXAMPLE:

The readability level indicated on the graph above is based on three samples with the following syllable and word counts:

	Syllables	Sentences
First hundred words	124	6.6
Second hundred words	141	5.5
Third hundred words	158	6.8
Average	141	6.3

Readability seventh grade (see dot plotted on graph)

Source: Fry, E. B. (2002). Readability Versus Leveling. *The Reading Teacher, 56*(3), 286–291.

CONTEXT

The context of the reading event is the climate of the classroom. Consider the scenario at the beginning of this chapter and think about the classroom context. The context includes teacher and student beliefs, type of literary event or interaction, student groupings, and other factors. Teachers' beliefs about teaching and learning are essential for creating an effective learning environment. Teachers who believe all students can be successful tend to focus on students' strengths instead of their weaknesses. They provide unison reading for all students so struggling readers can be a part of fluent reading experiences. They permit students to practice short poems or passages before they read in front of their classmates. They effectively use readers theater, giving long, difficult passages to fluent readers and short, repetitive passages to struggling readers. With these three types of reading experience, all readers achieve success in front of their peers.

Effective teachers understand the social aspects of literacy. Students need time to expand their ideas through discussion with peers. From those discussions they encounter different points of view and new ideas. Students often connect that information to some aspect of their own lives. Thus, effective teachers use discussions instead of simple questions to engage students in higher-level thinking activities. Teachers may ask students to consider whose voice was not presented in the story, or what information was not given in the passage, or how different the story would be if told from the antagonist's point of view.

As a teacher, try to create an environment where there are frequent, sustained, and consistent opportunities for literary discussion (Schmidt et al., 2002). Use an array of class groupings, including homogeneous and heterogeneous small groups. One small homogeneous group setting is guided reading (see Chapter 6). Frequently change groupings, and shift heterogeneous groups so that struggling readers can listen to many different fluent readers. Give students opportunities to discuss stories and expository texts with many different thinkers. Change homogeneous groups based on the need; one group may comprise all those who need to be taught a particular skill. Groups will change frequently because students' needs change frequently.

TASK

Allington (2002) reports that effective literacy teachers engage students in reading or writing for 50 percent of the school day! Many of these teachers assign large blocks of time to literacy activities, usually 90 minutes. This reading block includes all types of interesting and authentic tasks—independent reading, reading along with audiobooks, paired reading, or guided reading. Students do not complete worksheets; instead they read a variety of texts—stories, mysteries, poems, plays, expository texts, and so on. Reading extends beyond books; they also read computer screens, children's magazines, newspapers, other students' stories, and posters. Not all students read the same text at the same time.

Foster higher-level thinking tasks through teacher–student and student–student exchanges. In such discussions, you should ask higher-level thinking questions that have no simple, correct answer. This permits students to think and express themselves logically. It also encourages students to question the authors and seek answers that will improve their comprehension.

Personalize tasks by responding to students' interests, needs, strengths, and weaknesses (Brozo, 2010; Allington, Johnston, & Day, 2002). Exercise control over tasks the students need to accomplish, but give them a choice of many texts to accomplish them. For example, if a struggling reader needs to improve her fluency, the teacher might provide 10 selections of easy reading material from which she is instructed to choose one or two.

Also engage students in longer tasks that integrate reading, writing, thinking, and listening, and give students opportunities to choose from a suggested list of activities. Make sure all tasks are meaningful and challenging enough so all students are developing and refining their literacy skills.

Students also require time for silent reading. Silent reading and oral reading make different demands on students. During oral reading, students must pronounce words correctly, read with expression, and comprehend. During silent reading, students must remain focused.

Independent reading allows students to master the tasks of skimming, abandoning, and scanning in selecting texts. When selecting a book for independent reading, students should skim the first page and the illustrations to see if they find the book interesting. If the book is not interesting or it is too difficult, they should know that abandoning it is a legitimate strategy. If they miss one word in ten then the book is probably too difficult for them to read independently. They need to learn to scan for specific information. They must identify capital letters quickly if they are trying to locate the name of a person or other proper noun, or numbers if they are locating dates.

During small group reading instruction, the class space and time should be set up so that students not working in the small group can work independently, with a tutor (see Chapter 13), or with a volunteer (see Chapter 11). This enables teachers to concentrate on the needs of the students in the small group without interruption from other students. Afterward, the teacher may allow the students to complete some literacy tasks independently (Fountas & Pinnell, 2006b). These tasks may include:

1. Reading self-selected texts and writing in a journal or logbook.
2. Listening to audiobooks and responding to questions, with or without a partner.
3. Reading in pairs.
4. Reading from a poem box and drawing a picture based on the poem.
5. Reading ebooks.
6. Buddy reading (see Chapter 13).
7. Rehearsing for readers theater.
8. Reading riddles on the bulletin board and writing answers.
9. Reading texts the class has written together.
10. Using "Record, Check, Chart" to increase reading fluency and rate. (See Chapter 10 and Appendices D.24 and D.25.)

CONCLUDING THOUGHTS

Reading is a complex process, and becoming proficient in any such process requires a lot of practice. Your responsibility as a teacher is to create a setting in which all students can be successful. In order to accomplish this consider (1) your own effectiveness, (2) the uniqueness of each student, (3) multifaceted strategies that will fit readers' needs, (4) methods of motivating and engaging students, (5) appropriate use of a variety of texts, (6) the context of the reading event, and (7) creating an environment conducive to learning and assigning meaningful and appropriate tasks. To be effective you will also need an understanding of (1) the reading process, (2) various assessment instruments, and (3) how and when to teach reading strategies so students will know how and when to use them independently. Finally, remember to have fun with language so your literary passion will be infectious!

Reflective Learning AT-RISK STUDENTS

Scenario. It is the end of May and Mr. Glass has just completed his first year of teaching. He taught seventh-grade language arts at a school in a low socioeconomic neighborhood. His classes were racially diverse, each with three to four students who were English learners. Most students came from single-parent homes in which the parent worked one or two jobs to support the family. None of these parents had attended college, and many did not complete high school. His students did not enjoy learning and often did not complete assignments. Their test scores at the end of the year indicated adequate yearly progress on the reading comprehension and writing test, but only by a small margin.

Mr. Glass is not content; he realizes he failed to motivate his students. He knows that you are in a teacher education program and asks you to help him compile a list of five to eight principles that he can embrace his second year so his next students will enjoy reading and become lifelong learners. He wants his students to dream of going to college.

QUESTIONS

1. After reading this chapter, compile a list of principles that will help Mr. Glass or any teacher motivate students to learn.
2. Discuss the scenario with classmates and seasoned teachers and ask them to share their lists. Do the comments from classmates differ from those of seasoned teachers?

CHAPTER THREE

ASSESSMENT

I hear, and I forget. I see, and I remember. I do, and I understand.

CHINESE PROVERB

scenario

Mr. Leu is excited about his first teaching position. He is one of eight third-grade teachers at Ranchlane Elementary, a large school with a diverse population. The school has two reading specialists and five reading interventionists. During the in-service days before the school year started, Mr. Leu learned that the reading specialists would be calling students out of each classroom to administer reading assessments and would share the results with the teachers after they scored them. The third graders are to be tested during the fourth week of school. Mr. Leu is relieved that he does not have to administer the tests, but he thinks that four weeks is a long time to wait to find out his students' reading levels, strengths, and needs.

During the first two weeks of school, Mr. Leu becomes aware of the wide range of reading abilities in his class and realizes he cannot wait for the test results from the reading specialists. He feels he needs to do some in-class assessments to immediately assess and address the strengths and needs of his students.

During one of his university reading classes, Mr. Leu had tutored a struggling third- grade student from the university lab school. He had been required to administer two miscue analyses as pre- and post-tests and to take a running record each session over the passage a student reread. He found both of those assessments to be great tools to help him understand his tutee's reading needs. He remembered that during the first miscue analysis his tutee, Alice, had enjoyed filming herself reading a passage using the computer's Photo Booth application. Alice liked watching and hearing herself read the passage. After that session, Mr. Leu used Photo Booth during each tutoring session to motivate Alice to listen to herself to determine if she misread any words and if she read with expression. Mr. Leu thought that his third-grade students would enjoy using Photo Booth as well. As a bonus, it would also allow him to later listen to and analyze the students' reading. He also decided to take a running record from one student during each guided reading circle. During the course of one week, he would have a running record and one other passage from each student that he could analyze.

Using an interactive whiteboard and his laptop, he demonstrated to the students how to use Photo Booth. He read a short passage without expression and making a couple of errors. He played it back and asked the students for comments. Many students noticed the errors, and one student commented that he sounded like he was not interested in the passage because his voice was monotone. Mr. Leu complimented them on their observations.

Mr. Leu explained that they would all have a chance to read a passage into Photo Booth during center time and would be able to self assess their reading. He laminated short passages of different reading levels. Students were instructed to record the passage and then listen to it. As they listened, they used a Visa pen to circle words they misread and to comment on their rate and expression. Mr. Leu was pleased to be able to assess their reading and that they were learning to assess themselves. The Photo Booth exercise allowed him to immediately begin tailoring instructional interventions to his students' strengths and needs. Of course, he was also eager to get the test results from the reading specialists.

guiding questions

As you read this chapter, consider the following questions:

1. Do you think it was prudent of Mr. Leu to informally assess students before he received the results from the reading specialist? Defend your stance.
2. What other methods could Mr. Leu have used to assess his students?
3. What reading assessments do you remember from elementary and middle school?
4. What is the difference between formative and summative assessments and between formal and informal assessments?
5. What are the possible strengths and weaknesses of each of the different formal and informal reading assessments?

INTRODUCTION

Mr. Leu understands the importance of assessing students. He and all classroom teachers can choose from many different assessment instruments, but he decided to use two that he knew how to administer and analyze. This chapter discusses a variety of formal and informal assessments.

The Buros Institute publication *Reading* (2002) identifies 102 different assessments that measure reading competencies and attitudes toward reading. The list includes inventories, achievement and aptitude tests, comprehension tests, decoding tests, and oral tests. With so many tests available, teachers must analyze the data from several tests to determine their students' strengths and needs. For example, teachers administer a wide variety of tests mandated by their particular state and school district, and they must review the results of these tests. In addition, teachers analyze the results of informal assessments used in developing instructional plans for their students.

The purpose of this chapter is not to debate the pros and cons of testing, but rather to (1) define terms associated with assessment; (2) describe the characteristics of standardized tests, including the differences between intelligence tests, achievement tests, and diagnostic tests; (3) list commonly used standardized tests; (4) look at a variety of reading assessments that indicate student growth in particular areas of reading; and (5) discuss in detail how to administer and score the various informal assessments used to identify literacy problems. This chapter will focus on informal assessment because these tests are beneficial to classroom teachers in identifying students' strengths and weaknesses and making plans for instruction. The many assessment procedures discussed in this chapter will help teachers to meet the increasing demands they face for accountability of student learning. Always keep in mind that assessments drive instruction.

DEFINING ASSESSMENT

"Assessing students' performance to guide instruction is a long-standing practice of classroom teachers and reading specialist" (Risko & Walker-Dalhouse, 2010, p. 420).

Assessment is the "process of gathering data in order to better understand the strengths and weaknesses of student learning, as by observation, testing, interviews, etc." (Harris & Hodges, 1995, p. 12). School districts and classroom teachers use two basic types of assessment, formal and informal. *Formal assessments* are standardized tests given under controlled conditions so that groups with similar backgrounds can be compared. *Informal assessments* are not standardized tests; rather, they record observations using anecdotal records, checklists, rubrics, portfolios, informal reading inventories, running records, and miscue analysis. Figure 3.1 presents various assessment types.

You will assess students using both formative and summative assessments. *Formative assessments,* as the term implies, are ongoing assessments, including observations in which teachers provide daily feedback to students so they know what to do in order to improve. *Summative assessments,* on the other hand, are given at the end of a designated time period and used to assess student growth and assign grades. Both kinds of assessment provide teachers with valuable information around which to plan instruction.

STANDARDS FOR ASSESSMENT

The National Council of Teachers of English (NCTE) and the International Reading Association (IRA) collaboratively wrote 11 Standards for Assessment of Reading and Writing, which can be used as a guide when planning assessment of your students' literacy. Figure 3.2 lists these standards, and Appendix A.1 provides a short explanation of each.

In addition, the Council of Chief State School Officers (CCSSO) and the National Governors Association (NGA) have drafted the Common Core State Standards (CCSS), explaining "These English language arts and mathematics standards represent a set of expectations for student knowledge and skills that high school graduates need to master to succeed in college and careers" (NGA & CCSSO, 2010, unpaged). One purpose for the CCSS is to provide a degree of continuity among states so that when students move from state to state, they will not be either ahead of or behind their new classmates. In conjunction with the CCSS, most states are adopting Common Core-influenced assessments. This next generation assessment program ranges far beyond the usual multiple-choice and short-answer questions to measure the full breadth and depth of knowledge and skills described in the standards. You will find all the CCSS, as well as additional information, at www.corestandards.org/assets/CCSSI_ELA%20Standards.pdf. Information about assessment systems and the CCSS can be found at www.edweek.org/media/ngaccsso_assessmentdesignpaper.pdf.

figure **3.1** Categories of assessments.

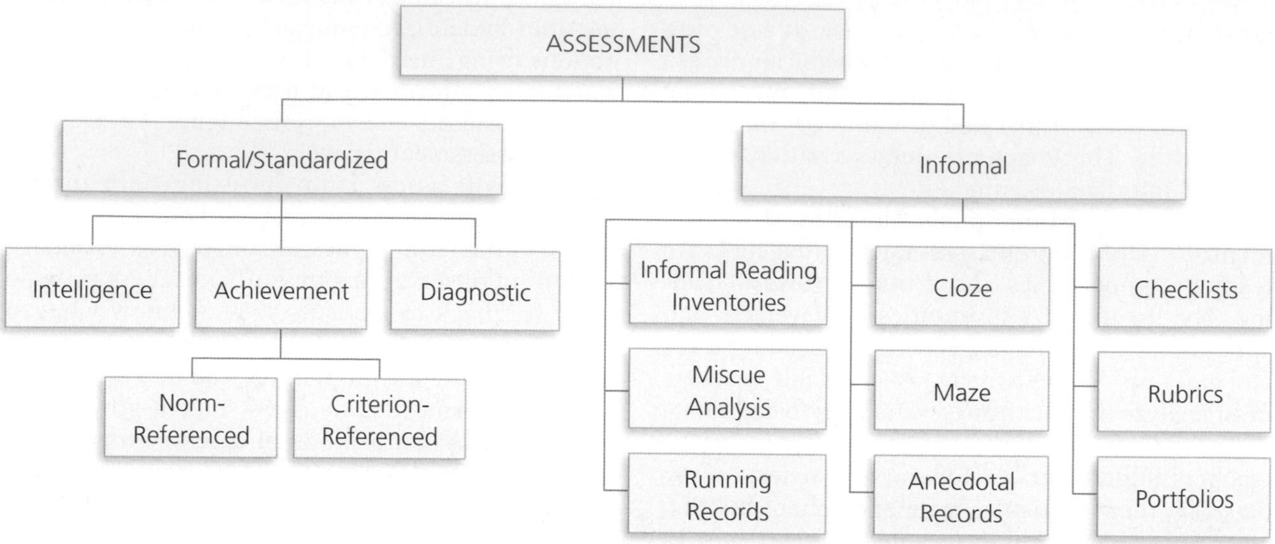

figure **3.2** NCTE/IRA Standards for Assessment of Reading and Writing.

1. The interests of the student are paramount in assessment.
2. The teacher is the most important agent of assessment.
3. The primary purpose of assessment is to improve teaching and learning.
4. Assessment must reflect and allow for critical inquiry into curriculum and instruction.
5. Assessment must recognize and reflect the intellectually and socially complex nature of reading and writing and the important roles of school, home, and society in literacy development.
6. Assessment must be fair and equitable.
7. The consequences of an assessment procedure are the first and most important consideration in establishing the validity of the assessment.
8. The assessment process should involve multiple perspectives and sources of data.
9. Assessment must be based in the local school learning community, including active and essential participation of families and community members.
10. All stakeholders in the educational community—students, families, teachers, administrators, policymakers, and the public—must have an equal voice in the development, interpretation, and reporting of assessment information.
11. Families must be involved as active, essential participants in the assessment process.

From *Standards for the Assessment of Reading and Writing* by the International Reading Association and the National Council of Teachers of English, Visit www.ncte.org/standards/assessmentstandards for the complete standards.

FORMAL/STANDARDIZED ASSESSMENT INSTRUMENTS

Figure 3.1 lists the three types of standardized tests: intelligence, achievement, and diagnostic. There are also standardized tests for English learners. Most schools administer standardized tests, and classroom teachers who suspect a student has a reading problem should use the student's standardized test score as a starting point for recommending individual reading tests.

Standardized tests have advantages and disadvantages. Two advantages of standardized tests are that (1) they indicate whether an individual student needs additional screening, and (2) they are designed for validity and reliability. *Validity* means the test measures what it claims to measure; *reliability* means it does so on a consistent basis.

Standardized tests have two primary disadvantages. First, because many questions are in a multiple-choice format, the student can guess the answer, which results in an inaccurate score. Second, students may be able to answer some questions without comprehending the passage. This is especially true for literal questions, which use the exact language of the passage. Consider this example: The passage the student reads includes the following sentence: "A favorite main dish in Louisiana is gumbo, a type of soup." One of the multiple-choice questions that follows the short passage is: "Gumbo is a type of (A) bread, (B) fish, (C) soup, (D) none of the above." Students may deduce that they merely need to find the word *gumbo* in the passage and look at the surrounding words to complete the answer.

Individual and Group Intelligence Tests

Intelligence tests determine the scholastic aptitude of students. While it is important for classroom teachers to understand students' potential, teachers must remember that some students with low IQ scores do not struggle with reading and some students with high IQ scores do (Barry, 1998). Intelligence test scores must be used with great caution because scores may differ depending on students' exposure to schooling and other cultural experiences.

The classroom teacher, who closely follows the script found in the testing manual, administers intelligence tests to a group or class of children. The teacher does not score these tests, but he or she can interpret the scores if instructed. One example of a group intelligence test given by the classroom teacher is the California Test of Mental Maturity. Because most students do not perform as well on group tests as they do on individual tests (Miller, 1988), most intelligence tests used in school are individual tests.

School psychologists or guidance counselors usually administer individual intelligence tests because of the complexity of administering and scoring the tests. Examples of individual intelligence tests are given in the box below.

Achievement Tests

Achievement tests measure the current level of a student's performance in a variety of areas, including reading, language arts, mathematics, science, and social studies. Each of these main areas has subtests; for example, the reading tests may include comprehension, vocabulary, phonics, subtests, and so on. There are two different types of standardized achievement tests—norm-referenced and criterion-referenced. All of these tests assess student achievement and are given under standardized conditions; however, their goals differ.

Norm-referenced tests

Norm-referenced tests are assessment instruments developed by publishers who administer them to

Examples of Individual Intelligence Tests

1. The Wechsler Intelligence Scale for Children—III, for students ages 6–17, and Wechsler Adult Intelligence Scale (WAIS) provide a verbal intelligence quotient (IQ), a performance IQ, and a full-scale or overall IQ. The Verbal Scale includes the following subtests: (1) general information, (2) comprehension, (3) arithmetic, (4) similarities, (5) vocabulary, and (6) digit span, which tests the individual's ability to recite digits forward and backward. The Performance Scale includes subtests for (1) picture completion—finding the missing part of a picture, (2) picture arrangement—or sequencing, (3) block design—a task that resembles a jigsaw puzzle, (4) object assembly—a timed assembly activity, (5) coding—which involves making associations, (6) mazes—finding one's way through a maze, and (7) symbol search—processing novel information.
2. Stanford-Binet Intelligence Scale for ages two through adulthood measures students' intelligence in verbal reasoning, quantitative reasoning, abstract/visual reasoning, and short-term memory. The subtests include vocabulary, comprehension, verbal absurdities, pattern analysis, matrices, paper folding and cutting, copying, number series, equation building, memory for sentences, memory for digits, memory for objects, and bead memory.
3. Peabody Picture Vocabulary Test—Revised, for grades Pre-K through 12 provides information about students' receptive vocabulary based on life experiences. This test can be useful with English learners because it assesses receptive vocabulary.
4. Slosson Intelligence Test (SIT) for Children and Adults measures the overall mental ability of both children and adults, but has no subtest scores. The test is a set of 10 graded word lists. The score is based on the student's ability to pronounce words at different levels of difficulty.

large populations of students from different geographic locations and socioeconomic backgrounds in order to develop norms. The norms are the average scores of the large population of students in each age group and grade level who take the test. That average score becomes the "measuring stick" by which to gauge the performance of other students who take the test. A norm-referenced test permits teachers to compare their students against the students used in the standardization sample.

The scores of norm-referenced tests provide a comparison of each child's achievement level to national norms. Results are reported in the form of grade equivalent scores, stanine scores, percentile ranks, and standard scores. Teachers need to accurately interpret and communicate the test scores for parents. Figure 3.3 explains the different types of scores. Figure 3.4 lists standardized, norm-referenced achievement tests with their reading subtests.

Norm-referenced tests exist for a variety of subjects, including reading, mathematics, social studies, and science. The reading sections of such tests often include subtests for word identification, vocabulary, comprehension, reading rate, and study skills.

figure **3.3**

Types of standardized test scores.

- **Standard scores** are transformed from raw scores using the standard deviation. The standard deviation is the number (usually ±1, 2, or 3) used to refer to the variability in the scores indicated by their distance from the mean, or average. Converting scores from raw scores to standard scores allows teachers to make comparisons between two dissimilar measures.
- **Grade equivalent scores** reflect the median raw score for a grade level. For example, a raw score of 126 with a grade equivalent of 6.4 indicates that the students used in setting the norm, whose median raw score was 126, were in the sixth grade, fourth month.
- **A percentile ranking** compares the student to other students her age. For example, if Jane has a percentile rank of 65 percent, it indicates that 35 percent of all students Jane's age had better scores than Jane, while 64 percent had worse scores than Jane.
- **Stanine scores** are much like percentiles; however, the stanine scores range from one through nine. Stanine scores are more general than percentile scores. Scores of four through six are average scores. For example, if Joe has a stanine of six, it indicates that his score is average when compared to all students at his same grade level who were used for establishing the norm. To find a stanine score for a particular test, the teacher needs to calculate the overall score and use the test's chart to convert the raw score into a stanine score. If the tests are graded by a testing company, the stanine score is given.

Criterion-referenced tests

Criterion-referenced tests assess the point at which the student has achieved mastery; these tests do not compare students to others with similar backgrounds. Criterion-referenced tests enable teachers to compare a student's performance to a predetermined goal. They help teachers determine whether a student has met the necessary criteria for mastery in a particular area or achieved competency on a specific reading subskill, for example. One advantage of these tests is that they help teachers identify areas of student weakness so they can plan instruction based on the students' needs. Teachers should realize, however, that subtests divide reading into fragments and do not approach it as a holistic process.

State-designed criterion-referenced tests. Many state departments of education have designed criterion-referenced tests that are aligned with their state standards (also called benchmarks or competencies in some states). Each state develops its own standards for each

figure **3.4**

Standardized norm-referenced achievement tests.

1. Iowa Test of Basic Skills (Grades K–8).
   Subtests: vocabulary, comprehension, listening, word attack, spelling, study skills.
2. Stanford Achievement Tests–Ninth Edition (Grades K–13).
3. Gates-MacGinitie Reading Tests (Grades K–12).
   Subtests: vocabulary and comprehension.
4. Metropolitan Achievement Tests–Reading (Grades K–12).
   Subtests: primer = listening for sounds; primary = word knowledge, word analysis; grades 1–12 = vocabulary and comprehension, spelling.
5. Comprehensive Test of Basic Skills, U and V (Grades K–12).
   Subtests: vocabulary, comprehension, word attack.
6. California Achievement Tests–Reading (Grades K–9).
   Subtests: vocabulary, comprehension, listening, spelling.

subject area. Language arts standards include those for speaking, listening, viewing, visually representing, reading, and writing. Subcategories address various areas of reading, writing, and the other components of the language arts. For example, one first-grade Oklahoma reading standard is Phonics/Decoding, and a subheading under that states that the student will use consonant sounds in the beginning, medial, and final positions to decode unknown words.

In order for U.S. school districts to qualify for federal funding, they must document student growth in the following five areas of literacy: phonemic awareness, systematic phonics, fluency, text comprehension, and vocabulary. One way to document student growth is through the administration of state-designed criterion-referenced tests at the beginning and end of the school year. Each state designs tests that reflect its state standards. Throughout the year, teachers can use checklists and/or rubrics based on the state standards to monitor growth patterns. (See sections on Checklists and Rubrics later in this chapter.)

State-designed criterion-referenced tests for English learners. In January 1974 the U.S. Supreme Court ruled in *Lau v. Nichols* that students who were not native English speakers had to receive instruction that they could understand. States are required "to have in place standards and assessments for the English language proficiency (ELP) of ELLs as well as having the capacity to ensure that ELLs meet the same challenging state academic content and student academic achievement standards as all students. Ensuring that ELLs are ready to meet this challenge requires standards and assessments that are rigorous and demanding but also sensitive to the linguistic and cultural backgrounds of this diverse group of students" (National Clearinghouse for English Language Acquisition, 2010). Some states have their own standards for English learners, but most states use or adapt the standards of Teachers of English to Speakers of Other Languages (TESOL). Figure 3.5 lists these standards.

Making sure English learners meet these standards is a challenging mandate for classroom teachers, as it includes assessing the growth not only of English learners' oral or social language, but also their growth in the main subject areas. School districts use standardized tests to determine if English learners are meeting these standards and if their programs are meeting the needs of English learners.

Familiarize yourself with the difficulties English learners encounter when they take standardized state and district tests. When assessing an English learner via these tests, take into consideration the student's background. For example, did she have a formal education in her native country? Did her native country use standardized tests? How long has she been in the United States? You can provide some accommodations for English learners when they take teacher-designed tests or standardized tests. O'Loughlin and Haynes (2004) recommend the following:

1. Make the language understandable.
2. Give English learners more time to take the test.
3. Give the test orally by reading the test to the student and permitting them to respond orally, or permit them to record their responses.
4. Give tests in the student's native language, if possible, to assess their content knowledge.
5. Allow the student to use spellcheck on essay tests.
6. On multiple choice tests, reduce the number of choices to two from the four or five on the original test.
7. On fill-in-the-blank tests, provide a word bank from which to choose.
8. If idioms are on standardized tests, interpret the idiom for the student.
9. Simplify directions and make sure the student understands them.
10. Use a peer interpreter to read the test to the student.

Three tests widely used to measure English learners' oral, reading, and writing skills are Pre-Language Assessment Scales–2000, Language Assessment Scales–Oral (LAS–O), and Language Assessment Scales–Read-

figure **3.5**

English Language Proficiency Standards.

Standard 1: English language learners communicate for social, intercultural, and instructional purposes within the school setting.

Standard 2: English language learners communicate information, ideas, and concepts necessary for academic success in the area of language arts.

Standard 3: English language learners communicate information, ideas, and concepts necessary for academic success in the area of mathematics.

Standard 4: English language learners communicate information, ideas, and concepts necessary for academic success in the area of science.

Standard 5: English language learners communicate information, ideas, and concepts necessary for academic success in the area of social studies.

ing/Writing (LAS–R/W). The Pre-Language Assessment Scales–2000 uses games, pictures, and stories to assess the pre-literacy skills of children ages four to six. The LAS–O and LAS–R/W (both group-administered tests) measure five areas of language development: sound/phrase recognition, sound/phrase reproduction, vocabulary, comprehension, and storytelling. The LAS–O is for preschoolers and up, while the LAS–R/W is for grades two and up. Because oral language development is crucial to developing reading skills (Helman and Burns, 2008), it is important that teachers monitor the oral language skills of English learners.

Informal assessments that are particularly helpful for literacy teachers to use with English learners will be discussed later in this chapter.

Diagnostic Tests

Diagnostic tests are standardized, but they differ from achievement tests in that they determine a student's strengths and weaknesses. In most school districts, primary students who score one year below grade level on achievement tests and intermediate students who score two or more years below grade level are given diagnostic tests.

Diagnostic reading tests include many subtests that cover a wide range of skills—visual and auditory discrimination, phonics skills, sound blending, word recognition, structural analysis, syllabication, scanning, skimming, contextual analysis, vocabulary, and comprehension. All of these subtests indicate a student's strengths and weaknesses, but none identifies the causes for the weaknesses.

Like all tests, diagnostic tests have advantages and disadvantages (Calkins, Montgomery, Santman, & Falk, 1998). The advantages include: (1) the fact that because they are standardized they are more valid and reliable than running records, miscue analyses, maze tests, and cloze tests; (2) they identify the student's reading level; (3) most are normed tests that can compare a student to others with similar characteristics; and (4) they identify a student's weaknesses. Disadvantages to diagnostic tests include: (1) they must be administered and scored by trained teachers; (2) the individual tests are time consuming to administer; (3) the tests may discriminate based on cultural differences; (4) some tests use nonsense words to evaluate a student's word identification skills, which may frustrate younger students; and (5) they are timed, which requires students to perform on-demand (Murphy, 1995).

Diagnostic tests can be given to groups or individuals, and all group tests can be administered to individuals. Even though classroom teachers do not administer the tests, they should be familiar enough with the reading diagnostic subtests to know the tasks they measure.

Oral reading tests

Oral reading tests assess an individual student's rate, accuracy, fluency, and comprehension (see examples in Figure 3.6). They are usually reserved for struggling readers because of the time it takes to administer them. Oral tests consist of graded passages that range from

figure **3.6**

Individual and group diagnostic tests.

INDIVIDUAL DIAGNOSTIC TESTS

1. Gilmore Oral Reading Test, evaluates the reader's accuracy, comprehension, and rate.
2. Gray Oral Reading Test, evaluates accuracy and comprehension, but not rate.
3. Woodcock Reading Mastery Test (Grades 1–12).
   Subtests: letter identification, word attack skills (with nonsense words), word comprehension (analogies), and passage comprehension. This test is easy for classroom teachers to administer and score.
4. Durrell Analysis of Reading Difficulties–Third Edition (Grades K–6).
   Subtests: pre-reading phonics inventories, auditory analysis of words and word elements, visual memory of words, pronunciation of word elements, listening, vocabulary, and spelling.
5. Gates-McKillop-Horowitz Tests (Grades K–6).
   Subtests: auditory discrimination, phonics analysis, structural analysis, vocabulary, and spelling.
6. Diagnostic Reading Scales (Grades 1–7).
   Subtests: 12 subtests on phonics analysis, word identification, oral reading, and silent reading.
7. Sipay Word Analysis Test.

All subtests evaluate word identification or phonics analysis skills.

GROUP DIAGNOSTIC TESTS

1. Stanford Diagnostic Reading Test; Red Level, Green Level, Brown Level, and Blue Level. (Levels range from primary grades through high school.)
   Subtests: auditory vocabulary, auditory discrimination, phonetic analysis, structural analysis, and comprehension.
2. Iowa Silent Reading Test (Grades 6–adult).
   Subtests: comprehension, vocabulary, reading efficiency, work–study skills.
3. Nelson-Denny Reading Test (Grades 9–adult).
   Subtests: vocabulary, comprehension, rate.

first- through eighth-grade levels. The student reads the passages until she reaches a ceiling level, which is called her frustration reading level. The teacher checks oral errors, which include substitutions, mispronunciations, omissions, insertions, repetitions, and hesitations, while the student reads. During this process the teacher learns the types of errors a student makes and how she handles unknown words. The teacher also notes the reader's expression and prosody, two aspects of fluency.

Diagnostic tests that assess reading components

Because school districts must show adequate yearly progress (AYP), many use assessments that monitor student growth in five components: phonemic awareness, phonics, vocabulary, fluency, and comprehension. Two such assessments are the Basic Early Assessment of Reading™ (BEAR®) and the Dynamic Indicators of Basic Early Literacy Skills (DIBELS).

The BEAR tests are group tests for kindergarten through third grade, whereas DIBELS assessments are individual tests for grades kindergarten through sixth grade. Both tests have pretests, midyear tests, and post-tests. They are given multiple times throughout the year to assess student progress so classroom teachers can provide instruction to those students who are lagging behind. Figure 3.7 lists the components assessed in each test for each grade.

Other formal tests also assess the five components. For example, the Comprehension Test of Phonological Processing (CTOPP) assesses students' phonological awareness, phonological memory, and rapid naming. There are two versions of this test—one for ages five and six and a second for ages seven through college age.

INFORMAL ASSESSMENT INSTRUMENTS

Informal assessments are not standardized or normed, and they do not compare one student to another. Rather, they serve the following purposes:

1. Gauge what an individual student can do as a reader and writer.
2. Diagnose reading problems.
3. Check the student's reading level.
4. Analyze which cueing systems students use when making sense of print.
5. Highlight a student's interests and attitudes toward reading and writing so teachers can find materials that interest the student.
6. Monitor growth.
7. Allow a student to reflect on literacy accomplishments.

figure **3.7**

Comparison of the components of reading that are assessed at different grade levels in BEAR® and DIBELS.

COMPONENTS	GRADE LEVELS K	1st	2nd	3rd	4th–6th
BEAR® (Published by Riverside Publishing)					
Reading Basics					
Concepts of Print	X	X			
Phonemic Awareness	X	X			
Decoding—Phonics and Word Recognition	X	X	X	X	
Decoding—Structural Analysis		X	X	X	
Vocabulary	X	X	X	X	
Language Arts					
Penmanship	X				
Sentence Structure		X	X	X	
Grammar/Usage		X	X	X	
Punctuation/ Capitalization		X	X	X	
Spelling	X	X	X	X	
Comprehension					
Listening	X	X	X	X	
Reading/Literacy Response		X	X	X	
Reading Fluency					
Letter Recognition	X				
Informational Passage	X	X	X	X	
Narrative	X	X	X	X	
Reading Rate		X	X	X	
Accuracy	X	X	X	X	
Oral Reading Skills	X	X	X	X	
Retelling	X	X	X	X	
DIBELS (Published by Sopris West Educational Services)					
Initial Sound (phonemic awareness)	X				
Letter Naming	X	X			
Phoneme Segmentation	X	X			
Nonsense Words (phonics)	X	X	X		
Oral Reading (fluency)	X	X	X	X	X
Retelling (comprehension)	X	X	X	X	X
Word Use (vocabulary)	X	X	X	X	X

8. Provide an opportunity for the student to set realistic goals.
9. Help a teacher plan for instruction.

It is helpful to discuss authentic assessment in relation to informal assessment. Authentic assessment measures literacy behavior in real-life situations (e.g., in the community or workplace). For example, an authentic assessment may measure a child's ability to comprehend the directions when constructing a model airplane. "Authentic assessment practices . . . hold enormous potential for changing what and how we teach and how children come to be readers and writers" (Allington & Cunningham, cited in Fountas & Pinnell, 2006b, p. 89).

Commonly used informal tests include emergent reading and writing instruments, informal reading inventories, miscue analyses, running records, cloze tests, maze tests, anecdotal records, checklists, rubrics, portfolios, interest and attitude surveys, and student self-assessments. All of these informal assessment instruments aid a teacher as she gains insight into her students' literacy processes. Informal assessment instruments differ "significantly from all other commonly used diagnostic and evaluative instruments in that the resulting analysis of reading proficiency is qualitative as well as quantitative" (Goodman, Watson, & Burke, 1987, p. 4).

Because the classroom teacher is usually the first to detect a student's struggle with reading, writing, speaking, listening, or visual literacy, it is advantageous for the teacher to administer and score the informal literacy tests so she can observe the student as he engages in literacy processes.

Using these and other classroom-based assessments effectively depends on the teacher's ability to select assessments based on instructional goals, frequently and systematically collect data, and immediately implement instructional interventions based on analysis of that data (Risko & Walker-Dalhouse, 2010).

Emergent Reading and Writing Instruments

Informal literacy assessment begins with young children. Many preschoolers and kindergarten children are assessed on their concepts of print. These assessments are administered individually to see what the child understands about reading and writing. One of the first instruments used to assess a child's concepts of print was Marie Clay's *Sand* (1993a), followed by her *Stones* (1993b), *Follow Me, Moon* (2000a), and *No Shoes* (2000b). The print size of these books is appropriate for young children and is intended to be used as a basis for asking questions about print. The books begin with the text and pictures written correctly and progress to pages with the words written upside down and with high-frequency words spelled incorrectly. As the adult shares the book with a child, the following print concepts are assessed (Los Angeles County Office of Education, 2000):

1. Does the child know which is the front of the book? Does she hold a book correctly?
2. Does the child know that the words, not the picture, is what is read when asked, "Where do I start to read?"
3. Does the child know that one reads from the top of the page to the bottom?
4. Does the child know that one reads the left-hand page and then the right-hand page? Can he point to where you go after completing the left-hand page?
5. Does the child know the return sweep concept? (Where do I go when I come to the end of a line?)
6. Can the child point from word to word?
7. Does the child know the difference between a word, a letter, and a sentence?
8. Does the child know that letter order is important and different in each word? (Does he recognize the misspelled words?)
9. Can the child identify the first and last letters in words?
10. Does a child recognize the difference between various end marks? Does she know the purpose of a period, question mark, and exclamation mark?

The child's answers to these questions reveal his depth of knowledge about print. As you can see, some questions are more advanced than others. For example, a child who can recognize when the text is written upside down or who can locate misspelled words is more advanced than one who merely knows how to hold the book correctly. See Figure 3.8 for traits of emergent and beginning readers. Teachers can assess most of the concepts of print by using any picture book along with the checklist in Appendix C.2, although most picture books do not have upside down text or misspelled words.

Although many of the reading concepts overlap with writing, Clay (2006) uses the following concepts and principles to assess early writing:

1. *Sign concept:* Child understands that writing conveys a message.
2. *Message concept:* Child understands that what is spoken can be written down.
3. *Copying principle:* When first learning to make letters, a child closely observes all of the lines, circles, and details of letters and words by copying them.

figure **3.8** Traits of emergent and beginning readers.

EMERGENT READERS

1. Understand that print carries meaning.
2. Understand directionality such as left to right, top to bottom, and front of book to back of book.
3. Use picture clues for meaning when pretend reading.
4. Use story-like language when pretend reading (e.g., "Once upon a time" or "There once was a").
5. Mime a reader's intonation.
6. Recognize environmental print.
7. Expect books to be enjoyable.
8. Can retell stories.

BEGINNING READERS

1. Understand that words are made up of letters and each letter makes a sound.
2. Understand that text has a space between words.
3. Read word by word.
4. Point to words when reading.
5. Can successfully read books with uncomplicated, monosyllabic words, such as Dr. Seuss's *Hop on Pop* (1963) and *One Fish, Two Fish, Red Fish, Blue Fish* (1960b).
6. Successfully read books with patterns.

4. *Flexibility principle:* Child learns how to change a letter's form while retaining its identity.
5. *Inventory principle:* Child lists what he knows about writing.
6. *Recurring principle:* Child writes repeatedly so producing patterns becomes habitual and the child feels competent.
7. *Generating principle:* Child combines or arranges elements of print in an inventive manner.
8. *Directional principle:* Child writes from left to right and from top to bottom.
9. *Reversing the directional pattern:* Child has not learned the importance of left versus right on a page.
10. *Contrastive principle:* Child can distinguish the differences between the shapes, meanings, and sounds in letters and words.
11. *Space concept:* Child understands that a space is needed between words.
12. *Page and book arrangement:* If necessary, child ignores directionality to use up leftover spaces.
13. *Abbreviation principle:* Child understands that letters construct words.

The checklist in Appendix C.3 assesses a child's concepts about writing based on Clay's principles, and the observational checklists in Appendices C.8 and C.9 assess a child's literacy habits at the early emergent and emergent literacy stages.

Informal Reading Inventories

Informal reading inventories (IRIs) are individual tests given by a classroom teacher. They generally include lists of leveled words or sentences and sets of graded reading passages with accompanying questions. Commercial IRI passages range from 50 to 250 words, depending on the grade level; thus, they take little time to administer. The passages, together with the retelling of main points and/or questions, measure the readers' comprehension and recall ability. Most commercial IRIs have three equivalent passages for each grade, accompanied by graded word lists. Two passages are narrative text and the third is expository text. This permits a teacher to use one of the narrative passages to test oral reading comprehension and the other for silent reading comprehension.

During an IRI, students are first asked to read words from a graded word list of the most frequently used words for the intended grade level. Word lists assess students' ability to read words out of context. After reading the word list, students silently read a short story or informational passage. Teachers are encouraged to give both a narrative and an expository passage so they can determine if the students comprehend one type of passage better than the other. After silent reading, the students retell the story or all they remember about the information. Teachers assess the silent reading by determining how many of the questions that accompany each story the students answer during the retelling. If the students do not answer many of the questions, the teacher asks questions to determine whether the students forgot to include the information or did not comprehend the passage. After the retelling, the students read the story orally. Teachers then ask the students if they remember anything else about the passage. If so, the students may still be at the stage of reading aloud in order to comprehend stories and information. Although many commercial IRIs suggest that teachers record the students' reading so they can analyze it later, some teachers do it while the student reads. While analyzing miscues (using the process discussed later), teachers determine the strengths and weaknesses of each student.

A teacher can also use the IRI to determine the student's comprehension score. The comprehension score is based on the reader's retelling. In the retelling, students should include an account of *who, what, where, when, why*, and *how*. A teacher determines how many of these six items were included in the retelling and then calculates the comprehension score. For example, if Joey recounts only *who* and *what* in his retelling of the story "The Pumpkin Man for Piney Creek" (by Darleen Bailey-Beard, 1995), he receives a comprehension score of 33 percent. The story is at Joey's frustration reading level. Figure 3.9 lists sample scoring criteria from the Ekwall/Shanker Reading Inventory, which defines the three reading levels for retelling.

Appendix A.2 lists commercial IRIs. Commercial IRIs also include forms used during a miscue analysis.

Miscue Analysis

Miscue analysis, designed by Yetta Goodman and Carolyn Burke (1972), is based on Kenneth Goodman's *Taxonomy of Reading Miscues* (1969). Goodman developed this taxonomy "by analyzing the degree to which unexpected responses or miscues change, disrupt, or enhance the meaning of a written text" (Goodman, Watson, & Burke, 1987, p. 5). He used the word *miscues* instead of *errors* "to eliminate the pejorative connotations of words such as *error* and *mistake* and to underscore the belief that all reading is cued by language and personal experience and is not simply random, uncontrolled behavior" (Goodman, Watson, & Burke, 1987, p. 5).

Types of miscues

When analyzing miscues, a teacher focuses on what type(s) of miscues—substitutions, mispronunciations, repetitions or insertions, and omissions—the reader makes.

Substitutions. There are many different types of substitutions. Sometimes a substitution is a word that does not resemble the written word, but it may mean nearly the same thing as the word in the text. For example, a student may read *frog* for the word *toad*. This type of substitution may occur if the student uses picture clues to help with unknown words; in this case the miscue reveals the student is reading for meaning. Other times, substitutions may not resemble or mean anything approximating the original word. For example, a student reads *cookie* for the word *catalog*. Obviously, when this occurs the student is not reading for meaning. A third type of substitution is a reversal. The text may read "Dad said" but the student recites "said Dad." The meaning remains intact despite the reversal of the two words.

Mispronunciations. Mispronunciations often reflect a student's dialect. For example, the student may pronounce *specific* as *pecific*, or *spaghetti* as *pashetti* or *breakfast* as *breafest*. Mispronunciations caused by dialects are not considered miscues (Goodman & Burke, 1972). Other times, a student's mispronunciations may result from accenting the wrong syllable. For example, "He will record his voice" becomes "He will record [accent on first syllable so it sounds like the noun form] his voice."

Repetitions/insertions. Repetitions are words the student repeats, and insertions are words the student adds to a text. The text may read, "The fisherman was hungry after his long day of fishing" and the student says, "The fisherman was very hungry after his long long day of fishing." Many times the student is reading for meaning and adds words for effect. Insertions of this type are miscues; however, they do not disrupt meaning.

Omissions. Omissions are words that the student drops from the text. Sometimes the student may not know the word and merely skips it. These types of omissions disrupt meaning. Other omissions may involve the elimination of commas and end marks. These also hinder comprehension. One omission that does not always hinder comprehension is the skipping of explanatory words in dialogue. For example, in the following sentence the student may omit *asked Dad*: "Will you," asked Dad, "please mow the lawn for me?" This type of miscue indicates a proficient reader (Goodman & Burke, 1972).

Figure 3.10 provides the unified set of conventions used for miscue analysis.

Preparing and administering a miscue analysis

A teacher can administer a miscue analysis using any text; however, as stated previously, commercial IRIs include passages and grids to facilitate the process. Advantages of using commercial miscue analyses include: (1) they have graded passages for both

figure **3.9**

Reading comprehension chart based on retelling.

Independent Reading Level	=	90% or better
Instructional Reading Level	=	60–89%
Frustration Reading Level	=	60% or less

Source: Shanker, J. & Ekwall, E. (2000). *Ekwall/Shanker Reading Inventory* (4th ed.). Boston: Allyn & Bacon.

figure **3.10** Conventions used for miscue analysis.

1. **Substitutions:** Write substituted word above actual word.	frog The toad leaped down the path.
2. **Mispronunciations:** Write mispronounced word above actual word.	countent I was content with my B on the test.
3. **Omission:** Circle omitted word.	Jane walked into the huge store.
4. **Insertion:** Use caret to show point of insertion; write word above.	new I want to go to the movies.
5. **Repetition:** Underline repeated words.	Dan's pet is a monkey.
6. **Long pauses:** Use "P" to show where pause occurred.	Molly wants a new P dollhouse.
7. **Self-corrections:** Use symbol and underlining as shown.	© Molly wants a new doll.
8. **Sounding-out words:** Write out approximate version of sounded-out word.	A-All-Al-i-ga-tors Alligators live in swamps.

narrative and expository texts; (2) they have graded word lists; and (3) they provide the passage from which the students read and a prepared script with a grid for the teacher's use. A drawback to commercial miscue analyses is the fact that the short passages lack the elements of a well-developed story or expository text. Weaver (2002) found that students make fewer miscues after reading approximately 200 words because they become familiar with the author's vocabulary and style. Teachers who would like to use longer passages to analyze their struggling readers can prepare and administer a miscue analysis on any story using the following steps:

1. Select an interesting story that has all of the elements of good literature or an expository passage taken from a well-written trade book. The story or passage should be at least 600 words in length and challenging to the reader, but not so difficult as to cause frustration.
2. Prepare the script using the blank form found in Appendix C.4.
3. Prepare a number of questions based on the story's setting, characters, and main events or the expository passage's main topic, supporting details, and key vocabulary.
4. Prepare a quiet reading station with the chosen selection (it can be the original text or a photocopied script) and a recording device.
5. Instruct the student to read the selection silently.
6. Ask the student to retell the story in as much detail as he can. Note which of your prepared questions the student answers in his retelling.
7. Have the student read the selection orally into the recorder. Inform her that you will not help; she must try to figure out the words or skip them and continue.
8. Ask the student to retell the story or passage again. Take notes on the prepared questions the reader answers in this retelling. (This step helps teachers determine whether a student's comprehension increases with oral reading.)
9. Dismiss the student and listen to the recorded selection, marking the miscues on the prepared grid. For example, if the miscue is an omission, mark an X in the "Omission" column. If the miscue makes sense grammatically, mark an X in the "Syntax acceptable" column. If the miscue disrupts meaning, mark an X in the last column.
10. Total the number of miscues in each column, making note of which type of miscue the student most often makes.
11. Calculate the total number of miscues that disrupt meaning and summarize the reading and retelling.
12. Decide which reading strategy you will teach first in order to increase the student's reading comprehension.

Figure 3.11 is a short example of an eighth grade student's reading of *The Jungle Book* (1894) by Rudyard Kipling.

figure **3.11** Grid for miscue analysis.

TEXT	Substitution	Mispronunciation	Insertion	Omission	Repeats	Self-correction	Syntax acceptable	Meaning disrupted
It was seven o'clock of a very				✓		✓	✓	
warm evening in the	✓						✓	
Seeonee hills when Father		✓					✓	
Wolf woke up from his day's	✓			✓			✓ ✓	
rest, scratched himself,		✓						✓
yawned, and spread out his			✓				✓	
paws one after the other to								
get rid of the sleepy feeling			✓				✓	
in their tips. Mother Wolf								
lay with her big gray nose								
dropped across her four								
tumbling, squealing cubs,								
and the moon shone into	✓						✓	
the mouth of the cave								
where they all lived.				✓			✓	
TOTAL MISCUES:	3	2	2	3	0	1	9	1

Notes: One miscue disrupted meaning.

Source: Text from Rudyard Kipling, *The Jungle Book* (1894).

Quantitative scoring

To obtain the quantitative score, the teacher calculates the number of words read correctly (words that do not disrupt meaning). The quantitative score is calculated using the following steps:

1. Count the number of words in the passage.
2. Count the number of miscues that disrupted meaning.
3. Subtract the number of miscues that disrupted meaning from the total number of words in the passage.
4. Divide the number of words read correctly by the total number of words in the passage.
5. Multiply quotient by 100 to get the percentage of the reading score.
6. Use the Reading Level Chart in Figure 3.12 to determine the reading level of that passage for the student.

For example, if Joey reads a passage of 500 words and makes 30 miscues that disrupt meaning, he reads 470 words correctly. To calculate the score, divide 470 by 500 and multiply by 100 to get 94 percent. Joey scores a 94 percent on the oral reading, which means the passage is at Joey's instructional level. This passage would be appropriate to use when teaching Joey new reading strategies. The criteria for the three reading levels are found in Figure 3.12.

figure 3.12

Reading level chart based on correct word identification.

Independent Reading Level	=	99%
Instructional Reading Level	=	90–98%
Frustration Reading Level	=	Below 90%

Scores set by the International Reading Association. Source: Harris, T., & Hodges, R. (Eds.) (1995). *The Literacy Dictionary: The Vocabulary of Reading and Writing.* Newark, DE: International Reading Association.

Qualitative analysis

The quantitative score of a miscue analysis may help a teacher determine the student's instructional reading level. However, the main purpose of a miscue analysis is to evaluate a reader's miscues "based on the degree to which the miscue disrupts the meaning of the written material" (Goodman, 1972/1997, p. 534). It is important for a teacher to assess a reader's strategies when encountering unknown words or those he uses to correct a miscue. This qualitative analysis of miscues "provides specific information regarding readers' strengths and weaknesses, which can be used to plan a personalized reading program" (Goodman, 1972/1997, p. 534).

In a qualitative analysis teachers ask the following questions about the students' miscues and use the following strategies to address them:

1. *Does the student insert or omit words?* Instruct him to point to words as he reads to avoid additions and deletions.
2. *Does the student guess at words by looking only at the initial letter sound?* Have her work on analyzing the entire word.
3. *Does the student read too fast or too slow?* Echo read with him. In echo reading, a teacher reads a phrase or sentence geared toward the student's grade level, and he repeats the phrase or sentence using the same speed and intonation as the teacher.
4. *Do the miscues disrupt meaning?* If so, repeat the phrase or sentence as the student read it, and ask if it made sense. Some students can determine whether a sentence makes sense when they hear it read by another person.
5. *Does the student pause for commas and periods?* If not, echo read or have the students snap their fingers each time they see a comma and clap their hands each time they see a period.
6. *Does the student have good intonation?* If the student reads in a monotone voice, ask her how she would say a particular sentence if she were talking to you. Or read a sentence to the student using correct intonation and have the student repeat it.

Retrospective Miscue Analysis

Retrospective miscue analysis, designed by Yetta Goodman and Ann Marek (1996), contains all the steps of a miscue analysis and adds steps following the recorded oral reading of a passage. The teacher finds a portion of the written passage with a number of miscues representative of the reader's miscues in general. She then cues the recording to that portion of the passage and asks the student to listen to his reading while following the script. The purpose is to determine if the student can locate his miscues—omissions, insertions, and so on—and articulate what type of miscues they are. The teacher and student then discuss the miscues and the ways the student can improve his reading. The teacher records this second session in a separate recording for further analysis. Retrospective miscue analysis is more than assessment; it becomes a powerful instructional tool when the student listens for his errors and attempts to understand if the error disrupted the intended message. When he listens to his reading, he also determines if he has read at an appropriate rate and if he has made the same type of errors throughout the passage (Goodman & Marek, 1996).

Running Records

Running records, designed by Marie Clay (2000c), are another type of informal assessment. The purpose of the running record is to give a teacher the opportunity to observe, score, and interpret a student's reading behaviors. As the name suggests, this tool provides a running record of the student's oral reading. The process involves three steps:

1. Recording the student's oral reading through check marks and other conventions.
2. Examining each error and determining which of the three cueing systems—syntactic, semantic, or graphophonic—the student used when making the errors.
3. Determining if the passage is at the student's independent, instructional, or frustration reading level.

Unlike the miscue analysis, a running record does not require the teacher to use a prepared script or a recording device. The only tools the teacher needs are a copy of a book from which the student reads, a pen or pencil, and a blank sheet of paper. In a running record, all words read incorrectly are called *errors* instead of *miscues*.

The goals of the running record and the miscue analysis are different. In the miscue analysis, the goals are to determine if the miscue disrupts the intended meaning of the text and if the student comprehends what he reads. The goals of the running record are to (1) determine a student's instructional level, (2) analyze cues used and cues neglected during oral reading, (3) analyze the student's strategic processing of a text through the teacher's interpretation of the strategies used during oral reading, and (4) use the results to guide individual instruction.

Quantitative analysis of running records

The marking conventions used for the quantitative analysis of running records are somewhat different from those used in a miscue analysis. The teacher makes a check mark (✓) for each word the student reads correctly. Figure 3.13 lists the conventions used to record a reader's oral reading, with examples. Each error is recorded above the word that appears in the text with a horizontal line separating the two words. In order for the teacher to relate the running record to the text, he makes the check marks on the record in the same pattern as the words on the page. For example, if the first page of the passage has three lines, with five words on each line, the teacher makes five check marks (if the student reads all words correctly) on three different lines. To keep track of page numbers, the teacher draws a line across the page for every new page and records the page number in the left column.

When scoring a running record, a teacher calculates the errors in the following manner:

1. Substitutions, omissions, insertions, and "tolds" each count as one error.
2. Multiple attempts count only as one error.
3. Self-corrections do *not* count as errors.
4. Repeats are *not* errors.

The percentage of correct words read correctly is calculated by (1) subtracting the number of errors from the total number of words in the reading, (2) dividing that remainder by the number of words in the passage, and (3) multiplying the answer by 100. For example, a passage has 200 words, and Jodi has 20 errors.

$200 - 20 = 180$

$180 \div 200 = .9$

$.9 \times 100 = 90\%$

Jodi reads 90 percent of the words correctly. Figure 3.14 provides a conversion table for a running record, and Figure 3.15 lists the reading level for the percentage of words read correctly. The passage that Jodi reads is at her instructional level.

figure 3.13 Running record conventions.

Correct reading	=	✓ ✓ ✓	
Omission (one error)	=	Child / text	— / very
Insertion (one error)	=	Child / text	very / —
Repeats (no error)	=	R (one repeat), R2 (two repeats)	R2 / The house
Self-corrections (no error)	=	misread sc / text	want/went / went
Appeal	=	— | A / Text	"What's that word?" / hurricane
Teacher told (one error)	=	— | / Text | T	long pause | / hurricane | (teacher gives word)

Try that again [TTA]: one error for the entire confusion (if a reader jumps a line or really gets confused).

figure **3.14** Conversion table for running records.

EASY READING LEVEL		INSTRUCTIONAL READING LEVEL		DIFFICULT READING LEVEL	
Error Rate	*Percentage (%) Accuracy Rate*	*Error Rate*	*Percentage (%) Accuracy Rate*	*Error Rate*	*Percentage (%) Accuracy Rate*
1:200	99.5	1:17	94	1:9	89
1:100	99	1:14	93	1:8	87.5
1:50	98	1:12.5	92	1:7	85.5
1:35	97	1:11.75	91	1:6	83
1:25	96	1:10	90	1:5	80
1:20	95			1:4	75
				1:3	66
				1:2	50

Source: Adapted from Schulman, M., & Payne, C. (2000). *Guided Reading: Making It Work.* New York: Scholastic.

figure **3.15**

Reading levels for percentage of words read correctly.

95–100%	=	Easy level
90–94%	=	Instructional level
Below 90%	=	Frustration level

Qualitative analysis of running records

The quantitative analysis of a running record identifies the reading level of the passage for a particular student, while the qualitative analysis determines which of three cueing systems—semantic, syntactic, and graphophonic—(note the pragmatic system is not analyzed during a running record) the student uses when encountering an unknown word and whether she self-corrects and monitors her reading. The quantitative analysis lets the teacher know if the reading material was too easy, too hard, or perfect for the instructional purpose, while the qualitative analysis helps a teacher decide which reading strategies to teach the student. The qualitative analysis helps the teacher determine which cueing system—semantic, syntactic, or graphophonic—the student uses while making each error.

Semantic system. If the student uses the semantic cueing system, the sentence will still make sense. The teacher asks herself, "Does this error make sense in the sentence and passage? Is the meaning the same?" If a student reads *house* instead of *home* in the following sentence, the meaning remains almost exactly the same: "We moved to a new home last fall."

Syntactic system. When the student uses the syntactic system, the error sounds correct in the sentence. The question the teacher asks is, "Does that sound right in the sentence?" The student who reads, "I got a valentine *for* my grandmother" instead of "I got a valentine *from* my grandmother" is using the syntactic cueing system. The reader changes the meaning of the sentence; however, the error fits the sentence structure.

Visual or graphophonic system. A student uses the graphophonic system when the word he reads erroneously resembles the word in the text. The error may share the same initial letter as the word in the text, or it may share other letters of the word in the text. The question the teacher asks is, "Does the error look like the word in the text?" For example, if Jodi reads *cap* instead of *cape,* she is using the visual cueing system.

Thus, when determining which cueing system the student is using, the teacher asks three questions: "Does it make sense?"; "Does it sound right?"; and "Does it look right?" During instructional time, the teacher prompts the reader to ask herself these three questions when encountering unknown words. Note that when administering a running record, the teacher focuses on the specific cueing system that the reader uses.

The teacher uses the acronym MSV (Meaning, Structure, Visual) to represent the three cueing systems. Notice the four columns marked E, SC, E, and SC on the right side of the scoring sheet in Figure 3.16. In the first E column, the teacher records the number of errors the reader makes in each line. In

figure 3.16 Running record of *Just Juice* by Karen Hesse.

TEXT	RUNNING RECORD	ANALYSIS Number E	Number SC	System Used E	System Used SC
PAGE					
12 While I stand in the raggedy	When/While ✓ ✓ ✓ ✓ r – r/raggedy	2		M S (V) M S (V)	
road, my sisters start walking	✓ ✓ s-sis/sc/sister ✓ walk/sc/walking		2		M S (V) M S (V)
to school without me, shoulder	✓ ✓ with/without ✓ show/shoulder	2	0	M S (V) M S (V)	
to shoulder, closing up the	✓ —/shoulder ✓ ✓ ✓	1	0	M S V	
little space where I had been	✓ s-sp/sc/space ✓ ✓ ✓ ✓	0	1		M S (V)
in the middle. Half of me	✓ ✓ mind/middle ✓ ✓ ✓	1	0	M S (V)	
wishes I was going down	✓ ✓ ✓ ✓ ✓	0	0		
that raggedy road with them.	✓ —/raggedy ✓ ✓ ✓	1	0	M S V	

M = meaning (semantic system); S = structure (syntactic system); V = visual (visual/graphophonic system); E = errors; SC = self-corrections

Source: Hesse, K. (1998). *Just Juice,* p. 12. New York: Scholastic. Reprinted with permission.

the first SC column, the teacher records the number of self-corrections the reader makes in each line. In the second E column, the teacher writes an MSV for each error the reader makes in each line. If a reader makes three errors in one line, the teacher writes three MSVs on that line and circles the cueing system the reader used for each error. Many times the reader uses more than one cueing system for each error. In those cases the teacher circles each letter that represents a cueing system used by the reader. In the second SC column, the teacher writes an MSV for each self-correction and circles the cueing system the reader uses for each self-correction. Figure 3.16 is a sample record for a student's reading of *Just Juice* (1998) by Karen Hesse. The story's original text is provided in the left column.

Once a teacher determines which cueing system(s) a student uses when reaching an unknown word, he can use these findings during instruction. For example, when Jodi, a struggling sixth-grade reader, reads *Just Juice* (Figure 3.16), she uses visual cues to self-correct. With two of the three self-corrections, she sounds out the word. During instructional time, the teacher will help Jodi develop strategies to use the other cueing systems that she currently does not use, such as reading to the end of the sentence and then going back to insert a word that makes sense. The student must determine if the inserted word begins with the same sound as the printed word. For example, the student may provide the word *winding* for *raggedy,* which makes sense, but the printed word begins with an *r.* The teacher prompts the student to use other clues to decode "raggedy."

As previously stated, running records can be tallied on a sheet of plain paper. However, for beginning teachers and tutors, the blank form in Appendix C.5 may prove helpful. The top of the form includes spaces for the reader's name, the name of the story, the quantitative score, and some general notes about the reading.

Cloze Test

The cloze test is another informal reading assessment. The purpose of the cloze test is twofold—for informal assessment and for instruction. When used for assessment, the cloze test helps a teacher to (1) understand how readers use context and background knowledge to figure out unknown words, and (2) determine if a text is too easy or too difficult for a particular reader. When used for instruction, the cloze test shows students how to use context clues and background knowledge to decipher unknown words. A cloze passage can be taken from any text, and the length of the passage is 125 to 500 words, depending on the reader's grade level. To construct a cloze test, delete every fifth word in the passage, while keeping the first and last lines intact. To calculate the reader's score, divide the total number of correct suggestions for missing words by the total number of blanks. For example, if there are 100 missing words and the student provides 80 correct responses, the student's final score is 80 percent.

The most valid scoring system for diagnostic purposes is to accept only the exact word (Ruddell, 1964). When using the cloze test for instructional purposes, synonyms are acceptable (Gillet & Temple, 2004). When determining the reading level, the following scale is used:

Individual reading level = 60–100%
Instructional reading level = 40–59%
Frustration reading level = Below 40%

Later chapters will discuss in detail and provide examples of how to use cloze tests in instruction.

Figure 3.17 provides a short example of a cloze test from Chapter One of *Little Men: Life at Plumfield with Jo's Boys* by Louisa May Alcott (1913). Because the reader has only 12 correct responses—approximately 46 percent—the passage is at the reader's instructional level. Because most of the responses make sense, the teacher concludes that student reads for meaning and will be able to comprehend the passage with some

figure 3.17 Sample cloze test.

CHAPTER 1

"Please, sir, is this Plumfield?" asked a ragged boy of the man who opened the great gate at which the omnibus left him.

"Yes; who sent you?"

"(Hello) ____1____ Laurence. I have got (a) ____2____ letter for the lady."

"(All) ____3____ right; go up to (the) ____4____ house and give it (to) ____5____ her; she'll see to (it) ____6____, little chap."

The man (talked) ____7____ pleasantly, and the boy (walked) ____8____ on, feeling much cheered (by) ____9____ the words. Through the (new) ____10____ spring rain that fell (on) ____11____ sprouting grass and budding (flowers) ____12____, Nat saw a large (green) ____13____ house before him—a (big) ____14____ house, with an old-fashioned (porch) ____15____, with wide steps, and lights (on) ____16____ in many windows. Neither (curtains) ____17____ nor shutters hid the (shiny) ____18____ glimmer; and, pausing a (second) ____19____ before he rang, Nat (saw) ____20____ many little shadows dancing (on) ____21____ the walls, heard the (cheerful) ____22____ hum of young voices, (and) ____23____ felt that it was (just) ____24____ possible that the light (and) ____25____ warmth and comfort within (would) ____26____ be for a homeless "little chap" like him.

"I hope the lady will see to me," he thought; and gave a timid rap with the great bronze knocker, which was a jovial griffin's head.

ANSWERS:

1. Mr.	2. a	3. All	4. the	5. to	6. you
7. spoke	8. went	9. by	10. soft	11. on	12. trees
13. square	14. hospitable-looking	15. porch	16. shining	17. curtains	18. cheerful
19. moment	20. saw	21. on	22. pleasant	23. and	24. hardly
25. and	26. could				

Source: Excerpt from *Little Men: Life at Plumfield with Jo's Boys,* by Louisa M. Alcott. Copyright © 1913, Little, Brown, & Co.

instructional help. If the teacher observes the student during the reading, she will be able to detect the strategies the student uses. Does he read to the end of the sentence to figure out the missing word? Does he read past the sentence to figure out the missing word? Based on observation, the teacher introduces the strategies not used by the student.

Maze Test

The maze test is much like the cloze test in purpose and construction. Its purpose is to allow younger students to demonstrate what context clues and background knowledge they use when they encounter unknown words. Like the cloze test, the maze test can be used for diagnostic and for instructional purposes. To construct a maze test, again delete every fifth word while keeping the first and last sentences intact. However, instead of leaving a blank, give students three choices. One choice is correct; one fits the sentence's syntax; and the third choice does not fit the sentence in any way. Figure 3.18 presents a short example from Paula Danziger's (2001) *A is for Amber: It's Justin Time, Amber Brown.* The maze test works best when the teacher observes the student during the process and notes whether the student rereads sentences, reads beyond the word choice, or reads beyond the sentence to figure out the word.

Anecdotal Records

Anecdotal records refer to notes a teacher makes about student behavior. Anecdotal records follow no criteria or standards; they are merely a teacher's observations about a student's habits, attitudes, or abilities. A teacher may record changes in attitude for one student and changes in the reading strategies for another. The notes can be taken in a number of ways. Some teachers keep anecdotal records in a file folder for each student; some use a three-ring notebook; and others maintain a computer file. Each teacher should select a method that is compatible with her organizational style, begin taking notes at

figure 3.18 Maze test for *A Is for Amber: It's Justin Time, Amber Brown* by Paula Danziger.

I, Amber Brown,
am one very excited six-year,
364-day-old kid.
I am so excited
1. 2.
(which, that, too) I am dancing with (your, two, my) toy gorilla.
3.
He is (a, that, for) two-year,
364-day-old gorilla.
4. 5.
I (have, got, by) him on my fourth (school, built, birthday).
6.
Tomorrow, July 7, is our (fun, birthday, bottle).
7.
Last year I was (seven, five, six) on July 7.
8. 9.
Next year (I, we, too) will be eight on (August 3, birthday, July 7).
This year I will be seven on July 7. (p. 5)

ANSWERS:

1. that	2. my	3. a	4. got	5. birthday
6. birthday	7. six	8. I	9. July 7	

Source: Excerpt from *It's Justin Time, Amber Brown*, text by Paula Danziger, illustrated by Tony Ross, copyright © 2001 by Paula Danziger. Used by permission of G. P. Putnam's Sons, a division of Penguin Young Readers Group, a member of Penguin Group (USA) Inc., New York, NY 10014. All rights reserved.

the start of the school year, and continue until year's end.

Mr. Jackson, a first-grade teacher, and Mr. Green, a second-grade teacher, both keep anecdotal records for their students. At the beginning of the year Mr. Jackson notes that Ali is shy and appears to have negative feelings about reading. As you read the anecdotal records for Ali in Figure 3.19, note how Mr. Jackson detects the problem that hinders Ali from becoming engaged in the reading activities. Figure 3.20 displays Mr. Green's notes (taken on a tablet computer) about Rosa, whose native language is Spanish. His notes are based on Rosa's reading habits. Mr. Green records the instructional strategies he uses to help Rosa become a more proficient reader. Notice that Mr. Green's notes are very detailed. Not all anecdotal records need to be so thorough.

Checklists

Checklists allow teachers to gauge students' literacy gains throughout the year. A checklist includes all traits the teacher expects students to display by the end of the school year. Each observation is dated; the checklist may include a column to mark "yes" if the trait is observed or "no" if it is not. Symbols may be used to show consistency of a trait (e.g., a plus sign means "always observed," a check means "sometimes observed," and a zero means "seldom observed"). Symbols may also be used to indicate degrees of mastery of a trait (e.g., a plus sign means "target," a check means "acceptable," and a zero means "unacceptable").

The objective of a checklist is threefold: (1) to assist a teacher as he observes a student's behavior or performance; (2) to assist a teacher as he plans for instruction; and (3) "to compare evidence of behavior

figure **3.19** Mr. Jackson's anecdotal record.

STUDENT: Ali GRADE: 1st

DATE:	COMMENTS
9-10	Ali readily went to the back of the group rug during shared book reading when other children pushed her. During the reading of the story, she did not pay attention and offered no comments to the class discussion.
9-12	Ali sat right in the middle of the horseshoe table during guided reading, facing me. She pointed to each word as we read in unison. She contributed to group discussion. She appears to have a speech impediment.
9-13	During guided reading, she sat at the end of the horseshoe table, next to me. She did not follow along with her finger. She did not read in unison with group and gave no comments during discussion.
9-17	During shared reading, she sat right in front of me and chimed in on "Catch me if you can." She added comments during discussion. She definitely has a speech problem. I referred her to Ms. Wilson, the speech teacher.
9-18	Ms. Wilson reported that Ali has a hearing problem. She called her mother. Ali reads lips.
9-19	During guided reading, Ali sat directly in front of me so she could hear and read my lips. She participated in unison reading and discussion. She told me she gets to go to the hospital to get her ears fixed.
9-24	Ali had tubes put into her ears.
10-1	During guided reading, she sat at the end of the table and participated. She told me she can hear now!
10-2	During shared reading, she sat at the back of the rug and chimed in and discussed questions with the group.

figure **3.20** Mr. Green's anecdotal record.

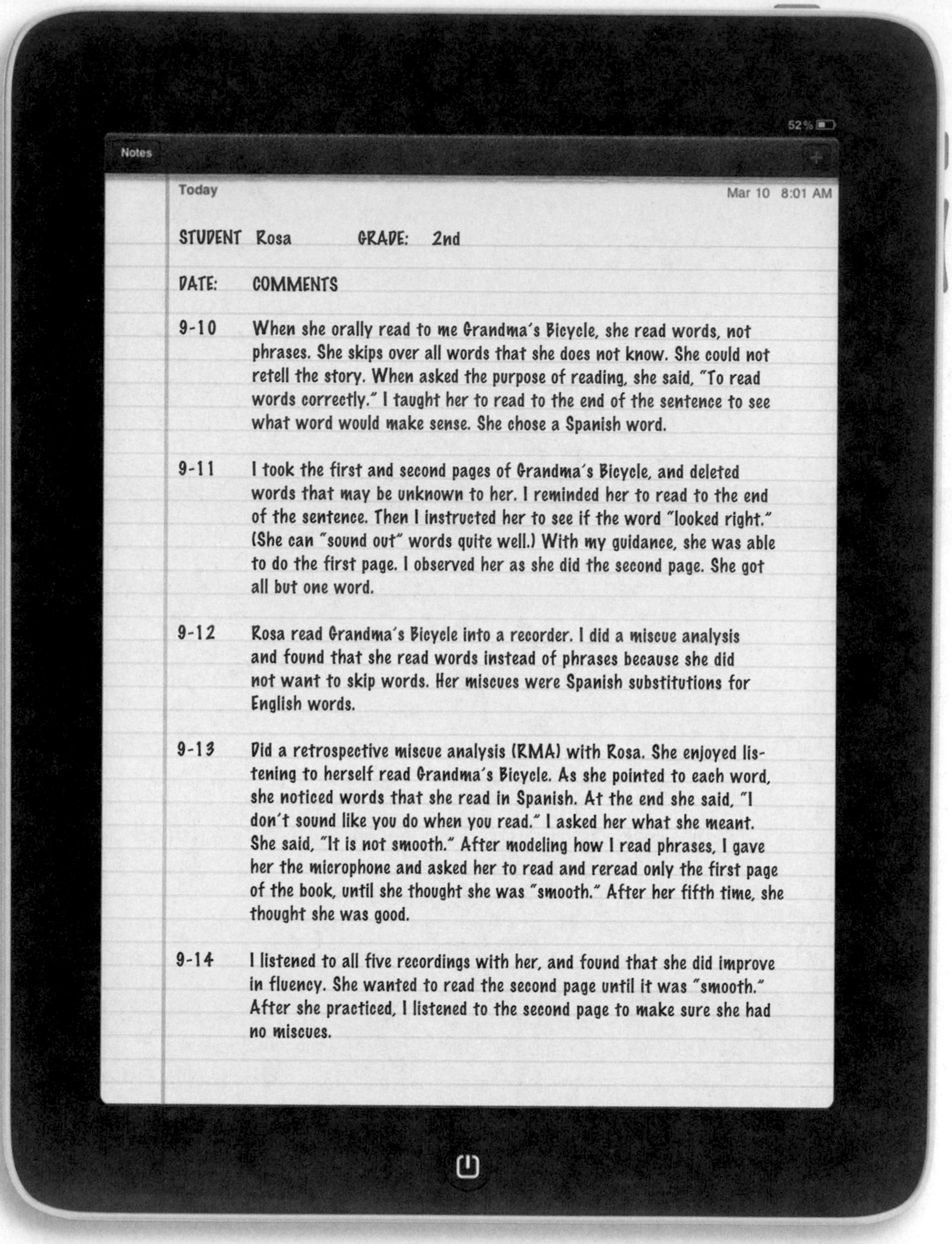
Notes

Today Mar 10 8:01 AM

STUDENT Rosa GRADE: 2nd

DATE: COMMENTS

9-10 When she orally read to me Grandma's Bicycle, she read words, not phrases. She skips over all words that she does not know. She could not retell the story. When asked the purpose of reading, she said, "To read words correctly." I taught her to read to the end of the sentence to see what word would make sense. She chose a Spanish word.

9-11 I took the first and second pages of Grandma's Bicycle, and deleted words that may be unknown to her. I reminded her to read to the end of the sentence. Then I instructed her to see if the word "looked right." (She can "sound out" words quite well.) With my guidance, she was able to do the first page. I observed her as she did the second page. She got all but one word.

9-12 Rosa read Grandma's Bicycle into a recorder. I did a miscue analysis and found that she read words instead of phrases because she did not want to skip words. Her miscues were Spanish substitutions for English words.

9-13 Did a retrospective miscue analysis (RMA) with Rosa. She enjoyed listening to herself read Grandma's Bicycle. As she pointed to each word, she noticed words that she read in Spanish. At the end she said, "I don't sound like you do when you read." I asked her what she meant. She said, "It is not smooth." After modeling how I read phrases, I gave her the microphone and asked her to read and reread only the first page of the book, until she thought she was "smooth." After her fifth time, she thought she was good.

9-14 I listened to all five recordings with her, and found that she did improve in fluency. She wanted to read the second page until it was "smooth." After she practiced, I listened to the second page to make sure she had no miscues.

over time and thus help determine student progress" (Cooper & Kiger, 2005, p. 31). To design a checklist, a teacher includes a list of competencies—often based on national or state standards or benchmarks—that all students are expected to attain by the end of the school year. The checklist may be used at the end of each quarter so the teacher can analyze which students are meeting the standards and which students need more instructional time and practice.

Figure 3.21 reproduces a standard from the Oklahoma Core Curriculum Guide. To illustrate the design of a checklist based on such state standards, Figure 3.22 shows a partial checklist that includes the main language arts standards for the second grade in Oklahoma. The Oklahoma Standards are called the Priority Academic Student Skills (PASS). The partial checklist was completed after the first grading period. The teacher could see which students were progress-

figure 3.21 Standard 5: Comprehension/critical literacy.

The student will interact with the words and concepts in a text to construct an appropriate meaning.

1. Literal Understanding
   a. Read and comprehend both fiction and nonfiction that is appropriately designed for the second half of second grade.
   b. Use prereading strategies to preview, activate prior knowledge, make predictions, use picture clues, and establish the purpose for reading (e.g., graphic organizers).
   c. Ask and respond to questions to aid comprehension about important elements of fiction and nonfiction.
2. Inferences and Interpretation
   a. Make inferences about events, characters, and ideas in fictional texts by connecting knowledge and experience to the story.
   b. Support interpretations or conclusions with examples taken from the text.
3. Summary and Generalization
   a. Retell or act out narrative text by identifying story elements and sequencing the events.
   b. Produce oral or written summaries of text selections by discussing who, what, when, where, why, and how to identify the main idea and significant supporting details of text.
4. Analysis and Evaluation
   a. Identify cause/effect relationships in text.
   b. Make comparisons and draw conclusions based on what is read.
   c. Describe character traits, changes, and relationships.
5. Monitoring and Correction Strategies—Integrate the use of semantics, syntax, and graphophonic cues to gain meaning from the text.

Source: Oklahoma State Department of Education. (revised 2002). *A Core Curriculum for Our Children's Future: Priority Academic Student Skills (PASS).* Oklahoma City: Author.

figure 3.22 Checklist for second grade, based on PASS.

TEACHER Mr. Reinhart DATE Jan.

\+ = always x = sometimes 0 = seldom/never

STANDARD	Hannah	Kent	Marc	Reed	Zack	Vanessa	Austin	Lauren	Adam	Merrick	Ryan	Emily	Rachel	Jacob	Chrystie	Miranda	Juanita	Riley
1. Read and comprehend fiction, suitable for grade level.	+	X	X	+	+	X	O	O	+	+	+	X	X	+	+	+	X	O
2. Read and comprehend nonfiction, suitable for grade level.	X	O	X	+	+	O	O	O	+	X	+	X	O	+	+	+	O	O
3. Uses prereading strategies to preview and make predictions.	+	O	X	+	O	O	O	O	O	X	+	O	O	O	+	+	O	O
4. Uses picture clues and graphic organizers as prereading strategies.	X	O	O	+	O	O	O	O	O	O	+	O	O	O	+	+	O	O

ing and who needed extra help. The complete checklist is located in Appendix C.6.

This particular checklist gives the date and the names of the students. The plus sign (+) indicates that the student performs the task all the time, an X indicates that the student performs the task sometimes, and a zero (0) means that the student does not perform the task. As you can tell, this type of assessment also provides a general assessment of the class. From this assessment, the teacher can readily note which standards no one in the class has met and thus need to be addressed.

Another checklist, based on the National Standards for the English Language Arts established by the National Council of Teachers of English (NCTE) and the International Reading Association (IRA) in 1996, is provided in Appendix C.7. This checklist is specific to one student and records the context in which each behavior was observed. The teacher may use this type of checklist to show the student and his caregivers his progress in meeting national standards. Checklists that do not include the context are more subjective and serve as general guidelines for teachers.

The Literacy Habits checklists in Appendices C.8–C.12 are intended for use with early emergent through proficient readers. A teacher may need to use two consecutive checklists to get accurate records of the student's behavior. Later chapters will discuss other checklists for assessing specific aspects of literacy.

Rubrics

A rubric "describes the knowledge and skills a particular project or performance demonstrates, based on specific criteria for quality work" (Fiderer, 1999, p. 5). Like checklists, rubrics list competencies that students are expected to master. Unlike checklists, rubrics are *scoring guides* for particular assignments or for an evaluation period within the school year. Most rubrics describe three or four levels of achievement or performance. Each level gives a detailed explanation of the degree of mastery and/or a numerical score. Often the same rubric is used for similar assignments throughout the year so it can document student growth in a particular area. The rubric in Figure 3.23, used at the end of each grading period, gives a detailed explanation of degrees of mastery. Like many rubrics this one is based on a state standard, in this case the Oklahoma Priority Academic Student Skills (PASS), Standard 5 for the second grade. The standard is printed in Figure 3.21.

The rubric in Figure 3.23 closely reflects the state standard, and using it helps the teacher focus on each item in the standard. Note that the rubric's target degree of mastery (5 points) corresponds with the state standard; the other two degrees of mastery—acceptable (3 points) and unacceptable (1 point)—represent the degree to which the student has met the standard.

If the teacher uses the same rubric each quarter, she can document each student's progress in reading comprehension. If the entire class is weak in one or two areas, she can readily tell which part of the standard she needs to emphasize with the class. The rubric will also identify the weaknesses of individual students.

Figure 3.23 presents Victor's rubric at the end of the first grading period, completed by his teacher after reviewing Victor's portfolios, running records, and miscue analyses for nine weeks. The teacher's comments at the end of the rubric summarize its contents. Obviously, at the end of the first grading period, no second grader would have reached the target degree of mastery in each part of Standard 5; therefore, Victor will not score a 42 percent for the grading period. Rather, the percentage helps Victor's teacher mark his growth from one grading period to the next. Some teachers may choose not to assign a number to degrees of mastery.

Rubrics for a variety of subjects can be accessed at http://Rubistar.4teachers.org. The rubrics at this site fall into eight main categories—oral projects, research/writing, work skills, multimedia, science, math, music, and art. There are rubrics in English, Spanish, and Dutch. The user can modify the rubrics to fit a particular assignment.

Portfolios

Portfolios are collections of students' work from the school year. They are useful tools to organize materials, document growth, and display exemplary work. Portfolios can be file folders, three-ring binders, or electronic files. It is helpful for each portfolio to include a log to record the title of the composition or passage read and the date it was completed. There are three types of portfolios—working portfolios, best-work portfolios, and growth portfolios. Any of these can be in an electronic rather than a physical format.

Working portfolios

Working portfolios organize a student's work-in-progress. For example, a working portfolio for reading may contain a recording that the student is using to increase reading expression, rate, or fluency. If a student is writing a research report, the working portfolio may contain prewriting graphic organizers; notes taken from sources; a list of sources; all

figure 3.23 Rubric for reading comprehension based on Standard 5 of the Oklahoma PASS.

SECOND GRADE

STUDENT: Victor GRADING PERIOD (1) 2 3 4 TOTAL SCORE: 23/55

	LEVEL OF MASTERY		
TRAIT	**Target (5 points)**	**Acceptable (3 points)**	**Unacceptable (1 point)**
1. Grade Appropriate Material	Reads & comprehends fiction and nonfiction at the assigned grade & month. ___	Reads & comprehends fiction & nonfiction at two or three months below grade level. X	Reads & comprehends fiction & nonfiction at more than three months below grade level. ___
2. Prereading Strategies	Always uses prereading strategies to preview, activate prior knowledge, make predictions, use picture clues, & establish the purpose for reading. ___	Sometimes uses prereading strategies to preview, activate prior knowledge, make predictions, use picture clues, & establish the purpose for reading. X	Seldom uses prereading strategies to preview, activate prior knowledge, make predictions, use picture clues, & establish the purpose for reading. ___
3. Questioning	Always asks & responds to questions to aid comprehension about important elements of fiction & nonfiction. ___	Sometimes asks & responds to questions to aid comprehension about important elements of fiction & nonfiction. ___	Seldom asks & responds to questions to aid comprehension about important elements of fiction & nonfiction. X
4. Inference & Interpretation	Always makes inferences about events, characters, & ideas in fictional texts by connecting prior knowledge to story. ___	Sometimes makes inferences about events, characters, & ideas in fictional texts by connecting prior knowledge to story. ___	Seldom makes inferences about events, characters, & ideas in fictional texts by connecting prior knowledge to story. X
5. Gives Examples	Always supports interpretations or conclusions with examples from the text. ___	Sometimes supports interpretations or conclusions with examples from the text. ___	Seldom supports interpretations or conclusions with examples from the text. X
6. Retells	Always retells or acts out narrative by correctly sequencing the events. ___	Retells or acts out narrative with some events out of order. X	Retells or acts out narrative with most events out of order. ___
7. Summarizes	Always produces oral or written summaries of text by discussing *who, what, when, where, why,* and *how* to identify the main idea and significant supporting details. ___	Sometimes produces oral or written summaries of text by discussing *who, what, when, where, why,* and *how* to identify the main idea and significant supporting details. X	Seldom produces oral or written summaries of text by discussing *who, what, when, where, why,* and *how* to identify the main idea and significant supporting details. ___
8. Cause/Effect	Always identifies cause/effect relationships. ___	Sometimes identifies cause/effect relationships. ___	Seldom identifies cause/effect relationships. X
9. Comparisons	Always makes comparisons & draws conclusions. ___	Sometimes makes comparisons & draws conclusions.	Seldom makes comparisons & draws conclusions. X
10. Descriptions	Always describes character traits, changes, & relationships. ___	Sometimes describes character traits, changes, & relationships. X	Seldom describes character traits, changes, & relationships. ___
11. Monitoring	Always integrates the use of semantic, syntactic, & graphophonic cues to gain meaning. ___	Sometimes integrates the use of semantic, syntactic, & graphophonic cues to gain meaning. ___	Seldom integrates the use of semantic, syntactic, & graphophonic cues to gain meaning. X

TEACHER COMMENTS:

Victor's strength is his ability to retell most of a story in order and list main events. He enjoys talking about characters. He uses graphophonic cues most of the time and sometimes uses syntax. Victor struggles w/expository text. He needs one-on-one attention while reading expository text that is at his instructional level.

drafts and revisions; the editing copy; and the final copy. After the teacher has assessed and discussed the process and result of the project, the final copy of the composition, poem, or report is placed in the growth portfolio.

Growth portfolios

Teachers usually have one growth portfolio for reading, one for writing, and another for math or other subjects. The growth portfolio contains final copies of the student's work along with their scoring rubrics.

Because they contain samples of a student's work over time, growth portfolios are valuable assessment tools for documenting achievement in reading and writing. For example, a growth portfolio may include an audio recording of the student's monthly reading. With each reading, the teacher includes a miscue analysis, a running record and/or anecdotal records, as well as checklists and rubrics used to assess the student's reading ability. The teacher then uses the recording to (1) discuss reading strengths and weaknesses with students and parents, (2) plan for future instruction, and (3) encourage readers' abilities.

Teachers can share the growth portfolios during parent–teacher conferences to illustrate the particular literacy skills the students are developing or need to develop. It will also help the teacher and caregiver identify the areas in which the child may need extra help. For example, if a second-grade student cannot retell a story in the correct sequence by the end of the third grading period, the teacher and caregiver know that they need to give the child opportunities to develop that skill. Portfolios are tools to encourage the caregiver and the child about the child's growth.

Best-work portfolios

If the student believes that an item represents his best work, he places a copy of it in his best-work portfolio. The best-work writing portfolio may contain poems, stories, reports, and newspaper articles, each accompanied by a self-assessment sheet explaining why the student believes it is one of his best works. The best-work reading portfolio may include selections from the student's favorite stories, poems, and other passages. The student reviews each selection and chooses to keep it as a favorite story, poem, or passage.

Electronic portfolios

The contents of electronic portfolios are usually the same as the file-folder and three-ring binder versions, but items are saved digitally. The electronic portfolio contains scanned forms, student writings, audio versions of students' readings, digital photographs, and videos. The material is stored electronically. Teachers and students must be able to use equipment such as scanners, digital cameras, video cameras, and portfolio software.

One flexible software program is the *Scholastic Electronic Portfolio*. The program permits the teacher to store text, record a student's readings, and make slide shows and videos. The program comes with a detailed manual for teachers.

Another software program that can be used in primary and middle school is *The Portfolio Assessment Kit,* produced by Super School Software. This program is designed for the Mac but can be transferred to PCs. It allows student writing to be stored and viewed easily; teachers can use it to scan rubrics, checklists, logs, and anecdotal records that can be shared with caregivers during conferences. All records can be viewed on the screen and printed out. A third software program, useful to elementary and middle school teachers, is *The Portfolio Builder for PowerPoint,* produced by Visions-Technology in Education. This program permits users to create graphics, sound, and video in addition to text.

Study the capabilities of several portfolio programs before you purchase one. Ask yourself, (1) What do I want to accomplish with the program? (2) Is it complicated and time consuming to operate? (3) Can students readily learn how to use it?

INFORMAL ASSESSMENT FOR ENGLISH LEARNERS

The two assessments for English learners discussed earlier, the LAS–O and LAS–R/W, measure general growth, but they are not diagnostic-oriented (Kuhlman, 2005). Classroom teachers, especially in grades four and up, require additional methods to measure English learners' literacy development in teacher-designed, subject-area tests such as science, social studies, math, and health education. Lenski, Ehlers-Zavala, Daniel, and Sun-Irminger (2006) suggest authentic performance assessments for this purpose.

Lenski et al. (2006) use Hurley and Blake's (2000) six guiding principles for teachers as they consider authentic performance assessments. They are:

1. Assessment activities should help teachers make instructional decisions.
2. Assessment strategies should help teachers find out what students know and can do . . . not what they cannot do.
3. The holistic context for learning should be considered and assessed.

4. Assessment activities should grow out of authentic learning activities.
5. Best assessments of student learning are longitudinal . . . they take place over time.
6. Each assessment activity should have a specific objective-linked purpose. (Lenski et al., p. 25)

Depending on the information teachers seek about an English learner, they can choose from several types of authentic assessments. The first type of authentic assessment measures an English learner's knowledge base. Teachers determine this knowledge base by interviewing the student, family members, former teachers, and any community worker who may have assisted in the student's literacy development. From these sources teachers determine what type of formal education (if any) the students have had or are receiving in their native language, including whether the students currently attend literacy classes in their native language. This assessment aids the teacher's understanding of the student's background. Never assume that all English learners with the same first language have had similar experiences.

The second type of authentic assessment permits students to demonstrate what they know using non-language methods. These include Venn diagrams, charts, drawings, PowerPoint presentations, or other multimodal methods. See Chapters 8 and 9.

The third type of assessment is observation. Teachers observe students' abilities and willingness to participate in literacy discussions and small group circles and work with their peers.

The language experience approach (LEA) is an instructional strategy that can also be used for assessment. The teacher writes the text as the student dictates the "experience"; then the teacher informally assesses the student each time he reads it back. The teacher assesses the correct pronunciation of words, the prosody, and fluency. The student may also note syntax errors that he made in the initial dictation.

To encourage students to self-monitor their development, teachers may have them write reflections on the LEA. Students may reflect how the content connects to another subject or how one story reminds them of another.

Teachers can also authentically assess English learners by modifying a teacher-created test. The following modifications from Lenski et al. (2006) are in addition to those listed earlier in the chapter:

1. Give the test orally. Assess content knowledge by reading the test to students and permitting them to answer orally. If the teacher wants to assess the student's reading ability, the student can read the text and answer the questions orally. Often students' reading (receptive) skills are stronger than their writing (expressive) skills. Letting them answer orally bypasses their weaker writing skills but allows the teacher to assess their stronger reading skills.
2. Give the test in small segments. English learners may read more slowly than other students and process information in their native language before answering in English. This takes more time than reading, thinking, and answering in English. Dividing the test into small segments will keep students from becoming exhausted and giving up on the task.
3. Use as many visuals as possible. The visuals can include photos, drawings, charts, diagrams, or any type of graphic organizer.
4. Permit students to use glossaries in English or in their native language.
5. Simplify vocabulary and sentence structures by using synonyms and simple sentences.
6. Simplify directions so English learners understand how to complete the assessment.
7. Write tasks instead of questions, using imperative statements. For example, instead of "Who signed the Declaration of Independence?" state: "Write the names of the men who signed (wrote their names at the bottom of) the Declaration of Independence."
8. Permit students to take breaks during the assessment. Tests in middle school often last the entire 45- or 50-minute period; allowing a small break for students to stretch or rest their eyes will prevent them from becoming exhausted and rushing to finish with the task.
9. Give double grades on essay tests, one for correct responses and another for grammatical correctness.

One free website designed to informally assess English learners in many different subject areas is http://world-english.org. This site has online assessment tests in vocabulary, grammar, reading comprehension, listening, writing, literature-based quizzes on Shakespeare and other novels, and WebQuests that assess world-content knowledge. The grammar tests assess student's knowledge in Standard English usage, while the reading comprehension tests require the student to read a passage and answer the questions. All these assessments begin at an easy level and become more difficult if the student's answers are correct. With some of the multiple-choice tests, if the student answers incorrectly, the same question appears later with the answers given in a different order. The computer indicates immediately if the answer is correct, and the student receives her score at the end of the test.

As discussed above, teachers and districts can use both formal and informal or authentic assessments to determine the individual literacy development of English learners and whether or not the district's literacy program is meeting these students' needs.

PERSONAL INTEREST SURVEYS

If you know each student's interests, you can provide them with more effective, individualized reading and writing opportunities that will motivate them to engage in the activities. Figure 3.24 is a personal interest survey for young students. The teacher should be the scribe so the student will express what he really likes without worrying about spelling or grammar. Try extending the interest inventory if the student expresses interest in things not on the survey. To illustrate how the interest survey can provide the student with more meaningful literacy experiences, Figure 3.24 suggests that Grey enjoys spending time with his grandpa. His teacher can then look for stories about grandparents, such as Tomie dePaola's *Tom*.

Personal interest surveys are also useful for older students. Some may enjoy informational books or magazines but dislike funny stories. Others may not like informational books but enjoy mysteries or other puzzle-like materials. Older students should complete the surveys themselves to ensure honest responses. If they give their responses verbally, they may tend to give what they believe is the "correct" answer, rather than an honest answer. Use the completed surveys to find materials that interest the students. Figure 3.25 contains a partially completed personal interest survey for older students; Appendix C.13 contains the full survey.

figure **3.24** Personal interest survey for young students.

MY FAVORITES!
By Grey

Foods:
pizza
grandpa's waffles

Snacks:
apples
grapes

Hunt for bugs

Swim by grandpa's house

Sleep over by grandpa's house

Read:
about snakes, bugs, wild animals

Don't like to write!

I am a star at Rollerblades.

I like to read alone.

I like to swim with friends.

I like to ride bike with my family.

My favorite things to do on Saturday and Sunday are rollerblade in the park with grandpa.

figure **3.25** Partial personal interest survey for older students.

NAME: LaVonda GRADE: 6 QUARTER: 1st

List more than one item for each category if you have more interests. Explain why you gave each response. For example, why do you enjoy researching (*your favorite topic*) on the Internet?

1. My favorite subjects in school are music and art because I like to sing and draw.
2. My least favorite subject in school is science because it is hard.
3. My favorite topic to research on the Internet is art galleries to learn about them.
4. My favorite topic to study in science is weather because it is interesting.
5. My favorite foreign country to study is Italy because I would like to go there.

ATTITUDE SURVEYS

Teachers must gain insight into their students' attitudes. Some are quite happy when someone else reads to or writes for them, but they dislike reading aloud or writing of any kind. When students have strong dislikes for reading and/or writing, you should attempt to understand why. They may find it boring or too hard, or they may be afraid of failure. You need to help students change these negative attitudes so they will not avoid these crucial activities. Once you understand what reading and writing events a student dislikes and why, you can help him build a more positive attitude.

Appendices C.14–C.18 include Reading and Writing Attitude Surveys for primary and older students. The scoring sheet found in Appendix C.16 can be used for the primary reading and the primary writing attitude surveys. The pre- and post-test scores are recorded on this sheet. To score them, the teacher gives four points for each circled happy character, three points for each circled somewhat-happy character, two points for each neutral character, and one point for each unhappy character. The higher the score, the more interest the student has in reading or writing.

"Collecting data about students is an empty exercise unless the information is used to plan instruction" (McKenna & Kear, 1990, p. 627). With any attitude survey, the quantitative score is not as important as the information the student shares about each statement. According to the criteria above, a score of 20 indicates that a student does not have a positive attitude toward any kind of writing, while a score of 80 indicates the opposite. However, one teacher discovered that one of her students circled the happy character only because it seemed friendlier than the others. Thus, teachers should take time to discuss the survey. The conversation may indicate that the student likes to write about himself or his pets, but dislikes composing letters to authors, thank-you notes, poems, or riddles.

It is also important to remember that attitude surveys do not indicate the sources of poor attitudes, nor do they give suggestions about instructional techniques that will change them (McKenna & Kear, 1990).

These surveys are effective pre- and post-tests. After a student is tutored by a teacher, paraprofessional, or adult volunteer, the surveys will hopefully reflect a change in attitude.

LITERACY SELF-PERCEPTION SCALES

Self-perception scales provide a picture of how students feel about themselves as readers and writers. The Reader Self-Perception Scale (RSPS; Henk & Melnick, 1995) and the Writer Self-Perception Scale (WSPS; Bottomley, Henk, & Melnick, 1998) have been validated systematically. Teachers conducting experimental studies and needing validated assessment instruments may find these useful. Both surveys, with the directions for administering, scoring, and interpreting them, are found in Appendices C.19 and C.20.

STUDENT SELF-ASSESSMENT

Assessment by a teacher is important, but self-assessment by students can also increase self-esteem and the motivation to read and write.

Book Logs

When students log the texts they read and indicate their likes and dislikes, they see themselves as having a voice in the reading process. These logs also help

figure 3.26 Book log for primary school student.

RECORD OF BOOKS Chao READ GRADE: 2

Circle the face that best shows how you feel about the book.

BOOK	AUTHOR/ILLUSTRATOR	COMMENTS
The Little Red Hen Makes Pizza	Philemon Sturges/Amy Walrod	☺ (😐) ☹
Gumbrella	Barry Root	☺ (😐) ☹
26 Fairmount Avenue	Tomie dePaola	(☺) 😐 ☹
Here We All Are	Tomie dePaola	(☺) 😐 ☹
Fables from Aesop	Tom Lynch	☺ 😐 (☹)

them determine their preferences for informational or narrative text, genre, and authors. The log in Figure 3.26 (also found in Appendix C.21) allows primary students to record their reading habits. At the end of a grading period they can check how many texts they read and note their favorite authors and illustrators.

Even young children have a preference for certain authors and illustrators over others. They can simply circle the face that fits their attitude toward the text. Figure 3.27 (also found in Appendix C.22) has a similar log form for more advanced readers. They also record the genre and how long it took them to read each text. In the Comments column, they can indicate if they would recommend the text to others or if they liked a particular character. This column is not intended to be used as a book report.

figure 3.27 Book log for older student.

BOOKS THAT Kalee READ GRADE: 5 QUARTER (1) 2 3 4

TEXT	AUTHOR	GENRE	DATE STARTED/ ENDED	COMMENTS
Mister and Me	Kimberly Willis Holt	Realistic fiction	8/24–8/26	Very easy reading. My mom is dating too and I know how Jolene felt.
Choosing Up Sides	John Ritter	Realistic fiction	9/1–9/5	I recommended this to Jack because his dad is a preacher.
Don't You Know There's a War On?	Avi	Realistic/ Historical fiction	9/10–9/12	It was so funny! I loved it!
Graveyard Girl	Anna Myers	Historical fiction	9/13–9/14	Loved it! But it was so sad! I cried.

My favorite book I read this quarter was Mister and Me

because my mom is dating again and I treat my mom badly too.

Skill Logs

When students log their skills, they have a repository of strategies to turn to when they struggle with a passage. For younger students, you can record the taught strategies during a teacher–student conference. Older students can record what they learned in the conference with the teacher, with a peer, or by themselves.

For students to record what they have learned to do as readers and writers is advantageous. When stumped on a task, they can look back at their log. It also gives them a record of what they have learned over a period of time. These sheets are also helpful during home–school conferences to show caregivers what a child has learned. Logs also let students list information about different genres and authors. The form in Figure 3.28 is a sample form for a second-grade reader. The form in Figure 3.29 is designed for older students to record details about genres and authors.

Reflection Logs

Teach your students to think about their reading habits. At the end of each quarter have them complete a form to summarize their thoughts, such as the one Sheila uses in Figure 3.30. (A blank form is in Appendix C.23.)

In the primary grades, the teacher confers with each student and writes the student's response to each statement. Older students write their responses before they meet with the teacher. Forms such as "My Thoughts About My Reading" challenge students to become lifelong reflective readers. Proficient readers reflect on aspects of texts they liked or disliked and think about why they prefer certain reading materials to others.

Accomplishment and Goal-Setting Logs

After students reflect on their reading habits and understand their preferences, they need to set literacy goals for themselves. Setting such goals gives students an active role in their literacy development. With the teacher's guidance, students should set realistic goals and determine how to accomplish them. A teacher can fill out the form with young students, while older students can fill out the form

figure 3.28 Skills list for primary school student.

FOR QUARTER 1 (2) 3 4

Things that Syndee learned to do as a reader.

1. Stop at the periods (.)
2. Point to every word as I read it.
3. Raise my voice with questions (?)
4. Get excited when I see !
5. Read to the end of the sentence when I come to a word I don't know. Then ask, "What word would make sense?" Also look at pictures.

figure 3.29 Skills list for older student.

FOR QUARTER 1 2 (3) 4

Things that Hayley learned to do as a reader.

1. Sometimes authors don't use explanatory words.
2. Authors can use flashbacks like movies do.
3. Authors use first person—you only know what that person thinks.
4. Authors use some real information in fiction.
5. Stories are interesting when authors use dialect.

figure 3.30 Reflection log.

MY THOUGHTS ABOUT MY READING

NAME Sheila GRADE: 6 QUARTER (1) 2 3 4

1. The informational books I read were about Composers and their compositions.
2. The novels I read were mostly (realistic, (historical), biographies, autobiographies, mysteries, science fiction, fantasy, folktales).
3. My favorite author is Avi.
4. The best book I read was Don't You Know There's a War Going On?
5. When I dislike a book, I put it back on the book shelf.
6. My favorite place to read is on my bed.
7. My reading habits at home are: I always read before I go to bed.
8. I do not enjoy reading books that are science fiction.
9. The book I recommended to my friends was Don't You Know There's a War Going On?
10. After I read a book, I like to talk about it with Megan.

themselves and then discuss it with the teacher. Allowing students to set their own goals empowers them and makes them more likely to strive for the goal than if they had no voice in the process. Encourage your students to reach their goals by discussing them periodically throughout the grading period. Figure 3.31 is a form that Ms. Walker uses with her fifth-grade students to record their accomplishments and goals. It clearly shows that India has been working on becoming a faster reader so she can read more books and that she knows how to accomplish that goal.

figure 3.31 Accomplishment and goal-setting log.

ACCOMPLISHMENTS AND GOALS FOR READING

NAME India GRADE: 5 QUARTER (1) 2 3 4

ACCOMPLISHMENTS	GOALS	WAYS TO ACHIEVE GOALS
I read 2 chapter books. Both—realistic fiction. I re-read almost all the poems from A Light In the Attic. I also read 2 folktales on the "Starfall" website.	Read at least 3 books—historical fiction. Read 2 comic strips from "Starfall" website.	Read at least 30 minutes each night and 1 hour on Sat. and Sun. Don't read books that are too hard for me. Read a book that someone else recommends so I know it's good. Ask teacher if I can go to computer lab during independent reading time.

TEACHER'S COMMENTS:

Student's Signature ______

Teacher's Signature ______

TECHNOLOGY AND ASSESSMENT

Reluctant readers often are motivated to tackle any task—even tests—on the computer because it is different from paper and pencil tests. The Internet provides free resources for teachers to assess students in different areas of literacy. Some free sites include:

- Frontline Phonics (www.frontlinephonics.com) offers a learning phonics assessment test.
- Test 4 Free (www.test4free.com) provides a reading aptitude test.
- Vocabulary Test (www.vocabtest.com) has vocabulary quizzes for grades 6 through AP senior level.
- Learningabled Kids (www.learningabledkids.com) assesses student decoding skills, fluency, and comprehension.
- World-English (http://world-English.org), mentioned earlier in this chapter, has assessments in many different literacy areas in which students receive direct feedback and scores.

Throughout the text, I will discuss other websites that assess different areas of literacy, such as phonemic awareness, phonics, comprehension, vocabulary, and spelling, through game-like activities.

CONCLUDING THOUGHTS

Assessment instruments, both formal and informal, come in many varieties. Formal tests are standardized, which means they are given under controlled conditions. Formal tests include intelligence, achievement, and diagnostic tests. Achievement tests measure the achievement level of the student and can be either norm-referenced or criterion-referenced. Norm-referenced tests compare the performance of a student to the group on which the test was standardized. Criterion-referenced tests measure a skill that the student is expected to have mastered. Diagnostic tests have many subtests that assess a student's strengths and weaknesses in particular areas.

Teachers use informal assessment instruments to (1) diagnose reading problems, (2) check the reading level of a student, (3) analyze which cueing systems students use when making sense of print, (4) understand student attitudes toward reading and writing and help identify materials that interest them, (5) monitor student growth, (6) provide opportunities for students to reflect on literacy accomplishments, (7) help students set realistic goals, and (8) develop plans for instruction.

Both types of tests are useful in measuring students' literacy skills. Formal test scores indicate general abilities in various areas of literacy. Informal tests, administered by classroom teachers, permit those teachers to observe students' behaviors while they make sense of print.

Rubrics, checklists, and anecdotal records serve as indicators of certain aspects of students' growth that cannot be measured on a test. Throughout this chapter and other chapters in this text, I have included checklists and rubrics for specific types of reading and writing activities. Many of the checklists, rubrics, surveys, and logs are designed to help you assess the entire reading process, which encompasses students' skills, attitudes, and interests. When teachers diligently assess the entire reading process, they can truly *teach the student, and not the method!* All of the checklists and rubrics in this text are provided only as suggestions. Feel free to create your own checklists and rubrics based on your curriculum and students' needs.

Reflective Learning TESTING

Scenario. After teaching first grade for a number of years, Grace Cho stayed at home with her son for several years. Last May Ms. Cho's family moved to a small town and she decided to return to teaching in order to get to know the community. She was excited when Mr. Day, the principal, told her she had the first-grade job, because the school has only one classroom per grade and she knew others had applied for the position. The interview had been brief because Mr. Day said her former school had recommended her highly. They never discussed new trends in education or testing.

Excited to teach again, Ms. Cho sets up her classroom the week before teacher orientation week. During teacher orientation, she keeps hearing about adequate yearly progress and DIBELS—terms new to Ms. Cho. There is no other first-grade teacher to help her understand how these items impact teachers, and she is hesitant to ask the other teachers for fear of appearing unqualified.

During the first week of school, Principal Day hands Ms. Cho a set of DIBELS and tells her he wants them administered, scored, and analyzed by the end of the third week so he can decide if he needs to hire a reading specialist that year. In reading the DIBELS instructional manual, she realizes the test needs to be administered individually. She is overwhelmed because she already has her curriculum planned for the first month.

QUESTIONS

1. Should Ms. Cho seek help from Mr. Day or from another teacher?
2. How can she learn about the impact of adequate yearly progress and tests like DIBELS?
3. What are your recommendations for classroom management as she administers the individual tests?

CHAPTER FOUR

PHONEMIC AWARENESS

Education is what survives after what has been learned has been forgotten.

B.F. SKINNER

Scenario

Ms. Reyes is a kindergarten teacher who knows how crucial it is to understand what each child knows about the letters and their sounds at the beginning of the year. She plays a game that identifies students who appear unable to distinguish sounds. The game format is ideal because most students perceive games as fun. Last year Ms. Reyes's students enjoyed playing various versions of the "train" game, with students listening carefully as the list grew longer and longer.

During the first week of school, Ms. Reyes gathers a group of six on the rug and explains that they are going to play a sound game. She says, "I will announce one sound of the alphabet, for example /d/, and I will begin with the sentence 'I know that *dog* begins with /d/.'" (Note: Ms. Reyes says the /d/ sound, not the letter name.) "I want the student next to me to repeat my sentence and my word, and then give another word with that sound. For example, the first student might say, 'I know that *dog* and *dirt* begin with /d/.' The second might say, 'I know that *dog, dirt,* and *dad* begin with /d/.'"

When Ms. Reyes is sure they understand the game, she asks if they are ready to play. She encourages each child to listen carefully so he or she can remember the words that have already been said. Then she begins with the following: "I know that *milk* begins with /m/." After one round and a few errors, the students say, "Let's do it again." In the first round some students repeat the same word as a classmate, but everyone except Brandon gives a correct response.

"Ok," Ms. Reyes says, "let's do it again with /b/." She begins, "I know that *bag* begins with /b/." The second round goes much better; however, Brandon is again the only student who gives an incorrect response.

During center time Ms. Reyes asks Brandon to join her for a game. She lays out picture cards of a clock, bell, and duck, and asks Brandon to pick up the card that begins with the /k/ sound. He picks up the bell card. She repeats the process two more times and each time Brandon is unable to pick up the correct card. (See Appendix D for picture cards.)

When Brandon's eighth-grade buddy comes to read with him, Mrs. Reyes gives Brandon and his buddy several old magazines and invites them to make their own alphabet book. She provides 10 index cards and one card with a big "B" on the front. She begins with "B" because it is the first letter of his name.

Brandon's job is to find pictures in the magazines that begin with the sound of his name and glue them onto the cards. Ms. Reyes instructs the eighth grader to emphasize the initial sound of the pictures to help Brandon determine if it begins with the same sound as his name. If the picture does not begin with the /b/ sound, the buddy is to say "Brandon" and the incorrect picture word (e.g., cake) and really emphasize the beginning sound, such as "C-C-C-C-Cake" and then "B-B-B-B-Brandon," so the initial sound of the word is exaggerated.

After a half hour, the eighth grader reports that at first Brandon had a difficult time choosing correct picture cards; but once he had Brandon say the words while exaggerating the beginning sound, he was able to quickly choose the last four picture cards correctly.

Ms. Reyes thanks the buddy and makes Brandon his own personal /B/ alphabet book.

guiding questions

As you read this chapter, consider the following questions:

1. Which dimensions of phonemic awareness are the focus of Ms. Reyes's lessons?
2. What assessments could Ms. Reyes use to measure Brandon's growth in phonemic awareness?
3. From your observations in classrooms or your own kindergarten days, what are some other game-like activities Ms. Reyes could do with Brandon? What are some activities she could do with the entire class?
4. Choose several activities from the chapter and think about how you would modify these activities for English learners.

INTRODUCTION

"Filling children's heads with rhyme is one of the easiest and most natural ways to focus their attention on the sounds of the English language."

BEAR, INVERNIZZI, TEMPLETON, & JOHNSTON, 2008, P. 111

Young children become aware of different and similar sounds within words by enjoying the alliteration, rhyme, rhythm, and onomatopoeia found in songs, nursery rhymes, poems, and children's literature. The teacher's responsibility is to provide opportunities for children to experience joy in using the English language. One way to fulfill this responsibility is to encourage children to play with language as they sing, chant, and read.

This chapter discusses a number of different topics surrounding phonemic awareness: (1) its definition, (2) its seven dimensions, (3) phonemic awareness and English learners, (4) what teachers should know about it, (5) methods teachers can use to introduce children to the sounds of our language, (6) types of phonemic awareness assessments, and (7) activities that help children become sensitive to the sounds within words.

As an adult who spends hours reading and writing, you may think phonemic awareness is a simple skill for younger children to develop. However, as you read this chapter, take time to reflect on the intricate characteristics of phonemic awareness to gain awareness of why some young children struggle with written language.

DEFINITION

According to the International Reading Association and the National Association for the Education of Young Children (1998), **phonemic awareness** is "a child's understanding and conscious awareness that speech is composed of identifiable units, such as spoken words, syllables, and sounds" (p. 4). Yopp and Yopp (2000) elaborate on this definition by characterizing phonemic awareness as "the ability to generate and recognize rhyming words, to count syllables, to separate the beginning of a word from its ending (e.g., the *st* from the *op* in *stop*), and to identify each of the phonemes in a word" (p. 30). Linguists disagree on the actual number of phonemes in the English language; this disagreement stems from distinct dialects, accents, and individual speech patterns. Figure 4.1 lists the 44 phonemes on which most linguists agree.

Phonemic awareness is not the same concept as **phonics**, which is the understanding that letters represent certain sound(s). Phonemic awareness tasks are aural and oral, while phonics focuses on written letters and the aural process. Students do not need to know letter names and their sounds in order to merely hear the sounds in a word. However, if they do know the letter names, teachers can facilitate their learning by highlighting the letters in their instruction.

DIMENSIONS OF PHONEMIC AWARENESS

According to Lane and Pullen (2004), Blevins (2006), and Yopp (2005), phonemic awareness consists of various dimensions; nevertheless, it is important to note that "there is no research to suggest that there is an exact sequence of acquisition of specific sounds" (Cunningham et al., 1998, p. 3). The following are seven dimensions of phonemic awareness:

1. *The ability to hear syllables within a word.* To assess children's ability to hear syllables, have them

figure 4.1 The 44 most common phonemes.

VOWEL SOUNDS

/a/	cat	/ā/	game	/ə/	aloft	/ô/	all
/e/	bed	/ē/	see	/o͞o/	spoon	/û/	bird
/i/	it	/ī/	I	/o͝o/	look	/â/	air
/o/	odd	/ō/	hole	/ou/	mouse	/ä/	far
/u/	under	/ū/	use	/oi/	toy, oil		

CONSONANT SOUNDS

/b/	boy	/k/	key	/s/	sun	/ch/	church
/d/	dad	/l/	log	/t/	tent	/sh/	shadow
/f/	fish	/m/	man	/v/	vest	/th/	thumb
/g/	game	/n/	nose	/w/	wagon	/th/	the
/h/	hat	/p/	pipe	/y/	yellow	/wh/	wheel
/j/	judge	/r/	rake	/z/	zipper	/zh/	pleasure
						/ng/	sing

Source: Adapted from W. Blevins (2001). *Teaching Phonics and Word Study in the Intermediate Grades.* New York: Scholastic.

first clap one-syllable words or names (e.g., Jim, Jane, Kim), and then progress to two-, three-, and four-syllable words (e.g., Ste-ven, Gin-ger, Kim-ber-ly, In-di-a, Ok-la-ho-ma).

2. *The ability to hear initial letter sounds or recognize alliteration.* This includes listing words like those Ms. Reyes asked her students to name. Most children enjoy adding to a list of words that begin with the same sound. For example, the teacher may say, "Sally sells seashells all begin with the /s/ sound. What other words, can you think of that begin with the /s/ sound?" Children with phonemic awareness will respond with such words as *silly, summer,* and *sun.*

3. *The ability to distinguish rime and rhyme.* The concepts of *rime* and *rhyme* are often confusing not only to students but also to educators. Words in the same rime family always end with the same letters (e.g., *sit, hit, fit*), while words with rhyme share the same sound but do not necessarily share the same ending letters (e.g., *great/late* or *bear/care*). Words in the same rime family also rhyme since they have the same ending (*fat, bat, sat*); however, words that rhyme are not necessarily part of the same rime family since they may end differently.

Words with rime have two parts—onset (the consonant or consonant blend at the beginning of the word), and rime (the ending letters that are shared). For example, in the words *cat* and *bat,* the *c* and the *b* are the onsets and the *at* in each of the words is the rime. Words with the same rimes are often referred to as *word families.*

The concepts of rime and rhyme may be difficult for some children to distinguish, but a wide array of books introduce them. (See Appendix A.7 for a list of books that highlight rime and rhyme.) Like many authors, Guarino (1989) emphasizes both rime and rhyme in her book *Is Your Mama a Llama?:*

> "Is your mama a llama?" I asked my friend Clyde. (rime, which also happens to rhyme)
>
> "No, she is not," is how Clyde replied. (rhyme)

4. *The ability to distinguish oddity.* Children's ability to identify words that begin with a different sound from the other words that the teacher pronounces is their ability to distinguish oddity. For example, the teacher might pronounce *man, money,* and *cat* and ask the children to listen and identify which word begins with the different sound.

5. *The ability to blend sounds together orally to make a word.* For this dimension, the teacher should again first work with onset and rime because they are larger units of sound. Students are able to control larger units of sound before smaller units or phonemes, which are the smallest units of sound (Blevins, 2006; Yopp, 2005). When working with blending, say the first sound (the onset) of a word (e.g., /s/) and have the students repeat it. Then say the rime (e.g., *at*), and ask them to repeat it. Then ask them to blend the two parts into one word. You may wish to work with one word family (e.g., the *at*

family) before moving on to another family. Appendix B.1 contains a list of word families commonly used in instruction.

Another aspect of the fifth phonemic awareness dimension is children's ability to blend individual sounds to form a word. With this task, the teacher begins with three-letter words that have the consonant-vowel-consonant (CVC) pattern, such as *big, fun, bat,* and so on. (Notice these words are members of word families, but at this point you are working with individual letters and not the onset, rime, or rhyme.) Articulate each sound separately, ask the student to repeat each sound, and then ask her to blend the three sounds together to form a word. An example of such an activity would be the following exchange:

Teacher: /s/

Student: /s/

Teacher: /a/

Student: /a/

Teacher: /t/

Student: /t/

Teacher: Now blend all three sounds together.

Student: *sat*

If students already know the names of the letters and the sounds of some letters, Ransom, Santa, Williams, and Farstrup (1999) recommend the teacher work with magnetic letters because this helps children's visual and auditory processes. If they do not know letter names, the teacher can simply emphasize the sounds within the words. Blending may be difficult for some children because this task involves working with language in an unnatural form, a form in which they have not heard words spoken (Smith, 1999). The section on phonemic awareness instruction later in this chapter will explain in greater detail why this task is difficult for many students.

6. *The ability to segment words orally.* Segmenting is different from blending. In blending, the task is to put sounds *together* to make a word *before* hearing the entire word. In segmenting, however, the task is to pull sounds apart *after* hearing the entire word. In segmenting, the teacher says the entire word—for example, *man*—and asks the children to say all three sounds in the word. An example of such an exercise is the following:

Teacher: I'm going to say a word that has three sounds in it. I want you to tell me the three sounds you hear. For example, in *cat,* I hear /c /, /a /, and /t/. Now I want you to tell me which three sounds you hear in *man.*

Student: /m/ . . . /a/ . . . /n/.

7. *The ability to manipulate sounds orally to create new words.* This task can be difficult for some children because they must focus on small parts of a word (Smith, 1999). **Manipulating** sounds involves the task of either substituting or deleting. **Substituting** is the act of replacing one sound for another sound in a word. For example, in substitution, the teacher says the word *Sam,* asks children to put an /h/ sound in place of the /s/ sound, and then asks them to pronounce the new word (*ham*). **Deleting** is the act of removing a sound from a word to create a new word. The sound can be either an initial or an ending sound. An example is to pronounce the word *beat* and then omit the /t/ sound to get *be.* Or, you could pronounce *beat* and then omit the /b/ sound to get *eat.*

According to Blevins (2006) children should master the first three of the seven dimensions of phonemic awareness by the end of kindergarten and the last four dimensions by the end of first grade. This does not mean, however, that one dimension needs to be mastered before working on the next.

PHONEMIC AWARENESS AND ENGLISH LEARNERS

When working with the seven dimensions of phonemes, be aware that phonemes differ from one language to another. As the number of English learners in U.S. schools grows dramatically each year, many classrooms have English learners from many different countries, while some schools have large populations of English learners from one country, particularly Mexico. All of these students must learn to produce the 44 most common phonemes of the English language to become fluent English speakers.

Many languages (e.g., Spanish, Italian, or Romanian) have fewer phonemes than English (Bear et al., 2007). Some English phonemes are unique to the English language, while other phonemes are unique to other languages. "A phoneme not present in one's native language is more difficult to hear and, in turn, produce" (Helman, 2004, p. 454). If you have ever attempted to say a phrase in Thai, Japanese, Korean, or Chinese, you may have found it difficult because Asian languages have many phonemes that are not part of the English language. You may have wondered how to place your tongue and lips to produce the unfamiliar sound. Similarly, many non-English speakers have difficulty producing phonemes that are unique to English. For example, Asian speakers have difficulty with the English phonemes that are produced with the tongue and lips (e.g., /v/, /f/, /p/, /d/) because they do not use the lips and tongue to produce phonemes when speaking their native language.

Native Spanish speakers, the largest group of second-language learners in the United States (U.S. Census Bureau, 2007), have difficulty with phonemes because English has 44 phonemes and Spanish has only 24. Spanish speakers, therefore, must learn to produce at least 20 new sounds. Figure 4.2 shows English phonemes that are not found in Spanish. Notice that the short vowel sound, the controlled-r vowel sounds, and the schwa vowel sounds are only English phonemes.

Many of the consonant blend phonemes are not Spanish phonemes. Any phoneme that is unique to English speakers may be difficult for native Spanish learners. Think of how difficult the following sentence would be for a native Spanish speaker (phonemes not found in Spanish are underlined): Robert spilled jelly on Ruth's treasure. When working with Spanish speakers, begin not with phonemes that are uncommon in Spanish, but rather with phonemes that are common in English and Spanish. Figure 4.3 shows the phonemes, represented by the English grapheme, common to Spanish and English. In Chapter 5, you will learn that even though some phonemes are common in both languages, the same letters may not represent the same phonemes. For example, the long /a/ phoneme is spelled with the letter *e* in Spanish, but in English the long /a/ is spelled many different ways (e.g., *cake, eight, they*).

Figure 4.4 lists English phonemes not found in Chinese, French, Greek, Italian, Japanese, and Native American languages. Notice how many languages do not have the schwa, /th/, /dg/, and /oo/ phonemes. As with Spanish speakers, when working with other non-English speakers always begin with the phonemes that are common in English and the student's native language, while being aware of why they may struggle with other phonemes.

Not only do languages have unique phonemes, but every language also has different phoneme placements within words. For example, phoneme placement within words varies between English and Spanish. In English all consonant phonemes, except /ng/ and the /h/, are placed anywhere within a word. However, in Spanish only five consonant phonemes (/l/, /r/, /d/, /n/, and /s/) are ever heard as ending sounds (Helman, 2004). Think of the difficulty native Spanish students have when repeating this sentence:

***figure* 4.2** English phonemes not found in Spanish.

short /a/	short /e/	short /i/	short /u/	schwa	/ar/
/er/	/ir/	/or/	/ur/	/j/	/r/
/v/	/z/	/th/ *thick*	/sh/	/zh/	/tw/
/qu/	/scr/	/spl/	/spr/	/str/	/squ/
/st/	/sp/	/sk/	/sc/	/sm/	/sl/
/sn/	/sw/				

Sources: Helman, L. A. (2004). Building on the sound system of Spanish: Insights from the alphabetic spellings of English-language learners. *The Reading Teacher, 57*(5), 452–460. Bear, D., Helman, L., Templeton, S., Invernizzi, M., & Johnston, F. (2007). *Words their way with English learners: Word study for phonics, vocabulary and spelling instruction* (4th ed.). Upper Saddle River, NJ: Pearson.

***figure* 4.3** Phonemes common in English and Spanish.

Note: These are represented by the English grapheme.

/b/	/d/	/f/	/g/	/k/	/l/	/m/	/n/	/p/	/s/	/t/	/w/
/y/	/ch/	long /a/		long /e/		long /i/		long /o/		/u/ as in *June*	
/pl/	/pr/	/bl/	/br/	/tr/	/dr/	/cl/	/cr/	/gl/	/gr/	/fl/	/fr/

Sources: Helman, L. A. (2004). Building on the sound system of Spanish: Insights from the alphabetic spellings of English-language learners. *The Reading Teacher, 57*(5), 452–460. Bear, D., Helman, L., Templeton, S., Invernizzi, M., & Johnston, F. (2007). *Words their way with English learners: Word study for phonics, vocabulary and spelling instruction* (4th ed.). Upper Saddle River, NJ: Pearson.

figure 4.4 English phonemes not found in the Chinese, French, Greek, Italian, Japanese, and Native American languages.

LANGUAGE	SOUNDS NOT PART OF THE LANGUAGE										
Chinese	b	ch	d	dg	g	long /a/	sh	s	th	v	z
French	ch	long /e/		j	ng	oo	th				
Greek	aw	long /e/		i	oo	schwa					
Italian	a	ar	dg	h	I	ng	th	schwa			
Japanese	dg	f	I	th	oo	v	schwa				
Native American *(some dialects)*	l	r	st								

Source: Cecil, N. L. (2011). *Striking a Balance: A Comprehensive Approach to Early Literacy* (4th ed.). Scottsdale, AZ: Holcomb Hathaway.

The cat and dog ate from the same dish. Again, begin with words that have common placement of phonemes in the two languages, and progress to those with unfamiliar placement.

WHAT TEACHERS SHOULD KNOW ABOUT PHONEMIC AWARENESS

A number of issues surrounding phonemic awareness have arisen in recent years: (1) Is phonemic awareness necessary for students to become proficient readers? (2) Do children benefit from intense, explicit instruction? (3) If not, then how do children become aware of the phonemes within words?

These issues are presented here so you can begin to formulate your own opinions. Ultimately, your opinion should be based on research and experience working with students of many different ages, backgrounds, and cultures. Ask yourself some of the following questions to help formulate your opinions:

1. How often has this child been read to by an adult?
2. How engaged in the reading process is this child when someone reads to him?
3. Do the child's parents or caregivers "play" with word sounds as they read to him?
4. Is the child a native English speaker?
5. Does the child have hearing problems?
6. Does the child have any speech impediments?
7. If the child is a reader, does he have a sense of the individual sounds within a word when he reads and writes?

Informed educators understand many points of view and form opinions about controversial issues only after they have examined the relevant research and worked with many types of readers. To help you consider the questions surrounding phonemic awareness, the next sections discuss differing perspectives about the topic.

Is Phonemic Awareness Necessary for Students to Become Proficient Readers?

Blevins (2006) and IRA/NAEYC (1998) argue that students must be aware that words are made up of distinct sounds if they are to become proficient readers and writers. Cunningham et al. (1998) suggest that phonemic awareness is necessary, but not sufficient, for producing good readers. They contend that "the precise relation between phonemic awareness abilities and reading acquisition remains under investigation" (p. 4). Cunningham (1990), Yopp and Yopp (2000), Blevins (1997), and IRA/NAEYC (1998) indicate that when children approach unfamiliar words, they learn to read them by understanding that they contain individual sounds and that every word is different. Otherwise, each new word must become a sight word—a word they automatically identify. Writing, they also suggest, requires that children understand words are composed of individual sounds. These experts do not conclude that children need to master all the phonemic awareness dimensions before they begin to read, only that they are able to detect beginning sounds to learn initial letter–sound relationships.

Many elementary teachers believe phonemic awareness instruction is important for reading achievement. These teachers emphasize the importance of the following elements of phonemic awareness, in which the child must:

1. Understand that a word is a series of speech sounds.
2. Be able to isolate a sound in a word.
3. Be able to blend individual sounds to form a word.
4. Be able to substitute sounds in a word to produce new words.
5. Be able to recognize common rhymes.
6. Be able to recognize syllables within words.

Lane and Pullen (2004) also argue that proficient readers need to understand how phonemes—the sounds of spoken language—are connected to the printed word.

Do Children Benefit From Intense, Explicit Phonemic Awareness Instruction?

Experts disagree. Smith (1999) believes phonemic awareness instruction is an educational hazard. He claims that teaching students to listen to individual sounds within words is impossible because such sounds are inextricably combined. One cannot separate the sounds from a word that has been uttered any more than one "can extract the ingredients from a cake that has been baked" (p. 153), and that there is "no more need to identify and classify individual letter sounds in order to understand written words than we need to identify and classify eyes, noses, and mouths before we recognize faces" (p. 151). Smith feels so strongly about phonemic awareness that he calls it "a spurious concept" (p. 150).

Taking the opposite view, IRA/NAEYC (1998) suggest that literacy does not develop naturally, and careful instruction in phonemic awareness is necessary for students to become literate. Cunningham et al. (1998) conclude that different children need different amounts and forms of phonemic awareness instruction. They find some children benefit when teachers combine text with phonemic awareness instruction, while others respond better when engaged in oral language experiences such as nursery rhymes, songs, chants, and other language play. The key is that a teacher engages the student while manipulating sounds within words. Cunningham et al. conclude that "instruction with print with explicit attention to sound structure in spoken words is the best vehicle toward [language] growth" (p. 3).

To date, no longitudinal study documents the effectiveness of intense, sustained phonemic awareness activities. However, the National Reading Panel conducted a quantitative meta-analysis evaluating the effects of phonemic awareness instruction on learning to read and spell, with the following results (Ehri et al., 2001):

1. It does impact children's awareness of sounds in letters.
2. It does impact children's reading comprehension and decoding.
3. It does impact normal children's spelling, but not the spelling of readers with a disability.
4. It is more effective when taught with letter names.
5. It is more effective when only one or two skills are taught in a session, instead of multiple skills.
6. It is more effective when conducted in small groups, rather than individually or in classroom settings.

If Not Through Intense, Explicit Instruction, How Do Children Become Aware of Phonemes Within Words?

Most researchers and educators agree that when students are actively engaged and involved in literacy activities, they become aware of the sounds within words (Cunningham et al., 1998; IRA/NAEYC, 1998; Taylor, Pressley, & Pearson, 2000). These activities include linguistic awareness games (such as those found in the last section of this chapter), nursery rhymes, poems, songs, rhythmic activities such as jump-rope jingles, and stories that use rhyme and onomatopoeia. Because phonemic awareness develops over time and through sustained exposure, students should have opportunities to develop it every day. Cunningham et al. (1998) found an estimated 80 percent of students develop phonemic awareness by the middle of first grade. The other 20 percent benefit from one-on-one language activities with an adult who actively engages the student in play with word sounds. These types of activities are found in the Intervention section of this chapter.

ASSESSMENT

Assessing a Child's Level of Phonemic Awareness

The first step in assessing phonemic awareness occurs during the "kid watching" that takes place during small-group language activities. For example, in the opening scenario Ms. Reyes notices while she is working with small groups that Brandon does not have the ability to clap the syllables of names or to recognize words that have the same beginning sounds. Following this observation, she assesses Brandon individually, using commercial and informal assessment instruments. Commercial phonemic awareness assessments available to teachers, based on the seven dimensions of phonemic awareness, include:

1. Lindamood-Bell Auditory Conceptualization Test (LAC-3). Hingham, MA: Teaching Resources Corporation.
2. Test of Phonological Awareness (TOPA-2+). Austin, TX: Pro-Ed.
3. Scholastic Phonemic Awareness Kit. New York: Scholastic.
4. Yopp, H. K. (2005). A test for assessing phonemic awareness in young children. In S. J. Barrentine & S. M. Stokes (Eds.). *Reading Assessment* (pp. 262–271). Newark, DE: International Reading Association.
5. Basic Early Assessment of Reading™ (BEAR®). Rolling Meadows, IL: Riverside Publishing.
6. Dynamic Indicators of Basic Early Literacy Skills (DIBELS). Longmont, CO: Sopris West Educational Services.

One easy informal phonemic assessment is the Quick Phonemic Awareness Assessment Device (Cecil, 2011; see Appendix C.24). Appendices C.25 and C.26 feature two assessments, one to use as a pretest before one-on-one time with the student, and the other as a post-test after spending individualized time with the student. Five correct responses for each task indicate the child has mastered the skill. Three or four correct responses indicate that he is developing the skill, and only one or two correct responses indicate he is having difficulty with the tasks. Remember, this is only an informal assessment to indicate a student's knowledge about the individual sounds within words. Not all seven of the dimensions of phonemic awareness need to be mastered before children can read, nor does a teacher need to assess all students. Only those children who would benefit from the assessment and the strategies need to complete it. It only measures children's capacity for hearing small units of sound within words. In addition, a teacher can easily make his or her own informal assessment by having students complete activities based on each of the seven dimensions.

Because most states require schools to document growth in phonemic awareness, primary teachers are advised to keep a class checklist based on the seven dimensions of phonemic awareness. Using this checklist, the teacher can monitor class growth in each area during each grading period. She can also use the checklist to form small groups based on the children's strengths and weaknesses. The checklist in Figure 4.5 reflects results at the end of the first quarter. It shows Reed is competent in all

figure 4.5 Checklist for phonemic awareness based on the seven dimensions, primary grades.

TEACHER Jones DATE 10/12

+ = always x = sometimes 0 = seldom/never

DIMENSION	Cooper	Cy	Reed	Melinda	Jami	Scott	Rebecca	Tim	David	Erin	Marie	Lori	Stacey	Terri	Aubree	Alea	Darci	Janelle
1. Ability to hear syllables within words.	X	+	+	X	+	X	+	X	+	O	+	+	O	+	+	X	+	+
2. Ability to hear initial sounds or recognize alliteration.	X	+	+	X	+	X	+	X	+	O	+	+	O	X	+	X	+	+
3. Ability to hear rhyming words.	X	+	+	X	+	X	+	X	X	O	+	X	O	X	+	X	X	+
4. Ability to distinguish oddity.	X	O	+	O	X	O	X	O	X	O	+	X	O	O	X	O	X	+
5. Ability to blend words orally.	O	O	+	O	X	O	X	O	X	O	X	X	O	O	X	O	X	X
6. Ability to segment words. * Drop beginning sound * Drop ending sound	O	O	+	O	O	O	O	O	O	O	O	O	O	O	O	O	O	O
7. Ability to manipulate sounds orally to create new words.	O	O	+	O	O	O	O	O	O	O	O	O	O	O	O	O	O	O

seven dimensions; Erin and Stacey are weak in all areas; and most of the students cannot manipulate sounds or delete an ending sound. A blank checklist is provided in Appendix C.27.

Assessing a Child's Growth in Phonemic Awareness

After a semester of reading to students in small groups, with an emphasis on listening to the sounds of our language, and after introducing various language activities, most students will show signs of growth in phonemic awareness. To assess their growth, you may use one of the assessment instruments listed above or you may use the post-test informal assessment instrument found in Appendix C.26. The scoring on the post-test is the same as the pretest. To document the phonemic awareness growth of the class, use the Phonemic Awareness checklist found in this chapter or design one that fits your needs.

INTRODUCING CHILDREN TO THE WONDERFUL SOUNDS OF OUR LANGUAGE

Jongsma (2000) points out that the building materials and tools of the English language are the eight parts of speech—adjectives, adverbs, verbs, pronouns, conjunctions, prepositions, nouns, and interjections—which are themselves filled with many wonderful sounds that add color and luster to our speech. She believes a teacher must help students develop an ear for the sounds within words. One way to do this is through language play. Teachers can engage students in language play through songs, nursery rhymes, poems, jump-rope jingles, riddles, jokes, tongue twisters, and stories because they are filled with words and phrases that emphasize the sounds and rhythms of our language. These words and phrases may fall into one of the following categories:

- alliteration (sentences or phrases that begin with same letter sound; e.g., *Silly Sally shines sea shells*).
- assonance (sentences or phrases that have repeated vowel sounds; e.g., *Aunt Bea flees when she sees bees*).
- onomatopoeia (words that sound like their meanings; e.g., *crackle, pop*).
- nonsense words (made up words e.g., *jabberwocky*).

Language learning begins with oral language; children first hear and speak words they will later learn to read and write. Children of all ages, beginning with the very young, should have many opportunities to play with language orally—to enjoy the sounds of words through alliteration (*Peter Piper picked a peck of pickled peppers*), rhymes (*Humpty Dumpty sat on a wall / Humpty Dumpty had a great fall*), and onomatopoeia (*Snap, Crackle, Pop!*) before they are asked to analyze words (Booth, 1999; Smith, 1999). Because language learning occurs when teachers engage students in language play (Cunningham et al., 1998; Foorman et al., 1991; Taylor et al., 2000), students should have many opportunities to engage in play-based aural and oral language activities.

Songs

Language activities can include singing, because many songs are filled with alliteration and rhyme. Teachers may want to develop a repertoire of songs that emphasize the sounds within words. Words and phrases such as "fid-dle-ee-fee," "chimney chuck, chummy chuck," and "swishy, swashy" in the delightful "Barnyard Song" (adapted by Glazer, 1973) delight young children. "Hush, Little Baby" (traditional) allows children to make up their own rhyming verses after they sing the first few. Following the seventh verse of "Hush, Little Baby," for example, you may make up your own verse (something like the eighth verse given below), and then invite the children create their own.

7TH VERSE:

If that dog named Rover don't bark,
Papa's gonna buy you a horse and cart.

8TH VERSE:

If that horse and cart won't run,
Papa's gonna buy you the golden sun.

There are many books of children's songs. *Wee Sing: Children's Songs and Fingerplays* (1979) by Pamela Conn Beall and Susan Hogan Nipp includes 73 classic children's songs with finger play directions and a CD (in case a teacher does not feel comfortable leading children in singing). Tom Glazer's *Eye Winker, Tom Tinker, Chin Chopper* (1973) is a collection of 50 musical finger plays with piano arrangements, guitar chords, and detailed directions for the finger plays. *Children's Favorites*, a CD produced by Music Little People (1987), also has a wide selection of songs for young children. Hilda Jackman's *Sing Me a Story! Tell Me a Song!* (1999) includes creative curriculum activities with many songs for young children. This book's songs are grouped into thematic units.

Nursery Rhymes and Poems

Children are often introduced to poetry through nursery rhymes chanted by their parents or caregivers. Continue to model the joy of hearing the sounds, feeling the rhythms, and telling the stories found in nursery rhymes. They abound with wonderful rhythm, rhyme, and onomatopoeia; think of the musical sounds in the words "Hickory, Dickory, Dock." The rhythm of the three words is triplet, triplet, quarter note, with an accent on the beginning of each word. To assist children in feeling the rhythm, add actions, such as the following:

"Hick" (right hand up) "ory" (right hand down)

"Dick" (left hand up) "ory" (left hand down)

"Dock" (both hands up in a v-shape and then down again)

"The mouse ran up the clock" (run fingers up the imaginary clock)

"The clock" (draw a circle with finger) "struck one" (hold up index finger)

"The mouse ran down" (run fingers down the imaginary clock)

"Hick" (right hand up) "ory" (right hand down)

"Dick" (left hand up) "ory" (left hand down)

"Dock" (both hands up in a v-shape)

"Humpty Dumpty" is another favorite nursery rhyme that evokes many characters and story lines in rhythmic rhyme. Again, body actions can help the children feel the beat of the syllables:

"Hump" (bounce once so the accent and syllable can be felt) "ty"

"Dump" (bounce once) "ty"

"Sat" (crouch in a sitting position) "on a wall."

"Hump" (bounce once) "ty"

"Dump" (bounce once) "ty"

"Had a great fall." (fall down)

"All the King's horses,"

"And all the King's men,"

"Couldn't put Humpty together again." (stay sprawled out)

In the foreword to *My Very First Mother Goose* (1996), Iona Opie suggests that Mother Goose nursery rhymes are "jollifications that cheer parents as well as children" (unpaged). She goes on to say that Mother Goose is "astonishing, beautiful, capricious, dancy, eccentric, funny, goluptious, haphazard, intertwingled, joyous, kindly, loving, melodious, naughty, outrageous, pomsidillious, querimonious, romantic, silly, tremendous, unexpected, vertiginous, wonderful, x-citing, yo-heave-ho-ish, and zany" (unpaged). Approach nursery rhymes with the same jolly spirit! The following selections, all found in *My Very First Mother Goose,* demonstrate the joyful language of nursery rhymes:

- "Down By the Station," with words and phrases such as *puffer-billies; puff, puff; peep, peep.*
- "Cackle, Cackle, Mother Goose," with rhyming words such as: *goose/loose* and *fellow/pillow.*
- "To Market to Market," with such words as *jiggety-jig.*
- "Horsie, Horsie," with words such as *clipetty-clop, swish, giddy-up.*
- "From Wibbleton to Wobbelton." The repetition of the two words in the title makes it a tongue twister.

Nursery rhymes and poetry are made more enjoyable when the author emphasizes the sounds of words as spoken by children. Sometimes these sounds are different from standard pronunciation. An example is George Ulrich's poem "My Tooth Ith Loothe" (1995), which envisions how a child might speak with a loose tooth:

My tooth ith looth! My tooth ith loothe.
I can't go to thcool, that'th my excuthe.
I wath fine latht night when I went to bed
But today it'th hanging by a thread! (p. 6)

Continue to use poems with first and second graders. Read them aloud, emphasizing the rhythm and engaging students in the sounds of the words and rhymes. In many of Jack Prelutsky's *Zoo Doings: Animal Poems* (1983), he uses words that are enjoyable to hear and even more fun to roll off the tongue. "Yickity-yackity yickity-yak, the yak has a scriffily, scraffily back!" begins one delightful poem about a yak. Later in the same poem, Prelutsky uses the phrase, "Sniggildy-snaggildy, sniggildy-snag." Children can have fun with these words and even change the beginning consonant to form a new tongue twister. Try changing the *y* in "yickity-yackity yickity-yak" to *j* or *l* or *s*, and the *scr* in "scriffily, scraffily" to a *tw* or *th*. Model these transformations to help children become aware of the sounds within words.

"The Giggling Gaggling Gaggle of Geese," in Prelutsky (1983), uses the title phrase 10 times in a short 5-verse poem. The words are as noisy as the geese and twist the tongue if the reader attempts to read it with speed. Again, you might change the beginning sound of "giggling, gaggling gaggle of geese" to a *ch* and say it fast!

Many poems use onomatopoeia, which naturally emphasizes the sounds of words. *Noisy Poems,* collected by Jill Bennett (1987), contains many delightful poems that emphasize the noisy sounds of our language. As you read these poems, take visible pleasure in their alliteration, assonance, onomatopoeia, rhyme, and rhythm. You can model how these sounds evoke laughter and other emotions by substituting different initial sounds for some words and by emphasizing how sounds create different moods. The following few lines of "Jazz-Man," from *Noisy Poems,* demonstrate how the poet Eleanor Farjeon uses onomatopoeia:

> Crash and
> Clang!
> Bash and Bang!
> And up in the road the Jazz-Man sprang . . .
> . . . Toot and
> Tingle!
> Hoot and
> Jingle!
> Oh, what a clatter! How the tunes all mingle! (unpaged)

Onomatopoeia, alliteration, rhythm, and rhyme are also found in classic children's nursery rhymes, such as "Horsie, Horsie":

> Horsie, horsie, don't you stop,
> Just let your feet go clipetty clop;
> Your tail goes swish, and the wheels go round—
> Giddy-up, you're homeward bound!

Poets also play with language by coining names and words to indicate the characteristics of people. One such poem is Helen Ksypka's "My Family of Dinosaurs," in *Miles of Smiles: Kids Pick the Funniest Poems, Book #3* (1998) edited by Bruce Lansky:

> My sister, finkasaurus,
> is a tattletaling skrew.
> My brother, Slobasarus,
> doesn't quite know how to chew.
> My mother, rushasaurus,
> Finds it hard to be on time. (p. 85)

To emphasize how the name of the person fits the personality, you might change the poem to read: "My mother, flowerasaurus / Grows flowers of every kind." Or, "My mother, jogasarus / Jogs both day and night." After you model some of these improvisations, encourage students to add their own.

Kenn Nesbitt's "Kangaroos," also from Lansky (1998), contains more coined words:

> If a person has four babies
> You would call them all quadruplets.
> If a kangaroo does likewise,
> Should you call them Kangaruplets? (p. 89)

Many poems are written in couplets—two lines that rhyme—which make it easy for children to hear the rhymes. An easy way to introduce children to couplets is through the nonsense poem "Mr. Backward" by Douglas Florian, in Lansky (1998). Read six lines and then ask students to insert a word that rhymes. It does not matter if the word is different from the original word used in the poem because the poem is full of nonsense:

> Mr. Backward lives in town
> He never wakes up; he always wakes down.
> He eats dessert before his meal.
> His plastic plants and flowers are real.
> He takes a bath inside his sink
> And cleans his clothes with purple ____ (ink). (p. 98)

By permitting the students to fill in the blank, you engage them in language play and emphasize the enjoyable nature of rhyme.

"Dainty Dottie Dee" by Jack Prelutsky, also found in Lansky (1998), likewise engages children with language play. This poem has alliteration, rhyme, onomatopoeia, and some great vocabulary:

> There's no one as immaculate
> as dainty Dottie Dee,
> who clearly is the cleanest
> that a human being can be,
> no sooner does she waken
> than she hoses down her bed,
> then hurries to the kitchen,
> and disinfects the ________ (bread). (p. 102)

Let the students supply the missing word to keep them fully engaged. You might also play with the squeaky, clean-sounding words that Prelutsky uses to show how clean Dottie Dee really is. Squeaky sounds include the /c/ and /t/ in *immaculate,* /t/ in *dainty,* /d/ and /t/ in *Dottie,* /d/ in *Dee,* /c/ in *clearly,* and /c/ and /t/ in *cleanest.* Emphasize these sounds as you read the poem.

A list of poetry and Mother Goose books is in Appendix A.4. Other books with rhyme are presented in Appendix A.7.

Jump Rope Jingles

Jump rope jingles (or chants) are full of rhythm and rhyme. They cater to kinesthetic learners because the children jump in rhythm with the syllables. Straight jumping, which is most appropriate for very young children, requires they jump once for every beat or syllable. Jump rope jingles also lend themselves to the addition of more rhyming verses by the children. A good example of this is the following jingle found in Joanna Cole's *Anna Banana: 101 Jump-Rope Rhymes* (1989):

I went upstairs to make my bed.
I made a mistake and bumped my head.
I went downstairs to milk my cow.
I made a mistake and milked the sow.
I went in the kitchen to bake a pie.
I made a mistake and baked a fly. (p. 17)

You can model adding to the jingle with lines such as the following:

I went to the closet to get my hat.
I made a mistake and stepped on the cat.

or

I went to town to buy a wig.
I made a mistake and ate a pig.

Another jingle in Cole's book that lends itself to adding rhyming verses is "Standing on the Corner":

Standing on the corner,
Chewing bubble gum,
Along came a beggar
And asked me for some. (p. 17)

Again, you can model additions to the jingle with verses such as the following:

Standing by the wall,
Playing with the ball,
Waiting for my uncle
To take me to the mall.

Have fun with jump rope jingles and with improvising verses. This activity should take place in a safe environment and children should feel comfortable adding their own verses. A safe environment means that the teacher and the children accept all student suggestions, even nonsense words, because they are a legitimate part of many jingles.

Tongue Twisters

Tongue twisters are a natural way to introduce students to alliteration. Not all the words in a twister need to begin with the same initial sound, but most of them should. An example of alliteration in a tongue twister is, "Peter Piper picked a peck of pickled peppers." Remember to emphasize the repeated initial sounds so students will develop an ear for words beginning with the same sound.

Challenging tongue twisters are found in *Ready . . . Set . . . Read!* (1990) compiled by J. Cole and S. Calmenson. One of these tongue twisters is "Fran fried five flat fishes" (p. 124). You can extend this tongue twister by adding to the sentence: "Fancy, frilly Fran fried five flat fishes on Friday." Another of the book's easily expanded tongue twisters is, "Sue saw sheep in shoes" (p. 125). Add the following words and attempt to say it really fast: "Silly Sally and sad Sue saw sheep in shoes and snakes in sneakers." More books with alliteration and language play are listed in Appendix A.7. After practicing tongue twisters with students, encourage them to create and share their own with their classmates.

Children's Literature

Engage students in additional language play by reading texts that feature rhyme, alliteration, and onomatopoeia. The teacher's responsibility is to focus on the sounds within words so students become engaged in the activity. Listening to these sounds should be an everyday activity for children. Do not be concerned if students do not hear all the intricate sounds of a particular passage at first; focus on making these language experiences positive so they look forward to more texts. Phonemic awareness will develop over time with continued exposure to and engagement in diverse language experiences (Cunningham et al., 1998).

Many of Dr. Seuss's books are filled with humor and rhymes, with the story line often taking a back seat to the sounds of the text. *Green Eggs and Ham* (1960) is filled with rhymes. Notice the rhymes are all couplets so the children can hear them easily.

I do not like them in a box.
I do not like them with a fox.
I will not eat them in a house.
I do not like them with a mouse.
I do not like them here or there.
I do not like them anywhere!

The more you read the story and encourage students to participate, the more fun they will have as the words roll off their tongues. You can always permit them to add their own verses, such as the following:

I do not like them in the mall.
I do not like them with y'all. (In a nice Southern accent!)

or

I do not like them on a log.
I do not like them with a frog.

or

I do not like them in a tree.
I do not like them with a bee!

Some authors use couplets in stories in which the primary emphasis is on plot; the rhyme adds to the tone of the story. Jez Alborough, in *It's the Bear* (1994), uses couplets that enhance the tone of an adventure about a mother with her child in a forest:

"A bear?" said Mom. "That's silly, dear!
We don't get great big bears around here.
There's just you and me and your teddy, Freddie.
Now let's all get the picnic ready."

Jill Sardegna, in *The Roly-Poly Spider* (1994), also uses couplets and dialogue to tell a delightful story about a spider:

The roly-poly spider once spun a sticky web,
Spun a sticky chair,
Two couches and a bed.
"Come visit me," she cried.
"I'm as lonely as can be."
But the roly-poly spider was hungry too—
You'll see.

Instead of using couplets, Irma Joyce, in *Never Talk to Strangers* (1967), uses three lines of rhyme before the repeated line of "never talk to strangers":

If you are hanging from a trapeze
And up sneaks a camel with bony knees
Remember this rule, if you please—
Never talk to strangers.

Other books with rhyme, alliteration, and language play are listed in Appendix A.7.

Many authors use multiple language elements to create a story's mood. Some use onomatopoeia, alliteration, and assonance, which add a range of sounds and moods to a story. A favorite board book of my young children is *Miss Spider's New Car* (1999) by David Kirk. The verbs and interjections are filled with onomatopoeia, which are written in brightly colored capitals. Here are a few sample lines:

It mustn't SCREECH (written in bright orange) or GROWL (written in blue) or WHINE! (written in green)

CHA-HISS! (written in orange) This speedster's charged with steam.

VA-ROOM! (written in bright pink) Slow down, I'm going to scream!

Students enjoy when you exaggerate the sounds of a car.

Eve Bunting's *In the Haunted House* (1990) uses couplets with alliteration, assonance, and carefully chosen words to conjure a scary setting:

There's a coffin-shaped tub, claw-footed and deep
and in it's a vampire who smiles in his sleep.

Ghosts swim in the hallway
Three witches appear
Bats hang by their feet
From the cracked chandelier . . . .
At the basin a werewolf is washing his snout
Sucking in water and spouting it out.

Emphasize the alliteration and assonance and discuss with the students how the sounds of the words add to the story's scary mood. For example, you might emphasize the clicking /k/ and /t/ sounds in *coffin-shaped, tub,* and *claw-footed* to mimic the eerie sounds of the haunted house. (Notice how an exaggerated /h/ sound in *haunted house* echoes the hollow sounds of the house!) Heighten the devious mood by drawing out the long /i/ sound in *vampire* and *smiles.* Forming your mouth into a wide smile on the long /i/ also adds to the mood. In the next setting, the alliteration of the /w/ in *werewolf washing* might evoke a feeling of fear or woe, and the /s/ sound in *washing, sucking,* and *spouting* suggests the hissing of the werewolf. These playful sounds help the students become conscious of sounds within words and to realize that the sounds of words in a story or poem help set the mood, just as much as the illustrations do.

In *Zin! Zin! Zin! A Violin* (1995), Lloyd Moss uses couplets, alliteration, and onomatopoeia to introduce orchestral and musical terms to young readers. Notice the light, high-pitched, flute-like sounds in the following passage:

Flute, that sends our soul a-shiver,
Flute, that slender, silver sliver.
A place among the set it picks
To make a young sextet—that's six.

In many books, characters' names have magical or musical sounds. Younger children enjoy the rhyming names of the different characters in Joan Powers's *Henny Penny* (1988): Cocky Locky, Ducky Lucky, Turkey Lurkey, Foxy Loxy, and Goosey Loosey. You can substitute other sounds to make your own names, such as Turkey Murkey or Ducky Mucky. The more you manipulate word sounds while reading stories, the more the students will become aware of the sounds in language.

Jan Brett's *Berlioz the Bear* (1991) also uses sounds to suggest the musical instruments played by the characters. Notice the /z/ sounds of the bass as the story begins:

Zum. Zum buzz. Zum. Zum. Buzz. Berlioz had been practicing for weeks, and now just when the orchestra was going to play in the village square for a gala ball, a strange buzz was coming from his double bass. (unpaged)

What more needs to be said about the wonderful language in children's songs, chants, poems, tongue twisters, riddles, and stories? Take advantage of it by reading with expression and playing with word sounds. Drawing attention to the sounds within words while taking pleasure in reading poems, riddles, stories, and other texts is the best way to develop children's phonemic awareness. Language play should take place in small groups or with individual students who lack a rich language background. Most of the activities described here can be conducted with students lacking a wide range of language experiences at home. They will need extra one-on-one experience with an adult who engages them while they play with language.

Intervention STRATEGIES & ACTIVITIES

The following section includes a number of activities that correspond to the seven dimensions of phonemic awareness. You may believe it is not necessary for students to develop all seven dimensions. However, some students, especially those who are inattentive in a large group, may benefit from these language activities, especially one-on-one or in a small group, which gives them more intensive exposure to language sounds (IRA/NAEYC, 1998; Taylor, Pressley, & Pearson, 2000). Many children become aware of the sounds of the English language through game-like activities and sustained exposure to singing and rhymes. Remember that games are a part of childhood play and meant for entertainment, not direct instruction. Therefore, the emphasis should not be on teaching phonemic awareness, but rather on playing with language in an enjoyable, relaxed manner. Instructions written for small groups can be modified for use with individuals and vice versa.

As mentioned earlier, some English sounds are not found in other languages. Also, because some sounds (e.g., /t/ and /d/; /b/ and /p/) are confusing even for native speakers, it is a good idea to present them several weeks apart (Vaughn et al., 2005). It is recommended that high-frequency sounds be introduced early (see Figure 5.5 and Appendix B.4).

Activities Emphasizing Syllables

When introducing activities that focus on the sounds within words, start with syllables because they are a larger part of a word than single sounds. During small group work, you may observe some students having difficulty clapping out the syllables in their names or keeping up with similar activities. If you administer the Pre-Assessment for Phonemic Awareness instrument and the student cannot complete the first task (clapping out syllables), engage him in one of the following activities to emphasize listening to syllables. For these activities, the student may benefit from a one-on-one tutoring setting.

CLAPPING SYLLABLES TO FAMILIAR SONGS AND RHYMES — GRADES K–2 — ACTIVITY

Teach the children the following rhymes, then have them clap their hands or slap their knees for each syllable. All of the following rhymes can be found in *My Very First Mother Goose* (1996), edited by Iona Opie and illustrated by Rosemary Wells.

- "Jack and Jill Went up the Hill." (Most words have one syllable.)
- "Little Boy Blue, Come Blow Your Horn." (Most words have one syllable.)
- "Hey Diddle, Diddle." (Many two-syllable words.)
- "Humpty Dumpty." (Many one- and two-syllable words.)
- "Down at the Station, Early in the Morning." (A great combination of one- and two-syllable words.)

ACTIVITY **CLAPPING SYLLABLES TO MULTISYLLABLE WORDS** GRADES 3–6

Older students also need to hear syllables within words as they analyze multisyllable words and write them. For this age group, find multisyllable words in poems that you read together. You say the multisyllable word and the student taps his fingers as he repeats the word. For example, *streptococcus* is a fun word in "My Brother Doesn't Like to Share" (Lansky, 2000). Say the word and have the student tap as he pronounces *strep-to-coc-cus.*

ACTIVITY **LET'S MAKE MUSIC** GRADES K–1

When the child can sing the following songs by heart, have her beat each syllable with a rhythm instrument as she sings. Choose instruments that produce a distinct beat, such as rhythm sticks, drums, triangles, and sand blocks. Shaking instruments such as maracas are not as good because the beat is not as distinct. All of the following songs can be found in Pamela Beall and Susan Nipp's *Wee Sing* (1979) songbook:

"The Eentsy Weensty Spider"	"This Old Man"
"Rain, Rain Go Away!"	"Teddy Bear"
"Twinkle, Twinkle, Little Star"	"Bingo Was His Name-o"

ACTIVITY **HOW MANY SYLLABLES IN THE ZOO?** GRADES K–1

Using the game board and picture cards found in Appendix D.3, have the student select a picture card from the stack. She says the word and claps the number of syllables. If she claps the correct number, she moves forward that number of spaces on the game board. If she claps the number of syllables incorrectly, she moves backward that number of spaces. You may need to help the student with unfamiliar animals.

Activities Emphasizing Initial Sounds

Listening for initial sounds in words is best developed when a teacher models writing during Morning Message and other writing experiences (Bear, Invernizzi, Templeton, & Johnston, 2006). However, if a student cannot distinguish the difference between sounds when most of his peers can, or if he cannot tell which two words begin with the same sound (task #2 on the Pre-Assessment Phonemic Awareness instrument), the following activities may prove helpful.

ACTIVITY **SOUND BOXES** GRADES K–3

Sound boxes, developed by Elkonin (1973), demonstrate how words are made up of smaller pieces. When working with sound boxes, begin with three-letter words in the consonant-vowel-consonant (CVC) pattern.

1. Fold up the bottom of a large sheet of construction paper to make a pocket and staple the ends. (See Figure 4.6.) Use different colors of paper to represent different sounds, although the same color does not always have to match a particular sound.
2. Place three different colored slips of paper in the pocket, one over "Beginning," one over "Middle," and one over "End." Because the focus is on sounds and not letter names, it is not necessary to put the letters on the slips of paper.

figure **4.6** Sound boxes.

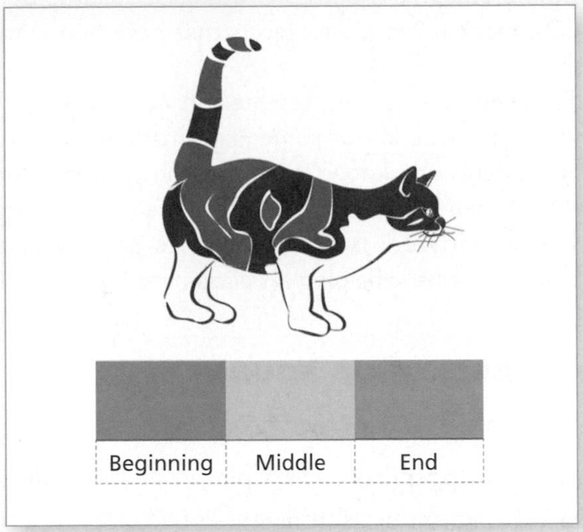

3. Select words systematically. McCarthy (2008) suggests teachers choose first from level 1 words, which are the easiest for young students to dictate, to level 3 words, which are a little more difficult.
   a. Level 1: words with 3 phonemes that begin with /s/, /f/, or /m/ because the "flow of breath is not constricted" (p. 347) as these sounds are made.
   b. Level 2: words with 3 phonemes that begin with /d/, /k/, or /t/. These phonemes are "stop-consonant sounds" that feature a distinct break between these initial phonemes and the next phoneme.
   c. Level 3: words that begin or end with a consonant blend, such as /gr/ and /mp/. Blends are so closely connected that young students have a difficult time segmenting them.
4. After sharing a song, poem, or book with rimes, select one word with the CVC pattern, such as *sun*. Bear et al. (2006) suggest singing the following song to the tune of "Are You Sleeping, Brother John?"

   Beginning, middle, end; beginning, middle, end.
   Where is the sound? Where is the sound?
   Where's the ssss in sun? Where's the ssss in sun?
   Let's find out. Let's find out. (p. 123)

5. After singing this verse, the child selects the position of the sound by selecting the first card. This activity can also be used when listening for final consonant sounds by changing the third line appropriately.

ALPHABET BOOKLETS

GRADES K–3 ACTIVITY

1. Give the child a magazine and have her find three or four pictures that begin with a designated consonant.
2. Have the child tear or cut out the picture and glue it onto a 3 x 5 index card.
3. Put the letter on an index card and use it as a cover for the booklet.
4. Make a booklet for each consonant by using a comb binding to secure the pages.

ACTIVITY

SPANISH/ENGLISH CONCEPT BOOKS

GRADES 1–3

Many concept books are bilingual (Spanish and English). These books are great to use when tutoring because most authors use objects that have phonemes common to both English and Spanish.

Recommended concept books are presented in Appendix A.8. You may pair two native Spanish speakers, one who knows some English and another who knows very little English. Instruct the student who knows some English to pronounce both the English and Spanish words, and then to have his buddy say the word in English. Explain to the "student teacher" how important it is for his buddy to pronounce the English word to the best of his ability because he is helping his classmate.

ACTIVITY

REMEMBER THE BEGINNING SOUND!

GRADES K–1

This activity is played like the popular Memory or Concentration game.

1. The picture cards (see Appendix D.4) are placed on the table or floor, face down.
2. The teacher and student take turns turning over two cards at a time. The player says the words on the cards; if the two words begin with the same sound, the player must isolate the beginning sound by saying it.
3. If the player recognizes that the words do begin with the same sound, the player keeps the two cards.
4. If the player does not pick up two cards that begin with the same sound or if the player does not recognize that the words begin with the same sound, the player turns the cards back over in their places.
5. The objective is for the players to collect as many cards as possible. Begin the first game with cards of two different letters and then proceed to cards with three and four different letters.

ACTIVITY

INITIAL SOUND BINGO

GRADES K–2

Make copies of the Bingo cards provided in Appendix D.5 and laminate them. Make more than one set if a large group is going to play. Call out words from the following list. Each participant puts a marker on any word that begins with the same letter sound. Participants try to get five in a row, in a vertical, horizontal, or diagonal line.

WORD LIST

basket	kick	tip	doughnut	potato
cards	love	very	farmer	rooster
dad	move	want	game	Santa
first	no	yell	jelly	telephone
go	pick	zip	lace	water
hard	rise	bump	mom	yellow
jump	stand	camel	nice	zap

Note: Because the game focuses on initial sounds, accept responses that confuse *c* and *k* words.

ACTIVITY

TOSS THE CUBE

GRADES K–2

Using cubes like those found in Appendix D.6, students toss a cube, say the sound the letter makes, and name one word that begins with that sound.

GO FISH

GRADES K–1 ACTIVITY

For kinesthetic learners in the semi-phonemic stage, Go Fish reinforces initial sounds of words. First, using pictures of objects known to students as "fish," attach a magnetic strip on their backs. Place the fish on a large piece of blue butcher paper. Have the students use the fishing pole (a stick attached to a piece of string, with a magnet as a hook) to fish for a word. Students then say the initial sound and name the first letter of the word. Appendix D.7 has templates of fish for each letter of the alphabet.

TONGUE TWISTERS

GRADES 2–3 ACTIVITY

For older students having difficulty distinguishing words with the same initial sound, reciting tongue twisters with the teacher often helps. Focus on saying them, not writing them. Most older students are familiar with "She sells seashells down by the seashore." You can improvise a tongue twister based on your name and then invite the student to create one based on his name. The focus is on hearing initial sounds, not identifying the letter names. For example, you might improvise, "Cute Katie Cauthrin couldn't cut carrot cake."

Activities Emphasizing Rhymes

Many students have a difficult time hearing rhymes. A teacher who is a good "kid-watcher" will be able to detect these students as she reads poems and stories; they will either not respond or will give incorrect responses. They often cannot complete the third task on the Pre-Assessment for Phonemic Awareness instrument. The following activities emphasize rhyme.

IDENTIFYING RHYMING WORDS IN POETRY

GRADES 1–8 ACTIVITY

One useful activity for any age student who cannot hear rhyme is for you to read an age-appropriate poem to students and ask them to listen for rhyming words. An example for younger students is "The Poet-Tree" in Bagert (1997), which includes three different words that have rhyme—*tree, knee, me*—in the first two lines.

Using poetry to help middle school students listen for rhyme can aid their spelling skills. Choose short poems intended for adolescents and instruct them to listen carefully for words that sound the same at the end. For example, "Good Models," a poem in Bagert (1997), is appropriate for older students because it references Elizabeth Browning, Emily Dickinson, and Walt Whitman. It includes the rhymes *frowning/Browning, change/strange, weird/beard,* and *rule/school.*

Verify that the student understands the rhyme by asking for another word that rhymes with *rule.* Then use one of Bruce Lansky's poems, whose humor appeals to middle school students, and ask the student to identify the rhyming words. Here are a few suggested poems, all from Bruce Lansky's *My Dog Ate My Homework!* (2009) collection. Each of these poems has the ABCB pattern.

"My Dog Chewed Up My Homework"
"Measles"
"There's a New Cook in the Cafeteria"
"Confession"
"A Bad Case of the Giggles"

ACTIVITY

HUMPTY DUMPTY BOARD GAME

GRADES K–1

After reading "Humpty Dumpty," assemble the game board provided in Appendix D.8 and follow these directions.

DIRECTIONS FOR HUMPTY DUMPTY

- The game is for two participants.
- Turn all Humpty Dumpty halves upside down.
- Assign one side of the board to each participant.
- Decide who goes first.
- The first participant picks up a Humpty Dumpty half, pronounces the word, and checks to see if there is a half on her side of the wall that rhymes with it. If the participant has a rhyming picture and can correctly match it with its half on her side of the board game, she receives another turn. If she does not have a match or cannot identify the matching piece, her half is again turned upside down and put back in the playing pack.
- The objective for players is to get all the matches on their side of the wall.

ACTIVITY

CLOWNING AROUND WITH RHYMING WORDS

GRADES K–2

Using the picture word cards in Appendix D.4 from the "Remember the Beginning Sound" activity, lay out the pictures for the following words:

dog	pig	boat	fan	king
ham	bat	cow	coat	sun
cat	fish	duck	nose	
cake	ball	goat	hand	
top	fox	box	frog	

The student picks up the card and names the picture. He then must name any word that rhymes with the picture. For example, if he picks the picture of the pig, he can say any word that rhymes with *pig*, such as *big* or *fig*. With each correct response, add one section of the clown (as shown in Figure 4.7) until the entire clown is complete.

figure **4.7** Steps for clown drawings.

Activity Emphasizing Oddity

To emphasize oddity, pronounce three words, two of which begin with the same sound and one of which does not (e.g., *milk, mom, table*). Ask the students which word is different. Those who have a difficult time with this tend to listen to the entire word rather than focusing on the initial sound. Students who do this may think that all the words are different. One-on-one time with the teacher, in which you emphasize the beginning sounds of the two similar words and then point out the beginning sound of the word of the different word, will help. Working with manipulatives, such as in the following activity, may make the task easier.

ODD-CARD OUT! GRADES 1–3 ACTIVITY

Using the picture cards from "Remember the Beginning Sound" (Appendix D.4), place three cards in front of the student. Two begin with the same initial sound, and the other is the "odd" picture card. The student must pick out the picture card that does not begin with the same initial sound as the other two.

As an example, place the cards with a picture of a fish, boat, and bat in front of the student. She must pick out the fish card as the "odd" card. Work with any particular sounds that give the student trouble.

Activities Emphasizing Blending

Blending is a skill that is needed when students begin to decode and encode unknown words. Most will learn to blend onsets with rime as the teacher plays with language in small groups. However, some students have difficulty blending because when decoding words, they often look for smaller parts within a word and then put the parts together. These children often struggle to complete the fifth task on the Pre-Assessment for Phonemic Awareness. The following activities emphasize blending.

CHILDREN ARE SOUNDS GRADES K–1 ACTIVITY

Some students learn best through kinesthetic activities. This activity will help both kinesthetic and visual learners; it is designed for small- or whole-group learning.

1. Call three students to stand in a straight line in the front of the group. You then stand behind them.
2. Assign each student a sound (e.g., first child is /h/; second child is a short /a/; and the third child is /t/).
3. Tell the group the sound of each student, and then ask the group to say the sounds as you point to each student. Point slowly at first and repeat a few times. Go faster each time.
4. Ask the group what word (e.g., *hat*) the three students represent.
5. Ask the group to say the three sounds again while you point, then give a swooping gesture to have the group say the word.
6. Repeat with other students and other words.

BLENDING WITH PUPPETS GRADES K–1 ACTIVITY

This activity works well with young English learners in the shy, silent stage, who may be reluctant to speak for themselves but willing to talk through a puppet (refer back to

Figure 1.4; Vaughn et al., 2005). The activity works best with one child, but can be performed with a small group of no more than five students.

1. Put on three finger puppets (any puppets will do) and explain to the student(s) that the puppets can only say sounds, no words.
2. Instruct the student(s) to listen carefully as the puppet says its sound. For example: Puppet #1 is /p/, Puppet #2 is a short /a/, Puppet #3 is /n/.
3. Have the student(s) repeat the sound as each puppet says its sound.
4. Repeat steps 2 and 3 a little faster each time.
5. Then ask the student(s) what word the three puppets make together (*pan*).

ACTIVITY **ONSET AND RIME BLENDING CARD GAME** **GRADES 1–3**

Use the words listed below from the picture cards provided in Appendix D.4. Place three cards in front of the student; for example, the cards with pictures of the fish, cat, and hat. Then say the onset "plus" the rime for one of the cards. For example, say, "I see a /k/ plus *at*." The student must pick up the cat card and say the word. Continue the activity by placing a new card with the fish and hat cards; for example, the bed card.

PICTURE CARDS TO USE

ball	cat	frog	key	net	rake	top
bag	cup	gate	king	nose	rat	vase
bat	dog	goat	lock	pail	ring	vest
bed	fan	ham	log	pan	rug	web
bee	fin	hand	map	pen	sink	well
box	fish	hat	mouse	pig	socks	wing
cake	fork	jar	nest	pin	sun	wig

ACTIVITY **BLENDING INDIVIDUAL SOUNDS CARD GAME** **GRADES 1–3**

Use the picture cards named below from Appendix D.4. Draw two cards and place them in front of the student. For example, the two cards may be the pictures of the bell and the bat. Ask, "Which picture is /b/ plus /a/ plus /t/?" (say each sound separately, but do not distort the sounds). The student must say the word and select the correct card.

PICTURE CARDS TO USE

ball (/b/ + /a/ + /l/)	cat	gate	log	pig	top
bat	coat	goat	lock	pin	tub
boat (/b/ + /o/ + /t/)	cup	gum	map	pipe	tie
bell	dog	ham	moon	rat	web
bed	dime	hat	net	rake	wig
bag	duck	jet	nose	road	zoo
box	fan	jug	nut	rope	
bee	fin	kite	pan	rug	
cake	five	key	pen	sun	

Activity Emphasizing Segmenting

Being able to segment sounds within words is an important skill as students begin to write. They pronounce the entire word as they start writing it, and then segment the sounds as they write each letter. When working in small groups, you may find a student who cannot detect individual sounds in words. Administer the Pre-Assessment for Phonemic Awareness instrument to determine his ability to segment words. If he cannot complete the sixth task, he may benefit from the following activity.

SEGMENTING INDIVIDUAL SOUNDS (CARD GAME) **GRADES 1–3** ACTIVITY

Use the same picture cards from Appendix D.4. The student draws a card from the deck and segments each sound of the word. For example, if she draws the picture card of the pig, she must say, "/p/ plus /i/ plus /g/."

Next, reverse roles with the student. Draw a card and say each individual sound. The student must determine if you are correct. Try making some errors to see if the student recognizes them.

Activities Emphasizing Deleting

Most students will be able to delete sounds as they participate in small group activities with the teacher. Use the sound box described earlier in this section and choose three-letter words in which the rime is a word by itself (e.g., *hit, fan, sat, Sam*). Place a "word" (three different colors of paper) in the sound box and review with the small group the sound for each slip of paper (e.g., first slip: /b/ sound, second slip: short /a/ sound, and third slip: /t/ sound). Then, remove the first slip of paper (the /b/ sound) and ask the group to pronounce the new word. During this activity watch closely for children who do not understand the concept, and conduct it again with them on an individual basis if necessary.

POP OFF THE BEADS! **GRADES K–1** ACTIVITY

Perform this activity using different colored pop beads with those who need one-on-one help deleting sounds from words. Each bead represents one sound within a word. When the child completes the activity successfully with manipulatives, try conducting it orally.

If the word has three sounds, give the student three connected pop beads. Say to her, "I'm going to say a word and ask you to take off one sound from the word. I want you to first say the entire word, and then I want you to pop off a bead and say the new word. For example, here are three beads. The three beads are the word *bat.* The first red bead is the /b/, the middle yellow bead is the short /a/ sound, and the last green bead is the /t/. Now I am going to take off the /b/ bead, and I have the word *at.* Now, I am going to let you do it." You can use any three-letter words from the following lists. When the child is comfortable working with three-letter words, you can add one bead and work with four-letter words.

SET #1	SET # 2	SET # 3
Late; take off /l/	Harm; take off /h/	Bin; take off /b/
Meat; take of /m/	Burn; take off /b/	Send; take off /s/
Ball; take off /b/	Cup; take off /k/	Hand; take off /h/
Bat; take off /b/	Chair; take off /ch/	Ledge; take off /l/
Ham; take off /h/	Fear; take off /f/	Wax; take off /w/
Beat; take off /b/	Bus; take off /b/	Pant; take off /p/
Bill; take off /b/	Nod; take off /n/	Mask; take off /m/
Sit; take off /s/	Link; take off /l/	Cash; take off /k/
Boar; take off /b/	Ditch; take off /d/	Dan; take off /d/
Cart; take off /k/	His; take off /h/	Fact; take off /f/

You can make more sets by using the rimes from the list above and adding new onsets.

ACTIVITY **CHILDREN AND SOUNDS** **GRADES K–1**

This activity is similar to "Children Are Sounds" and is good for kinesthetic learners. It also has students delete sounds.

1. Choose a three-letter word, such as *bat, sit,* or *ham,* and assign one letter sound to each child. For example, Carolyn is the /b/ sound, Victor is the short /a/ sound, and Juan is the /t/ sound.
2. Line up the three children in a row in the correct order: *b a t.*
3. Ask them the following set of questions.
   - What sound is Carolyn?
   - What sound is Victor?
   - What sound is Juan?
   - What word do the three sounds make?
   - Now let's have Carolyn sit down.
   - What word do Victor and Juan make?
   - Now let's have Carolyn stand back up. What word do we have now?

This activity can be done with any word in which one letter can be deleted to form another word (e.g., *sand, ball, Jill, sit, meat*). Words such as *right* and *sound,* of course, do not work.

Activities Emphasizing Manipulating

Learning to manipulate sounds within words aids students when they later need to find patterns within words to decode unknown words and spell new ones. Manipulating activities can be done in small groups. The following small group activity uses the sound box, discussed earlier in this chapter.

1. Assign a sound to each of the three slips of paper in the pocket (e.g., /f/ + /a/ + /n/), and pronounce the word with the students.
2. Remove the first slip of paper, the /f/ sound, replace it with another colored slip of paper, and call it the hard /c/ sound.
3. Ask the children what word the three sounds make. Take out the "c" slip of paper, replace it with yet another colored slip, and call it the /m/ sound. Have the children name the new word.

For those who do not respond correctly and also cannot complete the eighth task on the Pre-Assessment for Phonemic Awareness instrument, use the sound box during one-one-one time to complete the following activity.

ACTIVITY **MOVING THE TILES** **GRADES 1–3**

1. Cut seven 2 x 3 x 2 tiles from seven different colors of poster board. You can laminate the pieces so they can be used over a period of time.
2. Lay out three different colored tiles in front of the student (e.g., blue, red, and yellow). Assign a letter sound to blue (e.g., the /b/ sound), another sound to the red tile (e.g., the short /a/ sound), and a third sound to the third yellow tile (e.g., the /t/ sound).
3. Ask him to say the word that the tiles make.
4. Remove the blue tile and replace it with a white tile, calling it the /f/ sound. Again ask the student to pronounce the new word. Do this activity first with three tiles and later add the fourth tile to form four-letter words.

The following are lists of suggested words. Note that the child is to replace the initial sound of each of the words in the list with the sound of the letter that is on top of the list.

S	M	B	P	H
pat	late	late (bait)	sat	sat
pit	neat	meat	meat	pit
neat	ball	call	ball (Paul)	meat
ham	bat	sat	bat	Sam
boar	bake	cake	ham	late
bake	fan	fill	bill	neat
ring	cart	sit	sit	ball
round	night	soar	cart	cart (heart)
right	round	turn	cup	fill
		pear	bear	farm
		wig	wig	fair
		site		night (height)

PHONEMIC AWARENESS AND TECHNOLOGY

Many interactive websites encourage students to listen for phonemes. The following resources will assist you as you help students build phonemic awareness:

www.learningtoday.com/corporate/reading-games.asp

http://teacher.scholastic/com/clifford1/flash/phonics/index.htm

www.readinglady.com

www.readwritethink.org

www.pbskids.org

CONCLUDING THOUGHTS

Phonemic awareness is the ability to distinguish oral sounds and syllables within words. Children with this ability can distinguish initial sounds, determine how many sounds are in a word, manipulate sounds to create new words, delete sounds from a word to create a new word, and determine the number of syllables within a word. Most researchers and educators agree that proficient readers and writers need these skills; however, how teachers should facilitate these skills is open for debate. Some believe children must receive explicit instruction in phonemic awareness, while others believe that teaching phonemic awareness breaks language into too many parts, which makes language difficult for children.

Learn as much as you can about phonemic awareness and enjoy the wonderful sounds in the English language. Then, as you work with your students, you can instill in them the fun of listening to and manipulating sounds in words.

Reflective Learning — PHONEMIC AWARENESS

Scenario. Mr. Ross is certified to teach early childhood and elementary grades. After teaching fifth grade for three years, he is offered a kindergarten position and is thrilled to have a new challenge. Even though many of his students have spent time in daycare, he knows that he will be their first formal teacher because the district has no four-year-old program.

When Mr. Ross meets with the other kindergarten teachers in the fall, he is surprised to learn about the district's emphasis on phonemic awareness and that teachers are required to assess kindergarteners on it. The other kindergarten teachers tell him the principal, a former kindergarten teacher, is motivated to demonstrate that kindergarten students make adequate yearly progress in building phonemic awareness and that she will question him regularly on what he is doing to achieve that goal.

The results of the initial DIBELS assessment indicate that most of his students cannot clap syllables, many cannot give words that begin with the same initial sound, and no student can delete or manipulate sounds. Mr. Ross knows he needs to spend time helping students build their awareness of phonemes; however, he knows of no strategies to help build phonemic awareness.

QUESTIONS

1. What should Mr. Ross do first?
2. Do you think Mr. Ross should spend time each day with explicit instruction in phonemic awareness? Explain why or why not, as though you are addressing the parents of children in Mr. Ross's class.
3. What types of activities are most appropriate for kindergarten children, and which should Mr. Ross use?
4. Where should Mr. Ross go to get creative activities in all the five areas of phonemic awareness?
5. Is there a particular sequence of the five areas that Mr. Ross should use? Or should he engage the students in all five areas each day?

CHAPTER FIVE

PHONICS

Education costs money, but then so does ignorance.

SIR MOSER CLAUS

scenario

At the beginning of the fall semester at Neil Armstrong Middle School, reading interventionist Mr. Spearhead is assigned to work with Jesus, a seventh-grade English learner. Jesus has lived in the United States for four years and attended nine different schools before his father found steady work and enrolled Jesus at the school. During their first session, Mr. Spearhead observes the boy reading a short poem, "Bring Your Own Lunch" (Lansky, 2009), which has mainly one-syllable words recognizable to most seventh graders. The poem also has rhyming words (e.g., *lick/sick* and *ill/will*). When Jesus is unable to identify the rhyming words, Mr. Spearhead has Jesus tell him about his family, their favorite family activities, and his other schools. This allows Mr. Spearhead to assess Jesus's oral language, which he finds adequate for a fourth-year English learner.

During his second session with Jesus, Mr. Spearhead works with riming words. He reads three words (e.g., *hall, jump, fall*) and asks Jesus to repeat the words that rime. He cannot, so Mr. Spearhead writes *hall* and *fall* on a whiteboard and underlines the *all* in each word. Jesus catches on quickly and soon adds to the list with *mall, ball, call,* and *tall.* Mr. Spearhead begins with onset and rimes because there are 37 rimes that create nearly 500 words (Stahl, 1998), and Jesus recognizes analogies between shared rime spelling.

guiding questions

As you read this chapter, consider the following questions:

1. What do you know about phonics generalizations? Can you remember any jingles you learned about phonics?
2. What generalizations will be important for Mr. Spearhead to teach Jesus?
3. What principles of phonics instruction does Mr. Spearhead use with Jesus?
4. If you had a student with Jesus's abilities, what would you do to assess his knowledge of phonics?
5. In what specific additional activities would you engage your student?

INTRODUCTION

School districts must demonstrate student growth in phonics, as well as phonemic awareness, fluency, text comprehension, and vocabulary in order to qualify for federal funds. In 2003 the International Reading Association declared that explicit and systematic phonics instruction has long-lasting positive effects on students' reading ability (International Reading Association, 2003a).

Reading researchers and educators agree that phonics is important for readers as they attempt to understand how the sounds of language create words (Templeton & Bear, 2005; Cunningham, 2004; Fountas & Pinnell, 1999b; Smith, Walker, & Yellin, 2004). The big question that teachers face is "What is the most effective way to help students as they learn the letter–sound relationships?" Camilli and Wolfe (2004) contend that direct phonics instruction may aid some struggling young readers, "but only if embedded in a print-rich comprehensive literacy program and delivered in brief, individualized lessons" (p. 28). They found whole-class phonics instruction ineffective because some students already know and use the concept being presented, and other students lack the background knowledge to understand the concept.

Another debate is whether phonics instruction is needed for older students. Ivey and Baker (2004) argue that it is not. Instead, older students need strategies to develop vocabulary and make sense of text, not to understand letter–sound relationships. However, older English learners, such as Jesus in the above scenario, can benefit from explicit phonics instruction if it is not part of their background knowledge.

These questions and other issues surrounding phonics instruction are addressed in this chapter, including (1) what teachers need to know about phonics, (2) how students learn phonics, (3) how to teach phonics, (4) types of phonics assessments, (5) effective strategies for teaching phonics, and (6) computer programs that reinforce phonics.

DEFINITIONS

The **graphophonic system** is the relationship between the letters and their sounds. A **phoneme** is the smallest unit of speech sound (e.g., /l/, /m/, /b/, /sh/, /ch/, and so on). A **grapheme** is the written representation of the phoneme. A grapheme may be one letter or a cluster of letters. For example, the word *wish* includes four letters, three phonemes (/w/, /i/, and /sh/), and three graphemes (*w*, *i*, and *sh*). The cluster /sh/ makes one distinct sound. Our English alphabet is complicated because some letters have more than one sound. For example, each vowel has a long sound, a short sound, a schwa sound (a vowel sound that is articulated with the tongue in a neutral position, e.g., *a* in *a-gree*, and *e* in *chil-dren*), and a controlled *r* sound (the letter *r* follows a vowel and alters the vowel sound, e.g., *art* and *term*). Sometimes more than one letter represents the same sound. The /k/ sound can be represented by a *k* (kite) or a *c* (cake), and sometimes the *k* is silent (know). Because all elementary teachers work with struggling readers sometime during their teaching career, they should understand terms such as *grapheme* and *schwa* as well as other basic phonics terms. Terms associated with phonics are listed in the following box.

Phonics Glossary at a Glance

Accent: The vocal emphasis applied to syllables in words. In *ac-cent,* the first syllable *ac* is accented.

Affix: Meaning units (prefixes and suffixes) that are added to root or base words.

Analytic phonics: An inductive approach to analyzing a word. The whole word is first read, then each letter sound is analyzed to determine the pronunciation of the word.

Base: Also called the root part of the word. The part to which affixes are added.

Blend: Two or three consonants with closely related but separate sounds. Also called consonant clusters. (Two examples: /br/, /fl/.)

Closed syllable: Syllable that ends with a consonant sound. (Example: first syllable of *but-ter.*)

Cluster: See **blend.**

Compound word: Two words joined together to form a new word. (Example: *butterfly.*)

Consonants: The letters *b, c, d, f, g, h, j, k, l, m, n, p, q, r, s, t, v, w, x, y, z.*

Consonant cluster: Two connecting consonants that when blended together make a unique sound:

/br/ as in *brick*	/cr/ as in *crib*
/dr as in *drink*	/fr/ as in *frog*
/gr/ as in *grape*	/pr/ as in *prize*
/tr/ as in *tree*	/bl/ as in *block*
/cl/ as in *clock*	/fl/ as in *flag*
/gl/ as in *glue*	/pl/ as in *plane*
/sl/ as in *slime*	/sc/ as in *scar*
/sk/ as in *skate*	/sm/ as in *small*
/sn/ as in *snail*	/sp/ as in *spoon* and *crisp*
/st/ as in *star* and *mist*	/sw/ as in *swan*
/scr/ as in *screen*	/squ/ as in *squirrel*
/str/ as in *stream*	/spr/ as in *spring*
/spl/ as in *splash*	/thr/ as in *throne*
/nt/ as in *ant*	/pt/ as in *slept*
/rd/ as in *card*	/rk/ as in *park*
/sk/ as in *ask*	

Consonant digraphs: Two connecting consonants that make one sound:

/sh/ as in *sheep*
/th/ (voiced) as in *the*
/th/ (voiceless) as in *third*
/ch/ as in *cheese*
/zh/ as in *pleasure*
/wh/ as in *wheel*
/ng/ as in *ring*

Decoding: The process of identifying words by attaching appropriate sounds to corresponding letters or letter sequences.

(continued)

Phonics Glossary at a Glance, *continued*

Digraph: Two letters that represent one sound. (Examples: /ch/ in *church,* and /oa/ in *road.*)

Diphthong: Two connecting vowels that make a distinct sound, unlike either of the two vowels:

/ou/	as in	*cloud*	/ow/	as in	*now*
/oi/	as in	*oil*	/oy/	as in	*boy*
/au/	as in	*caught*	/aw/	as in	*lawn*
/ui/	as in	*suit*	/ew/	as in	*new*

Encoding: The process of attaching appropriate letters to sounds when writing.

Fricative consonants: When pronounced, they cause friction in the mouth (/f/, /v/, /th/, /z/, /s/, /zh/, /sh/).

Grapheme: Unit of writing that represents a phoneme.

Nasal consonants: When pronounced, the air is forced through the nose (/n/, /m/, /ng/).

Onset: The part of a word that precedes the vowel. (Examples: *p* in *pat* and *str* in *street.*)

Open syllable: Syllable that ends in a vowel sound. (Example: *ba* in *ba-by.*)

Phoneme: The smallest unit of sound. (Example: *fly* has three phonemes, /f/, /l/, and /y/.)

Phonetics: Study of speech sounds and the way these sounds are made.

Phonics: A way of teaching reading and spelling that stresses symbol–sound relationships.

Phonemic awareness: Awareness that spoken language consists of a sequence of phonemes.

Phonogram: The vowel and any letter that follows the beginning consonant. (Example: *am* in *Sam.*) Words that share the same phonograms are often called word families.

Plosive consonants: When pronounced, these consonants produce a burst of air (/b/, /p/, /d/, /t/, /k/, and /g/ as in *gate*).

Rhyme: Sound elements that consist of the same sound combination. (Examples: *fly* and *by, fox* and *socks.*)

R-controlled vowel: When the letter *r* follows a vowel and alters the vowel sound. (Examples: *art, term, girl, fort, burp.*)

Rime: The vowel and any letter that follows the beginning consonant. (Example: *am* in *Sam.*) Also called phonogram.

Schwa: Vowel sound that is articulated with the tongue in a neutral position. (Examples: /a/ in *a-gree,* /e/ in *chil-dren,* /i/ in *e-dit,* /o/ in *ed-i-tor,* /u/ in *un-load.*)

Short vowel: Vowel sounds that occur in words like *hat, men, fit, hop, but.*

Silent letters: Letters that make no sound. (Example: *k* in *knit.*)

Syllable: Combination of phonemes that creates larger sound units within words. All syllables have a vowel sound. (Example: *clut-ter* has two syllables.)

Synthetic phonics: Stringing isolated letter sounds together to create words. (Example: /c/ + /a/ + /t/ = cat.)

Vowels: These letters of the alphabet: *a, e, i, o, u* and sometimes *y* and *w.*

Vowel digraph: Two connecting vowels that make one sound. Examples:

ai	as in	*mail*	*ee*	as in	*see*
ea	as in	*ear*	*oa*	as in	*road*
ay	as in	*day*	*ey*	as in	*they*
ie	as in	*die*	*ei*	as in	*receive* or *eight*

Whole word approach: Learning new words by memorizing the entire word.

WHAT TEACHERS SHOULD KNOW

In 1995 Louisa Moats surveyed teachers' backgrounds in linguistics. She found that about 50 percent of the surveyed teachers could benefit from additional training in linguistics, especially phonics. Specifically, she determined that teachers with a basic understanding of linguistics could help struggling readers in the following ways:

- Interpret and respond to readers' errors.
- Provide clear and simple examples for decoding and spelling.
- Organize and sequence instruction.
- Explain spelling patterns.
- Integrate language instruction.

Remember that students may become confused by educational jargon and terms such as *consonant blends, clusters, digraphs,* and *diphthongs* (Cunningham, 2004). Therefore, much of the information in this section is designed to help you gain a better understanding of phonics, but the terms and "rules" are not intended to be taught to struggling readers, who may be overwhelmed or intimidated by the overload.

How Students Learn Phonics

English spelling has three layers: alphabetic, pattern, and meaning. *Alphabetic* refers to spelling words letter by letter from left to right. *Pattern* refers to understanding the major patterns of letters: CVC (*hat*), CVCe (*hate*), CVVC (*road*), and so on. *Meaning* refers to different spellings for the different forms of words, for example, *music* and *musical*. Children learn about these three layers through decoding (reading), encoding (writing), and teacher modeling.

Decoding words

The human brain detects patterns (Bear & Templeton, 1998; Cunningham, 2004). Therefore, young readers learn new words more easily by analyzing onset and rime than by attempting to make letter–phoneme correspondences. For example, it is easier for young readers to read *Sam, ham,* and *jam* when they recognize the rime *am* and add the onsets *s, h,* and *j*. When the rimes become longer than two letters, it is even easier for children because they see two parts instead of four or five. Take the *ound* rime in *found, sound, round,* and *mound* as an example. *Ound* is rather complicated to sound out as individual letters; however, if students know *ound* as one sound, they merely add the onsets—*f, s, r,* and *m*—to create the four words.

Young readers also use analogies to pronounce unknown words (Moustafa & Maldonado-Colon, 1999). For example, if beginning readers know that the letter *m* makes the /m/ sound in *mom,* they know they need to make the /m/ sound when they see the word *milk* for the first time.

Students learn to read by focusing on onset, rime, and the initial letter, and by considering the length of words (Cunningham, 2004). Emerging readers can recognize their classmates' names by looking at initial letters; when two names begin with the same letter, they can identify which name sounds longer. For example, they know that when they pronounce *Jill,* it is shorter than when they pronounce *Jeremy*. Therefore, when they see *Jill* and *Jeremy* in print, they can determine which word is *Jill* and which one is *Jeremy*.

Students learn decoding skills when the skills are introduced, taught, practiced, and reinforced within a context that is meaningful to them (Cunningham, 2004; Dahl & Scharer, 2000; Hiebert, 1999; Kane, 1999). When a teacher reads a text that interests students, they see "real" words at work and not nonsense words. When reading, you can help students discover simple examples of the various phonics concepts. Hiebert (1999) found that "[p]honics instruction disconnected from texts that children read contributes little to children's use of phonics strategies in recognizing words" (p. 556).

Encoding words

As students write their own texts, they learn to listen to the sounds within words when they break up words to encode them. They also learn (1) to read/write from left to right, (2) to read/write from top to bottom, and (3) that words have spaces between them. During this process students should write meaningful texts, not strings of nonsense words. Their words do not need to be spelled correctly; they will make approximations of correct spellings as they develop writing skills. Students who listen to sounds and make approximations as they write become better decoders when they read (Cunningham, 2004).

Teacher modeling

Students also learn phonics by observing teachers model and talk about their writing. Ask students to talk about the initial sounds, ending sounds, medial sounds, and the patterns within words as you write the morning message. Effective teachers choose texts that use rhyme. For example, Ms. Synder might choose Ludwig Bemelmans's *Madeline and the Gypsies* (1986) to emphasize the word families for words such as *side, land, bring,* and *went*. After the class reads the book, Ms. Synder writes these words one at a time on the board or flip chart and asks the children to think of other words that rhyme with them. As Ms. Synder writes the rhyming words, she notes how they share the same ending letters. She may also demonstrate how some words rhyme even though they do not have the same ending letters. For example, in the same story, Bemelmans uses the following rhyming words: *more/door, blue/new, girls/curls,* and *bread/bed*. Ms. Synder writes *more* on the board or flip chart and asks the students to recall other words in the book that rhyme with *more*. She writes them down and discusses the different spellings with her students in this guided discovery of rhyme.

English Spelling Patterns

English is "a complex system that is basically phonetic, but also relies upon patterns and meaning to provide an optimal system" (Johnston, 2001b).

Consonants

Many struggling readers and English learners have a difficult time distinguishing consonant sounds because they do not know the proper mouth position for each. Teachers who understand the position of the mouth and tongue for each sound can help students who struggle with correct pronunciation and spelling of words. Appendix B.3 provides detailed information about each consonant of the alphabet. Elementary students should not memorize or recite this information, but you may consult it in your effort to aid struggling readers. For example, after determining which letter sounds are problematic for a student, recite a word containing that letter sound to show the proper shape of the mouth as the sound is formed. The better you understand the English language, the more help you can offer struggling readers and English learners as they make sense of print.

Struggling readers may attempt to pronounce each sound of a **consonant cluster**—two connecting consonants that make a unique sound—separately. Help these students recognize consonant clusters as distinct sounds. The same is true of **consonant digraphs**, which are two connecting consonants with one sound (e.g., *sh* in sheep). Children need to recognize these digraphs as having one sound, instead of two distinct sounds.

Teachers working with struggling readers must also be aware of **allophones**, which are the slight variances of each phoneme. Allophones are caused by co-articulation. For example, the /m/ has a more distinct nasal sound in *mum* than in *most*. This is caused by the mouth positioning itself for the letter after the /m/.

Blevins (2006) found the nine consonant generalizations listed in Figure 5.1 have 95 to 100 percent utility.

Vowels

The vowels *a, e, i, o,* and *u* represent 19 different phonemes. This presents a challenge for struggling readers because with every vowel they encounter they must determine which sound it makes. Notice what happens to the sound of *o* as a different letter is added to *ho:*

hoe	hop	hoop	house
hope	hour	horse	hook
hoist	how		

It has at least nine distinct sounds. For this reason, synthetic phonics (teaching new words by adding one sound on to the next) may not be the best way to teach phonics.

The letter *y* is also used as a vowel when it appears at the end of a syllable or word. It usually has the long /i/ sound at the end of a syllable (*cycle*) or a one-syllable word (*by, fly*), and usually has the long /e/ sound at the end of a polysyllabic word (*funny, silly*). The letter *w* is also a vowel when it is used with another vowel (*low, now, flew, raw*).

Vowel sounds can be written many different ways. Figure 5.2 lists the possible spellings of the long vowel sounds and vowel diphthongs.

When working with English learners, help them understand how vowels are articulated in the mouth. Demonstrate the positions by first saying these long vowel words in this order—*beet, bait, bite, boat, boot*—in which the articulation is from front to back. When teachers talk about articulation of vowels, they also need to "describe the shape of the mouth, the openness of the jaw, and position of the tongue" (Bear et al., 2006, p. 145). Next, demonstrate short vowels by pronouncing these words in this order—*bit, bet, bat, but, bah.*

figure **5.1** Nine useful consonant generalizations.

1. Only one consonant is heard when two of the same consonants are side by side (*merry, ladder*).
2. *C* has the /k/ sound when it is followed by *a* or *o* (*cat, cot*).
3. *C* has the /s/ sound when followed by *e, I,* or *y* (*cent, city, cycle*).
4. The digraph *ch* is usually pronounced /ch/, not /sh/ (*chair, chocolate*).
5. When *c* and *h* appear next to each other, they always are a digraph.
6. When a word ends in *ck,* it produces the /k/ sound (*buck, shock*).
7. When *ght* appear together, the *gh* is always silent (*light, might*).
8. When *kn* appears at the beginning of a word, the *k* is always silent (*knee, know*).
9. When *wr* appears at the beginning of a word, the *w* is always silent (*write, wren*).

figure **5.2** Various spellings for long vowels and diphthongs.

LONG /A/ SOUND

a – came
ue – bouquet
ay – say
ey – they
ai – rain
ei – eight

LONG /E/ SOUND

e – be
ee – see
ea – eat
ey – key
ei – receive
ie – chief

LONG /I/ SOUND

i – bite
ey – geyser
igh – sight
ie – lie
ei – seismic

LONG /O/ SOUND

o – hope
oa – road
ow – know

LONG /U/ SOUND

u – use
ew – flew

DIPHTHONG /OI/ SOUND

oi – oil
oy – boy

DIPHTHONG /OU/ SOUND

ow – how
ou – house

CONTROLLED R

ar – arm
er – fern
ir – girl
or – for
ur – turtle

VARIANT /OO/ SOUND

oo – food
ui – fruit

VARIANT /OO/ SOUND

oo – foot

VARIANT /O/ SOUND

au – haul
aw – saw

Note the short /o/ is represented with an *ah*. The diagram in Figure 5.3 depicts where the vowels are articulated in the mouth.

Vowel diphthongs are two vowels placed together to create a sound different from either of the two vowels. When pronouncing a diphthong, the mouth changes positions as the sound is produced. Two common diphthongs are /oi/, spelled *oi* (*oil*) or *oy* (*boy*), and /ou/, spelled *ou* (*count*) and *ow* (*cow*). Also classified as diphthongs are the long *i*, pronounced /ie/, and the long *u*, pronounced /yoo/. Many Southerners transform their vowels into diphthongs; hence the Southern drawl. Appendix B.2 includes common diphthongs with an example and utility of each.

Vowel digraphs are two vowels placed together, but only the long sound of one of the vowels is heard. Many children are taught that "When two vowels go a walking, the first one does the talking." Weaver (2002) views this rule as not very helpful because it has so many exceptions. Appendix B.2 lists common digraphs with an example and the utility of each. The struggling reader should try different possibilities to see which one works or sounds best. When *r* follows a vowel, the vowel takes on an r-controlled sound. All five vowels can be controlled by the *r* (*care, fern, girl, corn, turn*).

Three other variant vowels are (1) /oo/ (*food*), (2) /oo/ (*book*), and (3) /o/ (spelled *a* as in *all*, *au* as in *author*, or *aw* as in *draw*). Generalizations about vowels that are helpful to struggling readers (Blevins 2006) are listed in Figure 5.4.

figure **5.3**

Articulation of vowel sounds.

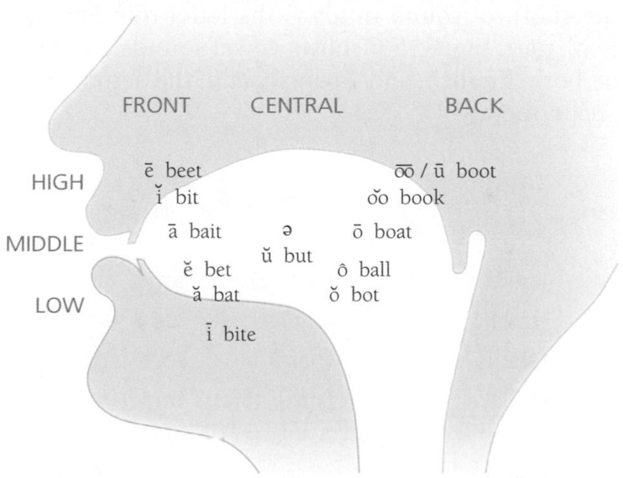

Source: Words their way: Word study for phonics, vocabulary, and spelling instruction (4th ed.) by Bear/Invernizzi/Templeton/Johnston, © 2006. Reprinted by permission of Pearson Education, Inc., Upper Saddle River, NJ.

Common spelling patterns in English words

Because the English language relies upon regular patterns of letters, it is advantageous for teachers to be familiar with these patterns in order to help read-

figure 5.4

Seven generalizations about vowels.

1. If a single vowel is followed by one or two consonants, it usually is short (*cat, cent, hop, cut*).
2. If the letter a comes before *l, u,* or *w*, it usually has the /o/ sound (*ball, caught, crawl*).
3. In the vowel digraphs *ai, ay, ee,* and *oa,* the first vowel is long (*bait, day, bee, road*).
4. The *y* usually represents the long /i/ sound in one-syllable words (*by, fly*).
5. The *y* usually represents the long /e/ sound at the end of a two-or-more syllable word (*happy, merry, sensibly*).
6. Some vowel spellings are used to distinguish word meanings (*meat/meet, red/read, beet/beat*).
7. In the word pattern (VCe) the *e* is often silent (*gave, time, cape*).

From *PHONICS FROM A TO Z,* 2/E by Wiley Blevins. Scholastic, Inc./Teaching Resources. Copyright ©2006, 1998 by Wiley Blevins. Reprinted by permission.

ers discover them (Bear et al., 2008; Cunningham, 2004; Fountas & Pinnell, 2008). Figure 5.5 lists 37 high-frequency spelling patterns.

English Learners and the Graphophonic System

Learning the sounds of English is not easy for English learners because English, like French, is a deep orthography. This means that the letter–sound relationship is not consistent (Helman, Bear, Invernizzi, & Templeton, 2008; Bear et al., 2007; Perez-Canado, 2005). For example, some consonants have two sounds (e.g., *c* and *g*), some phonemes can be represented by more than one grapheme (e.g., /f/ in *from* and *phone;* long /a/ in *maid, eight,* and *they*), and some consonants are silent if they precede a certain letter (e.g., *w* is silent when it precedes *r*, as in *write* and *wren,* and *k* is silent when it precedes *n* at the beginning of a word, as in *knee* and *know*). Other languages, such as Spanish, Italian, and Portuguese, are shallow or translucent orthographies, which means that their letter–sound relationships are quite consistent (Bear et al., 2007). The fact that it is a deep orthography is what makes learning to read English so difficult for English learners. And of course it takes longer for English learners whose native languages do not share our alphabet (e.g., Chinese, Vietnamese, Arabic, and Korean).

Because the largest population of English learners in the United States is composed of native Spanish speakers, you will likely have Spanish speakers in your classroom. Note that Spanish, like English, has three deviations. First, some phonemes are represented by more than one letter. For example, the /g/ is written g before the vowels *a, o,* and *u* and is written *gu* before the vowels *e* and *i*. The /k/ sound can be written as *c, k,* or *qu* (Perez-Canado, 2005). Second, one letter can have more than one sound. For example, the letter *c* has a /k/ sound before *a, o,* and *u,* and the /z/ sound before the vowels *e* and *i* (Perez-Canado, 2005). Third, some words share the same pronunciation. For example, *sac* and *saqu* are both pronounced /sak/. As discussed in Chapter 4, some phonemes are common in both English and Spanish; however, some of these phonemes are represented with different graphemes. For example, the short /o/ sound in *top* is the letter *a* in Spanish (e.g., *ajo*). Figure 5.6 shows vowel sounds common to both English and Spanish and the letters that create them.

figure 5.5 High-frequency spelling patterns.

ack (black)	ail (pail)	ain (train)	ake (cake)	ale (whale)	ame (game)
an (pan)	ank (bank)	ap (cap)	ash (trash)	at (cat)	ate (skate)
aw (claw)	ay (tray)	eat (meat)	ell (shell)	est (nest)	ice (rice)
de (bride)	ick (brick)	ight (night)	ill (hill)	in (pin)	ine (nine)
ing (king)	ink (pink)	ip (ship)	it (hit)	ock (sock)	oke (Coke)
op (mop)	ore (store)	ot (hot)	uck (truck)	ug (bug)	
ump (jump)	unk (skunk)				

Source: From Cunningham, Patricia M., *Phonics They Use: Words for Reading and Writing,* 3rd Ed. Copyright © 2000, pp. 63, 94. Reprinted by permission of Pearson Education, Inc., Upper Saddle River, NJ.

figure **5.6**

Vowel sounds common to English and Spanish.

ENGLISH VOWELS	SIMILAR VOWEL SOUND USED IN A SPANISH WORD	EXAMPLE SPELLING ERROR
a as in cake	e as in *hecho*	shek (shake)
e as in bean	I as in *ido*	spic (speak)
i as in like	ai as in *aire*	nait (night)
o as in hope	o as in *ocho*	flout (float)
o as in top	a as in *ajo*	jab (job)
u as in June	u as in *Usted*	flut (flute)

Source: Helman, L. A. (2004). Building on the Sound System of Spanish: Insights from the Alphabetic Spellings of English-Language Learners. *The Reading Teacher, 57*(5), 452–460.

PRINCIPLES OF PHONICS INSTRUCTION

Four key principles underlie phonics instruction:

1. Base instruction on what students know (Piaget & Inhelder, 1969).
2. Provide systematic instruction (International Reading Association, 2003a).
3. Use appropriate texts.
4. Embed instruction in meaningful contexts (Bear & Templeton, 1998; Cunningham, 2004; Dahl & Scharer, 2000; Hiebert, 1999; International Reading Association, 1997; Johnston, 2001b; Kane, 1999; Moustafa & Maldonado-Colon, 1999; Wagstaff, 1997/1998).

Principle One: Base Instruction on What Students Know

Effective teachers assess what students already know and build on that knowledge. Take the same approach with phonics instruction—begin with what students know. Assess students' knowledge during shared reading, interactive writing, and other literacy activities. Closely observe ("kid watch") what the students know about words. (In addition, you may use one of the other methods described in the informal assessment section of this chapter, such as word sorts or an IRI.)

Once you have a basic idea of students' literacy knowledge, place them in homogenous groups in order to provide appropriate instruction for each. The instruction for each group should be embedded in a meaningful context. Carefully select texts that permit students to examine both known words and new words appropriate for their developmental stage. As students examine text, encourage them to make generalizations about groups of words. Subtly guide students to articulate a "phonics rule" behind their generalization; their "rules" may be similar to the generalizations in Figures 5.1 and 5.4. Note that students may also find exceptions to these generalizations.

Principle Two: Provide Systematic Phonics Instruction

Systematic phonics instruction means teaching phonics in a planned sequence, using one of several approaches:

1. *Analytic phonics.* Teachers begin with students' sight words, known words developed from authentic reading, and then guide the students to analyze patterns and identify the phonics generalizations.
2. *Synthetic phonics.* Students convert letters into sounds and then blend the sounds to form a word.
3. *Phonics-through-spelling.* Students transform sounds into letters as they write; thus, they are engaged in many writing activities.
4. *Analogy phonics.* Students use parts of already-known words to identify unknown words.
5. *Phonics in context.* Students use sound–letter correspondences along with context cues to identify unknown words. This approach relies on students' knowledge of letter–sound relationships and patterns in words.
6. *Onset and rime phonics instruction.* Students recognize rimes and add the onset when reading new words. See the section "Decoding Words" earlier in this chapter.

Commercial phonics programs teach a sequence of concepts in each grade. Some phonics programs begin with the pair of voiced and unvoiced consonants, such as *b* and *p*. Other commercial programs begin with consonants that are distinctly different from one another, beginning with *l*. Rinsky (1993) suggests a sequence that teachers can use without purchasing a commercial phonics program. The sequence for grades K–3 is found in Figure 5.7.

Principle Three: Use Appropriate Texts

"At the earliest stages of reading acquisition—particularly with students who are first introduced to book reading in school—careful attention needs to be paid to the text of instruction" (Hiebert, 1999, p. 555). For example, texts used during shared reading events should meet the following criteria:

- Include predictable text

figure 5.7 A phonics sequence.

KINDERGARTEN

Begin phonemic awareness training during kindergarten and include sounds with and without letters, beginning with consonant sounds; introduce blending and segmentation skills; introduce a few high-frequency sight words; introduce onsets and rimes with a few short vowels. Start with the letters that are dissimilar, the most useful, and introduce the lowercase letters first. An acceptable sequence is:

m, t, a, s, I, f, d, r, o, g, l, h, u, c, b, n, k, v, e, w, j, p, y
T, L, M, F, D, I, N, A, R, H, G, B, x, q, z, J, E

FIRST GRADE

Review consonants and vowels and letter combinations, and introduce useful rules: endings (ing, er, s), consonant digraphs (two letters that cannot be separated): sh, ch, th, wh, ph; blending and segmentation skills reinforced, frequently used sight words, the final "e" rule, consonant blends (two consonants that can be separated): fl, fr, sl, sm, sn, sw, sc, sk, sp, sq, st; then bi, br, cl, cr, dr, gl, gr, pl, pr, tr, tw; then scr, spl, spr, str; the "ed" ending; then vowel digraphs *(ai, ay, ee, ea, igh, oa, ow, ew, oo, ow, ou, oi, oy, au,* and *aw),* r-controlled vowels *(ar, er, ir, ur,* and *or),* transformations of open and closed syllables (*me* becomes *met; go* becomes *got*) and generalizations for "y" at the end of a word.

SECOND GRADE

Complete highest-frequency words; review and complete single-syllable phonics patterns, then generalizations for *c* and g at ends of words; silent consonant clusters: *kn, wr, gn, mb, ght, ng, nk, tch;* continue word parts (prefixes and suffixes, root words) and dividing words into word parts or syllables.

THIRD GRADE

Reinforce syllabication and word parts, and introduce word derivatives (e.g., *interrogative* comes from the word *interrogate*).

Source: Rinsky, L. A. (1993). *Teaching Word Recognition Skills.* Gorsuch Scarisbrick: Scottsdale, AZ. Used with permission of the author.

- Have a smaller amount of text on each page
- Use large illustrations that support the text
- Appeal to children
- Are conceptually appropriate (texts that teachers can use to develop a concept, such as the topic for a unit, author study, or illustrator study)

In addition, reading researchers have found that during shared reading, it is most effective to use authentic children's literature with text that (1) is predictable, (2) uses phonograms, and (3) includes rhyming words (Cunningham, 2004; Fountas & Pinnell, 2006b; Hiebert, 1999; Kane, 1999).

1. *Predictable text.* Children enjoy stories with predictable text, such as *The Teeny Tiny Woman* (1986) by Jane O'Conner and *Hattie and the Fox* (1987) by Mem Fox. Students chime in as soon as they know words and refrains. Appendix A.7 lists books with predictable text patterns.
2. *Phonograms.* Books that emphasize phonograms (rimes following onsets) help students see patterns within words. As you read and discuss stories, students discover words that have the same letter patterns. Bill Martin, Jr. has written many books highlighting phonograms. Appendix A.7 lists others.
3. *Rhyming words.* Rhyming texts also draw attention to the sounds in words. Words that rhyme do not necessarily share the same letter pattern, as phonograms must (thus, *socks* and *fox* are rhyming words with different rimes). Draw attention to the difference between phonograms and words that rhyme. Appendix A.7 lists books that feature alliteration, phonograms, and rhymes.

Conversely, there is no research regarding the exclusive use of decodable texts for beginning reading instruction (Cunningham, 2004). Decodable texts, such as the *Books to Remember Series* by Flyleaf Publishing, are those written with words that closely follow phonetic rules or that feature words from one word family (e.g., "Dan can fan Nan").

Principle Four: Embed Instruction in Meaningful Contexts

Reading, writing, listening, and speaking activities that focus on meaningful tasks create meaningful contexts. Carefully select texts that children enjoy, have predictable patterns, and use words that help teach phonics concepts. Cunningham (2004) suggests engaging in the following series of activities to provide meaningful context:

1. Choose a book with predictable text that both the teacher and the students will enjoy.
2. Read and enjoy the text!
3. Act out the story or put on puppet shows. (Acting caters to kinesthetic learners and develops oral language skills.)
4. Have students discuss what they notice about words. (E.g., ask "Which ones begin with same letter?")
5. Play word games based on the story.
6. Add words from the story to the word walls.
7. Find rhyming words and words that end with the same spellings.
8. Have students write creative extensions of books that use predictable patterns. (For example, "I went walking. What did I see? I saw ______ looking at me.")

Another activity that teaches phonics in a meaningful context is to have students reread favorite predictable texts and then ask them to point to words that begin with certain sounds. Next, ask them to create a list of words that begin with that same sound. You may also give students words on index cards and ask them to match them with words in the text.

Students also learn phonics when they write meaningful messages (Bear & Templeton, 1998; Cunningham, 2004; Savage, 2001). They learn to break up words and listen for all the sounds when they write notes to friends, stories, log observations from experiments, and riddles. Effective teachers model "stretching out words" as they write morning messages and involve students in interactive writing. Students are less likely to listen for sounds in words when performing rote exercises such as copying words correctly. Writing skills are discussed in greater detail in Chapter 11.

ASSESSMENT

Informal Assessment

Ideally, phonics assessment is conducted in natural settings as you observe students making sense of letter–sound relationships as they read and write. However, for those who must record growth throughout the school year, a number of informal assessment instruments can help, including checklists, surveys, word sorts, rubrics, running records, miscue analyses, and inventories.

Checklists

The Checklist of Known Letter Names and Sounds, found in Appendix C.28, assesses a student's knowledge of letter names, letter sounds, and words with these sounds. The student reads from the Master Card, while the teacher records the responses on the Checklist. The student is asked (1) the names of the uppercase letters, (2) the names of the lowercase letters, (3) the names of the script letters, if appropriate, (4) the sound of each letter, (5) a word that begins with that sound, and (6) a word that ends with that sound. Figure 5.8 is the checklist that

figure **5.8** Sample checklist of known letter names and sounds for the beginning of the year.

STUDENT: Dustin DATE: 8–27

LETTER	UPPERCASE NAME	LOWERCASE NAME	SCRIPT NAME	SOUND	WORD WITH INITIAL SOUND	WORD WITH ENDING SOUND
K	✓	✓				
N	✓					
E	✓					
J	✓	✓				
A	✓					
T	✓	✓				
B	✓			✓	✓	
S	✓	✓		✓	✓	

Ms. McGee uses to assess Dustin's knowledge at the beginning of the year. She will use the checklist to record Dustin's growth throughout the school year. Two copies (one typeset and one in cursive) of the Master Card of Letter Names and Sounds, along with the score sheet, are located in Appendix C.28.

You will need to know your state's standards and design appropriate rubrics and checklists to chart the growth of your students. The partial checklist in Figure 5.9 is based on Texas's first-grade Standard 1.7: Reading/letter–sound relationships, which states: "The student uses letter–sound knowledge to decode written language" (Texas Education Agency, 1997, p. B-29). Mr. Francis, a first-grade teacher, uses this checklist to help him assess and monitor the growth of his students. At the beginning of the school year, he notes that many of his students know letter names and understand that words are composed of letters that represent sounds; however, only a few of his students know the letter–sound relationships of consonants and no student knows the relationship for the short vowel sound. The complete checklist, based on the entire Texas First-Grade Standard 1.7, is located in Appendix C.29.

Surveys

The Phonics Mastery Survey (Cecil, 2011) is an informal instrument for assessing various phonics elements. I do not advocate using nonsense words when teaching letter–sound relationships to students, but I do believe that using nonsense words to assess students tells me what they know about particular sounds of letters and how to blend those sounds. However, do not use this survey to assess students' sight word ability.

The Phonics Mastery Survey is designed to assesses a student's ability to recognize (1) consonant sounds, (2) rhyming words, (3) consonant digraphs, (4) long vowel sounds, (5) words with CVC patterns, (6) consonant blends, (7) other vowel sounds, and (8) syllables in words. The scoring and answer sheets for this survey are in Appendix C.30. This assessment is also appropriate for middle school students. Too often middle school teachers assume that all students know letter–sound relationships and can hear rhyme. This survey is easy to administer and does not include pictures that would make middle school students think it is too "elementary" for them.

Word sorts

Having a student perform a word sort task is another informal phonics skills assessment. When assessing a student's ability to sort words by initial, ending, or medial sounds, use picture cards that prevent the student from looking at the letters. When the student cannot see the words, you can determine if she knows letter–sound relationships. Give the student pictures beginning with two, three, or four different letters, identify the letters for her, and ask her to sort the picture cards according to the initial letters. As

figure **5.9** Letter–sound relationships checklist, first grade.

TEACHER M. Francis PERIOD 1 (2) 3 4

+ = always x = sometimes 0 = seldom/never

8-27 (Beginning of school)

SUB-STANDARD	Eric	Leah	Coby	Vanessa	Jocelyn	Hayden	Blake	Erin	Lindsay	Lesley	Cole	Shona	Ryan	Shannon	Casey	Warren	Brooke	Marsh
1. Names and identifies each letter.	+	+	+	+	+	+	X	X	+	+	+	+	+	+	X	+	X	+
2. Understands that written words are composed of letters that represent sounds.	+	+	+	+	+	+	X	X	+	+	+	+	+	+	X	+	X	+
3. Identifies letter–sound relationship for all consonants.	+	O	X	X	X	O	O	O	+	X	X	X	X	O	O	X	O	+
4. Identifies letter–sound relationship for short vowels.	O	O	O	O	O	O	O	O	O	O	O	O	O	O	O	O	O	O

a pretest, you may choose letters that have not been formally introduced; for a post-test, you may choose letters that have been explicitly taught. You can also assess a student's knowledge of ending sounds or medial sounds such as long and short vowel sounds. Appendix D.4 contains a set of picture cards.

Informal reading inventories

The informal reading inventory, running record, and miscue analysis are excellent devices to assess a student's ability to approach unknown words. As the student reads an unfamiliar text, observe what cueing systems he uses and what types of miscues he makes. Although these informal assessments take time to administer and analyze, they provide valuable information about students' phonics skills. (See Chapter 3 for a detailed discussion of these instruments.)

Qualitative Spelling Inventories 1 and 2

The Bear et al. (2008) Qualitative Spelling Inventories 1 and 2 assess students' capacity for encoding letter sounds. They test what students know about letter sounds as they write words. Chapter 12 describes the inventory and Appendix C.54 includes the two lists.

Formal Assessment

A number of standardized tests include phonics subtests; many of these use nonsense word lists. Remember, nonsense words will help you understand what the student knows about the sounds of letters and how to blend the sounds together, but they do not assess student's sight vocabulary. Figure 5.10 lists standardized tests with phonics subtests. Chapter 3 includes detailed descriptions of many of these tests.

figure **5.10** Standardized tests with phonics subtests.

1. Iowa Test of Basic Skills
2. Stanford Achievement Tests–Ninth Edition
3. Metropolitan Achievement Test–Reading
4. Comprehensive Test of Basic Skills, U and V
5. Phonics Criterion Test
6. Prescriptive Reading Performance Test
7. Stanford Diagnostic Reading Test–Red Level, Green Level
8. Woodcock Reading Mastery Test
9. Durrell Analysis of Reading Difficulties–Third Edition
10. Gates–McKillop–Horowitz Tests
11. Diagnostic Reading Scales
12. Sipay Word Analysis Test
13. Basic Early Assessment of Reading™ (BEAR®)
14. Dynamic Indicators of Basic Early Literacy Skills (DIBELS)

Intervention STRATEGIES & ACTIVITIES

Students learn about letter–sound relationships and patterns within words most effectively when they read and discuss books that interest them and engage in other meaningful literacy tasks. As you work with small groups and individual students, remember the five principles of phonics instruction: (1) it must be based on what the student knows, (2) it must be systematic, (3) it must be explicit and extensive (beginning with initial consonant sounds, onset and rime, and word patterns), (4) it must use appropriate texts, and (5) it must occur in a meaningful context. Therefore, base the following intervention activities on texts students have enjoyed and on words they have encountered in print.

Instruction must always be based on the student's needs. The following activities are systematic; they start with initial consonant sounds, move to onset and rime, and finish with word patterns. However, if a student masters initial consonant sounds but struggles with onset and rime, emphasize onset and rime activities. Students can perform these activities with a teacher, a trained tutor, an older book buddy, or a peer (see Chapter 13).

Activities Emphasizing Initial Consonant Sounds

During group time, if you notice a student who cannot name three or four words that begin with the same sound, engage her in one of the following activities in a tutoring setting or have a trained tutor who understands these activities work with her. Do not merely engage the child in the activity, but also determine why the student has a difficult time distinguishing initial sounds. You may find she has an auditory problem. Usually, however, you will find that young children who cannot distinguish initial sounds lack linguistic experience and simply need time with an adult to develop the skill.

The following activities focus on listening to the initial sounds of words.

ACTIVITY

WORD SORTING WITH PICTURES — GRADES K–1

Beginning readers need practice relating letters to their sounds. Word sorting with picture cards emphasizes letter-sound relationships.

1. Place two magnet letters on the desk.
2. Have the student sort pictures according to the initial letter sounds using the picture cards found in Appendix D.4. Work up to three or four letters with their corresponding cards when he demonstrates progress.
3. If a student continues to confuse two letter sounds (e.g., the /d/ and /t/ sounds), continue working with only those two letters.
4. Later, set out magnet letters that correspond to the ending sounds and ask the student to sort the pictures accordingly.

ACTIVITY

WORD SORTING WITH PICTURES FOR ENGLISH LEARNERS — GRADES 4–8

English learners enter U.S. schools in all grade levels. English learners, like native speakers, need time to learn letter-sound relationships. One of the first skills to focus on is listening for the initial sound of a word. Using the picture cards found in Appendix D.3 and D.4, have students sort the cards different ways. For example, first give the student pictures of objects that begin with two different letter sounds and ask him to sort the words into two piles according to the initial sounds. Next, give the student pictures of objects that begin with three different letter sounds and ask him to sort the words into three piles according to the initial sounds. Have the student name the object each time; this will also increase his vocabulary.

ACTIVITY

LISTEN FOR THE INITIAL CONSONANT BLENDS — GRADES 1–3

1. Using the picture cards and game board in Appendix D.9, turn all picture cards upside down in a pile. Decide which person should begin.
2. The first player picks up a picture card, pronounces the word for the picture, and correctly places the picture on the consonant blend space that corresponds to the initial consonant blend of the word.
3. If the player cannot place a card on the correct consonant blend space, the card is placed on the bottom of the pile.

Note: The goal is for students to fill all of the consonant blend spaces.

WORD WALLS — GRADES 1–2 — ACTIVITY

Create a word wall featuring all the letters of the alphabet. On a poster board or butcher paper, write all of the letters of the alphabet and add words that children want to remember or will use in writing or reading. In a tutoring setting, write the letters of the alphabet in order on slips of paper, place them in a file folder, and have the tutee add words she wants to remember below the appropriate letters.

PERSONALIZED WORD FAMILY DICTIONARY — GRADES 1–8 — ACTIVITY

Arrange a personalized dictionary with two major sections. The first section contains a page for each letter of the alphabet. The second section contains a page for each of the following common word families: *ack, age, ake, an, am, at, ight, ound, all, it, in, ill, ig, ell, ed, ead, ot, op, og, ad, ap*. The top of each page includes either a letter (in upper- and lowercase) or the name of the word family; for example:

Aa	**ack (back)**
after	lack
about	Jack
around	sack
alligator	smack

Students can add words as they find them in texts or hear them in conversation.

ALPHABIOGRAPHY — GRADES 6–8 — ACTIVITY

Alphabiography is described on the website ReadWriteThink.org (International Reading Association, 2010). This activity encourages middle school students to connect their personal lives with the alphabet. Students create an alphabet book by thinking of one event, object, friend, or attribute associated with their lives. They need one word for each letter of the alphabet. They can have the one word on the page and add narrative to make the booklet meaningful to share with classmates. For example, Juan may create a picture book about his new friends in the United States. For the letter "A," he may write, "My friend Ben likes apples." For the letter "B," he may write, "My friend Ben plays basketball." For the letter "C," he may write, "My friend Karl likes to play cards." For each letter, he writes a sentence based on his ability. More advanced students will write longer sentences. This activity can be found at: www.readwritethink.org/classroom-resources/lesson-plans/alphabiography-project-totally-937.html?tab=1#tabs.

ALLITERATION — GRADES 1–8 — ACTIVITY

In this activity, either you or the student can do the writing.

1. Share some familiar tongue twisters such as *Sally sells seashells down by the seashore,* or *Peter Piper picked a peck of pickled peppers,* and then share some not-so-familiar tongue twisters such *Peter Potter splattered a plate of peas on Patty Platt's pink plaid pants* (Rosenbloom & Artell, 1999, p. 219).
2. Create your own original tongue twisters, perhaps based on the student's name.
3. Ask what sound the student hears at the beginning of the words.

Some of these sentences will result in amusing tongue twisters that also help the student with articulation, such as *Happy, hungry Harry has hundreds of hamburgers* or *Brave Beverly Beaver blew blue bubbles.*

ACTIVITY **DOMINOES** **GRADES 2–4**

This activity is designed to help struggling readers focus not only on the initial sounds, but also on the ending sounds of words. Using the domino cards from Appendix D.10, participants match the ending consonant sound (not the letter) of one domino with the initial sound of the next word. For example, if one player lays out the cat domino, the next player must lay down a domino picture that begins with a /t/ sound. Play the game with the students or observe as they play together. Through observation, you will determine which letter sounds are troublesome for which students.

Activities Emphasizing Onset and Rime

Often a teacher will observe a student "sounding out" phonograms letter-by-letter, instead of recognizing the pattern within the phonograms. For example, the child may read this passage in the following manner: "Mike put his h-h-a-a-n-n-d hand in the s-s-a-a-n-n-d sand." This student would benefit from tutoring sessions with some of the activities presented in this section, which emphasize the recognition of onset and rime. Helping a student recognize onset and rime will result in quickly gaining a large bank of recognizable words. For young readers, begin with texts that have word families with two letters in the rime (e.g., the *an, at, am, up,* or *op* families), because they only need to recognize those two letters. Later, choose texts that have word families with more letters in the rime, such as the *ound* and *ight* families.

ACTIVITY **WORD FAMILY WORD WALLS** **GRADES 1–3**

A separate word wall can be used for all phonograms students discover in texts. Word walls with phonograms draw students' attention to patterns within words. Appendix B.1 lists common phonograms. Figure 5.11 shows a sample word wall.

figure **5.11** Phonogram word wall.

at	all	an	and
bat	ball	ban	band
cat	call	can	sand
fat	fall	fan	land

ACTIVITY **FIND THE MYSTERY WORD** **GRADES 1–2**

Use the word wall in your classroom for this activity, which is appropriate for whole group, small group, or individual instruction. The goal is for students to listen to the teacher for sound clues, put the sounds together, and name the word from the word wall. At the beginning of the year, use easy clues (initial sound, followed by medial sound, followed by ending sound). Later, try giving the sounds in a mixed order. Here is a mixed order example:

1. Instruct students to look at the word wall and to think, not say, the mystery word.
2. Give clues to the mystery word by saying, "I see a word that has a short /a/ sound." (Say the sound, not the letter name.) "This word begins with a /b/ sound. This word ends with a /g/ sound. If you know the word, whisper the word to your neighbor. What was the word, Robert?"
3. As the word wall grows, use words that have silent sounds or digraphs.

FLIP BOOKS — GRADES 1–2 — ACTIVITY

Often struggling readers do not see the common rime within word families. Teachers should show these students how the rime is a common factor in the entire "family" and how the onset changes the words. Explicit instruction in word families encourages readers to look for known parts within words. Again, use word families from texts that have been read in a tutoring or small group session. For example, after reading Dr. Seuss's *The Cat in the Hat,* have readers construct a flip book of all the *at* words.

1. To construct a flip book using sentence strips, neatly print *hat* on a strip and cut the word off the sentence strip.
2. Using the rest of the sentence strip, write the letters *b, c, f, h, m, p, r, s, v.*
3. Cut them up and staple them on top of the *h* in *hat.* Because *at* is a word, the top sheet should be blank.

See Figure 5.12 for an example. Using *The Cat in the Hat,* you can also construct a flip book for the *ump* family. Put the letters *h, c, gr, d, j, l, p, r, st,* and *th* on the pages. Because *ump* is not a word, the top page must have a letter.

figure **5.12** Sample flip books.

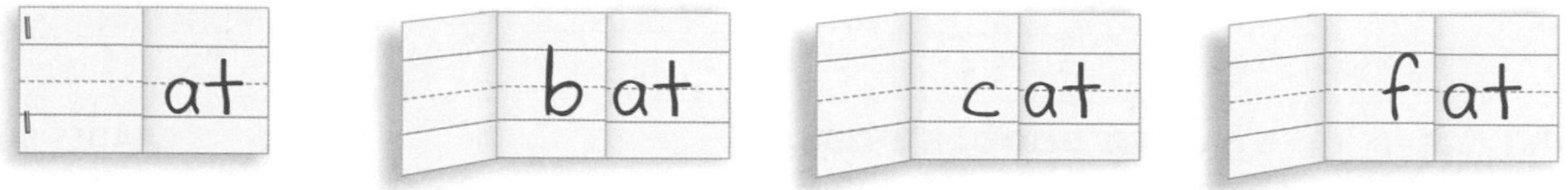

WORD FAMILY CONCENTRATION — GRADES 2–5 — ACTIVITY

The game Concentration teaches students to focus and remember. Cards can be based on any text the struggling reader enjoys. Work with the student to decide which words she wants to learn and remember. Make two 2-inch by 2-inch cards of the same word. If the book has phonograms, make the activity more challenging by having the student match phonograms (e.g., the *hat* card with the *cat* card). Participate in the activity with the student in order to understand what letter sounds or words are troubling her. Appendix D.11 contains two examples. The first, based on Nancy Shaw's *Sheep Out to Eat* (1992), is built on a number of different word families. The second is built on other homophones. It is not recommended that you use all the cards in each activity.

Activities Emphasizing Rhyme

Eventually students discover that not all rhyming words end with the same letter (e.g., *know/go, blue/shoe*). The following two activities focus on students writing their own rhyming verses.

ACTIVITY **RHYMING WORD CONCENTRATION** **GRADES 6–8**

Concentration is a game that middle school students can also enjoy. Many poems by Shel Silverstein and Bruce Lansky are humorous and include rhymes. After reading Lansky's (2009) "New Year's Resolutions" and "Someone's Toes Are in My Nose" have the student write each of the rhyming words—*better/letter, looking/cooking, stairs/chairs, sorrow/tomorrow, me/be, understand/band, truck/stuck, mad/had*—on a 3 × 5 index card. Then turn the cards over and challenge the student to find the matches as quickly as possible, or play the game according to the traditional rules.

ACTIVITY **PREDICTABLE RHYMING TEXTS** **GRADES 1–2**

Smith, Walker, and Yellin (2004) suggest teachers encourage students to write their own rhyming verses by using a template. First, teachers share any book with a predictable text, such as *Here Are My Hands* (Bill Martin Jr. and John Archambault, 1998, unpaged). After finding the rhyming words, provide a template that eliminates some of the words. Have students brainstorm words that could fit in each blank, then write a verse or two with them. Finally, invite students to write their own verses. Here is an example:

"Here are my eyes
For seeing and crying.
Here are my ears
For washing and drying" (Martin and Archambault, 1998, unpaged)

Template:

Here are my ________________
For ________________ and ________________.
Here are my ________________
For ________________ and ________________.

ACTIVITY **YANKEE DOODLE POETRY** **GRADES 6–8**

Middle school students can borrow writing and rhyming ideas from poets. After sharing two of Bruce Lansky's (2009) humorous poems, "Yankee Doodle's Monkey Ride" and "Yankee Doodle's Turtle Ride," invite students to brainstorm with you to write hilarious versions of this four-line verse. Write one or two together, then have them write their own and share them with the class. The above poems are both found in *My Dog Ate My Homework!* (Lansky, 2009).

Activities Emphasizing Word Patterns

Some students will continue to have difficulty recognizing word patterns, despite explicit demonstrations. You will identify these students by observing how they approach an unknown word; often they will sound out unknown words letter-by-letter. Students who have learned to recognize word families may tend to believe that all words will have onset and rime. Again, you will identify them by observing how they read. When they approach an unknown word, they will often sound out the first letter and then attempt to put all the other letters together. For example, they will attempt to sound out *hope* as *h- op*. Both these types of students will benefit from some individualized sessions working on word patterns.

The following activities are designed to help a student see patterns within words. The first pattern, consonant-vowel-consonant (CVC), is also found in many phonograms. However, the emphasis is now on the short vowel sound that is found in most CVC words. Some exceptions to this pattern that students may notice are words like *cow, how, few,* and *sew.*

SHORT VOWEL BINGO

GRADES 1–3 ACTIVITY

Play short vowel bingo with readers who struggle with short vowel sounds.

1. Duplicate a blank Bingo card (five columns with B, I, N, G, O as the column heads, and 5 rows, with a "Free Space" in the center block).
2. Write a list of 25 words with short vowel sounds on the board.
3. Instruct the students to write the list of words anywhere on their Bingo cards, leaving the Free Space blank.
4. Write the words on index cards, draw one from the stock, and read the word aloud.
5. Have the students place a marker on the word.

The goal is for a student to fill five spaces in a row, vertically, horizontally, or diagonally. If you laminate the cards before students write on them, the cards can be used for many different bingo games. (You may want to use erasable pens or pencils.) The following word list is from Kristen Hall's *A Bad, Bad Day* (1995) and Rex Schneider's *That's Not All!* (1993). Both are books for beginning readers.

bad	dad	bed	hit	what	can
bus	got	not	that	bug	rug
has	pet	let	hen	pen	den
cat	rat	dog	hog	bat	hat
pig	wig	run	fun		

THE MAGICAL E!

GRADES 1–3 ACTIVITY

The following activity builds on the CVC pattern and introduces the CVCe pattern. Using the cards in Figure 5.13, have the student first pronounce the short vowel word. Then have him move the "e" card to the end of the word and pronounce the new word, which has a long vowel sound. Choose words that are familiar to the student.

figure 5.13 Magical E! cards.

Activities Emphasizing Sounds Within Words

Students should learn to recognize long, short, controlled-r, and schwa vowels as well as the subtle differences between /b/ and /p/, /m/ and /n/, /f/ and /v/, and /t/ and /d/ sounds. You may notice that when some students approach unknown words, they cannot determine whether a vowel sound is long, short, schwa, or controlled by the letter *r*. Other students may consistently write a *t* when the correct letter is a *d*, or a *p* instead of a *b*. These students will benefit from tutoring sessions that feature some of the following intervention activities.

ACTIVITY

LISTEN TO THE VOWEL SOUNDS — GRADES 1–3

1. Create a board game by gluing a page of vowel squares (Appendix D.12) on each side of an opened file folder so both players can view the vowels right-side up.
2. Using the picture cards in Appendix D.12, place them face down in a pile.
3. Decide which student will begin.
4. The first player picks up a picture card, pronounces the word for the picture, listens to the medial vowel sound, and matches the picture with the correct vowel space.
5. If the player cannot place the card on the correct vowel space, the card is placed on the bottom of the pile.

The game is over when students fill all the vowel spaces.

ACTIVITY

COLLECTING VOWEL SOUNDS MADE WITH DIFFERENT SPELLINGS — GRADES 1–8

This activity will help students understand that a vowel sound may have different spellings (e.g., the long /a/ sound can be spelled *a, ue, ay, ey, ai,* or *ei*). Have students find words in their texts that use various spellings to represent the same letter sounds. One way to have students keep track of the words is by giving them one 4 × 6 index card for each specified vowel sound. For example, you might begin with all the spellings of the long /a/. Figure 5.14 shows a sample long /a/ card.

figure 5.14 Sample long /a/ card.

WORD SORTING WITH WORDS

GRADES 1–5 ACTIVITY

Word sorts can be done with words as well as pictures. Write 15 to 20 words on sentence strips and cut the strips into single-word sections. Let the students sort the words however they choose, by the number of syllables, initial sound, ending sound, vowel sounds, or shared sounds (rhymes). Ask students to explain their sorting strategy to you. The cards found in Appendix D.11 from the Concentration activity can be used for this, or you can use any words students find in their reading.

CHANGE HEN TO FOX

GRADES 1–4 ACTIVITY

This activity, created by Cunningham (2004), is based on *Hattie and the Fox* (1987) by Mem Fox, but it can be played with different words.

1. Instruct the students to write *hen* on the top line of their paper.
2. Have them change *hen* to *pen* on the next line.
3. Have them continue to change words using this sequence: *pen* to *pet* to *pit* to *sit* to *six* to *fix* to *fox.*
4. Have them discuss how changing one letter creates a new word each time. For example:

hen
pen
pet
pit
sit
six
fix

For a variation on this activity, write a word on the board (e.g., *lost*), and announce the class is going to change one letter at a time to get from *lost* to *find.* For example, write *lost* and directly below it write *los__*. Ask the students what letter will complete this word. Give students one word at a time so that they cannot look to the next line for the answer. Continue in this fashion until you reach the target word.

lost
los__
lo__e
l__ne
__ine
min__
__ind

The answers are *lose, lone, line, mine, mind, find.*

WORD LADDERS

GRADES 6–8 ACTIVITY

Rasinski (2005a, b) creates a more difficult version of Hen to Fox by having students add, delete, rearrange, or substitute letters to create words that correlate to a definition. The following activity encourages students to see how changing one or two letters results in a new word. This activity is based on the *ing* sound.

Write down *think.*

Delete two letters to create a word that refers to something used to write. (*ink*)

Add one letter to create a word that refers to what a person may do with his/her eyes. (*wink*)

Change one letter to create a word that names a part of a bird. (*wing*)

Add one letter to create a word that names a favorite piece of playground equipment. (*swing*)

Delete one letter to create a word that refers to a rock star's talent. (*sing*)

Add one letter to create a word that refers to the action of a bee. (*sting*)

Add one letter to create a word that refers to a part of tennis shoes. (*string*)

Activity Emphasizing Words Within Words

As most students begin to encode words, they start to recognize words within words; for example, *cap* is in *cape* (Bear et al., 2007; Gentry, 2004). Later, they understand that multisyllabic words may be made up of shorter words. This is especially true of compound words; for example, *butter* + *fly* = *butterfly*. However, you may observe students who continue to sound out words letter-by-letter. Again, these students need time with an adult who demonstrates the practice of recognizing smaller words within words. The following activity gives students an opportunity to see this process.

ACTIVITY **SECRET WORDS** **GRADES 2–8**

In this activity, give students a "secret word" from a topic they are studying (e.g., *metabolism, Revolutionary War, Independence, alliteration,* or *Thanksgiving*). Instruct them to find as many words as possible without using any letter twice. (If a letter appears more than once in the secret word, students may use each appearance one time.) For example:

Thanksgiving: an, at, has, gas, as, in, it, sit, thank, thanks, hang, gang, sin, sank, sink, kin

PHONICS AND TECHNOLOGY

One of my favorite interactive websites for K–2 students is ReadWriteThink.org, designed by the International Reading Association and the National Council of Teachers of English. The site permits teachers to type in literacy terms, such as *phonics* or *rhyme,* and click "interactive" to allow students to work on a particular phonics, rhyme, or other literacy skill. The six interactive phonics pages are ideal for helping K–2 students construct words, create an alphabet organizer, match pictures, play a word family sort, ABC match, and participate in word wizard. The pages are simple enough for young students to navigate. Another site that has multiple phonics games is PBSKids.org. This site includes music, animated characters, and voice instructions that guide students as they play the phonics games. This site has an application for use with tablets and iPads.

A Google search on "phonics" reveals even more sites that feature useful lessons for building phonic skills. Some of my favorites sites include:

www.learningtoday.com/corporate/reading-games.asp

www.starfall.com

http://teacher.scholastic.com/clifford1/flash/phonics/index.htm

www.learningplanet.com

www.suelebeau.com

CONCLUDING THOUGHTS

All teachers need to understand the graphophonic system that links letters with sounds. Insight into the unique sound structure of the English language will help you assess specific reading problems. Remember, phonics instruction must be based on what students know, and it should be systematic, explicit, and extensive. Strive to find appropriate texts and to teach phonics concepts in a meaningful context.

Reflective Learning ENGLISH LEARNERS

Scenario. After teaching for five years in her hometown, a small, rural community in Ohio, Ms. Synder moved to a large city in Texas. Anticipating that she would have Spanish-speaking students in her eighth-grade language arts class, she got out her college Spanish textbook and CDs over the summer to brush up on her skills. Although she was prepared for the new challenges of the position, she was still overwhelmed by the number of native Spanish speakers in her class. Five had been in the school system since first grade; three had been at the school for two years, and eight had moved to the United States during the summer. Ms. Synder determined the five students who had been in the system since first grade were on grade level in all subjects; the three students who had been at the school only two years had weak literacy skills and struggled to read stories, poems, and informational text. The eight new students had few English literacy skills, and she was not sure if they were literate in Spanish.

QUESTIONS

1. What assessments should Ms. Synder give the eight students?
2. What type of help should she give the three students?
3. What type of literacy instruction should she give the eight students because they are eighth graders and not first graders?
4. What should she do with the three students and eight students when the class is reading a novel?

CHAPTER SIX

WORD IDENTIFICATION

A teacher is one who brings us tools and enables us to use them.

RALPH WALDO EMERSON

scenario

Mr. Morris taught fifth grade for three years but moved to second grade this fall. He is amazed that one group of students confuses simple words such as *with, when, where, went,* and *who.* Often these students keep reading without realizing they have misread the word. From their retellings it is obvious they are reading words and not reading for comprehension.

Another group of students looks at him when they do not know a word. They expect him to say the word and do not even attempt to pronounce it themselves. Often these words have more than one syllable, such as *together, mountain, vacation,* and *important.* Mr. Morris knows both groups need extra help. The first group needs help learning simple sight words, and the second group needs help learning to recognize syllables within polysyllabic words. The second-grade teachers in his building have high school interns who are planning to be teachers, and Mr. Morris is lucky to have three interns working with him for an hour each day. For the students who do not recognize their reading errors, he makes a set of flash cards with the Fry phrases and sentences (see Appendix B.6). He sorts the cards into groups of five, beginning with the first five phrases. An intern keeps track of which words the students have learned.

For the students who do not attempt to pronounce unknown words, Mr. Morris, makes a set of cards with compound words, such as *butterfly, mailbox, backpack, piggyback, backyard, downtown, homework.* He instructs an intern to help the students look for two small words in the longer word. Mr. Morris also makes a set of cards for them, each featuring one element of a compound word. The cards include these words: *butter, fly, box, mail, pack, back, yard, piggy, down, town, work,* and *home.* Students are instructed to put two cards together to make one longer word.

Mr. Morris knows what both groups need in order to become fluent readers. He also knows that his interns are learning valuable strategies to use in their own classrooms someday.

guiding questions

As you read this chapter, consider the following questions:

1. Do you think it is necessary that young readers recognize simple words automatically?
2. How would you assess a student's ability to recognize sight words?
3. What other activities could Mr. Morris give the interns to help the group of students needing work in learning sight words?
4. What other activities could Mr. Morris have given to help the group needing work in learning to recognize syllables in polysyllabic words? What are some generalizations about polysyllabic words that could aid in his students' visual analysis of them?

INTRODUCTION

Although Mr. Morris understands the role of word identification in reading, he also knows the purpose of reading is not just to read words correctly but also to comprehend texts. One reads stories for entertainment, newspapers for current events, menus to satisfy appetites, poetry to feed the soul, expository texts to learn about interesting topics, instruction manuals to assemble items or operate tools, and text messages to communicate with friends.

In order to comprehend texts and enjoy reading, students should be able to instantaneously recognize a large bank of words and effortlessly analyze unknown words. This automaticity requires the brain to process both visual and nonvisual information (Smith, 2005). Every time a reader identifies a letter or word, the brain is involved in a decision, "and the amount of information required to make the decision depends on the number of alternatives there are" (Smith, 1978, p. 24).

Smith's (2005) research on the brain's role in the reading process reveals that the brain is capable of identifying only four or five random letters (e.g., *w, x, q, e, j*) per second. This is because when one letter is presented, the brain has 26 letters from which to choose. Thus, the brain takes approximately two seconds to identify five to eight random letters.

When letters are organized into a random list of words (e.g., *basket, board, sneeze, Iowa*), the brain approaches them as chunks of information, which permits a reader to identify two or more words (the equivalent of 10 to 12 letters) in one second (Smith, 2005). When the words are organized into grammatically correct sentences (e.g., *I love to read*), the brain can process four times the amount it can handle when identifying random letters. This gain occurs because readers make use of nonvisual information already stored in the brain. Readers' prior knowledge reduces the amount of information required to identify entire words. Being able to automatically identify words and being able to comprehend texts depend "on using visual information economically and using as much non-visual information as possible" (Smith, 1978, p. 33). "Tunnel vision," a state of incomprehension when faced with a text, occurs when the brain is overloaded with visual information. Beginning readers often find themselves paralyzed by tunnel vision because they read too slowly, attempting to sound out each word letter by letter. Tunnel vision also often occurs when readers lack background knowledge or when reading materials are too difficult. When readers encounter too many unknown words, they pay attention to the visual aspects of reading (the letters within words), which prompts the brain to process all of the letters separately.

It is imperative that students have the automatic word recognition and word analysis skills to comprehend text. Struggling readers find reading unpleasant because the task is laborious and embarrassing when they must read aloud in front of peers. Thus, they spend little time on it and do not receive enough practice to become fluent. Like any other skill, word identification requires practice. It is best if students develop this skill with a teacher who can assess their reading problems, teach appropriate strategies, and provide engaging activities.

In order for reading to become more pleasurable for struggling readers, they must develop the ability to automatically recognize a large bank of words, known as sight words (*at, the, of, have*). According to Pinnell and Fountas (2007), word recognition includes the following elements:

- Recognizing words without conscious attention
- Recognizing words without attending to every letter
- Using parts of words to quickly identify new words
- Connecting unknown words to known words (analogies)
- Connecting spelling with word meaning (homonyms, plurals, tenses, etc.)

Students achieve automatic word identification when they read full texts, not when they spend hours on drills with isolated word lists (Clay, 1991; Pinnell & Fountas, 2007; Taberski, 2000).

To identify words in full text, proficient readers use all four cueing systems—syntactic, semantic, pragmatic, and graphophonic—along with context clues and their receptive vocabulary. A good goal for corrective reading instruction is to have struggling readers (1) learn how to use the four cueing systems, (2) learn the components of word identification, and (3) increase their range of strategies for analyzing words.

Before you assess and assist struggling readers, you need to understand some basic concepts about the role of word identification in reading.

WHAT TEACHERS SHOULD KNOW

Students do not become proficient readers simply by memorizing lists of words or learning all of the combinations of letter–sound relationships. Instead, they "use visual information for print and graphics; put together the information to gain the literal meaning of the text; [and] remember it while reading, thinking beyond the text" (Pinnell, 2006, p. 79). Proficient readers simultaneously use their knowledge of the four cueing systems—syntactic, semantic, pragmatic, and graphophonic. Here is a brief recap of the concepts discussed in Chapter 2, related to their roles in word identification.

The Four Cueing Systems

1. Syntactic system. The **syntactic** language system is often described as the system of grammar and sentence structure. The sentence structure of English is unique. For example, when translating a sentence from German to English, you cannot simply substitute English words for German words to produce a meaningful, well-formed sentence. From birth, native English speakers automatically acquire the flow of English syntax when they communicate with adults. When reading, most children automatically use the syntactic system to identify familiar words and learn new ones. For example, even if proficient readers do not know the word *track*, they can use syntax to help them make sense of the sentence, "The train sped down the track." They will know that any verb such as *trampled, tried*, or *tackled* will not be appropriate here, because the determiner "the" is not followed by a verb. Proficient readers may not be able to explain the grammatical rule, but their prior knowledge of syntax will tell them that a verb does not make sense at the end of that sentence. Struggling readers, on the other hand, do not automatically use syntax in this way.

English learners know only the syntax or grammar of their native language and must learn a new syntax. Because no foreign language can be translated word-for-word into English, English learners cannot use context clues as readily as native English-speaking students. For this reason, English learners need to hear books read to them so they become familiar with the English syntax.

2. Semantic system. Semantic refers to the meanings of words, sentences, and longer passages in language. Many words have multiple meanings. For example, *run* can be a verb (Run as fast as you can!), a noun (The ski run is fast and challenging.), or a root word for a number of other words (runny, runner, running). In each instance, *run* has a different meaning. Struggling readers may recognize the word when it stands by itself, but they may have a problem recognizing *runner* and *runny* in a word list. However, if they read each of these words in a sentence, the context will help them identify the word. For example, most children would easily recognize *runner* in the following sentence because of the context: "As the race was about to begin, the runner waved to his dad." Also, most children would recognize *runny* in the following sentence because of the context: "The sick baby had a runny nose."

Homonyms are words that are spelled the same but have different pronunciations and meanings in different contexts. The words *minute, wind, read*, and *tear* are pronounced differently and carry different meanings in the following sentences.

The minute hand on the clock was stuck on seven.

The minute glove was too small for the giant's hand.

I love to feel the soft wind on my face.

Please wind the alarm clock.

You need to read two chapters tonight.

I read that book three times.

The child's tears cascaded down her face as the balloon floated above the roof.

Please do not tear any pages of the library book.

Readers know the correct pronunciation and intended meaning of these words only when they are used in context.

3. Pragmatic system. The **pragmatic system** refers to the situational context of a word, sentence, or passage. Readers' prior knowledge and previous experiences impact the pragmatic system because all readers' experiences are different. For example, students who live in the southern United States and who have never visited the northern plains might not appreciate a description of the bone-chilling winds of a blizzard as much as students who live in North Dakota. In fact, a southern student may lack a whole range of sights, sounds, and feelings that a North Dakota student associates with a blizzard. When a student from the South reads a story set in a blizzard, she may not automatically identify words such as *blizzard, parkas*, and *toboggans* with the same ease as students in the North.

4. Graphophonic system. The **graphophonic system** refers to relationships between letters and their sounds. Chapter 5 contains a detailed discussion of this cueing system.

Proficient readers use these four cueing systems automatically, and teachers should encourage early readers to use all cueing systems when they read (McKenna & Cournoyer-Picard, 2006).

Components of Word Identification

Automaticity is not only the ability to recognize a large bank of words by sight and to quickly decode unfamiliar words, it is also the ability to comprehend words in their context and thus comprehend passages. Both knowledge and skills are needed for automaticity. Students must know words and be able to use word analysis skills. See Figure 6.1.

Word knowledge

Students must have good receptive and expressive vocabularies. They need to know frequently used sight words (words that do not conform to pronunciation rules). They also need an extensive sight vocabulary, a large bank of words they recognize instantaneously.

Receptive and expressive vocabularies. Readers' vocabularies consist of two parts—their receptive vocabulary and their expressive vocabulary. **Receptive** vocabulary consists of the words students know in conversation and while reading texts. Students' receptive vocabulary is a result of their past experiences, conversations, and reading. Oral language in home and daycare experiences are the primary sources of students' receptive vocabulary (Molfese, Modglin, & Molfese, 2003; Kieffer & Lesaux, 2007; Wasik, 2006; Rasinski, Padak, Newton, & Newton, 2008). Because a large receptive vocabulary is essen-

figure **6.1**

The main components of word identification.

WORD KNOWLEDGE

Receptive vocabulary: a bank of words a student can understand during conversation; listening vocabulary

Expressive vocabulary: vocabulary students use during speech or writing

Sight words: words that do not conform to pronunciation rules

Sight vocabulary: words that students recognize in half a second or less

WORD ANALYSIS SKILLS

Context clues: rhetorical knowledge, schema, and picture clues that a student can use to figure out unknown words

Visual analysis of monosyllabic words: the ability to break words into smaller known parts to figure out unknown words

Blending polysyllabic words: the ability to blend the smaller parts (single syllables) of words together to make whole words

Structural analysis: the ability to distinguish frequently used prefixes and suffixes from root words and the knowledge of how they affect the meaning of words

Morphemic structure: Understanding how root words with different affixes (prefixes and suffixes) form different parts of speech (e.g., music, musician, musical/ magic, magician)

tial for successful reading and writing in school and all through life, it is essential that preschool children are immersed in environments where they interact with adults during play and reading/writing activities. Quality children's literature is a great source to increase students' receptive vocabulary.

Because receptive vocabularies are developed orally (in conversation and listening to quality literature), students need to be able to distinguish between phonemes that have fine gradations. Some of these phonemes include /b/ and /p/, /f/ and /v/, or short /i/ and short /e/. Beverly Wolf (2009) found that some of her students with oral- and written-language learning disabilities (OWL–LD) heard something quite different from what the teacher dictated. For example, when Wolf dictated "Rome wasn't built in a day," the student wrote "Row mustn' bill tinted a." When she dictated "Always be polite," the student wrote "Al waits beep a light." To determine if older students can distinguish sounds with close gradations, dictate short sentences that are appropriate for their writing ability.

Students' **expressive vocabulary** is often smaller than their receptive vocabulary and has two parts—one used in speech and one used in writing. Their oral expressive vocabulary is usually larger than their written vocabulary.

When students encounter new words in text and attempt to identify them, they are aided by their receptive vocabulary and their expressive oral vocabulary. If the unknown words are not part of either vocabularies, they will not recognize words as they attempt to pronounce them. Too often struggling readers have limited receptive and expressive oral vocabularies. These struggling readers are often children "who live in poverty and are exposed to fewer experiences than their middle-class counterparts" (International Reading Association, 2002).

Sight words. As stated previously, **sight words** are those that are immediately recognized as a whole unit; identification of sight words does not require word analysis. Sight words appear often in simple text (e.g., *the, to, you, there, one, once*). There are many sight word lists. See Appendix B.5 for Dolch's (1948) list. Cunningham's (2004) list of high-frequency words (see the box and Appendix B.4) also includes many sight words. As stated earlier, students learn words in context. For this reason, it is beneficial to use phrase lists made up of sight words. The Phrases and Short Sentences for Repeated Reading Practice list (Rasinski, 2003) is based on the Fry Instant Word List (2003) and is presented in Appendix B.6. I will refer to this list as the Fry Phrase List. Shanker and Ekwall's (2002) list of sight word phrases is another example.

Students should be introduced to sight words when they begin reading. Gunning (2001) contends that sight words are best learned using the whole-part-whole approach as demonstrated in the following activity. Note that the teacher and students first enjoy the poem as a whole, then work with individual sentences, phrases, and words, and finally put the words and sentences back together.

1. Using a short poem that students will enjoy, the teacher selects four or five sight words.
2. The teacher points to the words as he reads the poem.
3. The teacher reads the poem again, inviting the students to "chime in" on words or phrases they know.
4. After a number of readings, students are invited to read the poem independently.
5. The teacher writes each sentence of the poem on a separate sentence strip.

6. Students are asked to read the sentence strips and put them in order.
7. The teacher cuts the sentence strips into single words and ask the students to put the sentences back together.

The teacher might focus on four or five sight words and add them to the class word wall. When students write, they should be expected to spell the words that appear on the wall correctly.

Sight vocabulary. Readers' **sight vocabularies** are the words they recognize in half a second or less (Fry & Kress, 2006; Taberski, 2000). Each reader's sight vocabulary is unique because his or her personal experiences differ (Heath, 2004).

Native speakers and English learners develop their sight vocabularies in three ways (August & Shanahan, 2006; Helman & Burns, 2008; Nilsen & Nilsen, 2004):

1. *Known to unknown.* Alice may know the simple word *walk* and learn *walking* when it appears in a sentence. Alice is learning unknown words by focusing on the part of the word she does know.
2. *Simple to complex.* Dameon knows the word *volcanoes* and learns more complex scientific terms such as *lava* and *magma* when reading the text and captions under photographs on a website about this subject.
3. *Literal to metaphorical.* Jeremy understands what it is to cry tears and what rain is. When he reads the sentence "The clouds cried for hours yesterday," he understands and appreciates the personification of the cloud and rain.

High-Frequency Words

"One hundred words account for almost half of all the words we read and write. Ten words—*the, of, and, a, to, in, is, you, that,* and *it*—account for almost one-quarter of all the words we read and write" (Cunningham, 2004, p. 54). Many of these high-frequency words are difficult for children because they have no concrete meaning. However, students need to recognize these words automatically when they read and to spell them instantaneously when they write. Displaying these words on a word wall keeps them available to students as they read and write.

Appendix B.4 features the list of high-frequency words compiled by Cunningham (2004). Appendix B.5 includes the Dolch word list, a collection of high-frequency words.

Word analysis skills

When students encounter words that are not part of their word knowledge, they use certain skills to figure them out. They must be able to use context clues when they encounter unfamiliar words. They need skill in visual analysis and blending, and they need the ability to distinguish affixes and root words.

Context clues. When readers come to unknown words, they use context clues—rhetorical knowledge, schema, and picture clues. **Rhetorical knowledge** is readers' knowledge about story grammar, the structure of expository text, paragraphs, and so on. **Schema** refers to readers' knowledge of the world. Readers' background knowledge (or schema) is closely related to their receptive vocabularies (Wasik, 2006; International Reading Association, 2002). If the reader has background knowledge on the reading topic, unknown words will be easier to recognize. For example, if the teacher mentions that a passage is about pioneers, readers who have background knowledge about this topic will begin to think of prairies, mud houses, covered wagons, buffalo, and so on. When readers "sound out" any of these words they have never encountered in print, their background knowledge helps them. **Picture clues,** illustrations that help readers identify unknown words, are another type of context clue used by proficient readers. For example, readers may not recognize the word *iguana* in the text, but a picture may help them associate the word with the object. To aid struggling readers, teachers often use vocabulary words that will be found in the text during a pre-reading discussion of the pictures.

Visual analysis of monosyllabic words. When words cannot be determined from context clues, readers can use **visual analysis.** This skill involves breaking syllables into smaller, known parts. Proficient readers look for parts they know. For example, as discussed in Chapter 5, they will look for a rime within the syllable and then add the onset (e.g., *ight* + *fl* = *flight*). (See Appendix B.1 for common word families, or phonograms.)

For monosyllabic words that are not part of a word family, proficient readers look at the whole word, automatically say the sound of the vowel or vowel cluster, and then add the beginning and ending consonants (e.g., *ie* + *shr* + *k* = *shriek*). Struggling readers, however, tend to mechanically sound out the word from left to right (Rasinski & Padak, 2003). This may cause problems because the sound of certain letters changes as more letters are added to a syllable. For example, with the word *knee,* readers encounter a problem if they first sound out the /k/ in *knee,* because the *k* is silent when followed by *n.*

Visual analysis also involves knowing how polysyllabic words are divided into syllables. This knowledge aids students with pronunciation and spelling of words (Blevins, 2001).

The concepts (Blevins, 2001) listed in Figure 6.2 are consistent 95 to 100 percent of the time; thus they are valuable concepts to teach students to help them visually analyze words.

Blending polysyllabic words. Once readers recognize the smaller parts (single syllables) of words, they need to quickly blend these parts to make whole words. Accurate, quick blending is necessary for pleasurable reading. Struggling readers may recognize the parts but lack the skill to quickly blend the pieces back together (Bear et al., 2008). Instruction in blending should begin with word endings, such as *-ed, -ing, -ly, -er,* and *-est,* because readers frequently need to recognize only the base word and the ending. Next, introducing compound words helps readers understand that longer words often consist of smaller words. Words such as *butterfly, mailbox, tablespoon,* and *teacup* are long words to sound out letter by letter; however, quickly recognizing the smaller words within the longer ones and blending them together will enable students to identify these longer words automatically. After working with inflectional endings and compound words, students can work with other polysyllabic words.

Structural analysis. Young readers and writers first become aware of endings that are added to words, such as *s* to make plural nouns, and *ed* and *ing* to change verb tenses. As they begin to use more polysyllabic words, familiarize them with frequently used prefixes, suffixes, and root words. Recognizing these parts helps them see the structure of words. When students enter fourth grade with a limited receptive and expressive vocabulary, they are likely to struggle in content subjects (Chall & Jacobs, 2003; RAND Reading Study Group, 2002; Biancarosa & Snow, 2004). Kieffer and Lesaux (2007) suggest that in order for these students to be successful, teachers should focus on morphology (the study of the smallest units of words, such as prefixes, suffixes, and root words). They propose four principles of teaching morphology:

1. "Teach morphology in context of rich, explicit vocabulary instruction." Morphology study should be an important component of vocabulary study that includes explaining the meaning of words found in content areas and teaching word learning strategies, such as dictionary skills and using context clues.
2. "Teach students to use morphology as a cognitive strategy with explicit steps." Students must learn how to analyze words by finding the affixes and root, attaching the meaning of each of these parts, and then hypothesizing the meaning of the word in the context of the passage being read.
3. "Teach the underlying morphological knowledge needed in two ways—both explicitly and

figure **6.2** Generalizations concerning words that aid visual analysis.

1. Syllables have one vowel sound, even though there may be more than one vowel. (*bat, boat*)
2. Words with CVC or CVVC patterns are one syllable.
3. Words with multiple syllables have one syllable that is accented.
4. Compound words are broken between the two identifiable words.
5. Vowels in unaccented syllables have the schwa sound. (le-mon, a-bove)
6. When the first vowel in a word is followed by *th, ch,* or *sh,* these symbols are not broken when the word is divided into syllables, and they may go with either the first or second syllable. (e.g., fa ther)
7. If the last syllable of a word ends in *le,* the consonant preceding the *le* usually begins the last syllable. (e.g., ta-ble)
8. In most two-syllable words that end in a consonant followed by *y,* the first syllable is accented and the last is unaccented. (ba-by)
9. In most two-syllable words that end in a /r/ sound, the second syllable is unaccented. (teach-er)
10. When *tion* or *ture* is the final syllable in a word, it is unaccented. (e.g., *va-ca-tion*)
11. Consonant and/or vowel diagraph and diphthongs are never separated. (*black-mail, speed-way, fa-ther*)
12. Inflectional endings (*ly, ing, er*), prefixes (*pre-, be-*), and suffixes (*-tion, -ant, -able*) are often syllables.
13. When one consonant is found between two vowels (e.g., *o-pen*), the word is divided after the first vowel. The vowel in the first syllable is often long.

in context." Students should learn the meaning of common prefixes and suffixes by teachers teaching them explicitly. Students should also learn them through reading activities such as word hunts. During word hunts, students look for words with prefixes, suffixes, and root words and add them to the classroom word wall or their personalized dictionaries. Teachers also need to explain how words are transformed from one part of speech to another by changing the suffix (e.g., *necessary/necessitate; negate/negative*).

4. "For students with developed knowledge of Spanish, teach morphology in relation to cognate instruction." Comparing the spelling of cognates aids Spanish-speaking English learners in comprehending English text (Kieffer & Lesaux, 2007, pp. 139–142). For example, when the student reads *metropolitan,* she may recall the Spanish word *metropolitano* and recognize the meaning of the English word from the Spanish.

Appendix B.7 lists frequently used suffixes and prefixes with their meaning and examples.

Because 90 percent of English words with more than one syllable are derived from Latin words and about 10 percent of other polysyllabic words are derived from Greek words (Bromley, 2008), intermediate and middle school students who become familiar with these Latin and Greek words have an advantage. Appendix B.8 has a list of Latin and Ancient Greek word roots.

SEQUENCE OF WORD STUDY FOR ENGLISH LEARNERS

English learners also need to break down long words into smaller chunks and syllables (Kieffer & Lesaux, 2007; Bear, et al., 2007). Figure 6.3 provides a suggested sequence for teaching syllables and affixes to English learners.

ASSESSMENT

Because reading comprehension depends on automatic word identification and oral vocabulary among other factors, you must know how to assess the readers' oral vocabulary, their ability to identify unfamiliar words, and their sight vocabularies using both informal and formal assessment instruments.

figure 6.3 Suggested sequence for teaching syllables and affixes to English learners.

1. Inflectional ending *ing*
   a. For some single syllable words that end in a consonant and the vowel is short, the consonant is doubled before adding the *ing* (*hopping, sitting*).
   b. For some single syllable words with a short vowel that end in a consonant, only the *ing* is added (*walking*).
   c. For some single syllable words ending in silent *e*, the *e* is dropped (*hope = hoping*).
   d. For one-syllable words with a long vowel sound, only the *ing* is added (*sleeping*).
2. Inflectional ending/suffix *ed* can have different sounds: /d/ as in *died*, /t/ as in *laughed*, or /ed/ *wanted*
3. Plural endings (*s* or *es* have three possible pronunciations: /s/ as in *plants*, /z/ as in *zoos*, and /ez/ as in *faces*)
4. Compound words, such as *backpack, notebook*
5. Unusual plurals (*wives, children, oxen*)
6. Simple prefixes (*re, un, dis, mis*)
7. Diphthongs in one-syllable words (*oil, ought, taught, cow*)
8. Familiar vowel patterns in accented syllable: long vowel sound in accented syllable (*a-**lone***), and the short or schwa sound in unaccented syllable (*a-**lone***)
9. Less familiar and ambiguous vowels in two-syllable words (*mountain, powder*)
10. Final unaccented syllable with *er, or, ar* (*reporter, doctor, sugar*)
11. Initial hard and soft *c* and *g*: these letters followed by *a, u, o* are hard (*cat, cut, cot, gate, guy, go*); these letters followed by *e, i, y* are soft (*cent, city, cycle, gem, ginger, gym*)
12. Simple suffixes (*er, est, ier, iest, y, ly*)
13. Less frequent one-syllable homophones (*cruise/crews; aisle/isle*) and two-syllable homophones (*principal, principle*)
14. Less frequent one-syllable homographs (*bow/bow; wind/wind*)
15. Two-syllable homographs (***pre**sent/pre**sent***)
16. Spelling-meaning connection (*music/musical*)
17. Concrete and frequently occurring Greek and Latin word roots (*spect, struct, tele*).

Source: Bear, Donald R.; Helman, Lori; Invernizzi, Marcia R.; Templeton, Shane; Johnston, Francine R., *Words Their Way with English Learners: Word Study for Spelling, Phonics, and Vocabulary Instruction,* 1st ed., © 2007. Adapted by permission of Pearson Education, Inc., Upper Saddle River, NJ.

Informal Assessment

As discussed earlier, students' receptive vocabularies, their sight vocabularies, their ability to use context clues, their ability to use visual analysis in monosyllabic words, their ability to blend, and their knowledge of word parts all affect their capacity to automatically identify words. Informal assessments in evaluating students' abilities in each of these areas include the following.

Checklists

At the beginning of the school year, familiarize yourself with your state's literacy standards, especially those that address word identification. To ensure that all students become competent in these standards, design a checklist to informally assess each student's growth in this area. You may assess knowledge at the beginning of the year and at the end of each quarter. Students who lag behind the others should receive extra help in word identification. Students who are competent in all areas should perform other activities when the rest of the class is focused on word identification. The partial checklist in Figure 6.4, which is based on California's first-grade Standard 1.10: Decoding and Word Recognition, was completed by Ms. Henderson after the first quarter. From her review of this checklist, she realizes that Rosa and R. J. need more time working on word identification. Kim is competent in all areas; therefore, she gives him other reading materials during guided reading time. The entire checklist for this California standard is reproduced in Appendix C.31.

Assessing receptive vocabulary

A student's receptive vocabulary consists of words he recognizes when listening to speakers. The context for the conversation often helps him grasp the meaning. One way you can informally assess a student's receptive vocabulary is by having him read a passage at his instructional level. If he decodes a word and does not realize he has mispronounced it, the word may not be a part of his receptive vocabulary. For example, imagine that Jacob has never heard the word *signature;* when he encounters it in a text, he may pronounce it "sign-a-ture," with emphasis on the *sign,* with a long /i/, and never realize that he has mispronounced the word.

Assessing sight words

Many word lists are available to help you informally assess readers' sight words. The Dolch Basic Sight Vocabulary (see Appendix B.5) is commonly used, especially with first graders. The Fry phrase list (Rasinski, 2003; see Appendix B.6) is a good informal assessment tool because it consists of phrases. Many basal readers also have graded word lists for students to master by the end of the school year. You may use the list as a pretest at the beginning of the school year and as a quarterly assessment instrument throughout the year. Decide which list is appropriate for your struggling readers.

To use these lists as informal assessment tools, print the words or phrases on individual index cards. Number the cards in order of difficulty on the back, with number one corresponding to the easiest word or phrase. Prepare a scoring sheet that lists the words or

figure 6.4 Checklist for first grade, based on California's Standard 1.10.

TEACHER Ms. Henderson DATE 10/30/11

+ = always x = sometimes o = seldom/never

STANDARD	STUDENTS: Kourtlyn	Kim	Gillian	Quinton	R. J.	Arielle	Coy	Zachary	Rosa	Alexis	Gabrielle	Mat	Blake	Taylor	Teagan	Josh	Zeb	Tyler
1. Recognizes consonant blends.	X	+	+	X	O	X	+	+	O	X	X	+	X	X	X	O	X	X
2. Recognizes short vowel pattern: CVC	X	+	X	O	O	X	X	+	O	O	X	X	X	X	X	X	X	O
3. Recognizes long vowel patterns: CVCe and CV	X	+	X	O	O	X	X	X	O	O	O	X	O	X	X	X	X	O
4. Blends onsets with rime.	X	+	X	O	O	X	X	X	O	O	O	O	O	X	O	O	X	O

phrases in order. Figure 6.5 includes a partial sample based on the Fry phrase list. Appendix C.32 has a complete form that can be used for any list. Mark all correctly pronounced items with a plus sign (+) on the scoring sheet and missed items with a minus sign (–). If you are using a phrase list, all words in the phrase must be read correctly or the student receives a minus.

To administer the Fry phrase list, you may also have the student read the list into a recording device as you flash one card every two seconds. If a student misses five consecutive words, pause the exercise. You may also use the program found on http://np.harlan.k12.ia.us/reading_center.htm, which will flash the cards in two-second intervals. The goal is for every child to read each list that is appropriate for his grade with 90 percent accuracy (Shanker & Ekwall, 2002). The following commercial informal reading inventories have graded word lists. They can be used in the same way as the Fry phrase list; however, they provide a scoring sheet and a list from which the students can read. Note that not all of the words on these lists are sight words.

- Burns, P., & Roe, B. (2007). *Informal Reading Inventory* (7th ed.). Boston: Houghton Mifflin.
- Shanker, J., & Ekwall, E. (2000). *Reading Inventory* (4th ed.). Boston: Allyn and Bacon.
- Silvaroli, N., & Wheelock, W. (2011). *Classroom Reading Inventory* (12th ed.). New York: McGraw-Hill.

Assessing sight vocabulary

Informally assess struggling readers' sight vocabularies by having them read a passage at their instructional level. If their sight vocabulary is weak, they will read word by word or laboriously sound out every word to the point that they won't know what word they have read by the time they get to the last sound.

You can also informally assess each struggling reader's sight vocabulary by designing a personalized speed test. To do this:

1. Write three words of equal difficulty on a line.
2. Repeat this process to make at least 10 different lines. The first line should have the easiest words and the last line should have the most difficult.
3. Pronounce one of the words from the first line two times for the student.
4. Within five seconds, the student must circle the word you pronounced.
5. Repeat this process for the remaining lines.

Figure 6.6 provides a sample list for this activity.

figure **6.5** Scoring sheet for a sample phrase list using the Fry phrase list (Rasinski, 2003).

STUDENT Tyler GRADE 2nd

+ = yes – = no

WORDS	BEGINNING OF YEAR	1ST QUARTER	2ND QUARTER	3RD QUARTER	4TH QUARTER
The people	+				
By the water	–				
You and I	+				
He called me	+				
What did they say?	+				
No way	+				
One or two	+				
More than the other	–				
How many words?	+				
This is a good day	+				
Sit down	–				
But not me	+				

figure 6.6 Sight vocabulary assessment.

1. the	on	of
2. when	which	with
3. then	them	these
4. made	may	way
5. only	our	after
6. want	where	old
7. read	need	end
8. answer	animal	world
9. every	earth	never
10. example	important	together
11. children	river	second
12. mountain	enough	idea

Remember that sight vocabulary assessment must be quick and accurate. The following graded word lists can also be used for sight vocabulary assessment:

1. ESA Word List
2. *Basic Elementary Reading Vocabulary* by Harris and Jacobson
3. DLM's Word Radar, software by Chaffin, Maxwell, and Thompson

Assessing context clues

Students' background knowledge impacts their ability to use context clues. You can informally assess readers' background knowledge in a number of ways. The first way is to ask the student to "read" the pictures in a text. While discussing the pictures, listen to his technical vocabulary. If he does not use any specific terms and relies on words like *things* or *whatchamacallit,* you can assume the reader is not familiar with the topic.

You can also assess a reader's ability to use context clues through a cloze test. When completing a cloze test, readers read for meaning as well as recognize the missing word. (To construct a cloze test, see the instructions in Chapter 3.) A cloze test should be administered orally so you can analyze the reader's ability to fill in the blank correctly, and then ask why she chose a particular word. If the reader makes wild guesses, you can infer that she is not using context clues.

The running record (also discussed in Chapter 3) is another way to assess if and how students use context clues. Use it to determine if readers use picture clues or context clues to help them with unknown words.

Assessing visual analysis

One informal way to assess readers' ability to analyze monosyllabic word parts is to give them a list of words that highlight onset and rime. Pronounce either the onset or the rime of each word, and allow five seconds for students to circle the word part you pronounced. Figure 6.7 presents a small sample list for the reader and a list of sample answers.

To informally assess readers' visual ability to analyze polysyllabic words, ask yourself the following questions while observing how they analyze unknown words:

- Do the readers attempt to sound out the words letter-by-letter?
- Do they segment the words into syllables?

figure 6.7 Words with onset and rimes.

LIST FOR READER

1. bill	6. found	11. top	16. sand	21. man
2. light	7. pup	12. see	17. hay	22. pack
3. ham	8. flat	13. hill	18. sound	23. stop
4. land	9. fan	14. might	19. cup	24. bee
5. may	10. back	15. clam	20. hat	

UNDERLINED PART PRONOUNCED

1. bill	6. found	11. top	16. sand	21. man
2. light	7. pup	12. see	17. hay	22. pack
3. ham	8. flat	13. hill	18. sound	23. stop
4. land	9. fan	14. might	19. cup	24. bee
5. may	10. back	15. clam	20. hat	

- Do they segment the word into the correct syllables?

Assessing blending

To assess a reader's ability to blend word parts, first assess auditory blending skills by saying two parts of a word and having the reader put the two sounds together. You might begin with monosyllabic words by pronouncing *fl* and then *ight*. The reader should pronounce *flight*. Proceed to two-syllable words (e.g., *pic* + *nic* = *picnic*), then progress to three- and four-syllable words.

Next, assess students' visual blending abilities by writing the parts of words on separate cards and having the students push the cards together and pronounce the word. For example, with monosyllabic words, one card might have a *c* and another card an *at*. Students move the cards together and pronounce *cat*. With polysyllabic words, each card displays a syllable of the word; one card has *moun* and the other has *tain*. Students put the cards together and pronounce *mountain*. See the Intervention section of this chapter for sample cards.

Assessing structural analysis

To informally assess readers' ability to analyze word structure, observe as they encounter words with prefixes and suffixes. Does the reader automatically pronounce the prefix and suffix as separate syllables? For example, on the word *unending*, does the reader automatically pronounce *un*, or does she attempt to sound out the *u* and then the *n*? Does the reader pronounce *ing* as one syllable?

You can also give the student a list of words with prefixes and suffixes (Gipe, 1995). See Figure 6.8 for an example. Pronounce either the prefix, suffix, or root of the word and allow five seconds for the student to circle that part. Allow no more than five seconds because word identification must be instantaneous.

Formal Assessment

Figure 6.9 lists diagnostic tests that include subtests that assess oral language, phonic skills, structural analysis, blending, visual and auditory discrimination, sight word recognition, and syllabication skills.

figure **6.8** List of words with prefixes and suffixes.

LIST FOR READER

1. recalls	5. smiled	9. smallest	13. unopened	17. jumpy
2. unless	6. hopeless	10. bigger	14. unnecessary	18. weakness
3. before	7. careful	11. friendly	15. prettiest	19. reading
4. coming	8. running	12. quicker	16. unfriendly	20. teacher

UNDERLINED PART PRONOUNCED

1. recalls	5. smiled	9. smallest	13. unopened	17. jumpy
2. unless	6. hopeless	10. bigger	14. unnecessary	18. weakness
3. before	7. careful	11. friendly	15. prettiest	19. reading
4. coming	8. running	12. quicker	16. unfriendly	20. teacher

figure **6.9** Diagnostic tests used to assess sight words.

1. Diagnostic Reading Scales (individual test): Decoding skills and word recognition.
2. Gates McKillop-Horowitz Reading Diagnostic Test, Second Edition: Word recognition, phonics, syllabication, producing letter sounds, letter naming, blending, word analysis, and use of context clues.
3. Gray Oral Reading Tests, Third Edition: Word recognition in context.
4. Gilmore Oral Reading Test: Word recognition in context.
5. The Durrell Analysis of Reading Difficulty, Third Edition: Word analysis in isolation and in context.
6. Diagnostic Reading Scales, Revised: Word analysis in isolation and in context.

Intervention STRATEGIES & ACTIVITIES

Word identification skills should not be taught through isolating worksheets (Bear et al., 2008; Bloodgood & Pacifici, 2004; Pinnell & Fountas, 2007; Rasinski & Padak, 2003; Taberski, 2000), but rather in context—for example, while reading good literature or while writing a letter. A primary goal of teaching word identification skills is to help struggling readers gain automatic word identification. "The best way to develop fast and accurate perception of word features is to engage in meaningful reading and writing, and to have multiple opportunities to examine those same words out of context" (Bear et al., 2008). Having struggling readers memorize lists of words is fruitless. Rather, help them learn how to think about words by looking for familiar parts within words. Many words can be identified as part of a word family, and sometimes there are familiar short words in longer words, such as *chimpanzee,* which contains *pan,* or *scare,* which contains *s* + *care*. When segmenting a longer word, the result is sometimes several smaller, connected words. Consider *attendance,* which segments into *at* + *ten* + *dance*. In this word and others like it, the smaller words must be blended together quickly to form the longer word. When teaching word identification skills, teachers need to incorporate reading and writing activities, and during the editing portion of the writing process, they need to examine spelling patterns and spelling–meaning relationships (Bloodgood & Pacifici, 2004). All of the strategies and activities discussed in this section can be used in small group settings. However, it is strongly recommended that these activities be primarily used in tutoring sessions so teachers can focus on what the one student knows about word identification. All instruction should take place while working with authentic literature and writing tasks. Feel free to use the suggested texts for these activities, or choose those that interest the struggling readers. Assisting students to discover patterns within monosyllabic words and morphological relationships helps them unlock pronunciation, spelling, and meaning of words (Blevins, 2001).

The activities in this section are divided into the following categories: (1) small group activity for teaching word identification skills; (2) activities emphasizing receptive and expressive vocabularies; (3) activities emphasizing sight words; (4) activities emphasizing sight vocabulary; (5) activity emphasizing context clues; (6) activities emphasizing visual analysis of monosyllabic words; and (7) activities emphasizing blending polysyllabic words and structural analysis. First assess struggling readers as they read and write, then emphasize the specific skills that meet their particular needs. The first activity is designed for small groups; the others can take place either in small groups or during one-on-one instruction.

Small Group Activity for Teaching Word Identification Skills

During the first benchmark tests at the beginning of the year, you may identify students who are below benchmark and could benefit from word identification activities. To use your classroom time effectively, teach concepts to small groups who need to develop similar skills. Observe and assess what each student does when faced with unknown words during these sessions and modify your instruction as needed. Guided reading is a popular small group instructional strategy designed for teachers to work with students of similar strengths.

ACTIVITY **GUIDED READING** **GRADES 1–6**

In guided reading the teacher works with a small group of students who read at the same level and use similar reading processes (Fountas & Pinnell, 2006b). For these activities, use leveled books that offer a minimum of new concepts to learn, and take time to teach one or two new concepts in each session. The premise of guided reading is for students to experience new texts that they can read at once with minimal support. Your role is to teach strategies and skills and how to use them successfully during independent reading.

The guided reading lesson follows a specific format:

1. Select a text that offers one or two new concepts. The text might be in a large book format so that all children in the group can see it clearly.
2. Introduce the book by talking through the pictures, using the vocabulary of the text. For example, if the story is about a humungous bear but the children use the word *big* in the discussion, introduce the word *humungous* during further discussion.

A Guided Reading Session

Mr. Francis is supervising a small group activity in which students are quietly reading aloud to themselves Meish Goldish's *Step Inside the Rain Forest* (1993). He notes the children struggle with the word *sloth,* an unfamiliar animal, and *chimpanzee,* a longer word for this group of readers. When the children use picture clues for this word, some say, "ape," while others say, "monkey." When they have completed the story, Mr. Francis writes *sloth* on the whiteboard.

Mr. Francis: What parts do you see in this word?

Children: A *sl* and a *th.*

Mr. Francis: Good. What sound does *sl* make?

Children: /sl/.

Mr. Francis: Good! What sound does the *th* make?

Children: /th/.

Mr. Francis: Good! Do you think the *o* makes a short or long sound?

Carla: A short sound because there is no *e* at the end of the word.

Mr. Francis: Now let's blend the three parts together.

Children: /sl/ . . . /o/ . . . /th/.

Mr. Francis: A little faster now.

Children: *Sloth* (as Mr. Francis quickly moves his finger under the letters).

Mr. Francis: Now turn to page 11 and let's read that page together.

Children: A sloth—it doesn't walk on the ground.

Mr. Francis: Great! We also know that monkeys and apes are incorrect words because these animals can walk on the ground. Now let's look at this word. (He writes *chimpanzee* on the board.) Again, some of you read *ape* and some of you read *monkey.* The animal on page 13 looks like a monkey or ape. But let's look at the letters of the word. What sound does *monkey* start with?

Children: /m/.

Mr. Francis: Correct! This word (pointing to *chimpanzee* on the board) does not begin with the /m/ sound or the letter *m.* What sound does *ape* begin with?

Carla: A long /a/ sound.

Mr. Francis: Correct! These letters (points to the *ch*) do not make the long /a/ sound. What word do you see in this long word?

Colin: I see *pan.* (He points to it.)

Brian: It's *chimpanzee!* A chimpanzee is like a monkey, and that has *pan* in it. Listen, *chim pan zee.*

Mr. Francis: Great job! Let's read that page together.

Children: Bats and snakes and chimpanzees.

Colin: Mr. Francis, you spelled it wrong. It has an *s* on the end.

Mr. Francis: Thanks for catching that Colin. What does that *s* mean?

Colin: That there are more than one.

Mr. Francis: Great job! Colin saw a smaller word in *chimpanzee* and Brian, you recalled that a chimpanzee is like a monkey. Today, boys and girls, you learned how to find smaller parts in words, like in *sloth* and in *chimpanzees.* Now, let's read the entire book together.

3. After you talk through the entire text, give each child a copy of the book. Instruct them to look at the pictures again, and perhaps ask them to find a particular word on a particular page.
4. Next, instruct the students to read the book aloud quietly to themselves. Watch for words they find difficult.
5. After the reading, make a list on a whiteboard of words they found difficult. Now teach them an appropriate word identification skill (e.g., structural analysis) and ask them to apply it to the given word.
6. Read the text in unison with the students.
7. Sometimes you might invite students to respond to the book to assess their comprehension. Other times you may include writing, drama, or art extensions to complement the book. However, not every book works with such extensions.
8. Ask a student to stay so you can make a running record of his reading.

Read the scenario in the box on the previous page and examine how Mr. Francis teaches several word identification skills during a guided reading session.

Fountas and Pinnell's *Guided Reading: Good First Teaching for All Children* (2006b) offers more detail on how to conduct a guided reading session.

Activities Emphasizing Receptive and Expressive Vocabularies

During discussions you may observe a student whose receptive and expressive vocabularies are very limited. The student may use general terms such as *thing* for common objects, like the wheel of a car. Or he may not know the specific names of familiar animals. Take time to discuss books and pictures with him, using specific words and prompting him to join in. The following two activities should be conducted in a tutoring session so you or the tutor can adapt the activity to the student's individual needs.

WORDLESS BOOKS — GRADES 1–8 — ACTIVITY

"Reading" a wordless book is one way to build a struggling reader's receptive vocabulary and schemata. The "reading" becomes a discussion when a teacher also comments on the pictures, using specific terms or a more advanced vocabulary than a reader has. Appendix A.5 presents a list of wordless books that encourage this kind of discussion, and Appendix A.6 presents some appropriate material for content area learning. Some of the books in the list are intended for younger students, while some, especially those in Appendix A.6, are complex enough for middle school students. One example is the complex wordless book *Zoom* (1995) by Istvan Banyai, in which the illustrations involve multiple shifts in perspective. After viewing the first picture in the book, a middle school student may say that it depicts a bird. As the student turns to the second page, you may agree but say that it is a rooster because of the colorful crown. As you continue through the book, if the student calls the cruise ship a boat, you can explain the difference. As you discuss the pictures, write each specified word on an adhesive label and stick it to the appropriate page so the student can later go through the book and read these words back to the tutor.

PICTURE BOOKS — GRADES 1–3 — ACTIVITY

Jan Brett's books have detailed pictures and borders. Often the borders are stories within the main plot or details that supplement it. Using one of Brett's books, you can help a struggling reader "read" the pictures before tackling the text. Use specific vocabulary so she hears potentially challenging words before she attempts to read the text. For example, while discussing the pictures in Brett's *Armadillo Rodeo* (1995), use words such as *lizard, hand-tooled, chili, arena, jalapeno,* and *fiddles,* which may be unfamiliar to the student. When she reads the book, she will refer to the discussion and picture clues to help decode the unfamiliar words. Additional titles by Jan Brett are listed on her website (www.janbrett.com), and she includes many useful ideas for using her books with children.

ACTIVITY

USING PICTURES TO ENHANCE THE EXPRESSIVE VOCABULARY OF MIDDLE SCHOOL STUDENTS

GRADES 6–8

Brod Bagert's (2006) *Hormone Jungle: Coming of Age* poetry book has a drawing on each page that can be used to enhance the expressive vocabulary of middle school students. Read the title of the poem and then invite the student to explain the drawing, many of which are abstract. For example, the poem "The Gap" features a drawing of the right half of one face and the left half of another. The right-half face has a heart drawn over it. Ask the student to explain why she thinks the artist drew that picture for that poem. (This poem is written from a female's perspective so this activity works best with a female student.) As you ask "why" questions, the student will be developing an expressive vocabulary as she tries to explain herself. An appropriate poem for boys is "The Girl-Crazy Alien Body Snatcher," featuring a drawing of an alien-looking male with four wings; one wing has a mask of a devil and one wing has three moons on it. The male has his hand up in the air as if he is in a dilemma. Ask "why" questions such as, "Why do you think the illustrator drew an alien-looking male?" and "What is meant by the four wings?," giving him time to find words to express his thoughts.

The wordless book *Ben's Dream,* which includes illustrations of famous places such as the Leaning Tower of Pisa and Big Ben in London, may also be used with middle school students. Ask students to describe the places in as much detail as they can. If students are unfamiliar with these places (they are listed on the book's final page), encourage them to use the place name as a search word and read more about it online.

Activities Emphasizing Sight Words

Sight words do not follow phonetic rules, yet they are found in every story. Students who do not recognize sight words quickly fall behind the rest of the class. If you notice some students who continue to struggle with sight words such as *the, of,* and *once* during group time, schedule one-on-one time with them. The goal is enabling each student to recognize sight words automatically. If a child needs more time than others to gain proficiency at the task, have her work with a tutor.

ACTIVITY

MATCH THE WORD

GRADES K–1

1. After reciting a poem or song with sentence strips, place them in a pocket chart.
2. Give the student a card with one of the sight words from the text.
3. Ask the child to place the card over the correct word in the sentence strip. This will be easy for most children, but some will not take enough time to examine the letters within words.

This activity can also be used with big books by writing the sight word on a sticky note and asking the child to place it over the word in the book. Later, you can say a sight word and ask the child to point to the word in the text.

DOLCH LIST BINGO **GRADES 1–5** ACTIVITY

The Bingo cards in Appendix D.13 use the words from the Dolch word list. When playing Bingo, call out each word twice and allow only five seconds between each word. Remember, with word identification, automaticity is the goal.

Activities Emphasizing Sight Vocabulary

As you observe students in small groups, you will notice some struggle with words that are not difficult for others. These words are frequently necessary to understand a particular passage. For example, when reading about natural disasters, students need to quickly and automatically recognize words such as *hurricane, volcano, tornado,* and *earthquake.* Students who cannot do this may become frustrated and give up. These students will need one-on-one time for activities that will help them develop their sight vocabularies. The following activities should be conducted in tutoring sessions.

UNSCRAMBLE THE SENTENCE **GRADES 1–2** ACTIVITY

Read a short poem and then write each line on a separate sentence strip. After reading "Perfect Children" (1997) by Brod Bagert, for example, write the following four lines on four separate sentence strips:

1. | We | children | are | sweet. |

2. | We | children | are | nice. |

3. | We | always | say | "please." |

4. | At | least | once, | maybe | twice. |

After the student can comfortably put the four lines in the correct order and read each sentence while pointing to each word, cut each line into individual words and have her put the sentences back in the correct order.

PERSONALIZED FLASH CARDS **GRADES 1–8** ACTIVITY

As you and a student read books that contain vocabulary specific to the topic of the book, he may encounter difficult words that he sounds out every time they appear. For middle school students, these words will be found in the content materials. Have a stack of index cards handy to write down words that the reader needs to remember. The stack of personalized cards should be no more than 10 to 12 in number. The goal is for the reader to recognize those words quickly by sight. When these words are mastered, place them in the "known" stack. Students find it satisfying to see their stack of "known" words grow.

ACTIVITY

PERSONAL WORD WALLS

GRADES 1–5

To help a struggling reader create a meaningful word bank, create personalized word walls on card stock or a piece of paper. One of Mr. Morris's students created the following list as she read various books about birds, adding words that she found tricky: *bulbul, extinction, emu, ganets, molting, osprey, preening, plumage.*

ACTIVITY

UNSCRAMBLE THE WORD

GRADES 1–2

1. After reading a book with the student, select some nouns from the text that the student wants to remember or that are new vocabulary for him.
2. Write out the words, using half-inch squares for each letter and cut them out.
3. Give the student the squares for one word and have the student unscramble it.
4. Repeat for all the words.

This activity is useful for assisting tactile learners. The sample cards found in Figure 6.10 are based on *Curious George Visits the Zoo* (1985) by H. A. Rey.

figure **6.10** Unscramble the letters.

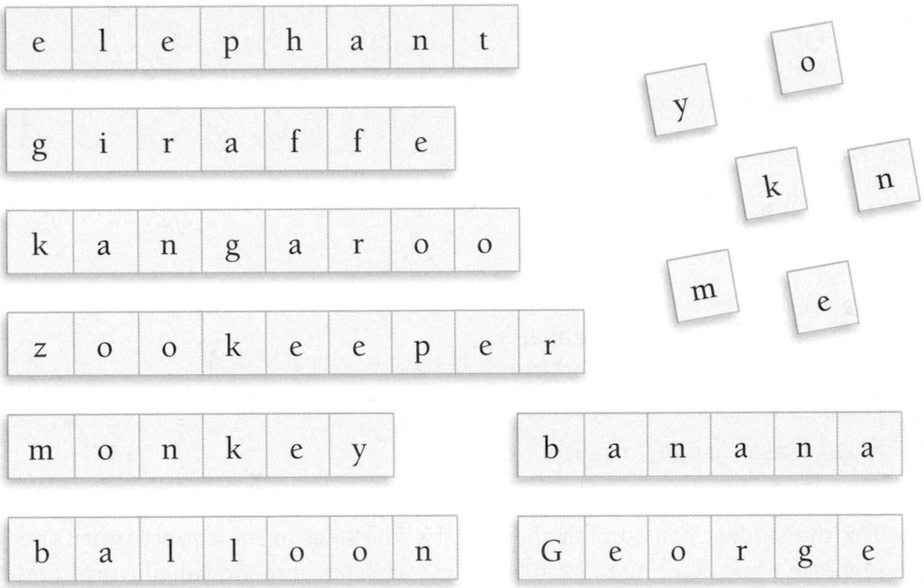

ACTIVITY

TECHNICAL TERMS

GRADES 2–8

Many concept books feature vocabulary words that are specific to the book's topic. To familiarize a student with this specialized vocabulary, first ask the student what she knows about the topic. Then create a word-web for the book's key terms. This will aid the student as she learns to recognize the words before reading the text. The web in Figure 6.11 is drawn by Ms. Inoue for her second grader, Ben, as they discuss his knowledge of the rain forest. She asks him if he has seen TV shows about the rain forest or if he has read about the rain forest at home. After Ms. Inoue marks down the words that Ben contributes, she adds a few more she knows he will encounter in the text. After the

figure 6.11 Sample word-web.

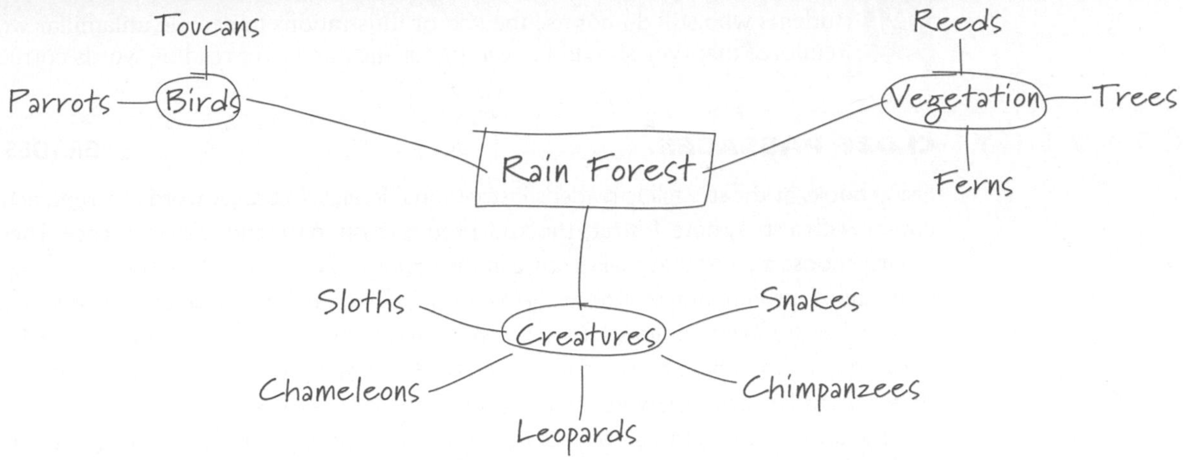

discussion, she has Ben read the words in the web. This gives him an opportunity to see these potentially difficult words in print before he reads the text.

Jon, an eighth grader, is very interested in Greek mythology, but when he begins researching mythological figures online, he is surprised to find so many categories. With the help of a high school buddy, he creates the web organizer found in Figure 6.12.

figure 6.12 Organizer of Greek gods, semi-gods, monsters, and heroes.

The Olympian Gods	Semi-Gods and Spirits	Monsters and Creatures	Greek Heroes
Aphrodite	Furies (Erinyes)	Centaurs	Achilles
Apollo	Graces (Charities	Cyclopes	Agamemnon
Ares	Fates (Moirae)	Giants	Heracles
Artemis	Muses	Satyrs	Jason
Thena	Nymphs		Odysseus
Demeter	Sirens		Theseus
Dionysus			
Hades			
Hephaestus			
Hera			
Hermes			
Hestia			
Poseidon			
Zeus			

Source: www.greek-gods.info

Activity Emphasizing Context Clues

While emphasizing context clues during guided reading sessions, you may observe students who still do not use the text or illustrations to decode unfamiliar words. Reinforce that they should be reading for meaning over reading words correctly.

ACTIVITY **CLOZE PASSAGES** **GRADES 1–8**

Using books at the struggling reader's instructional level, select a key word in a sentence and cover it with a sticky note. Instruct the student to read on to the end of the sentence. Then ask him to choose a word that makes sense in the context of the sentence. If the student has no suggestions, prompt him to look at the pictures for clues. (Choose a book with vivid illustrations to help younger students.) If you are working with an older student and the book has no illustrations, simply have him read to the end of the paragraph to determine the correct word. After the student selects a word, he can take off the label and see if he was correct.

For a variation on this activity, photocopy a short passage at the student's instructional level. Delete every fifth word or every key word and have the student fill in the deleted words. As you observe the student, look for context clues to help her select the correct word.

Activities Emphasizing Visual Analysis of Monosyllabic Words

Students who continue to struggle with word families often do not recognize smaller elements within monosyllabic words; if they do, they often cannot quickly blend the two parts together. Use the following activities in tutoring sessions to help struggling students learn to automatically blend onsets with rimes.

ACTIVITY **TOSS THE CUBE** **GRADES 1–3**

This activity helps a student develop the ability to create words with a given set of letters. Using three to five letter cubes (found in Appendix D.6), the student tosses the cubes and creates words from the letters. He gets one point for each word he creates. To make the activity more difficult, set a time limit for each toss.

Activities Emphasizing Blending Polysyllabic Words and Structural Analysis

In your small groups you may notice one student continues to sound out words letter-by-letter instead of breaking them into familiar parts, such as prefixes, root words, and suffixes. This chapter emphasizes techniques you can use to help them see these parts within words. Working with prefixes, suffixes, and base words can be extremely helpful for a struggling student. First graders can benefit from recognizing word endings (e.g., *ing, ed, ly, er,* and *est*), while older students, especially middle school students encountering polysyllabic words, can work with prefixes, root words, and suffixes. Assess what a student knows and continue to develop the skills she needs for success.

ACTIVITY **COMPOUND WORDS** **GRADES 2–4**

Read a book with a variety of compound words and then create cards that display the words that make up each compound word. These cards will help students to see how many compound words they can form by putting the cards together. Time students to make this exercise

figure 6.13 Compound words that correlate with *The Jolly Postman,* by Janet Ahlberg.

post	man	card	age	box	pal
pen	mail	box	bag	office	truck

more challenging. One book that features many compound words is *The Jolly Postman* (1986) by Janet Ahlberg. Some words that relate to the postal service are found in Figure 6.13.

AFFIXES WORD STUDY

GRADES 1–2 ACTIVITY

Select texts with words that have a number of affixes. First read the book for enjoyment and then discuss the words that have affixes. When selecting texts for English learners, refer to the sequence for teaching syllables and affixes to English learners (Figure 6.3). The list progresses from most commonly found suffixes to words with Greek and Latin bases. A good example for this exercise is Sam McBratney's *Guess How Much I Love You* (1994) because it uses many past tense verbs and *ing* verbs: *listening, stretching, reached, swinging, laughed,* and *touched.* Notice these words have endings that do not share letters with the base word (e.g., *listen + ing; swing + ing*). At first exclude words with double consonants and words in which the base word and the suffix ending share letters. For example, words such as *hopping* and *tumbled* should be avoided because in *hop,* the *p* is doubled to form *hopping,* and in *tumbled* the root word (*tumble*) and ending (*ed*) share the *e.*

In the building blocks activity, write all of the base words, suffixes, and prefixes from a passage on sentence strips of different colors. For example, write all root words on blue strips, prefixes on green strips, and suffixes on orange strips. Then cut up the words and affixes and have the readers form as many words as possible by putting the pieces together. Figure 6.14 presents a sample list of words and affixes.

figure 6.14 Root words and affixes.

ROOT WORDS	work	walk	friend	slow	clear	clean
	quick	fore	behave	to	take	lead
PREFIXES	un	mis	in	be		
ENDINGS	ing	ly	ed	er	s	

ACTIVITY

PERSONALIZED WORD-PART DICTIONARIES: AFFIXES AND ROOTS

GRADES 3–8

When working with older students, help them see the parts as well as the definition of each part. Using Appendices B.7 and B.8, have students make personalized dictionaries that are divided into three sections—one for prefixes, one for suffixes, and one for root words. Each affix and root word should be given a half page so there is room for students to add new words. This personalized dictionary, like all dictionaries, must include the definition of each affix and root word. When reading, students need to be encouraged to add words to their dictionaries. For example, when a student comes across the word *irresponsible* in a story, he can add the word to the *ir-* page and put the definition in his own words.

ACTIVITY

MORPHOLOGY RUMMY

GRADES 6–8

Many middle school students enjoy playing cards with friends. The following Morphology Rummy game is adapted from Homophone Rummy (Bloodgood & Pacifici, 2004). Using the template provided in Appendix D.15, make 50 copies each of the root, suffix, and prefix cards for 150 cards total. Use Appendix B.8 to select the words and affixes for your cards.

On 25 of the cards write a different root word on two diagonal corners so the cards resemble playing cards (see Figure 6.15). Then create 25 additional cards providing the definitions for the 25 root words. Thus, the original card may have *aqua* on its diagonal corners, while its mate has the definition *water* on its corners. Follow the same procedure for creating the prefix and suffix cards and the cards with their meanings. Create a deck of 50 root word cards, 50 for prefixes, and 50 for suffixes. (You may make more cards, but make sure each root, prefix, or suffix card has a matching definition card.) The object for student players will be to find as many matches (a root word card and its definition card) as possible. When two cards are matched, the player discards them. The goal is to be the first player to discard all his or her cards.

Directions:

1. Give each player five to seven cards, depending on how many cards you made and on the number of players.
2. Place the remaining cards in a draw pile, with the top card lying face up next to the pile. The upturned card is the discard pile.
3. The player to the left of the dealer draws a card from the draw pile or the discard pile. If the card from the discard pile is chosen, the player must have a match for it. For example, if a player draws a root word card, then she must have the card with the root word's meaning in her hand.
4. Players lay down any matching pair in their hand when it is their turn.
5. When players make a match they must say the root word, prefix, or suffix, read the definition, AND give a word that uses that root word, prefix, or suffix. If the player cannot give a word, the player to the left of the player may attempt to give a word. If that second player can give a word, he keeps the match; if he cannot give a word, the match is placed on the discard pile.
6. To signify the end of a turn, the player discards a card from his or her hand by placing it on the discard pile.
7. Players can challenge a word at any time by consulting a dictionary.

8. If the discard pile contains a card a player needs in order to create a match for a card he has in his hand, he must pick up all the discarded cards on top of the one he wants and keep them. At the end of his turn, he must discard one card.
9. The game is over when one person gets rid of all his or her cards.
10. The winner is the person with the most matches.

figure **6.15** Sample morphology rummy cards.

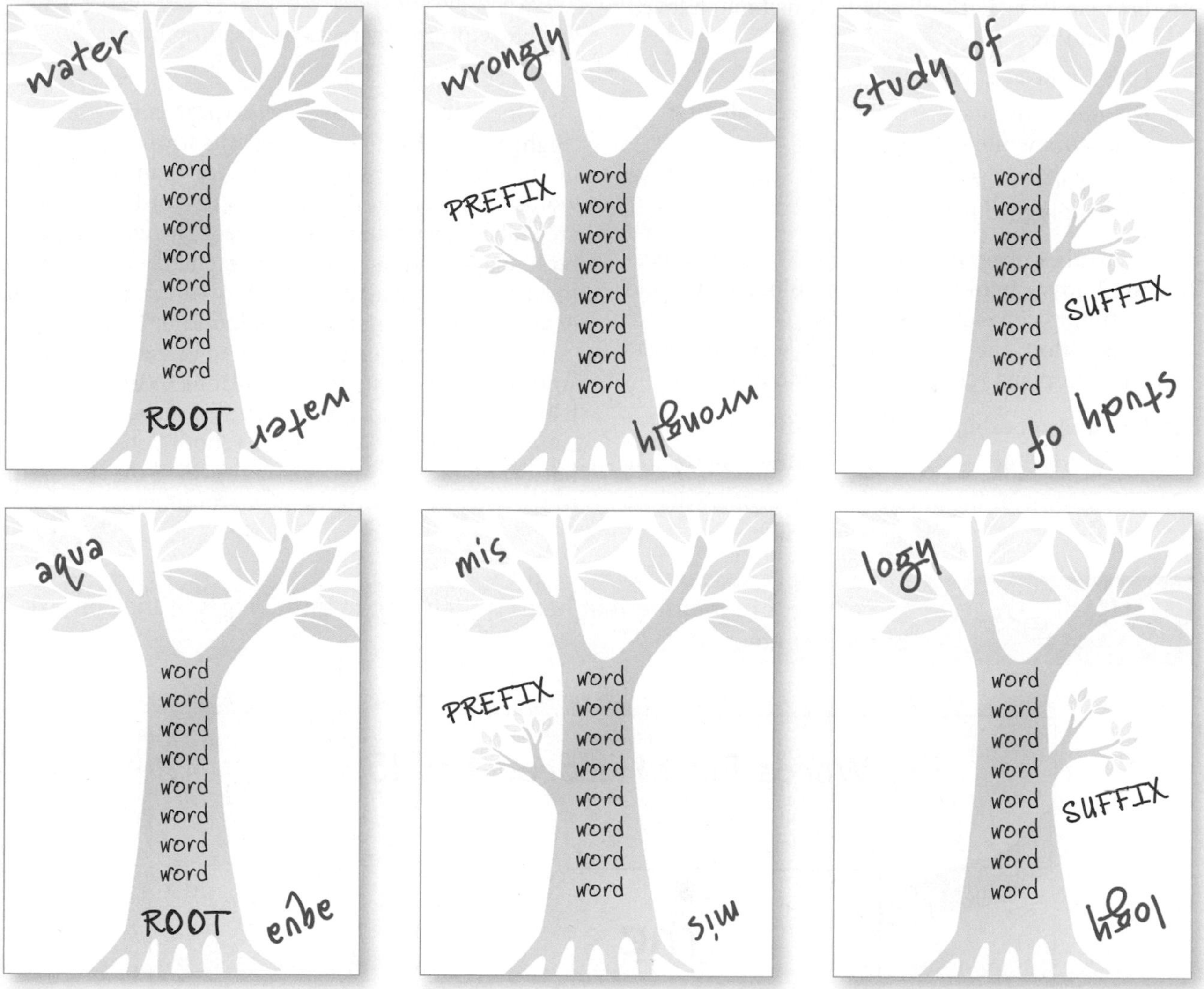

WORD IDENTIFICATION AND TECHNOLOGY

Computer activities motivate many children to read, and a number of interactive books are available to aid children in word identification. The Discis Series, for example, allows students to click the mouse once to hear the pronunciation of unknown words and twice to hear the definition. (See Appendix A.11 for a list of titles.)

Living Books offers a wide selection of interactive books that help children master unknown words. Text is highlighted in phrases so children can follow along. Students control the turning of each page so they do not become lost. Titles available from Living Books are listed in Appendix A.11.

Listening to an audiobook while following a printed text is an excellent way for students to increase their ability to identify unknown words.

See Chapter 8 for a thorough discussion of using audiobooks.

Scholastic Publishers offers the following CDs/DVDs with interactive books and strategies to increase students' word identification skills:

- *Phonics Readers*. Includes 72 interactive books on 12 CDs.
- *Phonics Booster*. Offers interactive books on 16 CDs.
- *Let's Go Read 1*. 175 lively lessons build a love for reading.
- *Let's Go Read 2*. Nine interactive stories.
- *Dinosaur Adventure 3-D*. Learn facts about dinosaurs while solving puzzles.
- *I Spy Spooky Mansion* ("Mystery Bins"). Offers challenging riddles.

Two other programs to increase word identification are I Spy School Days ("Wood Block City") and Inspiration ("Vocabulary Template").

In addition, the ReadWriteThink.org site offers three lesson plans related to word identification.

1. Learning Vocabulary Down by the Bay
2. Active Reading Using the Enormous Watermelon
3. Word Sorts for Beginning and Struggling Readers

Many websites allow students to read books online. Some sites are programmed with digitized speech so the student can place the cursor over the word and hear its pronunciation.

My favorite interactive websites to help build word recognition skills include:

www. readingrockets.org
www.funbrain.com
www.prongo.com
www.starfall.com
www.primarygames.com/reading.htm
www.pbskids.org

One site (www.candohelperpage.com, click on "Sight Vocabulary") helps students learn sight words in the context of sentences rather than as isolated words. Words from the Fry Instant Word List (1980) are embedded in simple sentences. The word appears both in a box and in a simple sentence below it. Digitized speech is available to help with pronunciation. A sample page from the site is found in Figure 6.16.

Be sure students know how to operate programs so they do not waste time. Continue to browse publisher websites and catalogs to stay current on educational software. When your school considers new hardware, be sure any existing media you still want to use will work with the new equipment.

figure **6.16** Screenshot of a website that helps students learn sight words in the context of short sentences.

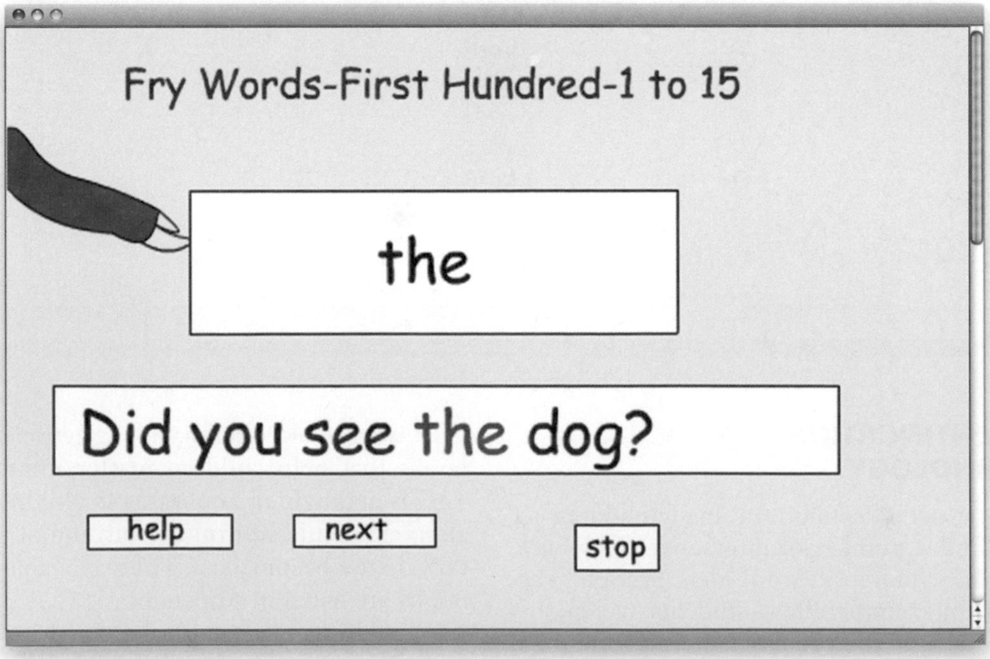

Source: www.candohelperpage.com

CONCLUDING THOUGHTS

Automatic identification of words is a necessary skill for reading comprehension. Many readers struggle with sight words and others lack vocabulary to read about specified topics. To address these problems, teachers must (1) help students see patterns in words rather than having them memorize long lists; (2) help struggling readers recognize onset, rime, prefixes, suffixes, and root words to increase their sight vocabularies; and (3) help students use context clues when they encounter unknown words, because many words are not phonograms and do not have prefixes or suffixes.

Throughout this chapter the emphasis has been on the importance of students automatically recognizing a large bank of words, especially those found most frequently in a given text. Read and reflect on the following scenario and answer the questions. Then discuss the scenario with classmates and, if possible, a reading specialist who works with English learners.

Reflective Learning ENGLISH LEARNERS

Scenario. For five years Mr. Perez has taught fourth grade in a small Midwestern town. Last January a new company moved into town, along with many families who were not native English speakers. Mr. Perez had no English learners in his first five years of teaching. However, this year he has five. Two students' native language is Mandarin, and three students' native language is Spanish. During the summer, all five students attended a reading camp that focused on the alphabet, its sounds, and nouns and verbs used in daily conversations. When they started school in August, all five could identify the letter names, give the common sound for each letter, give at least one target word that began with the sound (e.g., b = /b/ and *bat* begins with *b*), and read and write common nouns and verbs used in daily conversation (e.g., types of foods and verbs such as *run, walk, smile*). However, Mr. Perez realizes they struggle with common words such as *with, went, off, the, is, was,* and *saw.*

QUESTIONS

1. What type of assessment should Mr. Perez give these five students to assess their ability to read sight words?
2. What type of small group instruction should Mr. Perez give these students?
3. What type of individual strategies should he teach these students?
4. Because his time is limited, what do you suggest he does to give these students the maximum help they need?

CHAPTER SEVEN

VOCABULARY BUILDING

The limits of my language are the limits of my mind.
All I know is what I have words for.

LUDWIG WITTGENSTEIN

scenario

Mrs. Lopez, the principal of an inner-city school, overhears some of the fifth-grade teachers in the lounge discussing their students' difficulties in reading and understanding science materials. She decides to remind the teachers how readers' vocabularies affect their comprehension. At the fifth-grade team meeting, Mrs. Lopez gives the teachers the following passage from her old music harmony textbook:

> If the root of a triad remains stationary while its third and fifth rise one degree and return, a six-four chord is formed. This type differs from the appoggiatura type in that it is weak rhythmically and the sixth and fourth must enter from below in the manner of auxiliary tones. A simple analysis of one root for all three chords is always possible, the sixth and fourth being nonharmonic tones. (Piston, 1962, p. 108)

Then Mrs. Lopez asks them to write a short summary, explaining it in their own words. The teachers object, saying they cannot complete the task because they have little background knowledge about music and are not familiar with the terms *root, triad, six-four chord,* and *appoggiatura.* Ms. Ling comments that she is not even sure of the paragraph's main topic. Mrs. James surmises the topic is music because of two words: *tone* and *rhythmically.*

Next, Mrs. Lopez gives the teachers this paragraph:

> The French system was an extension of Franconian principles. The long, the breve, and the semibreve could each be divided into either two or three notes of the next smaller value. The division of the long was called mood, that of the breve time, and that of the semibreve prolation; division was perfect if it was triple, imperfect if duple. (Grout, 1964, p. 79)

Again, the teachers do not comprehend what they have read. No one knows the word *prolation.* At first Mrs. James thinks the paragraph is about the French government because of the words *Franconian, system,* and *principles.* However, the word *notes* in the second sentence convinces her this paragraph must also be about music. She has no idea that it, in fact, has to do with rhythm, because she does not know the terms *quarter note* and *eighth note*. Mr. White, who has a strong background in phonics instruction, thinks the paragraph has to be about marking vowels in words because of the term *breve.* Finally, Mrs. Lopez explains the reason for the exercise: She has heard the teachers complain about students not being able to comprehend science texts. She reminds them that science texts are dense with new vocabulary and with common words that have multiple meanings. When students encounter many new vocabulary words and do not have background knowledge of the topic, they may struggle to comprehend the text. She suggests that they, as a school community, focus on building students' vocabulary. She asks volunteers to find strategies that have proven successful for large group instruction, small group instruction, and for tutoring. She also asks for ideas about ways to motivate students to learn new words. The volunteers will share the activities with the entire faculty at their meeting in September. After reading the passages with unfamiliar vocabulary words, the teachers understand the importance of vocabulary building and 15 teachers volunteer.

guiding questions

As you read this chapter, consider the following questions:

1. If you were one of the teachers in Mrs. Lopez's school, what strategies would you recommend for large group instruction? For tutoring sessions?

2. Would you recommend that a list of vocabulary words be assigned each week? If so, why?
3. How would you recommend that teachers select the vocabulary to teach?
4. If there are English learners at Mrs. Lopez's school, what specific vocabulary building strategies would you recommend for this group of learners?
5. What would you recommend that your fellow teachers do to motivate students to become interested in new words?

INTRODUCTION

Roughly 800 new words are added to the English language each year, and in the twentieth century alone the language grew by an estimated 90,000 words (Ayto, 1993; Riverdeep.net, 2000). Have you learned that many new words within the last twelve months? Out of the words you have learned recently, how many are new to the language and how many are from your course work? It is important for teachers to consider how to motivate students to learn new words. "In order to comprehend, students must know the meanings of words they read" (Richek, 2005, p. 414). To really comprehend the meanings of words, students need to process the words "deeply and repeatedly" (Richek, 2005) in different contexts, and if the word has multiple meanings students need to be exposed to the various definitions of the word (Mason, Stahl, Au, & Herman, 2003). Students need to "own" the word in order to understand and use it in different context. Townsend (2009) contends that in order for middle school students, including middle school English learners, to "own" words they need less memorizing and more meaningful, engaging, collaborative learning experiences that cater to their social needs. Vocabulary building must be an activity that is enjoyable for students of all ages so they will find joy in learning new words and will be looking for new, "spicy, tasty words" (Baumann, Kame'enui, & Ash, 2003) that roll off the tongue.

Therefore, it is imperative for teachers to understand how (1) proficient readers naturally enrich their vocabulary, (2) to explicitly teach vocabulary, (3) to meet the vocabulary needs of English learners, and (4) to assess struggling readers' vocabulary. This chapter examines these four issues and discusses various interventions to use with elementary and middle school students.

GENERAL BACKGROUND

Research indicates a strong correlation between readers' vocabulary knowledge and their reading comprehension (Armstrong, 2004; Blachowicz & Fisher, 2005a; Cooper, 2006; Juel & Deffes, 2004). Baumann, Kame'enui, and Ash (2003) conclude that students' knowledge of words is the single greatest predictor of their reading comprehension. Whether students are learning language arts, math, science, or social studies concepts, comprehension of content depends on word knowledge. In addition, according to August and Shanahan (2006) and August, Carlo, Dressler, and Snow (2005), vocabulary knowledge and narrative comprehension (see Chapter 8) are important precursors for literacy skill for bilingual students.

Heilmann, Miller, and Dunaway (2010) found a relationship between children's vocabulary and narrative organizational skills, which includes telling the three main parts of a story—the problem, attempts to solve the problem, and the outcome. In a study with four-year-olds and kindergarten students, Puccelli and Paez (2007) found that Spanish-speaking kindergarten students' Spanish and English oral language affected their storytelling ability in kindergarten and first grade. Students who scored high in kindergarten on the picture vocabulary subtests of the Woodcock Language Proficiency Battery–Revised 1991 scored higher on the beginning reading scores in first grade compared to students who scored low on the same test.

Proficient readers tend to have a large working vocabulary; therefore, comprehension comes easily for them. However, students who have a limited vocabulary often struggle with reading because even when they decode words correctly, they do not understand them.

Environment affects children's vocabulary. By age three, children from privileged families (those with higher incomes and higher parental education) have heard 30 million more words than children from under privileged families (those with lower income, lower parental education) (Hart & Risley, 2003). Linguistically advantaged children enter first grade knowing approximately 20,000 words, while linguistically disadvantaged children know only 5,000 words (Juel & Deffes, 2004). Mothers in a higher socioeconomic status usually have a postsecondary education and know the importance of reading to and discussing books with their children, taking them to story time at the public library or local bookstore, and modeling good reading habits. These same mothers have a robust oral vocabulary, which they impart to their children through everyday activities.

Children who have conversations with adults who have a rich vocabulary naturally learn a wide range of words, whereas children who lack such an environment have fewer opportunities to hear and learn new words. Compare the different conversational environments of the two young children in the sample sentences below:

> Adult speaking to Susie: I need to inflate the balloon.
>
> Adult speaking to Mary: I need to blow up the balloon.
>
> Adult speaking to Susie: Watch the yellow duckling go swoosh as it submerges its head into the water.
>
> Adult speaking to Mary: Watch the yellow ducky put its head into the water.
>
> Adult speaking to Susie: Listen to the chirping of the cardinal.
>
> Adult speaking to Mary: Hear the bird singing.
>
> Adult speaking to Susie: I appreciated the daisies you gave me.
>
> Adult speaking to Mary: I love the flower you gave me.

In a meaningful context, Susie is learning words such as *duckling, submerge, appreciate,* and *chirping,* and specific names for birds and flowers. In contrast, even though Mary is conversing with adults, she is not developing an advanced vocabulary.

INCREASING STUDENTS' VOCABULARY

The average high school senior has a vocabulary of approximately 40,000 words (Nagy & Herman, 1987). This means that from grades one through twelve, students learn approximately 2,700 to 3,000 new words a year, or seven words a day (Snow, Burns, & Griffin, 1998).

Beck, McKeown, and Kucan (2002) defined three word tiers. Tier one words are common words used in everyday conversation (e.g., *house, car, run, sleep*); tier two words are less frequent but interesting words that transcend content (e.g., *persuade, parched, exhausted*); and tier three words are those associated with particular content (e.g., *pandemonium, psycholinguistic*). In classroom conversations, teachers should explicitly teach and use tier two words so students hear them daily. Soon, the students will begin to use them in conversation and they will recognize them in print. Tier three words are those usually learned through explicit instruction when studying content area subjects.

Knowing a word, however, is more than merely understanding when someone says it. Aspects of knowing a word include:

1. Knowing how to pronounce it correctly.
2. Knowing its relationship to other words.
3. Knowing its connotation in different contexts.
4. Knowing how to use it in multiple settings.
5. Knowing how to use it when writing.
6. Knowing its multiple meanings.
7. Knowing its morphology (derivation) (Juel & Deffes, 2004; Kieffer & Lesaux, 2007).

Ways of Increasing Vocabulary

Researchers refer to children's awareness of new words and their desire to learn and use them in speaking and writing as "word consciousness" (Graves & Watts-Taffe, 2002). The major avenues of students' vocabulary growth are life experiences in and out of school, vicarious experiences, and explicit instruction, which includes activities involving word play (Blachowicz & Fisher, 2005b; Yopp & Yopp, 2007).

Life experiences

Students learn the meanings of words that are used in their communities. Students from rural areas understand terms such as *barns, silo, combines,* and *corncribs;* students from urban areas understand words such as *skyscraper, taxi,* and *subway.* They learn these words through daily interaction in their communities. Students from different communities also learn different meanings for the same words. To rural students, an elevator may be a large tower used to store grain, while to the urban student an elevator is a boxlike enclosure that carries passengers between different floors in a building.

Children and adults constantly learn new words through new experiences. On a person's first visit to a Mexican restaurant, he learns the differences between *tacos, burritos, quesadillas,* and *tortillas.* A trip to the ocean introduces children to the terms *low tide, high tide,* and *sandbar.* Cooking helps them understand the difference between *creaming, grating,* and *blending.* A trip to a large department store introduces children to different categories of products and the various items found in each department. In all these experiences, adults need to draw children's attention to the words and their meanings so they become conscious of the new words. As mentioned earlier, students immersed in vocabulary-rich environments naturally take ownership of a broad spectrum of words.

Vicarious experiences

The second way students' vocabulary increases is through vicarious experiences. Such experiences might include viewing educational videos and television and reading a variety of texts. These media take students places they have not visited in person.

Educational videos and television shows increase students' vocabulary through technical terms used to explain concepts. Many movies and most television shows, however, do not increase students' vocabulary, because these shows often focus on everyday life issues that only reflect what students already know (Rasinski & Padak, 2004).

Researchers have found that students' vocabulary develops through reading (Mason, Stahl, Au, & Herman, 2003; Yopp & Yopp, 2007; Beauchat, Blamey, & Walpole, 2009; Nagy & Scott, 2004). High-quality poems and books offer the greatest opportunity to learn new words because the "authors choose vocabulary that is rich and interesting—words that create a particular mood, feel, or texture" (Rasinski & Padak, 2004, p. 138). When listening to stories and poems above their reading level, students' vocabularies increase because they hear new words in context and become familiar with their pronunciation and meaning (Yopp & Yopp, 2007; Rasinski & Padak, 2004).

Poems have especially rich language. Jack Prelutsky (1990b) introduces readers to vivid vocabulary in many of his humorous poems. In "The Turkey Shot Out of the Oven," he uses phrases such as "partly *demolished* a chair," "It *ricocheted* into a corner," "completely *obscuring* the room," "It *blanketed* every appliance," and "thought with *chagrin* as I mopped." The poem is easy for students to grasp and the italicized words in the quoted phrases add to readers' vocabularies. In another poem, "Floradora Doe" (1984), Prelutsky introduces the reader to many synonyms for talked—*recited, chatted, murmured, yammered, babbled, lectured, whispered, tittered, gossiped, prattled,* and *regaled.*

Trevor Harvey, in his poem "The Curse of the Foul-Smelling Armpit" (1998), also uses a rich vocabulary to explore the odor of the infamous armpit. In this short poem, Harvey introduces students to seven useful words—*lurks, unsuspecting, despair, frantic, foul, performance,* and *grungy*—that are easily understood in the context of the poem. Of course, poetry is read for more than increasing students' vocabulary, but discussing a poet's diction is a crucial part of analyzing and enjoying a poem.

Authors of stories and novels also use a rich, descriptive language to paint scenes for readers. In Chapter 7 of *26 Fairmount Avenue,* Tomie dePaola (1999) talks about "driving on the sea of mud" and "squishing through all the muddy water." In the same chapter, he introduces the reader to the concepts of *guardian angels* and *nor'easters.* In *Beauty,* Bill Wallace (1988) carefully chooses the following words to describe a rat: "A huge, gigantic rat was hiding under the sack. He glared up at me with his beady, ratty eyes. His scaly, ratty tail was curled up behind him" (p. 83). The words *gigantic, glared, beady,* and *scaly* provide a disturbing word picture of this creature. After reading short passages such as these with your students, explain unfamiliar words and discuss how the author's word choice contributes to the mood of the story and creates a vivid picture in the reader's mind.

In her books on the parts of speech, Ruth Heller also uses distinctive vocabulary to create pictures in the reader's mind. *Many Luscious Lollipops* (1989) includes the words *star-spangled, asteroidal, mesmerizing, soggy, remarkable,* and *regal.* In *A Cache of Jewels* (1987), she introduces students to new words or words used in new ways:

Cache of jewels (Students may be familiar with the homophone *cash.*)

Batch of bread

School of fish (Students may only be familiar with the *school* house.)

Gam of whales

Bevy of beauties

Muster of peacocks (Teachers may need to explain the difference between *muster* and *mustard.*)

Host of angels

Kindle of kittens

Pod of peas

Parcel of penguins (Students may recognize the word as a package.)

Coven of witches

Drift of swans (Students may be familiar with *drift* used as a verb.)

Brood of chicks

Clutch of eggs

Pride of lions (Students may be familiar with *pride* used as an adjective.)

Lock of hair (Students may be familiar with "Lock the door" or "The lock on the door.")

Army of ants

In *Some Smug Slug* (1996), P. D. Edwards also uses evocative vocabulary to introduce young readers to alliteration. Words include *sauntered, slithered, snickered, sapphire, swooshing, shrieked,* and *scurrying.* As students hear the words in context, they become familiar with their pronunciations and meanings. You can explain these words by acting them out and then inviting students to do the same so they remember the word. After sharing these books and discussing the words, invite the students to "Saunter and not scurry in the halls!" instead of commanding them to "Walk in the halls!"

The Internet introduces students to new vocabulary words, just as traditional sources do. The level of vocabulary varies with the type of passage they are reading. If they are researching how animated movies are created, they will learn words such as *optical illusion, footage, flip book,* and *film stock*. When teachers use these new words in daily conversation, students begin to take ownership of them in their own conversations. Learning new words should be an adventure for students and not a boring task!

Explicit instruction

Lehr, Osborn, and Heibert (2005) estimate that students learn approximately 3,000 new words each year through life experiences and vicarious experiences, but other research shows students' vocabulary also grows through explicit instruction (Manyak & Bouchereau-Bauer, 2009; Carlo et al., 2004; Townsend, 2009; Flynt & Brozo, 2008). Most students can easily learn eight to ten words each week through explicit instruction. So, which eight to ten words should be taught and how should they be taught?

Selecting vocabulary for explicit instruction. Staudt (2009) suggests that teachers ask the following questions when choosing words for study:

1. Does the word have multiple meanings? (e.g., Please sit on that *chair*. I was asked to *chair* the meeting.)
2. Does it function as multiple parts of speech? (e.g., Please *present* your gifts to the queen. I love the *present* I got from my sister.)
3. Does it have an affix or root word that will help the student segment the word? (e.g., *unpredictable*)
4. Does the word have an affix or root base that the student knows? (e.g., *audio* from the base *aud* which means *hear* or *listen*)
5. Can the word be easily confused with another word? (e.g., *fleece* and *fleas*)
6. Does the word have a common onset and rime? (e.g., *fright/flight*)
7. Is the word an adjective or the comparative or superlative degree of that adjective? (e.g., *happy/happiest*)
8. Is there a synonym or antonym the student knows? (e.g., *happy* for *exuberant*)
9. Is the word used figuratively? (e.g., Heaven's tears fell softly on my cheek.)

Also teach content words necessary for students to understand the concepts they are studying and other general words that students must know as they read more difficult texts (Beck, McKeown, & Kucan, 2002).

Guidelines for explicit instruction of vocabulary. Explicit instruction need not mean giving students a list of words to look up in the dictionary and memorize. Flynt and Brozo (2008) give teachers six guidelines for introducing vocabulary in content subjects:

1. Selectively choose words students need to know to understand the content.
2. Expose students to these selected words multiple times and use them in discussion. Require students to use vocabulary when they discuss the content.
3. Teach students to infer word meaning by looking for context clues and word parts (affixes and root words).
4. Use vocabulary maps and word association to demonstrate the relationships among words.
5. Teach students how to do a morphemic analysis on words.
6. Teach students multiple meanings of words.

As mentioned before, vocabulary words are best learned naturally through direct experiences (Rasinski & Padak, 2004). However, many academic (tier three) words cannot be conveyed in an everyday setting. Most new concepts students learn in school are introduced through textbooks and trade books, and each new concept includes a set of vocabulary words. Consider a few of the terms associated with the geologic concepts of volcanoes and caves: *eruption, lava, magma, stalactite,* and *stalagmite.*

When teaching new words explicitly in the context of the topic being studied, be a cheerleader as students pronounce new words, learn their meanings, and use them in different situations. Because words with multiple syllables are often difficult to pronounce, provide many opportunities for students to practice fluent pronunciation. Have them pronounce the new word a number of times so it flows smoothly off their tongues. I have found that having students tap out syllables with their fingers as they pronounce a new word helps break it into smaller pieces. When students can pronounce the word, explain it by naming a familiar synonym or by linking it to a concept the students understand. After students grasp the meaning of the new word, explain how it is used in different situations.

Give students time to play with new words in a risk-free environment. "Jazz-Man," a poem by Eleanor Fargeon in *Noisy Poems* (Bennett, 1987), features a number of challenging words—*mingle, accordion,*

Semantic Complexities of English

Older elementary and middle school students need to understand that words and word phrases can have more than one meaning. Encourage students to reflect on the semantic complexities of English as they play with ambiguous language (Sterling-Honig, 2007; Zipke, 2008). Consider the double meanings of the following sentences:

1. Kids make nutritious snacks (Zipke, 2008).
2. When a clock is hungry, it goes back four seconds.
3. A chicken crossing the road is poultry in motion.
4. A bicycle cannot stand alone because it is two tired.
5. What is the definition of a will? It is a dead give away.
6. Bakers trade bread recipes on a knead to know basis.
7. A boiled egg in the morning is hard to beat. (Sterling-Honig, 2007, p. 600)

Share these examples with your students to illustrate the multiple meanings of English words.

and *pandemonium*. This last word is difficult for some children to pronounce because it has five syllables. For explicit instruction, first pronounce the words and have the students repeat them, tapping their desks with each syllable. Then explain the meaning of the three words as used in the poem. *Mingle,* the easiest word of the three, means "mixed together" in this poem; however, this definition alone is not enough. Also explain how the term is used in daily conversation. For example, students *mingle* in the halls, meaning they do not move in straight lines. Instead they shift around, bumping into and talking over each other; the scene of mingling students may be noisy and chaotic. *Accordion,* a concrete noun, may be easier for students to understand when you point to a picture of the instrument and explain how it is played. *Pandemonium* is somewhat harder to explain. You might first say it means noise. However, pandemonium is more than mere noise; it is chaotic noise and movement. Convey this by having the students picture themselves in the gym with no teacher in sight; the noise and commotion quickly become loud and boisterous. This is the beginning of *pandemonium.* Give students time to discuss the word, enjoy its sound, and use it in sentences so they can take ownership of it.

Use explicit instruction not only to teach new words, but also to teach word-learning strategies, such as how to use morphological knowledge, how to use a dictionary to find the origin of words and their multiple meanings, and how to collect new words that they have heard or read. Students should also receive explicit instruction in context clues, word hierarchies, and language concepts, which will be discussed in more detail in the next sections.

Explicit instruction in context clues. One way to teach students how to learn the meaning of words is to focus on contextual clues. Start by teaching them to read to the end of the sentence and then guess what the word may mean. Sometimes they may need to read to the end of the paragraph to get the meaning of the word. Point out that many authors define words in the text. They use various techniques to include a synonym or definition of the new term in the sentence. Figure 7.1 lists various examples of how authors share the meanings of unknown words with the reader. You should explain the different ways authors may define words in their texts by using specific examples from the students' reading. Many ebooks and websites provide the aid of giving definition of words. Show students how they can click on the word, and the pronunciation and definition will be given.

As an example of teaching a student to use context clues, consider the word *brusque*. It may be new

figure 7.1

Ways that authors define words within texts.

Definition in an appositive phrase: The *waif,* a *homeless child,* longed for a ten-speed bicycle.

Definition within the sentence: A *vagabond who wanders from place to place* is also called a tramp.

Synonym: Mary does not *procrastinate* because she never *postpones* her assignments.

Antonym: After the storm, the *wild* sea became *serene.*

Situation: Juan will be the *valedictorian* speaker because he *ranks first* in the senior class.

Ann is so vain; she is constantly bragging about her excellent grades and good looks.

to fifth graders; however, they can get a good idea of its meaning when reading the following paragraph:

> "What's wrong with Joan?" Lynn asked.
>
> "I don't know. Why?" Deena replied.
>
> "Last night she was so brusque. When I saw her in the grocery store and asked her how she was, she replied, 'None of your business!' and stomped away."

After reading this short passage to the students, ask them what they think the word means. Most students will guess that it means "rude." By affirming their guesses, you will teach them that readers often learn new words from the context of the passage without using the dictionary. Repeat this procedure with examples from the material the students are currently reading. Once the students can pronounce a word and understand its meaning, invite them to use it in a sentence to demonstrate they understand it. Saying the word a number of times and using it in a sentence gives students a sense of ownership.

Explicit instruction in word hierarchies. In all content areas, especially social studies and science, students need to understand the hierarchy of words that organize most informational materials. Some words are headings and other words fit under those headings. Still other words make up subheadings and individual topics. In teaching this concept to students, begin with an idea they already understand, such as departments within a department store. Through games and team activities, students can have fun learning about word hierarchies. The Intervention section of this chapter discusses gamelike activities involving categorization. The purpose of these exercises is to help students understand the hierarchy of concepts that will later help them with vocabulary building in various subjects.

Explicit instruction in language concepts. Understanding some basic language concepts is advantageous for students as they build their vocabularies. Give students direct instruction in all of the concepts found in Figure 7.2, and explain more about them when they encounter them in texts. After that encourage them to find examples as they read and use them as they write their own texts. Figure 7.3 lists texts that emphasize many of the concepts defined in Figure 7.2. Direct instruction in these concepts should take place in a fun environment so students learn to enjoy language and vocabulary building.

Meeting the Vocabulary Needs of Struggling Readers

Struggling readers often have a limited vocabulary, which may be a result of limited early language experiences. Blachowicz and Fisher (2005b) note the vocabulary disparity between young children who come from homes rich in conversation, experiences, and lap-reading, and children who come from less language-rich home environments. When students with underdeveloped language enter school, it is the teacher's responsibility to immerse them in

figure 7.2 Language concepts and examples.

Synonyms: Words that have the same or nearly the same meaning.

raven and *black*

Antonyms: Words that have opposite meanings.

mingle and *separate*

Homophones: Words that sound the same but may be spelled differently and have different meanings.

would and *wood; which* and *witch*

Neologisms: New words that enter our vocabulary through extensive usage or for new inventions.

bytes, silicon

Portmanteaus: New words formed by combining two existing words and omitting some of the letters.

breakfast + *lunch* = *brunch; smoke* + *fog* = *smog*

Acronyms: Words formed from initials of other words.

NATO = North Atlantic Treaty Organization

Euphemisms: A more pleasant sounding word used in place of a word with negative connotations.

administrative assistant instead of *secretary*

Oxymoron: Two contradictory words or ideas used together in a word or phrase.

jumbo shrimp; awfully good; plastic silverware

Regionalisms: Words associated with particular geographic regions.

couch or *sofa; pop* or *soda; griddle cakes* or *pancakes*

Puns: Humorous expressions that highlight the multiple meanings of a word or two words that sound alike.

He *ran* up the flag. Rain is saved in *cloud banks.*

Onomatopoeia: Words that sound like their meanings.

Sploosh went the fish through the water!

figure 7.3 Books emphasizing various language concepts.

VOCABULARY

Four Famished Foxes and Fosdyke by P. D. Edwards (1995). New York: Harper Collins. (Alliteration; vocabulary building)

Some Smug Slug by P. D. Edwards (1996). New York: Harper Collins. (Alliteration; vocabulary building)

A Mink, a Fink, a Skating Rink: What Is a Noun? by B. Cleary (1999). Minneapolis, MN: Carolrhoda Books, Inc. (Nouns; vocabulary building)

Hairy, Scary, Ordinary: What Is an Adjective? by B. Cleary (2000). Minneapolis, MN: Carolrhoda Books, Inc. (Adjectives; vocabulary building)

A Cache of Jewels and Other Collective Nouns by R. Heller (1987). New York: Grosset & Dunlap. (Nouns; vocabulary building)

Many Luscious Lollipops: A Book About Adjectives by R. Heller (1989). New York: Grosset & Dunlap. (Adjectives; vocabulary building)

HOMONYMS AND PUNS

The King Who Rained by R. Gwynne (1970). New York: Simon and Schuster.

A Chocolate Moose for Dinner by F. Gwynne (1976). New York: Trumpet Club.

A Little Pigeon Toad by F. Gwynne (1988). New York: Trumpet Club.

IDIOMS

In a Pickle and Other Funny Idioms by M. Terban (1983). New York: Clarion Books.

Mad as a Wet Hen! And Other Funny Idioms by M. Terban (1987). New York: Clarion Books.

Punching the Clock: Funny Action Idioms by M. Terban (1990). New York: Clarion Books.

Amelia Bedelia series by P. Parish. New York: Harper Collins. (also emphasizes homonyms and puns)

OTHER

A Word Wizard by C. Falwell (1998). New York: Clarion Books. (Anagrams)

Guppies in Tuxedos: Funny Eponyms by M. Terban (1988). New York: Clarion Books. (Eponyms)

What's a Frank Frank? Tasty Homograph Riddles by G. Maestro (1984). New York: Clarion Books. (Homographs)

What's Mite Might? Homophone Riddles to Boost Your Word Power! by G. Maestro (1986). (Homophones)

Noisy Poems edited by J. Bennett (1987). New York: Oxford Publishing Services. (Onomatopoeia)

Opposites by M. Novick & S. Harlin (2001). San Diego, CA: Advantage. (Synonyms and antonyms)

rich language experiences. To help these students acquire the vocabulary necessary for academic success, Blachowicz and Fisher suggest teachers include four practices in their vocabulary instruction:

1. Develop a love of words through word play. Permit students to post interesting words on a bulletin board and have them explain to the class where they encountered the words and what they mean. Also, play word games and provide age-appropriate crossword puzzles.
2. Deliver rich instruction by teaching words they need to know to understand a passage, discussing the words with the students, revisiting the words often.
3. Teach strategies so students can decipher new words as they encounter them. Teach word parts (prefix, suffix, root word) and how to use dictionaries or glossaries.
4. Engage students actively in a wide range of texts by providing literature circles, guided reading groups, shared reading, and book clubs. Also, allow the students to show the meanings of words, such as the difference between *surprised* and *stupefied.*

Other experiences that create a language-rich environment include, but are not limited to, experiments, field trips, videos, the Internet, and audiobooks or ebooks. During the field trips and after viewing videos, conversation between adults and students is important. Be sure to use the pertinent technical terms and invite students to pronounce the words with you. Lev Vygotsky's (1962) theory of the zone of proximal development stresses the importance of students interacting with someone who thoroughly understands the concept being learned. As discussed in Chapter 1, the "zone" is the gap between what students know or can express on their own and what they know when working and talking with an informed adult. According to Vygotsky, what students understand today when working with an adult, they will understand by themselves in the future. For this reason, it is important that during and after all of the learning events listed here, students are given ample opportunity to ask questions and discuss new concepts.

Meeting the Vocabulary Needs of English Learners

The vocabulary needs of English learners must also be addressed in the classroom. The English learner population continues to grow. The Center for Public Education reported that in 2007, five percent of the K–2 population were English learners who did not know enough English to function in a regular classroom. English learners are often diagnosed as learning disabled when, in fact, they may only lack the vocabulary to read grade-level texts (August, Carlo, Dressler, & Snow, 2005; Carlo et al., 2004). Research indicates that many English learners lack the depth of understanding and the vocabulary they need to comprehend grade-level texts (August, Carlo, Dressler, & Snow, 2005; Puccelli & Paez, 2007). These students, however, do not need to spend vocabulary-building time memorizing definitions of words; they need learning experiences that are engaging and meaningful. They need games that are fun and collaborative because students are social and enjoy activities with peers. Teamwork provides English learners a risk-free environment because they are not evaluated individually. They also benefit from studying words that appear in various content materials. When students reach the upper grades, such words often have multiple meanings, but with "specific meanings in different contexts" (Townsend, 2009, p. 243). For example, *function* has one meaning when referring to a computer, but has a totally different meaning when referring to a school activity (e.g., a school *function*). The Intervention section of this chapter discusses engaging, fun strategies for middle-school English learners.

English learners from high socioeconomic status (SES) families outperform English learners from low SES families, and they perform as well or better than native English-speaking students from low SES families (Krashen & Brown, 2005). This indicates that socioeconomic status correlates with students' vocabulary and success in school more so than whether they are English learners. Schools cannot change the SES of their students, but teachers can provide all students, both native speakers and English learners from all socioeconomic levels, with a literacy-rich environment in order to narrow the achievement gap between all students.

Manyak and Bouchereau-Bauer (2009) outlined the following ways teachers and schools can help English learners acquire in-depth word knowledge:

1. Schools must implement vocabulary instruction that builds from one grade to the next.
2. Teachers must teach high-frequency words in phrases so students are introduced to the way they will encounter new words.
3. English learners also need to learn higher-level or academic English words.
4. English learners must learn strategies that help them infer word meanings.
5. English learners benefit when teachers use real objects, visual images, graphic organizers, and drama to teach new words and their definitions.
6. Teachers should read informational books and engage students in activities that will help them learn new words. Some strategies will be discussed in the Intervention section of this chapter.

Furthermore, in vocabulary instruction with English learners, effective teachers use many gestures and facial expressions, and they encourage students to ask questions so they can clarify the meaning (Vaughn et al., 2005). Like all students, English learners need repeated exposure to the words and benefit from acting out the words. For example, they can demonstrate with their body the difference in such verbs as *melt, shrink, stretch,* and *bounce.* (See the Total Physical Response activity in the Intervention section of this chapter.) When students are emotionally engaged, they are more likely to understand and remember the words.

As stated earlier, knowing a word is more than pronouncing it correctly. It implies the user knows its literal meaning, connotations, part or parts of speech, synonyms and antonyms, and multiple forms (e.g., *music* = noun; *musical* = adjective). In addition, English learners must understand how words relate to one another (the relationship between *helmet* and *football,* for example) and how words differ from one another (the difference between *chilly* and *cold*). They also must know how to use the words in oral and written expressions.

Another way to help English learners' build vocabulary is to examine the cognates—words with similar spellings and meanings across languages—that their language shares with English (Puccelli & Paez, 2007; Carlo et al., 2004). For example, when working with Spanish-speaking students, you can examine the overlap between the spelling and pronunciation of words such as *coincidencia* and *coincidence, industrioso* and *industrious,* and *afortunado* and *fortunate.* Write the English word on one side of a 3 × 5 index card and the Spanish word on the other. On the Spanish side have the student draw a picture to depict the word's meaning or write its meaning in Spanish. Over time the student builds a deck of personal vocabulary words. Bear et al. (2007) suggest teachers have students sort picture cards of a bank, some music notes, a park, a train, a computer, and a telephone—see the activity in the Intervention section of this chapter.

Accepting Students and Their Limited Vocabulary

When working with students who have underdeveloped oral language skills, accept their vocabularies and be patient as they learn new words. Also, work to develop their oral and aural language abilities and their reading skills simultaneously. Students with weak language experiences should not be isolated from their classmates but be included in small group and large group learning situations so they can hear words in meaningful contexts. However, students with underdeveloped language skills must have realistic expectations about their learning rate (Wilson & Cleland, 1989). Therefore, provide these students with special help in a risk-free environment that focuses on their strengths and successes and minimizes their weaknesses. This chapter includes strategies that can be used in these tutoring settings.

ASSESSMENT

Much vocabulary assessment is initiated by teachers closely observing students' oral language capabilities in conversation and in small groups and when reading new passages. When teachers detect students with limited oral vocabularies, they can choose from a number of assessment instruments.

Informal Assessment

You can frequently determine a pre-reader's weak vocabulary through conversation. Pre-readers with limited vocabulary often do not use specific terms in conversation. They may call any form of money—nickels, dimes, and quarters—just *money*. Sedans, SUVs, and dump trucks are all *cars*. If you detect a weak vocabulary in a student, perform the following assessment using pictures from magazines mounted on construction paper. The pictures might be of different types of vehicles (cars, pickups, semi-trucks, recreational vehicles, and so on), various types of workers (firefighter, police officer, farmer, nurse, doctor, dentist, and so on), or numerous kinds of animals or plants. Prepare a checklist of the objects and then either name the object and ask her to point to the word, or invite her to name all the different items in the category (e.g., *tulips, sunflowers, roses, daisies*) that she knows. If the student is weak in naming specific objects, arrange for a tutor to take time to "talk" with him about pictures in books or about more mounted magazine pictures with specific names of the items written on them. Later, he can go through this collection of pictures and practice reading the names.

Other informal vocabulary assessment instruments are the cloze test for older students, maze tests, zip tests, and synonym tests for younger students, and checklists based on state standards.

Cloze tests, discussed in Chapter 3, indicate whether students have the requisite vocabulary background for a particular passage. From this test, the teacher can then determine if students know specific terms related to the topic or if they merely know general ones. For example, in a passage about the jungle, the teacher might delete the word *panther*. The rest of the sentence indicates the animal is a panther and not a lion; however, the student's response is *lion*. The teacher concludes the student's vocabulary lacks the word *panther*.

In maze tests, also discussed in Chapter 3, students are given three possible answers to fill blanks in sentences. When teachers attempt to assess students' technical vocabulary on a topic, they make one of choices for the blank the general term and one choice the specific term. The third choice is not associated with the topic. Teachers can then determine if students are familiar with the specific term. For example, a passage might be about a farm with horses and include pictures of horses. The maze sentence reads "Mary wanted to ride the (animal, horse, zebra)." The synonym cloze test is another form of maze test. A synonym is added above the deleted word and three choices are provided for each deleted word. The synonym gives readers an excellent clue, but teachers can still assess students' technical vocabulary. The following is an example:

hungry
The basketball player was (ravenous, exotic, zealous) after the game.

The zip test, designed by Blachowicz and Fisher (2005a), can be used for assessment as well as instruction. In this test the words chosen for deletion are masked with blank labels. The readers attempt to supply the word and then "zip" off the label to receive immediate feedback. This permits teachers to assess students' vocabulary and students to continue reading with a sense of understanding.

Checklists based on state standards can help teachers assess students' vocabulary growth throughout the year. You can use this type of checklist at the beginning of the year to assess what they know and at the end of each quarter to assess which students need extra help with vocabulary. The partial checklist in Figure 7.4 is based on data from Ms. Lorenz's first-grade class. It appears from

***figure* 7.4** Vocabulary growth checklist for first grade based on Florida's state standards.

TEACHER Ms. Lorenz   Date 10–7

+ = always   x = sometimes   o = seldom/never

STANDARD	Amy	Leigh	Marisa	Lauren	Candace	Kas	Kirby	Katie	Carly	Faith	Summer	April	Hunter	Logan	Brett	Zachary	Allie	Andy
1. Identifies and sorts common words into conceptual categories.	+	+	X	X	X	X	X	X	X	+	X	+	+	+	+	X	+	+
2. Determines the correct meaning of words with multiple meanings in context.	+	+	X	X	+	+	+	X	X	+	X	+	+	+	+	X	+	+
3. Uses the meaning of individual words to predict meaning of unknown compound words.	X	O	X	X	O	O	O	O	X	O	O	X	+	+	+	X	X	X
4. Determines the meanings of unfamiliar words by using a beginning dictionary, illustrations, and digital tools.	+	+	X	X	X	+	+	X	X	X	X	X	+	+	+	X	+	+

Source: Florida Department of Education, www.floridastandards.org/Standards/FLStandardSearch.aspx

the checklist that after the first quarter most students in the class use their knowledge of individual words with compound words to predict meanings and that they have learned to use suffixes to determine word meanings. The complete checklist in Appendix C.33 is based on Florida's state standards for the first grade.

Formal Assessment

Most formal vocabulary assessments are multiple-choice tests. Some require students to match a word with its definition. Others ask students to choose the one word out of three that best fits the sentence (e.g., "John took the [escalator, generator, mobile] to the third floor in the department store.").

The Peabody Picture Vocabulary Test–Revised (Dunn & Dunn, 1997), discussed in Chapter 3, is an individual test that assesses students' receptive vocabulary. The test has four pictures on a page. The teacher says the word corresponding to one of the pictures and the student must point to the correct picture. The test begins with simple noun pictures that most students know—words such as *car, ball, money,* and *mail.* The test becomes progressively more difficult through the use of words such as *attire, incisor, convergence,* and *bumptious.* The Expressive Vocabulary Test (Williams, 1997) assesses students' expressive vocabulary. Figure 7.5 lists some other formal reading tests that have vocabulary subtests.

***figure* 7.5**

Formal reading tests with vocabulary subtests.

STANDARDIZED ACHIEVEMENT TESTS

Iowa Test of Basic Skills (Grades K–8)
Stanford Achievement Tests–Ninth Edition (Grades K–13)
Gates-Mac-Ginitie Reading Tests (Grades K–12)
Metropolitan Achievement Tests (Grades K–12)
Comprehensive Test of Basic Skills, U and V (Grades K–12)
California Achievement Tests (Grades K–9)

GROUP DIAGNOSTIC TESTS

Stanford Diagnostic Reading Test (Grades 1–12)
Iowa Silent Reading Test (Grade 6–Adult)
Gates-Mac-Ginitie Reading Tests (Grades 1–9)
Nelson-Denny Reading Tests (Grade 9–Adult)

INDIVIDUAL DIAGNOSTIC READING TESTS

Woodcock Reading Mastery Test (Grades 1–12)
Durrell Analysis of Reading Difficulties–Third Edition (Grades K–12)
Gates-McKillop-Horowitz Tests (Grades 1–12)

Intervention STRATEGIES & ACTIVITIES

Teachers need to use a wide variety of strategies to prevent students from becoming complacent about word study. It is also important that teachers enjoy word study and make it engaging for students (Baumann, Ware, & Carr-Edwards, 2007). As noted earlier in this chapter, learning words in an isolated context is rarely beneficial. The practice of giving students 10 vocabulary words on Monday and testing them on Friday often leads to frustration and no sense of personal ownership of the words. Words learned in the context of a social studies or science unit or from stories and poems are words students will use and remember. All of the strategies explained in this section should be associated with topics being studied.

VOCABULARY BOOKMARKS

GRADES 4–6 ACTIVITY

Draw students' attention to new vocabulary words as they listen to a teacher read and as they read independently. One strategy to increase upper elementary students' expressive and receptive vocabulary is to have them "collect" interesting words and make a bookmark with the words and definition (Baumann, Ware, & Carr-Edwards, 2007).

During shared reading and independent reading, invite students to note descriptive verbs such as *saunter, slithered,* and *lollygag.* Then have them create a bookmark that includes the information seen in Figure 7.6.

Alternately, during independent reading students can create a specific vocabulary bookmark that they keep with the book and refer back to as they continue reading. See Appendix D.16 for a template.

figure **7.6**

Sample vocabulary bookmark.

Name: Kaylee Date: January 15

VOCABULARY BOOKMARK

Title: Ruby Holler

Author: Sharon Creech

Word: Worrywart

Definition: Someone who worries unnecessarily about some small incident that might happen.

Sentence: "Listen to us," Sairy said. "A couple of worrywarts."

PREDICT-O-GRAM

GRADES 4–6

Predict-o-grams (Nicholson, 1998) encourage students to predict the meaning of words before reading a story or novel. Teachers present the unfamiliar words to the students; the students predict whether the words relate to a character, setting, or plot; and then they place them under the appropriate heading. For example, students might predict that the author uses the word *eccentric* to describe a character. When they encounter the word in the passage, they either confirm or correct its meaning.

FIGURATIVE SPEECH

GRADES 4–8 ACTIVITY

Authors spice up their narratives and poems with many types of figurative language. Introduce figurative language, give examples, write original examples, and encourage students to find all of the following in the text they are reading: synonyms, antonyms, homophones, alliteration, slang, similes, metaphors, hyperboles, idioms, oxymorons, homographs, acronyms, and personification. Create a word wall where students can add their original creations or ones they find in books. Christopher Paul Curtis' books *Bud, not Buddy* (1999) and *The Watsons Go to Birmingham – 1963* (1995); and Richard Peck's *A Long Way from Chicago* (1998) have many slang words and examples of figurative speech that pique students' interest. For example, Curtis describes Ma's reaction to the toady-frog on her lap this way: "[she] jumped straight out of the rocker. Yarn and needles and buttons and the toady-frog and the half-know sweater flewed all over the stoop like your guts do after you been hoop snake bit! Ma's knitting spectacles jumped partway up her forehead and she started hopping up and down and slapping at her skirt like it's afire" (p. 14). Also, in Curtis's *Elijah of Buxton* (2007) Mr. Leroy tells the title character: "You got to always keep in mind, Elijah, that I'm growned and you ain't. You got to always 'member that we gets 'long just fine but I ain't your friend. I cares 'bout you like you's my own boy, but you always got to give me my respect" (p. 100).

ACTIVITY

LANGUAGE EXPERIENCE APPROACH (LEA)

Language experience approach (LEA) can be traced back to the late 1930s (Lamoreaux & Lee, 1943). LEA was widely used in New Zealand in the late 1960s and 1970s (Ashton-Warner, 1963; Holdaway, 1979) as an effective technique to introduce children to their oral vocabulary in written form. In the 1970s Roach Van Allen (1976) used it as an approach to teaching literacy in the United States. Today, LEA is used in many different contexts. LEA views reading, writing, and the other language arts as interrelated, and it uses students' experiences as the basis for reading materials.

For example, after a student or a group of students and the teacher share an experience (a science experiment; a schoolyard safari focused on environmental noise or identifying types of trees, flowers, or insects), they discuss what they have seen. The teacher uses technical terms, and the student begins to use them as well. Then the teacher serves as a scribe as the student creates a word-web about the experience. Next, the student dictates sentences to the teacher about the experience. The teacher writes the text exactly as the student dictates it. He reads the passage back to the teacher. If the student thinks the sentence doesn't sound right, he may ask to change it so it is more grammatical. When used for vocabulary instruction, the purpose of the LEA is for a student to dictate a passage that includes words from his expanding vocabulary and then read it back to the teacher. This activity can also be done with a small group of students.

The following six ideas are variations of the LEA and can be done with individual struggling readers. The teacher acts as the scribe for each activity, while the student reads and rereads the passage.

Wordless Books — GRADES 1–8

Wordless books are useful for students with limited language experiences and students who are learning English (see Appendices A.5 and A.6 for title lists). Some wordless books, such as *Deep in the Forest* (1976) by Brinton Turkle and *The Bear and the Fly* (1976) by Paula Winter, are appropriate for younger children, while older children enjoy *Freefall* (1988), *Tuesday* (1991), *Sector 7* (1997), *Flotsam* (2006), and *The Three Pigs* (2001) all by David Wiesner. (Wiesner's books appeal to upper elementary and middle school students because of their more developed plots.) When using wordless books, talk through the book a number of times with the student. During these discussions, point out different aspects of the pictures while introducing new words to the student. Then have the student dictate the story to you. Using adhesive notes, post the text on each page. Finally, have the student read her story a number of times in order to learn the new vocabulary words in print.

Science Experiment — GRADES 1–3

After reading *The Empty Pot* (1990) by Demi, help your students plant lima beans in clear plastic cups. Each day have them dictate notes on their observations and discuss it with them. Use technical terms such as *soil* (instead of *dirt*), *seed* (instead of *bean*), *sprout, embryo,* and *root.* Each day the students should read back over their previous entries. Note: lima beans grow quickly so students with short attention spans see results fast.

Listening Walk — GRADES 1–3

After reading *The Listening Walk* (1961) by Paul Showers, take a walk on the playground or in the school hallways with your students and discuss what you hear. Strive for vivid descriptions so their vocabulary is enriched (e.g., *chatter* of voices, *squeaky* wheels, *screeching* tires, *whirling* water sprinklers, and so on). Put each idea into a sentence so the text becomes predictable. For example, in the school you can begin each sentence with "In the hallway, I hear ____________ and ____________." Out on the playground, the sentence pattern can be: "Outside my school, I hear ____________ and ____________."

Schoolyard Safari — GRADES 1–4

In the fall or spring when there are signs of changing seasons, take your students outside and write a book based on the following pattern. Encourage vivid use of adjectives (e.g., *decomposing* leaves, *howling* winds, *multicolored* hues, or *budding* blossoms).

On the playground, I see ____________, ____________, and ____________.
On the playground, I hear ____________, ____________, and ____________.
On the playground, I smell ____________, ____________, and ____________.
On the playground, I feel ____________, ____________, and ____________.

Total Physical Response — ENGLISH LEARNERS GRADES K–6

As the name suggests, Total Physical Response (TPR), developed by James Asher (1982), is a strategy that emphasizes using the body to "act out" the word or phrase so that it is easy for English learners to understand its meaning. If a student has limited English skills, it is important that the teacher use TPR to demonstrate the meaning of common commands the student must know. TPR steps include the following:

1. Pronounce the vocabulary word and then use actions to demonstrate its meaning.
2. Repeat the word and actions.
3. Invite the students to perform the action simultaneously with you.
4. Say the word or phrase without doing the action but have the group do it.
5. Say the word or phrase and ask an individual student to do the action.

Following is an example of a teacher using TPR with a small group of kindergarten English learners who have never cut with scissors. The key vocabulary concepts the teacher wants the students to grasp are *scissors, cut,* and *kite.*

Teacher: Take a scissors. (*Action: takes a scissors from the center of the table.*)

Teacher: Take a scissors. (*Action: repeats taking a scissors from the center of the table.*)

Teacher: Take a scissors. (*Action: teacher and students each take a scissors from the table.*)

Teacher: Take a scissors. (*Action: the students, without the teacher, take a scissors from the table.*)

Teacher: Juan, take a scissors. (*Action: Juan takes a scissors from the table.*)

Teacher: Take a scissors and paper and cut the paper. (Students already know the word *paper.*) (*Action: teacher takes scissors and paper and cuts a blank sheet of paper.*)

Teacher: Take a scissors and paper and cut the paper. (*Action: teacher takes scissors and paper and cuts the paper.*)

Teacher: Take a scissors and paper and cut the paper. (*Action: teacher and students take scissors and paper and cut the paper.*)

Teacher: Take a scissors and paper and cut the paper. (*Action: students, without the teacher, take scissors and paper and cut the paper.*)

Teacher: Marie, take a scissors and paper and cut the paper. (*Action: Marie takes a scissors and paper and cuts the paper.*)

Teacher: Take a scissors and a paper with a picture of a kite and cut out the kite. (*Action: teacher takes a scissors and a piece of paper with a picture of a kite and cuts out the kite.*)

Teacher: Take a scissors and a paper with a picture of a kite and cut out the kite. (*Action: teacher takes a scissors and another piece of paper with a picture of a kite and cuts out the kite.*)

Teacher: Take a scissors and a paper with a picture of a kite and cut out the kite. (*Action: teacher and group of students take a scissors and a piece of paper with a picture of a kite and cut out the kite.*)

Teacher: Take a scissors and a paper with a picture of a kite and cut out the kite. (*Action: group of students, without the teacher, take a scissors and another piece of paper with a picture of a kite and cut out the kite.*)

Teacher: Rose, take a scissors and a paper with a picture of a kite and cut out the kite. (*Action: Rose takes a scissors and a piece of paper with a picture of a kite and cuts out the kite.*)

Once the students know a number of commands or phrases, the teacher can assess their knowledge of the words by giving all of the words or phrases and asking the students to perform the task.

Categorizing

GRADES 2–8

Older students especially need practice in categorizing to connect known words to unknown words. This activity provides main headings of areas students have studied and asks them to name as many items as possible for each category. Figure 7.7 includes some examples.

figure 7.7 Categorizing.

Name as many items as possible for each category.

AIR TRANSPORTATION	WATER TRANSPORTATION	ROAD TRANSPORTATION	DOGS
airplane	ship	bike	Collie
hot air balloon	boat	car	Retriever
space ship	wave runner	truck	Labrador
helicopter	sail boat	RV	Poodle
	ocean liner		

POETS	AUTHORS	GENRE	MINERALS
Bruce Lansky	Avi	poetry	iron
Shel Silverstein	Gary Paulsen	science fiction	nickel
Brog Bagert	Anna Meyer	realistic fiction	zinc
	Richard Peck	historical fiction	copper
	Sharon Creech	drama	
	Lois Lowry	biography	
	Linda Sue Parks	autobiography	

VEGETABLES	FRUITS	CARBOHYDRATES
carrot	apple	bread
potato	orange	rice
squash	banana	pasta
pea	peach	cereal
corn	pear	

POSSIBLE SENTENCES

GRADES 2–8 ACTIVITY

This activity, designed by Moore and Moore (1986), is a strategy to preview new words from a story, concept book, or informational text.

1. Explain six or seven new words to the students.
2. Give them an additional six or seven words they already know.
3. Ask them to write sentences using two or more of the words from the two lists in each sentence.
4. After they read the passage you have been previewing, have them decide which of their sentences are "true" in regard to word usage.
5. Ask them to change the sentences so all information is correct.

Figure 7.8 shows an example of words and sentences appropriate for Tomie dePaola's *Clouds* (1984). Both Nathaniel and Anton are applying what they know about clouds, and both will need to modify their sentences after they read the book.

figure **7.8** Possible sentences based on new vocabulary.

NEW VOCABULARY WORDS	KNOWN WORDS
cumulus	clouds
stratus	rain
cirrus	weather
nimbostratus	thunder

Nathaniel's sentences: We can tell what kind of weather is coming by looking at the clouds. Cumulus and stratus clouds bring us rain. Cirrus and nimbostratus clouds bring us thunder and storms.

Anton's sentences: Some clouds do not bring bad weather, but other clouds do bring us bad weather. Cumulus clouds are just white, pretty clouds that come on sunny days. Stratus clouds look like rib cages and bring us rain. Cirrus and nimbostratus clouds are black clouds that bring us thunder and hurricanes.

ANALOGIES

GRADES 3–8 ACTIVITY

Standardized tests often assess students' vocabulary through analogies; therefore, it is advantageous to introduce struggling readers to analogies they will encounter in these tests. Analogies are written as *A* : *B* :: *C* : *D* (say, "A is to B as C is to D"). Analogies display the ways that words are related. Following are six relationships that elementary students are asked to complete on standardized tests:

1. Part to whole: *Leaf* is to *tree* as *hand* is to *human.*
2. Synonym: *Black* is to *raven* as *red* is to *crimson.*
3. Antonym: *Black* is to *white* as *up* is to *down.*
4. Action: *Bird* is to *fly* as *fish* is to *swim.*
5. Cause and effect: *Hurricane* is to *wind* as *blizzard* is to *snow.*
6. Geography: *London* is to *England* as *Washington, D.C.* is to the *United States.*

Once students are familiar with analogies, they can write their own. Writing analogies helps students understand the words at a deeper level. Students must be able to justify each analogy by explaining the relevant relationship. The following are examples of analogies written by fourth graders who were studying analogies before they took standardized tests. The teacher knew that if students could write their own, they would better understand how to complete them on the test.

Cloud is to sky as dew is to ______ (grass or earth).

Seed is to apple as pit is to ______ (cherry, peach, apricot).

Barn is to cow as ______ is to bird (nest).

This next set would be appropriate as samples to use with middle school students.

Fragrance is to stench as sour is to _________(sweet).

Plankton is to microscopic as redwood is to _________(gigantic).

Football is to touchdown as hockey is to ________(goal).

ACTIVITY **ORIGIN OF WORDS** GRADES 3–8

Exploring the origin of words with struggling readers interests them in new vocabulary, especially if you choose familiar words with interesting origins. Students and teachers may find it fascinating that candy is named after the 17th-century Prince Charles de Conde (pronounced con-DAY), who loved sugary treats. His chef glazed bits of meats and vegetables with egg whites, sugar, and nuts so the young prince would eat the "healthy" foods. Older struggling readers may enjoy learning how the bikini swimsuit got its name, and younger children may enjoy learning how hamburgers and sandwiches got their names. *Guppies in Tuxedos: Funny Eponyms* (1988) by Marvin Terban explains the origins of many words that are familiar to all students.

Often schools are named after national or state heroes. Exploring the background of these heroes can also be fun. For instance, many schools named after heroes in the Oklahoma City area have some interesting stories–Angie Debo Elementary, Cooper Middle School, Gene Autry Elementary, Sequoyah Middle School, and Cheyenne Middle School. Encourage students to learn about local heroines or heroes and create books about them. You might also encourage them to research the origins of words that interest them and write their own booklets. "Exploring the origin of words with students helps them develop indelible memories as they link specific words with stories of the words' origin" (Rasinski & Padak, 2003, p. 147).

ACTIVITY **CROSSWORD PUZZLE** GRADES 2–8

Many students enjoy doing and making crossword puzzles. Crossword puzzles most often focus on definitions or synonyms; however, you can construct them using antonyms. The best crossword puzzles are those based on words found in books that students have read. Marguerite Lewis (1986) collected a book of crossword puzzles based on Caldecott winners. Each puzzle is shaped like the main topic of the book. For example, the puzzle for *Tuesday* (1991) by David Wiesner is in the shape of a frog.

Many online resources allow you to create crossword puzzles easily. To create a simple puzzle by hand, select the words that are important for the reader to remember, identify shared letters among them, and assemble them in the form of a puzzle. Using large-ruled graph paper makes this task easier. Then assign numbers to the blanks and write the definitions based on the numbers in the puzzle. See Figure 7.9 for a completed crossword puzzle using the language terms from Figure 7.2 (created using PuzzleMaker.com). This puzzle is for fifth-grade students.

figure **7.9** Crossword puzzle based on literary terms.

ACROSS

1. Words associated with particular geographic regions.
5. New words that enter our vocabulary through extensive usage or for new inventions.
8. A more pleasant sounding word used in place of a word with negative connotations.
10. Words that have opposite meanings.

DOWN

2. Two contradictory words or ideas used together in a word or phrase.
3. Words that mean the same or nearly the same.
4. New words formed by combining two existing words and omitting some of the letters.
6. Words that sound like their meaning.
7. Word formed from the initial letters of other words.
9. Humorous expressions that highlight multiple meanings of a word or two words that sound alike.

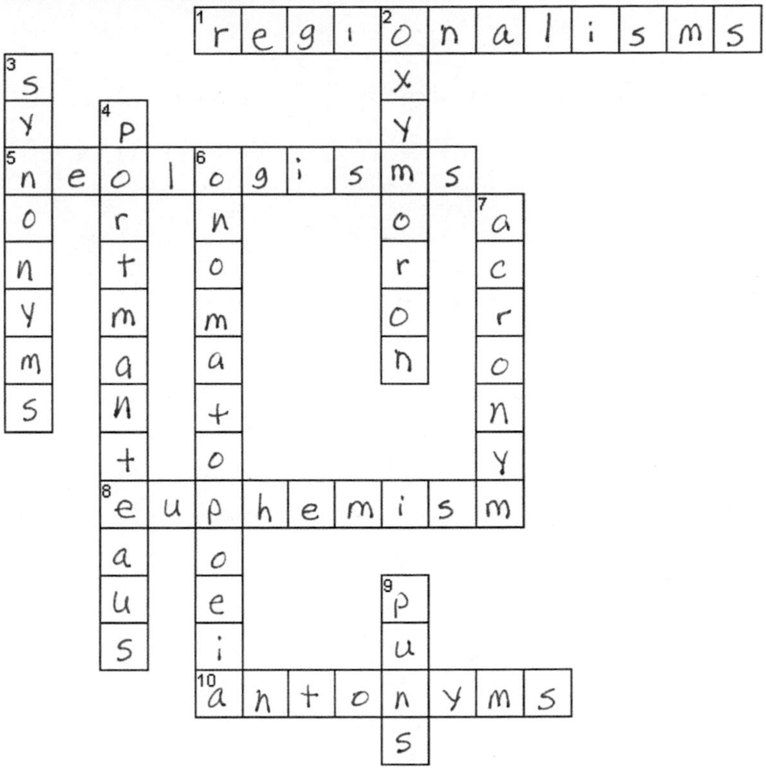

SYNONYM/DEFINITION CONCENTRATION — GRADES 2–8 — ACTIVITY

For this activity first read and discuss with students a story or informational book that includes new vocabulary. The purpose of this version of Concentration is to have students match the word with its definition or its synonym.

1. During the reading, explain any vocabulary word that students do not understand.
2. After reading the book, choose 10 to 15 important words from the text and write them on square cards.
3. Create an equal number of cards with a synonym or concise definition of each word.
4. Turn all 20 to 30 cards face down.
5. Have a student turn over the cards one by one and match the words with the correct synonym or definition.

This activity can be used to prepare students for a test over a unit or chapter. Two or three students can engage in this activity, or a teacher or tutor can watch and encourage a student as she matches the terms. Mr. Watts designed the cards in Figure 7.10 as a way for his sixth-grade students to recall the terms they learned during their unit on mythology.

figure 7.10 Sample synonym/definition Concentration cards.

Achilles	Amazon	Agamemnon	Atlas	Cassandra	Electra
Helen of Troy	Hercules	Jason	Muses	Odysseus	Paris
Pegasus	Penelope	Phoenix	Priam	Prometheus	Saturn
Greek warrior who could be killed only by a wound to the heel.	Female Greek warriors who were powerfully built and ferocious.	Greek king who led his men in the Trojan War.	Giant who could hold earth and sky on his shoulders.	Prophet in Troy whom no one believed.	Agamemnon's daughter, who helped kill her mother.
Daughter of Zeus and Leda.	Son of Zeus and Alcmene, who showed his strength doing the impossible.	Greek hero who found the golden fleece of a magical ram.	Nine daughters of Zeus and Mnemosyne, each representing a different art.	Greek, also called Ulysses.	He killed Achilles with an arrow.
Winged horse that flew above the earth.	Wife of Odysseus; symbol of fidelity.	Bird that could set itself on fire.	King of Troy.	Giant who stole fire from gods and gave it to humans.	Father of Jupiter.

ACTIVITY **COGNATE PICTURE CARDS (Adapted from Bear et al., 2007)** **GRADES 1–5**

As stated previously, one way to help build English learners' vocabulary is to have them examine cognates their languages share with English. The following activity uses picture cards of several common cognates in various languages including Spanish, German, Italian, French, Norwegian, and Dutch.

1. Use the picture and cognate cards for a bank, some musical notes, a park, a train, a computer, and a telephone, found in Appendix D.17.

2. Have the students sort the cards, placing the cognates together with the appropriate picture card. Because the words are similar in spelling, students should be able to correctly match the words and pictures.
3. Help students practice pronouncing the various words.
4. Ask them what they notice about the words and discuss how cognates can help them as they learn new languages.
5. Have them perform an Internet search to hunt for the cognates for bank, music, park, train, computer, and telephone in other languages. They may also search for other cognates, such as coincidence, industrious, and fortunate.

MULTIPLE MEANING RACETRACK — GRADES 2–5 — ACTIVITY

Multiple Meaning Racetrack highlights the multiple meanings of commonly used words. The goal is for struggling readers to provide as many definitions as possible for a set of words chosen by the teacher.

1. Duplicate the racetrack in Appendix D.18 on stock card paper and laminate it.
2. Make a list of words that have multiple meanings and have been introduced to the students in various texts. Your list might include:

run	box	wind	chair	grate
bow	tire	hanger	frog	wing
exhaust	ring	minute		

3. Write the words on index cards.
4. Have players draw cards from the deck and give as many definitions as possible. Players move their game pieces one space for each correct definition. If a player gives an incorrect definition, he must move one space backward.
5. As on any racetrack, drivers may encounter other obstacles!

HINK PINKS — GRADES 2–8 — ACTIVITY

Riddles increase students' creative thinking. Hink pinks are word riddles that have two-word answers that rhyme. The two words each have one syllable. The following are hink pinks:

What is an unhappy father called? *A sad dad.*

What did the fish say to the bait? *Squirm worm.*

What is a sneaky insect called? *A sly fly.*

Hinky pinkies are like hink pinks, but the answers are two-syllable words. Here are some examples:

What is messy writing? *A sloppy copy.*

What is a thicker arachnid? *A wider spider.*

What do you call a carpenter? *A hammer slammer.*

Hiniky pinikies have answers with three syllables. Examples are:

What do you call a soft, deluxe place of execution? *Velveteen guillotine.*

What do you call an evil clergyman? *Sinister minister.*

By folding an index card in half, students can create these riddles for classmates. They write the question on the top fold with the answer inside. Writing hink pinks encourages students to think of rhyming words and to understand syllables.

Some middle school students may benefit from language play involving hink pinks, especially if they struggle with spelling. Recognizing that words that end in the same sound (e.g., *clown* and *brown*) may have the same spelling can assist them with spelling words. When reading hink pinks they will readily recognize that other times words with the same ending sounds are not spelled the same. Older students who have trouble with rhyming may enjoy reading and later writing hink pinks. Give samples of hink pinks and encourage students to write and post them on a classroom hink pink poster.

Another activity with hink pinks involves the poem "Home Poem Or, the Sad Dog Song" by J. Patrick. The teacher reads the beginning of each line and the student provides the rhyming word after the colon. Students do not need to read the poem, only to listen and give the rhyming words. The entire poem is printed in Paul Janeczki's *A Foot in the Mouth: Poems to Speak, Sing, and Shout* (2009). Three sample lines from the poem follow:

Home of the frog: *log.*
Home of the mole: *hole.*
Home of the ants: *pants.*

ACTIVITY **LEXICAL AND STRUCTURE RIDDLES** GRADES 5–8

Zipke (2008) states the importance of older students understanding that words and word phrases can have more than one meaning. Riddles manipulate language by relying on multiple meanings of words, metaphors, and idioms.

Zipke designs two kinds of riddles with humorous answers. The first, lexical riddles, are those in which one word of the answer is a homonym. For example, "Why are fish so smart? Because they swim in schools" (p. 131). The second type is the structural riddle, in which the reader must decipher the non-preferred meaning in the question. For example, "How do you make a hot dog stand? You take away its chair" (p. 131). For English learners and struggling readers, you can draw a picture of a person attempting to make a hot dog stand upright to make sure students understand the riddle's humor.

To have students write their own riddles, Zipke (2008) gives the following steps. She suggests that teachers walk through the steps with a small group of students first to monitor their comprehension of the concept.

1. Collect all words associated with a topic that interests students (e.g., baseball).
2. Have students generate a list of words associated with baseball (e.g., bats, ball, diamond, coach).
3. Instruct students to look for homonyms in the list (e.g., *bats* can be a stick or a flying creature; *diamond* can be a field on which baseball is played or a precious gem).
4. Have the group write a riddle for each homonym: Write a question that is about one meaning of the word, and an answer that is about the other meaning of the same word. (E.g., "Why do spiders like baseball? They are good at catching flies.")

After students understand the steps, invite the students to write and share riddles based on vocabulary in their content area subjects.

ACTIVITY **WORD EXPERT CARDS** GRADES 6–8

Word Expert Cards (Richek, 2005) encourage students to become an expert in a word and then to teach the word to peers. Before reading a story, novel, or content area passage, teachers choose new key words and assign one or two words to each student. The student looks up each word's definition, states it in his own words, finds synonyms and antonyms, and uses the word in a sentence. After you approve their answers, give each student a 4 × 6 index card and instruct them to fold it in half so it resembles a booklet. On the cover they write the word in large print and illustrate it. Inside they write the definition, synonym, antonym, and the sentence. On the back they write their name and the title of the novel, story, or content area passage. Students then teach their words to classmates. An effective method is to form groups of three with each taking turns teaching her word. Then they rotate to different groups until everyone has taught his or her word to the entire class. Or you can have students create a slideshow presentation with a voiceover of their word booklets.

COLLABORATIVE ACTIVITIES — GRADES 6–8 ENGLISH LEARNERS — ACTIVITY

Middle school English learners need less memorizing of academic (content area) word lists and more meaningful, engaging learning experiences (Townsend, 2009). Middle school students are social and enjoy being with friends; capitalize on this preference by choosing collaborative activities. Picture Puzzlers and the following five activities are especially good for middle school English learners. To effectively monitor students' development, divide them into small groups.

For Picture Puzzlers (Townsend, 2009), teachers select pictures that represent abstract terms. For example, the word *function* is an abstract term. Teachers find pictures of objects that have a function, such as a computer, desk, notebook, and screwdriver. The small group discusses the function of each of the pictures. Then students add the word to their personalized dictionary using their own words and illustrating it with a drawing.

MUSIC PUZZLERS — GRADES 6–8 ENGLISH LEARNERS — ACTIVITY

To play Music Puzzlers (Townsend, 2009), teachers select several favorite songs of the group of students to discuss a word found in multiple disciplines. For example, in many classes students are asked to interpret, compare, or contrast different topics. For the word *interpret,* students interpret the song; for the word *contrast,* students explain how the song is different from another song; and for *compare,* they compare the song to another song.

MATCHING GAME — GRADES 6–8 ENGLISH LEARNERS — ACTIVITY

In the Matching Game (Townsend, 2009), teachers put selected words on individual 2 × 3 cards. The definitions of the words are written on a second set of cards, and a sentence with a blank where a word fits is placed on a third set of cards. For example:

> *Word:* Octagon
>
> *Definition:* An octagon is a shape that has eight sides and eight angles.
>
> *Sentence:* A stop sign is in the shape of a(n) ______________.

Give some students a word card, some a definition card, and some a sentence card. The goal is for students to find the matches for their card. Then the trio performs a skit to dramatize their word, and the rest of the class guesses the word. Other times the small group can draw a picture instead of acting out the word. For variation, the game can be played in silence, or a word card can be taped to a student's back and she must determine what it is by asking questions of the others in the group. With so many possible variations, students will not become tired of playing the "same old game again."

ACTIVITY **TWO CUBE GAME** **GRADES 6–8 ENGLISH LEARNERS**

When playing the Two Cube game (Townsend, 2009), create two cubes using the template in Appendix D.6. Tape target words on each side of one of the cubes, and instructions on each side of the other cube, such as "draw a picture," "write a sentence," "act it out," and so on. A small group of students rolls the cubes and performs the action while the class tries to decipher the word.

ACTIVITY **PICTIONADES** **GRADES 6–8 ENGLISH LEARNERS**

Pictionades (Townsend, 2009) is a combination of Pictionary and Charades. Students are divided into two teams. A student from team A draws a word card from a pile. The student acts out the word and draws a picture of it so his team can guess the word in one minute or less. Then one student from team B draws a word card and acts it out and draws a picture for her team. The team that guesses the most words wins the game. You can also play the game without making it a competition.

ACTIVITY **ACTION JEOPARDY** **GRADES 6–8 ENGLISH LEARNERS**

In Action Jeopardy (Townsend, 2009), set up a game board, which can be a large poster board divided into five columns and four or five rows. Label the columns with the following categories: definition, synonym, antonym, sentences, and context. In each row write a definition, a synonym, an antonym, a sentence with a blank that needs to be filled in with the focused word, and the topic in which the word would be found. Each row becomes more difficult and the points increase, just like on the Jeopardy TV game show. Students work in three teams as they choose the answer and state the question in one minute or less. Use words students need to learn for their content areas. The following websites offer free game boards to simplify the set-up: http://quizboxes.com, http://jc-schools.net/tutorials/PPT-games, and http://warp.byu.edu/jeopardy. Some of these sites enable you to post the game board on an interactive whiteboard, and some allow you to include images or MP3 files in the game.

VOCABULARY BUILDING AND TECHNOLOGY

Many ebooks provide CD-ROMS featuring verbal word pronunciations and definitions as students read along. Acha (2009) conducted research in which second-language third and fourth graders read a story from a computer program in which there were twelve new concrete nouns presented in three ways: verbal annotation, visual annotation, or verbal and visual annotation. Results on both the immediate post-test and the delayed post-test given two weeks later indicated that students had better recall when words were given only in verbal annotation. Acha concluded that processing multiple visual cues simultaneously may be an overload on students' cognitive abilities.

Discis Knowledge Research's electronic books can be set to read to the student or the voice can be turned off while the student reads the text from the screen. When reading the texts by themselves, students can click once for the pronunciation of an unknown word and twice for its definition. The program keeps track of these words, and the list can later be used for review. The Living Books series by Broderbund (see Appendix A.12) highlights the text as the computer "reads" the book. When readers click on various objects in the picture, the objects become animated. The animation is intended to aid students in learning the meanings of unfamiliar words. Many of the ebooks also include games that aid vocabulary building, spelling, writing, and comprehension. The games make learning enjoyable for students.

A helpful website for building English learners' vocabulary is www.languageguide.org/english/. It features categories (e.g., human body, foods, family, time) with many familiar words in each. The student places the cursor over the image and receives the spelling and pronunciation of the word. This is a good program to use at a center so English learners can practice their pronunciation and build their vocabulary of common words.

Another great site for customizing games is www.point4teachers.com. You can create Jeopardy games on an interactive whiteboard or on PowerPoint. The original music from the TV game accompanies the SMARTBoard version.

The site www.discoveryeducation.com/freepuzzlemaker will help you create crossword puzzles based on any unit of study.

CONCLUDING THOUGHTS

Research indicates that readers' vocabulary knowledge is strongly correlated with their reading comprehension, which makes assessing and facilitating students' vocabulary growth essential.

Students build their vocabulary through life experiences, vicarious experiences, and explicit instruction. Many students' vocabularies are weak because they lack life experiences and vicarious experiences, which leaves them without the vocabulary necessary to comprehend grade-level texts. Work with these students in a meaningful context, focusing on building their vocabularies. Discuss topics using content-specific terms, have students pronounce the words correctly, discuss the definitions, and use the new words until they have ownership of them. Remember that many students love to play games with peers; therefore, turning vocabulary building into a game makes learning fun.

Reflective Learning — VOCABULARY BUILDING

Scenario. Mr. Stone teaches sixth-grade science in an urban Iowa school. Each year, many of his students struggle with the assigned textbook because of their limited vocabularies. It is August and he has just received his four class lists for the year. Because he considers himself a reading teacher as well as a science teacher, he checks his new students' scores for the reading and vocabulary subtests on the Iowa Basic Skills Test. He discovers a wide range of scores on the reading comprehension subtest, but most scores on the vocabulary subtest are below grade level. Only 5 percent of the students have scored at or above grade level on the vocabulary subtest.

QUESTIONS

1. Mr. Stone understands that his students' vocabulary skills are low. What large group activities would be appropriate to motivate them to learn the words necessary to comprehend the science concepts?
2. What small group activities would you suggest Mr. Stone use, and how would you manage the classroom so all groups remain engaged during the entire period?
3. What individual activities would you suggest Mr. Stone use to engage students to build their vocabulary?

CHAPTER EIGHT

COMPREHENSION OF NARRATIVE TEXT

Only the curious will learn and only the resolute overcome obstacles to learning.

EUGENE S. WILSON

scenario

Mr. Bradley has been teaching eighth-grade language arts for four years. His students score higher than the other eighth graders in his district on the state criterion-referenced reading test. However, he is not as concerned about their state test scores as much as he is that his students are content to read stories and novels without empathizing with the plight of the characters. For example, when discussing *Elijah of Buxton* (Curtis, 2007), students focus on the slang and humor rather than on the plight of the African Americans seeking refuge in Canada during the time of slavery. For his students that was a long time ago, far removed from their lives full of technology, the Internet, social networking, cell phones, and texting. His goal for the coming year is to raise his students' awareness of injustices found in the United States today and throughout our history as they read stories and novels.

During the summer as he is catching up with his journal reading, he comes across the article "Critical Literacy as Comprehension: Expanding Reader Response" (McLaughlin & DeVoogd, 2004) in a back issue of the *Journal of Adolescent and Adult Literacy.* The article piques his interest, and he browses through the International Reading Association's Reading Online articles on the same subject. He reads "Song lyrics as text to develop critical literacies" (Lloyd, 2003). Mr. Bradley realizes he can develop his students' critical literacies by having them examine the author's perspective in a passage and consider whose voice is silenced. He decides to begin with song lyrics. From all the iPods in his students' ears, he assumes they love music. He personally is bothered by the middle school culture in which students strive to out-dress one another, coming to school with many new outfits and bragging about how inexpensive they are. He is aware that many of these clothes are made in foreign countries, where child labor laws are not in effect. As a fan of Ken Medema's songs, which highlight social injustice in today's society, Mr. Bradley decides to share with his students Medema's "Storm the Gate."

He plays the song while the students read along with the lyrics. When it is over he asks them to read the last verse again:

> "In a sweat shop in the city
> The pregnant woman cries.
> She can't keep up the pace anymore,
> No matter how hard she tries.
> And my daughter buys those discount clothes
> So cheap she won't think twice." (Medema, 1997)

Then he asks if they know where their clothes were made. They check each other's labels in their shirts and are surprised to find that most were made in foreign countries. He then asks if they know what sweatshops are. A few students have some idea, but they are not exactly sure. For homework he has the class search online to find out more about sweatshops.

The next day students come to class with many different articles describing the terrible working conditions and low wages found in these shops. The students are appalled. Without any prompting from Mr. Bradley, they decide to write a class letter to the two discount department stores from which most of their clothes were purchased. They decide to pair up in order to peer critique the letters before sending them. In the letters they share the information they have found online and ask the manager if he can get the CEO of the company to consider purchasing clothes from places other than foreign sweatshops. Mr. Bradley is surprised at the students' reactions. He is especially amazed at how struggling readers became excited about finding online information about sweatshops and child-labor laws. Even though the reading level for some of the articles was high, his students worked hard to understand them so they could contribute to the class discussion and add their comments to the letters.

Mr. Bradley wants his students to understand that prior to the passing of child labor laws in the United States, working conditions in U.S. factories were also deplorable. He invites students who want to learn more about this to read Katherine Paterson's *Lyddie* (1991), a young adult novel about one young woman's experience working in a factory in the 19th century.

guiding questions

As you read this chapter, consider the following questions:

1. How would you define critical literacy?
2. What reading comprehension strategies were students asked to use in Mr. Bradley's critical literacy lesson?
3. What other comprehension strategies might Mr. Bradley have included in the lesson?
4. What guiding questions might Mr. Bradley give to students before they begin reading the novel *Lyddie?*
5. What strategies and activities could Mr. Bradley use as a follow-up to his students reading the novel?
6. In what ways could he motivate students to take action after reading the novel?

INTRODUCTION

Comprehension is the main purpose of reading, yet many struggling readers fail to comprehend what they read. Comprehension is an active process that requires complex, higher-level thinking skills, and in the case of narrative text, it "is based on the ability to encode and retrieve the basic building blocks (propositions) of sentences and relate the meaning within them to scenes and stories from a text" (Rose, Parks, Androes, & McMahon, 2000, p. 4). Research indicates that readers use the following strategies to comprehend text: draw inferences, predict, self-monitor, retell and summarize, draw conclusions (Fortenberry & Fowler, 2006/2007), activate prior knowledge, use knowledge of text structures (Mills, 2009), and visualize before, during, and after reading (RAND Reading Study Group, 2002; Guerrero, 2003; Sadoski & Paivio, 2001). Readers also need to generate their own questions such as "What is my opinion?" or "Does this support my prior knowledge?" Soalt (2005). To comprehend text on a deep level, they need to have the background knowledge (RAND Reading Study Group, 2002), adequate vocabulary (McKeown & Beck, 2004; RAND Reading Study Group, 2002), and motivation (Guthrie, 2003).

As Mr. Bradley already knows, comprehending a text goes beyond the literal level; comprehension includes being able to read critically. In order to comprehend text at a critical level, students need to have an appropriate vocabulary, be able to visualize times and places beyond their present world, and consider the author's perspective and the voices of those not represented in a story. To help students comprehend at this level, teachers, especially in primary grades, must read and discuss stories with their students that are conceptually challenging, so they can take "an active stance toward constructing meaning" (Beck & McKeown, 2001, p. 10). Most students can do this in a large or small group setting and learn from both activities. Others, however, require a one-on-one setting in which such stories are read to them. These may be students who have few opportunities at home to read and discuss stories with adults, so they may be lacking a narrative vocabulary or a sense of story grammar. Other students, including many who have attention deficit disorder (ADD) or attention deficit hyperactivity disorder (ADHD), have a difficult time focusing in a large group. Therefore, teachers should scaffold struggling students as they begin to decode and comprehend text. Like all readers, struggling readers need to experience success as they engage with texts (Brown, 1999/2000).

For students to develop reading comprehension skills, they need long periods of time for independent reading of texts that interest them and are on their reading level (Ivey & Fisher, 2005). Teachers of all grades should help students find their reading level and provide a wide range of narrative texts. Effective teachers encourage readers to be adventurous and try different genres, but students should always be permitted to read texts of their choice in independent reading time.

Upper elementary teachers will focus on strategies, such as making inferences, visualizing, and setting a purpose for reading, to help students become more proficient. However, they should never teach skills in isolation (Ellery, 2005) because even older students cannot transfer strategies taught in isolation to reading full texts (Rhodes, 2002).

As noted earlier, comprehension has many elements and is intertwined with other reading knowledge and skills—decoding, vocabulary, fluency, prior knowledge, and so on. This chapter discusses the complex process of reading comprehension by examining (1) the relationship of comprehension to other reading skills, (2) reading comprehension strategies, (3) critical literacies, (4) the characteristics of poor versus good comprehenders, (5) informal and formal diagnostic and assessment instruments, (6) English learners and narrative text, and (7) intervention strategies and activities to aid and develop comprehension. The focus of this chapter will be primarily on the skills and strategies needed to comprehend narrative text, while Chapter 9 focuses on skills and strategies that are unique to comprehending informational text. Both types of text require many of the same skills, and those skills are discussed in this chapter.

READING SKILLS

Comprehension of narrative text is complex, just like a car is complex. Readers require fundamental skills to comprehend text, just like a car requires fundamental parts in order to move down a road. A car requires four tires, an engine, a steering wheel, and a chassis; readers need decoding skills, fluency skills, and an adequate vocabulary.

Decoding

Recognizing familiar words automatically and decoding unknown words quickly are essential skills for comprehending text (Brown, 1999/2000; Richek, Caldwell, Jennings, & Lerner, 2006; Vaughn et al., 2000). If students focus all their energy and concentration on decoding, they have no energy left for comprehending. A reader's decoding ability helps him pronounce terms automatically that may be part of his aural vocabulary. When he hears himself say these words, he understands them. Struggling readers who cannot effectively decode do not have the benefit of hearing the word. Also, because decoding a word takes so long, struggling readers become discouraged by the length of time it takes to read each assigned passage.

Decoding skills include the knowledge of letter–sound relationships, consonant blends, consonant digraphs, vowel digraphs, and diphthongs. Equally important is the ability to analyze words, because many technical terms have multiple syllables. Readers who can easily break words into syllables and who know the meanings of basic prefixes, suffixes, and root words read faster and become less discouraged than readers who lack these skills. For example, the word *transferable* may be a long word for a third-grade reader. However, if she can readily recognize the prefix (*trans*) and the suffix (*able*) and identify the meanings of each part, she can easily figure out the meaning of the entire word.

Chapter 6 discusses in detail how readers learn to recognize and decode words. That chapter also provides strategies to help struggling readers with decoding.

Fluency

Fluency implies a reader can accurately and automatically recognize a large bank of words; read at an appropriate rate, which is about 75 words per minute with 98 percent accuracy (Rasinski & Padak, 2003); and read with expression. However, students with these traits do not necessarily comprehend everything they read (DeKonty-Applegate, Applegate, & Modla, 2009). Some studies show that growth in fluency correlates with growth in comprehension (Flood, Lapp, & Fisher, 2005; White & Swanson, 2007; Griffith & Rasinski, 2004); however, in most of these studies comprehension was measured by standardized multiple-choice literal questions (Keehn, 2003; O'Connor, White, & Swanson, 2007) or on retellings (Keehn, 2003). As discussed earlier, we know that comprehension goes beyond the literal level. Chapter 10 discusses the components of fluency at length.

Vocabulary

A large listening vocabulary is necessary for comprehension (Beck & McKeown, 2001; Oster, 2001; Vaughn et al., 2000). When students attempt to decode written words already in their listening vocabulary, they recognize and grasp their meanings more quickly (Beck & McKeown, 2001). When readers attempt to decode words that are not in their listening vocabulary, they may not even know if they are words. One way to increase a struggling reader's vocabulary is to discuss the topic of a story before reading it, using the new words the reader will encounter. When introducing each new word, write it on the board and have students say it so they are more likely to recognize the word in text (Beck & McKeown, 2001). Unknown words are frequently important to the meaning of a story. Stop and discuss unknown words when reading aloud in order for children to understand words in context. For example, in *The Old Woman Who Lived in a Vinegar Bottle* (1995) by Margaret MacDonald, two words important to the story's meaning are *content* and *complaining*. Make sure students understand these words by providing examples of each, because examples are easier to understand than abstract definitions. Chapter 7 discusses strategies for building struggling readers' vocabularies.

READING COMPREHENSION STRATEGIES

Reading comprehension requires many strategies. A reader needs all of these strategies and each strategy depends on the others; all must work concurrently for the reader to attain comprehension. These components are listed in Figure 8.1.

Before Reading Strategies

Comprehension strategies that come into play before reading include predicting and setting a purpose.

Predicting

Predicting is a higher-level thinking skill that requires readers to perform many different tasks simultaneously. Students who predict draw on background knowledge, supply details, and then try to determine whether their prediction was correct. Good readers make predictions automatically, while struggling readers often make no attempt to predict what will happen next in the story (Hurst, 2000; Santoro, Chard, Howard, & Baker, 2008; Oster, 2001). Introduce a new text to students by previewing the title, author, and illustrator to decide if they have read texts with similar topics or by the same author or illustrator. For example, a teacher who has shared Kevin Henkes' *Lily's Purple Plastic Purse* (1996) and *Julius: The Baby of the World* (1995) shows the students *Lily's Big Day* (2006) and asks them what they think Lily will do in this book. One way to encourage struggling readers to predict is to have them look at the cover illustration (without reading the title) and ask what they think the story is about. Predictions may include details that are not in the story, which later gives students an opportunity to evaluate and adjust their predictions with the benefit of hindsight. For example, the teacher is about to read *The Old Woman Who Lived in a Vinegar Bottle,* a book in which a fairy grants the old lady of the title her wish for a bigger house each time the fairy visits her, the conversation may go as follows:

figure **8.1** Strategies for comprehension.

- Finding main ideas/story elements
- Predicting
- Making inferences
- Setting a purpose
- Self-monitoring
- Generating visual images
- Drawing conclusions
- Summarizing
- Retelling
- Comparing and contrasting
- Interrelating ideas
- Connecting appropriate background knowledge to new information
- Understanding characters' motives
- Sequencing events
- Self-questioning
- Analyzing text for story elements—character, plot, setting, theme, style, point of view
- Synthesizing
- Retaining information from one reading to the next
- Elaborating author's intent
- Understanding purpose

Sources: Doty, Popplewell, & Byers, (2001); Dowhower (1999); Duffy-Hester, (1999); Manning (2001); NEA Today (2001); Rose, Parks, Androes, and McMahon (2000); Vaughn et al. (2000).

(Note: the cover of the book features an elderly woman with white hair pulled back in a bun, looking into a large bottle. Also on the cover are a small fairy and a chicken.)

Teacher: Whom do you think this story is about?

Student: An old lady, a fairy, and a chicken.

Teacher: Why do you think the lady is old? (Nudge the student to make inferences.)

Student: Because her hair is white and she has it pulled back like the old lady who lives in my building.

Teacher: Do you think she is happy?

Student: No.

Teacher: Why not?

Student: Because I think she wants a chicken.

Teacher: Do you think she will get a chicken?

Student: Yes, I think the fairy will give her one.

Teacher: Let's see if you are correct. The title of the book is *The Old Woman Who Lived in a Vinegar Bottle.*

Student: See! I was right! She is an old lady. But why would she want to live in a vinegar bottle? It must be a big bottle!

Teacher: Yes, you are right; she is an old lady. Let's find out why she lives in an old vinegar bottle, and let's see if it is a large bottle.

Predicting engages students in the reading task. The idea that the old woman wants a chicken is incorrect, but the fairy does make the old woman happy. This is an excellent book to read while students continue to confirm predictions and make new ones. The book has repetitive text and a plot that is easy to follow: The woman constantly asks the fairy for bigger houses, but is not content until the fairy returns her to the vinegar bottle.

If your students depend too much on a picture book's illustrations for their predictions, merely read the title without revealing the cover and ask them what they think may happen in the story (Brown, 1999/2000). With younger students this may be a hard task because they enjoy the illustrations and rely on them for help with comprehension. In these discussions, always ask "why" questions and ask students to support their answers. Keep in mind that simply reading the title of the book *The Old Woman Who Lived in a Vinegar Bottle* while not allowing students to see the illustrations may elicit an entirely different conversation.

Teacher: This book is called *The Old Woman Who Lived in a Vinegar Bottle.* What do you think the story is about?

Student: A woman who lives in a vinegar bottle. (A very literal answer to a very literal question.)

Teacher: Why do you think she lives in a vinegar bottle?

Student: What's a vinegar bottle? (Good! The child recognizes her lack of prior knowledge.)

Teacher: Vinegar is a sour liquid used to make pickles.

Student: Phew! Does it stink like pickles?

Teacher: Vinegar doesn't smell very good. So why do you think the woman lives in the vinegar bottle?

Student: Because she was old and mean and someone didn't like her so they first made her drink the vinegar and then they made her small and then they put her into the bottle so she couldn't be mean anymore.

This student has a complete but inaccurate plot in mind. However, that is fine because she will change her predictions as the story unfolds. The teacher has engaged the student in the thinking process, which is the purpose of predicting.

Predicting helps readers interrelate ideas through the reading of a story. They begin to understand that reading is more than just reading words correctly. Begin predicting activities with stories having simple, predictable plots in order to give students a better chance of success with their predictions (Brown, 1999/2000). Stories with repetitive text are helpful because students can join in on repeated phrases and learn to recognize unfamiliar words. Appendix A.7 has a list of books with repetitive texts and predictable plots.

Teachers in the middle school can also use the book's cover and title to get students to predict what it may be about. For example, a discussion of *Head Above Water* (Rottman, 1999) may go like this:

Teacher: From the title and illustration on the cover, can you predict what the novel will be about?

Student 1: It looks like a girl swimming.

Student 2: No, I think the girl is struggling to get out of the water.

Teacher: Why do you think that?

Student 2: Because her hands are above her head like she is reaching upward.

Student 1: Yes, but she has goggles on and from her facial expression it does not look like she is struggling.

Student 3: I think the title implies that she is in deep trouble and she is attempting to get out of trouble. You know how we sometimes say, "I need to get my head above water," meaning I need to get out of trouble.

Student 4: I never heard of that, but I do think she is trying to get out of trouble because I read *Hero* (1997) and *Rough Waters* (1997) also by S. L. Rottman and her books are about teens who are in some type of life trauma. They are really good books.

Student 5: Are there some chapter titles so we can get a better idea?

Teacher: No there are no chapter titles, but let's read the first page and see if we can tell if any of the predictions are correct.

After reading the first page, the students agree that it is about a swimmer and she is in trouble because she is late for practice. This type of discussion engages middle school students in predicting the plot before they even read one page.

Setting a purpose

Setting a purpose is an important part of reading comprehension that occurs before reading. After reading the title of a text, readers should ask themselves what genre the text belongs to. The primary purpose of reading narrative text is to find out who did what, when, where, and why. In both fantasy and realistic fiction, readers usually attempt to understand the protagonist's conflict and how the conflict is resolved. In historical fiction, readers attempt to answer the same questions while learning more about the time and place in which the story is set. In a mystery readers usually attempt to find clues in the text about how the protagonist will identify a criminal or resolve a problem.

During Reading Strategies

During reading comprehension strategies include making inferences, self-monitoring, visualizing, and connecting prior knowledge to text. Santoro et al. (2008) suggest that teachers use a consistent strategy to discuss the text until students become proficient in using it. Students can then use the strategy during independent reading.

Making inferences

According to Cooper and Kiger (2005), one of the most significant strategies for comprehension is the ability to make **inferences.** Making inferences is the process of judging, concluding, or reasoning indirectly from the information available. Most of the information needed for making inferences comes from students' background knowledge (Santoro et al., 2008). Pose questions that will activate students' knowledge and prompt them to make inferences, for example, "Have we ever read about a similar plot in another story?" "Have you ever experienced a similar incident?" "Have any of you ever visited this country in which the story takes place?" These questions help students make three types of connections: text-to-text, text-to-self, and text-to-world (Santoro et al., 2008). By answering these questions they connect their prior knowledge to the events of the story. This connection helps students make inferences. It is easy to see that inferring is also a higher-level thinking skill. Proficient readers readily combine their prior knowledge and then draw conclusions that are not stated in the text. Struggling readers often find this task difficult (Flynt & Cooter, 2005).

Many teachers understand inferential thinking but find it difficult to formulate inferential questions. May (2001) suggests that teachers "listen within our heads to the author and infer the messages left between the lines" (p. 114). May contends that authors "subconsciously leave empty slots for your imagination to fill in" (p. 114), and teachers need merely look for what the author omitted when they attempt to devise inferential questions.

Readers can make inferences before and after reading a story, but they must often make inferences about how characters feel based on how they act or what they say. At other times, readers make inferences about characters from what other characters say about them. Authors invite inferences because they want to show, not tell, readers about a character or a scenario and want them to use their imaginations. Teachers can facilitate students' ability to make inferences by asking open-ended questions. Katie Couric gives many opportunities for readers to imagine what kind of character Lazlo is in *The Brand New Kid* (2000). While reading this story to a struggling reader, you might ask him how Lazlo feels when he is ignored. The story does not explicitly describe Lazlo's feelings. Stop reading from time to time and ask inferential questions. The reader may need to draw on personal experience to infer how Lazlo feels when he is ignored. The following presents a passage from the book with some possible inferential questions:

> . . . all morning long, they kept shooting him looks.
>
> They headed to gym class, a quick softball game.
>
> When they went to pick teams, no one mentioned his name. (unpaged)

> Teacher: What do you think it means to "shoot him looks"?
>
> What kind of looks are they?
>
> What happens earlier in the story to let you know how Lazlo feels?
>
> Can you shoot me that type of look?
>
> What does it mean when the narrator states that "no one mentioned his name"?
>
> Do you know how it feels when no one calls your name to be on the team?
>
> How did that make you feel?
>
> Do you think Lazlo feels the same way?

Reading students books such as this one and discussing the implicit aspects of characterization, setting, and plot can strengthen students struggling with inferential strategies. This approach prompts them to connect their own knowledge to what they learn from the text. Strive to ask probing questions that will help readers grasp characters' motives and elicit their empathy or understanding. Always ask students why they have particular reactions to characters or events; the "why" questions give readers a chance to practice their higher-level thinking skills. More activities for increasing readers' ability to make inferences will be discussed in the Intervention section of this chapter.

Self-monitoring

Self-monitoring is yet another important strategy of reading comprehension (Santoro et al., 2008). According to Fountas and Pinnell (2001), **self-monitoring** is the ability of readers to check "whether their reading sounds right, looks right, and makes sense" (p. 312). Good readers can hear whether each word they read fits the syntax of the sentence. They automatically stop when it doesn't sound correct. Struggling readers, on the other hand, may pronounce words that are not real words or they may grasp at words that do not make sense in the sentence. By helping struggling readers to self-monitor these simple tasks, you help them notice their errors. Stop such a student at the end of a sentence, reread the sentence the way the student read it, and ask, "Did that sound correct? What word doesn't sound right or make sense?" These prompts help readers understand that what they read must match the print and make sense.

The main goal of self-monitoring is to make sure readers are making sense of what they have just read and are connecting previously read information to the current passage. Therefore, periodically stop a student and ask him to retell what they just read. If the reader cannot do this accurately, have him read the passage again and retell it. If this fails, read the passage aloud and ask the student to retell it. If he can then retell, this suggests that he may be spending too much energy on decoding, which is causing comprehension to break down. When this happens, choose an easier text or spend more time reading stories to them, discussing the story as it unfolds.

A student may add information to a retelling that is not in the story. In such cases, ask her where in the story she found the information. If it came from the story's illustrations, you may conclude this reader used the entire text to comprehend. However, if she cannot locate the source of the information, find out if the student is making an inference from background experience or knowledge. The goal is to help students focus on the events of the particular story that is being read. Modeling the think-aloud strategy (see the activity in this chapter's Intervention section) is one way to help students with self-monitoring.

With longer chapter books, readers should self-monitor their comprehension from one sitting to the next. Sometimes a day or two will pass before they resume reading. Or, as with the popular Harry Potter series, a couple of years may lapse before the author publishes a new volume. With longer texts or text series, readers need to relate ideas from chapter to chapter and book to book. For example, in the Harry Potter series, the Dursleys are introduced at the beginning of the first book, but they do not return until the second book. Readers learn some new information in the second book about how Harry differs from the Dursleys. Readers need to be able to interrelate all of this information in order to understand the characterization and the plot of the series. Struggling readers often have trouble relating information from one chapter or book to the next.

Visualizing

Visualizing the imagery and events of the story as it unfolds is another critical strategy necessary for comprehension (Beck & McKeown, 2001; Gregory & Cahill, 2010; Fountas & Pinnell, 2001; Guerrero, 2003; Sadoski & Paivio, 2001). Students should visualize the scene so vividly that they can almost hear the surrounding noises and smell the scents. They should imagine what each character looks like, how he or she walks or runs, and how the character speaks. Is the character's voice nasal or sweet? Husky or weak? For example, in *The Brand New Kid* (2000), the narrator describes the lunchroom in the following manner:

> As Lazlo was leaving the line with his tray
> Someone tripped him, his food it went every which way.
> The students all froze as they saw Lazlo's face
> With French fries and Ketchup all over the place.
> (unpaged)

After reading this passage and without revealing the pictures, ask the struggling readers questions regarding details the author leaves to the reader's imagination:

> What kind of tray was he carrying, plastic or metal?
> Were there any items besides French fries and ketchup on the tray?
> Do you think Lazlo fell to the floor or did he just stumble and drop his tray?
> Describe the mess on the floor.
> How do you think they looked?
> What smells are in the cafeteria?
> What type of floor did the cafeteria have?

Good readers will visualize Lazlo falling or stumbling and can imagine the entire scene because good readers can visualize the details of a story (Guerrero, 2003; Sadoski & Paivio, 2001). Struggling readers have trouble with visualization. Gregory and Cahill (2010) suggest teachers ask these students "I wonder" questions. For example, while sharing *Epossumondas Saves the Day* (Salley, 2006), the teacher may ask: "I wonder what sodysallyraytus does for a birthday cake"; "I wonder what a hissy fit looks like"; "I wonder what it would look like if a snapping turtle really ate a person"; or "I wonder what kind of gifts a possum would get for his birthday." After modeling some "I wonder" questions, encourage students to ask similar questions as other books are shared.

Connecting prior knowledge to texts

Connecting background knowledge to the text you are reading is another strategy for comprehension. There are three types of background knowledge: (1) literary background, or text-to-text connection; (2) world knowledge, or text-to-world connection; and (3) life experiences, or text-to-self connection (Gregory & Cahill, 2010). Each of these is discussed below.

Literary knowledge or text-to-text connection. Literary knowledge includes what readers know about story elements—setting, characters, plot, climax, resolution, point of view, style, and theme. Struggling students often need help understanding these elements as they learn to become independent readers (Fountas & Pinnell, 2001; Gregory & Cahill, 2010; Staal, 2000). One way to help struggling readers discover story elements is by reading stories and completing story webs with them. Staal's Story Face strategy (2000) is a web technique that helps readers identify the main elements of the story. One eye on the "face" represents the story's setting, with eyelashes composed of adjectives that describe the setting. The other eye is the main character(s), with eyelashes composed of adjectives that describe these character(s). The nose is the conflict. The events are arranged in the shape of a mouth, which forms a smile if the story has a happy ending and a frown if it has a sad ending. See Figure 8.2 for an example.

Literary knowledge also includes an understanding of various genres and how they are similar and different from one another. For example, the fantasy genre often includes talking animals and stories that begin with "Once upon a time." Young proficient readers may not always know the names of different genres, but their previous exposure helps them recognize the components of a fantasy, a mystery, realistic fiction, or historical fiction. Struggling readers, on the other hand, will not know to look for clues when reading a mystery; when reading historical fiction, they will often not be able to separate historical facts from fictitious details the author has added to enhance the plot. They may also find it difficult to differentiate between fantasy and realistic fiction because in fantasy, animals and objects often exhibit human behaviors and emotions. Help readers recognize the differences between fantasy and realistic fiction by having them complete a Venn diagram that shows the commonalities between the two genres and the conventions that are unique to each.

Another facet of literacy knowledge is making connections between texts. Proficient readers can easily make connections from one text to another (Gregory & Cahill, 2010). For example, if you share *If You Give a Pig a Party* (Numeroff, 2005) to your class one week, and three weeks later read *If you Give a Cat a Cupcake* (Numeroff, 2008), proficient readers will readily connect the two books and explain how they are similar in plot, language, and even illustrations.

World knowledge or text-to-world connection. The second aspect of background knowledge is readers' knowledge of the world. This knowledge enables readers of fantasy, for example, to distinguish between fact and fiction. For example, when hearing *Epossumondas Saves the Day* (Salley, 2006), proficient readers will know, based on their world knowledge, that it is impossible for a snapping turtle to swallow whole an alligator and two people. However, even proficient readers might not understand the setting of the story if they have never been to Louisiana. Story settings are often beyond the readers' world of experience, so you may need to introduce them to nuggets of basic geography, history, or anthropology for them to appreciate the locale. For example, consider the following opening sentence of a story: "Once upon a time in the Arctic, lived seven polar bears." The author assumes readers know the Arctic is a cold, snowy place and that polar bears live there. Readers with rich background knowledge can visualize the setting and know something about the characters from that first sentence. Those with weak background knowledge will need your help to understand the setting so they can appreciate the story. In many stories, the setting plays a pivotal role in the problem. Think-alouds (discussed in the Intervention section of this chapter) help struggling readers by providing background knowledge about settings beyond their communities. In the story about polar bears, you might use the think-aloud strategy by stopping after the first sentence and offering the following comments:

> Teacher: Wow! This story makes me shiver because I know the Arctic has lots of snow and ice. Does it make you cold too?
>
> I wonder if it's sunny or cloudy. What do you think?
>
> If it's sunny, the glare would hurt my eyes. Would it hurt your eyes too?
>
> I know polar bears love the cold, but I wonder if these are friendly or mean bears. Do you know if polar bears are friendly or mean?

figure **8.2** "Sad" story face.

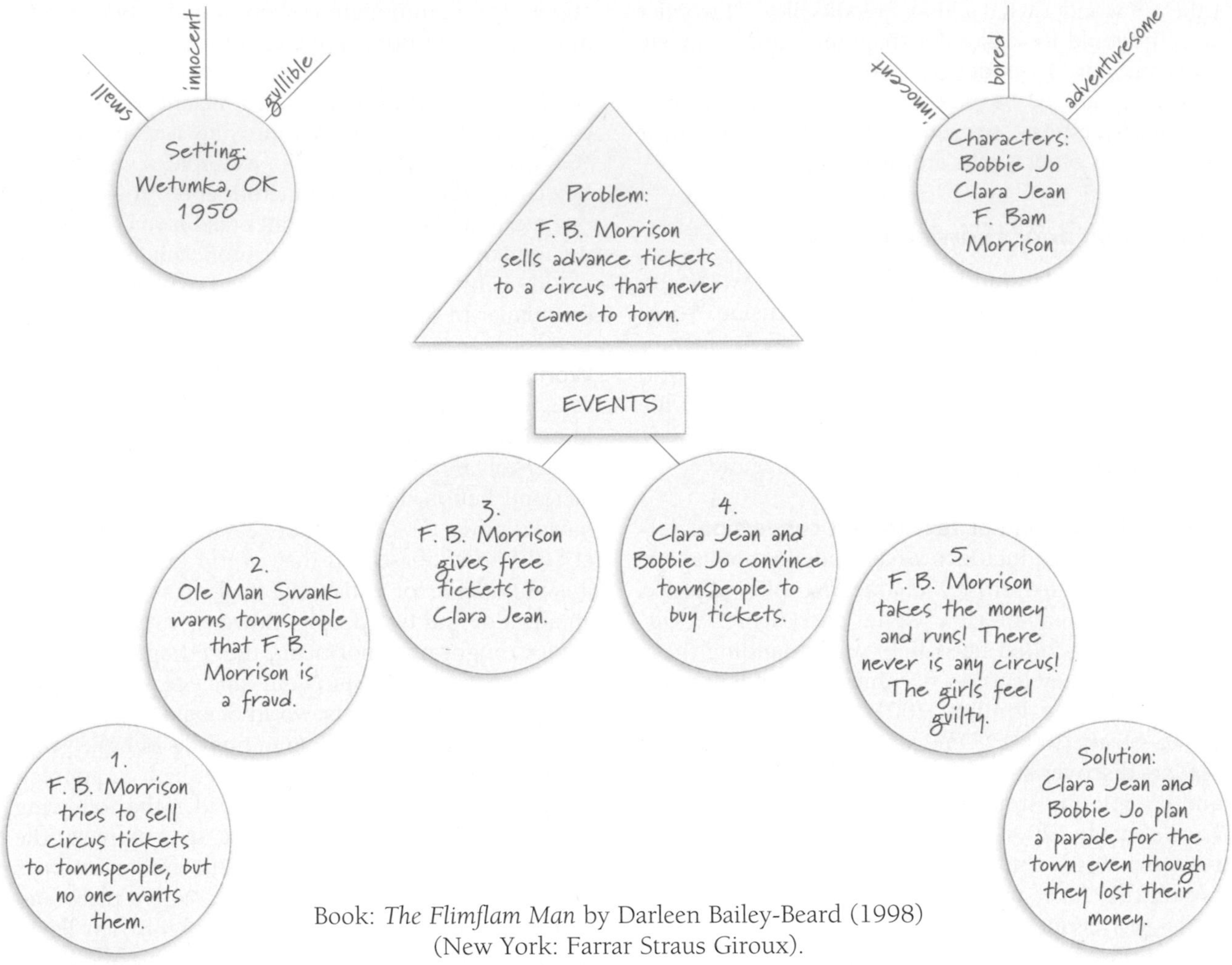

Source: Staal. L. A. (2000). The Story Face: An adaptation of story mapping that incorporates visualization and discovery learning to enhance reading and writing. Adapted from a graphic by Paula Clifford and Doug Ritsema. *The Reading Teacher, 54*(1), 26–31.

With each question, you can solicit information from readers in order to find out what they know and provide information about what they don't know. The reader may know something about the Arctic and polar bears from a television show, but the child may not know if the bears are aggressive. The think-aloud strategy engages struggling readers in the comprehension process before reading the story.

If you had merely read the first sentence without discussing it, the struggling reader may not comprehend the story, because most authors assume that the reader will supply much of the background information.

Life experience or text-to-self connection. The third component of background knowledge is one's life experience in terms of family, community, and other social interactions. All these experiences help readers construct meaning when they encounter new stories. A reader whose family member has suffered a stroke will have a better understanding of Tomie dePaola's *Now One Foot, Now the Other* (1981b). Readers who have watched a parent struggle with depression or who have lived in a foster home may have a richer appreciation for Patricia MacLachlan's *Mama One, Mama Two* (1982).

All readers have previous life experience, but proficient readers are able to make connections between their personal experiences and the story. For example, J. W., whose grandfather recently suffered a stroke, reads about Bob's stroke in Tomie dePaola's *Now One Foot, Now the Other* (1981b) and asks, "Why is Bob sick just because he cannot move his arms and legs?

Why can't he talk? Why wouldn't Bob know who Bobby was?" From these questions, J. W.'s teacher knows he is not connecting his background knowledge to his reading, because J. W. often talks about his grandpa's inability to walk, talk, and recognize him. Poor readers such as J. W. often miss connections that will seem obvious to proficient readers.

On the other hand, readers may encounter comprehension problems if they rely too much on personal experiences (Beck & McKeown, 2001). Both types of reading problems—not connecting previous experiences or relying too much on such experiences—make comprehension difficult. In such cases, teachers can use text-talks (Beck & McKeown, 2001). Text-talks are described in the Intervention section of this chapter. When readers depend too much on previous personal experiences, teachers ask students to find the sentences in the text that support their comments.

After Reading Strategies

Comprehension strategies after reading include retelling, drawing conclusions, and elaborating the author's intent.

Retelling story elements

Retelling is more than listing the events in a story. Retelling is the readers' ability to name the main characters, state the problem, and relate events that lead to the climax and resolution. This process requires students to (1) understand the vocabulary and language in order to comprehend the meaning, (2) apply decoding skills for unknown words, (3) understand the chronological order of events, and (4) understand the author's intended message (Mills, 2009; Lapp, Fisher, & Johnson, 2010). Proficient readers are good at retelling stories.

Unskilled readers, on the other hand, may be able to tell who did what, but not in the correct sequence of events. They may relate the climax first and then what leads up to it. Often they cannot remember where and when the story takes place. For example, Cloe, a struggling reader retelling Paula Danziger's *It's Justin Time, Amber Brown* (2001), states that Amber Brown gets a watch and a walkie-talkie for her birthday. Cloe does not relate that it is Amber's seventh birthday and she wants the watch so she can tell how late Justin is when he comes over to play. Cloe also fails to relate that Justin is late the day before Amber's birthday because he is writing a card and wrapping her gift—the walkie-talkie. Cloe only relates what gifts Amber receives. A more skilled reader would relate the story from beginning to end, summarizing the main points of the plot.

When students struggle to relate the plot in sequence, construct a set of four index cards with one of these questions on each card: "Where?", "When?", "Who?", and "Did what?" Display each card in order after reading a story. Use this technique for a period of time, then remove the cards and ask the students to retell the story. Retelling events in sequence is an important skill in exploring fiction, and it will also serve students later when relating scientific phenomena and historical events.

Drawing conclusions

Drawing conclusions demonstrates a student's ability to answer higher-level thinking questions. The main conclusion question is "Why?" The answers to these questions are not stated in the story, but students who comprehend the stories draw conclusions based on textual clues or previous experiences. Struggling readers will have trouble doing this because they cannot find the answer stated in the text. For example, while retelling Linda Sue Park's *A Single Shard* (2001), the proficient reader will be able to explain why Tree-ear is faithful in delivering the delicate celadon ware for Min even though the journey is dangerous. The proficient reader realizes Tree-ear does this because Min's destiny will be determined by his delivery of the ware, and because of the lessons his friend Crane-man has taught him. The struggling reader, when asked why Tree-ear is faithful to his task, may say, "because Min tells him to do it."

Elaborating on the author's intent

After reading a story discuss the author's intent. Did the author write the story to make readers laugh, inspire them, teach a lesson, relate historical information, or explore another culture? Teach students to consider the author's perspective as well as other perspectives by examining stories written from opposing points of view. One way to get students to understand different viewpoints is to read and discuss *The True Story of the Three Little Pigs As Told by A. Wolf* (Scieszka, 1995) or *Twice Upon a Time: Rapunzel: The One with All the Hair* (Mass, 2005). In *The True Story of the Three Little Pigs,* the wolf attempts to convince readers that he had a cold and his sneezes were the cause of the Pigs' houses falling down; of course, after that he could not let good pork go to waste. In *Twice Upon a Time,* the story shifts between the voices of the prince and Rapunzel. Even young students recognize that both these stories have perspectives different from those of traditional fairy tales. After discussing these stories, invite students to choose another fairy tale and rewrite it from a different perspective.

COMPREHENSION AND CRITICAL LITERACY

As stated previously, comprehending a text goes beyond the literal level; it includes being able to read critically, as Mr. Bradley—the teacher in the opening scenario—knows. It means understanding the possibly biased language authors sometimes use, the author's perspective and use of figurative language, and a willingness to take action if the reader is moved by the author's message. Comprehending at this level refers to the critical literacy theory (DeKonty-Applegate, Applegate, & Modla, 2009).

Critical literacy was introduced in Chapter 1 as a theory that focuses on sociopolitical issues of our society. Its goal is for teachers to "encourage students to recognize connections between their lives and the lives of real or imagined story characters . . . [and] to explore authors' possible biases, and to reflect on how to take social action to create a more compassionate world" (Richards, 2006, p. 193). Critical literacy helps students "develop a critical awareness that texts represent particular points of view while often silencing other views" (Ciardiello, 2004, p. 138). Nieto (1996) believes that if teachers do not engage their students in critical literacy, "they receive only a partial and biased education" (p. 312).

Critical Literacy Themes and Topics

Teachers can examine six themes with students as they comprehend text at this deeper level. The themes are:

1. recognizing social barriers, or ways that barriers have been broken, between race, age, religions, ethnic groups, social classes, and gender;
2. examining multiple perspectives of historical events throughout history;
3. examining authentic voice by critically looking at the language of the text and exploring how different cultural groups can use language to change situations;
4. juxtaposing two contrasting texts;
5. finding one's identity by discussing differences within the classroom and examining ways to overcome any existing prejudices; and
6. finding ways to take action (Ciardiello, 2004; Ciardiello, 2010; Soares & Wood, 2010).

Possible topics to be read and discussed with students are (1) westward expansion by White Americans from the point of view of native tribes; (2) Chinese immigrants detained on Angel Island during the early 20th century; (3) slavery in the United States; (4) Native American children taken from their homes and enrolled into American boarding schools; (5) the civil rights movement; (6) the fight for the vote in the early twentieth century by women and minorities; (7) internment of Japanese Americans during World War II; and (8) outsourcing of U.S. jobs. These are only a few of the many possible topics from which to choose. You may find additional topics for critical literacy units through an Internet search. Many sites are available, some offering unit plans.

Teachers engage students in reading about and discussing these critical literacy topics so they become citizens who empathize with others through their actions. The Intervention section of this chapter includes specific activities that encourage such discussions and actions.

Questions to Encourage a Critical Stance

Critical literacy "is a dynamic process that examines relationships, expands our thinking, and enlightens our perceptions as we read the word and the world—as we read from a critical stance" (McLaughlin, & DeVoogd, 2004, p. 55). When students read from a critical stance, they not only understand the words, but they are also "'reading the world' and understanding a text's purpose so readers will not be manipulated by it" (McLaughlin & DeVoogd, 2004, p. 53).

To encourage upper elementary and middle school students to take a critical stance, pose the questions presented in Figure 8.3 after reading a novel, short story, a traditional text, e-text, song lyric, or poem. Consider these questions as springboards. Always encourage students to raise questions about a story or novel.

Scaffold students' discussions as they consider these questions. Prompt them to use a variety of comprehension strategies, such as predicting, connecting background knowledge to present text, using the correct meaning of words, and self-questioning. Also encourage students to read additional stories with similar themes so they are exposed to a variety of perspectives. It is important to guide the discussions, listen to all students' ideas, encourage students to listen and respond to other classmates' ideas, and not force opinions on the students.

SKILLED VERSUS UNSKILLED COMPREHENDERS

What is the difference between a skilled reader and an unskilled reader? First, skilled readers have a purpose for reading, such as for information, enjoyment, adventure, or to understand historical eras. Second, skilled readers know how to accomplish goals through creating story maps or journaling. Third, as they read, they monitor themselves and use effective strategies, such as those discussed in the previous section, when comprehension breaks down. This comes so naturally that they are not even aware

figure **8.3** Example questions to encourage students to take a critical stance.

1. Is the setting integral to the story?
2. Does the plot present a problem that is unique to a particular race, ethnic group, or gender? If so, whose perspective does the author give? Is any group's voice silenced? If so, how do you think they would tell the story?
3. Is the story or novel a work of historical fiction? If so, whose perspective does the author give? Could the story be told from a different perspective?
4. What seems to be the primary purpose for the story? To entertain? To inform? To help readers understand a particular problem of a group of people? Or some other purpose?
5. From what point of view is the story told? If it was told from a different perspective, would the story change drastically?
6. Is there any language, figurative or literal, that persuades readers to "feel" any particular way?
7. Does the story provoke you to take action for or against a cause? If so, what are some appropriate ways to take action?

they are using strategies. Finally, at the end of reading, they determine whether they accomplished their goal. Skilled readers use higher-level thinking skills to interpret, analyze, and evaluate the text as they read.

Skilled readers also have the ability "to provide sequenced explanations, logical arguments, grounded interpretations, and abstract analysis" (Jacobson et al., 2001, p. 2). Figure 8.4 summarizes behaviors and characteristics of proficient readers, and Figure 8.5 summarizes some common habits of struggling readers. It is important for teachers to be able to assess readers' strengths and weaknesses.

figure **8.4** Behaviors and characteristics of proficient readers of narrative text.

1. Reads for details about description of setting and character.
2. Makes inferences readily about characters' reactions and how characters feel, based on their actions.
3. Visualizes how the setting looks, smells, and feels, and imagines in detail the physical features of characters.
4. Brings in appropriate prior knowledge about periods of history or details of settings.
5. Predicts by looking at the illustrations and by evaluating the action that has taken place.
6. Summarizes in sequence the events in the plot and identifies setting and main characters.
7. Self-monitors and thus slows down or rereads a passage when having trouble understanding motive or plot.
8. Becomes engrossed in funny stories enough to laugh aloud—in sad stories enough to cry.
9. Uses many strategies to read unfamiliar words and to follow the plot.
10. Understands new vocabulary through context clues or by using the dictionary.
11. Possesses a broad vocabulary that helps elucidate the setting of the story.
12. Integrates relevant text information with background knowledge without that knowledge distorting an understanding of the text.
13. Understands metaphors and figurative language that the author uses; understands how an author employs figurative language for effect.
14. Rereads to clarify ideas when comprehension clashes with background information or previous predictions about the plot.
15. Develops valid interpretations of the theme that elucidate the author's purpose.
16. Remembers content of previous reading sessions when reading longer chapter books or books in a series.
17. Synthesizes information from similar stories. For example, if reading a number of retellings of the same fairy tale, the reader can explain how they are similar.
18. Decodes unknown words automatically by looking at patterns within one-syllable words and finding syllables in multi-syllable words.
19. Supplies necessary details from background knowledge when the author assumes readers have relevant information.
20. Draws conclusions about the mood, style, and theme that demonstrate the author's intent.

Sources: Hurst, C. O., 2000; Jitendra, A., Hoppes, M., & Xin, P., 2000; Jongsma, K., 2000; Oster, L., 2001.

figure 8.5

Behaviors and characteristics of a poor reader.

1. Focuses exclusively on pronouncing words.
2. Remembers small, unimportant details.
3. Relies too much on picture clues.
4. Lacks appropriate background knowledge.
5. Has a limited vocabulary.
6. Doesn't recognize failures of comprehension.
7. Doesn't connect prior knowledge to text.
8. Has difficulty drawing inferences.
9. May lack decoding skills. (Some poor comprehenders have good decoding skills.)

Source: Richek, M. A., Caldwell, J., Jennings, J., & Lerner, J. W. (2006). *Reading Problems: Assessment and Teaching Strategies* (5th ed.). Boston: Allyn & Bacon.

In the next section, I will discuss formal and informal assessments of comprehension.

ASSESSMENT

Any oral assessment of comprehension is beneficial to teachers because they can observe what readers do during the reading process. Good inflection, appropriate pace, and adherence to punctuation and dialogue indicate comprehension (Vaughn, et al., 2000). You can also observe what readers do when they encounter unknown words. Comments made by students during reading or during retelling indicate their level of comprehension.

There are formal (standardized) comprehension tests and many types of informal tests. I recommend the informal tests in order to get a deeper understanding of readers' methods of comprehending texts.

Informal Assessment

Informal reading inventories

An informal reading inventory (IRI) determines a student's reading level. However, IRIs can also be used to compare the student's silent reading to her oral reading comprehension. First have the student read a passage silently and retell the story; then have her read a grade-equivalent text orally and retell that story. Most commercial tests have questions that should be answered by the student in the retelling. Compare the number of questions answered in the retelling after the reading of each story. After the retelling, ask her the questions she left unanswered to determine whether she comprehended that aspect of the story.

Miscue analysis

Miscues are oral divergences from the written text (Goodman et al., 1987). Ask one major question concerning each miscue: "Did the miscue disrupt meaning?" When working with a student, analyze which type of miscue most often disrupts meaning and then work with the student to eliminate that miscue. Miscues that disrupt meaning will most certainly hinder comprehension. See Chapter 3 for instructions on how to administer miscue analyses and a grid to record and analyze miscues.

Retrospective miscue analysis

The retrospective miscue analysis (RMA) can be used for instructional purposes and for assessment (Goodman & Marek, 1996). During the RMA session, a reader listens to a recording of his or her reading while following along in the text. The teacher asks the reader if the miscues disrupt meaning.

The RMA "seeks to empower readers to view reading miscues as repeated attempts to predict meaning and to make sense of text" (Moore & Aspegren, 2001, p. 2). Use the RMA to analyze critically and constructively the entire reading process—in other words, to analyze what students do when they recognize their miscues (Martens, 1998; Moore & Aspegren, 2001; Goodman, K., 1996).

Running records

Running records can also be used to assess comprehension when used for more than cueing errors. The purpose here is to analyze the errors to determine which language system—syntax (sentence sense), semantics (meaning), or graphophonic (visual)—students use (Clay, 2000c). If the analysis indicates that a student uses only visual clues, the student will need instruction in developing the skills to read for meaning. You may also use running records to help determine whether a student's inflection and pace hinder or aid comprehension. For example, proficient readers raise their voices when they read questions, they make a slight pause for commas, and they read at least 75 words per minute, which is considered to be a good reading rate. See Chapter 3 for instructions on how to administer and analyze running records.

Retelling

Retelling, the act of relating the most important events of the story, is an important indicator of reading comprehension (Allinder, 2001; Cooper, 2006;

Dowhower, 1999; Fountas & Pinnell, 2001; Jitendra, Hoppes, & Xin, 2000; Rose et al., 2000). Retelling can be used for assessment and instruction. (See the description of retelling in the "After Reading Strategies" section earlier in this chapter.) Retellings give you insight into readers' thinking and sequencing skills and their ability to restate the main points of the story. Retellings give students opportunities to reflect and discuss the complete text (Doty, Popplewell, & Byers, 2001), rather than merely answer questions that cover one aspect of the story.

Think-alouds

Jongsma (1999/2000) suggests that think-alouds "offer excellent opportunities for teachers to assess students' developing comprehension processes" (p. 310) because they help teachers gain insight into how students process texts. Although teachers commonly use think-alouds as a strategy to model how students should make sense from text, once teachers have modeled the process, student think-alouds can also be used for assessment.

To use a think-aloud for assessment, see if students (1) predict upcoming actions, (2) visualize settings, characters, and events, (3) make inferences, and (4) self-monitor when comprehension breaks down.

Cloze and maze tests

As discussed in Chapter 3, cloze and maze tests can be used to determine whether a passage is at a student's easy, instructional, or frustration reading level. Cloze and maze tests are also good tools for diagnosing and assessing reading comprehension (Gillet & Temple, 2004).

Gillet and Temple (2004) found cloze tests to be particularly worthwhile for assessing comprehension because it requires readers to focus on the entire meaning of the passage in order to fill in missing words. Teachers can observe students in action as they construct meaning in the cloze test. Questions to ask while observing students complete this activity include:

1. Does the reader give up when he or she does not know the word?
2. Does the reader make wild guesses?
3. Does the reader go back to the beginning of the sentence to fill in the blank?
4. Does the reader read to the end of a sentence before filling in the blank?
5. Does the reader read to the end of a paragraph and then come back to the blank to fill in the word?

The Intervention section includes a discussion on how to use the cloze test to teach comprehension.

Rubrics

Rubrics, especially those based on state standards, are another way to ensure that all students are attaining the competencies needed for the criterion-referenced tests that many states use to document reading growth. The rubric in Figure 8.6 is based on the Illinois State Standards for Early Elementary School English/Language Arts. Instead of comprising individual grade-level standards, these particular Illinois standards are grouped together as "early elementary," considered in most schools to be grades one through three. The rubric is based on Standard 1, sections 1.C.1a through 1.C.1d. Notice in this example that Joshua, a third grader at the end of his second quarter, can only sometimes orally retell the story and make accurate predictions with evidence from the text. Obviously, Joshua needs some extra help in reading and interpreting stories.

Appendix C.34 contains a blank version of the rubric found in Figure 8.6. Two other rubrics not based on any particular state standard are also included: Appendix C.35 is a rubric to use for assessing students' narrative reading skills (Narrative Reading Rubric), and Appendix C.36 is designed for assessing general reading (General Reading Rubric).

Computer programs as assessment tools

Software tutorial programs can be used to assess students' current reading level and track their progress. These programs also define the level of text appropriate for students' independent and instructional reading. These programs save teachers time by providing summaries that can be shared with the parents. Such software programs include the following:

1. Accelerated Reader program, distributed by Renaissance Learning.
2. Scholastic Reading Inventory program, distributed by Scholastic.
3. SuccessMaker, distributed by Computer Curriculum Corporation.
4. Launch Pad, distributed by Learning Advantage.
5. LeapTrack, distributed by Leapfrog Schoolhouse.
6. Reads, distributed by Mindplay.

In the Accelerated Reading and Scholastic Reading Inventory programs, students read a trade book and take a computer-guided quiz. The computer grades the quiz and generates a score. In most of these programs, students fill in the blank with an appropriate word (as with a cloze test) and the computer indicates if the answer is correct. Most of the questions are literal, thus the tests measure a student's basic comprehension of the story, but not whether the student can make inferences.

figure 8.6 Rubric for narrative reading comprehension.

STUDENT Joshua GRADE 3 GRADING PERIOD 1 (2) 3 4

TRAIT	TARGET (5 POINTS)	ACCEPTABLE (3 POINTS)	UNACCEPTABLE (1 POINT)
	LEVEL OF MASTERY		
1. C.1a Verify predictions	Responds to questions that reflect higher-level thinking (e.g., analyze, synthesize, infer, and evaluate). ___	Sometimes responds to questions that reflect higher-level thinking (e.g., analyze, synthesize, infer, and evaluate). ___	Seldom responds to questions that reflect higher-level thinking (e.g., analyze, synthesize, infer, and evaluate). X
	Generates questions that reflect higher-level thinking (e.g., analyze, synthesize, infer, and evaluate). ___	Sometimes generates questions that reflect higher-level thinking (e.g., analyze, synthesize, infer, and evaluate). ___	Seldom generates questions that reflect higher-level thinking (e.g., analyze, synthesize, infer, and evaluate). X
	Uses evidence in text to support predictions and conclusions. ___	Sometimes uses evidence in text to support predictions and conclusions. X	Seldom uses evidence in text to support predictions and conclusions. ___
1. C.1b Themes and topics	Makes interpretation of text with text-based support. ___	Sometimes makes interpretation of text with text-based support. ___	Seldom makes interpretation of text with text-based support. X
	Identifies author's lesson, either stated or implied. ___	Sometimes identifies author's lesson, either stated or implied. ___	Seldom identifies author's lesson, either stated or implied. X
1. C.1c Compares reading selections	Compares/contrasts themes, topics, and story elements. ___	Sometimes compares/contrasts themes, topics, and story elements. ___	Seldom compares/contrasts themes, topics, and story elements. X
	Uses text information to make connections to other situations. ___	Sometimes uses text information to make connections to other situations. ___	Seldom uses text information to make connections to other situations. X
1. C.1d Summarization	Retells in written form the main points of the story. ___	Sometimes can retell in written form the main points of the story. ___	Seldom can retell in written form the main points of the story. X
	Retells orally the main points of the story. ___	Sometimes can retell orally the main points of the story. X	Seldom can retell orally the main points of the story. ___
			TOTAL SCORE: 13

SCORING:

28–45 pts = competent in narrative comprehension (end-of-year goal)
10–27 pts = becoming competent in narrative comprehension (midyear goal)
1–9 pts = unacceptable; needs intense instruction

Based on Illinois Early Elementary School English/Language Arts Standards 1.C.1a–1.C.1d, at www.isbe.state.il.us.

Effective teachers administer a variety of informal assessments in order to evaluate a struggling reader's skills and weaknesses. They then demonstrate an appropriate strategy and permit the individual reader to practice the strategy while they watch. Teachers must be knowledgeable about a variety of reading strategies in order to choose strategies that will help a particular reader. Many of the activities in the Intervention section focus on teaching various comprehension strategies.

Formal Assessment

Standardized achievement tests measure the current level of students' performance in a variety of areas including reading comprehension. However, because many achievement tests are group tests, they are not designed to diagnose individuals (Gillet & Temple, 2004). Nonetheless, teachers can look at student reading subtest scores to get a benchmark level for how an individual student scored in comparison to his grade level. Some commonly used achievement tests are the current edition of the Metropolitan Achievement Test, the Comprehensive Test of Basic Skills, the Iowa Tests of Basic Skills, and the Stanford Achievement Test. See Chapter 3 for a complete list of formal student comprehension assessments.

ENGLISH LEARNERS AND NARRATIVE TEXTS

Instructional Recommendations

The reading development of English learners is somewhat different and requires a modified type of instruction. It should be explicit, in-depth, conducted at a slower pace, and provide many opportunities for discussion and physical response (see discussion of TPR in Chapters 1 and 7). When sharing a picture book, teachers should browse the book by "reading" the pictures and allowing these students ample time for discussion so they develop their oral language skills concurrently with their comprehension skills. They should participate in collaborative conversations about stories they have heard or read (Beckman-Anthony, 2008). Collaborative conversations occur when English learners are able to discuss open-ended questions in small groups where the teacher is an observer and not the leader. Some open-ended questions include

- "What do you think about . . . ?"
- "Have you ever had the same problem as in the story?"
- "What other action could the main character have taken to solve the problem?"

When English learners discuss these open-ended questions in risk-free small groups, they comprehend the story on a deeper, more meaningful level than the literal level (Beckman-Anthony, 2008; Bouchereau-Bauer & Manyak, 2008).

Selecting Narrative Texts

Choosing the appropriate text is also an important element when working with English learners. First, choose texts that are age appropriate and interesting to the students. Second, the texts must be quality literature with intriguing plots and well-developed characters. Because English learners' reading abilities are as varied as those of English language readers, teachers must make books for all of the reading levels accessible in the classroom. Picture books are great for English learners because they are written on many grade levels and cover topics interesting to all ages.

Vardell, Hadaway, and Young (2006) provide the following guidelines when choosing texts for English learners:

1. Provide texts based on the students' cultures. Topic familiarity will help them identify with the characters and comprehend the story line. Figure 8.7 lists the traits of quality multicultural books.
2. Choose texts with chronological story lines. Flashbacks are more difficult to follow.
3. Avoid stories with idioms and other colloquial expressions.

figure **8.7**

Traits of quality multicultural books.

1. Exhibit high literary quality
2. Contain no distortions or omissions of history
3. Contain no negative or inaccurate stereotypes of minorities
4. Free from derogatory overtones (e.g., words such as *savage* or *primitive*)
5. Portray genuine, complex lifestyles
6. Contain dialogue that represents oral tradition, if appropriate to the culture
7. Confirm that all groups can be successful
8. Portray roles of females, elders, and families accurately
9. Free from situations anyone might find embarrassing or offensive
10. Written and illustrated by members of the group represented, or by those qualified to represent the culture
11. Contain illustrations depicting genuine individuals
12. Portray minorities as leaders who can solve their own problems
13. Present heroines and heroes whose struggles for justice are appropriate to their culture
14. Written no earlier than the late 1970s

Source: Johnson-Higgins, J. (2002, January). *Multicultural children's literature: Creating and applying an evaluation tool in response to the needs of urban educators.* New Horizons of Learning. Available online: http://education.jhu.edu/newhorizons/strategies/topics/multicultural-education/multicultural-childrens-literature/. Retrieved February 28, 2010.

4. Choose themes that are based on (a) fitting in, (b) adjusting to a move, (c) being different, or (d) finding one's niche in society, if they seem appropriate for the student.
5. Choose texts that also "teach" survival topics, such as days of the week, months, foods, weather, types of clothing, occupations, and family members.
6. Choose predictable story lines so students can guess what will happen with each turn of the page.
7. Choose texts with illustrations that advance the story.

See Appendix A.9 for a list of suggested bilingual English–Spanish narrative picture books and Appendix A.10 for a list of multicultural picture books. Figure 8.8 shows a translation into Mandarin of a page from *The Empty Pot* (1990) by Demi.

figure **8.8**

Translation of page 1 in Demi's *The Empty Pot.*

A long time ago in China there was a boy named Ping who loved flowers. Anything he planted burst into bloom. Up came flowers, bushes, and even big fruit trees, as if by magic!

很久以前，中国有个小男孩叫"平"，他非常爱花。不论他种什么都会很繁盛，长出各种花儿，灌木，甚至很大的果树，就好象魔术一般！

很久以前，中国有个小男孩叫"平"，他非常爱花。 不论他种什么都会很繁盛，长出各种花儿，灌木，甚至很大的果树，就好象魔术一般！

(Top translation = handwritten; bottom = typed.)

TEACHING COMPREHENSION STRATEGIES

Studies show that teaching comprehension strategies to students directly does enhance reading comprehension (Flynt & Cooter, 2005; Allinder, 2001; Beck & McKeown, 2001; Gauthier, 2001; Jitendra, Hoppes, & Xin, 2000; Vaughn et al., 2000). Therefore, effective teachers know many strategies and match them to the needs of each struggling reader.

Before examining activities to use with struggling readers, consider the following question: Is explicit instruction in comprehension strategies necessary? The answer differs between good and poor comprehenders. Swanson and De La Paz (1998) concluded that good comprehenders know what strategies to use without recalling having learned them. However, struggling readers do not necessarily know when to use the strategies that they have been taught. The goal is to demonstrate how and when students need to apply strategies, explaining what strategies to use before, during, and after reading. First explain and then demonstrate all of the strategies in the following intervention section, while engaging in a text. Next, guide the students through passages as they read and use the strategy until they demonstrate proficiency in it (Lapp, Fisher, & Johnson, 2010; Flynt & Cooter, 2005). Then monitor the students as they use the strategy during independent reading. Focus on one instructional strategy for a minimum of three weeks. Instead of peppering students with a different strategy with every new passage, you need to "marinate students in the new skill if it is to become permanent knowledge" (Flynt & Cooter, 2005, p. 775).

When teaching comprehension strategies to struggling readers, remember the following:

- Teach in context.
- Use simple, easy-level reading material.
- Individualize! (This is the most important factor.)
- Choose an appropriate strategy for that material.
- Teach the strategy explicitly.
- Model the use of the strategy.
- Have the reader practice it under your supervision.
- Give appropriate feedback.
- Provide numerous opportunities for the student to practice the strategy so he or she can self-regulate.
- Don't present multiple strategies at one time.
- Have the student verbalize the steps of the strategy, explaining when it should be used.

The following section includes a number of activities to be used before, during, or after reading with students who struggle with comprehension. Remember that comprehension strategies should be explicitly taught (Ciardiello, 1998).

Intervention STRATEGIES & ACTIVITIES

The International Reading Association and the National Council of Teachers of English deem it important that all readers, including struggling readers, be able to apply a wide range of strategies for comprehension (IRA/NCTE, 1996). In the 1960s and 1970s, the trend was to teach subskills through direct instruction and then have students master each subskill while reading a short passage. However, research now indicates it is more effective to teach skills to students in context, at moments when they can make an active choice to use them to aid comprehension of that particular text (Beck & McKeown, 1991; Dowhower, 1999; Fountas & Pinnell, 2006b; Hamilton & Kucan, 1997). The comprehension strategies in this section should be taught in context when struggling readers need them. Each strategy should be explicitly explained and demonstrated by the teacher using the story that is being read.

Some of the activities presented in this section extend through all of the stages of reading, while others are intended for a specific stage. Make sure you are familiar with many types of activities, that you understand the needs and interests of the students, and then apply the activity that best fits the need of each reader. Many of these activities can be used in large or small groups. However, it is suggested that these activities be used in a tutoring setting so they fit the needs of individual struggling readers.

Strategies and Activities to Use Before, During, and After Reading

PAIRING NONFICTION AND FICTION TEXTS — GRADES 3–8 — ACTIVITY

Build comprehension by creating units in which you read aloud nonfiction texts to provide background information about a topic that appears in a story or novel that students will read (Soalt, 2005). Discuss how authors of fiction use facts to shape their story. If students have the background knowledge (the facts) about a topic discussed in a story, they may become motivated to read the story or novel. For example, middle school students who first read *Chinese Immigrants 1850–1900* (Olson, 2001) will have the background knowledge to understand Yin's *Coolies* (2001). For younger students, teachers can share Micucci's *Life and Times of the Ant* (2003) before reading *Two Bad Ants* (Van Allsburg, 1988). Through discussion of both books, students are able to better discern fact from fiction.

Santoro, Chard, Howard, and Baker's (2008) research confirms that this read-aloud strategy was effective with English learners. They incorporated comprehension strategies and vocabulary building strategies as they conducted read-alouds with science and social studies informational and narrative text with first graders. They found that using the two types of text in tandem built background information about many social studies and science topics. For example, during a science unit on reptiles they used *A True Book: Sea Turtles* (Lepthien, 1997) and *Albert's Impossible Toothache* (Williams, 2004). For a social studies unit, they used *I Am Rosa Parks* (Parks & Haskins, 1999) and *Daisy and the Doll* (Medearis & Medearis, 2005). While reading both fiction and informational books, teachers used the following during, before, and after reading strategies, shown in Figure 8.9.

figure 8.9 Before, during, and after reading strategies used while reading fiction and informational texts (Santoro et al., 2008).

BEFORE READING

- Identify the purpose for reading; is it fiction or nonfiction?
- Review the title, author, and illustrator and decide if they have read similar books or books by the same author or illustrator.
- Predict what the book may be about by looking at the title, and pictures. With young children, teachers can do a picture walk/talk of the entire book.
- Describe any key vocabulary words that are needed to understand the text.

DURING READING

- Use a consistent strategy to discuss the text until students become proficient in using it (e.g., story elements such as main characters, supporting characters, setting, problem, attempts at solving problem, climax, resolution; and K-W-L charts for informational books).
- Use open-ended questions.
- Make connections, such as text-to-text, text-to-self, and text-to-world.
- Make inferences based on background knowledge.
- Self-monitor by going back or slowing down when comprehension breaks down.
- Look for new vocabulary and talk about meaning as used in the text.

AFTER READING

- Retell the main points—characters, setting, main points of plot, ending of fiction, and two or three main points of nonfiction.
- Review and extend new vocabulary found in text.

ACTIVITY

THE MEMPHIS COMPREHENSION FRAMEWORK — GRADES 4–6

The Memphis Comprehension Framework is a research-based framework shown to be effective with grades four through six (Flynt & Cooter, 2005). In this framework, teachers use fiction and informational books to teach concepts. The framework has three steps:

1. Preplanning: Select an age-appropriate comprehension skill or strategy and use it for a minimum of three weeks.
2. Focused read-aloud and discussion: Read a story based on the concept once a week, and read informational texts based on the topic twice a week. Teach unfamiliar vocabulary words before, during, and after each reading. All readings should be 10–15 minutes daily. Follow each read-aloud with a group discussion that encourages higher-level thinking (see Figure 8.10 for examples of questions to start such discussions); encourage students to justify their answer or stance. During discussion, create a graphic organizer to show relationships among concepts. Chart unfamiliar vocabulary words on the graphic organizer to show relationships between words and the topic.
3. Engage in a three-level retelling:
    - Level 1 is a guided oral retelling in which students are encouraged to retell the information in a logical sequence.

figure 8.10 Higher-level discussion questions for the unit on World War II.

1. We have read as a class a number of fiction books about World War II. Compare and contrast the experiences of Milkweed, living in Poland, and Sevrine, living in France. Which of the main characters had a harder time surviving daily life? Give reasons for your stance.
2. Ann in *When Hitler Stole Pink Rabbit* had very different experiences than did the children in *The Story of Friedl Dicker-Brandeis.* Explain how their experiences were different and give some reasons why you think this was so.
3. *Every Day Lasts a Year: A Jewish Family's Correspondence from Poland* is nonfiction, and *Milkweed,* also set in Poland, is fiction. Do you think Jerry Spinelli used accurate information in *Milkweed?* Why or why not? Explain.

- Level 2 is a graphic organizer retelling in which students use the graphic organizer that was created during the focused read-aloud and discussion time.
- Level 3 is a written/graphic retelling in which the students create their own graphic organizers and write a summary.

The following pages show example materials from a seventh-grade unit on the Holocaust. For the unit, Mr. Greenberg selected fiction and nonfiction in the form of both picture and chapter books with a range of reading levels. He selected these books because they were set in Germany, Poland, France, Switzerland, and Czechoslovakia. See Figure 8.11 for a list of the books he selected. One of Mr. Greenberg's students, Michelle, created the graphic organizer and retelling depicted in Figure 8.12.

figure 8.11 Fiction and nonfiction books for a unit on the Holocaust.

FICTION:

Kerr, J. (1971). *When Hitler Stole Pink Rabbit.* New York: Putnam & Gosset Group.

Polacco, P. (2000). *The Butterfly.* New York: Philomel Books.

Spinelli, J. (2003). *Milkweed.* New York: Alfred Knopf.

NONFICTION:

Browning, C. R., Hollander, R. S., & Tec, N. (Eds.) (2007). *Every Day Lasts a Year: A Jewish Family's Correspondence from Poland.* New York: Cambridge University Press.

Glick, S. (2003). *Heroes of the Holocaust.* San Diego, CA: Lucent.

Gross, E. B. (2009). *Elly: My True Story of the Holocaust.* New York. Scholastic.

Krinitz, E. N. & Steinhardt, B. (2005). *Memories of Survival.* New York: Hyperion Books for Children.

Rubin, S. G. (2000). *Fireflies in the Dark: The Story of Friedl Dicker-Brandeis and the Children of Terezin.* New York: Holiday House.

figure **8.12** Michelle's graphic organizer and retelling of Patricia Polacco's *The Butterfly.*

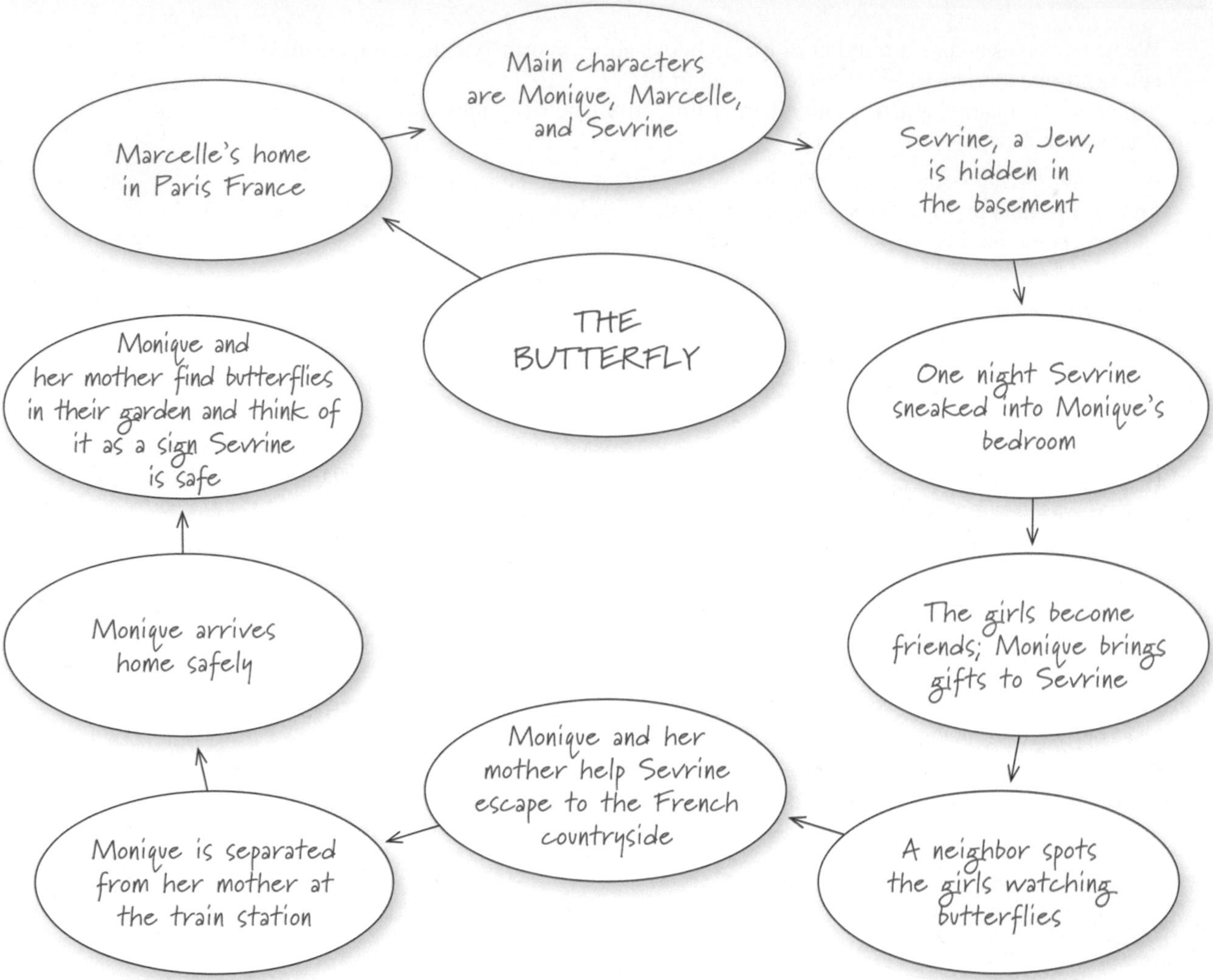

When? World War II.

Where? France, at Marcelle Solliliage's home, an underground safe haven for Jews escaping to freedom.

Who? Monique (young French girl), Marcelle (her mother), Nazi soldiers, Sevrine (a Jewish girl hiding in Monique's basement).

Main Problem: Jews were being taken from homes and shipped to "camps."

Sequence: Monique noticed Sevrine one night in her bedroom.

Monique kept taking things, including butterflies, to Sevrine to enjoy.

Neighbor spotted the two girls at the bedroom window.

Marcelle and husband, dressed like a nun and priest, fled on foot with the girls to the French countryside.

Another family met them on the way and took Sevrine to another place.

At the train station Monique was separated from her mother.

Monique made it back to her house without her mother.

Her mother found her safe at home.

Climax: Monique and her mother spotted butterflies in their garden in the spring; they saw it as a "sign" that Sevrine was safe.

figure **8.12** Continued.

Retelling: Monique and her parents lived in Paris during World War II. They provided a hiding place for a Jewish girl who was the same age as Monique. First, Monique did not know who Sevrine was, but her mother told her Sevrine was hiding in a secret room in their basement. Monique and Sevrine became friends and loved to watch the butterflies from Monique's bedroom window.

One day a hateful neighbor spotted two girls at the window (he knew his neighbor had only one girl). Monique told her mother, and that night they fled on foot to the countryside where another friendly person helped Sevrine get to Switzerland. When Monique and her mother were returning to Paris, they became separated in the crowd at the train station.

Monique took the train to Paris and walked the two miles to her home. Later her mother arrived home too.

The next spring, Monique and her mother found hundreds of butterflies one day in the garden. They saw that as a good sign that Sevrine was safe.

REPEATED INTERACTIVE READ-ALOUD — GRADES PRE-K–8 — ACTIVITY

This strategy is a research-based approach that aids students in Pre-K through eighth grades. One story or book is read three different times. Each read-aloud includes analytic talk, which involves students making predictions and "inferences that explain a character's motivation or connect events from different parts of the story" (McGee & Schickedanz, 2007, p. 742). With each reading the talk is more in-depth. Figure 8.13 is a framework of a repeated interactive read-aloud based on three readings.

figure **8.13** An example repeated interactive read-aloud.

	FIRST READING	SECOND READING	THIRD READING
Introduction of Book	By looking at title and book cover, predict what story is about.	Have student talk about the characters and what they did in the story.	Have students tell you what the problem was and how it was resolved.
Reading of Book	Focus on new vocabulary words or words that are important to the story. Comment on what the protagonists is thinking and feeling throughout the story. Ask students why they think the character is thinking or feeling that.	Using the same vocabulary words, review meaning and give more verbal definition. Comment on what other characters are thinking or feeling throughout the story. Ask students why they think these characters are feeling or thinking that way.	Before reading a double page, ask the students to retell what has happened on that page. Point out the focused vocabulary words in the text. Ask students to think of other times they hear that word.
Discussion After Reading	Ask "why" questions and be sure students explain. Use follow-up questions if necessary to get students to explain their stance.	Ask other "why" questions or "What would have happened if . . . .?"	Ask a different "why" question, or "What would have happened if . . . ?" Get students to extend their explanations.

Adapted from L. McGee & J. Schickedanz (2007). Repeated interactive read-alouds in preschool and kindergarten (p. 747). *The Reading Teacher, 60*(8), 742–751.

ACTIVITY

STORY LINES

GRADES 3–6

The story line is a strategy to use with struggling readers who enjoy making up their own stories. This strategy connects writing, predicting, reading, and validating. The book on which the story line is based must be new to the readers. Here is the process:

1. On a piece of paper, list 10 to 15 nouns as they appear in the story.
2. Have students write short stories using those nouns in the given order. The story must have a beginning, a middle, and an end.
3. Ask students to read their stories aloud.
4. Have either you or your students read the original story and compare it to their versions.

This strategy can be used with any story. Figure 8.14 includes a list of nouns found in Tomie dePaola's *Fin M'Coul* (1981) and a student story based on *Fin M'Coul.* If you know the real story, you will recognize that this story does not follow the original plot. However, the student did include a setting, characters, a conflict, and a resolution. A student will enjoy reading the real story and comparing it to his own.

figure **8.14** Creating a story line: Nouns and student story.

Giant	Earthquake	Cradle
Knitting	Charm	Bread
Causeway	Thread	Teeth
Thunderbolt	Cheese	Tea
Bread	Brass finger	

Sample Story

Once upon a time in a far away place lived a lady giant who earned her living by knitting. She lived by a causeway; her name was Thunderbolt because she could produce a thunderbolt any time she wanted to bake bread. Sometimes she baked bread so that it was hard enough to cause an earthquake. But one time, she baked soft bread and used her bread as a charm to lure a young wicked prince to her cottage. The prince was very proud and always wore red threads between his teeth although no one knew why he wore it.

The lady giant knew that this young prince loved bread with cheese more than any other food. So she took a large chunk of cheese, put a brass finger into the cheese and placed it in a cheese cradle. She baked a loaf of soft bread and invited the prince in for some bread and cheese. (She knew he would not be able to resist the offer.) As he bit into the cheese, he bit into the brass finger which caused all of his teeth to fall out. Straightaway he lost all of his handsome looks and could only drink lukewarm tea after that day. But after that day, he no longer was wicked; he treated all of his people with respect. All of the people thanked lady giant for a job well done.

Strategies and Activities to Use Before Reading

ALTERNATE WRITING

GRADES 3–6 ACTIVITY

This strategy combines reading and writing. Alternate writing creates a story written by a teacher and a struggling reader. It helps students acquire literary knowledge, such as elements of a story—setting, characters, conflict, climax, and resolution—and thus aids comprehension. Alternate writing is a pre-reading activity that helps readers understand the beginning, middle, and end of stories. Use paper or a computer as you complete the following steps:

1. Agree with the student on a topic and a title for her story.
2. Write the first sentence of the story.
3. Have the student read your sentence and then add a sentence.
4. Then, you read the first two sentences and add the third sentence. Take turns writing sentences until the story is complete.
5. Discuss story elements with the student as she writes her sentences.

All good stories begin with a setting and a problem and include roadblocks as well as a resolution. The focus throughout the writing should be on comprehension, not correct spelling.

The following is an example of an opening sentence for an alternate writing story. Note that the teacher does not name the frog. This permits the student to write a sentence about the frog's name or to begin describing the place.

Once upon a time, in a far away place, there lived a sad frog.

DIRECTED LISTENING-THINKING ACTIVITY (DL-TA)

GRADES 1–3 ACTIVITY

A directed listening-thinking activity (DL-TA) is used before (and during) the reading, with the teacher doing the reading. You may use this strategy in two ways. One way is as follows:

1. Read the title without showing the cover picture to the students.
2. Ask them to predict what will happen in the story.
3. Read a little of the story and have the students validate the prediction.
4. Ask the students to predict what will happen next.

These steps continue to the end of the text. The second way to use this strategy is the following:

1. Show the picture on the cover without reading the title.
2. Have the students predict what will happen in the story.
3. Read the title, turn to the first page, show the pictures on the first open page, and ask the students to make predictions about what will happen on that page.
4. Read that page as the students validate predictions.

These steps continue to the end of the book. Note that the second way of doing the activity can also be done using an ebook and an interactive whiteboard.

ACTIVITY **DIRECTED READING–THINKING ACTIVITY (DR–TA)** GRADES 1–3

Directed reading–thinking activity (DR–TA) is used before (and during) reading. It differs from the DL–TA in that here the students do the reading. Students look at the cover of the book, read the title, and predict what will happen in the story. Students then read to validate their predictions. This cycle continues as students read the book, with readers using chapter titles, illustrations, and so forth, to make predictions.

With the DR–TA you can also cover up the words of the book and allow readers to make predictions based solely on the pictures. Then they expose the words and find out whether their predictions were accurate.

Strategies and Activities to Use During Reading

ACTIVITY **TEXT MAPPING** GRADES 6–8

Lapp, Fisher, and Johnson (2010) believe students must become proficient in one comprehension strategy and able to use it independently before they learn a new strategy. Text mapping improves and expands students' comprehension and oral retells. First, teachers model filling in the map as they read and discuss a passage with students. Then they guide students to complete a map by themselves. Later, students complete maps while reading with no guidance from teachers. See Figure 8.15 for an example. Appendix D.19 is a blank version of this form.

figure **8.15** Text mapping example.

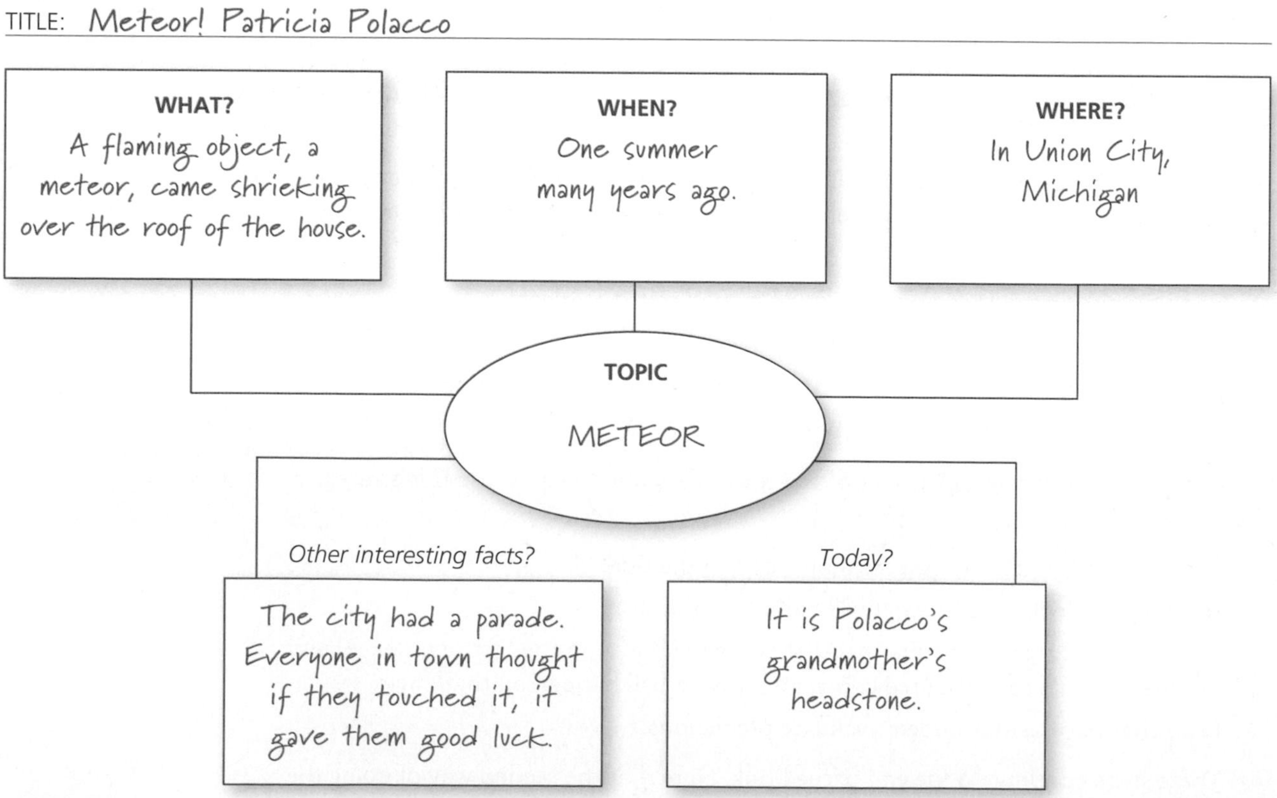

RECIPROCAL QUESTIONING

GRADES 1–6 ACTIVITY

In this strategy the student and teacher take turns asking each other questions. After you and the student read to a certain point in the story, instruct the student to ask you a literal question. You then ask the student a literal or inferential question. Then read another section of the story and repeat the process. Because most children ask literal questions, you can model higher-level thinking by asking inferential and evaluative questions. See Figure 8.16 for an explanation of the different kinds of questions.

figure **8.16** Types of questions.

1. **Literal questions.** Literal questions can be found on the page; the purpose of a literal question is to check a reader's ability to recall information stated in the book. For example, one literal question from *Possum Magic* (1983) by Mem Fox is "What could Hush do when she was invisible?" The answer is stated in the story.
2. **Inferential questions.** The answers to inferential questions are not written verbatim in the text. In order to answer inferential questions, a student needs to read between the lines. For example, one inferential question from Patricia Polacco's *Thank you, Mr. Falker* (1998) is "Why did tears come to Mr. Falker's eyes when Trisha did learn to read?" The answer for this question is not stated directly in the story; however, there is a correct answer to the question, and a reader who comprehends the story will understand why Mr. Falker cries.
3. **Critical questions.** Critical questions require a reader to analyze and synthesize in order to give a correct answer. A critical question may require a student to gather information from a number of books or from her personal experiences.
4. **Evaluative questions.** Evaluative questions have no right or wrong answer. A reader gives his own opinions, but must provide sound reasoning. One example of an evaluative question from *Possum Magic* is "What would have happened to Hush if Grandma Poss could not make Hush visible again?" There is no correct answer; however, if a student comprehends the story and draws on his past experiences, he will have a plausible answer.

Critical and evaluative questions require a student to read past the words on the page.

THINK-ALOUD FOR NARRATIVE TEXT

GRADES 1–5 ACTIVITY

Although a think-aloud can be used for assessment, it can also be used first by you to verbalize your thoughts and then by students as they read and make sense of a text. When you verbalize your thoughts while reading, you permit the students to understand the strategies you use to comprehend texts. As you read, you can comment on or question the text, bringing your "prior knowledge to bear, or making inferences or predictions" (Oster, 2001, p. 64). You then have the students practice the strategy as you observe and scaffold their thought processes as necessary. Be sure to model a think-aloud using a book that is conceptually challenging to the readers. The following is an example of a teacher modeling a think-aloud, using Patricia MacLachlan's *Mama One, Mama Two* (1982). The teacher's thoughts are presented in italics and brackets.

> Maudie heard the baby cry in the middle of the night. *[I wonder how old Maudie is and how old the baby is. I wonder if the baby is sick.]* She got up and walked through the moonlit hallway to the room. *[I wonder if she is angry that the baby woke her up.]* The baby reached out and curled his fingers around hers. *[I see the baby is a boy and that he likes Maudie.]* "Are you awake, too?" asked Katherine in the doorway. *[I wonder who Katherine is. From the picture, I think she is Maudie's mother. However, if it is Maudie's mother, she probably wouldn't be called Katherine.]* She held the baby's night bottle of milk. *[I guess the baby is hungry, not sick.]*

Later in the story we read:

> "Tell me the story again," said Maudie, "the story about Mama One, Mama Two." *[I wonder what Maudie means. Is she talking about Katherine? Is Katherine not her real mother? Who are Mama One and Mama Two?]*

This process demonstrates to struggling readers that the teacher also asks questions as she reads and makes and confirms predictions. After you have modeled this strategy, give struggling readers an opportunity to practice it with a book on their instructional level they have not yet read.

ACTIVITY

THINK-ALOUD MYSTERY — GRADES 6–8

With this strategy, teachers create short "stories" in which each sentence reveals another aspect of a story or mystery. Teachers should write the "story" so the ending sentence brings some element of surprise. Students hear one sentence at a time and explain what they have learned from that sentence and predict what they think will happen next. In this strategy, students (1) relate prior knowledge to text information, (2) predict through the use of their background knowledge and text cues, (3) question and reread when they are confused, (4) create mental pictures of the information or action of the story, and (5) seek outside help from other sources if a word is unfamiliar (Smith, 2006).

- In a group of two or three students, read a short passage one sentence at a time.
- After each sentence ask students what they learned from that sentence and how they arrived at their conclusions.
- Students may change their minds about any conclusions drawn from previous sentences if the information in a subsequent sentence suggests they have made incorrect predictions.

Smith (2006) includes the following think-aloud mystery about sports.

1. The players all came out eager to begin the winter game.
2. One team wore gold, black, and white uniforms, the other, black, orange, and white.
3. It was obvious that all the players were strong and fit. Quite a few of them were very big, too.
4. When the game began, I was glad they wore protective gear because the game was very rough.
5. The sound of the crowd almost drowned out the noise of the helmets and body pads hitting into each other as the teams played.
6. Pittsburgh and Philadelphia might both be cities in Pennsylvania, but their teams fought furiously against each other in the icy cold.
7. One team scored a goal, Mario Lemieux raised his stick in triumph, and the fans went wild.

A Flyer vs. Penguins hockey game is always fun (p. 767).

The first sentence tells students the passage is about a winter sport. From their background knowledge they recall all the winter sports they know, such as basketball, skiing, snowboarding, and so on. The teacher then reads the second sentence, and the students refine their prediction based on the new information it provides. After hearing the sixth sentence, students who are familiar with hockey may correctly predict the game and solve the mystery.

Here is another example.

1. The Chair stands alone in the corner.
2. A clock hangs on the wall opposite the door.

3. In the middle of the room stands a long, narrow table that will seat 12 people.
4. When the clock strikes 2:00, there is a rap at the door.
5. The Chair says, "Come in."
6. The twelve jury members file into the room and take places around the table.

Because the story is read to them, students may think the word *chair* in the first sentence is the object one sits upon. Not until the fifth sentence do they realize the chair is a person, but they still do not know what that person is in charge of. In the last sentence students realize the *chair* is the person in charge of the jury.

"AND THIS IS THE REST OF THE STORY" GRADES 3–5 ACTIVITY

In this strategy a teacher reads the story and stops at a critical point such as the climax. The student then tells the rest of the story. For the student's ending to be plausible, he must have comprehended the story up to that point and be able to make inferences as he thinks about the ending. After he predicts the ending, the teacher finishes the story. The students finds it enjoyable to compare his ending to the author's. Good stories to use with this strategy include:

Cloudy with a Chance of Meatballs (1978) by Judi Barrett
Show and Tell (1991) by Elvina Woodruff
The Popcorn Shop (1993) by Alice Low
Vanishing Pumpkins (1996) by Tomie dePaola
Strega Nona's Magic Lessons (1982) by Tomie dePaola

A variation of this strategy is called "What If?" Instead of having the students write their own ending, they read to the end of the story and write a different ending by asking, "What if such and such happened?"

TEACHER-MADE AUDIOBOOKS GRADES 1–3 ACTIVITY

Marie Carbo (1996a) suggests creating read-along audiobooks that allow you to record the story at a pace slightly slower than normal. These are especially useful for English learners and struggling readers. Students are invited to read along with the audiobook. To create a read-along audiobook, do the following:

1. Select a story or passage that is at the student's instructional level.
2. Record only one short selection into an audio file. Do not put more than one story in a file even if the passage is very short, because students must be able to quickly find the starting point.
3. Read the story at a pace that allows the reader to point to each word and read along.
4. Be sure to include a turn-the-page signal with a pause long enough to allow the reader to turn the page.

Teacher-made audiobooks have many advantages. You can create them to fit a particular reader's interest and read them at a pace that allows the student to follow along. Audiobooks can transcend the mere read-along when you add cues that prompt students to stop and respond to reflective questions. If two children listen together, they can stop the recording after each question and discuss the question together. If they disagree on an answer, have them replay the audiobook until they can discern who is correct.

If you do not have time to create read-along audiobooks, Figure 8.17 lists companies that sell them.

figure 8.17 Publishers of read-along audiobooks, with examples of available titles.

Newbridge
www.newbridgeonline.com

1. *Spinning a Web*
2. *Out of Space*
3. *A Butterfly Is Born*
4. *Amazing Water*
5. *Sink or Float?*
6. *An Apple a Day*

Sundance
www.sundancepub.com

1. *Making Friends with Samson*
2. *The Fine Line*
3. *Two Hours with Tilly*
4. *Sticky Fingers*
5. *Mug Shots*
6. *Chocolate Chuckles*

Scholastic
www.scholastic.com

1. *Caps for Sale*
2. *City Mouse-Country Mouse*
3. *Henny Penny*
4. *Little Rabbit's Loose Tooth*
5. *More Spaghetti, I Say!*
6. *Is Your Mama a Llama?*

ACTIVITY

TEXT-TALK

GRADES 2–5

First introduced by Beck and McKeown (2001), text-talks require a specific kind of text and talk. Beck and McKeown suggest all texts should be "conceptually challenging to require grappling with ideas and taking an active stance toward constructing meaning" (p. 10) and all talk or discussion between the teacher and reader should require the reader "to make sense of ideas that are about something beyond the here and now" (p. 10). Text-talks should be based on the following format:

1. Read a section of the story without showing the pictures.
2. Pose open-ended questions that focus on text ideas and encourage inferential thinking. The open-ended questions should encourage language development.
3. Have the child attempt to answer the questions.
4. If necessary, scaffold the child's thinking by posing more open-ended questions using the language of the book. Scaffolding is an important process as you provide information that the child has not provided.
5. Show pictures of that section of the story to encourage more discussion.
6. Repeat steps 1–5 with each section of the story until you reach the end.

Using the language of the story during text-talks will encourage students to use the story's vocabulary later in retellings and summarizations.

ACTIVITY

WORDLESS BOOKS FOR DEVELOPING INFERENTIAL READING

GRADES 2–6

While "reading" wordless books, students need to make inferences about characters, plot, and motives. They need to connect sets of pictures to make a story. Drawing inferences and connecting information to previously read information are two components of comprehension.

To use this strategy, read the title and have the student skim each page of the entire book. Then, have the student start from the beginning and "read" each page. If the story does not make sense, ask her to "read" the page again. Use wordless books to develop inferential reading skills by asking students to add more detail to their stories. For example, concerning *Tuesday* (1991) by David Wiesner, you may ask what the man who is eating the midnight snack is thinking when he sees frogs flying past the window, or why the old lady did not wake up when the frogs watched her television.

Appendix A.5 offers a list of wordless books that can be used for this strategy.

Strategies and Activities to Use After Reading

REPEATED READINGS

GRADES 2–6 ACTIVITY

Repeated readings both by the teacher and the struggling reader have been shown to increase comprehension. Repeated readings by the teacher gives such readers an opportunity to understand multiple layers of meaning in favorite stories. Through these readings and the discussions that follow, readers begin to make inferences about characters' motives and how the setting affects the action. Repeated readings allow students to focus less on decoding words and more on comprehending the story (Brown, 1999/2000; Pearson & Fielding, 1991).

DIFFERENT PERSPECTIVES: DIARY ENTRIES

GRADES 4–8 ACTIVITY

All texts are embedded with multiple meanings. Teachers need to guide students to draw conclusions about the author's perspective, position, and power (Clarke & Whitney, 2009).

Clarke and Whitney (2009) found that this strategy facilitates students' ability to comprehend multiple perspectives by reading about an historical account often omitted in history books. For example, students in the upper grades have studied about Columbus's voyages to the New World; however, Jane Yolen's (1992) *Encounter,* a story told from a Taino Indian boy's perspective, introduces students to the Native Americans' point of view about the white man coming to their land. For example, Greg is a sixth grader involved in a collaborative social studies and language arts unit on Columbus. After Greg's class has read *Encounter,* Mr. Grigg, his language arts teacher, invites them to write diary entries representing different perspectives. Greg, a shy student, writes a diary entry of Whitecloud, a young Taino Indian, and Columbus. Figure 8.18 shows examples of Greg's diary entries.

figure **8.18** Diary entries of Whitecloud and Columbus.

Whitecloud's Diary	Columbus' Diary
October 10, 1492 I had a bad dream last night during the thunder storm. Three winged birds rode the wild waves in our bay.	October 10, 1492 We need to find land soon. So many of my people are sick. Our food is low and getting stale and rotten.
October 11, 1492 I had the same bad dream last night. This time I heard the winged birds' voices. I think this is a bad omen. I even saw their sharp white teeth.	October 11, 1492 I looked through my spy glass today and I saw land in the distance! I think we have finally sailed to India! I told my people! There was great happiness! I told them to gather the gifts that we had taken with us to give to these people.

(continued)

figure 8.18 Continued.

October 12, 1492

I again had a restless night, and when I left my hammock to walk the beach, I saw a great canoe with white sails. I went to tell our chief not to welcome the strangers, but he told me that it is our custom to welcome all who come to our village.

All the strangers looked like parrots with their bright clothes. They did not look human with their ivory skin.

I warned my people not to welcome them because funny sounds came from their mouths.

They gave us strings with smooth balls, with many colors on them. We gave them spears so they could fish. During the feast that we shared with them, I looked into their chief's eyes and they looked threatening. His smile was a wicked smile; I again went to my chief to warn him, but he pushed me aside because I was only a child. I remembered my dream and left the feast to pray to my zemis.

October 12, 1492

We landed today on the shores where people with very dark skin welcomed us! But we do not understand them; they speak a different language. But they appear friendly enough because we exchanged gifts. We got spears and bouncy balls for the beads we had given them. They made a feast for us of orange potatoes, bread and fish. They gave us tobacco leaves to smoke, but they were strong and caused many of us to cough. This was a GOOD day!

October 13, 1492

I was taken with four other young boys to the stranger's canoe. They are taken us to far away. I MUST escape even if I have to jump into the cold waters! I MUST get back to my people! I knew these strangers were bad people! What is going to happen to me?

October 13, 1492

I am taking five of these young boys with me as we continue to search these strange shores. I am taking these young boys because they are healthy and they will be able to talk to any other of these people on this strange land that is not India like I thought it would be.

ACTIVITY PAINTING MENTAL PICTURES — GRADES K–2

This activity is based on research suggesting that comprehension requires readers to visualize the characters, setting, and action of a story (Gregory & Cahill, 2010). Teachers read a story without showing the pictures and then invite students to share a mental picture from the story with a classmate. After they share their mental pictures, they draw those pictures. Finally, the students compare their pictures with the book's illustrations.

SPIN THE DISCUSSION — GRADES 1–8 — ACTIVITY

In lieu of using literal questions, teachers can use the following prompts to discuss books, allowing students to learn from others and demonstrate their comprehension of story (Blum, Koskinen, Bhartiya, & Hluboky, 2010). Teachers make a spinner with the following prompts in the four sections:

1. Tell in your words what happened.
2. Tell your favorite part.
3. Say what this book reminds you of.
4. Add something new to the story.

After reading a book to a small group, invite one student to flick the spinner to begin a discussion. Other students can add to that discussion or take a turn with the spinner to start a new discussion.

GRAPHIC ORGANIZERS FOR NARRATIVE TEXT — GRADES 2–8 — ACTIVITY

The general term *graphic organizer* includes all types of story maps, charts, webs, diagrams, or any visual representation of a story's content. Some graphic organizers chart the beginning, middle, and ending of the story. Most include the setting, characters, problem, main events, and resolution. Previously in this chapter, we discussed The Story Face by Staal (2000). Figure 8.19 includes examples of three types of graphic organizers. When selecting one for a struggling reader, consider her age, her reading ability, and the purpose for using the strategy. For each one of these organizers, first model how to fill in the structure and then monitor the student as she begins to use it.

figure **8.19** Types of graphic organizers.

STORY MAP (based on *The Wren* by P. Polacco)

SETTING: **Time** Long ago **Place** Ukraine

CHARACTERS: Luba
Luba's parents
The wren w/magical powers

PROBLEM: Wren will grant any wish to Luba. Luba doesn't want anything. However, her parents want a bigger farm, but are never content.

ACTION: Wren gives Luba's parents each of the following after her parents become unhappy:

1. Bigger house on fertile land
2. Manor with large estate
3. Palace and rulers of the Ukraine
4. Become Tsar & Tsarine of all Russia
5. Become Emperor & Empress of the world

They want to become Gods.

OUTCOME: Wren knows that Luba does not like her parents' last wish. Wren returns them to their former poor dacha on a small piece of poor land. — But they are happy!

Source: Basic story map adapted from J. David Cooper, *Literacy, Helping Children Contract Meaning,* 4th ed. Copyright © 2006 by Houghton Mifflin Company.

(continued)

figure 8.19 Continued.

STORY WEB (based on *Henny Penny*)

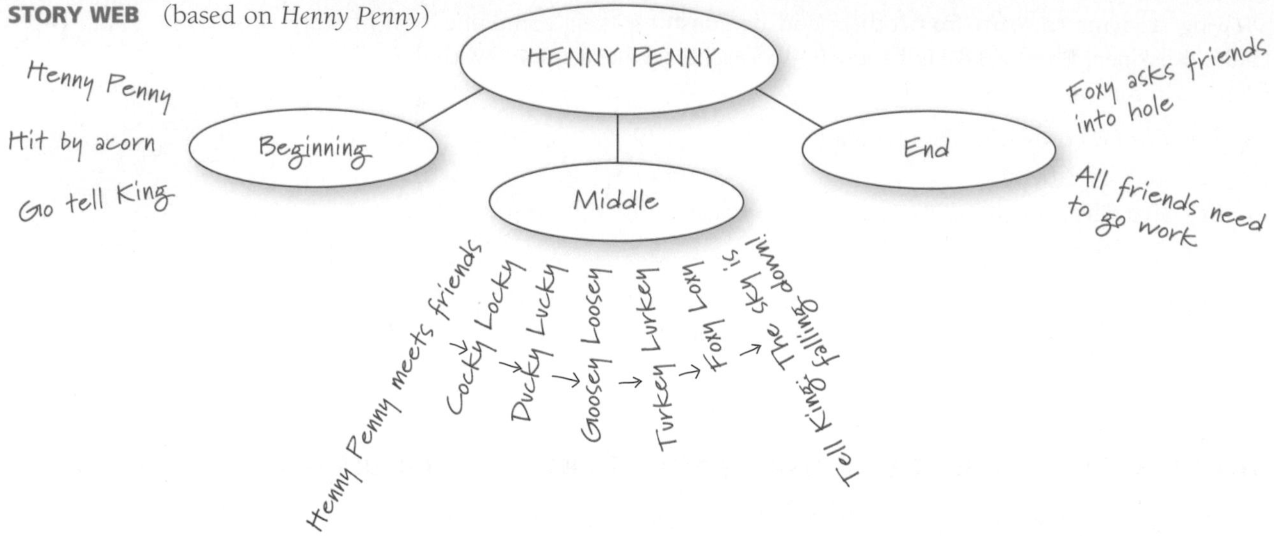

MT. PLOT (based on *The Old Woman Who Lived in a Vinegar Bottle* by M. R. MacDonald)

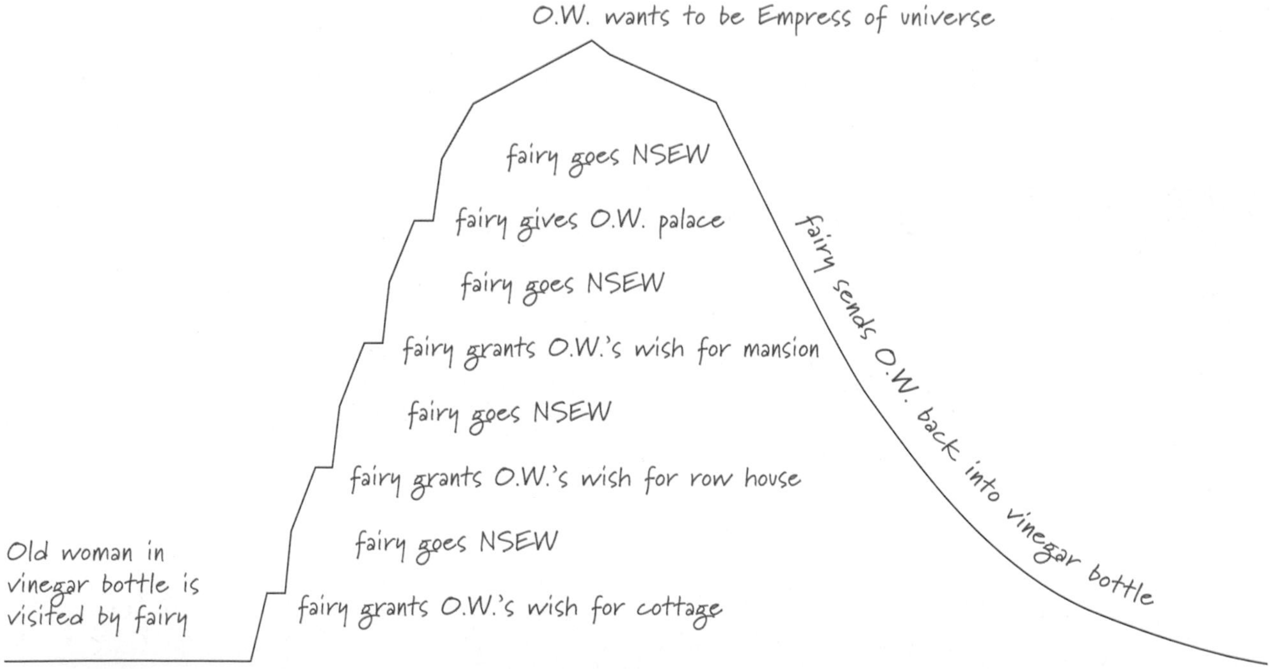

ACTIVITY **RETELLING WITH PUPPETS** **GRADES 1–4**

Retelling a story using simple stick or sack puppets helps readers with sequencing and recalling main points. When children act out the story, they draw inferences about a character's vocal quality and motives, and puppets facilitate this process. Create a puppet for each character and have students manipulate all the puppets in the retelling. One enjoyable story for young children to retell with puppets is *The Little Old Lady Who Was Not Afraid of Anything* (1986) by Linda Williams, but many of students' favorite stories can be retold with puppets.

QUESTION CONNECT TRANSFORM (QCT) GRADES 6–8 ACTIVITY

Richards (2006) developed this critical literacy strategy to help middle school students "enhance their critical literacy abilities" (p. 194). After reading an historical story or novel, the teacher engages the students in questioning (Q) "the moral and ethical dimensions of issues presented in the historical fiction" (p. 194). Second, the students are asked to connect (C) the story to their lives. Finally, the students are asked to think how they might transform (T) any inequities that were presented in the novel and are still prevalent in today's society. See Figure 8.20 for a student example.

figure 8.20 Student journal using QCT with Katherine Paterson's *Lyddie* (1991).

Questioning the moral issue: I question why Lyddie's employer had her and other employees work for low wages in deplorable working conditions at the mill. I also question how the owner got away with forcing the girls into having sex with him and then firing them if they became pregnant.

Connecting the story to my life: I never had to work in such deplorable conditions, but I do remember when men were paid more than women for teaching the same grade.

Transforming the unjust wages: I could have told a judge about the deplorable working conditions and demand he make the owner install air vents so the girls did not have to breathe the textile dust. I could have gone to other places of employment to see if the wages were similar to the ones in the mill. I could have gone to a pastor to explain how the owner was sexually abusing the girls and asked him to confront the owner. I could have gone to the local newspaper and submitted a letter to the editor about the deployable working conditions, low wages, and the owner's abuse of the employees.

CHARACTER PERSPECTIVE CHART GRADES 4–6 ACTIVITY

Many stories depict conflict between the goals of two characters. For example, in Anna Harwell Celenza's *The Farewell Symphony* (2000), Joseph Haydn and his 22 musicians have a goal to return to their families in Austria after spending a long summer in Hungary providing music for Prince Nicholas. Prince Nicholas's conflicting goal is to remain at his Hungarian summer palace long into the fall and have the musicians play at all of his parties. Shanahan and Shanahan (1997) introduce the Character Perspective Chart, which follows a story map from two characters' points of view. Shanahan and Shanahan believe this type of chart helps readers draw inferences about the goals of each character. Figure 8.21 features a character perspective chart of *The Farewell Symphony*.

figure 8.21 Character perspective chart of characters in *The Farewell Symphony.*

Haydn & Musicians	MAIN CHARACTER	Prince Nicholas
Palace in Hungary	SETTING	Palace in Hungary
Haydn and musicians want to return to Austria.	PROBLEM	Nicholas wants to stay in Hungary.
Go back to Austria	GOAL	Stay in Hungary
Musicians ask to go home.	ATTEMPTS	Prince says later.
Musicians beg for their families to join them.		Prince says there is no room in the palace.
Musicians say they are going home.		Prince says he will fire them if they do.
Haydn writes the Farewell Symphony to show Prince the anger of the musicians.		Prince was upset with the angry music.
Musicians play with passion.	OUTCOME	Prince is filled with compassion and permits them to go home.
Reward awaits those who are faithful.	THEME	Think of others' feelings.

ACTIVITY VENN DIAGRAMS FOR NARRATIVE TEXT GRADES 2–6

One aspect of comprehension is being able to compare and contrast information. Venn diagrams are often used for this task. This strategy has been effectively applied to fairy tales that have been retold by various authors and illustrators. You and a student may read two versions of the same tale and then compare the versions by completing a Venn diagram. Figure 8.22 shows a diagram comparing Jan Brett's *The Mitten* (1989) and Alvin Tresselt's *The Mitten* (1964).

figure 8.22 Venn diagram comparing two versions of *The Mitten.*

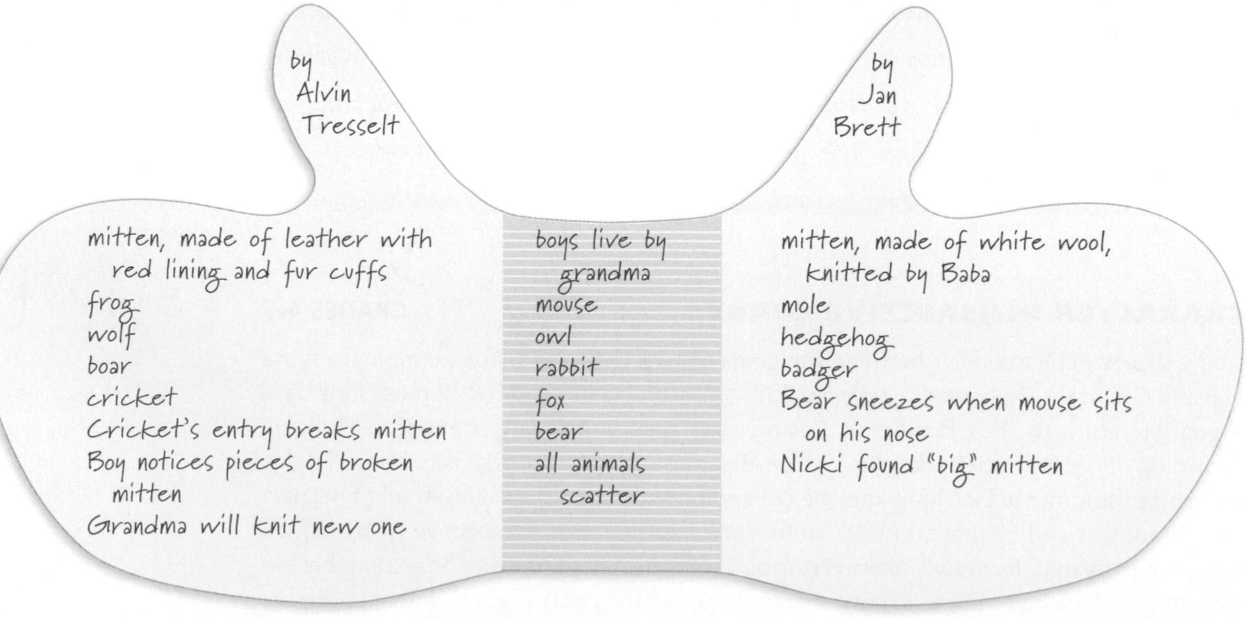

CHARACTER SKETCH

GRADES 3–5 ACTIVITY

This strategy encourages readers to visualize the characters by providing graphically inclined students an opportunity to connect their artistic ability with reading.

To use this strategy, read a story to students without showing the pictures and then have them draw a picture of the characters. Ask them to explain the reasons for their depictions.

COMPREHENSION OF NARRATIVE TEXT AND TECHNOLOGY

Computers and e-readers fascinate many students. Reluctant readers often become interested in reading through the use of these new devices (Sibenaller, 2001). Doty, Popplewell, and Byers (2001) found that students who read interactive ebooks "obtained significantly higher scores than students who read the print version of the storybooks" (p. 3). Ebooks for younger children are interactive in a number of ways. The reader narrates the story as the text is highlighted and users can click on the various characters and objects in the pictures; the talking characters and moving objects expand the story.

Select ebooks with caution. Some are so entertaining that students become overly involved with the animation and do not follow the story line. Other ebooks are not engaging, and students lose interest. When selecting ebooks, make sure the program aids student learning, particularly for struggling readers and English learners. Quality ebooks scaffold students by providing them the opportunity "to master tasks that they would not be able to accomplish independently" (Shamir & Korat, 2006, p. 2). A good ebook allows students to build on their present knowledge through active involvement with the story. Scaffolding is accomplished if the ebook both provides narration and permits students to turn off the narration, and when it pronounces unknown words and gives definitions when students click on the words. Ebooks help students build knowledge when they permit students to click on pictures to demonstrate an action or a character's mood and when they engage users in open-ended activities. The narrative ebook form in Appendix D.20 will help you evaluate particular features of ebooks. Shamir and Korat (2006) suggest a score of 69 out of 92, or 75 percent, makes an ebook acceptable.

The following sites offer free e-texts. Some of the sites feature e-texts with digitized speech. Others allow students to click on an unfamiliar word and hear its pronunciation and definition. Still other sites are text only. The following sites have print sizes appropriate for the grade level of the book:

www.magickeys.com/book Books for all ages, including young adult books.

http://en.childrenslibrary.org Books in many languages.

http://kids.nypl.org Access to any book in the library for those with a New York City Public Library card.

http://pbskids.org Favorite books for young children, such as the Clifford series.

www.childrensbooksonline.org Mother Goose rhymes read by the computer.

www.readingrockets.org Books, podcasts of children's authors, and reading guides.

www.storylineonline.net Videos with celebrities reading books; students follow along with on-screen text.

www.starfall.com Leveled books for students which allow readers to click on unfamiliar words and hear the correct pronunciation.

www.eduplace.com/tales Wacky web tales for students.

www.brainpop.com Teaches students how dialogue is written in novels, comics, and movie and TV scripts.

www.mightybook.com Over 800 animated stories and songs for students to read.

www.roythezebra.com A reading website that can be used on a whiteboard with the class.

http://bygosh.com/childrensclassics.htm Includes many favorite classics such as *Peter Rabbit* and *Alice in Wonderland,* with first edition illustrations.

If a school has extra funds, e-readers or tablet computers are great for expanding classroom libraries. Books purchased online for these devices can be cheaper than the printed copies.

The Readwritethink.org site is created and maintained by the International Reading Association and the National Council of Teachers of English. It includes many wonderful literacy activities for students of all ages. One activity that encourages students to consider multiple perspectives of a story is "Fractured Fairy Tales," in which students create an alternate version of a popular fairy tale. Teachers may complete this activity with struggling readers to help develop their critical thinking skills, or small groups of students can create a fairy tale and then share it with the class.

CONCLUDING THOUGHTS

Comprehension of narrative text is a skill needed by students in all grades. Most students are able to achieve comprehension by listening to and reading stories written at their instructional level. However, some students struggle with narrative comprehension.

After reviewing your students' standardized tests scores, you will likely notice those who struggle with comprehension. You can administer a number of different informal reading instruments to help you understand the causes of each student's struggle. After determining the strengths and weaknesses of a student, choose from a number of strategies to engage the student in authentic reading and writing tasks. Teachers can also engage students in higher-level thinking and reading skills as they guide them through various critical thinking activities.

Reflective Learning — CRITICAL LITERACY

Scenario. Ms. Williams teaches fifth grade in a small, rural Southern town with a student population that is 99 percent Caucasian and one percent African American. She has only two African-American students in her class. This is her first year at this school, but she previously taught for five years in a diverse urban school. She always taught a unit on the Newbery winner Christopher Paul Curtis in her previous school and wants to do so again. Because she has heard some racial comments around the small town, she thinks this will be a great unit to introduce her students to the inequalities that many Americans endure, but she does not know how to approach the subject. She does not want to be didactic, and she really wants her students to think for themselves about the injustices that African Americans continue to suffer. When she introduces Christopher Paul Curtis, no one has read any of his books or heard of him.

QUESTIONS

1. Considering the students and their parents may have some racial prejudices, would you advise Ms. Williams to teach this unit? Give reasons for your stance.
2. Assume she does teach the unit. What activities would you suggest Ms. Williams use to meet her goals of avoiding didacticism and having her students discover for themselves the injustices perpetrated upon African Americans throughout history?
3. What opening activity would you suggest Ms. Williams use to motivate students to read Curtis' books?
4. Which of Curtis' novels do you think Ms. Williams should assign? Why?
5. What other books on the same topic might you suggest Ms. Williams use with this unit? Why would these books be good for fifth graders?

CHAPTER NINE

COMPREHENSION OF INFORMATIONAL TEXT

Teaching means helping a child realize his potential.

ERICH FROMM

scenario

Malcolm, an eighth-grade student, moved with his family from Kenya three years ago. His social studies teacher reports that he listens carefully in class, contributes to class discussions, performs reasonably well on chapter tests, and writes acceptable papers. However, when he takes the state criterion-referenced social studies test at the end of the year, he does very poorly. His scores on that and other state tests require him to attend summer school before he can advance to high school the following fall. During the summer he has seven weeks of social studies, science, and English. During the last week of summer school, he will be required to take the tests again. The teachers, the school counselor, and the principal notice that Malcolm, who was a very happy young man during the school year, appears to be depressed at the beginning of summer school. Ms. Hull, the principal, calls Malcolm into her office during the second week of school to discuss what is bothering him. During the conversation, Malcolm mentions that he is dumb. The principal assures him this is not the case because the teachers mentioned how much he contributed in class and how well he did on chapter tests. "Yes," he says, "but I did not pass the state tests." "Well," Ms. Hull asks, "Do you think I am dumb?" "Oh, no, ma'am! You're smart!" Then she asks, "Do you think I could pass a test that was written in Swahili?" Malcolm gives her a strange look and asks, "Do you know Swahili?" "I do not know one word of Swahili," answers Ms. Hull. "And I know I would not pass a test that was written in Swahili. Malcolm, you are not dumb, you need help with your English and reading informational text. So instead of going to class each day, I am going assign you a personal reading specialist who will help you with your English, vocabulary, and comprehension of informational text as you study each of your subjects, including social studies. Do you think that will help you?" "Oh, yes, ma'am! And thank you, Ms. Hull! I know that will help!" As he walks out the door with a grin on his face, he says, "Ms. Hull, if you would like to take a test in Swahili I could arrange for one."

guiding questions

As you read this chapter, consider the following questions:

1. Which factors within Malcolm as a reader, his environment, or the text he is reading may be affecting his comprehension of informational text either positively or negatively?
2. What qualities should the reading specialist working with Malcolm look for in the informational texts she assigns to him?
3. What are some ways the reading specialist can help Malcolm understand and remember important concepts related to his social studies texts? His science texts?
4. What specific intervention strategies and activities might the reading specialist use with Malcolm?

INTRODUCTION

You may have heard of the "fourth-grade slump." This is the year the students' undeveloped vocabulary, weak comprehension skills, and lack of motivation begin to affect content-area reading (RAND Reading Study Group, 2002). In grades one through three teachers help students develop such skills as decoding, word recognition, and vocabulary as students read both fiction and nonfiction (Brozo & Flynt, 2007). If students like Malcolm lack these fundamental reading skills, reading becomes a difficult task and they enter a "slump" of not trying.

The slump is caused by exhaustion as their underdeveloped skills leave them ill-prepared to learn dense new content material. For these students to be successful, they must continue to learn reading strategies that help them with decoding, vocabulary, and other skills as their teachers motivate and engage them in content reading (Brozo & Flynt, 2007). Teachers can begin motivating students by providing an abundance of interesting texts at different reading levels so struggling readers can learn the content while reading texts at their independent reading level. If the books are at their reading level, they expend their energy learning the content, not attempting to read and comprehend the text. After students have read different books about the same topic, teachers can encourage collaboration so they can learn from one another.

Fortunately, many teachers have begun to supplement the assigned textbook with trade books and the Internet. Both can be more engaging and challenging than textbooks. They are engaging because they provide detailed information about one topic and use photographs or detailed illustrations to explain it. They are more challenging for a number of reasons. First, trade books often include excerpts from primary sources, such as personal letters, newspaper articles, and diaries. Poor comprehenders find these primary sources challenging because they frequently contain archaic words and writing styles. Second, trade books and the Internet can be more challenging because they may present conflicting information, forcing students to evaluate the writers' credentials. Finally, when readers gather information from multiple sources, they must synthesize it (Afflerbach & VanSledright, 2001).

FACTORS AFFECTING THE COMPREHENSION PROCESS

Factors from three distinct sources affect the comprehension process of informational text. These sources are (1) factors within the reader, (2) factors within the reader's environment, and (3) factors within the text. Understanding the complexity of these factors gives teachers a better understanding of why some readers may struggle with reading in general and expository text in particular.

Factors Within the Reader

Basic reading skills are necessary to comprehend all types of text (narrative, expository, poetry, drama, and so on). These basic skills include the following:

- The ability to recognize a large bank of sight words.
- The ability to decode unknown, one-syllable words.
- The ability to analyze words with multiple syllables.
- The ability to read at an adequate rate.
- The ability to recognize when comprehension breaks down.
- The ability to choose an appropriate strategy when comprehension breaks down.
- Ability to make predictions and confirm or reject predictions when necessary.
- Ability to summarize.
- Ability to connect prior knowledge to text.
- Ability to self-question when confused or curious.

When comprehending informational text, a reader must also have the following:

- Knowledge of organizational patterns of expository text.
- Adequate background knowledge of the topic being read.
- Knowledge of specific terms associated with the topic.
- Ability to analyze the author's purpose and credentials.
- Ability to synthesize similar information from various sources.

Other factors that affect a reader's ability to comprehend informational text are her prior knowledge and experiences and her personal attitudes and interests.

Prior knowledge and experience

Prior knowledge includes all of life's experiences—walks with adults through woods and parks, or trips to a zoo, a museum, or the ocean. All experiences that take students out of their immediate surroundings help them develop a broader view of the world in which they live. Through many such experiences, they are introduced to new concepts in a natural setting. This knowledge aids reading comprehension (Richek, 2005; August & Shanahan, 2006; Richardson & Morgan, 2005). Some students come to school never having left their local community. Their background knowledge gained through firsthand experience is limited. Consider the contrast between Sally, who has never been outside her community, and George, who has traveled with his family to a wide variety of places in his home state, across the United States, and to other countries. These trips have afforded George many different firsthand experiences, all of which have enriched his vocabulary and knowledge of the world.

When George and Sally's fifth-grade social studies class studies the Middle Ages, George has an advantage over Sally and the other students.

The teacher, Mr. Black, chooses Philip Steele's *I Wonder Why Castles Had Moats and Other Questions about Long Ago* (1994) as one of the books to read to the students. Mr. Black asks them what a moat is. Sally, who knows about castles from fairy tales featuring queens, kings, princes, and princesses, predicts that a moat is someone who works for the royal family. Billy, who is fascinated with the castle dungeons and weapons, thinks a moat is a type of weapon used in the dungeons. However, George has visited castles and knows that the moat is the water—sometimes natural, sometimes man-made—that surrounds the castle and protects its inhabitants from outside invaders. George gives additional details, explaining how castles were built on high hills and on rivers so the inhabitants of the castle could better defend it from enemies. George is able to picture new information about the Middle Ages more readily than the other students. George's interest in the Middle Ages is also greater than the other students' because of his experiences.

Because prior knowledge is based on all of one's personal experiences, it includes one's experience with informational text. Students who have had a parent or other adult read and discuss expository texts with them understand that not all books tell a story. They understand that some texts teach them about the world or provide important information for everyday use. As concept books are read to children, they are introduced to technical vocabulary that is unique to the particular topic. Obviously, these children have an advantage over children who have never had informational texts read to them. Richardson and Morgan (2005) suggest that students with a broad background and understanding of the world will have an easier time comprehending texts than students with a more limited background.

Interests and attitudes

A positive attitude toward learning and reading is key to being a successful lifelong learner. A positive attitude often originates in the home; conversely, factors at home may cause students to develop a negative attitude toward learning and reading. Parents who cannot read obviously do not read to their children. Parents who had bad experiences in school often express negative opinions of school and teachers, and children often embrace these negative attitudes. Teachers need to counteract these negative attitudes by believing such students can achieve academic success. Sometimes the key to success is finding a subject that truly interests the student.

Not all students are interested in the topics that interest the teacher, and it is fine for students to be passionate about a topic that makes the teacher squirm. If students are exclusively interested in snakes and bugs, the teacher should find books on those topics and read them with the students. Encourage expository reading by eliciting students' interests through discussions of what they do in their spare time and what they would like to do when they become adults.

Richardson and Morgan (2005) argue that poor readers need encouragement and a positive support system. You can offer encouragement and support not only by helping students find books and Internet sites on topics that interest them, but also by making sure these sources are at their easy reading level so they are not discouraged by overly difficult texts. The Assessment section of this chapter discusses how to assess reader interests, and Appendix C.37 contains an Interest Inventory that will aid you in learning more about your students' interests.

Many factors affect readers' comprehension of informational texts. Figure 9.1 lists some characteristics of skilled and unskilled expository readers.

Factors Within the Reader's Environment

Home

Of the three environments most students inhabit—home, community, and school—the home most affects reading comprehension and provides the foundation upon which attitudes toward reading are built. Richardson and Morgan (2005) argue that students who are good comprehenders have parents who read and discuss many different types of texts with their children, and have books, magazines, and other informational materials available in their home. The parents also view and discuss videos, articles on the Internet, and educational TV programs with their children. They make good use of the community's library by checking out informational videos and trade books, and by using the Internet in the library if they do not have access at home. Many parents model the love of learning new things by reading, viewing, and discussing complicated ideas and facts with their children; these children have a great source of prior knowledge from which to draw when reading informational texts.

Unfortunately, not all students come from language-rich home environments. Many homes have no access to books, magazines, or the Internet. Their parents do not take them to the library to check out books or to participate in educational programs. These parents may not recognize the importance of reading skills for their children, nor do they read for enjoyment themselves. Many poor comprehenders also have poor oral skills because they do not have adults with whom they converse. These students

***figure* 9.1** Characteristics of skilled and unskilled readers of informational texts.

SKILLED READERS

1. Know purpose for reading (e.g., to find comparisons, understand details).
2. Know whether their purpose for reading was fulfilled.
3. Recognize a large bank of words automatically.
4. Analyze technical words with ease.
5. Possess background knowledge of many topics and make use of it when reading.
6. Have an advanced vocabulary about many topics.
7. Make inferences about information in the passage.
8. Use fix-up strategies when comprehension breaks down.
9. Are flexible in the use of strategies.
10. Paint mental pictures of the topic.
11. Recognize the organizational structure of text (e.g., cause/effect, comparison/contract, sequence, definition).
12. Build relationships between larger units of text (e.g., relate information among chapters or books).
13. Know where to go for more information if passage is not clear (e.g., go to Internet, databases, or other books).
14. Use appropriate graphic organizers to summarize and to remember text.

UNSKILLED READERS

1. Are often poor decoders.
2. Give up when the passage is not clear.
3. Lack word analysis skills.
4. Have limited background knowledge.
5. Do not relate limited background knowledge to the passage.
6. Have limited vocabulary.
7. Cannot monitor comprehension.
8. Cannot make inferences.
9. Do not create mental pictures of the passage's topic.
10. Do not recognize the organizational structure of text.
11. Do not build relationships between larger units of text.
12. Have poor summarizing skills.
13. Do not acquire strategic strategies; must be taught how, when, and where to consistently use appropriate comprehension strategies.

Sources: Anders & Lloyd (1996); Bos & Vaughn (1994); Gipe (1995); Kletzien (1991); Oakhill & Patel (1991); Richardson & Morgan (2005); Swanson & De La Paz (1998); Symons & Pressley (1993); Winn, Graham, & Prock (1993).

have parents who talk to them, but not with them. They do not watch or discuss educational TV programs together, read together, explore topics on the Internet, or take nature walks together. Chapter 14 will address in detail the correlation between home experiences and reading comprehension.

Community

The second environment that affects reading comprehension is that of the community. Consider two contrasting communities with comparable financial resources—Educationwise and Noread. The leaders of the little town of Educationwise love to learn new things and want the young people in their community to learn about the world in which they live. After all, their wheat crops are exported to all parts of the world! Educationwise's community library is a great source of information because the community leaders understand the importance of providing funds for the library. This library has a vast selection of books, DVDs, and computer programs. The many computers offer free access to the Internet. This library also has many Saturday and after-school programs, such as story time, and focused studies on particular topics, authors, and genres. The Educationwise Public Library also provides classes that teach a range of crafts and skills from different cultures. The library staff welcomes children and young adults and encourages them to "hang out" in the library. The community also provides summer day camps in the local parks. The young people from Educationwise, who have access to a library and many community programs, have the opportunity to develop a rich vocabulary and background knowledge on many topics.

Noread is in the same state as Educationwise. Noread has town leaders who do not see the importance of widening their children's horizons and so, even when funding is available, choose to allocate it elsewhere. This town's library is in a small, dilapidated building and houses outdated books. It has no computers or DVDs. It provides no Saturday or after-school programs or summer day camps to explore nature. In fact, it does nothing to entice young people to come and explore its paltry resources. The children and young adults from Noread have few opportunities for outside enrichment. Its leaders do not understand how this lack of resources affects children's reading, their academic achievement, and success in life.

A community can provide many resources that support the public schools and students' learning. All of these resources enrich background knowledge and encourage them to read more about the topics that interest them.

School

The third influential student environment is the school, and the most important aspect of the school is the classroom. The most important aspect of the classroom is the teacher. A successful teacher is one who:

1. Models a love of reading and learning new things.
2. Expects all students to succeed.
3. Accepts all students as they are and does not assign blame for a student's lack of skills.
4. Encourages risk-taking, which happens when there is:
   - Little emphasis on grades.
   - No ridicule from other students.
   - Appropriate praise for good attempts.
   - Tolerance for mistakes.
   - Appropriate and timely feedback, given in a constructive and caring manner.
5. Asks higher-level thinking questions in addition to literal questions with correct answers.
6. Uses a variety of activities to teach students how to read expository text (see the Intervention section of this chapter for example activities).
7. Provides materials for all reading levels.

Effective, positive teachers provide a wide variety of learning materials on a wide variety of topics. Their classrooms contain programs and software that appeal to many interests and do more than simply enhance skills. Hands-on stations allow students to conduct experiments. Old appliances (with electrical cords cut off) are disassembled and reassembled so students can figure out for themselves how they work. These teachers understand that hands-on experiences enhance the background knowledge students use to comprehend informational texts. They also understand that many struggling readers first need hands-on experiences to entice them to read about the topic.

Factors Within the Text

Teachers include more quality nonfiction trade books, computer programs, and Internet resources in their classrooms today than they did a decade ago (Palmer & Stewart, 2005).

These instructors realize that reading informational texts requires more than decoding skills and literal comprehension. Using a variety of reading materials requires students to (1) synthesize information, (2) analyze authors' credentials, and (3) apply critical-thinking skills when confronted with conflicting information. Struggling readers are often not expected to use these higher-level thinking skills. Too often they are asked to perform only lower-level thinking tasks because teachers are convinced they are incapable of higher-level thinking. Yet this is not true; struggling readers need only the opportunity to develop these skills. One way to develop them is to help them understand the organizational structure of expository texts and to increase their technical vocabulary on specific topics. In the following sections, I first examine the organizational structure of expository text and then discuss how to analyze informational trade and textbooks to select the best ones for your class.

ORGANIZATIONAL STRUCTURE OF EXPOSITORY TEXT

Expository text may be challenging for some students who have little difficulty with narrative text because its organizational structure is different. When reading fictional stories, students become familiar with settings, characters, and plots, and focus on conflicts that need to be resolved. Expository texts omit many elements of fictional narratives, thus students must develop a new schema to grasp how the information is organized. The eight commonly used organizational patterns in expository texts are chronology or sequence, description or enumeration, listing, classification or hierarchy, comparison/contrast, cause/effect, problem/solution, and persuasion.

Authors of informational text use key words for the various text structures. Knowing these key words can help students understand how the text is organized. Figure 9.2 lists words associated with the various text structures. Graphic organizers also help students to understand the organizational patterns in expository text. The Intervention section of this chapter contains an activity for creating graphic organizers and sample organizers for the various organizational patterns.

figure 9.2 Key words associated with text structures.

DESCRIPTION (ENUMERATION)	TIME FRAME (CHRONOLOGY)	COMPARE/CONTRAST	CAUSE/EFFECT & PROBLEM/SOLUTION
to begin	on a specific (date)	however	because
first	not long after	but	since
secondly	now	as well as	therefore
next	as	on one hand/on the other hand	consequently
then	before	not only/but also	as a result
finally	after	either/or	leads to
most important	when	while	nevertheless
also	following	although	accordingly
in fact	soon	unless	if/then
for instance	later	similarly	thus
for example	finally	yet	thereby

Source: Neufeld, P. (Dec. 2005/Jan. 2006). Comprehension Instruction in Content Area Classes. *The Reading Teacher, 59*(4), 302–312. Reprinted with permission of the International Reading Association via Copyright Clearance Center.

Chronology or Sequence

A text that presents information in a chronological or sequential pattern features events that happen in a particular order, and the order is important to understanding the information presented. In chronological texts, the information is often organized around dates. Usually the dates are explicitly stated, but sometimes the author gives only the number of years between events. With this type of text, students must make inferences to attach dates to the events. David Adler, in *A Picture Book of Benjamin Franklin* (1990), includes dates and phrases that represent the passage of time. Following are some examples:

> Benjamin Franklin was born in Boston, Massachusetts, on January 17, 1706.
>
> Benjamin began school when he was eight years old.
>
> When Benjamin was ten, he began to work in his father's soap-and-candle shop.
>
> When he was twelve, his father put Benjamin to work in a print shop.
>
> (unpaged)

From this information, the student can infer the following facts:

1706	Benjamin Franklin was born.
1714	He began school.
1716	He quit school and began working in soap-and-candle shop.
1718	He began working in print shop.

Description or Enumeration

If the organizational structure of the text is description, the author explains an event, an object, or a phenomenon in detail so the reader can better understand it. Notice how Seymour Simon describes the sperm whale in *Whales* (1989):

> The sperm whale is the only giant among the toothed whales. It is the animal that comes to mind when most people think of a whale. A sperm whale has a huge, squarish head, small eyes, and a thin lower jaw. All the fist-sized teeth, about fifty of them, are in the lower jaw. The male grows to sixty feet long and weighs as much as fifty tons. The female is smaller, reaching only forty feet and weighing less than twenty tons. (unpaged)

Simon paints a picture with words, and it is the reader's responsibility to transform those words into a mental picture. In this example, the reader must draw a mental picture of a square head with a thin lower jaw and small eyes in order to understand what a sperm whale looks like. The reader also needs to picture teeth the size of human fists. Proficient readers will do this without assistance. They may use a specific strategy, such as slowing down or rereading the passage, in order to create the picture in their minds (Bos & Vaughn, 1994). Struggling readers often read the words without picturing these images. Teachers should assist them in painting these mental pictures. Strategies for this kind of visualization are discussed later in the chapter.

In the following example from *I Wonder Why Castles Had Moats and Other Questions About Long Ago*, the author paints a picture so that readers can imagine the events and images of a Japanese *No* play.

> *No* are Japanese plays in which actors wear masks and move very slowly, telling story-poems through mime and dance. (p. 27)

As discussed earlier, background knowledge is very important for comprehension of expository texts. It is clear here that readers will benefit from background knowledge about mime and story-poems in attempting to learn about *No* plays. Writers who use description and enumeration expect readers to bring the background knowledge to the reading event because it is cumbersome to explain every concept in detail. Teachers may need to demonstrate mime and read a story-poem in order for struggling readers to understand the author's description of *No*.

In enumeration, an author states a concept and then elaborates on it. In the text *Frogs* (1996), written for young readers, Carolyn MacLulich explains how a frog makes a croaking sound:

> Male frogs make a croaking sound. They puff up the vocal sac under their chin, which makes the sound louder. (p. 13)

Texts for older readers have more detailed descriptions. Notice how Seymour Simon enumerates the process by which the mother whale feeds her calf:

> The mother squirts milk into the young calf's open mouth forty times a day. The milk is rich in fat and energy. Each feeding is very brief, because the baby must surface for air. But in a few seconds, the baby drinks two or three gallons of milk. In one day, a baby whale drinks more than 100 gallons of milk and may gain as much as 200 pounds. (unpaged)

Listing

In this third type of organizational structure, authors may merely list all of the things that fall into a particular category. In *Frogs* (1996), Carolyn MacLulich lists all of the things frogs eat:

> Frogs eat insects, spiders and worms. Some frogs eat larger animals, such as lizards, mice or even other frogs. (p. 12)

In the emergent reader book *Who Lives in the Rainforest?* (1998), Susan Canizares lists the inhabitants of a rainforest. Each type of creature is pictured on its own page with a simple two-word phrase. The text begins with the question "Who lives in the rainforest?" The following are some of the answers to this question:

> Iguanas do.
> Snakes too.
> Jaguars do.
> Pumas too.

This simple list with the colorful photographs of each creature intrigues even the emergent reader to find more information about rainforest creatures.

Classification or Hierarchy

Scientific texts often use classification to show relationships among concepts. Notice how Mary Cerullo explains the categorical relationships among dolphins, whales, and humans in *Dolphins: What They Can Teach Us* (1999):

> Dolphins are small, toothed whales. They belong to the group known as cetaceans (from the Latin word *cetus,* meaning large sea animals), which includes all whales, dolphins, and porpoises . . . Dolphins and humans have a lot in common, we are both mammals. (pp. 4–5)

This text requires higher levels of thinking because readers need to see the main classification with the families under it. Struggling readers will need help to understand how whales, dolphins, porpoises, and humans are related to each other.

Comparison/Contrast

In a comparison/contrast text, authors explain a concept by showing how one event, subject, or object is similar to or different from another. Comparison/contrast helps readers better understand concepts when authors directly present the similarities and differences between the two items. Sandra Markle, in *Outside and Inside Sharks* (1996), explains how sharks differ from fish:

> Look at the reef shark and the soldier fish. They are both fish. They both need oxygen, a gas in air and water, to live. And they both have special body parts called gills that carry oxygen from the water into their bodies. But there are differences between sharks and other fish. A shark's gills are in separate pouches with slits opening to the inside and outside of its body. The soldier fish, and other fish like it, have gills grouped in one chamber. . . . A shark's tail usually has a top part that is longer than the bottom. Other fish usually have tails with two equal parts. But the biggest difference between sharks and other fish is on the inside. (p. 5)

Cause/Effect

Cause/effect passages are often found in science texts to explain what causes natural phenomena. For example, Jenny Wood, in *Caves: Facts and Stories and Activities* (1990), explains how caves form:

> The process of making a cave takes thousands of years. It starts when surface water trickles down through tiny cracks in the rock. The water contains a gas called carbon dioxide which is absorbed from the air and this forms a mild acid that eats away the limestone. As it travels underground, the water continues to eat away some of the rock, forming passages and caves. (p. 4)

In *Volcano: The Eruption and Healing of Mount St. Helens* (1986), Patricia Lauber explains what causes a volcano to erupt.

> Beneath the crust is a region called the mantle. It is made of rock that is very hot. Rock of the mantle can flow, like thick tar. The crust floats on the mantle. . . . The plates are in motion, moving a few inches each year. . . . There are places where plates pull away from each other. Here molten rock wells up and sometimes volcanoes erupt. (pp. 51–52)

Notice that in both of these passages, readers need to be able to mentally picture the action as it happens. Struggling readers who cannot do this will have great difficulty with cause/effect texts. These readers should be taught to recognize the signal words authors use to indicate relationships between causes and effects.

Problem/Solution

Another organizational structure commonly found in expository texts is problem/solution. Often the explanation of a problem will expand for a number of pages before the solution is stated. In *Children of the Dust Bowl: The True Story of the School at Weedpatch Camp* (1992), Jerry Stanley devotes the first chapter to naming all of the problems the Okies endured during the 1930s before he offers a possible solution to the Okies' problems—moving to California. With this text, it is useful for teachers and students to make a list of all the problems that Oklahoma faced during the 1930s. In this way, the students will better understand why much of the state's poorer population migrated to California. The text explores the following problems in detail:

- Small farms
- Great Depression
- No irrigation
- Wheat prices low
- No reservoirs or canals
- Dust storms
- No rain
- Bankruptcy
- Crops shriveled
- Foreclosures on mortgages; evictions from homes

Finally, the text offers the solution many Oklahomans chose by describing how they loaded their possessions on trucks and moved to California, seeking a better life for their families.

Persuasion

Persuasion is a type of writing designed to change readers' minds or thinking. Teachers will usually need to specifically point out to struggling readers how authors attempt to persuade them. As you recall from the discussion in Chapter 1 on critical literacy, teachers can guide students to consider the author's point of view and language in persuasive texts about a particular topic. You can also advise students to consider other possible points of view. For example, some authors attempt to change readers' thinking about environmental issues such as offshore oil drilling, the harm of logging, and the need to protect wildlife. To do this they will use vivid adverbs, adjectives, and other powerful words, or offer a personal assessment of the topic. Notice Todd Wilkinson's persuasive technique in *Bison for Kids* (1994). The underlined words are examples of subtle persuasion; the last sentence, however, is emphatic rather than subtle.

> What happened after that is a <u>sad</u> story. People killed millions of buffalo for food and hides. Settlers <u>slaughtered</u> them to make room on the Great Plains for cattle. One of the most famous bison hunters was William "Buffalo Bill" Cody, who delivered mail for the Pony Express and shot bison to feed railroad workers. He killed thousands of bison. As a result of the <u>over hunting</u>, only a few hundred wild buffalo were left in the United Stated at the end of the 1800s. <u>Bison needed to be protected fast!</u> (pp. 15–16, emphasis added)

Sometimes authors use more forceful techniques to persuade readers to accept their point of view. Point out these techniques to your students.

Propaganda is a persuasive technique that involves the distortion of facts or manipulation of readers. Propaganda is prevalent in advertisements, so smart readers understand these techniques. Listed below are seven propaganda techniques accompanied by brief descriptions.

- *Name calling:* denouncing one product or person to promote another.
- *Card stacking:* giving one side of the story or telling half-truths. Note: advertisements for pre-

scription medications now are required to list negative side effects as well as benefits.

- *Plain folk:* using ordinary people to promote a product.
- *Glittering generalities:* stating a list of positive attributes without giving any specific details.
- *Testimonial:* using a popular person to promote a product that he or she uses.
- *Transfer:* using a popular person to promote a product that is not associated with his or her job or ability.
- *Bandwagon:* an attempt to convince consumers that "Everyone is doing it, so you should do it too."

Sequence for Teaching Expository Text Organizational Patterns

When introducing an informational text pattern to students, the following sequence of instruction may be used (adapted from Tompkins, 2002):

1. Introduce the organizational pattern (e.g., comparison/contrast or sequence) by explaining when and why writers choose this particular structure.
2. Point out the key words associated with the structure (e.g., *because, therefore, as a result, first, next, after that*) and share an example of text using these key words. (Refer to Figure 9.2.)
3. Model ways students can determine text structures when key words are not used (e.g., look at the table of contents and headings).
4. Introduce a graphic organizer for the pattern.
5. Read aloud a section of a book illustrating the text structure.
6. Ask students to listen for and identify the key words in the selection.
7. Using a whiteboard or overhead projector, have the class complete a graphic organizer illustrating the pattern type.
8. Ask students to work in pairs to locate an example of the structure in other informational texts.
9. Have students identify the key words and create a graphic organizer for their informational text.

ANALYSIS OF INFORMATIONAL TEXTS

In recent years, a great variety of nonfiction trade books have become available for all reading levels. Teachers and publishers find that even young students enjoy learning information about their world. When selecting nonfiction books for the classroom, review lists of award-winning titles:

Orbis Pictus Award (www.ncte.org/awards/orbispictus)

Sibert Medal (www.ala.org)

Children's choice (www.reading.org/resources/booklists/childrenschoices.aspx)

When analyzing any type of informational text—trade books, textbooks, e-texts, or websites—consider a number of elements: visual appeal, text features, author's writing style, use of technical vocabulary, and assumptions about readers' background knowledge (Gill, 2009).

Eye Appeal

When examining a text or a website, do the same thing students do when they first look at a book—thumb or scroll through it to see if it looks interesting. Visual appeal is an important characteristic of informational texts; attractive books and websites entice students to read (Stephens, 2008; Gill, 2009). An appealing text has the following traits:

- Appropriate print size for grade level
- Generous margins and white space
- Attractive, up-to-date graphics and photographs that represent both genders and different ethnicities
- Charts that are easy to read
- Pages or screens with the appropriate amount of text with pictures, graphs, and so on (Those filled with text scare young readers!)
- Many subheadings so no passage is too long
- No more than 7 or 12 words per line so the readers' eyes do not make unnecessary movements
- Not too many different ideas on one page so readers are not overloaded with information
- Graphics are located near the corresponding text (Hindes, 2007)

Traditional Book Features

Good textbooks have specialized features that aid reader comprehension, and many trade books also have these features: a table of contents, a glossary, questions at the beginning and end of each chapter, and highlighted vocabulary words. Examine these features to see if they will be useful to readers.

The table of contents should give an overview of the text and depict the relationships among the various topics. The table of contents represents the progression of topics through the text. For example, a table of contents for a history book should indicate whether the text is organized chronologically or by topic. Figure 9.3 shows a table of contents for one chapter of a science textbook. Notice how all of the subheadings support the main topic of the chapter: Changes in the Earth's Surface. Also notice how each *figure* **9.3** Sample table of contents.

Unit C Earth Science

	SCIENCE AND TECHNOLOGY	C2
CHAPTER 1	**Changes in the Earth's Surface**	C4
EXPLORE ACTIVITY	**Exploring Rocks Formed from Molten Rock**	C6
READING FOR SCIENCE	**Identifying the Main Idea**	C7
LESSON 1	**How Do Volcanoes and Earthquakes Change the Earth?**	C8
LESSON 2	**What Landforms Are on the Earth's Surface?**	C14
INVESTIGATE ACTIVITY	**Making a Model of a Landform**	C18
LESSON 3	**How Do Water and Wind Change the Earth's Surface?**	C20
LESSON 4	**How Can Living Things Affect the Earth's Surface?**	C24
	Chapter Review	C28

"Lesson" topic is presented in the form of a question. Good readers will infer from these questions that volcanoes, earthquakes, and wind cause changes in the Earth's surface. You may need to read a table of contents with your struggling readers so they learn how to make inferences about terms and headings. Asking the struggling student questions about these items also will activate his or her background knowledge.

Many textbooks and trade books have a glossary and an index. The glossary gives readers the definitions of words as they relate to the text. The index helps readers locate the pages that include discussion about particular concepts or vocabulary words. A good informational book highlights new vocabulary terms, either by defining new terms in the margin or using boldface or italics within the body of the text and embedding its definition. See Figure 9.4 for an example from the same science textbook.

Good textbooks for elementary and middle school grades include some thought questions at the beginning and end of each chapter. These questions should be literal, inferential, or critical/evaluative (see Chapter 8). For example, in *Bison for Kids* a literal question is, "What are wisents?" The answer is stated in the text,

figure **9.4** Sample definition of terms.

How Volcanoes Form

Hot, melted rock and gases are bursting out of the volcano in the picture. A **volcano** is a special type of mountain with an opening, or vent, at its top. Thousands of years ago, this volcano did not exist. So what happened to form this volcano?

GLOSSARY

volcano (vol kā′ nō), a type of mountain that has an opening at the top through which lava, ash, or other types of volcanic rock flows

Glossary

which provides a definition of wisents. An inferential question is, "Why was it not possible for bison and cattle to live on the Great Plains together?" A critical/evaluative question is, "Was it wrong for settlers to kill bison for food and hides? Support your answer."

Figure 9.5 has an example from the same science textbook that presents main questions with supporting questions under each main heading. Figure 9.6 provides an example of the questions often found at the end of a chapter. Take time to evaluate the questions in a text. Are all three types of questions represented?

Electronic Text Features

Electronic texts, including online texts and ebooks, have features that differ from those of traditional text, and students may need help in using these features. Whether accessed online, on an e-reader, mobile device, or computer, electronic texts typically contain hyperlinks to related material that supports the topic or provides more in-depth information. Links are often indicated by their blue or red text.

Many electronic texts permit readers to click on vocabulary words; clicking provides an audio pronunciation of the word and its meaning for that

figure 9.5 Pre-reading questions.

INQUIRING ABOUT
Changes in the Earth's Surface

LESSON 1
How Do Volcanoes and Earthquakes Change the Earth?

- How do volcanoes form?
- How do volcanoes change the earth?
- How do earthquakes change the earth?
- How do scientists study volcanoes and earthquakes?
- How can you be safe during earthquakes?

LESSON 2
What Landforms Are on the Earth's Surface?

- Where are some landforms?
- What are some kinds of landforms?

LESSON 3
How Do Water and Wind Change the Earth's Surface?

- How does weathering change rocks?
- How does erosion change the earth?

LESSON 4
How Can Living Things Affect the Earth's Surface?

- How do plants and animals change the earth?
- How do people change the earth?

Copy the chapter graphic organizer onto your own paper. This organizer shows you what the whole chapter is all about. As you read the lessons and do the activities, look for answers to the questions and write them on your organizer.

figure 9.6 End of chapter questions.

LESSON 1 REVIEW

1. How does a volcano erupt?
2. How do volcanoes change the earth?
3. How do earthquakes change the earth?
4. How do scientists study earthquakes and volcanoes?
5. What are some ways to stay safe during an earthquake?
6. **Main Idea** Read the material on page C10. What is the main idea of this material?

context. Some electronic texts have audio and/or videos to help explain concepts.

Many websites provide expository text for all reading levels. These electronic texts give students access to a wide variety of topics; however, they may need more guidance as they read online. Walk students through a website, showing them electronic text features and demonstrating how to use the back button. A good website for such a demonstration is the National Geographic site, www.kids.nationalgeographic.com/kids. On the opening page students are given a list of possible activities and topics: games, videos, animals and pets, photos, countries, fun stuff, community, news, animal jams, and little kids. The reading level is for upper elementary or middle school students. Figure 9.7 shows the opening page. Preview as many Internet sites as possible so you know whether they are at your students' reading level.

Online electronic texts do not usually have a table of contents or an index to help readers locate information. Therefore, it is important that each page on the screen has main headings and subheadings of

figure **9.7**

National Geographic Kids website.

Source: www.kids.nationalgeographic.com/kids

larger print and/or a different font so students can see the material's organization. Because Internet sites are not evaluated by trusted experts as most trade books and textbooks are, you must also teach students how to evaluate the information they find. Have them first check the information using their background knowledge; does the information conflict with what they already know? They can also verify accuracy by checking other sources, both traditional text and other websites. They can determine whether the site's information is current by checking the date on which the information was posted. Students should find out who the author is and with what organization, if any, the author is affiliated. Teach critical-thinking skills as you help students find biases in the information. The Library of Congress website, www.americaslibrary.gov/cgi-bin/page.cgi, is an excellent source for information that does not contain errors.

Karchmer (2001) found that most reputable websites include the following:

1. The author's credentials with an e-mail address for personal websites.
2. The address, telephone number, and e-mail address for organizational websites.
3. Complete citations of quoted material.
4. Endorsements from respected organizations.
5. Links only to reputable sites.

Of course, you must caution students about inappropriate websites. Most schools use blocking software to keep the Internet safe for students. Some teachers prescreen sites and permit students to use only those sites they deem appropriate.

The informational electronic text form in Appendix D.21 will help you evaluate websites and other forms of electronic text. Its questions were compiled from several checklists and are intended for use by the classroom teacher (Cecil & Gipe, 2009).

Writing Style

Writing style includes such aspects of writing as presentation of facts, grammatical structure, sentence length, tense, mood, and voice. These aspects affect the readability of a text. Palmer and Stewart (1997) found that many textbooks are cold, clinical, and present facts in an encyclopedic manner. They call this type of textbook "a parade of facts." This type of writing is not engaging and difficult to comprehend because the reader must process too many facts at once.

Textbooks may also feature poor grammar, which can cause comprehension problems. For example, the ambiguous pronouns in the following sentence obscure the writer's meaning: "Remove the plastic lids from the cans and throw them away." Should one throw away the lids or the cans?

Other times a text is composed of short, simple sentences that show no relationship among the ideas. Notice the choppy sentences used in *Sam the Sea Cow* by Jacobs (1979).

> One manatee turns to face Sam.
>
> He puts his snout right up to Sam's.
>
> They rub noses.
>
> They rub whiskers.
>
> The manatees begin to twist and roll.
>
> They pop up and down.
>
> They play follow-the-leader.
>
> They swim off together. (pp. 42–43)

Readers may not understand that the manatees become friends and swim off together.

Some texts have so many embedded phrases that readers have trouble identifying the main idea. Examine the following paragraph and note how many ideas the brain must process.

> The bones of whale's skull form huge upper and lower jaws. Each tooth in this sperm whale's jaw weighs more than half a pound. Whales have external ears, very little hair, and no sweat glands. A thick layer of fatty tissue beneath their skin, called blubber, helps insulate them against the cold water and also stores energy. Whales were once hunted mostly for their blubber, which was boiled down to whale oil aboard the whaling ships and used as fuel in oil lamps. (Simon, 1989, unpaged)

Texts in the passive voice are more difficult to comprehend than those in the active voice. Notice how the following two sentences convey the same message, but the active voice in the second sentence makes comprehension easier because the action is more vivid and direct.

> The fish was safely reeled in by two sailors, struggling not to fall out of the heaving boat.
>
> Two sailors, struggling not to fall out of the heaving boat, safely reeled in the fish.

Use of Technical Vocabulary

In addition to a complex writing style, the technical vocabulary used in expository texts may be overwhelming for struggling readers. "Students' comprehension is greatly influenced by their vocabulary knowledge" (Richardson & Morgan, 2005, p. 242). Good authors understand this and use writing techniques to help readers understand technical terms.

Having readers look up unknown words before they read the passage is nonproductive (Weaver, 2002). However, readers benefit by having teachers explain the ways new technical words are defined within the passage. Authors sometimes give a definition first and then state the vocabulary word. For example, in *Bison for Kids* Wilkinson explains wisents in this manner: "Huge ancestors of the modern bison, known as the wisent (VEE-SENT), roamed far and wide" (p. 12). Wilkinson even indicates how the word is pronounced by using parentheses and capital letters. Simon uses the same technique in *Whales* by setting off the technical term in commas:

> A whale's nostril, called a blowhole, is at the top of its head. A whale breathes through its blowhole. (unpaged)

Authors sometimes introduce a term and then set off the definition in commas: "Dolphins are remarkable mimics, copying others' behavior and sounds" (Cerullo, 1999, p. 18). Others provide definitions by setting them off with a dash: "This humpback whale is breaching—jumping almost clear out of the water and then crashing down in a huge spray of foam" (Simon, 1989, unpaged).

Most authors use a mix of techniques. In the following example Philip Steele (1994) uses a sentence to describe one term, an appositive phrase to describe another, and a participial phrase to explain the last term:

> Minarets are the tall slender towers on mosques, the building where Muslims pray to God. They, too, point to heaven. At the top of the minaret is a balcony, where a man called a muezzin stands to call people to prayer. (p. 13)

Like many authors, Wood (1990) uses boldface to draw attention to new words and then states definitions immediately after: "Another group of scientists who are interested in caves are **geologists.** Geologists study caves, rocks, soil, mountains, rivers, oceans, and other parts of the Earth" (p. 23). Watt (1993) uses boldface to indicate that the word is included in the glossary at the back of the book.

You must explicitly teach struggling readers about the techniques authors use to define new words, because they do not necessarily recognize them on their own (Fisher, Frey, & Lapp, 2008).

Author's Assumption of Readers' Background Knowledge

Authors tend to choose words that will best describe an event, an action, or a phenomenon; however, unfamiliar vocabulary may make the passage difficult for struggling readers. Be on the lookout for words that may cause problems for readers with a limited vocabulary. When reading the following passage, struggling readers may not create the appropriate mental picture of the swimming dolphins because they do not know the words *proportioned* and *penetrate*.

> You have to watch a dolphin swim for a few seconds to see that it is perfectly proportioned to penetrate the wave. (Cerullo, 1999, p. 10)

When reading the next passage, readers' comprehension may break down because they cannot pronounce *Cetaceans* and *cetus;* they will probably not know that *Cetaceans* is a classification based on the Latin root *cetus*. Teachers should explain these facts to struggling readers.

> [Dolphins] belong to the group known as Cetaceans (from the Latin word *cetus,* meaning large sea animal), which includes all whales, dolphins, and porpoises. (Cerullo, 1999, p. 4)

Authors may assume readers have sufficient background knowledge to fully comprehend the text and visualize its images. In the following passage, readers need to know the location of several countries to know what is meant by the word *Ring* in the phrase *Ring of Fire*.

> Some of these volcanoes are on the ocean floor. Others are on land. Most of the land volcanoes circle the Pacific Ocean. They run from South America to Alaska to Japan, Indonesia, and New Zealand. Together they are known as the Ring of Fire. (Lauber, 1986, p. 51)

Some authors do not provide enough illustrations, graphs, charts, and photographs to explain the text. The paragraph above would be easier to comprehend if the author had included a map of that area with the ring of volcanoes clearly marked.

Authors can aid readers' comprehension by organizing materials in a cohesive manner, using clear diagrams and charts, and writing literate sentences. Figure 9.8 presents considerate versus inconsiderate characteristics of textbook styles. As you critique textbooks, you may want to add to the list. In addition, you may use the checklist provided in Appendix D.22 for textbook evaluation.

Readability

Readability is often determined by formulas that approximate the reading level of texts. The formulas are based on the number of syllables and the sentence length within passages. (See Chapter 2 for a description of the Fry Readability Formula.) The assumption is that shorter words and sentences are easier to comprehend. However, teachers must also look at the vocabulary used in the passage, because new readers may often know its four- and five-syllable words but not its one- or two-syllable words. Consider the words *hippopotamus* and *rhinoceros* to the words *brusque* and *crux*. According to a readability formula, *hippopotamus* and *rhinoceros* would make the passage's reading level higher than the passage with the one-syllable words. Yet students are likely familiar with the animals but not the other two words. Teachers also understand that concrete words such as *butterfly* and *astronaut* are easier to understand than abstract words such as *transformation* and *prejudice*.

figure **9.8** Considerate and inconsiderate textbook styles.

CONSIDERATE

1. Organization of text's structure is clear to reader
2. Concepts are logically, clearly explained
3. Main ideas are explicitly stated
4. Subtopics relate and support main idea
5. Appropriate signal words are used for each type of text (e.g., sequence = *first, second*)
6. Clear pronoun/antecedent agreement
7. Necessary background information is provided
8. Definition of new term is clearly stated
9. New concepts are clearly and concisely explained
10. Visual aids complement text

INCONSIDERATE

1. No logical text structure
2. Ungrammatical sentence structure
3. Sentence length is long
4. Lack of pictorial aids
5. No use of subordinating conjunctions to show relationships
6. Ambiguous pronouns
7. Assumption of advanced background knowledge
8. New vocabulary is not defined
9. Information presented in encyclopedic fashion
10. Pages of text without visual aids

Sources: Ambruster, B. (1996), Considerate text. In D. Lapp, J. Flood, & N. Farman (Eds.), *Content Area Reading and Learning: Instructional Strategies* (2nd ed.), pp. 47–58. Boston: Allyn & Bacon; Olson, M. W. & Gee, T. (1991), Content reading instruction in the primary grades: Perceptions and strategies, *The Reading Teacher, 45,* 298–307; Palmer, R. & Stewart, R. (1997), Nonfiction tradebooks in content area instruction: Realistic and potential, *Journal of Adolescent and Adult Literacy, 40*(8), 630–642; Richardson, J. & Morgan, R. (2005), *Reading to Learn in the Content Areas* (3rd ed.), Belmont, CA: Wadsworth Publishing Co.

A *butterfly* and *astronaut* can be seen and felt, while a *transformation* and a *prejudice* cannot. Thus, formulas should not be the sole determinant of a textbook or trade book's readability, but they can provide an approximate reading level when used with a checklist like the one found in Appendix D.22.

ENGLISH LEARNERS AND EXPOSITORY TEXT

Instructional Recommendations

English learners deserve special consideration when reading from informational books. They first need to understand the academic vocabulary in order to comprehend the information. Like Malcolm in the opening scenario, English learners may have an oral vocabulary that exceeds their receptive (reading/hearing) vocabulary. You will need to scaffold these students as they "read" informational books. First work on building their vocabulary. English learners should know the word, meaning they should be able to pronounce it correctly, give a definition in their own words, and use the word in multiple ways. You may need to read the text with these students while they discuss the information and pictures. The pictures will help them with comprehension. Use as many visuals as possible; the visuals can be pictures, gestures, pantomime, and facial expressions. To engage them while you are reading, ask them to listen for the key words and raise a finger when they hear them. Technical terms often have many syllables, so these students may need time to hear and practice the pronunciation. Give English learners opportunities to ask questions and restate the information. It is also advantageous for teachers and students to read the text in unison so the students can practice phrasing and intonation.

English learners should also receive small group instruction "to assist . . . in building and extending vocabulary and improving their listening comprehension and oral expression" (Vaughn et al., 2005, p. 63). Base small group instruction on regular classroom materials to prevent a disconnect between small group and large group topics. However, you may choose easier books so the English learners can more readily grasp the concepts. Divide the passage in small sections of about 200 to 250 words and read only one section a day. The rest of the small group time should be used to discuss the passage—each student should be given an opportunity to discuss or explain the concept presented in their reading. This practice builds their confidence so they are later willing to express their ideas in the larger group.

Consider the following small group session between Mr. Chung and four of his third-grade English learners. The third graders are studying a unit on creatures of the seas. Mr. Chung is sharing Melvin and Gilda Berger's information book *Sharks* (2003) with the group because it is short, with only one or two sentences per page, but very interesting to third graders.

Mr. Chung: The book we are going to read is *Sharks* (pointing to the word on the cover) by Melvin and Gilda Berger (pointing to the names on the cover). Look at the shark's big mouth (pointing to the shark's mouth) and big eye (pointing to the shark's eye). Let's read this book together.

Mr. Chung and group: "Here comes a shark."

Mr. Chung: What do you see?

Juan: Shark big mouth.

Mr. Chung: The shark does have a big mouth. (Notice how Mr. Chung extends Juan's sentence.)

Mr. Chung: Now turn the page (as he turns his page). Let's read.

Mr. Chung and small group: "Fun Fact: If sharks stop swimming, they sink."

Mr. Chung: Do you know what stop swimming means?

(He can tell from their facial expressions that they do not understand.) Moving his arms as if he is swimming, he says, "I am swimming." Then he stops moving his arms and says, "I stop swimming. Do you understand?"

The students nod their heads "Yes" and move their arms and repeat: "I am swimming." They stop moving their arms and repeat: "I stop swimming."

Mr. Chung: Do you know what sink means?

They shake their heads "No."

Mr. Chung fills a large glass with water and puts a paper clip into the water and says, "The paper clip sinks." He then puts a small square piece of paper in the water and says, "The paper floats." He points to the paper clip and says, "Sink" and then to the paper and says, "Float."

The small group says both words, "Sinks! Floats!"

Mr. Chung moves his arms as if he is swimming. Then he reads: "If the sharks stop swimming, they sink." (Mr. Chung stops moving his arms and falls to the floor.)

The group mimics Mr. Chung and repeats the sentence.

Mr. Chung knows that for students to comprehend the information in the book, he has to act out the words and have the students model the actions. Because they are in a room by themselves, Mr. Chung is not embarrassing any of the students in front of their peers. He continues reading and discussing each page, because he wants each student to comprehend the information, not just read words.

English learners need to develop vocabulary and reading skills in content areas to be successful in school. Too often teachers focus only on reading the material, which results in the struggling readers and English learners not getting practice in reading this type of material (Ogle & Correa-Kovtun, 2010). To develop skills in reading informational texts, they have to read materials on their independent level or instructional level so they can focus on the information, not on the decoding. They also need ample opportunity to discuss materials so they learn to pronounce the words and internalize the information. Like all students, when English learners verbalize the information, they solidify the material in their minds (Ogle & Correa-Kovtun, 2010; Mills, 2009; Wolf, Crossen, & Resnick, 2004). They also need to be in small groups, as Mr. Chung knows, where they are free to discuss the topic and activate prior knowledge. Small groups enable them to make inferences, create mental pictures, and ask questions, instead of just answering questions with the group (Mills, 2009). Encourage them to ask questions when they do not understand a concept. Just like all students, they need explicit instruction in using many text features (captions, graphs, table of contents, glossary, and index). English learners also need to read and think critically by being encouraged to state their point of view concerning material that impacts their lives.

Like Malcolm in the opening scenario, English learners in middle school are attempting to learn advanced concepts and pass state-mandated tests while still learning the language. Sheltered instruction (see Chapter 1 for a detailed discussion on sheltered instruction) is "specially designed academic instruction in English" (Marino-Weisman & Hansen, 2007, p. 181). The goal of sheltered instruction is to teach content and academic language simultaneously to a small group. The teacher speaks slowly and uses gestures or pantomime as Mr. Chung did in the previous example when explaining new concepts. Because middle school textbooks use complex sentences that may be written in the passive voice, teachers and students should create graphic organizers of the information as they read. This activity will help English learners see the relationship between concepts. It is important to keep English learners engaged during instructional time, so students can also create a graphic organizer as the teacher creates it. After reading, discussing, and creating a graphic organizer related to a passage, invite the small group of students to role-play the concepts. This allows them to practice the vocabulary and gives the teacher an opportunity to informally assess their English growth and understanding of the concepts.

For example, if students are studying the life cycle of a seed, the teacher and students can first draw a graphic organizer showing the cycle. (See Figure 9.9 for a sample.) Then the teacher can role play how the tiny seed sprouts through the earth and becomes a small plant. She starts in a crouching position with her head between her knees and slowly raises her head up. Next, she role plays how the plant grows, blossoms, and becomes a fruit. She slowly stands up, stretches out her arms with fists clutches, and then finally opens her palms and fingers wide. Then through pantomime a student pretends to pick the fruit, cut it open, find a new seed, and plant that seed in the ground.

Many content area vocabulary words are abstract; for example, social studies introduces *liberty, responsibility, democracy, freedom,* and *government.* Reading selections usually offer no visual clues to help English learners understand these abstract concepts. Therefore, introduce only the words needed for that day's lesson instead of all the words for the unit. However, one fun way to engage students in reviewing all the vocabulary words for a unit is to play Jeopardy. (Build your own game board for free at http://jeopardylabs.com.) You can have students compete in teams of two; collaboration and competition are both activities that middle school students enjoy.

Singing "enhances personal expression, builds community, and connects reading and writing" (Bintz,

figure **9.9** Graphic organizer of the life cycle of a seed.

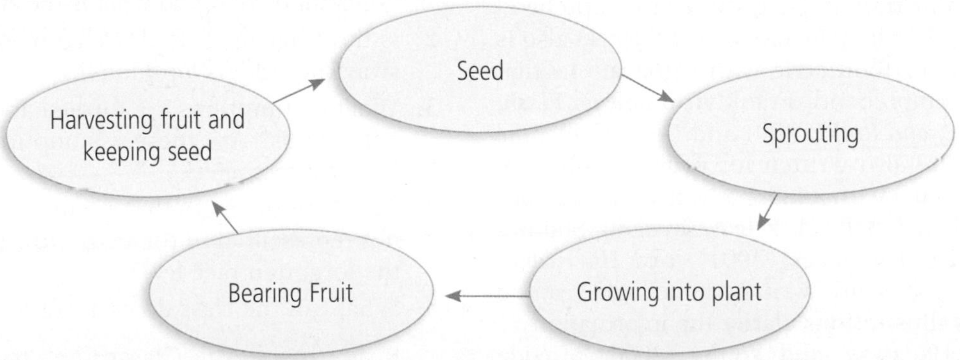

2010, p. 683). Singing helps facilitate phonics, phonemic awareness, rhymes, memorization, and vocabulary; therefore, it is a wonderful tool to use to help English learners (and others) to learn and remember science or social studies concepts. Bintz (2010) suggests that teachers write parodies of songs with content information. For example, while learning about clouds, he wrote a song to the tune of "London Bridge Is Falling Down" with a verse about cirrus clouds:

> "Cirrus clouds are made of ice
>
> Seen before, rain or snow,
>
> Cirrus clouds are made of ice
>
> Clouds, thin and wispy" (p. 684).

English learners are absorbing concepts, vocabulary, and English as they have fun singing with their classmates. Teachers can pair English learners with native speakers and have them write their own songs based on a concept they are studying.

Selecting Informational Text

What should a teacher consider when choosing informational texts for English learners? First, the books must be quality literature; they must contain accurate information, define technical terms, and feature illustrations that complement the text. Second, the books must be age appropriate and fit with the students' comprehension level. Because some English learners may not have the language skills to read or comprehend classroom science and social studies textbooks with technical information and vocabulary, you may want to choose trade books that deal with the same topic. Many authors write on a given subject, but for different grade levels. This makes it easy for teachers to choose books on a particular subject that accommodate a wide variety of reading levels. For example, when presenting a unit on weather, you can choose Gail Gibbons' *Weather Words and What They Mean* (1992) and *Weather Forecasting* (1993). Gibbons delivers the information in cartoon-style pictures. Her colorful and detailed illustrations help students comprehend the concepts. Tomie dePaola's *Clouds* (1984) also is written in the cartoon style with explanations that are easy to comprehend. Franklyn Branley's *Flash, Crash Rumble, and Roll* (1999) and *Down Comes the Rain* (1997) are also written for young children. If you have students with a more advanced vocabulary and comprehension level, select Seymour Simon's *Storms* (1992), *Tornadoes* (2001), and *Hurricanes* (2002). His books are written at a high reading level, but his illustrations clarify the information.

Vardell, Hadaway, and Young (2006) provide the following guidelines for selecting informational trade books for English learners. They should:

1. Have reference aids (glossary, index, table of contents).
2. Be well organized (sequence, cause/effect, problem/solution, enumeration, and so on).
3. Have charts, graphs, diagrams, photographs, or illustrations with useful captions.
4. Fit the students' background knowledge, focusing on appropriate vocabulary and reading level.
5. Contain plentiful white space; some information books with pages full of text are written for advanced grade levels.
6. Introduce new vocabulary words in boldface type or highlighted text.

DEVELOPING CRITICAL LITERACY WITH EXPOSITORY TEXTS

In Chapter 8, I discussed the importance of developing students' critical literacy because "critical literacy challenges status quo and clarifies connections between knowledge and power" (Soares & Wood, 2010, p. 488). I discussed how teachers can use historical fiction to create units that aid students in better understanding events in history. In this section I will discuss how critical literacy can be developed using expository texts in social studies, because "it is through the content of social studies that students make sense of their lives" (Soares & Wood, 2010, p. 487). Social studies gives students the opportunity to look at current events critically by questioning "truths, sources, and evidence" (Soares & Wood, 2010, p. 487). As students read about current and historical events they need to discuss the political, sociocultural, historical, and economic forces that affect their lives—and then question them—in order to become aware of their social responsibilities (Soares & Wood, 2010). Your goal is to prompt students to respond to information rather than be passive consumers of it.

After reading an expository text with students, lead a discussion that considers the following five aspects central to a critical literacy focus:

1. Does the author present dominant or the minority's point of view and what is the author's intent?
2. Is the language biased? What words are used to sway the readers' opinions?
3. What assumptions are formed about the different groups? Are these assumptions unfair and harmful to society?
4. Are there any races that are in the classroom but not represented in the text? How do students of the forgotten race feel?
5. What can the class do as a call to action?

Read "Inside the Classroom" to see how Ms. Nickel used the U.S. war in Afghanistan to prompt her eighth-grade class to take action.

Inside the Classroom

A SOCIAL STUDIES LESSON WITH A CRITICAL LITERACY FOCUS

Ms. Nickel, a seventh-grade social studies teacher, learns toward the end of the school year that she will have two Afghan immigrants in her class in the following fall. The school has students of many different races and ethnic groups, but these will be the first students from the Middle East. The two have been in the United States for five years but have just moved into the school district. Records indicate the students are high performers, yet shy. Ms. Nickel, whose father served a tour of duty in Afghanistan, is passionate about the Afghan people living in a free and democratic world. She understands that in her urban classroom some students may not share her feelings, because many have parents serving in the military in Iraq and Afghanistan. Ms. Nickel reads some articles in her professional journals about critical literacy. She decides it is her responsibility to get her class to welcome the new students, but she knows this will not happen simply by reminding them of her one rule: all students must respect each other and their property.

In past years when Ms. Nickel discussed current events with her middle school students, she found that many of them who claimed to be open-minded were really very close-minded about certain topics, or they parroted their parents' opinions. She wants to change this; she wants her students to read different accounts of current events and discuss them before they form opinions.

Throughout the summer she collects articles about the Afghan war from her local newspaper. She notices that some authors write in a manner intended to sway readers' opinions and ideas about the war.

During the first four weeks of school, Ms. Nickel explains the concept of critical literacy to her students and has them consider the authors' biased language and perspectives and the voices not represented by the authors. Because this is her first time teaching critical literacy, she decides not to begin with the Afghan war, but with another topic that resonates with her students: the Oklahoma Land Run, a state-required topic for her grade.

Her class, which includes three Native American students, becomes passionately engaged as they discuss whose voices were silenced during the settlement of their native Oklahoma and during the Trail of Tears. After these discussions, Ms. Nickel decides they are ready to consider the war in Afghanistan.

During the fifth week of school after the two new students have been accepted by the class, Ms. Nickel gives them all a copy of an article about a recent skirmish between U.S. and Afghan troops in which one of the soldiers killed was an Oklahoman.

The students react immediately to the following sentence: "Still, they feed on larger doubts about the ongoing massive recruiting among a largely illiterate population—many of whom are accustomed to holding a gun but not to rigid military discipline" (Associated Press, 2010, p. 10A). One student responds, "How can they say *illiterate?* They do not know our classmates!" Others discuss how some readers would believe that statement because they do not know their friends. One of the Afghan students shyly offers that in some cases the statement may be true because not everyone has the opportunity to go to school in Afghanistan. That is the reason their families came to the United States. His classmates were amazed; they could not imagine not going to school. One student, who had read *Three Cups of Tea* (Mortenson & Relin, 2006), tells the class about the Pennies for Peace project. The students are so enthusiastic that they ask Ms. Nickel if they can have a jar in the hallway and collect pennies until the end of the school year. The students agree to be responsible for rolling the change at the end of each week. Ms. Nickel is not only pleased with the way her students engage with the topic, becoming critical readers as they consider the author's perspective, the loaded language, and the silenced voices, but she is also thrilled to see her students take action by implementing the Pennies for Peace project.

ASSESSMENT

Reading expository text takes the same skills that are needed to read narrative texts. Readers must have a large bank of words they recognize on sight. They must have good decoding skills for encountering technical terms. They need to understand letter–sound relationships, digraphs, diphthongs, consonant blends, and syllabication for decoding. If a reader struggles with decoding, the teacher should determine what aspect of decoding is the problem. (Refer to Chapters 5 and 6 for ways to assess a reader's decoding and word analysis skills.) After assessment, teachers assist the readers as they build the necessary skills to master expository texts.

Informal Assessment

Informal reading inventories

As mentioned in Chapter 8, informal reading inventories (IRIs) can be used to assess oral and silent reading comprehension. IRIs include expository as well as narrative passages that can be used to assess a student's comprehension of informational text. Chapter 3 has more information about IRIs.

Rubrics

Designing rubrics based on state standards helps teachers monitor individual student growth in comprehending expository text. The partial rubric in Figure 9.10 is based on Colorado's standards for the fourth grade. Notice that at the end of the second quarter, Wade sometimes uses effective strategies to comprehend expository text and sometimes can identify supporting details and main ideas; however, he cannot summarize long text passages or draw inferences. Most of his classmates can do these things, so his teacher is concerned about his progress. She discusses the situation with Wade's mother, and they decide that Wade will benefit from weekly tutoring sessions with a paraprofessional.

figure **9.10** Rubric for reading comprehension based on fourth-grade reading standard for Colorado.

FOURTH GRADE

STUDENT *Wade* TOTAL SCORE *11* GRADING PERIOD 1 (2) 3 4

TRAIT	LEVEL OF MASTERY TARGET (5 POINTS)	ACCEPTABLE (3 POINTS)	UNACCEPTABLE (1 POINT)
Uses full range of strategies (skims, scans, self-monitors)	Always uses appropriate strategies to comprehend texts (skims, scans, self-monitors). ___	Sometimes uses appropriate strategies to comprehend texts (skims, scans, self-monitors). _X_	Seldom uses appropriate strategies to comprehend texts (skims, scans, self-monitors). ___
Identifies main ideas with supporting details	Always identifies main ideas with supporting details. ___	Sometimes identifies main ideas with supporting details. _X_	Seldom identifies main ideas with supporting details. ___
Summarizes long expository texts	Always summarizes long expository texts. ___	Sometimes summarizes long expository texts. ___	Seldom summarizes long expository texts. _X_
Draws inferences	Always draws inferences using contextual clues. ___	Sometimes draws inferences using contextual clues. ___	Seldom draws inferences using contextual clues. _X_
Sets purpose	Always sets purpose for reading. ___	Sometimes sets purpose for reading. ___	Seldom sets purpose for reading. _X_
Uses text features	Always uses text features (bold print, subheadings, etc.). ___	Sometimes uses text features (bold print, subheadings, etc.). ___	Seldom uses text features (bold print, subheadings, etc.). _X_
Sequential order	Always identifies sequential order in expository text. ___	Sometimes identifies sequential order in expository text. ___	Seldom identifies sequential order in expository text. _X_

Source: Based on Colorado's State Standards for Fourth Grade.

Running records and miscue analysis

Using informational texts for running records and miscue analyses will help you determine which cueing systems the students use while reading informational passages. A reader may use the same systems she does for narrative text or she may approach informational text in a different way. For example, she may use more visual clues, such as dividing words into parts, instead of using semantic clues, such as relying on background information. Chapter 3 discusses how to administer, score, and analyze both of these assessment instruments. Many commercial miscue analyses have one informational passage for each grade level.

Cloze and maze procedures

Often teachers find that most students are able to read a book or passage; only one or two students struggle with the text. There are two other ways to determine whether a text is at the easy level, the instruction level, or the frustration level for a student: the cloze test and the maze. Each of these assessments helps determine the appropriateness of a particular book for a particular student. See Chapter 3 for detailed description of these two tests.

Assessing reading interests

When working one-on-one with a struggling student, attempt to get him "hooked on reading." The student may enjoy stories but dislike informational books. Choosing a topic that interests him is essential; when possible let him choose the topic. First make sure the book is on the reader's instructional reading level. If the student is a reluctant and struggling reader, try choosing a book that is on her easy reading level so she experiences success. Determine a student's interests by developing an interest inventory that prompts her to think about her personal interests. Figure 9.11 shows a partially completed interest survey that will help a teacher select appropriate informational texts. Appendix C.13 has a blank survey.

Assessing background knowledge

Teachers must assess students' background knowledge to determine whether they are comprehending informational material. One way to assess this aspect of reading is to give students a list of major concepts from a passage, and ask them what they know about each. Another way to assess background knowledge is by using a K-W-L chart (refer to Figure 9.22).

Talking Drawings is another informal assessment used with kindergarten and first-grade students to assess their prior knowledge (Paquette, Fello, & Renck-Jalongo, 2007). Most kindergarten and first-semester first graders cannot take a paper-and-pencil test. From this assessment, teachers learn what prior knowledge students have about a topic and any misconceptions they might have. Teachers can also assess students' listening skills as they listen to their peers explain their drawings and students'

figure **9.11** Sample interest survey.

NAME: Matt AGE: 10 DATE: 9/20

THINGS THAT INTEREST ME

These questions are about your interests! You can list more than one thing for each question.

1. What is your favorite topic to study in science? hurricanes and earthquakes
2. What topic in science that you have not studied do you wish you could study? How space ships stay up in space
3. What sport would you like to read about? Basketball
4. Who is your favorite athlete? I don't have one
5. What would you like to learn about him/her? X
6. Do you watch any nature or discovery shows on TV? If so, are they about animals, earthquakes, hurricanes, different places in the world, space? earthquakes and space

Source: Adapted from McCormick, Sandra, *Instructing Students Who Have Literacy Problems*, 5th ed., © 2007, p. 170. Reprinted by permission of Pearson Education, Inc., Upper Saddle River, NJ.

oral vocabulary as they explain their own drawings. Following are the steps for Talking Drawings.

1. Tell students the topic that they are going to study, such as farm animals.
2. Invite them to draw a picture depicting what they know about the topic. For example, students would be invited to draw pictures depicting objects they would find on a farm.
3. Have students share their drawings with peers.
4. Read the text(s), using the directed-reading-thinking activity.
5. After the reading, have students draw a new picture or modify their first drawing. Encourage students to label parts of their drawing. Offer assistance with spelling if the child insists on correct spelling.
6. After all students have completed their drawings, again ask them to share with their peers the differences between the two drawings and explain what they learned from the text(s).

Vocabulary assessment

Knowing a vocabulary word is more than being able to recite its definition. It means being able to use the word and explain it to others. Informational books are dense with technical terms. The goal is to encourage students to "own" a word so they can use the specific term instead of the phrase, "this thing." According to Dale, O'Rourke, and Bamman (1971), there are four levels of knowing a word:

1. I've never seen or heard the word before.
2. I've heard it, but don't know what it means.
3. I recognize the word in context.
4. I know and can use it.

Dale, O'Rourke, and Bamman. (1971) suggest four methods a teacher can use when assessing readers' vocabulary knowledge:

1. Ask students to give the definition orally or in writing.
2. Have students complete a multiple-choice exercise.
3. Have them complete a matching exercise.
4. Ask students to check words they know in a list.

For the first method choose a list of new words from a passage. The readers then explain the terms in their own words. You can readily determine on what level readers know the word. I suggest you not use multiple-choice and matching exercises, because readers may resort to guessing.

In the fourth method, students are merely indicating if they know or do not know the meaning of the word. If this is done as a pre-reading task, take time to explain the words that are needed to comprehend the passage. If this exercise is done as a post-reading task, evaluate how well readers comprehend the concepts.

Assessing readers' growth

The most accurate assessment of students' growth in reading expository text comes through careful observation over a long period of time in a variety of settings—one-on-one tutoring, independent reading, and large and small group participation. The assessments must include all types of informational reading materials—textbooks, trade books, computer programs, age-appropriate Internet sites, magazines, and instructions (e.g., for board games, science experiments, arts and crafts projects).

When struggling readers do not recognize their own miscues, they continue to plod along. The goal for every reader is to become self-monitoring. One way to assess readers' self-monitoring growth is to have a child read a passage of expository text into a recording device and have the student play it back and identify his own errors. Teachers should be silent observers, allowing the student to find his own the errors. The goal is for him to recognize reading miscues as he makes them.

Many students are critical of themselves and have a poor self-concept. For these students to find their own errors may be counterproductive. In such cases, first record a passage that is at the reader's level and include some deliberate miscues. Then the student can listen to the recording while following the script, listening for your errors. When you make the recording, read a little slower than normal and very distinctly, so students can hear the errors. Closely observe them during this activity, and then discuss the miscues afterward. When students are comfortable with this procedure, they can then record their own readings.

To record struggling students' reading growth throughout the school year, use the recordings and a checklist similar to the one found in Appendix C.38 or the rubric found in Appendix C.39. Remember to date the checklist so there is a record of when the readers accomplished each task. The checklist can also help you write short-term goals for readers if it is used once a week or every other week.

Formal Assessment

Two types of standardized tests that assess students' reading comprehension are achievement tests and criterion-referenced tests. Many of the reading subtests that measure comprehension have informational passages as well as stories. As you will recall from Chapter 3, achievement tests measure the current level of students' performance in a variety of areas, including reading. There are three different types of standardized achievement tests—reading readiness, norm-referenced, and criterion-referenced. Only norm-referenced and criterion-referenced tests have comprehension subtests with informational passages. The following is a list of norm-referenced and criterion-referenced tests with comprehension subtests.

STANDARDIZED NORM-REFERENCED ACHIEVEMENT TESTS

1. Iowa Test of Basic Skills (Grades K–8)
2. Stanford Achievement Tests (Grades K–13)
3. Gates-MacGinitie Reading Tests (Grades K–12)
4. Metropolitan Achievement Tests–Reading (Grades K–12)
5. Comprehensive Test of Basic Skills, U and V (Grades K–12)
6. California Achievement Tests–Reading (Grades K–9)

STANDARDIZED CRITERION-REFERENCED TESTS

1. Comprehensive Test of Basic Skills–Reading, Expanded Edition (Grades K–12)
2. Phonics Criterion Test (Grades 1–3)
3. Prescriptive Reading Performance Test (Grades 1–12)

Also recall that the No Child Left Behind Act prompted state departments of education to design criterion-referenced tests that are aligned with their state standards (also called benchmarks or competencies in some states).

Critical Literacy Assessments

If teachers engage their students in critical literacy, it is best also to assess students' critical thinking skills (interpretation, inference, evaluation, analysis, self-regulation, and deductive and inductive reasoning), because these are the skills used in critical literacy studies. Most critical thinking tests are not subject specific, but rather assess students' general critical thinking skills such as ability to interpret and make inferences, engage in deductive and inductive reasoning, evaluate arguments, and evaluate if arguments are consistent. A few critical thinking tests are appropriate for elementary and middle school students.

The James Madison Test of Critical Thinking Form B from the Critical Thinking Co. is intended for middle school students and above. This test assesses a wide range of students' critical thinking ability such as interpreting complex texts; clarifying issues and arguments; distinguishing issues, claims, conclusions, and premises; evaluating whether an argument is strong or weak; evaluating claims for consistency and relevance; evaluating whether a deductive argument is valid; and discerning whether pairs of claims are consistent, contrary, contradictory, or paradoxical. All of these skills are needed as students engage in critical literacy as they read informational books. This test is available as software that tracks students' scores.

The California Critical Thinking Test M 1B, available from Insight Assessment, assesses students in grades 3 through 5, while the California Critical Thinking Test M20/M25 assesses students in grades 6 through 9. Both assess students' inductive and deductive reasoning skills as well as their ability to analyze, draw inferences, and evaluate everyday situations. There is a computer-based version as well as a print version.

The Cornell Critical Thinking Test, Level X and Level Z, for grades 5 through 12, available from The Critical Thinking Co., assesses students' critical thinking ability. Level X tests inductive reasoning, deductive reasoning, and ability to identify assumptions. Level Z assesses students' semantic ability and ability to make predictions for planning. The test is a software package that self-times, self-grades, and does all the record keeping for teachers.

Because each of these assessments measures different aspects of critical thinking, you must determine what skills you want your students to develop and then choose an assessment based on those goals.

Intervention STRATEGIES & ACTIVITIES

Teachers must explicitly teach reading strategies, model using them (Fisher, Frey, & Lapp, 2008), and guide students as they become "marinated" in them (Flynt & Cooter, 2005) so using them during reading becomes automatic. In a recent study of students in grades 3–8, Fisher, Frey, and Lapp (2008) identified 25 effective teachers. These teachers used shared readings to model four categories of strategies: comprehension and vocabulary strategies, understanding text structure strategies, and using text features strategies. For comprehension strategies, teachers modeled how they activate prior knowledge, summarize, infer, predict, clarify, question, visualize, synthesize, evaluate, monitor, and connect passages to the world, other text, and personal experiences. When they modeled vocabulary strategies, they looked at word parts (affixes, roots, cognates, word families), used context clues, and used other resources, such as peers, dictionaries, glossary or the Internet. To model understanding text structure, they and their students created graphic organizers to illustrate relationships between ideas in compare/contrast, problem/solution, cause/effect, sequencing, and descriptive texts. Finally, to model how to use text features they explained in detail how to read headings and captions; how to study illustrations, charts, tables, and graphs; how to review bold or italic words as important vocabulary; how to use the table of contents to predict main ideas and supporting ideas; and how to use the index to find a word in the text.

The following activities will help students develop strategies for reading expository text.

Strategies and Activities to Use Before, During, and After Reading

ACTIVITY

TEXTMASTERS

GRADES 4–8

Textmasters (Wilfong, 2009) brings literature circles to textbook reading. These textbook circles can be formed in a regular classroom or used by reading specialists as they work with small groups of four upper elementary or middle school struggling readers. Like literature circles with fiction, a teacher assigns one task to every member of the group. One student is the discussion director, who is responsible for formulating discussion questions. The second student, the summarizer, is responsible for summarizing the passage. The third student, the vocabulary "enricher" finds important words and gives definitions for each. The fourth student, the webmaster, is responsible for creating a graphic organizer of the information.

The students have 20 minutes to read the passage silently and complete their assigned task. Then the group spends the next 20 minutes discussing each task and questioning and challenging each other. The last 10 minutes is used for self reflection on how they and their peers performed for the day.

If this is completed in the classroom, each group thinks of unique ways to present its material (e.g., dramatic performance, song, multimedia or art project, Jeopardy game) to the whole class or another audience. Wilfong (2009) found the following advantages to this strategy when used in the classroom.

1. Social learning caters to middle school social needs; students learn from each other especially during discussion and performance time.
2. Students are engaged because they have a duty to perform for their group.
3. Students learn to do different tasks for each session; they learn to take on different leadership roles with peers.
4. They understand the responsibility of being a member of a group.
5. Scores can go up during the research project. For example, Wilfong (2009) found the average score was 86 percent on the first chapter. On the second chapter the scores rose to 89.3 percent.
6. Students take responsibility for their learning instead of expecting teachers to lecture to them.

SCIENCE EXPERIMENTS, CRAFTS, AND MATH GAMES

GRADES 2–5 ACTIVITY

One way to show struggling readers the importance of reading expository text accurately and interpreting it correctly is to have them read about and perform simple science experiments, craft and art projects, or math games. You may use the Personal Interest Survey (see Appendix C.13) to see which area interests the students most. Often struggling readers are tactile and kinesthetic learners, and experiments, crafts, and games meet their need to move around and use their hands. Reading directions emphasizes the importance of being able to read and comprehend accurately. Permit students to do the experiment, craft, or game just as they understand it from reading the directions, so they learn by trial and error the importance of reading directions correctly. Provide inexpensive and safe materials so any possible misinterpretations of directions results in no great harm. Science experiments are also wonderful ways to incorporate writing as the students can make predictions and keep a log of changes throughout the experiments. Read the accompanying factual reports of experiences college tutors had when working with tutees. All names are fictitious.

An excellent book to use for science experiments is Janice Van Cleave's *200 Gooey, Slippery, Slimy, Weird and Fun Experiments* (1993). Florence Tempo's *Origami Magic* (1993) is a great book to use for origami. For the struggling reader who has a love for math, there are math learning games and math mysteries that students must carefully read in order to solve the mystery or play the game. Two good books that incorporate reading with math are Marcia Miller's *Quick and Easy Learning Games: Math* (1996) and Mark Illingworth's *Real-life Math Problem Solving* (1996). These and other helpful books are listed in Figure 9.12. Read the vignettes in the box on the following page to see how science experiments can be used to motivate reluctant readers.

figure 9.12 Science, math, and art books that can be used to emphasize the importance of comprehension.

Churchill, R., Loeschnig, L., & Mandell, M. (1998). *365 More Simple Science Experiments with Everyday Materials.* New York: Black Dog & Leventhal Publishers.

Gilpin, R., & Pratt, L. (2008). *The Usborne Big Book of Science Things to Make and Do.* Tulsa, OK: EDC.

Illingworth, M. (2000). *Real-Life Math Problem Solving: 40 Exciting, Classroom-tested Problems with Annotated Solutions.* New York: Scholastic.

Knapp, Z. (1995). *Super Math Tricks: Solve Every Challenging Math Problem and Become a Super Sleuth Detective!* Los Angeles, CA: Lowell House Juvenile.

Miller, M. (1999). *Quick-and-Easy-Learning Games: Math.* New York: Scholastic.

Urton, A. (1992). *50 Nifty Origami Crafts.* Los Angeles, CA: Lowell House Juvenile.

Van Cleave, J. (2002). *204 Sticky, Gloppy, Wacky and Wonderful Experiments.* New York: John Wiley & Sons.

Wagner, K., & Racine, S. (2008). *Everything Kids Astronomy Book.* Avon, MA: Adams Media.

Watt, F. (1999). *The Usborne Book of Art.* New York: Scholastic.

Wiese, J. (1995). *Rocket Science: 50 Flying, Floating, Flipping, Spinning Gadgets Kids Create Themselves.* New York: John Wiley & Sons.

Wiese, J. (1996). *Detective Science: 40 Crime-solving Case-breaking Crook-catching Activities for Kids.* New York: Scholastic.

Active Learning

VIGNETTE 1

As part of a course requirement, Mary, an elementary education major, was assigned to work with Joe, a third grader, twice a week. Each tutoring session was 50 minutes long. After being encouraged to use science experiments with Joe, Mary found a recipe to make slime. Mary was convinced Joe would love the experiment because he loved science and working with his hands. Mary made sure the steps for the recipe were written a little below Joe's reading level to ensure success.

Excited, Joe carefully read and followed each step. However, he misread the amount of water he had to add. Mary remembered from the discussion in her college class that it was important for the student to perform the experiment based on his interpretation of the instructions if he was to learn the importance of reading instructions carefully. Therefore, Mary let Joe proceed. Needless to say, Joe's slime did not come out with the desired consistency.

However, desirable learning did occur. On his own Joe said, "Wow! I must have read something wrong! Let's reread the directions." When he got to the step for adding water he realized he read the amount incorrectly. He said, "Man, I'm not ready to be a rocket scientist if I make a mistake on something so simple!" Joe was not discouraged. He made a plea: "I promise to read the directions better if you let me do this again." Of course, Mary did. The small amount of white glue and borax powder Joe wasted was worth the learning experience.

VIGNETTE 2

Bob, an elementary education major, was assigned to work with George, a very active third-grade reader. George could not sit still for any length of time. In fact, in the middle of a paragraph he would stand up as he continued to read. Because he was so active George often omitted words or even lines, which made his comprehension very poor. Bob also noticed that George's fingers were in constant motion as he read and that George's drawings were very detailed and advanced for a third grader. George indicated on an interest survey that he loved art. Bob decided to try some origami with George.

Wanting George to be successful, Bob wrote the directions for constructing an origami frog at George's easy reading level. George carefully read and reread the directions as he meticulously followed each step. The frog was neatly constructed, and it jumped! Afterward George asked, "Where did you get these directions? I want to do more of these." Bob showed George the book. George picked up another piece of paper, read the directions from the book (which Bob thought were too difficult for George to read), and made a box that could be inflated. Throughout the semester, George wanted to do origami during every session. He did not care that he had to read the instructions in order to correctly construct each object.

Bob also used George's interest to help his writing skills. George did not like to write. However, when Bob invited George to write in his own words some of the instructions for his favorite origami structures so he could share them with friends, George readily agreed. Through the writing experience, George learned the importance of writing directions clearly so others could understand them.

ACTIVITY READ-ALOUDS — GRADES K–6

All teachers, especially those who teach grades K–3, should give students more access to expository texts. One way to do this is through read-alouds. During a read-aloud, a teacher can show students how expository texts differ from narrative texts and what strategies she uses to make sense of expository text.

First, write on the board any new vocabulary words related to the topic that the students will hear in the text. Pronounce the words and give the students ample time to repeat them until their pronunciation is correct. If necessary, give a short explanation of the word. Also before reading, you can activate students' prior knowledge by creating a K-W-L chart (see the explanation later in this section). While making the K-W-L chart, encourage students to generate questions about the topic and list things they would like to learn.

While reading the expository text, show your students how the pictures, charts, and figures are used to explain concepts and to give additional information. Also explain that with expository text you do not need to start at the beginning and read each page. Demonstrate how to use the index to find and read only relevant pages. Also show how on some pages the information is given in boxes and that the order in which one reads them does not matter.

Read-alouds should not be limited to trade books—newspapers, magazines, or websites can pique students' curiosity of current events. Demonstrate how you find an article that interests you, and how you connect the new information to your prior knowledge. *The Washington Post* "KidsPost," available online at www.washingtonpost.com.kidspost, features current events and other related articles that interest students in grades 3–8.

Magazines in which to find articles include the following Scholastic publications:

1. *Clifford the Big Red Dog* (PreK–K): an interactive magazine that promotes development of early learning skills.
2. *Let's Find Out* (K): articles about science, social studies, and language arts topics that reinforce the five essential reading components as identified in the No Child Left Behind Act.
3. *Let's Find Out Spanish* (PreK–K)—the Spanish version of *Let's Find Out.*
4. *Scholastic News Magazine* (different magazine for each elementary grade from 1–6): each issue has high-interest articles about current events.
5. *Scholastic News Bilingual* (different magazine for each elementary grade from 1–6): each Scholastic magazine is bilingual; students read a page in English and flip the magazine upside down to read the same article in Spanish. Each month has two issues—one issue focuses on science topics and one issue focuses on social studies.
6. *Storyworks Magazine* (3–6): each issue is fully illustrated, original children's literature that has engaging reading and writing activities based on the issue's story.

Magazines for older students include:

Faces: features people of many cultures.

Cobblestone: features articles about American historical events.

Footsteps: features articles about African Americans and their contributions to American culture.

Dig: features articles about archaeology.

Cricket: includes classic literature and invites students to submit poetry and essay for different contests.

After reading an expository text selection, help the students create graphic organizers to show the relationships between the concepts and help them remember the facts.

PARTNER READING AND CONTENT TOO (PRC2)

ENGLISH LEARNERS GRADES 4–8 ACTIVITY

English learners need practice reading expository text that includes technical vocabulary. Partner Reading and Content Too (PRC2) is a strategy in which two English learners collaborate on reading a text together. The teacher is the silent observer and cheerleader.

First the partners preview the book or passage by discussing the pictures and their captions. Then the partners read a two-page spread silently. After each is finished, each partner rereads his page (their side of the text) again and writes two questions to ask his partner. After both have completed their reading and writing their questions, the first partner reads his page orally and asks his questions. The two students discuss the information and answer the questions. Then the second partner reads his page orally and they discuss that information and answer his questions. At the end of each two-page spread, they write down important vocabulary terms in their personal notebook and write definitions in their own words.

ACTIVITY GRAPHIC ORGANIZERS FOR EXPOSITORY TEXT GRADES 2–5

"Mapping is thinking: constructing and creating the organizational design of ideas, selecting the information that is relevant and sorting this into its proper place, relating all facts to the whole and relating facts to other facts, and finally responding with personal reaction to the material" (Hanf, 1971, p. 229). Graphic organizers map how ideas are connected in the expository text. Heubach (1995) found that graphic organizers helped poor readers comprehend the material, which improved their attitude about informational books. Of course, educators know that when readers' attitudes improve, they will spend more hours reading.

As discussed earlier in this chapter, expository text is usually organized in specific patterns, and graphic organizers show how the information within a particular passage is related. Each expository pattern has a different type of graphic organizer. Mosenthal (1994) found that direct instruction in text organizational patterns before, during, and after reading improves comprehension and aids contextual understanding.

It is important to note that all graphic organizers should be concise, clearly depict relationships, and not be cluttered. At first you should model how to construct the correct type of organizer and map the information. Later you can construct the organizer and have the student map the information. Graphic organizers can be used as a prereading strategy to see what a student already knows about the topic. During reading, the information can be filled in as the reader learns new facts. After reading, the child can use it for recalling the information. Figures 9.13 through 9.21 show graphic organizers that can be used for each organizational pattern.

- *Chronology or sequence.* The timeline in Figure 9.13 is based on David Adler's *A Picture Book of Benjamin Franklin* (1990). The graphic organizer in Figure 9.14 depicts the butterfly's cycle.
- *Description or enumeration.* Figure 9.15 is based on William George's *Box Turtle at Long Pond* (1989).
- *Classification.* A graphic organizer used to show classification should clearly indicate the hierarchy of various categories. Figure 9.16 depicts the three levels of government.
- *Comparison/contrast.* Various organizers may be used to show comparisons and differences between two entities. Figures 9.17 and 9.18 show two different types.
- *Cause/effect.* Figure 9.19 depicts the acts of nature that cause a volcano. The information is taken from Fiona Watt's *Earthquakes and Volcanoes* (1993).
- *Problem/solution.* The problem/solution graphic organizer in Figure 9.20 is based on Jerry Stanley's *Children of the Dust Bowl* (1992).
- *Persuasion.* A teacher can use any advertisement from a magazine or newspaper to show how corporations persuade consumers to buy their products. The advertisement for Tums shown in Figure 9.21 is an example of card stacking.

figure 9.13 Graphic organizer: Timeline.

Born in Boston	Went to school	Worked in soap-and-candle shop	Worked in brother's print shop	Opened own print shop	Got married	Published *Poor Richard's Almanac*	Represented colonies in England	Represented colonies in France	Helped write peace treaty	Delegate to Constitutional Convention	Died in Philadelphia
1706	1714–1716	1716–1718	1718–1723	1728	1730	1732–1758	1765–1775	1776–1785	1782	1787	1790

Timeline based on Adler, D. (1990). *A Picture Book of Benjamin Franklin.* New York: Trumpet Club.

figure **9.14** Graphic organizer: Sequence.

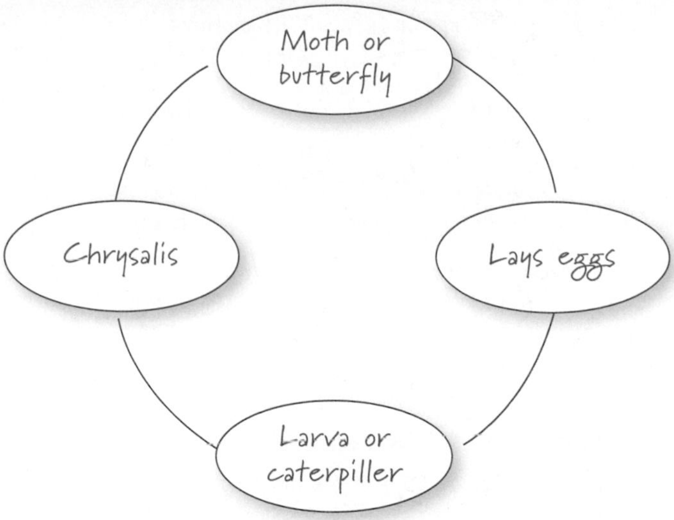

figure **9.15** Graphic organizer: Description or enumeration.

Organizer based on George, W. (1989). *Box Turtle at Long Pond.* New York: Trumpet Club.

figure **9.16** Graphic organizer: Classification.

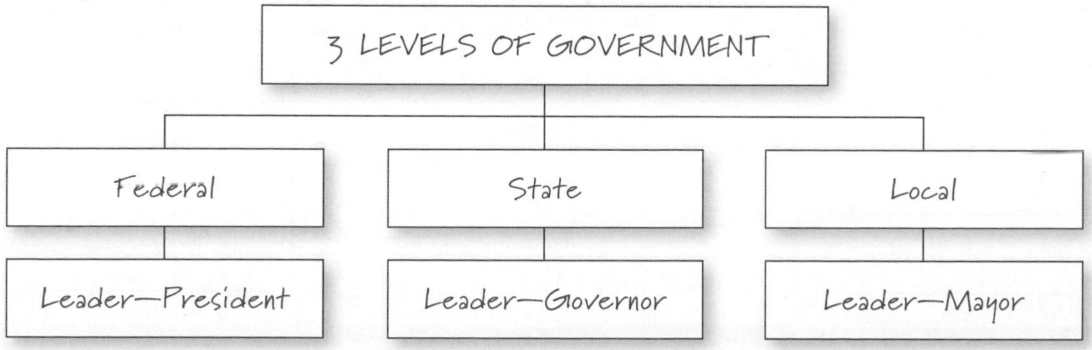

figure **9.17** Graphic organizer: Comparison/contrast (Venn diagram).

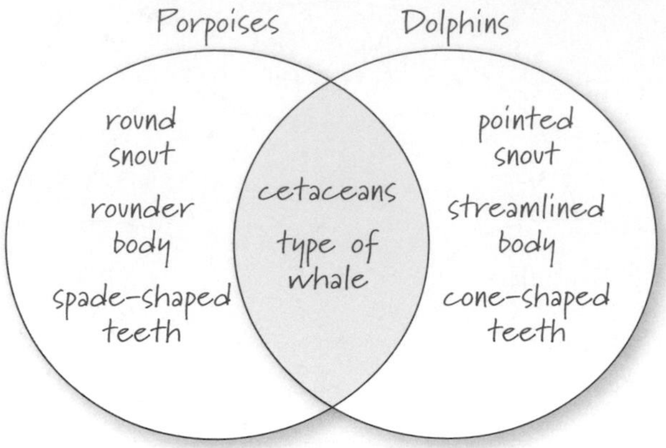

Organizer based on Cerullo, M. (1999). *Dolphins: What They Can Teach Us.* New York: Scholastic.

figure **9.18** Graphic organizer: Comparison/contrast.

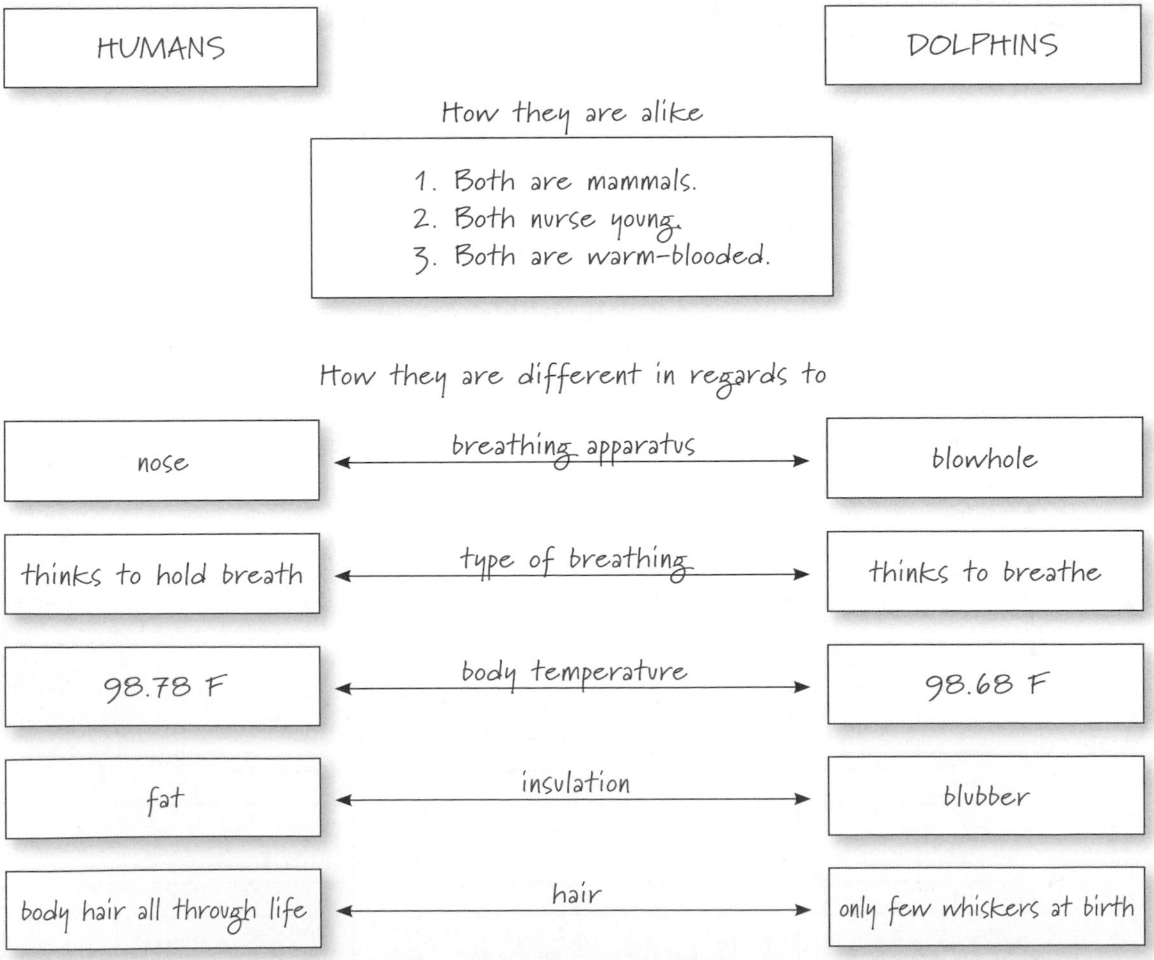

Organizer based on Cerullo, M. (1999). *Dolphins: What They Can Teach Us.* New York: Scholastic.

figure 9.19 Graphic organizer: Cause/effect.

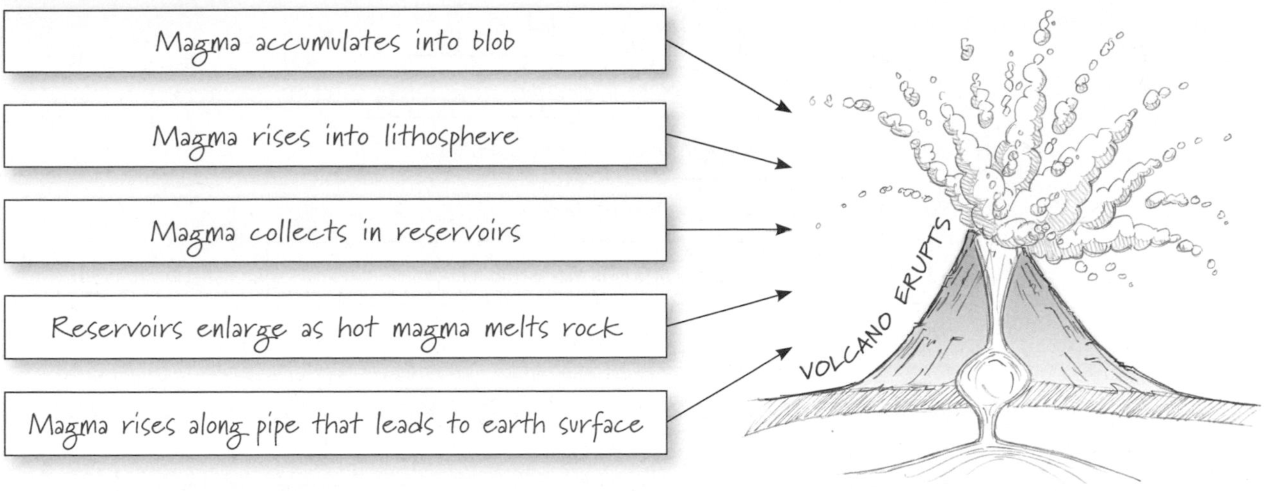

Organizer based on Watt, F. (1993). *Earthquakes and Volcanoes.* New York: Scholastic.

figure 9.20 Graphic organizer: Problem/solution.

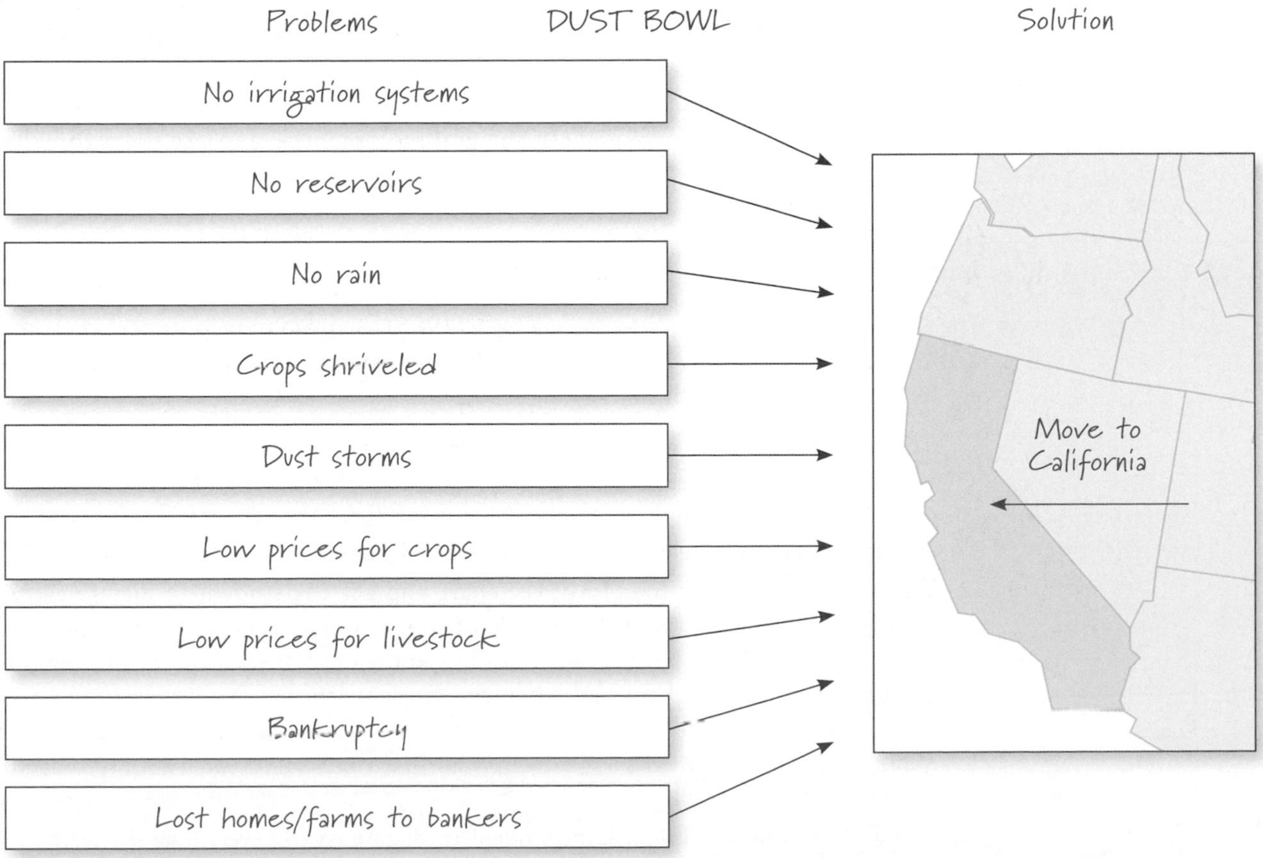

Organizer based on Stanley, J. (1992). *Children of the Dust Bowl: The True Story of the School at Weedpatch Camp.* New York: Trumpet Club Special Edition.

figure **9.21** Graphic organizer: Persuasion.

card stacking/glittering generalities

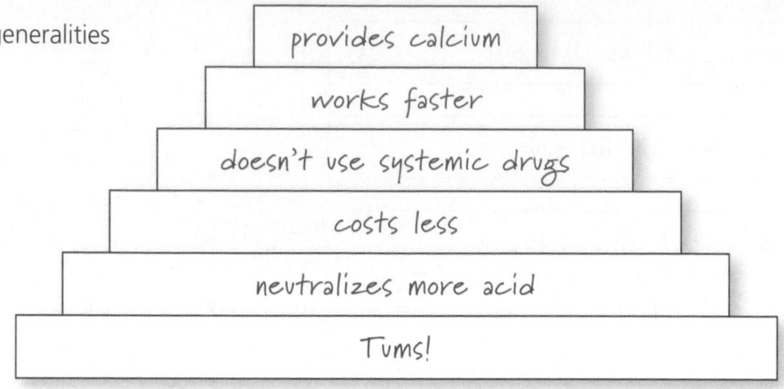

ACTIVITY

LESSON CYCLE

GRADES 5–8

Montelong, Herter, Ansaldo & Hatter (2010) suggest teachers working with one struggling student or a small group use the following cycle for comprehension of expository text. First introduce the main vocabulary words necessary to make sense of the information. Next teacher and students read the passage in unison and discuss the information, agreeing on what type of text structure the author used and identifying the signal words used in the passage. For example, if the information is given in sequential order, the author will use signal words such as *first, next, finally*. Then teacher and students complete a graphic organizer as they read. (See Figures 9.13–9.21 for examples of organizers for each type of text.)

Students create their own copy of the graphic organizer and use them to write a summary.

ACTIVITY

K-W-L

GRADES 2–6

The K-W-L method, developed by Donna Ogle (1986) as an aid to help students become active readers of expository text, is often used in classrooms, but it is also a useful strategy for a teacher to use with a struggling reader.

1. To construct a K-W-L chart, divide a piece of paper into three columns as in Figure 9.22. Label the first column K, which stands for WHAT I KNOW ABOUT THE TOPIC. Label the second column W, which stands for WHAT I WANT TO LEARN. The third column, labeled L, stands for WHAT I LEARNED.
2. Write the topic across the top of the chart and ask the student to dictate everything she knows about it. Take the role of scribe yourself so the student does not withhold information because she does not know how to spell words. During the discussion, find out where and when the student learned the information. It is interesting to learn, for example, if a struggling reader has learned about bats, sharks, or whales from viewing educational programs on TV or from listening to books read by an adult.
3. Using the second column, ask the student to dictate to you everything she wants to learn about the topic. From this step you may find that although the text matches the student's reading level, it may not contain any new information and thus bore her. In such cases, find more appropriate materials for the reader at her instructional level.

4. After reading the passage have the student tell you what she learned. (Later, have the student write the K-W-L chart, permitting her to use inventive spelling or look up the words.)
5. Now go back to the first column to see if all the background knowledge is accurate. Then refer to the second column to see if the student learned everything she wanted to. If not, the two of you may want to seek another source on the same topic.

K-W-L is a helpful strategy to use with a struggling reader because it permits a teacher to determine the student's background knowledge. K-W-L also actively involves the student in the reading process by encouraging him to think about what he would like to learn. Finally, K-W-L indicates if the student comprehended the material. As a variation to keep students interested in this widely used activity, create the chart in the shape of the topic being discussed (e.g., a whale, tree, building).

figure **9.22** Comprehension strategy K-W-L on caves.

K	W	L
1. Caves are hollowed into rock. 2. There are many different kinds. 3. They have water in them. 4. They are dark inside. 5. You can get trapped in them. 6. They have many tunnels.	1. Do they all have bats in them? 2. Do they all have snakes in them? 3. What are the things that hang down called? 4. Can you breathe in them?	1. Some caves are made from red-hot flowing lava. 2. Stalactites hang down from ceiling. 3. Stalagmites build up from floor. 4. Geologists study caves. 5. All caves are cold and damp. 6. Bears hibernate in caves. 7. Some caves have bats.

Chart based on Wood, J. (1990). *Caves: Facts, Stories, and Activities.* New York: Scholastic.

GUIDED READING STRATEGY — GRADES 2–5 — ACTIVITY

Bean and Pardi (1979) developed the guided reading strategy (GRS) for struggling readers. This strategy uses text features and includes steps to encourage a struggling reader to remember the topics that were discussed. These are the steps for the GRS:

1. Together with the student read chapter titles, subheadings, and vocabulary lists found at the beginning or end of the chapter as well as graphs, maps, picture captions, and chapter questions.
2. Close the book and have the reader dictate everything she remembers to you while you record what she says.
3. Have the student open the text to check if the information is correct and what is missing. Update the list.
4. Discuss the information with the student.

5. Together, organize the information into a graphic organizer.
6. Have the student silently read the entire passage.
7. Give the student a 10-item quiz on the material.
8. A week later, give the student another 10-item pop quiz.
9. Discuss the results of the quizzes with the student.

ACTIVITY **INFERENCE TRAINING** GRADES 2–5

If a struggling reader does not connect book knowledge with everyday experiences, then learning seems irrelevant. Inference training stresses the importance of a student relating the information to her personal life (Anthony & Raphael, 1996). The following is an example of a teacher and a student engaging in inference training:

Teacher: Today we are going to read about hurricanes. Do you know anything about a hurricane?

Student: No.

Teacher: Have you ever heard of a tornado?

Student: Oh yes! My grandpa's house blew away in a tornado!

Teacher: What caused his house to blow away?

Student: Really strong wind!

Teacher: Well, a hurricane is somewhat like a tornado. Both have strong winds and both are natural disasters, meaning that nature causes them and not humans. Today we are going to read about the hurricane named Andrew. Look at the pictures and tell me where you think it took place.

Student: Some place by an ocean and where there is this kind of tree (pointing to a picture of a palm tree).

Teacher: That's correct. Do you know what this tree is called?

Student: No.

Teacher: A palm tree.

Student: Oh, I think they are in places where it is hot all year long.

Teacher: Yes, they are. Where do you think the Andrew hurricane was?

Student: I think it was in Texas because it is hot there all the time and I think it is on the ocean.

Teacher: It is hot in Texas most of the year, but we will have to read and see if Andrew was a hurricane in Texas. When do you think Andrew happened?

Student: I think it was in the 1800s; long before there were weather people.

Teacher: That is an interesting observation; we'll have to read about it and see if that is true. Do you think it was a bad one?

Student: It looks like everything was destroyed and some people were killed (as she looks at the pictures).

The student reads the passage to the teacher, affirming or changing predictions as she reads. The student will learn that many aspects of her predictions were incorrect, but she was correct about some people dying.

After reading the passage, the teacher relates the information to the student's personal experience. Students from the Midwest can distinguish hurricanes from tornadoes by looking at the endurance of the storms, the wind speeds, and the rainfall.

QUESTION-ANSWER-RELATIONSHIPS (QARs) GRADES 3–8 ACTIVITY

Kinniburgh and Shaw (2009) expanded Raphael's (1986) question-answer-relationship strategy in science class by having students classify questions into four categories: (1) literal questions that are found in the text in one place, (2) literal questions that are found in the text, but students need to search several places to find the answer, (3) inferential questions that require students to use the text and their background knowledge, and (4), inferential questions that require students to use only their background knowledge. Make four columns on a whiteboard, poster board, or sentence pockets for younger students and write questions for the four categories you will ask before, during, and after the reading. During each phase, read the questions and ask students to decide in which category the question should be placed. Then they answer the question. If the answer is found in the text, students must state where they found the answer. After all the questions are discussed, the teacher assigns another passage from the Internet or another book and has the students write questions for each category. Kinniburgh and Shaw (2009) found that students were able to answer more questions correctly because they were required to think if the question was literal or inferential and if the answer was found in the text or if they had to use their background knowledge (refer back to Figure 8.16).

Following are some example questions based on the online article "Far-Out Foods," found at http://magma.nationalgeographic.com:

- Literal question, found in one place: "What is an anthropologist?"
- Literal question, found in a number of places: What insects are good for people to eat?
- Inferential question, using the text and background knowledge: "Are termites nutritious?"
- Inferential question, using only background knowledge: Is it possible that Americans consume insects without even knowing they did? If so, when or how?

Strategies and Activities to Use Before Reading

SURVEY OF TEXT FEATURES GRADES 1–8 ACTIVITY

This strategy allows you help a student examine the features of a textbook to predict what he will learn. (Some trade books have the same features.) First, encourage him to look for the text features that aid the reader. Using the table of contents, for example, helps struggling readers sort out main ideas from unimportant details (Bluestein, 2010). It can also help them to identify and follow the text's organizational structure. By looking at a detailed table of contents, teachers can help students create timelines if the information is given in chronological order. For chapters organized descriptively, comparatively, or according to some other system, teachers and students can create graphic organizers gleaned from the headings and subheadings (see Figures 9.13–9.21). Next you can ask the student to predict what he thinks he will learn from reading the selected passage. You can activate his prior knowledge by asking the student if he knows anything else about the topic. If there is a glossary or index, assist the student to understand how helpful these two sections of the text are. While reading, if he cannot figure out the definition of a term from context clues, he simply needs to check the glossary for a definition or look in the index to see where else that topic is discussed in the text.

Then turn to a selected chapter and help the student read the captions of the pictures. Again, the purpose is to generate interest and activate prior knowledge. Sometimes by talking about a picture, you introduce vocabulary that will be a part of the reading material. A student will then have heard the terms in context before reading the passage.

After previewing the pictures, help the student read chapter headings and subheadings to help him predict how they are related to one another. Lastly, read with the student any questions at the start of the chapter. If there are none, then the student should read the questions at the end of the chapter. This will help the student focus on the main points of the chapter. Reading all of the text features will help a struggling reader to become familiar with vocabulary and the topic before he attempts to read.

ACTIVITY

PRE-READING PLAN (PReP) GRADES 2–6

Pre-reading plan is a questioning strategy used to activate prior knowledge and to develop a student's interest in the topic (Anthony & Raphael, 1996). The following is an example of a discussion between teacher and student before they read *Caves: Facts, Stories, Activities:*

Teacher (asking general questions about caves): Have you ever heard of stalactites and stalagmites?

Student: I think so.

Teacher: What do you think they are?

Student: I think they are the icicles that are in caves.

Teacher: Do you know anything else about them?

Student: I think the stalagmites hang from the cave and the other ones come out of the floor of the cave.

Teacher: Where did you learn all that?

Student: I saw a show on TV about going down into a cave. It was really cold and dark in it.

Teacher: That sounds interesting. I think the stalagmites come out of the cave's floor and the stalactites hang from the ceiling. But let's read and find out for sure which is correct.

Student: I think you are right. I remember the man hit his head on a stalactite and it was hanging from the ceiling.

PReP is especially helpful to correct a student's misconceptions about a particular topic.

Strategies and Activities to Use During Reading

ACTIVITY

THINK-ALOUD FOR EXPOSITORY TEXT GRADES 2–5

The purpose of the think-aloud strategy is for a teacher to model to students what proficient readers do to make sense of a text (Davey, 1983). In this strategy, you should choose a passage that has new vocabulary and unfamiliar information, and then perform the following steps:

1. Read the title or heading of the passage and make predictions about the topic. "I think this will be about _____" or "I think I will learn_____" or "This subheading tells me I will also learn_____."
2. Describe the images that come to mind as you read the passage. For example, "I can almost feel (or hear or see or smell) _____."
3. Give analogies that relate the material to your personal life. "I (saw/heard/tasted/felt) _________ that is very similar to (topic of passage)."
4. Verbalize passages or phrases that you don't understand. This helps the student understand that proficient readers do not need to know everything to succeed.
5. Demonstrate the strategy you use to understand the passage (e.g., rereading, looking at a diagram or picture, looking up a word in the glossary, or reading ahead to see if the concept is explained).

Figure 9.23 is an example of a think-aloud using the section "Running Rivers" (pp. 30–31) in John Farndon's book *All About Planet Earth* (2000).

After you model a think-aloud, have the student do a think-aloud while you observe. The think-aloud should become a regular habit for struggling readers.

figure 9.23 Think-aloud based on John Farndon's *All About Planet Earth.*

1. The title "Running Rivers" tells me I will maybe learn why rivers run, where they come from, and where they go.
2. I could almost hear the noise of the "Thundering Water."
3. It reminds me of noise at Niagara Falls. I could not even hear my sister talking to me when we went to Niagara Falls even though we were standing right by each other. It also smelled like rain water as it roared over the ledge.
4. I still don't understand why a river winds. I would think that the closer it got to the sea, it would just go straight. I wonder if I can find out some more information about why rivers wind instead of going straight.
5. This diagram helps me better understand the three reaches of a river and how it becomes broader. I am surprised that many rivers don't become so broad in the lower reaches that they become lakes.

Based on Farndon, J. (2000). *All About Planet Earth.* New York: Anness Publishing.

CHECKLIST

GRADES 2–5 ACTIVITY

The checklist strategy allows students to see reading as an active process, in which they constantly analyze what is being read. You can model the process for students using the following steps:

1. Prepare statements about a passage that are either true or false.
2. Together with students read the statements before beginning to read the passage.
3. As you read, place a (+) before each true statement.
4. At the end of the reading, go back and reword the false statements to make them true. If necessary, you and the students should reread the material.

Figure 9.24 is a checklist that a teacher and student completed while reading "Into the Bat Cave" from Jenny Wood's *Caves* (1990).

figure 9.24 Checklist for *Caves* by Jenny Wood.

\+ 1. Bats live in colonies.
\+ 2. Bats live in caves.
– 3. They sleep during the night.
– 4. Bats are almost deaf.
– 5. Bats have excellent eyesight.
\+ 6. Echolocation is continuous high-pitched sounds.
\+ 7. Glowworms are found in New Zealand caves.
\+ 8. A glowworm's rear end gives off light.
– 9. Glowworms trap flying insects in their mouths.

CORRECTION OF FALSE STATEMENTS

3. Bats sleep during the day.
4. Bats have excellent hearing.
5. Bats are almost blind.
9. Glowworms trap insects with sticky threads that they have spun.

ACTIVITY **REQUEST** GRADES 3–6

ReQuest is a good strategy for struggling readers because the teacher and students reverse roles. The students ask you the questions, and you provide the answers. The following steps are used with ReQuest:

1. Together with students, silently read a paragraph.
2. Have the students ask you a question that can be answered after reading the passage. It is the students' responsibility to clearly state the question. If it is not clearly stated say, "I don't understand the question."
3. If the question cannot be answered from the material read, ask students to help you find the answer.

This strategy is especially enjoyable for students if you occasionally give an incorrect response. You, of course, are checking the students' comprehension. This activity teaches students to formulate good questions and that the answers to some questions are right there in the book, while others demand they "read between the lines." Ciardiello (1998) found that when students formulate questions, they internalize new information and use higher-level thinking skills.

Strategies and Activities to Use After Reading

ACTIVITY **SCANNING** GRADES 3–5

Provide opportunities for students to practice scanning while they find answers to textual questions. Too often struggling readers begin looking for an answer by reading from the beginning of the passage. This is time consuming and unnecessary. Teach them instead to check headings to determine if the answer can be located in a particular section. If the question asks for a date teach students to scan the page for numerals, such as 1776 or 2002. If the question asks for a name, the students should be taught to scan the page for the capital letters of proper nouns. Struggling readers need to remember that definitions can often be located by boldface or italic text. These dates, names, and definitions are easy for the eye to locate when scanning the printed page. Demonstrate to struggling readers what to do when looking for dates, names, and definitions. Then have them practice the strategy with you.

ACTIVITY **LEARNING LOGS** GRADES 2–6

Learning logs are an after-reading strategy that connects reading and writing and are associated with all types of informational texts, including textbooks, trade books, computer programs, Internet sites, and magazines. With learning logs, students recall what they have read and then articulate it in a concise summary. After you have read and discussed a text with students, have them close all reading materials and write about what they have learned. Carefully analyze what the students write to see if they recall the main ideas or unimportant details. Determine if the students can explain concepts in logical order. You can also determine if the readers understand the new strategy. As an additional task, have the students exchange logs with a partner to share information. Figure 9.25 presents a learning log entry and the teacher's analysis. This student has just read *Octopus' Den* (1997) by Deirdre Langeland. Figure 9.26 is a science log of a second-grade student.

figure **9.25** Learning log entry and analysis.

March 1: Octopus

An octopus eats crabs and glass. He has funny eyes. He squirts ink. He eats snakes and apples. I learned how to draw a circle with lines.

Teacher Analysis

The following information is incorrect. The octopus does not eat glass or snakes. The text states: "When he is sure it is safe, Octopus snakes an arm toward the piece of glass and snatches it back to the safety of the rock. For a moment he investigates it, the suckers on his arms tasting [not eating] the new object and feeling its shiny-smooth surface."

The last statement in the log is also incorrect. The text states: "The tiny opening is the size of an apple." The octopus does not eat apples.

Obviously, this reader reads concrete words and paints mental pictures of those objects, which causes the reader to see the octopus eating snakes and apples. It is apparent that the reader is not aware that these words have multiple meanings and uses.

(From the student's final statement, the teacher also realizes that the child does not know the term *graphic organizer*.)

figure **9.26** Sample science log, second grade.

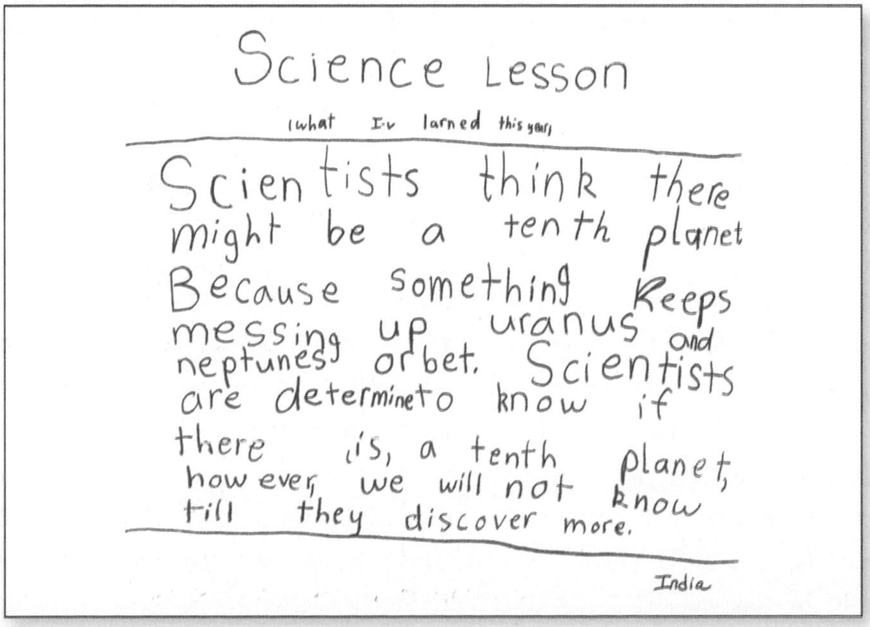

Science Lesson

(what I-v larned this year)

Scientists think there might be a tenth planet Because something Keeps messing up uranus and neptunes orbet. Scientists are determineto know if there is, a tenth planet, how ever, we will not know till they discover more.

India

ACTIVITY COLLABORATIVE APPROACH GRADES 3–8

Meyer (2010) suggests the reading workshop format used with fiction reading should also be used with expository texts. This strategy is based on Vygotsky's (1978) social learning theory and the evidence-based approach of the QAR (Raphael & Au, 2005). In the reading workshop, all students read the same expository text—from either a trade book or the Internet—based on the topic they are studying in the textbook, such as natural disasters or the U.S. Civil War. Students write three types of questions on three different sticky notes after they have read the passage. The first is a "burning question," something about a definition of a word or clarification of the text. The second is a "wondering question," which begins with "Perhaps . . . ," "Could . . . ," "I wonder . . . ," "What could?", or "What if . . . ?" The third is a clever connection thought. These statements begin with "This reminds me of"; "I remember when"; "Another text like this is"; "I didn't realize that"; or "Ah ha!"

After all the sticky notes are posted to a board that has three columns, students discuss their questions, answer them, or find answers to them.

ACTIVITY QUESTION CONNECT TRANSFORM (QCT) FOR EXPOSITORY TEXT GRADES 6–8

This instructional strategy (Richards, 2006) was introduced in the Intervention section in Chapter 8, but it can also be used with expository text. The teacher guides the students to question the moral issue surrounding the topic of a text. The students then connect that issue to their own lives and write about how they can take action to help transform society.

For example, after reading the online article "Space Junk" found at http://magma.nationalgeographic.com/ngexplorer/1005/articles/mainarticle.html, Ms. Synder asked her students to write what about the moral issues raised in the article. Figure 9.27 shows Dan's response to the three-part QCT.

figure 9.27 Sample response to QCT.

Question: I do not believe it is right for humans to pollute space with rockets used to place satellites in space.

Connect: I have not personally shot a rocket into space, but many times my neighbor has tossed Styrofoam cups and hamburger wrappers on our lawn. It is messy so my dad makes me clean it up.

Transform: I can write my U. S. Congress members and share the ideas from this article and ask them to write a bill to eliminate unnecessary rockets so we do not add to the space trash that is already up there. I could write a poem about all the space waste and ask our local newspaper to print it on the front page. I could also write our state's science department at the research university and ask them to research how we can collect trash that is in space.

COMPREHENSION OF EXPOSITORY TEXT AND TECHNOLOGY

Our increasingly global world makes Internet proficiency mandatory. Students must be able to comprehend and respond to informational text found on the Internet, and doing so requires different reading comprehension strategies. Henry (2006) found that students should possess the following basic skills when using the Internet. Students need to know how to:

1. Locate materials.
2. Identify important questions.
3. Use search engines and select search words.
4. Refine search words so they are specific as possible.
5. Read and evaluate the short descriptions found in search engine results and then use only the sites that address their topic.
6. Evaluate the site's or author's credibility, because anyone can post information on the Internet.
7. Use the "back" button to go from one link to the next.
8. Read and comprehend the text. Often, Internet text is too advanced for elementary students.
9. Take notes from the sites.
10. Synthesize material from the various sites.
11. Cite sources.

Appendix C.40 contains a checklist based on Henry's findings that you can use to assess a student's basic Internet skills.

In addition to assessing basic skills, teachers can assess students' online reading comprehension to determine which students need additional assistance. Online reading comprehension assessments (ORCAs) are one method for measuring students' ability to comprehend online resources. ORCAs are curriculum-based measurements that capture "'real-time' online reading skills and strategies" (Coiro, 2009, p. 60). They present reading passages accompanied by multiple questions in a web-based environment. Using software programs such as Camtesia or I Show U, teachers can record a student's actions and comments as she reads the passage and completes the questions. They can then use online tools such as Survey Monkey to compile student responses and review the videos to determine how their students are reading online. If teachers wish to create their own ORCAs, Coiro recommends they construct short challenges using an online quiz format that require students to

- Use a search engine to locate information
- Check information with another source
- Evaluate the information's accuracy
- Determine the author's or website's purpose and how it influences the information provided.

If the assessments indicate your students need work in navigating and comprehending material online, one method you can use to teach effective Internet skills is the Internet scavenger hunt. Three good sources for any beginner are:

1. Internet Treasure Hunts for English learners (http://iteslj.org/th)
2. Scavenger Hunts: Searching for Treasures on the Internet (www.education-world.com/a_curr/curr113.shtml)
3. A search on the term *webquest* in Google returns appropriate websites on a wide range of topics that interest students. The sites lead the students through a complete study of the topic.

Because Internet sites are not objectively evaluated by trusted experts, you must also teach students how to evaluate the information they find. Teach your students to compare their background information about the topic and information found in other sources with the information found on the particular site. They can determine whether the site's information is current by checking the date on which the information was posted. Students should find out who the author is and with what organization, if any, the author is affiliated. You teach critical-thinking skills as you help students find biases in the information. The Library of Congress website, www.americaslibrary.gov, is an excellent source for accurate information.

Karchmer (2001) found that most reputable websites include the following:

1. The author's credentials with an e-mail address.
2. If the website is posted by an organization, its address, telephone number, and e-mail address.
3. Complete citations of quoted material.
4. Endorsements from organizations.
5. Links only to reputable sites.

Of course, when using the Internet, you must caution students about inappropriate sites. Many schools use blocking software to keep the Internet safe for students. Some teachers pre-screen sites and permit students to use only those they pre-screen. See Appendix D.23 for a checklist for evaluating e-text.

Many informational ebooks are available on topics that interest elementary students. Use these with struggling readers to encourage problem solving and comprehension skills. Because choosing appropriate ebooks is not always an easy task, use the evaluation form in Appendix D.21.

Some excellent Internet sites for expository texts are:

http://kids.nationalgeographic.com/kids
www.kidsbiology.com
www.readwritethink.org
http://water.epa.gov/learn/kids
www.sciencekids.com
www.apples4teachers.com/science
www.brainpop.com/science
www.kidsknowit.com

I also recommend the Concepts of Comprehension Assessment (COCA)™ website at http://msu-larc.educ.msu.edu/what-we-do/projects/mai-coca, which contains an assessment of informational reading comprehension designed for first and second grade students. It measures four factors: comprehension strategy use, vocabulary strategy use and knowledge, knowledge of informational text features, and comprehension of graphics in the context of text. Also recommended is the Intelligent Tutoring for Structure Strategy (ITSS) website at www.poisonfreehosting.com/itss.br.psu.edu. This site provides a tutorial for teaching students how to use a passage's expository structure as an aid to comprehension.

CONCLUDING THOUGHTS

This chapter introduced assessment and reading strategies to aid in students' comprehension of expository text. Teachers are responsible for using these assessments regularly and explicitly teaching such strategies to struggling readers based on their assessment results. Reflective teachers must also analyze which strategies are best for each particular reader. Teachers must also engage their students in critical literacies as they read nonfiction.

Reflective Learning ENGLISH LEARNERS

Scenario. Hiroki, a fifth-grade student from Japan, arrived in the United States with his parents at the beginning of the school year. Hiroki's father is working on an advanced degree at the local university and reads and speaks English fluently. Hiroki's mother is literate in Japanese, but does not read English. Hiroki understands some oral English, and his father says Hiroki can read second-grade English materials. Ms. Johnson, his teacher, knows it is important for Hiroki to learn science and social studies concepts in addition to increasing his literacy skills. Hiroki's father has told Ms. Johnson that Hiroki is very interested in outer space and in studying inventors.

QUESTIONS

1. What assessment could Ms. Johnson administer to determine Hiroki's reading level?
2. What can Ms. Johnson do to help Hiroki develop his literacy skills?
3. What strategies can Ms. Johnson use to teach the content area concepts to Hiroki?
4. What small group activities would benefit Hiroki?
5. What websites would you recommend Ms. Johnson show Hiroki so he can research his two areas of interest—outer space and inventors?

Chapter Ten

FLUENCY

A teacher who is attempting to teach without inspiring the pupil with a desire to learn is hammering on cold iron.

HORACE MANN

"Will's life was the American dream.
He was rich in friendship, fortune, and fame.
But he always loved people—all people—
With a grin on his face and a smile in his heart.
'I never met a man I didn't like.'" (n.p.)

scenario

Thus ends Zach's flawless, fluent reading of *Will Rogers* (Keating, 2001). Abby, his tutor, is perplexed because Zach's mother said he needed help in reading. She explained to Abby that the fourth grader was getting poor grades in science and social studies, and his teacher said it was because of his reading. So when he finishes the book, Abby compliments him on his excellent reading. However, when she asks him what the book was about, he says, "Will Rogers."

"What did you learn about Will Rogers?" Abby prompts.

"He must be a cowboy because of the picture on the front cover."

"Is there anything else you remember?"

"Not really."

Abby reads the first page to Zach and then asks what he knows about Will Rogers.

"He traveled all over the world and he never met a man he did not like." This is exactly all the information shared on page one.

"Great! Now you reread the second page and let's see what we learn."

Again Zach reads the page without any errors, but he cannot provide any details about the information.

Abby knows some students read fluently without comprehending a passage. She figures this is the case with Zach and knows she has hard work ahead of her.

guiding questions

As you read this chapter, consider the following questions:

1. Do you believe that all fluent readers comprehend what they read?
2. Why would it be important to assess Zach in not just rate but in all components of fluency? What assessments would you recommend Abby use for this purpose?
3. Do you know what strategies to teach Zach so he not only reads fluently but also comprehends what he reads?

INTRODUCTION

Fluency, the ability to read with automatic word recognition, expression, and meaning, is a critical component of reading instruction (Allington, 2006; Rasinski & Lenhart, 2007; Griffith & Rasinski, 2004; DeKonty-Applegate, Quinn, & Applegate, 2008). Since the release of the National Reading Panel report (NRP, 2000) and the reauthorization of the Individuals with Disabilities Education Act (IDEA) in 2004, fluency assessments and instructional strategies have received much attention (Moore & Hinchman, 2006; Rasinski & Padak, 2005; Valencia et al., 2010; Dekonty-Applegate, Applegate, & Modla, 2009). However, teachers report that many of their most fluent readers do not comprehend what they read (DeKonty-Applegate, Applegate, & Modla, 2009). How can this be? Part of the answer may be that since the passing of the two federal acts, student's words correct per minute (WCPM) is commonly used to show student growth in fluency. Teachers have students read passages multiple times to increase their WCPM rate. High WCPM scores are equated with fluent reading. However, fluency involves much more than reading rate (Deeney, 2010; Johns, 2007; Rasinski & Lenhart, 2007).

Reading ability for both children and adults is measured by fluency—but what does fluency entail?

Listeners know that fluent readers read at a good pace. They attend to the punctuation in sentences; their voices rise for question marks, pause for commas, and increase in volume for exclamation marks. Fluent readers recognize words automatically and quickly decode unknown words. They slow down when needed. Audiences enjoy listening to fluent readers because they interpret the text with expression. When struggling readers read in a slow, staggering, monotone voice, however, audiences have a difficult time listening to and comprehending the text. Disfluency is not only a problem for the audience; it also causes comprehension problems for the reader.

Disfluency causes readers to become self-conscious of their reading, and they soon learn to avoid reading in public. Readers who are not fluent also read less because it takes them longer than proficient readers to read a passage (Allington, 2000). Because reading takes so much time, they become discouraged and avoid it altogether.

Comprehension is the main purpose for all reading, and fluency is important for comprehension. This chapter presents two definitions of fluency and the four main components of fluency that are recognized by most researchers and educators: rate, automaticity or accuracy, prosody, and comprehension (Rasinski & Lenhart, 2007; DeKonty-Applegate, Applegate, & Modla, 2009; Johns, 2007; Valencia et al., 2010). It also presents various instruments used to assess fluency and numerous strategies that have proven to be effective with individual struggling readers and small groups.

WHAT IS FLUENCY?

NAEP defines fluency as the ease or naturalness of reading. The key elements include

1. grouping or **phrasing** of words as revealed through the intonation, stress, and pauses exhibited by readers;
2. adherence to author's **syntax**; and
3. **expressiveness** of the oral reading-interjecting a sense of feeling, anticipation, or characterization.

Figure 10.1 presents the NAEP fluency scale. Students at levels 3 and 4 are generally considered to be fluent, and those at levels 1 and 2 non-fluent.

Two other aspects of oral reading measured in the NAEP assessment are **accuracy** and **rate. Accuracy** is determined through an analysis of students' oral reading deviations from the words in the text (misread words), and **rate** is measured in terms of words-per-minute.

The next section discusses the four main components of fluency recognized by most researchers and educators (Rasinski & Lenhart, 2007; DeKonty-Applegate, Applegate, & Modla, 2009; Johns, 2007; Valencia et al., 2010): rate, automaticity or accuracy, prosody, and comprehension.

figure 10.1

NAEP's oral reading fluency scale.

LEVEL 4

Reads primarily in larger, meaningful phrase groups. Although some regressions, repetitions, and deviations from text may be present, these do not appear to detract from the overall structure of the story. Preservation of the author's syntax is consistent. Some or most of the story is read with expressive interpretation.

LEVEL 3

Reads primarily in three- or four-word phrase groups. Some smaller groupings may be present. However, the majority of phrasing seems appropriate and preserves the syntax of the author. Little or no expressive interpretation is present.

LEVEL 2

Reads primarily in two-word phrases with some three-or four-word groupings. Some word-by-word reading may be present. Word groupings may seem awkward and unrelated to larger context of sentence or passage.

LEVEL 1

Reads primarily word-by-word. Occasional two-word or three-word phrases may occur—but these are infrequent and/or they do not preserve meaningful syntax.

Source: U.S. Department of Education, National Center for Education Statistics. *Listening to Children Read Aloud, 15.* Washington, DC: 1995.

COMPONENTS OF FLUENCY

In order for students to become fluent readers, teachers need to help them develop the four components: rate, automaticity or accuracy, prosody, and comprehension. Furthermore, to develop automaticity readers need to master four subskills: (1) phonological, (2) word identification, (3) word analysis, and (4) semantic. The majority of readers assessed as having reading difficulties lack one or more components of fluency (Wolf, Miller, & Donnelly, 2000). Allington (2006) and Fountas and Pinnell (2006b) describe the traits of fluent readers versus disfluent readers. They are summarized in Figure 10.2.

figure 10.2

Traits of fluent readers versus disfluent readers.

FLUENT READERS

1. Use knowledge of language to keep reading.
2. Use an appropriate reading rate.
3. Slow down to solve problems.
4. Have automatic word recognition.
5. Have automatic word analysis skills.
6. Use intonation to convey meaning.
7. Adhere to punctuation cues.
8. Use knowledge of story structure and expository text to keep reading.
9. Reproduce the natural phrasing of the text.

DISFLUENT READERS

1. Lack knowledge of language skills.
2. Read word-by-word.
3. Think fast reading is good reading.
4. Have a poor bank of sight words.
5. Lack word analysis skills.
6. Lack expression.
7. Omit punctuation.
8. Lack prior knowledge of story structure and expository text structure.
9. Lack the ability to phrase text appropriately.

Sources: Allington, R. L. (2006). *What Really Matters for Struggling Readers: Designing Research-based Programs.* (2nd ed.). Boston: Pearson/Allyn & Bacon. Fountas, I. D. & Pinnell, G. S. (2006). *Guided Reading: Good First Teaching for All Children.* Portsmouth, NH: Heinemann.

Rate

A slow rate is one of the most common indicators of inefficient reading (Rasinski, 2000). Reading researchers have varying opinions about what constitutes an appropriate reading rate.

In 2005, Hasbrouck and Tindal (2006) collected data from school districts in 23 states. They collected students' fluency scores as measured by words correct per minute for students in grades 1–8 during three different times of the year—fall, winter, and spring—because oral reading fluency increases throughout the school year. Figure 10.3 shows the scores for each grade at each scoring time, with students categorized into 10th, 25th, 50th, 75th, and 90th percentiles. Teachers can use these norms as a way of diagnosing students' reading rates in comparison to the norm for their grade and time of the year (fall, winter, or spring). Obviously, if a student's reading rate is in the 10th percentile, he will need intervention. Teachers can also use the table to determine if students are making adequate yearly progress. Remember, however, these norms only reflect students' correct words per minute and does not reflect their prosody and comprehension at those reading rates.

Oral reading rate is calculated by counting how many words the student reads in 60 seconds. To find the most accurate rate for a student, have the student read at least three timed passages on the same easy reading level, and then average the reading rates. The silent reading rate is calculated by multiplying the total number of words read by 60 and then dividing that number by the total number of seconds it takes the student to read the passage.

$$\text{Silent reading: } \frac{\text{Number of words read} \times 60}{\text{Number of seconds to read}} = \text{WPM}$$

Teachers working with struggling readers, who typically read at a slow pace, need to establish short-term, attainable goals. The reading material must be at the easy reading level at first and at the instructional level later. As illustrated in the opening scenario, comprehension is the purpose for reading; therefore, a fast reading rate can never substitute for comprehension. Help struggling readers understand that proficient readers slow down when the passage is difficult to comprehend and speed up when the text is easy to comprehend.

Automaticity/Accuracy

Rate and fluency depend on **automaticity**, which is "the ability to engage and coordinate a number of complex subskills and strategies with little cognitive effort" (Allington, 2006). One of the reading theories associated with fluency and its importance to comprehension is that of S. J. Samuels (1979/1997). Samuels' automaticity theory has two components: (1) accuracy of word recognition and interpretation of punctuation and (2) reading rate. Samuels argues that readers who recognize words effortlessly can devote all of their mental energies to comprehension, while readers who struggle to decode words and interpret punctuation have fewer cognitive resources available to process meaning. Readers who struggle with word recognition spend much of their mental ability on remembering letter–sound relationships or on breaking words into smaller chunks. If the reader slows down to sound out a word, her rate decreases drastically.

figure 10.3 Oral reading fluency norms, grades 1–8.

		FALL	WINTER	SPRING
GRADE	PERCENTILE	WCPM	WCPM	WCPM
1	90	N/A	81	111
	75	N/A	47	82
	50	N/A	23	53
	25	N/A	12	28
	10	N/A	6	15
	SD		32	39
Count [Students]			16,950	19,434
2	90	106	125	142
	75	79	100	117
	50	51	72	89
	25	25	42	61
	10	11	18	31
	SD	37	41	42
Count [Students]		15,896	18,229	20,128
3	90	128	146	162
	75	99	120	137
	50	71	92	107
	25	44	62	78
	10	21	36	48
	SD	40	43	44
Count [Students]		16,988	17,383	18,372
4	90	145	166	180
	75	119	139	152
	50	94	112	123
	25	68	87	98
	10	45	61	72
	SD	40	41	43
Count [Students]		16,523	14,572	16,269

		FALL	WINTER	SPRING
GRADE	PERCENTILE	WCPM	WCPM	WCPM
5	90	166	182	194
	75	139	156	168
	50	110	127	139
	25	85	99	109
	10	61	74	83
	SD	45	44	45
Count [Students]		16,212	13,331	15,292
6	90	177	195	204
	75	153	167	177
	50	127	140	150
	25	98	111	122
	10	68	82	93
Count [Students]		10,520	9,218	11,290
7	90	180	192	202
	75	156	165	177
	50	128	136	150
	25	102	109	123
	10	79	88	98
	SD	40	43	41
Count [Students]		6,482	4,058	5,998
8	90	185	199	199
	75	161	173	177
	50	133	146	151
	25	106	115	124
	10	77	84	97
	SD	43	45	41
Count [Students]		5,546	3,496	5,335

WCPM: Words correct per minute *SD:* Standard deviation Count: Number of student scores

Source: J. Hasbrouck and G. Tindal (2006). Oral reading fluency norms: A valuable assessment tool for reading teachers. *The Reading Teacher, 59*(7), 636–644. Reprinted with permission from the International Reading Association via Copyright Clearance Center.

Recognizing common words

One of the subskills of automaticity is the ability to recognize common words, often referred to as *sight words,* that appear in almost all texts (see Chapter 6). Some examples of sight words are *have, done, live,* and *come.* Chapter 6 has more information on sight words and strategies to develop a reader's bank of sight words.

Associating letter/letter combinations with their sounds

A second subskill of automaticity is the ability to associate letters or letter combinations (e.g., /sh/, /wr/, /oi/) with their sounds. For example, fluent readers recognize the /sh/ in *shake* as one sound, while too often disfluent readers will attempt to sound out the word letter by letter: /s/ + /h/ + /a/ + /k/

+ /e/. This subskill includes familiarity with the various sounds the vowels make and when the various vowel sounds are used. The proficient reader quickly recognizes that adding an *e* to *cap* makes the *a* into a long *a* sound and changes the word to *cape*. They quickly recognize the subtle differences between the two vowel sounds of the words *pin* and *pen*. They understand and recognize vowel digraphs, diphthongs, and consonant clusters (see Chapter 5).

Recognizing chunks/syllables within words

A third subskill of automaticity is the ability to quickly analyze unknown words by recognizing chunks, or syllables, within words, such as onset and rime, prefixes, suffixes, and root words. When readers recognize onset and rime, they quickly combine two sounds instead of sounding out three or more sounds. For example *hat* = /h/ + /at/ for readers who recognize onset and rime, while disfluent readers sound out the three letters: /h/ + /a/ + /t/. Readers who see the syllables within unknown words also cut down on reading time. For example, readers who recognize *transportation* as *trans + por + ta + tion* have a faster reading rate than readers who attempt to sound out every letter (*t+ r + a + n + s + p + o + r + t + a + t + i + o + n*). With a polysyllabic word such as *transportation,* it takes readers such a long time to sound out each letter that they often forget the beginning sound by the time they get to the last letter. It is very difficult to remember the sounds of 14 letters and then blend them back together. In fact, with the word *transportation,* readers produce the wrong sounds if they sound out the individual letters of the last syllable. They need to recognize *tion* as /shun/ instead of /t/ + /i/ + /o/ + /n/. For more information on prefixes, suffixes, root words, and blending, see Chapter 6.

Recognizing the meanings of words

A fourth subskill of automaticity is the ability to recognize the main meaning of words as well as the multiple meanings of these words. Readers who know the meaning of *crimp* read on when they encounter it in this sentence: "Fisherman Joe's job was to crimp the fish as Fisherman Mike tossed them to him." Some readers may be able to pronounce *crimp,* but do not know its meaning. They will slow down their reading rate when they get to the word because their comprehension breaks down.

Knowing multiple meanings of common words is also a part of this subskill. Take, for example, the multiple meanings of *frog.* When students read, "Mother has a frog in her throat," they must realize that Mother is hoarse—she does not have a green creature in her throat. If they do not realize that Mother has a sore throat, comprehension breaks down, which also hinders the reading rate. Chapter 7 has more information on building readers' vocabularies.

Phrasing or Prosody

Another component of fluency is a reader's ability to recognize phrases instead of seeing each word in isolation. Some readers recognize words quickly and have a good understanding of multiple meanings, but others are cautious and read words instead of grouping them into phrases. Recognition of phrases, also called **prosody**, greatly increases readers' fluency. Consider the following two readings of the same sentence. The first reader reads the sentence word by word. . . .

> The . . little . . girl . . with . . the . . pink . . bow . . was . . playing . . with . . her . . new . . doll.

The second reader automatically recognizes prepositional and other phrases and reads the sentence as follows:

> The little girl
> with the pink bow
> was playing
> with her new doll.

Reading word-by-word may be a result of struggling readers receiving poor instruction. Struggling readers often spend more time reading orally than proficient readers who mostly read silently—which is faster than oral reading (Allington, 2006). Struggling readers are also interrupted more often and more quickly than proficient readers when reading aloud (Allington, 2006). Struggling readers are taught to stop when they do not know a word, which, of course, slows down their reading process. The teacher or a classmate may provide the unknown words instead of sharing strategies for figuring them out.

Other teachers get in the habit of affirming each word a struggling reader says correctly. These students learn to wait for confirmation after each word (Allington, 2006). Consider the different length of time it takes two different students to read the following two sentences:

> Student #1: The
> Teacher: un-hunh.
> Student #1: elephant
> Teacher: Yes.
> Student #1: was
> Teacher: un-hunh.
> Student #1: the
> Teacher: un-hunh.

Student #1: first

Teacher: Good.

Student #1: animal

Teacher: Right!

Student #1: in

Teacher: un-hunh.

Student #1: the

Teacher: mm-hmm.

Student #1: parade.

Teacher: Good. Read on.

Student #2: The elephant was the first animal in the parade.

Be conscious of your actions when working with struggling readers. Instead of giving them an unknown word, have them skip it, read to the end of the sentence, and then go back to see what word makes sense in the blank. The student confirms the word is correct by seeing if her choice matches the spelling of the word in the text.

Parsing phrases

Students who read words instead of phrases need to be taught to parse phrases correctly. You may conduct a number of activities to help with phrasing. First, you can give students texts written at their easy reading level that are composed of natural phrases. For younger students, you can use many of Dr. Seuss's books, which are formatted in short, readable phrases. For example, the following page of *I Can Read With My Eyes Shut!* (1978) features phrases written in a natural, conversational form:

If you read with your eyes shut
you're likely to find
that the place where we're going
is far, far behind. (unpaged)

The first page of *Oh, The Thinks You Can Think!* (1975) is written and formatted in the same manner:

You can
    think up
        some birds.
That's what you can do.
You can think about yellow
or think about blue. (unpaged)

Teaching students to group words in phrases increases their rate of reading and helps them comprehend connected thoughts.

For older students, choose short poems written in a natural style. Notice how each line of the Bill Dodds's poem "Big Mary," in Lansky (1998) and found in Figure 10.4, is a natural phrase. Later, teachers can mark texts with arches to represent phrases, or put phrases within slash marks. See Figure 10.5 for an example. You can then model the phrasing and have students echo it. After the echo reading, students practice reading the text with the marked phrases on their own until they become comfortable (see the Intervention activity on echo reading later in this chapter). You can mark longer phrases after students learn to read the short ones.

figure **10.4**

Poem with natural phrasing.

BIG MARY

Mary had a little lamb,
a little toast,
a little jam,
a little pizza
and some cake,
some French fries
and a chocolate shake,
a little burger
on a bun.
And that's why Mary
weighs a ton.

Source: Copyright © 1998 by Bill Dodds. Reprinted from *Miles of Smiles* with permission from Meadowbrook Press.

figure **10.5**

Sample poem with marked phrases.

"Momma's sewing machine / clanked all week long. / Sometimes I woke up / and heard the Singer / before the morning sawmill whistle blew. / And sometimes / I fell asleep at night / listening to the rhythm / of the foot pedal / hitting the floor. But tonight was Friday / and we were going / to the picture show./ So Momma tucked the machine away / in a corner / like a broom / waiting to be used again."

Source: From *Mister and Me* by Kimberly Willis Holt, illustrated by Leonard Jenkins, copyright © 1998 by Kimberly Willis Holt, text. Used by permission of G.P. Putnam's Sons, a division of Penguin Young Readers Groups, a member of Penguin Group (USA) Inc., 345 Hudson St., New York, NY 10014. All rights reserved.

Expressive reading

Expressive reading is another aspect of prosody. Reading with expression is about making written words sound like speech. Many young children enjoy hearing the deep voice of Papa Bear, the melodic voice of Mama Bear, and the high, squeaky voice of Baby Bear in "Goldilocks and the Three Bears." Older children enjoy hearing ghost stories from a storyteller with a scary voice. An expressive voice makes a story come alive! Fluent readers distinguish the various voices in dialogue and are able to "project the natural pitch, stress and juncture of the spoken word" (Richards, 2000, p. 534). Disfluent readers do not distinguish between different voices in dialogue; instead they read every word in the same tone without expression. Note that expressionless, monotonous readers often read words correctly, but may not be comprehending the passage. Anyone who reads: "Ouch! You got my finger pinched in the door!" in a monotone voice does not comprehend the passage.

When fluent readers express the tone and message of a passage, they emphasize important words, slow down for suspenseful passages, and change volume to convey the mood. Those who read with expression indicate they comprehend the author's intended message. Read the following passage from *Daisy Comes Home* (2002) by Jan Brett two different ways: first in a monotone voice and then with the intended expression, responding to the exclamation marks, the italics, and the two speakers. Notice the difference in the meaning between the two readings.

> The fisherman ran after them, furious. "Stop!" he yelled at Mei Mei. "That's *my* hen!"
>
> "Finders keepers!" Mei Mei called over her shoulder.

To teach expressive reading first model this skill and then assist struggling readers through echo reading and unison reading. Readers' comprehension, rate, prosody, and expression increase through "teacher-directed lessons in which children spend maximum amount of time engaged in reading connected text" (Stahl & Kuhn, 2002, p. 582).

Selecting appropriate material for expressive reading is crucial. During the teacher-directed lessons, the material should be at the instructional level of the student, and during individual practice reading time the material should be at the reader's easy level. The passages should be complete stories or chapters from a chapter book. When modeling, be sure to select materials that have lots of expressive dialogue or suspenseful narration.

Linda Williams's *The Little Old Lady Who Was Not Afraid of Anything* (1986) has excellent passages to model expression for younger children. The beginning of the story presents the peaceful scene of the Little Old Lady leisurely walking through the forest at night, when "Suddenly she stopped!" (Long pause) "Right in the middle of the path were two big shoes. And the shoes went CLOMP! CLOMP!" When you model this short passage, use appropriate expression and then discuss what you did with your voice to make the story interesting. Then invite students to read it with you using the same expressions. After they can imitate your expressions, have them practice it individually.

With older students, take passages from chapter books that have extensive dialogue. Dialogue works well because most struggling readers can imagine the voices of different people. First, model reading the passage with appropriate expression and then invite students to read it in unison with you. If the passage has dialogue with two characters, assign the two characters' parts to two groups of students while you read the explanatory words and narrative.

Figure 10.6 features a short selection from Karen Hesse's (1998) *Just Juice*. The passage is divided into three parts—for the teacher, Group 1, and Group 2. This selection, like all selections used for beginning expressive instruction, does not have difficult vocabulary. This particular selection needs to be read with expression in order to convey first the encouragement and then the despair of the father (Group 2), and first the fear and then the kindness and encouragement of Juice (Group 1).

Punctuation

Another topic related to prosody and reading with expression, punctuation helps writers convey their message and readers to interpret it. Students who read fluently understand and respond to the punctuation marks. Notice how punctuation changes the message of the following sentences:

> Woman without her man is nothing!
>
> Woman: without her, man is nothing.
>
> Slow children playing.
>
> Slow! Children playing.

Many struggling readers do not read commas or end marks (Fountas & Pinnell, 2006b). Without observing these punctuation marks, their comprehension breaks down. Notice the differences between the following two sentences. The first reader omits the commas and believes that the author is asking for two kinds of juice. The second reader understands that the author is referring to three kinds of juice.

> Reader #1: Please give me cranberry apple and orange juice.

figure 10.6 Selection for expressive instruction from Karen Hesse's *Just Juice.*

TEACHER:	I hang out at the door to Pa's shop awhile, then hop over the timber frame and come in.
GROUP 1 (Juice):	"You think Ma had trouble with the truck?"
TEACHER:	I ask.
GROUP 1:	"You think she got stuck in the mud?"
TEACHER:	Pa takes his cap off and rubs his head.
GROUP 2 (Pa):	"I don't think so, honey. She'll be back soon. Don't worry."
TEACHER:	But I am worried.
GROUP 1:	"Were they mean to you at the town offices, Pa, when you were there?"
GROUP 2:	"They were nice enough. But they thought I was some stupid because of not reading those letters. I guess they were right, too. I am stupid."
GROUP 1:	"You're not stupid, Pa. No more than I am. Miss Hamble says some of us are wired up different inside our brains. You and me, we just have a different kind of wiring. You know?"

(pp. 129–130)

Source: Adapted from *Just Juice* by Karen Hesse. Scholastic Inc./Scholastic Press. Copyright © 1998 by Karen Hesse. Reprinted with permission.

> Reader #2: Please give me cranberry, apple, and orange juice.

When readers omit periods, comprehension and reading rate also quickly deteriorate. Once comprehension breaks down, the student reads words and not complete thoughts. The following passage is from Jan Brett's *Daisy Comes Home* (2002). The punctuation has been dropped to indicate how it might sound to a reader who omits punctuation.

> Dawn broke over the Gui Mountains as the basket drifted along the river branches brushed against it fish swam silently by and birds flew overhead suddenly Daisy felt a thump. (unpaged)

How difficult was it to grasp the meaning of the passage? Did you have to read the passage twice to comprehend what was happening?

When fluent readers encounter ellipses, they know it indicates a pause for emphasis. Consider the sentence from *The Old Woman Who Lived in a Vinegar Bottle* (1995) by Margaret MacDonald: "There sat the old woman . . . complaining." The ellipses tell the reader that the author intends a pause between the words *woman* and *complaining* to emphasize the action, complaining.

Parentheses indicate less important material, which may suggest that readers pause and read the words with a lowered voice. Notice in the following sentence how the author uses parentheses to help readers understand the term *readers theater*. The phrase is set off with a pause after *theater* and the phrase is read in a lowered voice.

> Readers theater [pause, and with lowered voice] (conveying drama through vocal expression rather than acting) [pause and return to natural voice] is a great activity to develop fluency.

When teaching students to respond to punctuation, explain the purpose of punctuation marks and model the pauses and vocal inflections when "reading" them. For many beginning and older students, echo reading and unison reading are good strategies to help develop an awareness of punctuation marks. As you can see, prosody includes many different, yet related, skills.

Comprehension

Researchers and educators understand the connection between fluency and comprehension. Reciprocal theory suggests the relationship between fluency and comprehension is give-and-take rather than unidirectional. Correlation studies conducted on fluency and comprehension indicate that when fluency increases, comprehension increases and vice versa (Flood, Lapp, & Fisher, 2005; Griffith & Rasinski, 2004; O'Connor, White, & Swanson, 2007).

However, when DeKonty-Applegate, Applegate, and Modla (2009) conducted a study with 60 primary grade students, 57 intermediate grade (4–5) students, and 54 middle school and high school (grades 6–12) students to determine if there is a correlation between a high level of fluency and a high degree of reading comprehension, they found that one third of students who were classified as fluent readers struggled with comprehension. They discovered that many students were assessed on fluency based only on their rate, accuracy, and prosody; their fluency scores did not reflect their comprehension. In other words, these students were not as fluent as their scores indicated.

Since the implementation of the NCLB Act and reauthorization of IDEA, many schools have been assessing students' fluency by having them read from a commercial test or a classroom text. Teachers have students read for one minute, subtract any misread words, and produce words correct per minute (WCPM). A study done by Valencia et al. (2010) with students in grades 2, 4, and 6 compared these one-minute assessments with assessments designed to measure combined aspects of fluency, such as rate, accuracy, prosody, and comprehension. The results indicated that fluency assessments that "include multiple indicators of oral reading fluency provided a finer-grained understanding of oral reading fluency and fluency assessment, and a stronger predictor of general comprehension" (p. 270).

Chapters 8 and 9 discuss the many subskills of comprehending narrative and expository texts.

FLUENCY INSTRUCTION

As mentioned earlier in this chapter, the poor instruction given to struggling readers may be a source of their disfluent reading. Often teachers give a different type of instruction to fluent readers than they do to disfluent readers. Although this is not intentional, teachers' lack of expertise in working with struggling readers may be the cause of the discrepancy (Allington, 2006). Figure 10.7 compares characteristics of instruction typical for fluent readers to the instruction typical for disfluent readers.

Research-Based Guidelines for Fluency Instruction

In order for teachers to avoid poor instructional practices, they must understand what reading researchers have discovered regarding specific types of instruction and the kinds of materials to use with struggling readers. Figure 10.8 lists some research findings related to fluent reading. The studies reveal eight principles that should guide fluency instruction (Rasinski, 2003).

1. Students need to hear fluent reading.
2. Students need to have direct instruction in fluency with feedback.
3. Students need support while reading. Support can be unison reading or reading along with an audio recording.
4. Students need opportunities to repeat readings. However, all repeated readings need a purpose or goal! Some benefits of repeated readings are (a) readers increase rate and accuracy, (b) readers better understand phrasing, and (c) readers increase their comprehension.
5. Students need specific instruction to learn phrasing skills.
6. Students need easy reading to practice fluency.
7. Students need time to work on increasing their reading rate and fluency.
8. Disfluent students should not be embarrassed by being forced to read in front of peers.

figure **10.7** Typical instruction given to fluent and disfluent readers.

INSTRUCTION OF FLUENT READERS	INSTRUCTION OF DISFLUENT READERS
1. Given materials that are easy or on their instructional reading level.	1. Given materials that are too difficult.
2. Given time to read silently.	2. Asked to read orally, which slows down rate.
3. Are expected to self-monitor.	3. Interrupted more often.
4. Taught strategies to see groups of letters within words.	4. Encouraged to sound out words letter by letter.
5. Are expected to self-correct; only interrupted at end of sentence.	5. Interrupted when error is made.
6. Asked to cross-check when they misread.	6. Given words with no strategies.

Source: Adapted from Allington, R. L. (2006). *What Really Matters for Struggling Readers: Designing Research-based Programs.* (2nd ed.). Boston: Pearson/Allyn & Bacon.

figure **10.8** Research related to fluent reading.

FINDINGS	STUDIES
1. "Guided repeated oral reading and repeated reading provide students with practice that substantially improves word recognition, fluency, and—to a lesser extent—reading comprehension" (National Reading Panel, pp. 3–20).	The National Reading Panel (2000); Samuels (1979/1997); Dowhower (1989); Duffy-Hester (1999); Fox & Wright (1997); Fuchs, Fuchs, Mathes, & Simon (1997); Sindelar, Monda, & O'Shea (1990); Young, Bowers, & MacKinnon (1996); Kuhn (2000); Allington (2006)
2. Assisted reading at the appropriate rate increases word recognition and fluency.	Carbo (1978, 1998); Richards (2000); Stahl & Kuhn (2002); Stahl, Heubach, & Cramond (1997); Mastropieri, Leinart, & Scruggs (1999); Matthew (1997); Morris & Nelson (1992); Sippola (1997); Taylor, Hanson, Justice-Swanson, & Watts (1997); Koskinen, Blum, Bisson, Phillips, Creamer, & Baker (1999)
3. Fluency affects comprehension.	Allington (1983, 2006); Anderson (1981); Duffy-Hester (1999); Rasinski & Padak (1994, 2003); Rasinski, Padak, Linck, & Sturtevant (1994); Vaughn (2000); Reutzel & Hollingsworth (1993); Young, Bowers, & MacKinnon (1996)
4. Dyad reading increases fluency.	Oliver, Wilcox, & Eldredge (2000); Vaughn et al. (2000); Topping & Ehly (1998); Moore & Hinchman (2006)
5. Cross-age tutoring is an effective strategy to increase fluency of both readers.	Taylor, Hanson, Justice-Swanson, & Watts (1997); Fox & Wright (1997)
6. Readers theater exercises improve fluency.	Moore & Hinchman, (2006); Gill (2000); Ivey & Broaddus (2000); Koskinen, Blum, Bison, Phillips, Creamer, & Baker (1999); Larkin (2001)
7. Choral reading improves fluency.	Hadaway, Vardell, & Young (2001)
8. Prosodic instruction improves fluency.	Allington (2006); Anderson (1981); Bray, Kehle, Spackman, & Hintze (1998); Rasinski (2004); Schreiber (1991); Young, Bowers, & MacKinnon (1996)
9. Guided reading is an effective instructional practice to increase fluency.	Fountas & Pinnell (2006b); Fawson & Reutzel (2000)
10. Specific instruction in fluency is beneficial for readers in all grade levels.	Allinder (2001); Moore & Hinchman (2006); Vaughn, Mathes, Linan-Thompson, & Francis (2005)
11. Instruction focused on semantic and syntactic cues helps readers with the interpretation of author's intended meaning.	Allington, (2006); Gill (2000); Moore & Aspegren (2001)
12. Instruction in morphological strategies (e.g., recognizing affixes and root words) aids automaticity.	Kane (1999)
13. Instruction in self-monitoring (analyzing one's own rate, accuracy, and expression) increases fluency.	Moore & Aspegren (2001); Goodman & Marek (1996)
14. Readers' rate affects comprehension.	Rasinski (2003); Harris & Sipay (1990); Samuels (1979/1997); Allington & Cunningham (2002)
15. Unison reading is effective instruction for English learners.	Vaughn, Mathes, Linan-Thompson, & Francis (2005)

Fluency Instruction for English Learners

English learners need support not only as they learn new words, but also as they strive to become fluent readers. When instructing English learners in fluency follow these steps.

1. Read a short passage to the student that is on his instructional level.
2. You and the English learner read the passage together.
3. The English learner reads the same passage by himself so you can assess his progress.
4. With the same passage, time the English learner's reading and record his rate.
5. The English learner practices to increase rate and improve intonation.
6. The English learner listens to a recording of his reading to self-assess. (See Appendix C.44 for a checklist the student can use.)

ASSESSMENT

Teachers need to recognize which of the subskills is causing problems for a struggling reader's fluency. You can use both informal and formal assessment instruments to diagnose fluency. Following are some formal and informal assessments. Listening to students and using the informal assessment instruments are the most useful ways to diagnose fluency problems. However, many school districts require the use of formal assessment instruments for the student to receive help from federally funded programs.

Informal Assessment

Teachers can informally assess fluency through observation and anecdotal records. It is easy to detect disfluent reading by watching and listening to a reader: They often point to each word; they tend to read word-by-word; they read at a slow pace and lack intonation. They often reread words and phrases and do not recognize when they mispronounce words. They often mumble because they lack confidence to articulate. Readers who fall 20 to 30 percent below the average rate (refer back to Figure 10.3), usually require additional instruction (Rasinski, 2003).

Checklists

The checklist found in Appendix C.41 shows four stages of reading fluency. If the checklist is used throughout the school year, the progression from one stage to the next should be evident. The Fluency Checklist for Narrative Text found in Appendix C.42 is simple enough for students in grades 2 through 8 to use as they assess their own reading on a recording.

Students can also assess their own fluency using a simple checklist like the one in Appendix C.43 (Cecil, 2011). Go over the questions with your students first. Then, the student can read a passage into an audio recorder and play back his reading while answering questions in the checklist. Alternately, students can take turns assessing each other using the form during partner reading.

Running records and miscue analysis

Running records and miscue analyses, both discussed in detail in Chapter 3, are also used to analyze fluency. The purpose of both of these informal reading assessments is for teachers to examine the graphophonic, semantic, and syntactic clues the reader uses. The teacher calculates what type of errors or miscues the reader most often makes. Mispronunciations indicate that readers lack graphophonic knowledge or word analysis skills. Substitutions for words indicate that readers lack the basic vocabulary needed for that text. Students who do not read punctuation or read in a monotone voice are most often disfluent readers. By administering the running record and miscue analysis, teachers can target the fluency skill the reader lacks and teach strategies that will aid him.

Retrospective miscue analysis

The retrospective miscue analysis discussed in Chapter 3 helps a student assess her own fluency. As the student listens to her reading, have her time it to check the rate. If the rate is very slow, have her practice reading the passage and record it again to see if the rate improves. The student should also be taught to analyze her expression and phrasing while listening to the recording. The Fluency Checklist for Narrative Text found in Appendix C.42 is simple enough for students in grades 2 through 8 to use to assess their own reading.

Rubrics

Applegate, Quinn, and Applegate designed a rubric that rates several aspects of fluency including oral reading, intonation, punctuation, and pacing. The rubric is found in Appendix C.43.

Rubrics based on state standards are yet another useful way for teachers to assess a student's fluency and rate. Most states find that fluency is an important component of reading and that fluency includes many other reading skills—word analysis, vocabulary, and automaticity—although many states have only a few standards that specifically relate to fluency. For example, Illinois has two benchmark indicators for fluency. The two benchmarks are reflected in the rubric in Figure 10.9.

Informal commercial assessments

Reading Fluency Monitor, published by Read Naturally, is an instrument that permits teachers to assess students' progress during the school year. Read Naturally recommends teachers assess students' three times a year—fall, winter, and spring. It includes grade-level passages for grades 1–8. A software program allows teachers to easily report and keep records.

Formal Assessment

Diagnostic tests, which are norm-referenced and standardized, are given to students who show signs of reading difficulty. There are a number of diagnostic tests that measure fluency by calculating rate and/or accuracy. They include the following:

1. **Stanford Diagnostic Reading Test.**
   Levels four and up measure rate.
2. **Gray Oral Reading Tests.**
   This test focuses on oral accuracy and speed, and results in an oral reading quotient.
3. **Gilmore Oral Reading Test.**
   This test measures reading rate separately from comprehension.
4. **The Durrell Analysis of Reading Difficulty.**
   This test assesses oral fluency by counting the oral reading miscues. Rate is not measured.
5. **Diagnostic Reading Scales.**
   This test assesses oral fluency by counting the oral miscues. Rate is also measured.
6. **Woodcock Reading Mastery Test.**
   The three subskills of fluency measured in this test are word identification, word attack, and passage comprehension. Rate is not measured.
7. **Testing of Reading Fluency (TORF).**
   The student is timed as he reads for one minute, and the teacher calculates the number of words read correctly. The score is the average of three readings.
8. **AIMS Standard Reading Assessment Passages (RAPs).**
   Teachers can use this assessment with grade-leveled passages to assess students' oral reading fluency. RAPs is field-tested and validated. Internet-based software allows teachers to collect and report data.

One negative aspect of these formal assessments is that they assess only rate and accuracy. Informal assessment allows the teacher to analyze all four components of fluency: rate, automaticity, prosody, and expression, which gives them a comprehensive measure of a student's fluency.

figure **10.9** Rubric for reading comprehension based on Standard 1.B.1d for early elementary school English/Language Arts, state of Illinois.

STUDENT: Jake GRADING PERIOD 1 ② 3 4 TOTAL SCORE 4

	LEVEL OF MASTERY		
TRAIT	**TARGET (5 POINTS)**	**ACCEPTABLE (3 POINTS)**	**UNACCEPTABLE (1 POINT)**
Fluency and Accuracy	Always reads with rhythm, volume, and flow that sounds like everyday speech. ___	Sometimes reads with rhythm, volume, and flow that sounds like everyday speech. ___	Seldom reads with rhythm, volume, and flow that sounds like everyday speech. X
	Reads orally age-appropriate text at instructional level with 90% accuracy. ___	Sometimes reads orally age-appropriate text at instructional level with 90% accuracy. X	Seldom reads orally age-appropriate text at instructional level with 90% accuracy. ___

Intervention STRATEGIES & ACTIVITIES

Several activities in this chapter's Intervention section teach effective fluency to English learners, including readers theater, echo reading, and choral reading.

Direct instruction in fluency can take place in various settings. Some strategies are best practiced in a tutoring setting, while others are best practiced in small groups so students can benefit from peer interaction. The following strategies are divided into two categories—strategies for tutoring settings and strategies for small groups and peer practice settings. All fluency strategies should be taught using whole texts that interest the student.

Strategies for Tutoring Settings

The following strategies, designed for use in tutoring sessions, permit you to focus on the unique needs of the disfluent reader.

ACTIVITY **ECHO READING** **GRADES K–4**

Echo reading involves a teacher reading a short phrase or sentence and the student echoing the phrase back, using the same rate and intonation. It is important for the teacher to interpret the passage with the author's intended meaning. To introduce echo reading, choose a short poem or passage that presents natural phrases on single lines. For example, Nancy White Carlstrom's *Guess Who's Coming, Jesse Bear* (1998) for younger students and Karen Hesse's *Come On, Rain!* (1999) for older students both use poetry to tell their stories. To echo read these books, you read a line and emphasize the underlined words, and the student echoes it using your rate and intonation. The slashes indicate where you stop and allow the reader to echo.

Echo reading is especially effective with English learners because they see the words and hear the correct intonation. Stress correct intonation when English learners echo the phrases and sentences.

Guess Who's Coming, Jesse Bear

Wednesday /

I <u>count</u> and <u>look</u> and then <u>sit</u> down. /

She <u>knows</u> she <u>never</u> will be <u>found</u>. /

At <u>hiding</u> Sara is the <u>best</u>. /

It gives us <u>both</u> a little rest. /

(Unpaged)

Come On, Rain!

"Is there <u>thunder</u>?" Mamma asks. /

"No <u>thunder</u>," I say. /

"Is there <u>lightning</u>?" Mamma asks. /

"No <u>lightning</u>," Jackie-Joyce says. /

"You <u>stay</u> where I can <u>find</u> you," Mamma says. /

"<u>We will</u>," I say. /
"<u>Go on</u> then," Mamma says, /
<u>lifting</u> the glass to her <u>lips</u> to take a <u>sip</u>. /(unpaged)

Echo reading can be enjoyable for both you and the students when you practice small segments of passages that you both enjoy.

PREVIEW-PAUSE-PROMPT-PRAISE (PPPP) STRATEGY

GRADES 1–5 ACTIVITY

The preview-pause-prompt-praise (PPPP) strategy developed by Topping and Ehly (1998) can be used by teachers, reading specialists, adult volunteers, and trained para-professionals.

1. During the *preview* segment, ask the reader to predict what will happen in the story based on the title and book cover.
2. Begin reading in unison with the student until she taps the desk to indicate that she wishes to read by herself.
3. When the student makes an error, pause three seconds or wait until the student gets to the end of the sentence.
4. If the student does not self-correct in three seconds or by the end of the sentence, give two prompts: "Let's read that again" and if the student still does not self-correct, tell her the word.
5. Begin again to read with the student until she taps the desk.
6. If the student does self-correct after three seconds, praise her, and read with her again until she taps the desk.
7. After she completes the passage, talk about her favorite parts with her.

This strategy focuses on fluency because the teacher reads along with the student, and it focuses on comprehension by emphasizing predictions before reading and in discussion afterward.

ORAL RECITATION LESSON (ORL)

GRADES 2–5 ACTIVITY

The oral recitation lesson (ORL) developed by Reutzel and Hollingsworth (1993) was designed for a classroom setting with second graders. However, you can modify this strategy to work with any struggling reader who lacks comprehension and prosody skills. Choose material at the student's instructional level. Passages with repeated refrains, cumulative episodes, rhyming patterns, or poetry are good. The ORL has two major components: the first is direct instruction by the teacher; the second is indirect instruction. The following are the steps for the direct instruction:

1. Read and discuss the story with the student completing a story map (see Chapter 8).
2. Ask the student to write a summary using the story map.
3. Model expressive reading.
4. Have the student practice by reading chorally with you.

The indirect instruction occurs when the student practices the short passage in a "soft reading voice" while you check progress in accuracy and fluency. After the student has "polished" the passage, he can perform it for a small group or for the class.

ACTIVITY

CARBO RECORDED-BOOK METHOD

GRADES K–3

Research indicates that children benefit from assisted reading. Reading along with audiobooks increases a reader's fluency, word identification, and comprehension (Allington, 2006; Carbo, 1998; Koskinen et al., 1999). However, too often commercial read-along audiobooks proceed too quickly for most struggling readers to follow along with the recording. The Carbo Recorded-Book Method is a technique for using teacher-produced audio texts. The teacher selects interesting reading material that is at or a little above the reader's reading level. The passage is recorded (1) at a slow pace, (2) in short, natural phrases, and (3) with excellent expression.

The purpose of this method is to produce recordings that permit the disfluent reader to read along successfully. After reading along with them at school, the students take the recordings home for more practice and to involve their parents in the learning process. See Chapter 8 for a discussion of teacher-made recordings.

ACTIVITY

RECORD, CHECK, CHART

GRADES 2–8

Record, Check, Chart, designed by Allington (2006), is a type of repeated reading that students can use independently to improve their accuracy. The student reads from a photocopy of a passage, which is either a story or a poem, and performs the following steps:

1. The student reads the passage into a recording device.
2. While following the text, the student listens to the recording and marks each word read in error with a black pen.
3. Without replaying the recording, the student reads the same passage into the recording again.
4. While following the text, the student listens to a second reading and checks each error with a green pen.
5. Without replaying the recording, the student reads the same passage into the recording device.
6. While following the text, the student listens to the third reading and checks each error with a blue pen.
7. Using the chart found in Appendix D.24, the student tallies the number of errors for each reading. Figure 10.10 is a partially completed example of Amy's reading of *Secret Soup* (1989) by Jenny Hessell. The little book has 51 words.

figure **10.10** Record, check, chart.

STUDENT Amy

Story	1st reading errors	2nd reading errors	3rd reading errors	Teacher's comments
1. Secret Soup	~~||||~~ ||| 8	~~||||~~ 5	||| 3	Had difficult time w/mushroom and lunch

Teacher Overall Comments:

The student's goal is to make fewer errors with each repeated reading. You can check the accuracy by listening to the three recordings. If the student misses some of the errors, listen to the recording with him, stop it when you hear an unmarked error, and ask him to listen closely to as he follows the text. The student can take the chart and recording home in order for the parents or caregivers to listen to it with him.

FLASH CARDS — GRADES 1–5 — ACTIVITY

Flash cards using key words found in a given passage allow students to practice sight word recognition, a subskill of automaticity. When preparing the flash cards, place the key word in a short sentence so the student can see the word in context (Nicholson, 1998). However, do not use a sentence from the book, but rather one that relates to the student's life experience. For example, the words *worried* and *proud* appear multiple times in *A Fine, Fine School* (2001) by Sharon Creech. Examples of cards with these words in sentences are the following:

> I was <u>worried</u> I would get an F.
>
> I was <u>proud</u> of my new book.

The goal is for the student to recognize the underlined word immediately and read the sentence fluently in one phrase.

Strategies to Use with Small Groups

Many fluency strategies are designed for use with a small group because by practicing together, they encourage and support each other's fluency. Teach the following strategies to a small group and then give the group ample time to practice the strategy. Encourage members to support each other in order to create a safe reading environment.

FLUENCY DEVELOPMENT LESSON (FDL) — GRADES 1–3 — ACTIVITY

One strategy to use with a small group is the fluency development lesson (FDL), designed by Rasinski et al. (1994), who found that nearly all students who used this strategy three to four times a week developed fluency. The lesson is 10 to 15 minutes in length. Choose short passages of 50 to 185 words that are at the students' instructional level. Then complete the following steps:

1. Give a copy of the passage to each student.
2. Read the passage while the students follow along.
3. Discuss story content and the quality of your reading (e.g., reasons for pausing or changing rate).
4. With small groups of students, read the passage chorally (in unison) or antiphonally (you read a phrase or sentence, and the students echo it)
5. Group the students in pairs and have each student read the passage three times to his or her partner.
6. Ask individuals or small groups to volunteer to perform the passage for the class.
7. Have students take the passage home and read it to their parents. Appendix D.26 can be sent home with the student in order for the parents to log the child's fluency. Figure 10.11 is a partially completed example.

***figure* 10.11** Sample fluency log.

Books I Can Read By Jeff W.

	TITLE	AUTHOR	PARENTS' COMMENTS	START DATE	NUMBER OF TIMES READ
1.	Fox on Stage (250 words)	James Marshall	We worked on expression. But book was too long.	9/8	1
2.	Get-up Machine (115 words)	Sunshine Book	I read a phrase and he repeated it (1st time). 2nd time he read by himself.	9/10	2
3.	Henry, Mudge, & the long weekend (250 words)	Cynthia Rylant	He loved the book and wanted to practice it w/expression.	9/12	4
4.	How to Make Salsa (192 words)	Book Shop	Information book was more difficult to get expression. He read words.	9/15	1
5.					

ACTIVITY **SPEECH READING** **GRADES 6–8**

Rasinski and Lenhart (2007) suggest that fluency is more than reading at a fast pace. "Authentic fluency instruction should include opportunities for students to practice their reading so they learn to use the various prosodic tools—phrasing, intonation, and expression—at their disposal (p. 18). Having students practice reading famous speeches, such as President Kennedy's inaugural address ("Ask not what your country . . .") or Martin Luther King, Jr.'s "I Have a Dream" speech, gives them opportunities to develop their fluency and public speaking skills. Speed was not the goal of either President Kennedy or Dr. King; they used different rates, pauses, and intonation to convey ideas they hoped would spur listeners to action.

ACTIVITY **TELLING JOKES** **GRADES 5–8**

Telling jokes helps students develop correct prosody so listeners get the punch line (Ness, 2009). Prosody includes (1) ability to emphasize appropriate words, (2) ability to use appropriate intonation, (3) ability to use punctuation appropriately, (4) ability to interpret characters' emotions, and (5) ability to pause at phrase boundaries. In order to tell a joke effectively readers need to have good delivery so those listening get the humor. Readers of jokes must adhere to punctuation, intonation, and phrasing (Ness, 2009). Collect books of jokes and help students with intonation, punctuation, pause, and interpretation and then let them read the jokes to friends in small groups. These are great for struggling readers because jokes are short and they can practice before they read them to peers. Joke books with appropriate humor for students include:

Brewer, P. (2003). *You must be joking! Lots of cool jokes, plus 17 1/2 tips for remembering, telling, and making up your own jokes.* Battle Creek, MI: Cricket.

Terban, M. (2007). *Eight ate: A feast of homonym riddles.* New York: Scholastic.

Weitzman, I. (2006). *Jokelopedia: The biggest, best, silliest, dumbest joke book ever.* New York: Workman.

SUPPORTED-READING STRATEGY — GRADES 2–3 — ACTIVITY

Morris and Nelson (1992) found the following supported-reading strategy increased second graders' reading ability when used three days a week for six months. In this strategy, instructional-level reading material is used in a three-day cycle. The focus is on comprehension first, expression second.

DAY 1

a. Read and discuss story elements (setting, characterization, plot, climax, resolution, theme, style, point of view) with students.
b. Together with students echo read segments of the passage, focusing on expression.

DAY 2

a. Have students read in pairs with each student reading alternate pages.
b. Have the pairs practice a short passage of their choice, focusing on expression.
c. Partners read their passages to each other and critique each other's expression. Partners may use the fluency checklist used for retrospective miscue analysis that is in Appendix C.42.

DAY 3

a. Ask individuals to read to you while you check for accuracy and expression.

DYAD READING — GRADES 2–3 — ACTIVITY

Another type of paired reading exercise that focuses on fluency is dyad reading. Dyad reading is unison reading with a buddy. The buddies share the same copy of text. One reader is usually somewhat stronger than the other. The readers sit side-by-side and take turns reading aloud, rotating after every paragraph. When a reader finishes a paragraph she summarizes it for the listener, who adds details not mentioned by the reader. Then the reader and listener switch roles. Dyad reading is most effective with reading material two grade levels above the reader's instruction level (Oliver, Wilcox, & Eldredge, 2000). The lead reader is responsible for setting the pace and pointing to each word while the buddies read.

REPEATED READINGS — GRADES 1–8 — ACTIVITY

Many of the strategies already discussed include repeated readings. Studies show that repeated readings increase students' fluency (Allington, 2006; Gill, 2000; Moore & Hinchman, 2006; Samuels, 1979/1997) and accuracy (Samuels, 1979/1997). However, in order for repeated readings to be effective, they need to have a clear purpose (e.g., to increase rate, to increase accuracy, to improve phrasing, to increase comprehension). Repeated readings can be performed with an individual reader or with a small group of readers. Readers theater and choral reading also provide purposeful repeated readings and are effective for any grade.

ACTIVITY **POETRY PARTY** **GRADES 2–6**

Poems are a wonderful way to help students develop fluency. They are short, and students need to comprehend them to communicate their message to an audience. A good way to foster a love of poetry in the class is to have a Poetry Party, in which students read a favorite poem they have practiced. Demonstrate how not to read a poem (in a monotone voice) and how to read a poem (with appropriate expression and correct pauses and rate so the audience understands its essence). Most elementary students enjoy the humorous poems of Shel Silverstein, Jack Prelutsky, and Bruce Lansky. Some collections of my favorites are the following: Shel Silverstein's *Where the Sidewalk Ends* (1974), *A Light in My Attic* (1981), *Falling Up* (1996); Prelutsky's *The New Kid on the Block* (1984), *Something Big Has Been Here* (1990b), *A Pizza the Size of the Sun* (1994); Arnold Lobel's *The Book of Pigericks* (1983); Jill Bennett's collection *Noisy Poems* (1987); Brod Bagert's *Rainbows, Head Lice and Pea-Green Tile* (1999); David Roessel and Arnold Rampersad's *Poetry for Young People: Langston Hughes* (1994); Mary O'Neill's *Hailstones and Halibut Bones* (1961); Patrick Lewis' *A Hippopotamustn't* (1990); and Bruce Lansky's (editor) *Miles of Smiles: Kids Pick the Funniest Poems, Book 1, Book 2, Book 3* (1996, 1997, 1998), and *If Pigs Could Fly . . . and Other Deep Thoughts* (2000). See Appendix A.4 for a list of poetry anthologies.

ACTIVITY **READERS THEATER** **GRADES 1–8**

Young and Rasinski (2009) use readers theater to develop fluency. They conducted a study with 29 second graders in a Title I school, which included nine English learners. The study researched whether readers theater instruction (1) motivated students to perform for others, (2) increased students' prosody, (3) instilled confidence in students as they performed, (4) built social skills among students as they practiced and encouraged each other to use correct expression, and (5) helped struggling readers learn to read with meaning. The study revealed a 20 percent overall improvement in students' ability to read with expression that reflected the meaning of the text. The readers theater was a part of a balanced literacy program.

The following websites offer free scripts to use for readers theater.

www.aaronshep.com/rt

www.fictionteachers.com/classroomtheater/theater.html

www.readerstheatre.ecsd.net/collection.htm

www.readinglady.com

www.readingonline.org/electronic/elec_index.asp?HREF=carrick/index.html

www.teachingheart.net; click on "readers theatre"

www.timelessteacherstuff.com

www.timrasinski.com/presentations/readers_theater_1-4.pdf

Readers theater is appropriate for all ages (Larkin et al., 2000), but especially for older students (Moore & Hinchman, 2006) and for English learners (Vaughn et al., 2005). You may assign parts with longer segments to more proficient readers and shorter segments to struggling readers. For the strategy to aid fluency development, schedule time for the group to discuss how they want to interpret the script. Then give them ample time to practice their lines by themselves and then with the group. Set aside blocks of time over a period of a couple of days for the group to work on expression and fluency. All readers theater activities should result in performances. The performance can be for other classmates, other classes, or parents.

CHORAL READING

GRADES K–8 ACTIVITY

Like readers theater, choral reading is a group activity. Unison reading, a form of choral reading in which children speak the same lines together, is especially effective with English learners. English learners hear other students pronounce the words, allowing them to practice rapid and accurate reading without fear of failure. Choral reading selections, however, do not transform texts into scripts. The purpose of choral reading is to read the selection with the interpretation intended by the author or poet. The passage is divided among a number of readers. Each reader is responsible for using vocal expression to communicate the meaning of the selection to the listeners. Poems are often used for choral reading because they come alive when read aloud. When conducting a choral reading, use the following format:

1. Read the poem to the students.
2. In a second reading have the students echo read, using your rate and expression.
3. Read the selection in unison with the students.
4. Discuss the meaning of the selection, noting rhyming words, word patterns, and word meanings.
5. With the help of students, arrange the selection as a choral reading.

Figure 10.12 shows an example of a poem arranged as a choral reading.

Impress reading is a type of unison reading that involves both teacher and student. Use a passage at the student's instructional level. When the two of you begin reading the passage, your voice should be dominant. As the student becomes more familiar with the vocabulary and the style of the passage, make your voice softer and allow the student's voice to become dominant.

figure **10.12** Example of choral reading.

The First Two Verses of "SPAGHETTI, SPAGHETTI!" by Jack Prelutsky

ALL VOICES:	Spaghetti! Spaghetti!
VOICE 1:	You're WONDERFUL (draws out the word) stuff,
VOICE 2:	I LOVE (draws out the /ah/ sound) you, spaghetti.
VOICE 3:	I can't get enough.
VOICE 4:	You're covered (voice rises and falls as if covering) with sauce,
VOICE 5:	and you're sprinkled (staccato voice) with cheese (draws out the /e/ sound)
ALL VOICES:	Spaghetti! Spaghetti!
	Oh, give me some more, please (in a plaintive voice).
ALL VOICES:	Spaghetti! Spaghetti!
VOICE 1:	Piled (draws out the long /i/) high (voice moves up in pitch) in a mound,
VOICE 2:	you wiggle (makes hand wiggle) you wriggle (makes body wiggle),
VOICE 3:	you squiggle (shaky voice) around.
VOICE 4:	There's slurpy (draws out the /slur/) spaghetti
VOICE 5:	all over my plate,
ALL VOICES:	Spaghetti! Spaghetti!
	I think you are GREAT! (emphasize *great*)

Those new to choral reading may wish to begin this activity with poems written for two or more voices, such as Paul Fleischman's Caldecott winning *Joyful Noise* (1988), which features poems about insects, and *I Am Phoenix* (1985), which features poems about birds. His book *Big Talk: Poems for 4 Voices* (2000) is uniquely formatted, using four different colors to depict the four voices. The poems can be read with four individual voices or four groups. Theoni Pappas's unique poetry book *Math Talk* (1991) is written for two voices and presents poems about easy mathematical concepts such as numbers, circles, and fractions, as well as more advanced concepts, such as radicals, tessellations, and infinity.

Some poems suitable for choral reading are the following:

Sara Holbrook's "Copycat" and "The Dog Ate My Homework."

Douglas Florian's "Delicious Wishes," "School Cafeteria," and "Twins."

Carol Diggory Shields' "Clock-watching."

Janet Wong's "Face It."

Karla Kuskin's "The Question."

Websites that focus on poetry and have poems that are suitable for choral reading include:

www.wings.buffalo.edu/epc

www.pw.org

www.poetrymagazine.com

http://potatohill.com

Books that do not feature action explained by narrators also make good choral reading selections. Books that have a question and answer format, such as *Mama, Do You Love Me?* (1991) by Barbara Joosse, are excellent for two groups or for two voices. Small groups give younger, struggling students the support they need to build confidence. Struggling readers should be placed with more proficient readers. Here is a short example of choral reading using *Mama, Do You Love Me?*

GROUP 1: Mama, do you love me?

GROUP 2: Yes, I do, Dear One.

GROUP 1: How much?

GROUP 2: I love you more than the raven loves his treasure, more than the dog loves its tail, more than the whale loves his spout. (unpaged)

Zin! Zin! Zin! A Violin (1995) by Lloyd Moss can also be divided into a number of voices, with each playing the part of a different instrument. The poem for each instrument gives students an opportunity to develop expression and fluency. Phrases such as "soaring high and moving in with Zin! Zin! Zin!" invite readers to change the pitch of their voices with each Zin! The evocation of the low trombone's "mournful moan" encourages the reader to draw out these words in a soft, low voice. Later, the same reader might raise and lower the pitch of his voice when "high notes go low." To choral read this text, first model the change of pitch, volume, and rate for each instrument and invite the students to echo read. Demonstrate how varying the rate, pitch, and volume helps you interpret the meaning of the selection.

Like all repeated readings, choral readings must be practiced in an environment that is enjoyable and relaxing. The materials for choral reading must be (1) engaging and inviting for students to use expressive voices, (2) manageable at the instructional level of the students, and (3) short enough so students can repeat their readings a number of times during one reading session.

Choral readings increase fluency and comprehension because the repeated readings have a clear purpose. The short-term purpose is having fun with language, and the long-term purpose is performance. Choral readings also encourage cooperation in small groups. Remind participants to help each other with fluency so the result is entertaining for the audience and instructive for the performers.

RHYTHM WALKS

GRADES 1–4 ACTIVITY

Many struggling readers need motivation because reading is a daunting task for them. Rhythm walks are collaborative, kinesthetic, fun ways to get students engaged by moving around as they read cards taped to the floor (Peebles, 2007).

1. Choose a short poem, story, or informational passage.
2. Analyze the text for natural phrases.
3. Laminate large pieces of rectangular card stock paper.
4. Using an erasable marker, write phrases on the rectangular pieces. The letters on the card should be at least 1½ inches tall so students can easily read them while walking.
5. Place the rectangular pieces in curvy order around the room, about one step from the other.
6. Students line up.
7. One student reads the first card, then moves on to read the second and third cards. When she gets to the fourth card, the second student begins on the first card. The second student proceeds to second, third, and fourth cards before the third student starts, and so on. The students' reading will resemble a musical round.
8. Encourage students to read each card with expression, such as tiptoeing on *whisper* and stomping on *shout.*
9. After a number of rhythm walks on a passage, students can read in unison from the original text.

FLUENCY AND TECHNOLOGY

Students can listen to audiobooks to build fluency by either following along with the text or reading along with the narrator. The Living Books and Discis Books series feature a wide variety of titles. Appendix A.12 lists titles in both series.

The speech recognition program Reading Assistant Expanded Edition by Scientific Learning is a tool students can use to practice reading a story a number of times to build fluency. The program offers four or five stories covering a number of different topics. Students can choose to have the story read to them, or they can read the story into a headset microphone. When the student reads the story, the program (1) recognizes mispronounced words and says the correct word, (2) highlights words that were mispronounced, (3) gives the definition of any word, (4) plays back the recorded reading so students can hear themselves, (5) permits students to reread the story so they can work on their fluency, (6) charts words read per minute for each reading so students can see their fluency growth, (7) provides a quiz that checks comprehension, and (8) grades the quiz and charts the score. The quiz, however, is mostly composed of literal questions, which do not challenge higher-level thinking skills. A Spanish button allows students to click on an English word and hear it pronounced in Spanish. The company features a demo story on its website (www.scilearn.com/products/reading-assistant/) so you can see how the program works.

Read-along Radio Dramas, published by Balance Publishing Company, are intended for small group reading. The stories are radio plays performed by a professional cast that include sound effects like ones used in old-time radio dramas. They come with read-along scripts and a variety of student activities. The program helps students develop comprehension by requiring them to visualize the action. After listening to these, students can produce their own radio dramas with accompanying sound effects.

CONCLUDING THOUGHTS

Fluency is an important aspect of reading and is comprised of four major components: rate, automaticity/accuracy, prosody, and comprehension. Research indicates a correlation between comprehension and fluency; therefore, teachers should not rely solely on a student's wcpm to measure fluency. You can use fluency-enhancing strategies that are designed for individuals or for small groups. First model the strategy and then provide ample time for the individual or group to practice it. Many of these strategies result in a performance for peers, other classes, or for parents.

Reflective Learning READING SPEED AND COMPREHENSION

Scenario. Mr. Gonzales is a reading specialist in a large urban middle school. He is assigned to work with sixth-grade students who are below grade level in reading comprehension. At the beginning of the year he works with small groups of eight, but after the first quarter another reading test determines that four of the students are still two grade levels behind. Each of the four now come in for individual sessions.

The first time he asks Sage to read, he reads very quietly (almost mumbling) and very fast. Mr. Gonzales is not sure Sage read accurately because his voice was so soft. After Sage reads the short passage on vampire bats, Mr. Gonzales asks him what he thinks makes a good reader. Sage says that Kimberly, a girl in his class, is a good reader and she reads really fast.

Mr. Gonzales then asks Sage to retell the passage. Sage says it is about bats but gives no more information. Mr. Gonzales asks what he learned about the bats, but Sage cannot relate any facts.

QUESTIONS

1. What strategies should Mr. Gonzales teach Sage? Explain why you think these strategies would be appropriate.
2. How can Mr. Gonzales get Sage to understand that fast reading is not necessarily good reading?
3. What specific strategies would you use with Sage to get him to comprehend the text?
4. Since Sage believes fast reading is good reading, what strategy would you use to get Sage to read fluently?

CHAPTER ELEVEN

WRITING

Only the educated are free.

EPICTETUS

scenario

Mr. Burns is an eighth-grade language arts teacher who loves to write, and his goal each year is to get his students to love writing. He uses the writing workshop as his framework, and his students always produce some interesting tall tales, stories, poems, and plays. However, he is baffled each year when his students do not perform well on the state-mandated writing test. After the second year of lower-than-expected scores, he analyzes the situation and comes up with a solution. He looks at what the students are required to do on the writing test and realizes that the test asks students to complete tasks they never do in the writing workshop. The test gives students a topic and a set amount of time to complete the task. He now knows he has to prepare his students for that type of writing—writing on demand!

During the summer he turns to his professional journals to find a strategy to help his students gain higher scores on the test. He feels the test scores do not reflect their ability to write, because they never wrote under those conditions in the classroom. In the *Journal of Adolescent and Adult Literacy,* he reads an article about Quick Writes (Mason, Benedek-Wood, & Valasa, 2010). He decides to use two Quick Write strategies mentioned in the article, the POW strategy and the TREE strategy (see the Intervention section of this chapter for details) for 15 minutes every Wednesday. Because he does not teach social studies or science, he needs the help of those teachers. Before the school year starts he talks with the social studies and science teachers in his building and tells them about his plan. He asks for their help in providing a topic each week related to what the students are studying in social studies and science. He will create a prompt from those topics and have the students write for 15 minutes.

Mr. Burns introduces the POW strategy at the beginning of the year and has the students use it for nine weeks. Then he introduces the TREE strategy and uses it for nine weeks. During the second semester, he switches them again. He shares the students' writings with the science and social studies teachers. They are amazed at how much the students have improved with these Quick Writes over the year. They are not surprised when they see the state test results; the writing scores are greatly improved over the previous years.

guiding questions

As you are read this chapter, consider the following questions:

1. What writing skills do Mr. Burns's students learn from participating in writing workshops? What skills do they learn from the Quick Write strategies?
2. If Mr. Burns wants to incorporate more technology in his writing workshops, what recommendations would you suggest to him?
3. For the English learners in his class, what practices should Mr. Burns incorporate in his writing instruction?
4. How might the 6 + 1 Trait Writing Assessment and Instruction Framework help his students with expository writing? With narrative writing?

INTRODUCTION

Mr. Burns believes that students should love writing as much as reading. He also understands that students need time to engage in various types of writing activities so they develop this love and do well on state-mandated tests.

Elbow (2004) argues that "very young children can write before they read, can write more than they can read, and can write more easily than they read—because they can write anything they can say" (p. 9). Researchers Calkins (1983), Graves (1983), and Weaver (1996) emphasize the importance and interrelationship between reading and writing.

The Secretary of Education's Reading Leadership Academy suggests that reading and writing "depend on fluent understanding and use of language at many levels. Each enhances the other" (Learning First Alliance, 2000, p. 21). Recent research also supports the conclusion that reading and writing enhance one another (Bear, Invernizzi, Templeton, & Johnston, 2006; Fountas & Pinnell, 2001; Fried, 2006; Ferreiro, 2003; McCarrier, Pinnell, & Fountas, 2000; Wood-Ray, 2006; Turbill, Bean, & Fox, 2006). Effective teachers understand, however, that good writing does not "just happen" because students read and reflect. The two processes are as "separate as they are same" (Johnston, 2000/2001, p. 377). Learning one skill does not guarantee that a student will automatically learn the other. Therefore, effective teachers include extended periods of time for students to write in their class schedules. Many use the writing workshop model that Mr. Burns uses and which is described later in this chapter. They also understand that writing is a process and students deserve a choice of topics and genre; they explain the writing process and expect their students to use it during writing workshop.

Today's classrooms have an ever-increasing number of students who are not native English speakers. Teachers must take these English learners' special needs into consideration as they plan their writing instruction. Most English learners acquire oral communication skills in about two years, but it takes five to seven years for most English learners to develop academic skills such as reading and writing (Cummins, 1981). Teachers must be familiar with the developmental writing stages of these students and know strategies that will help them become fluent writers. Research shows that English learners, like native English students, use the writing process to express themselves and that the writing workshop provides a safe environment in which they can develop their writing skills (Dworin, 2006; Rubin & Carlan, 2005).

The Internet has brought changes to writing instruction. No longer are students writing only with paper and pencils and sharing their work with peers. Today's students use computers to create compositions that include art, photographs, and/or music, and they recognize their audience spans the globe when they post their writing online.

In this chapter, discussion focuses on (1) the similarities and differences between reading and writing; (2) the developmental writing stages; (3) tips for helping struggling writers during the five steps of the writing process; (4) writing digital text and publishing on the Internet; (5) the challenge of working with second language learners; and (6) assessments and strategies for struggling writers.

THE READING–WRITING CONNECTION

Similarities in Reading and Writing Cognitive Processes

Reading and writing are complex cognitive developmental processes with aspects that occur before, during, and after each distinct reading or writing task (Rumelhart, 2004; Adams-Just & Carpenter, 2004; Hughes & Searle, 2000; Rymer & Williams, 2000; Kintsch, 2004; Fried, 2006; Weaver, 2002). When students read and write, they use cognitive processes such as gathering ideas, questioning, and hypothesizing. Reading requires students to gather background knowledge and connect it to the new information they are processing. Writing requires they synthesize their thoughts to articulate a message in print. Readers question the author in order to better understand the passage, and writers question whether their thoughts are clearly articulated. Readers need to hypothesize as they read. A substantial part of comprehension involves inferring what the author implied in a passage or predicting what is coming next in a passage. Writers also hypothesize about what their audience will know regarding the topic of their work.

Reading and writing depend on the same cognitive systems—semantic, syntactic, graphophonic, and pragmatic. Earlier chapters discussed these systems as they relate to reading. Their relationship to writing is presented later in this chapter.

Similarities in the Goals of Reading and Writing

Reading and writing not only share many of the same cognitive processes, they also share many of the same goals or skills. Pinnell (1999) compiled the following list of seven goals/skills for students as they read and write:

Goal/Skill 1: Have students automatically recognize or write words without conscious awareness.

Goal/Skill 2: Have students read and write words without focusing on every letter.

Goal/Skill 3: Connect unknown words to known words.

Goal/Skill 4: Focus on chunks of words.

Goal/Skill 5: Use root words to help determine meaning.

Goal/Skill 6: Connect spelling with meaning (e.g., homophones).

Goal/Skill 7: Focus on the main purpose of reading and writing, which is to communicate meaning.

Differences Between Reading and Writing

There are two big differences between reading and writing. First, reading is considered a receptive language art because it involves receiving a message; writing is considered an expressive language art because it involves creating and conveying a message. Second, readers must comprehend what others have written; writers must know their audience, choose the genre that best expresses their ideas, choose words that will allow the audience to understand the message, and choose how to share their writing. A third difference is that readers decode words; writers encode words automatically so they can spend their energy on expressing themselves, not on spelling words correctly.

WRITING INSTRUCTION

Writing instruction has changed during the last decade. The current trend is to provide students blocks of time to write on topics of their choice and give them peer and teacher feedback (Wolf & Wolf, 2002). Teachers also understand that students must learn to use computers effectively while writing (Read, 2005; Richardson, 2005) and how to write for a global audience (Ohler, 2005/2006). Despite teachers who provide the time and tools, many native English students and English learners still struggle with writing because they equate writing with creating stories and using correct spelling and punctuation (Read, 2005).

This discussion of writing instruction first describes the language systems that cause writers problems. Then it reviews the developmental writing stages of emergent writers and English learners and concludes with a discussion of the writing process.

Components of Writing

Students struggle with five aspects of language when they write—graphic, semantic, graphophonic, syntactic, and pragmatic (which relates to audience) (Zecker, 2001). Note that the graphic component is a language system unique to the writing process.

Graphic. The graphic aspect of writing involves knowledge about how to form the 26 letters of the alphabet. Students need to form letters correctly and write legibly in order for others to understand their writing. Some emergent and even older students struggle with letter formation, along with the directionality and the spacing of letters and words.

With the use of computers and other hand-held technologies, many students—even first graders—learn keyboarding skills. Some schools understand the importance of good keyboard skills and have added keyboarding to the elementary curriculum. Correct keyboard skills prevent students from falling into the habit of typing with one or two fingers, which slows down their ability to transfer their thoughts into text.

Semantic. The English language is symbolic. Words, made up of letters, represent objects, actions, and abstract ideas. Very young children sometimes think big objects call for big words. They make large scribbles for a cow because it is a big animal, and they make small scribbles for ant because it is small. As they learn letters, they may string many letters together for the word *horse,* and only a few letters for the word *mosquito* because of the physical size of each creature (Zecker, 2001). The concept that letters form words, which represent ideas, is quite complex for young children.

As students progress in their writing, they are not concerned about the length of the words but about the use of vivid verbs, adjectives, and adverbs, which make their passages easier for readers to understand the intended message. They also learn that figures of speech used appropriately make their writing more interesting for readers.

Graphophonic. Students need to learn letter–sound relationships and how one sound may be written in a number of ways (e.g., the long /a/ sound can be written as *a, ey, ay,* and *ei*). Learning all the possible letter–sound relationships is a complex cognitive process. They sound out the word for encoding by learning about patterns within words and how to break multisyllabic words into smaller parts (Bear, Invernizzi, Templeton, & Johnston, 2006; Fountas & Pinnell, 2001; Fresch, 2000; Hughes & Searle, 2000; Johnston, 2000/2001). Struggling writers often have trouble with irregular spellings and require explicit instruction in common word patterns (Cunningham, 2004; Bear, Invernizzi, Templeton, & Johnston, 2008; Hughes & Searle, 2000).

Syntactic. Writers, especially English learners, have a lot to learn about how to write a good sentence. They must learn how to be concise and how to organize ideas into paragraphs. They need to know how to structure a composition or story so it is easy and enjoyable for the reader and how to organize expository material in the appropriate text structure (e.g., cause and effect, enumeration, etc.). They need to understand the different forms of various genres. Many writers struggle with these tasks and need practice with immediate feedback from teachers (Spence, 2010).

Stages of Emergent Writing

In an effort to understand the very beginning stages of writing, Zecker (2001) studied young children and found seven stages of emergent writing. Most children pass through these stages, but at different rates and different ages. Some young children are given "writing" utensils and taught how to form letters early in life. These children have an advantage over those who do not receive these opportunities before they enter school. Zecker found that children who are taught to listen to sounds within words and to connect sounds with letters will also advance through the stages faster than children who have not had such opportunities.

The seven stages of the emergent writer are listed and described in Figure 11.1, and Figure 11.2 presents a sample of each stage.

Because writing is a skill, it can be developed. Therefore, teachers need to understand everything they can about the writing stages and how to aid struggling writers as they attempt to develop better skills. Writing activities should be developmentally appropriate for particular students. A number of different activities are provided in the last part of this chapter. The following paragraphs describe activities appropriate for the drawing, invented spelling, and conventional stages of writing.

Activities appropriate for the drawing stage

When students are in the drawing stage, teachers may ask students to "read" their stories aloud and then write a short caption for the student, preferably a sentence, under the picture. Teachers can then read the sentence to the student, pointing to each word as they read it.

figure **11.1**

Zecker's seven stages of emergent writing.

1. *Drawing:* Pictures that represent the word; child can tell stories that fit pictures.
2. *Scribbling:* The lines and marks do not resemble the forms of any letters; no directionality to the writing.
3. *Letter-like forms:* Lines and marks resemble letters.
4. *Letter strings:* "Words" have repeated patterns or include letters that the child knows. Letters do not correspond to any text.
5. *Copying:* The child copies from environmental print.
6. *Invented spelling:* The child begins to connect letters to some of the sounds heard in words. (In Chapter 12, I will explain the various stages of inventive spelling.)
7. *Conventional spelling:* Students spell most words correctly and use the correct format for each genre.

Source: Zecker, L. (1999). Different texts, different emergent writing forms. *Language Arts, 76*(6), 483–490.

Activities appropriate for the invented spelling stage

For students in the invented spelling stage, teachers can write interactively with them. Interactive writing is an event in which teachers and students "share the pen" (Clay, 1993c; Fountas & Pinnell, 2001; Wall, 2008; Weaver, 2002). It is based on Vygotsky's (1978) theory of the zone of proximal development, which states that what students can do with an adult today, they can do independently in the future. See the activity in the Intervention section of this chapter for the interactive writing procedure.

Most students are successful when interactive writing is conducted in small groups. However, other children need one-on-one interactive writing sessions with the teacher. It is important that students generate the ideas for the writing exercise. Young students need to know the focus of writing is composing, not spelling words or filling in blanks. Interactive writing is also an appropriate strategy to use with English learners because the writing task is shared (Wall, 2008).

figure 11.2 Graphic examples of writing stages.

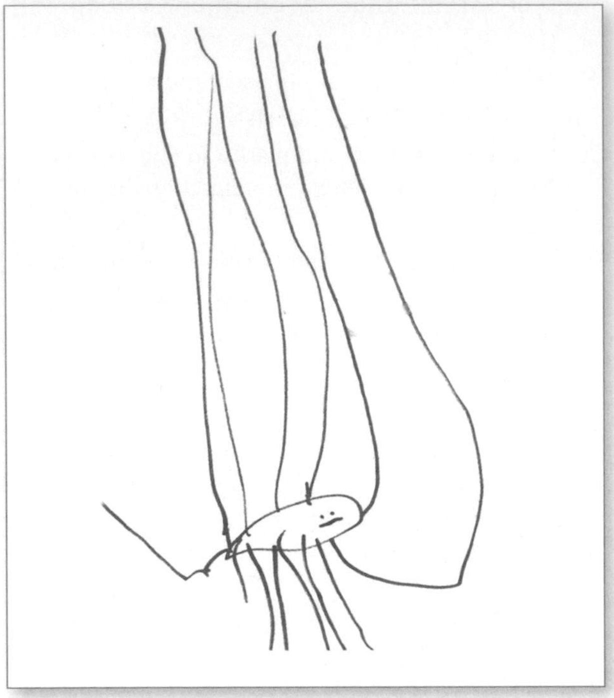

Stage 1: Drawing
Sydney's spider that bites. Age 2

Stage 2: Scribbling
Grey's scribbles. Age 2

Stage 3: Letter-Like Forms
Sydney's bugs. Age 3

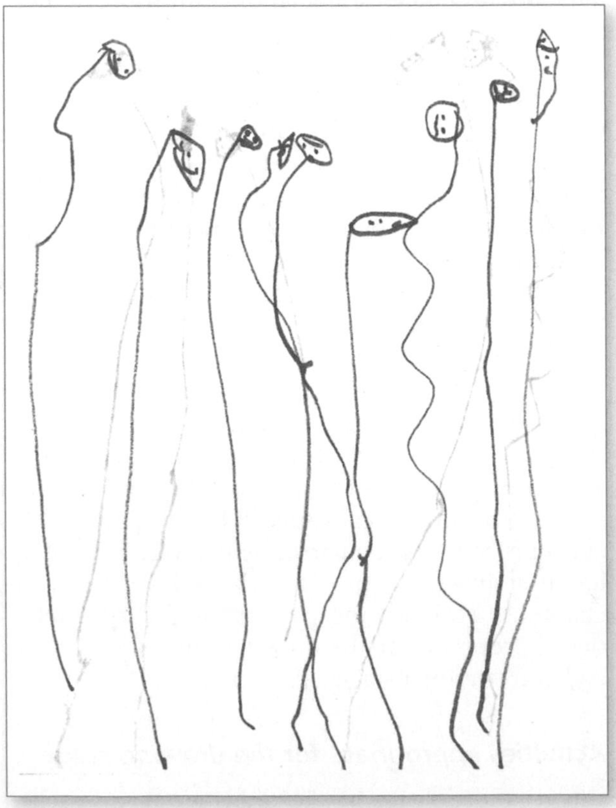

Stage 4: Letter Strings
Sydney's snakes. Age 3

figure **11.2** Continued.

Stage 5: Copying
Grey copying from Hide-and-Find. Age 5

Stage 6: Invented Spelling
Grey's scorpion. Age 5

Stage 7: Conventional Spelling
India's story of the Four Princesses. Age 7

Activities appropriate for the conventional stage

As struggling students progress to the conventional writing stage, teachers can use the Reading Recovery method with sound boxes (Clay, 1993c). In Reading Recovery, students write a "story" (usually only one or two sentences) on the bottom section of a double folded slip of paper. The top section of the paper is reserved for students to try out possible spellings of unknown words. For example, Billy has visited his grandpa over the weekend and wants to write: "My grandpa said his dog Bo was ornery when it got out of the backyard." Billy notes how his grandpa said *ornery,* and he likes that word. Ms. Grimes, his teacher, knows the sentence will challenge Billy because he does not know how to spell *ornery* or *grandpa.* Ms. Grimes aids Billy as he writes his "story." Their writing task is explained in Figure 11.3. Notice that on the top half of the paper, Ms. Grimes draws the sound boxes for *grandpa* and *ornery*. She asks Billy what sounds he hears. Billy has learned how to draw out the sounds of words as he listens for each letter sound. The numbers under each box indicate the order in which Billy hears the sounds. When Billy gets to the word *ornery,* Billy gives an *e* for the final *y*, so the teacher asks Billy what other letters can stand for the long /e/ sound at the end of words. With the teacher's prompting, Billy spells the word *ornery* correctly.

Billy is willing to put much effort into his "story" because he has a personal interest in it. Notice all the strategies Billy used to write his sentence. When he came to the two new words, Ms. Grimes taught him to draw a line and continue to write the words he did know so he would not lose his train of thought. When spelling *his,* he used his previous knowledge of patterns within words. When spelling *said,* he referred to a book where he had read the word. When he spelled *when,* he consulted his personal word wall. Ms. Grimes has taught Billy several strategies he can use when he writes independently. Ms. Grimes also understands that he still needs prompting so he does not become discouraged.

Activities that connect reading and writing are also appropriate during the conventional stage of writing. As students clarify and question their writing content, they become more critical readers and better writers (Kara-Soteriou, Zawilinski, & Henry, 2007; Mason, Benedek-Wood, & Valasa, 2010; Frye, Trathen, Schlagal, 2010). Explore and evaluate texts with students so they understand how published authors

figure **11.3** Billy's writing task.

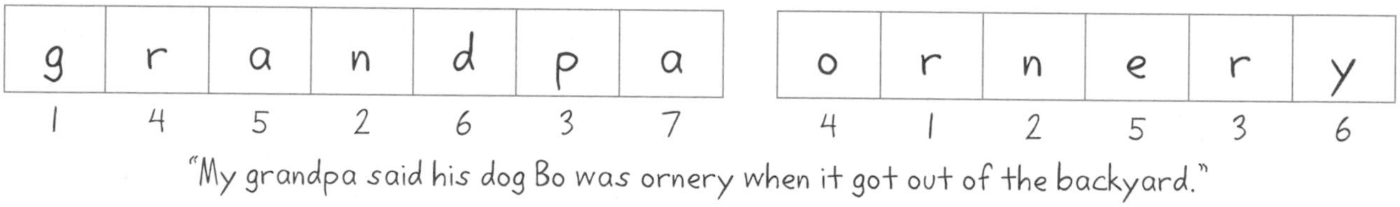

1. Billy knows *my* and writes it correctly.
2. Billy does not know *grandpa,* so Ms. Grimes suggests they draw a blank line and come back to it later.
3. When Billy attempts to write *said,* he quickly refers back to the book they have just read because he knows that *said* was in the story.
4. Billy sounds out *his* and knows that it is an /h/ sound before *is*.
5. Billy has no problem with *dog*.
6. Billy correctly sounds out *Bo,* but does not capitalize it. But with Ms. Grimes's question, "What do you do with the first letter of names?" Billy quickly made the *b* a capital letter.
7. Billy has no problem with *was*.
8. When he gets to the word *ornery,* Ms. Grimes again suggests that he draw a long line and come back to that word.
9. When Billy comes to the word *when,* he consults his personal word wall and finds *when* on it.
10. Billy has no problems with "he got out of the."
11. Billy writes *backyard* as two words. Ms. Grimes explains that *backyard* is a compound word and was one big word. Billy is pleased with the big word he now writes correctly.
12. After the sentence is complete, they return to the word *grandpa.* Ms. Grimes draws the sound boxes and helps Billy spell it correctly.
13. Then they return to Billy's new word and use the sound boxes to spell it correctly. By drawing out the sounds as he says the word, Billy is able to hear the sounds and spell *ornery* correctly. He decides to add that "fun" word to his word list. He also decides to add *grandpa* because he says he will be writing more stories about grandpa.

write. Encourage students to use some of the same techniques their favorite authors use. Some reading–writing ideas for the conventional writing stage are listed in Figure 11.4. These tasks should first be completed with a teacher, then students should be encouraged to engage in them during writing workshop.

figure **11.4**

General ideas to connect reading and writing.

1. Read poems that follow a pattern (e.g., acrostic, diamante, cinquain, haiku, or tanka) and write a poem based on that pattern.
2. Write a play based on a short favorite scene in a story or a fable. The plot is already organized for the student.
3. Write text for wordless books.
4. Use graphic organizers to summarize information from expository texts. (This makes it more difficult for students to plagiarize when they write summaries.)

Writing Stages of Bilingual Spanish–English Writers

In an effort to understand writing development in English learners and how it compares to that of English-speaking students, Rubin and Carlan (2005) analyzed 100 samples they obtained from Spanish–English bilingual students. Students ages 3 to 10 were asked to draw a picture, explain the picture to their tutor, and then to write in both Spanish and English an explanation of the picture. When they compared the developmental writing stages of English-speaking students (Gentry, 1982; Rubin & Carlan, 2005) to that of the Spanish-speaking students (Ferreiro & Teberosky, 1979, 1982), Rubin and Carlan discovered the unique developmental writing stages for bilingual Spanish–English students. Figure 11.5 shows the relationship among the three groups of writers.

Rubin and Carlan were amazed to learn that during the precommunicative stage, the bilingual Spanish–English students wrote the same string of letters for the English text as they wrote for the Spanish text; however, they read their sentences in Spanish and then in English, using the correct words.

figure **11.5** Summary and comparison of stages of writing development among English-speaking, Spanish-speaking, and bilingual children.

Monolingual English speakers' stages of writing development (Gentry, 1982, 2000)	Monolingual Spanish speakers' stages of writing development (Ferreiro & Teberosky, 1979, 1982)	Bilingual Spanish-English speakers' stages of writing development
Precommunicative stage Know the difference between writing and drawing. Write with scribbles, mock letters, and real letters unconnected to sounds.	Levels 1 & 2 Know the difference between writing and drawing. Write with scribbles, mock letters, and real letters unconnected to sounds.	Generally the same as monolingual English and Spanish, except some children will write the same letter symbols in both languages but read them differently in English and in Spanish.
Semiphonetic stage Letters are written to represent some of the sounds in words.	Level 3 Each syllable in a word is usually represented by a vowel.	Generally similar to monolingual English, except some children will write the same words in both languages but read them differently in English and Spanish.
Phonetic stage Letters are written to represent most sounds in words.	Level 4 Letters are written to represent most sounds in words.	Generally similar to monolingual English and Spanish. Some errors exist because of different letter–sound relationships in the two languages.
Transitional stage Letters are written according to common spelling patterns and include silent letters.	No corresponding level.	Similar to English monolingual stage with some errors caused by different letter–sound relationships in the two languages. Vocabulary and sentence structure become more complex.
Conventional stage Writing is generally correct.	Level 5 Writing is generally correct.	Writing is generally correct. Vocabulary and sentence structure become more complex.

Source: Rubin, R., & Carlan, V. G. (2005). Using writing to understand children's literacy development. *The Reading Teacher, 58*(8), 728–739. Reprinted with permission of the International Reading Association via Copyright Clearance Center.

During the semiphonetic stage, the bilingual Spanish–English students used both vowels and consonants for syllables, even though Ferreiro and Teberosky found Spanish-only writers used a vowel for each syllable. In this stage, some bilingual Spanish–English students wrote the same letters for the English text as they did for the Spanish text, while some students started to use different letters for the two languages.

In the phonetic stage, bilingual Spanish–English writers knew that words are written differently in English and Spanish. Like English-only writers, they omitted silent letters (e.g., *lam* for *lamb*) and sounds that are difficult to hear (e.g., *stad* for *stand*). In this stage the bilingual students used their knowledge of Spanish spelling. For example, the letter *i* in Spanish makes the long /e/ sound. They might write *si* for *sea* or *bi* for *bee*. They would often write *do* for *the* because the Spanish language does not use the initial /th/ sound. These bilingual students also confused the /v/ and /b/ because the /v/ in Spanish is similar to the English /b/.

During the transitional stage, bilingual Spanish–English students often put the adjective after the noun instead of in front of the noun like most English writers do. This again shows how these students used their knowledge of Spanish to write English text. Also in this stage, students insert Spanish words when they cannot think of the English equivalent. Perez-Canado (2005) found this to be a common writing habit of bilingual Spanish–English writers.

Based on the developmental writing stages of bilingual students, teachers should incorporate the following practices suggested by Rubin and Carlan (2005).

1. Provide extended periods of time to write and allow a personal choice of topic and genre.
2. Encourage students to use both languages so you can understand the student's development.
3. Emphasize that students should write original thoughts, not copy words or worry about spelling.
4. Have students read to you what they have written so you can help them develop their English vocabulary.
5. Value what bilingual students write, even if it is not lengthy.
6. Have bilingual students explain how they write and choose topics so you can understand their thinking.
7. Encourage students to use background knowledge when writing.
8. Teach spelling patterns within words and show students where to find correct spellings (e.g., on the classroom's word walls or in books) instead of having students memorize spelling lists.
9. Assess growth by looking at all student writing samples and then praise them for the progress they are making.

In addition, interactive writing is an effective instructional method to use with English learners.

English learners may require extra time to complete a composition even though their finished piece may be shorter than the other students' pieces. When writing expository text, English learners need to

- have more time to read and study the sources
- be permitted to read sources in their native language when possible
- write while they are learning English
- be able to choose their topics
- learn to write for a variety of purposes
- have opportunities to write about their families and cultures (Spence, 2010).

As teachers read English learners' compositions, they need to analyze the piece by asking some or all of the following questions.

1. What voices are represented in the piece?
2. What did I learn about the student as a person?
3. What did I learn about the student as a writer?
4. What instruction does this student need to develop strengths and address some weaknesses?

Skilled Versus Unskilled Writers

When working with struggling writers, understand the difference between skilled and unskilled writers. Figure 11.6 lists the characteristics of skilled and unskilled writers.

The Writing Process and Writing Workshop

Many teachers understand that writing is a process as described by Graves (1990, 1991, 1994); the stages of this process will be discussed below. Because writing is a process, teachers use the writing workshop practice outlined by numerous researchers (Atwell, 1987; Calkins, 1994; Hansen, 1987). The writing process itself and as used in writing workshop are effective means to help second language learners (Dworin, 2006; Rubin & Carlan, 2005) as well as English-speaking students. The writing workshop has six essential elements: (1) schedule regular, sustained writing sessions, (2) give students choices, (3) give teacher and peer feedback, (4) establish a structure, (5) build a cooperative learning community, and (6) provide mini-lessons for direct, explicit instruction. The underlying premise of the writing workshop is that all writ-

figure 11.6 Characteristics of skilled and unskilled writers.

SKILLED WRITERS	UNSKILLED WRITERS
1. Find out more about the topic than is needed.	1. Write only what they know.
2. Delete information when needed.	2. Do not plan.
3. Evaluate passages for clarity.	3. Do not reflect on what they have written.
4. Write with audience in mind.	4. Have no idea of audience.
5. Search for more information when needed.	5. Lack organization.
6. Spend time planning.	6. Very seldom delete material.
7. Have an inner voice.	7. Lack detail and elaboration.
8. Organize material.	8. Spend a short amount of time on composition.
9. Include details and elaborate.	9. Struggle with mechanics.
10. Spend a substantial amount of time on composition.	10. Emphasize form instead of content.
11. Self-edit.	11. Lack knowledge of the writing process.
12. Are concerned about content.	12. Do not research topics.
13. Proofread their own work.	13. Do not proofread.

Sources: Harris, 1997; Hughes & Searle, 2000; Turbill, 2000.

ers need regular, sustained time for writing. Student writers need to be able to choose their topics and the genres. Traditionally, teachers assigned class-wide topics in which students may have had little interest. As for structure, many writers favor a predictable environment in which they write at the same time every day. Writing workshops also emphasize the importance of community. Teachers foster a supportive environment where students freely share their thoughts with peers without the fear of being ridiculed. Sharing ideas with an audience that extends beyond the teacher is an important aspect of writing. Teachers also need to share their expertise with students in mini-lessons.

Graves (1990) argues that accomplished authors go through five steps as they produce manuscripts: prewriting, drafting, revising, editing, and publishing. These steps are discussed below. Just because you schedule time for writing does not ensure that all students will develop good writing skills. Give extra assistance to struggling writers and teach them how to complete each of the process's five steps (Graham & Harris, 1997). Provide this help in a tutoring session or in a very small group if you can. See the Intervention activities at the end of this chapter.

Prewriting stage

During the prewriting stage of either expository or narrative text, instruct struggling writers on how to choose a topic, how to research that topic, how to brainstorm possible subtopics, how to structure their material, and how to tailor their writing to their audience.

Choosing a topic. Help students who are going to write an expository text find a topic that really interests them so they will be more likely to take ownership of their writing (Graham & Harris, 1997). Also help students select topics that give them a chance to learn. Struggling writers often think they need to know everything about a topic in order to write about it; however, knowing too much about a topic negates the need to research it. A valuable part of writing expository text is exploring and researching new topics.

When helping young students choose a subject for a narrative text, ask them what kind of characters they want to write about. If they offer no ideas, brainstorm with them about all possible characters they could have in a story. Refer to some favorite stories for ideas. For example, if Sally loves Norman Bridwell's *Clifford the Big Red Dog* series, suggest that she use Clifford or another dog as a character. Then you and Sally can brainstorm a list of all the things Clifford could do or the problems Clifford could encounter. Next, together determine the step-by-step plot. Complete all the planning before Sally begins to write. Struggling writers need to understand that brainstorming is an important part of writing. The Intervention section of this chapter provides other activities to help students choose a topic.

Structuring the material. Prewriting is a time to make a plan. When writing expository text, students can use a graphic organizer to create a structure for their passage. After they have chosen their topics, pose questions designed to make them consider all its aspects.

Then they create a graphic organizer based on these questions, thus giving them a focus. As discussed in Chapter 9, students should choose a graphic organizer based on the organizational pattern they will use in their text to show how the information will be related. After they have created their organizer and list of questions, students read different sources to answer only those questions. Graphic organizers also keep students from copying (plagiarizing) complete paragraphs from books or the Internet by making them write phrases instead of complete sentences.

Students can also use expository frames to help them organize their material (see the Intervention section for activity). These frames are also based on the organizational patterns of expository text as well as the signal words commonly used in the pattern (see Chapter 9). Use the expository frame activity in the Intervention section of this chapter to help your students write informational text.

Help students write captivating stories by having them create storyboards that organize the story's elements as part of their prewriting process (Ohler, 2005/2006). Even if the end product will be presented with digital enhancements, it will flop if it does not contain all the elements of a good story. According to Ohler (2005/2006) a good story includes the following:

1. A call to adventure—the main character encounters an interruption in his or her life. For elementary students, they can draw from personal physical or emotional interruptions, such as breaking an arm the day before going to camp or moving to a new school.
2. Problem/solution involving transformation—the main character solves the problem by acquiring skills, maturing, or discovering the root of the problem. Then, the character applies a solution.
3. Closure—the story comes to some resolution, which, like life, may be happy or unhappy.

A sample storyboard applying these key elements is shown in Figure 11.7, and a blank template is included in Appendix D.27.

figure **11.7** Sample storyboard showing the key elements of a story.

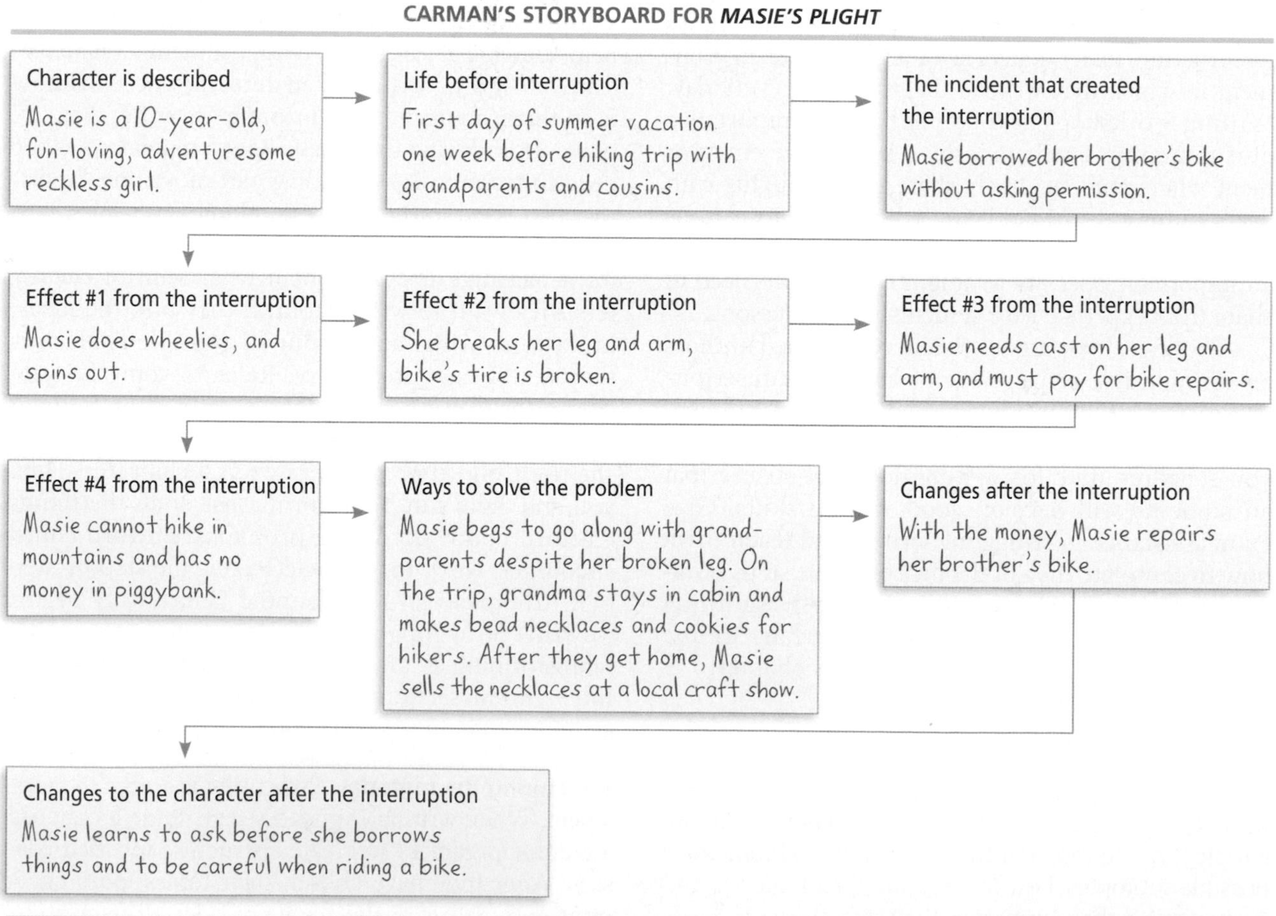

For students lacking a good sense of plot, use wordless books, such as *Carl's Afternoon in the Park* (1991) by Alexander Day, to help them structure the narrative. This book and the others listed in Appendix A.5 have no words after the first page but present a clear sequence of events that thrill most children. Ask students what is happening on each page, and help them write their answers on sticky notes as part of the prewriting process. Use wordless books with one student at a time because they often have different ideas about the story lines (see the activity in the Intervention section).

Writing to an audience. Another aspect of prewriting is defining the intended audience. Help struggling writers understand the importance of knowing who their audience is before they write. They need to estimate the audience's background knowledge during the writing process. Good writers know that readers bring some information to the text, while other information must be explained explicitly and concisely by the author. They must also decide if the passage should be formal or informal. For example, writing a letter to the president of the United States requires more formal language than texting friends. When the audience is forgotten, the writing often lacks a clear purpose. Students should choose the format for their composition based on the audience.

Drafting

Students often think form is more important than content while composing a first draft (Wood-Ray, 2006). Assure them that spelling and mechanics do not matter during this stage. Initially, you may need to do interactive writing with the student to keep her from becoming discouraged. By sharing the pen, students write more text in a shorter amount of time than they would by themselves. Teachers need significant patience as they work with struggling writers; sit with them and ask probing questions to keep the process moving. Let them know they may find it necessary to do more research or to do more imagining. Once a writer begins the first draft, it does not imply she will never return to prewriting activities.

Revising

"The ability to revise is significant because it helps the writer reflect and clarify his or her thinking with the goal of improving the writing" (Dix, 2006). Struggling writers do not see the significance of revising and often lack the ability to do it effectively, rendering their revisions superficial. Pose questions to prompt the writer to add, delete, reword, and/or reorganize sentences or longer passages. Queries such as "How big? When? How? Why? Where? What kind? What color or shape? Whose?" will get the writer to add information. If she cannot answer these questions, have her go back to the prewriting stage, find the information, and then do some more drafting. Writing is recursive, requiring one to go back to previous stages occasionally.

Deleting text is often more painful than adding text, so teachers need to help writers see its importance. Ask the writer why she included a section, or show how she has drifted from the main purpose and should delete a passage or use it in a different story or informational piece.

Introducing a writer to a thesaurus will help him see how vivid words make the piece more exciting and sophisticated. Help writers reorganize the piece by creating graphic organizers (a step that should be a part of prewriting) for informational passages and a storyboard (another prewriting device) for narration. Creating the story or essay in pictorial form helps young writers to see the importance of organizing the material so readers are able to easily follow the passage.

Editing

It is best to have students self-edit first (Hughes & Searle, 2000; Turbill, Bean, & Fox, 2006), then have a peer edit the piece, then have the teacher edit one more time before giving the composition back to the student (Moore-Hart, 2005). A wall chart with an editing or proofing checklist helps make students responsible for analyzing various aspects of a manuscript. Figure 11.8 is a checklist that writers can use to evaluate their own work and, later, have a peer evaluate it. Items that students check are based on the rules that have been taught during minilessons. The main categories are (1) capitalization rules, (2) punctuation rules, (3) paragraphing, and (4) spelling. You may need to go through the checklist with struggling writers first and then watch as they fill it out. It is important to teach struggling writers to become independent proofreaders.

Publishing

All students, even struggling writers, need to see their writing published and share it with an audience that extends beyond the classroom teacher. Giving students special stationary cards to write thank-you notes to the cafeteria workers, to parents who sponsored a skating party, or to senior citizens who supervised a field trip helps them realize their writing must be correct and neat. Someone is going

figure 11.8 Checklist for proofreading (second grade).

Student ____________________ Date ____________________

Title ____________________

CAPITALIZATION:

_____ First words of all sentences
_____ Proper nouns (names of people and places, titles of books, musical works, etc.)
_____ Proper adjectives

PUNCTUATION:

_____ All sentences end with a period, question mark, or exclamation point.
_____ Commas
_____ Quotation marks around dialogue (what characters say)

PARAGRAPHING:

_____ Each new idea begins a new paragraph
_____ Indented for each new paragraph
_____ Only one idea in a paragraph
_____ Ideas well developed in paragraph
_____ In dialogue, each time a speaker changes, there is a new paragraph.

SPELLING:

_____ Check every word closely
_____ Use word wall when in doubt
_____ Check spelling in another book
_____ Use dictionary

Student's Signature ____________________

Classmate's Signature ____________________

to read their note. Figure 11.9 shows thank you notes written by first graders to a student teacher on her last day in the classroom.

Consider publishing a classroom poetry book. Students contribute a poem for which they have received peer and teacher feedback. Have them verify that their poem's mechanics are correct and then neatly rewrite or type it before it is added to the class book.

You can do the same thing with informational books. Each student can research one or two aspects of a topic and then write a passage about what they have learned. They can illustrate the passage to

figure 11.9 Thank you notes written by first graders.

further explain the concept. Contributing one page to a book is not a daunting task for any student. All the student-created books become a part of the classroom library and can be read often by the teacher or classmates. If there is one class book for every student by the end of the year, hold a lottery to determine who gets to keep which book.

Every classroom with Internet access now has multimedia publishing capabilities at its disposal (Richardson, 2005). As of 2005, 100 percent of public schools in the United States had Internet access and 94 percent of classrooms had instructional access (Wells & Lewis, 2006). The term *Web 2.0* is sometimes used to refer to sites on which students can create, edit, manipulate, and collaborate online (Handsfield, Dean, & Cielocha, 2009). Students can write stories, poems, and essays and post them at www.fanfiction.net or on blog sites and then other students from around the world who read the stories can post comments. Figure 11.10 shows the opening paragraph of an 87-page story written by an eighth-grade student, along with excerpts from two student responses he received. The two responses illustrate authentic writing. Notice how honest the comments are; these responders are not writing to please a teacher; they are writing to give a critique and receive clarification for their queries.

Figure 11.11 lists websites and online references for Web 1.0 and Web 2.0 tools.

Publishing beyond the boundaries of the classroom can motivate struggling writers (Sylvester, Greenidge, 2009). Struggling writers share common traits. Their stories usually lack details and figurative language. They may be poorly organized at both the sentence and paragraph level and are often dotted with spelling and mechanical errors. Yet these students do not spend any time revising their stories, and they are reluctant to delete material even if it does not support the story (Sylvester & Greenidge, 2009). They usually are apathetic and do not take any pride in sharing their stories with peers. Digital storytelling may be the one activity that removes the apathy and motivates them to create dynamic stories, because they get to combine traditional story writing with new literacies (Sylvester & Greenidge, 2009). See the Writing and Technology section later in this chapter for more information on digital storytelling.

Bilingual students will also have a sense of accomplishment when they see their stories or informational passages on the Internet (Dworin, 2006). Teachers should also take advantage of sites that encourage students' pieces. Poets such as Jack Prelutsky (2006) encourage students to write poems (see http://teacher.scholastic.com/writewit/poetry/) and Prelutsky even provides warm-up exercises. He offers the first few lines of a humorous poem and invites students to complete it. He also encourages students to write original poems and submit them.

Evaluating Writing Instruction

If you desire to be an effective writing instructor, evaluate your own performance in five different areas (Barr, Blachowicz, Katz, & Kaufman, 2006).

figure **11.10** Excerpt from "Through a Dragon's Eyes by Garath Half-Elven," and student comments on the story.

SUNDAY, OCTOBER 16, 2011, 4:34PM

Posted by: Jack

I flew over the dusty plain, watching the scene unfold beneath me. On my back, Rhovanir drew his long blade. The elaborate hilt glinted in the sunlight. He was my Rider, and he had always been there. Ever since I was a hatchling, he watched over me, the last dragon in all of Eldareht. The Elves on the battlefield below were fully engaged, their blades adorned with goblin blood. They fought side-by-side with the Men of Thelduin, attempting to stem the flow of the goblin warriors that so foully desecrated the Sacred Land. I hunger for their blood.

. . .

Add Comment (2)

COMMENTS

Posted by: Kari on Monday, October 17 , 2011, 11:32AM

I like this. It seems almost like a snippet from a larger story . . . my only complaint is the characters have odd names and I get them confused. But that is small. Overall, good job!

Posted by: Justin on Monday, October 17, 2011, 2:07PM

hmm . . . this is a good story but I'm confused about where and when it is set. Is it set in Algaesea or not? And what timeframe is it set in? I'm confused . . . .

figure **11.11** Websites and online references for Web 1.0 and Web 2.0 tools.

TOOL TYPE	WEBSITE
Graphic novels and comic books	• www.scholastic.com/graphix/ includes graphic novels/comic stories that students can read and discuss with others on a discussion thread • www.plasq.com/ Offers an online space for users to develop graphic novels and comic books
Digital storytelling and video sharing	• www.VoiceThread.com A space for creating and sharing digital stories that use text, voice, and pictures and can be shared for collaboration • www.TeacherTube.com Online video streaming site. Videos can be viewed, uploaded, downloaded, and embedded into wiki pages
Mapping and webbing	• www.mind42.com • www.mindmeister.com Online collaborative mind-mapping applications • www.gliffy.com A collaborative space to create flow charts and diagrams
Collaboration	• www.docs.google.com Open source office applications for individual or collaborative use. Collaboration can be simultaneous • www.wikispaces.com • www.educationalwikis.wikispaces.com Spaces for free educator wiki development and collaboration
Blogging	• www.blogger.com • www.edublogs.org Spaces to develop and house blogs • www.bloglines.com An online space to manage your blogroll (blogs you read) and share your blogroll with others. Includes an option to create your own blog
Social networking/ bookmarking	• www.diigo.com • www.delicious.com Spaces where you can keep all your bookmarks so they can be tagged, accessed from any computer, and shared. Diigo also has options for setting up groups (for projects, classes, etc.) and functions to highlight and place notes on bookmarked web pages • www.ning.com Online space to create a social network, including groups, messaging, and collaboration
Global classroom collaboration	• www.flatclassroomproject2008.wikispaces.com/ Global student collaboration project
For more Web 2.0 resources and information	• www.go2web20.net/ • www.cooltoolsforschools.wikispaces.com/ • www.teachweb2.wikispaces.com/

Source: Handsfield, L., Dean, T., Cielocha, K. (2009). Becoming critical consumers and producers of test: Teaching literacy with Web 1.0 and Web 2.0. *The Reading Teacher, 63*(1), pp. 40–50. Reprinted with permission of the International Reading Association via Copyright Clearance Center.

The five areas are (1) classroom environment, (2) instruction, (3) class schedule, (4) professional role model, and (5) professional growth.

1. **Classroom environment.** When evaluating the classroom environment, periodically make sure all materials (computers, printers, pens, pencils, paper, pencil sharpener, folders, staplers, paper clips) are available and operational. The classroom also needs to be a print-rich environment. Provide an abundance of posters for class word walls, personal word walls, dictionaries, personal dictionaries, and thesauruses, and post rules on mechanics and standard usage. To build a genuine classroom community, provide a risk-free environment. Students must be accepting of each others' work. Students need to be taught first how to state specific aspects of their peers' writing that they like and then to offer some constructive suggestions for improvement. Comments should begin with phrases such as "I like how you . . . ." When they offer suggestions, have them begin with phrases such as "Have you thought about . . . ." Model these two steps in one-on-one conferences so students learn to imitate them.

2. **Instruction.** Instruction should include whole-class instruction, small group instruction, and individual instruction. Whole-class instruction can occur during mini-lessons that begin the writing workshop time. The mini-lesson should be approximately five to seven minutes (Atwell, 1987; Hansen, 1987) and should teach a skill or concept that the entire class needs to know. The mini-lesson is for group learning and should not be preparation for a worksheet that the students must complete. The concept shared in the mini-lesson should be one that students will be able to use later in their individual writing. Small group instruction is best conducted in guided writing groups where you can focus on one area in which all members are weak (Fountas & Pinnell, 2001). This instruction is explicit, with you modeling the skill, guiding the students in group practice, and then supervising the group as they practice the skill independently. Individual instruction should occur at the "teachable moment." When a student is writing and you are conferencing with the student, attempt to convey a concept or skill that the student needs at that moment. Teachers need to evaluate themselves, making sure that they engage in all three types of instruction.

3. **Class schedule.** Check your class schedule to make sure all students have a sustained, regular time to work on writing. The length of time must be developmentally appropriate for the student's age. Time must be given for a mini-lesson, self-selected writing, guided writing, conferencing, and the author chair (from which students share writing with classmates).

4. **Professional role model.** Teachers are professional role models, and therefore you need to model writing for your students. Share your own writing with students so they see you as a teacher. When you comment on the word choice of published authors or how an author describes something, students become more conscious of how professional authors write. You should also demonstrate a think-aloud on spelling of words, both known and unknown, and engage the students in word play.

5. **Professional growth.** Professional growth includes reading books and professional journals on writing research, attending workshops and conferences, conducting workshops, writing collaboratively with other professionals, and sharing personal writing successes with colleagues.

6 + 1 TRAIT WRITING® ASSESSMENT AND INSTRUCTION MODEL

Designed by the Northwest Regional Education Laboratory (http://educationnorthwest.org; 1998/1999), 6 + 1 Trait Writing® Assessment and Instruction is a framework for assessing, talking about, and organizing writing. Students and teachers at all levels use these traits to discuss the qualities of writing. Even primary-grade students can learn the language as they engage in the writing process.

The Traits

The 6 + 1 Traits are (1) idea/content, (2) organization, (3) voice, (4) word choice, (5) sentence fluency, (6) conventions, and (+1) presentation. Since the traits all interlock with one another, it is difficult to describe one trait without referring to another trait. However, here is a brief description of each.

Idea/content

This trait focuses on the content or message of the passage. Is it a mystery story to entertain, a political essay to persuade, or an informational passage about whaling? The content must be interesting and age appropriate. It should provide well-developed and appropriate details, such as clues in a mystery, reasons for a scientific phenomenon, or examples of types of jungle creatures. The content must have a clear focus. All the information in expository passages should support the whole, and all parts of a story should be important to the plot, with unrelated or unnecessary information omitted. The content must be original or at least presented in a fresh way. In expository writing, readers expect the author to have credibility by being knowledgeable about the topic either through experience or through research. Those reading a passage desire to learn something new; therefore, the writer must give information that is beyond the obvious.

Organization

The flow of the passage must be logical. In longer passages, the beginning paragraph typically states the purpose of the passage and must grasp the reader's attention. The middle of the passage needs a logical flow. Some information is best told in a sequential manner, while other information is best told from least important to most important. The writer must know "when to slow down and elaborate, and when to pick up the pace and move on" (Northwest Regional Educational Laboratory, 2001, p. 1). The concluding paragraph must signal to the reader that it is the end of the passage.

Voice

This trait refers to the way the writer "speaks" to the reader. It is the "flavor" the writer gives to the passage. In expository or persuasive passages, the writer's passion for the topic becomes obvious through his or her voice, which is reflected in wit, descriptions, figures of speech, style, and word choice (the fourth trait). Voice is what distinguishes one writer from another, and is often the trait that keeps readers coming back to a writer. Share one or two of Mo Willem's pigeon books to show students an author with a unique voice. He creates a distinct voice through his use of word bubbles and illustrations that enable the pigeon to carry on the conversation with the reader.

Word choice

This fourth trait is closely intertwined with voice. Vivid nouns, verbs, and adjectives help readers visualize descriptions of objects, settings, and characters. Unique, colorful words paint pictures in the readers' minds. Good writers choose words that show rather than tell the action of the narrative. For example, instead of stating: "The young man was angry," an author can write: "Jon stormed into the room, threw his backpack on the floor, kicked over a chair and yelled, 'It was not my fault!'" In expository writing, technical terms with good descriptions help readers better understand the concept. Writers who choose words carefully do not use clichés and jargon; instead they use unique figures of speech such as metaphors, similes, personification, and onomatopoeia that bring information or scenes, characters, and action alive for the readers.

Sentence fluency

Fluent writers work at varying sentence length and use a variety of sentence types, including

- *Simple sentence:* One independent clause or a group of words that can stand by itself.
- *Compound sentence:* Two or more independent clauses connected with a semicolon or coordinating conjunction.
- *Complex sentence:* One independent and at least one dependent clause that cannot stand by itself such as "because it rained last night."
- *Compound complex sentence:* At least two independent clauses and at least one dependent clause.

In expository text, writers use transitional words and phrases to connect thoughts within and between sentences, paragraphs, and chapters. In narrative text, dialogue is used to help reveal characters' feelings and thoughts, to show rather than tell the action, and to move the action along. When read aloud, a fluent passage is pleasant to hear.

Conventions

This sixth trait refers to the technical or mechanical part of writing. Is the paragraphing correct? Is the passage free of spelling, punctuation, capitalization, and usage errors? Mechanical errors distract readers, so passages free of mechanical errors permit readers to remain focused on the content. If the writer uses dialect for effect, the word's spelling should closely resemble its pronunciation so the reader does not have to stop and figure it out.

Presentation

The "plus 1" trait is the presentation of the passage, which refers to the formatting—the amount of white space, the width of margins, the font, the size of the print, the placement of words, and the illustrations that accompany the text. The presentation may be the first trait readers consider when they look at a passage. How small is the font? How much text is on a single page? Are the margins wide enough for making notes?

Just as the cover of a DVD attracts viewers as they select a movie, so a written passage needs eye appeal. The reader may expect to see graphs, charts, photographs, and/or illustrations to help explain an expository text. Even primary students need to know that presentation is important when writing for a audience other than just the teacher.

Teaching the 6 + 1 Traits

Every piece of writing includes all these traits. Primary grade teachers need to explain each trait during mini-lessons or guided writing sessions so students become aware of its importance. One way to introduce a trait in a mini-lesson is to choose a short passage from an age-appropriate book and discuss how the author made the passage unique and inviting. Because these traits are found in all types of passages, teachers should use examples of narrative and expository text and poetry from quality children's literature so students become conscious of how these traits are used in all types of writing. See the Intervention section for activities that teach the 6 + 1 Traits.

Assessing Writing with the 6 + 1 Traits

In order for students to develop all these traits, they must all be a part of assessment. As with all skills writing skills develop through practice, and an appropriate rubric reflects students' stages of development. The 6 + 1 Trait rubrics provided by teachers from Sheboygan Falls, Wisconsin, can be used for informative and narrative writing (www.mshogue.com/ce9/rubrics/rubrics.htm). Instead of the point-based categories used in the samples, teachers may use qualitative categories such as *Exemplary*, *Acceptable*, *Developing*, and *Unacceptable*. You may also create your own rubrics using the template found at http://rubistar.4teachers.org/index.php?screen=CustomizeTemplatePrint.

An abbreviated version of the 6 + 1 assessment developed by the Northwest Regional Educational Laboratory is presented in Appendix C.45.

ASSESSMENT

Informal Assessment

In addition to using the 6 + 1 Traits for assessing (see Appendix C.45) students' writing, teachers can use the methods of informal assessment discussed below.

Portfolios

The authentic way to assess student writing is by having students compose a passage based on a topic that interests them, and the authentic way to document students' writing growth is through the use of portfolios. The writing portfolio includes writing attitude surveys, writing self-assessment surveys, spelling inventories completed periodically throughout the year, and samples of the student's work with scoring rubrics. Rubrics used throughout the year document growth; other rubrics are designed for a particular type of composition. I believe the best way to assess writing growth is through students' compositions, therefore the focus of the next two sections is on developing rubrics, which is a form of informal assessment.

Assessing the writing process with rubrics

When using the five steps of the writing process, teachers need to assess students' processes as well as their products. Rubrics force teachers to examine many aspects of the process. In designing a rubric for the writing process, all five steps of the writing process must be considered, and rubrics must also be appropriate for the developmental stage of the students. The best rubrics are those designed by teachers for their own classrooms, because they know the developmental stage of their students and what standards the state requires for each grade level. Appendix C.46 is an example of a rubric for assessing the writing process in the primary grades and Appendix C.47 is an example of a rubric for assessing third graders. Both may be used as springboards for teachers who have never developed scoring rubrics. Both are designed to be used over the entire year and should illustrate each student's improving scores. When you use a rubric that documents growth, you can quickly detect in which areas each student needs to improve.

Assessing writing products with rubrics

Each assignment calls for its own rubric. Narrative and expository writing are very different from each other; scoring rubrics should reflect these differences. Consider the students' developmental writing stage when developing the rubric; no teacher expects the same quality of writing from a first grader as she would from a fourth grader.

Two sample rubrics are included in Appendices C.48 and C.49. One is for fourth-grade story writing, the second one is for a fourth-grade research report. Figure 11.12 contains a rubric for a sixth-grade research project. This rubric states the expected performance for three levels of mastery. The rubrics in Appendices C.48 and C.49 give ratings of *excellent* to *poor* with a number assigned to each rating (e.g., *excellent* corresponds to five points). The story-writing rubric in Appendix C.50 includes detailed criteria for awarding points. Many students appreciate knowing the exact requirement for each part of the assignment and expect to be graded fairly. Providing specific criteria helps the teacher be consistent in the grading process. Appendix C.51, Research Report Rubric, is intended for fifth- or sixth-grade students who are expected to use the Internet to gather information.

Another way to design rubrics is to weigh each component of the writing product differently. For

figure **11.12** Assessment rubric for first quarter research project, sixth grade.

STUDENT: *Char* DATE: *November 11*

TOPIC: *Weather balloons* TOTAL SCORE: *28*

	LEVEL OF MASTERY		
TRAIT	**TARGET (5 POINTS)**	**ACCEPTABLE (3 POINTS)**	**UNACCEPTABLE (1 POINT)**
1. Accessing information	Selected the best sources for the topic. ___	Selected some good sources for the topic. _X_	Did not select appropriate sources for the topic. ___
2. Sources used	Used 2 sources (library, database, credible Internet site) to research topic. ___	Used 1 of the 2 sources (library, database or credible Internet site) to research topic. _X_	Used only 1 source (library, database or Internet) to research topic but the source was not credible. ___
3. Authors used	Used as least 1 primary & 4 secondary sources to gather information. _X_	Used only 1 primary & 3 secondary sources. ___	Used 3 or fewer sources to gather information. ___
4. Note taking	Used at least 3 strategies to aid comprehension of difficult material. ___	Relied on 1 or 2 strategies to aid comprehension of difficult material. _X_	Used no organizational strategies to aid comprehension of difficult material. ___
5. Use of reference features	Used 2 or more reference features of printed text, such as citations, endnotes, & bibliographies, to locate relevant information about topic. _X_	Used at least 1 reference feature of printed text, such as citations, endnotes, & bibliographies, to locate relevant information about topic. ___	Used no reference features of printed text, such as citations, endnotes, or bibliographies, to locate relevant information about topic. ___
6. Analysis	Determined the appropriateness of an information source for the topic. ___	Determined the appropriateness of some of the information sources for the topic. _X_	Did not determine the appropriateness of any information source for the topic. ___
7. Citations	No more than 2 citation errors. ___	3 or 4 citation errors. ___	More than 4 citation errors. _X_
8. Content	Had 3 or fewer main ideas with no supporting details. ___	Had 4 or 5 main ideas with at least one or two supporting sentences for each idea. _X_	Had 6 or more main ideas with fully developed supporting sentences. ___
9. Paragraphs	1 topic per paragraph & logically organized. ___	1 topic per paragraph but not logically organized. _X_	More than 1 topic per paragraph. ___
10. Capitalization	No capitalization errors. ___	1 or 2 capitalization errors. ___	More than 3 capitalization errors. _X_
11. Punctuation	No punctuation errors. ___	1 or 2 punctuation errors. ___	More than 3 punctuation errors. _X_

NOTE: THERE WILL BE ONE POINT TAKEN OFF FOR EVERY SPELLING ERROR! (Start by using your spell check!)

TEACHER'S COMMENTS:

You used some good sources and included interesting information. Concentrate on details such as spelling and punctuation, too!

example, in the rubric for stories you may choose to assign five possible points for characterization, five points for setting, but only two for character motivation. This may be because the class has examined vivid literary descriptions of characters and settings and your goal is for them to create similar descriptions. You may have mentioned but not emphasized character motive in class and not told students that they had to include descriptions of the characters' motives. To design a rubric with different values for each component of the story, list the possible points after each component, as in the example below.

COMPONENT	POINTS
1. Description of setting	(5 points)
2. Description of characters	(5 points)
3. Motives of characters	(2 points)

The sample sixth-grade research rubric found in Figure 11.12 is based on Oklahoma's state standards that focus on conducting and writing a research report. Mr. Harmon, who designed the rubric for the first quarter, did not use the state's standards as the sole measure for assessing the research paper. He realizes that no student will be competent in all of the standards under the heading of *research* so early in the year. Therefore, he creates a rubric based on the criteria set for the first research paper of the school year. It requires students to use at least two different techniques to find sources. His students already know how to use the databases in the library so he introduces them to finding credible Internet sources for a research paper. This first paper requires five sources, including one primary source, and he teaches them how to use direct quotations and citations in the exposition. He encourages his students to carefully read and analyze each source. He does not teach them how to synthesize the information, which is another part of the standards on research; he plans to do this next semester. Notice his emphasis on correct spelling.

Assessing multimedia projects with rubrics

Teachers who assign multimedia projects may use a rubric like the one found in Appendix C.52 for assessment. This rubric is designed for a group project and can be modified online to fit specific assignments. Other multimedia and classroom website rubrics are available online.

Attitude surveys

In addition to process and product, teachers also need to assess students' attitudes toward writing—how they perceive themselves as writers and their views on the process and the product. Many times students' attitudes toward writing is their greatest obstacle to their success. Appendices C.15 and C.18 include a writing attitude survey for younger students and one for older students. Another excellent survey that has been tested for reliability and validity is the Writer Self-Perception Scale (WSPS) designed by Bottomley, Henk, and Melnick (1998).

The WSPS measures the affective elements related to writing. It assesses four categories of self-perception:

1. *General progress:* A student's perception of his/her past and present performance.
2. *Observational comparison:* How the student compares him/herself to others.
3. *Social feedback:* The student's perception of others' work.
4. *Physiological state:* A student's internal feelings while he/she writes.

The scale is designed for students in grades four through six.

The WSPS is made up of 38 simple statements that are easy to read. One of the statements is general ("I think I am a good writer") and each of the other 37 statements represents one of the five categories. The responses are based on the five-level Likert scale: "Strongly Agree," "Agree," "Undecided," "Disagree," and "Strongly Disagree." Some sample statements follow:

- "I write better than other kids in my class." [observational comparison]
- "I need less help to write well than I used to." [general performance growth]
- "I choose the words I use in my writing more carefully now." [specific performance improvement]
- "My teacher thinks my writing is fine." [social feedback]
- "When I write, I feel calm." [physiological]

Each of the five areas on the WSPS has a different number of questions; the scoring guide indicates which statements belong in each category. A score in any category that is "slightly below, equal to or slightly greater than the mean indicates a normal range" (Bottomley, Henk, & Melnick, 1998, p. 294). Scores lower than this range are a cause for concern; scores higher than the normal range indicate the student has a positive self-perception of his writing.

The WSPS has been tested for validity and reliability with 964 students in grades 4, 5, and 6. Correlation among the five scales ranged from .51 to .76, showing significant relationships and scale distinctiveness. It also demonstrated strong reliability characteristics. The WSPS with scoring sheet and the directions for administering, scoring, and interpreting it are provided in Appendix C.20. It may be photocopied for classroom use.

Self-assessment instruments

Fountas and Pinnell (2001) designed a self-assessment writing and spelling instrument for grades three through six. It is published in its entirety in *Guided Readers and Writers Grades 3–6: Teaching Comprehension, Genre, and Content Literacy*. This self-assessment asks the students about their writing habits, such as what kind of writing they have completed and what their favorite piece is. It also asks them what they do well as a writer and how they have improved throughout the grading period. The last questions allow the students to reflect on the mechanical aspects of writing and ask what conventions they use very well. Appendix C.53 contains a self-assessment instrument for writing and spelling.

Formal Assessment

Standardized tests such as the Iowa Test of Basic Skills, Comprehensive Test of Basic Skills, California Achievement Test, and Metropolitan Achievement Test have subtests for language, which usually means grammar. In each of these subtests, students are asked to find the segment of the sentence that has some type of a mechanical error. The error can be related to punctuation, capitalization, or usage. This type of testing assesses the student's ability to edit a product, not her ability to write. However, because writing is now generally viewed as a meaning-making process, educators realize they must assess the process as well as the product.

Many state departments of education also recognize the weakness of these standardized tests to assess students' ability to write; therefore, they have created standardized rubrics to assess students' writing. In many states teachers know the rubric benchmarks and focus their students' writing on scoring well on them. Some educators believe these students' writing now rigidly conforms to the rubric, making it "more uniform and much less interesting" (Strickland et al., 2001, p. 1).

Intervention STRATEGIES & ACTIVITIES

The strategies in this section focus on connecting reading and writing. Many struggling writers do not enjoy writing because they do not know what to write about, they see writing as a big task, and they struggle with spelling. For these students, begin with small tasks that connect reading to writing. Interactive writing activities make writing tasks manageable and less intimidating for students and give you opportunities to model writing strategies.

ACTIVITY

INTERACTIVE WRITING ("SHARING THE PEN") GRADES PRE-K–2

Interactive writing is a collaborative strategy involving a teacher and student working together to create a written piece. The teacher asks a student what he would like to write about concerning an event they shared (e.g., a story they read together). The student then dictates a sentence with the teacher writing most of it. As she writes she asks the student to listen to the beginning sounds of words, which she stretches so he can distinguish them. She also invites the student to write the letters he knows. While he writes the teacher emphasizes the letter-sound relationships. As the student learns more letter-sound relationships, the teacher gradually turns "the pen" over to him so that he can write more, until the teacher is adding only a few unknown words.

Variation for English Learners GRADES 1–8

English learners need opportunities to engage in many writing activities. Sharing the Pen in a small group is one way they can write a passage with the help of classmates (Wall, 2008). The small group can use Sharing the Pen with any type of writing; the group decides what they will write and students take turns writing the passage. The passage should be on a whiteboard or interactive whiteboard so all members can see the scribe. The students not holding the pen help the writer with spelling, punctuation, word choice, and so on.

QUICK WRITES (WRITING ON DEMAND) GRADES 5–8 ACTIVITY

As mentioned in the opening scenario, many students struggle with state-mandated writing tests that require them to write to a given prompt for a predetermined amount of time. If students are used to the writing workshop, they may have a difficult time writing under those conditions. In the scenario Mr. Burns used two writing strategies—POW and TREE, presented below—in addition to writing workshops (Mason, Benedek-Wood, & Valasa, 2010). When using these two Quick Write strategies, the teacher selects the topics and gives students 10 minutes to complete the task.

POW

POW can be used when the prompt asks students to write what they know about a certain topic. POW stands for

- Pick your ideas,
- Organize your thoughts, using notes, and
- Write your ideas

POW can be used when students are learning new material; it encourages them to plan their passage by making notes about their main ideas, organizing them into a logical sequence, and then using them to write the passage.

TREE

When students need to respond with a persuasive passage, they can use TREE. TREE stands for

T = write a **topic** sentence that states your point of view;

R = state the **reasons,** at least three, for your stance;

E = **explain** each of the reasons with details that have been learned from the reading material; and

E = **end** your passage by writing a good summary sentence.

ACTIVITIES FOR 6 + 1 TRAITS OF WRITING GRADES 3–8 ACTIVITY

Teachers want to build on what students can do, one step at a time. The best way to do this is to focus on one trait at a time and revisit traits that have already been taught. When teaching the traits to any struggling writer, whatever the student's age, begin with the first trait—ideas and content—and then emphasize subsequent traits one at a time.

Ideas and Content

Many students struggle with getting ideas down on paper and expressing ideas that are beyond the obvious.

For primary grades: Ask students if they have a pet, a favorite sport, or a best friend. Invite them to write four or five sentences about the topic. When they have completed the task, ask them to read their passages to you individually. After each reading ask questions that will lead to additional information. For example, following is a student's description of his dog.

My dog is my friend. We play together. He goes with me all over. He likes me.

After listening to the passage, the teacher asks questions that will prompt the student to add details. Here is a sample of the conversation. As the student responds to the questions, the teacher records the answers on a separate piece of paper.

Teacher: It sounds like you really like your dog. What kind of dog is he?

Student: He is a lab.

Teacher: What color is he?

Student: He is brown, I think they call it chocolate.

Teacher: Is he big or small?

Student: He's really big and strong. He once licked my face and pushed me over because he is so strong. But he's not mean. He was just happy to see I was home from school.

Teacher: You wrote that you play together. Tell me some things you play.

Student: He loves it when I throw a ball and he gets it for me. I am also teaching him to catch a Frisbee. If I throw it low, he can catch it. We also play hide and seek. I hide his rubber bone, and then he finds it. Sometimes we just lie in the grass and look at the clouds.

Teacher: You wrote that he goes everywhere with you. Where are some of your favorite places to go?

Student: He likes to go walk with me and my mom. But mostly we just play in the yard together. Oh, and he loves to come in my bedroom and he sleeps there.

Teacher: You wrote that your dog liked you. What does he do that really shows you he likes you?

Student: He wags his tail when he sees me and just follows me all over the house. Oh, and he loves to lick my face. But I don't mind.

Show the student your written notes and discuss how many details he shared about his dog. Then ask the student to write about his dog again and add the details so he can share the passage with his classmates during "Author Chair" time. Most struggling writers will not resist adding details if you provide the correct spelling of all the words. Not knowing how to spell often hinders a student from writing details.

For an upper elementary or middle school grade: Use the same approach as for younger students, but ask them to write about a favorite book character, sport hero, rock star, or actor.

Trait 2: Organization

Work one-on-one with students so each gets feedback about the organization of their passage. Because organization is essential for sequential or chronological passages, invite students of any age to write in paragraph form—not numbering format—about how they prepare their favorite sandwich. Older students can write how-to procedures for more complicated tasks, perhaps connected to a hobby or sport. When the student finishes writing, have her read the passage out loud and then ask questions that will help her rewrite the passage if necessary, using appropriate sequence.

Trait 3: Voice

This strategy can be used in grades two through middle school. Using the "Friendly Letter" strategy and the example of the letter found in Figure 11.18, discuss with students the sentences in which Betsy asks if the Little Pigs want her to take pork chops to barbeque or if they did not eat pork. Ask students if they think those sentences reveal Betsy's sense of humor (you may need to discuss that pork is pig meat). Or do they think Betsy is being cruel by suggesting pork chops? Help students see that the rest of the letter is friendly, so the author is showing her sense of humor. Discuss how these two sentences create a "voice" for the letter because the thoughts expressed are unique. Once students understand the humor, invite them to write a letter to another fairy tale character, either inviting the character to a party or accepting an invitation to a party. Encourage students to think of creative ways to write their letters; that is, to think of one or two sentences that will set theirs apart from everyone else's. When they have finished, have each student explain which sentence he or she worked on to reveal a unique voice. Because many struggling writers are concerned only with writing the required number of sentences or paragraphs and not about giving voice to their writing, you may need to work with them individually.

Trait 4: Word Choice

Because diamante and cinquain poems are terse, they are great forms for helping writers with word choice. Using the example of the diamante poem "Pizza" or the cinquain "Novels" found in the poetry activities on pages 310–313, discuss with students what word or words they would want to change in the poem to make it better. This is an easy task for students of all ages because they have a starting poem and they get to be the "editor" who improves it. After they have made their changes, invite them to write a cinquain or a diamante of their own; both forms depend on the poet's word choice to be effective.

Trait 5: Sentence Fluency

Most struggling writers write short, simple sentences. To teach students how to combine ideas, present a short passage such as "My cat is white. My cat also has black on it. My cat eats a lot of food. He is fat." Then invite students to be editors by helping you combine some of the ideas into a single sentence. Remind students they must keep all the author's ideas. Coach a student until she writes a sentence such as the following: "My white and black cat is fat because he eats so much." Point out that she made a more fluent sentence by using one coordinating conjunction and one subordinating conjunction. Have students reread each passage, the first with four sentences and the final with one sentence, to see if they can hear how the final passage sounds better and still contains all the ideas in the original sentences. After working with an example, have students read one of their recently written passages and consolidate the sentences without deleting any ideas.

Trait 6: Conventions

Teachers in all grades should post a large-print checklist chart somewhere in the classroom that can easily be seen by all students. The checklist could list common capitalization, punctuation, and grammar rules that are appropriate for the grade level. When you are reading a student's passage and see a mechanical error, direct her to the checklist. If you find a misspelled word, circle it so she can use resources such as word walls, dictionaries, and personalized dictionaries to correct it. If your classroom has a computer, teach students to use the spell check. The goal is for all students to become their own editors.

Plus 1 Trait: Presentation

Students writing for an audience other than the teacher need to understand the importance of presentation. Display a short poem on the computer and instruct them how to highlight a passage and then change the font, type size, and color. Demonstrate how they can even highlight the first letter of the poem or the first letter of each line and change the size, font, and color so that the initial letter is distinctively different from the rest of the passage. Also show them how to add clip art to illustrate a poem or passage. Older students can add audio (e.g., music) or video to their poems using programs such as PowerPoint, Photo Story, and Soundslides. Most students enjoy working on presentations to give their poems and other passages eye-catching appeal.

ACTIVITY

USING CONCRETE EXAMPLES OF AUTHORS' WRITING

GRADES 5–8

Help students with their narratives and poems by developing writing workshop mini-lessons in which they share effective examples from authors' published works (Kara-Soteriou, Zawilinski, & Henry, 2007). The following books include examples of many different authors' styles.

1. Two books that share different types of poetic forms are *Jazz ABZ* (Marsalis, 2005) and *A Kick in the Head: An Everyday Guide to Poetic Forms* (Janeczko & Raschka, 2005). In *Jazz ABZ* Marsalis writes for the letter V: "her vestal vexing vigorates my soul and voids the vagrant values that restrain my heart" (n.p.). *A Kick in the Head* includes the poem "Ode," which uses vivid adjectives: Shoes are "rain-beaten, sun-beaten"; and "Villanelle" contains strong verbs such as "lurking, smirking" and "what is *plaguing* you." Descriptive words create images in a reader's mind.

2. *Hey, There, Stick Bug!* (Bulion, 2006) is a multi-genre book that features poems about different bugs and facts about them. You can use this book to demonstrate how students can write on the same topic across genres—poetry and expository text.

3. *Red Sings from Treetops: A Year in Colors* (Sidman & Zagarenski, 2009) is another book of poems that show how authors use vivid adjectives to paint pictures in readers' minds. In "Fall" Sidman writes: "Green is tired, dusty, crisp around the edges. (In fall, / the wind feels Black: / star-spangled, full of secrets" (n.p.).

4. *City I Love* (Bennett-Hopkins & Hall, 2009) is a book of poems integrating social studies and writing. The poems take students on an international tour of cities around the world. They "travel" to New York City, San Francisco, Tokyo, Cairo, Johannesburg, and Rio De Janeiro. The end pages feature a map of the world with the cities marked.

5. *Eats, Shoots and Leaves: Why, Commas Really Do Make a Difference!* (Truss & Timmons, 2006) is a great book for demonstrating the importance of using commas correctly. Each double page has the same sentence punctuated two different ways to illustrate how the meaning changes when commas are moved or removed (e.g., "The student, said the teacher, is crazy" and "The student said the teacher is crazy" [pp. 19–20]).

6. Harrison (2008) in *Pirates* uses poetry to spark students' imaginations in writing a sequence of poems that tell the story of pirates or some other person, object, or event of the sea. An example is "Through the Glass." Harrison writes: "in these waters, / let fog be our friend, / wrap us in its blanket / cold and gray as a cemetery, / cloak our secret journey home / heavy with gold for the king" (n.p.).

ACTIVITY

GUIDED WRITING

GRADES 1–6

Guided writing is based on the same format as guided reading (Fountas & Pinnell, 2001). A teacher works with a small group of students who have the same writing needs. The teacher presents a concept or skill and then guides students as they apply it. The lesson is based on the needs of the group. For example, the teacher may work with one group of students who struggle with certain homophones, while another group may need help with quotation marks. Some concepts taught in guided writing are listed in Figure 11.13. Guided writing differs from the traditional method of "teach and drill" because it does not follow a script or predetermined sequence. The teacher imparts what the students need to know when they need to use the skill. However, the sequence of a guided writing lesson does follow the format of traditional teaching. The teacher:

1. teaches the concept
2. demonstrates how to use it
3. guides students as they practice it
4. expects students to use it in independent writing

Students should keep a personal record of conventions learned in guided writing sessions so they can refer to them when they work independently (Calkins, 1994). Figure 11.14 is a log sheet for doing just that. Guided writing also helps a teacher manage class time because she works with small groups instead of individual students.

figure **11.13** Concepts to teach in guided writing.

1. Capitalization rules
2. Punctuation rules
3. Vivid noun choice and usage
4. Vivid adjective choice and usage
5. Vivid verb choice and usage
6. Character description (appearance, speech, dress, actions)
7. Pronoun–antecedent agreement
8. Subject–verb agreement
9. Creating clues for mysteries
10. Back flashes
11. Creating good topic sentences
12. Adding and sequencing details
13. Transition words/signal words

figure **11.14** Sample log sheet for writing conventions.

Skills Marcie **learned in Guided Writing**

SKILL	DATE
1. Don't put "and" between all ideas.	9-7
2. Instead of short sentences, use comma with "and."	9-12
3. Begin new paragraph with new idea.	9-15
4. Use "return" key to begin new paragraph.	9-16
5. Make stories become real with quotations.	9-23
6. Use verbs other than "said" in dialogue.	9-30

MT. PLOT

GRADES 1–3 ACTIVITY

Responding to stories by creating story maps is one way to connect reading and writing. It also gives a topic to students who have "nothing to write about." Some story maps are described in Chapter 8. Mt. Plot is a story map that records main events of a story with distinct roadblocks (refer back to Figure 8.19 and see Appendix D.28 for a blank example). The plot obstacles are written going up the side of the mountain, the climax is written at the peak, and the resolution is written going down the other side.

ACTIVITY

EXPOSITORY FRAMES (CECIL, 2011)

GRADES 2–3

Expository frames help students understand expository structure by providing a systematic way to write about content material they have read. This is also an effective way to introduce young students to expository writing (Cudd, 1990). Expository frames provide a scaffold for creating different ways to organize text.

1. Write a simple paragraph about a topic that lends itself to sequential ordering, using the signal words *first, next, then,* and *last.*
2. Copy the sentences onto sentence strips.
3. Review the topic and logical sequence of events with the class.
4. Have the students arrange the sentences in correct order in a pocket chart.
5. Read the completed paragraph together.
6. Have the students reorder the paragraph on their own and paste it on construction paper in paragraph form.
7. Invite the students to illustrate the details or some important part of the paragraph.

Gradually introduce a sequentially ordered expository frame for the students to complete independently, as in Figure 11.15.

figure **11.15** An expository text frame for sequence.

First, the gardener needs to prepare the ground by hoeing the soil.

Second, the gardener digs one-inch-wide rows across the garden.

After this, the gardener plants the seeds one inch apart.

Next, the gardener gently covers the seeds.

Then, he waters the garden.

Finally, he enjoys the flowers.

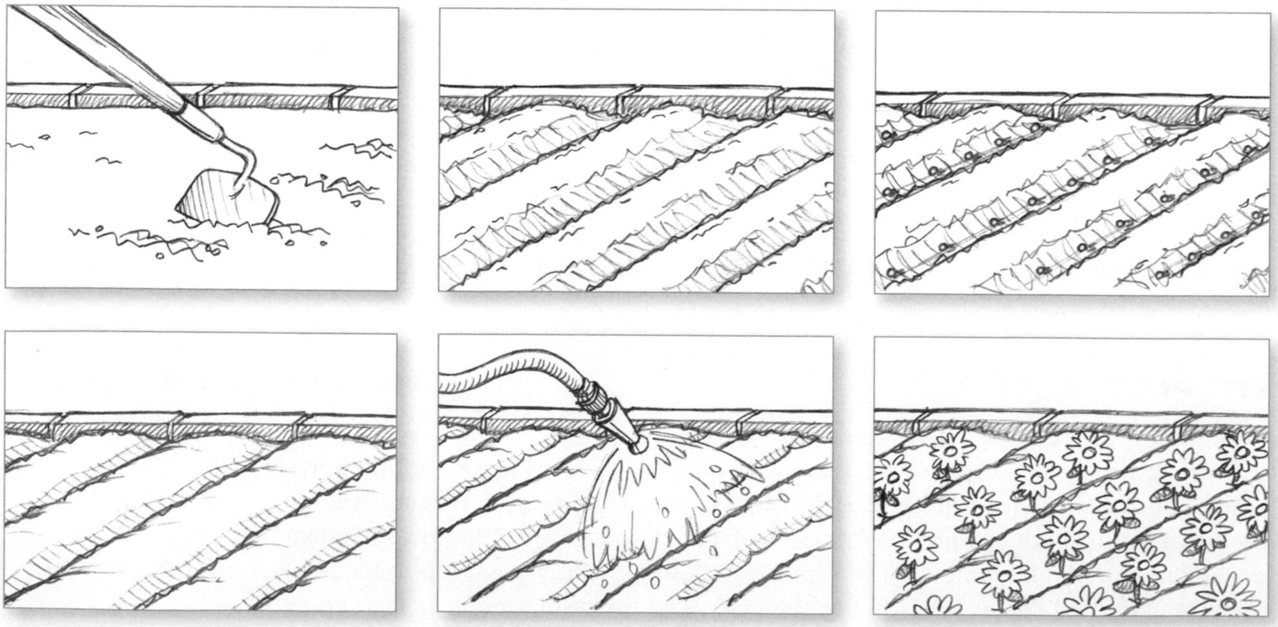

Other frames using different organizational models, such as cause/effect patterns, problem/solution patterns, and comparison/contrast patterns, are also helpful for assisting students writing expository text. Figure 11.16 is an example of a comparison/contrast pattern, and Figure 11.17 is an example of an enumeration pattern.

figure 11.16 A child's expository frame for comparison/contrast.

(Title)

Comparing Insects with Spiders

Insects differ from spiders in many ways. First, insects fly while spiders don't. Second, insects don't spin webs but spiders do. I think the easiest way to tell an insect from a spider is to count the legs. A spider has eight legs. An insect only has six.

Source: Nancy Cecil, *Striking a Balance: A Comprehensive Approach to Early Literacy,* Fourth Edition. Copyright © 2011 by Holcomb Hathaway (Scottsdale, AZ).

figure 11.17 A child's expository frame for enumeration.

Trees are useful in many ways. For example, ____________________

____

Also, ____________________

In addition, ____________________

Finally, ____________________

Source: Nancy Cecil, *Striking a Balance: A Comprehensive Approach to Early Literacy,* Fourth Edition. Copyright © 2011 by Holcomb Hathaway (Scottsdale, AZ).

PARODIES

GRADES 1–2 ACTIVITY

Books with repetitive text give students a springboard for writing. Give students a basic formula for the sentences and ask them to fill in the blanks with their ideas.

It Looked Like Spilt Milk (1947) by Charles Shaw is a good choice for a parody for young students. First, give students a blue piece of construction paper with a drop of white poster paint. Using a straw, the children can blow the white paint around to create an image. On the bottom of the page, write: "It looked like a ____________, but it wasn't a ____________." Students fill in the blanks based on the image they created.

For a parody of *I Went Walking* (1996) by Sue Williams, write the first phrase: "I went walking. What did I see? I saw a ____________ looking at me." Students can first draw a picture and then fill in the blank with a word. Encourage students to copy the phrase and add more pages to the story.

For a parody of *Brown Bear, Brown Bear, What Do You See?* (1983) by Bill Martin, you can also write the formula phrase the first time: "Brown Bear, Brown Bear, what do you see? I see a ____________________ looking at me." Students can complete the first page with a picture and a word and go on to write more pages for the story on their own. Having students draw a cover for the story on a piece of construction paper gives them the successful feeling of writing a book!

Older students, after reading stories like *The True Story of the Three Little Pigs* (1995) by John Scieszka, can write their own "true stories" of any fairy tale character. They can write the true story of the wolf who visited Little Red Riding Hood or the true story of the Giant in Jack and the Beanstalk.

ACTIVITY SEQUELS — GRADES 2–6

Help a student predict what might happen to a book's characters after the end of the story. Books such as *Nana Hannah's Piano* (1996) by Barbara Bottner invite a sequel with its ending, "I'm trying out for the Little League soon. I have a new piano teacher who lives next door and likes potato dumplings." Ask the student to predict how well the team will play, to describe the new piano teacher, and to explain why the teacher likes potato dumplings. *Show and Tell* (1991) by Elvira Woodruff suggests a sequel with its illustration of a twisted fork on the final page. An older student may be able to write a sequel to Demi's *The Empty Pot* (1990) by explaining what happens when Ping becomes the new emperor. Books such as *Eloise* and *Madeline* invite students to imagine more adventures for these two characters.

ACTIVITY ACROSTIC POEMS — GRADES 1–4

Acrostic poems are formed by writing a single word or short phrase vertically and using its letters to start the horizontal lines of the poem. Following is an example of an alphabet acrostic poem on spring.

Sailing kites on a warm afternoon
Planting young flowers
Raking old, dead leaves
Irises bobbing their purple faces in the breeze
Narcissus swaying to the rhythm of the woodlands
Getting out of school for an entire week!

After reading informational text, invite students to write an acrostic poem that conveys detailed information (Frye, Trathen, & Schlagal, 2010). Encourage students to use alliteration, assonance, and metaphors and/or to answer the five W's: *Who? What? When? Why?* and *How?*

Tornadoes
Twisting, twirling, threatening tornado
Ominous black clouds dipping down to touch earth
Rotating winds at 200 to 300 miles per hour
Nothing can withstand the tornado's force
All-time worst tornado outburst on April 3–4, 1974
Destroying everything in its track
Organized when warm, moist ground air rushes upward to kiss cool dry air
Every continent except Antarctica can have a tornado
Spawned by giant thunderstorms called *supercells*

CINQUAIN POEMS

GRADES 2–5 ACTIVITY

A cinquain is a five-line poem that follows a grammatical formula. The formula is somewhat flexible and two versions appear below. The first formula is easier for young students because they do not need to count syllables.

FORMULA 1

Line 1: a one-word subject
Line 2: two adjectives describing the subject
Line 3: three verbs that describe actions of the subject
Line 4: four words expressing a feeling or observation about the subject
Line 5: one word that renames the subject

FORMULA 2

Line 1: a one-word subject with two syllables
Line 2: four syllables describing the subject
Line 3: six syllables describing an action
Line 4: eight syllables expressing a feeling or an observation about the subject
Line 5: two syllables describing or renaming the subject

AN EXAMPLE OF FORMULA 1

Connie
Humorous, kind
Biking, swimming, running
Always there for me
Friend

AN EXAMPLE OF FORMULA 2

Novels
Thin, thick, old, new
Inviting me to read
They carry me to new places.
Best friends

DIAMANTE

GRADES 2–5 ACTIVITY

A diamante is a seven-line poem that follows a formula and is written in the shape of a diamond. This poem helps students focus on parts of speech and antonyms. The formula is as follows:

Line 1: One noun subject
Line 2: Two adjectives describing the subject on line one
Line 3: Three participles (ending in "ing") that describe the subject
Line 4: Four nouns; the first two nouns relate to the subject in first line; the third and fourth nouns relate to the antonym in line seven
Line 5: Three participles (ending in "ing") that tell about the antonym in line seven
Line 6: Two adjectives describing the antonym in line seven
Line 7: An "antonym" of line one (The term *antonym* is used loosely in this case. Many nouns do not have a true antonym and the poem will use a word that, in students' minds, contrasts with the noun in line one.)

EXAMPLE: Pizza
Delicious, spicy
Bubbling, steaming, tantalizing
Cheese, mushrooms—scraps, litter
Molding, rotting, decaying
Smelly, yucky
Garbage

ACTIVITY **BIOPOEMS** **GRADES 4–8**

Students in upper elementary grades who have studied famous inventors, explorers, or historical figures, can write biopoems (Fordham, Wellman, & Sandmann, 2002). Following is the template for the poem and an example.

Line 1: First name
Line 2: Four traits that describe the character
Line 3: Relative (brother, sister, daughter, etc.) of
Line 4: Lover of _______ (list 3 things or people)
Line 5: Who feels _____________ (3 items)
Line 6: Who needs _____________ (3 items)
Line 7: Who fears _____________ (3 items)
Line 8: Who gives ____________ (3 items)
Line 9: Who would like to see ___________ (3 items)
Line 10: Resident of _____________
Line 11: Last name

EXAMPLE: BIOPOEM OF BENJAMIN FRANKLIN

Benjamin
Inquisitive, precocious, practical, witty
Brother of seventeen siblings
Lover of literacy, experiments, and country
Who feels passionately about freedom of speech, science, and the Constitution
Who needs books, adventure, and humor
Who fears the British, slavery, and tariffs
Who gives the world bifocals, public hospitals, lightning rods, and public libraries
Who would like to see "truth spoken in every instance," "no one speaking ill of others," and "everyone doing good to Man"
Resident of Philadelphia
Franklin

Biopoems can also be used to encourage collaboration among classmates (Moore-Hart, 2005). Students interview each other and write a poem about their classmate, using the template below for their patterned poem.

Name
Who . . .
Relative of . . .
Lover of . . .
Who needs . . .
Who fears . . .
Who would like to see . . .
Who attends . . .
Last name.

ACTIVITY **FIBBIN POEMS** **GRADES 1–8**

Fibbin poems are named after Fibonacci, an influential mathematician in the Middle Ages who discovered number sequences (Bintz, 2010). Students from grades one through eight often enjoy working with a pattern in poetry, such as a numerical sequence. They can write about any topic. The older students' poem will tend to be more sophisticated than younger students' poems.

The Fibbin poem follows a number sequence:

Line 1: one syllable
Line 2: one syllable
Line 3: two syllables (the sum of lines one and two)
Line 4: three syllables (the sum of lines two and three)
Line 5: five syllables (the sum of lines three and four)
Line 6: eight syllables (the sum of lines four and five)
Line 7: thirteen syllables (the sum of lines five and six)
Line 8: twenty-one syllables (the sum of lines six and seven)
And so on.

After completing eight lines, students can reverse the pattern by having line nine contain twenty-one syllables, line ten contain thirteen syllables, and so on until the poem ends with the last two lines of each one syllable.

Example:

Pete
Sprete
Athlete
Plays baseball.
Best pitcher in town!
Easily strikes out ten batters!
Twas only in his dreams that he was such a great star!

FRIENDLY LETTERS

GRADES 2–3 ACTIVITY

This strategy teaches students the correct format for friendly letters and how to write with a particular audience in mind. For example, after reading *Yours Truly, Goldilocks* (1998) by Alma Flora Ada, students can write a letter to one of their favorite fairy tale characters. Figure 11.18 is a sample of a third grader's response to Pig One, Pig Two, and Pig Three's invitation to a house-warming party. The writer has been told that Goldilocks, Baby Bear, Little Red Riding Hood, and Peter Rabbit will all be attending.

figure **11.18** Response to the three little pigs' invitation.

April 10, 2012

Dear Little Pigs,

I was so happy to get your invitation to your house-warming party for Goldilocks.
She is one of my very best friends. And I have always wanted to meet Little Red Riding Hood and Peter Rabbit.
I have met Baby Bear. He is so sweet.
Please let me know if you would like me to take some pork chops to barbeque.
Or don't you eat pork? If you want me to take some lettuce and carrots,
I can buy some from my neighbor Mr. MacGregor.
Have a great day! Thanks for inviting me.

Love, your friend,

Betsy

If this task is daunting for a student, use the interactive approach by sharing the pen with him as he writes his letter.

ACTIVITY

WORDLESS BOOKS

GRADES 2–5

Wordless books aid students who cannot think of a plot for a story because the story line is already suggested. Students can easily progress through all the steps of the writing process. First, they can "read" the pictures with you and discuss the plot. Next, they can jot down possible ideas for each page. Then, using sticky notes of different colors, they can write the first draft on each page. After that they should reread their story and make revisions, adding or deleting as necessary; have students edit using a different color pen so marks will stand out, attending to grammar, punctuation, capitalization, and spelling. Students write the final draft on yet another set of sticky notes and share the story with their classmates. Appendix A.5 lists a number of wordless books. It is important to select a book that is appropriate for the particular student.

ACTIVITY

NOUN STORIES

GRADES 3–5

Before reading a book with students, choose 7 to 10 nouns that appear in the story. Write the nouns in a column in the sequence that they are found in the book, but keep the book's title a secret. Have students write a story using the nouns in the same order. After students share their stories, read the book so they can compare their stories to it. Following are nouns from Darleen Bailey-Beard's *Twister* (1999).

Swing	Hail
Wheelbarrow	Candle
Guacamole	Cellar
Raindrops	Cobwebs
Lightning	Sunshine
Thunder	

ACTIVITY

CLASSROOM ALPHABET BOOKS

GRADES K–6

Share some alphabet books featuring states (e.g., *M is for Magnolia: A Mississippi Alphabet Book* [Shoulders, 2003]; *B is for Bluegrass: A Kentucky Alphabet Book* [Riehle, 2002]) with the class. Each student chooses one letter of the alphabet, finds a point of interest from the state that corresponds to it, and researches it. They write a short paragraph and draw an illustration that supports their fact. For example, Jack, a fourth-grader in Stillwater, Oklahoma, began his C page with "C is for Cowboys, the best basketball team in the state." He researched the team's statistics for the past 50 years to find out how many national titles they had won and which Cowboys got drafted by the NBA. It became a favorite page for the boys in his class.

You may also create class alphabet books about national parks, sea creatures, or the national monuments in Washington, D.C., by having students choose one alphabet-related aspect of the large topic, research it, and write one page for the class book.

This activity can be adapted for grades K–2 if the books are written as a class.

ACTIVITY

CREATING BROCHURES

GRADES 4–8

Groups of students can create brochures about a science experiment (Duke, Purcell-Gates, Hall, & Tower, 2006). It should be an experiment they conducted in class or performed at home with a parent. The brochure should list the materials needed and the steps required to perform the experiment. They can illustrate the steps to make them easier to follow and conclude with an explanation of the experiment's results. Teachers can laminate these brochures and keep them at the science center for other students to use.

SENTENCE COMBINING — GRADES 2–5 — ACTIVITY

Struggling writers often write in short simple sentences. To help students begin to write extended sentences, Saddler (2005) suggests using kernel sentences in which the teacher gives a simple subject and predicate (e.g., The tree stood.). Then, the teacher models one or more of the following steps with the students. Primary students can do the first steps, but steps five through seven are intended for upper elementary students.

1. Insert adjectives and adverbs (words that answer what kind, how many, which one, whose, when, how, and where).

   My neighbor's old tall oak tree on the hill stood swaying in the wind.
2. Produce compound subjects and objects.

   The oak tree and elm tree stood erect and waved to all the children.
3. Create compound sentence with coordinating conjunction.

   The oak tree stood erect, while the weeping willow stooped over in the wind.
4. Add possessive nouns.

   My neighbor's oak tree stands at the edge of our property.
5. Create complex sentences by using subordinating conjunctions.

   Because our neighbor's oak tree stands on our property line, they allow me to climb it.
6. Add relative clauses to show relationships.

   The old oak tree that stands in my neighbor's yard is one hundred years old.
7. Add appositives.

   The oak tree, my neighbor's "friend," shades him during the hot afternoons.

USING COMPUTERS FOR AUTHENTIC WRITING TASKS — ACTIVITY

Blogs — GRADES 4–8

These online journals can increase the depth of your students' responses to reading. As they write entries, encourage students to (1) relate a story to personal experiences, (2) explain how a text is similar to other texts by the same author or by other authors, (3) explain how a book is similar to a movie, and (4) describe favorite passages. Blogging is a useful way to motivate reluctant writers to respond to their reading because they often enjoy using technology (Zawilinski, 2009). Blog entries are usually short, so students are not overwhelmed attempting to compose long passages.

Teachers first need to explain the mechanics of blog postings. Set up a classroom blog and invite students to dialogue with classmates about a chapter book or novel they are reading in class. The teacher poses the queries and students respond. As students become familiar with the process and format of blogging, invite them to post their favorite poem or story so they can be read by classmates and even parents (if they are allowed access to the blog).

One website that offers teachers and students a free blog without advertisements is www.edublogs.org. The directions for setting up the blog page are very easy to follow.

figure **11.19**

Wikispaces.

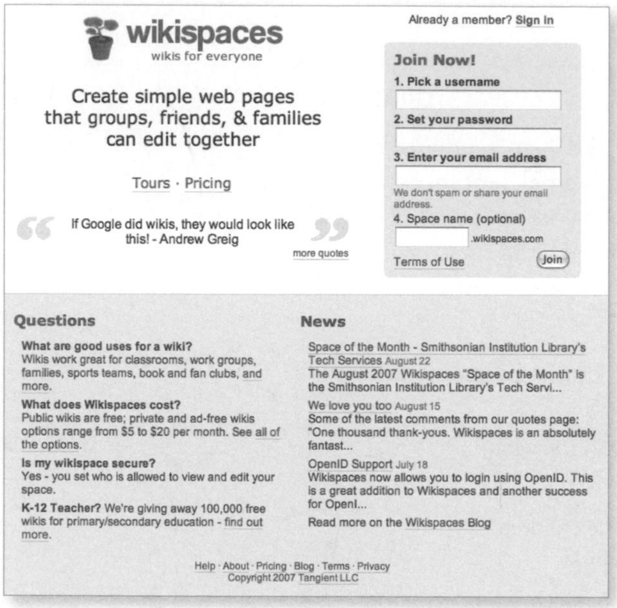

Wikis — GRADES 5–8

Your students may be familiar with wikis, a type of website designed using server software so the site's content can be edited by anyone who accesses it. The most famous wiki is Wikipedia, the free, collaborative Internet encyclopedia. Some wikis, such as Wikispaces, however, are more geared to classroom use (see Figure 11.19). Students can post information on wikis and then have others edit the post by adding or clarifying the information; or they themselves can edit a posting. For example, students in Oklahoma City can search for wiki sites about the 1995 bombing of the city's federal building. They may have information to add because they have family members who experienced the bombing, or, after visiting the Oklahoma City National Memorial and Museum, they want to add interesting facts not yet included on the site.

Blogs and wikis are great tools for teaching critical thinking skills—is the information presented factual, truthful, speculative, or erroneous? Anyone can post anything on these sites, so students must be armed with the ability to tell the difference between good and bad information.

International Pen Pals — GRADES 3–8

Writing letters to international pen pals gives students "an opportunity for authentic and meaningful writing" (Barksdale, Watson, & Park, 2007). Such letters motivate students to adhere to punctuation, capitalization, and spelling. They are invested in the content as they share their favorite foods, stories about their family and school, and details about the sports they play. International pen pals also prompt students to learn about geography, other cultures, and school settings that may be very different from their own. Students are motivated to answer their pen pal's questions and read more about their country. Of course, teachers will need to choose a school in which most students speak English. In many countries, English is the official language for business and education, but even many non-English-speaking countries have schools for English-speaking students from abroad. Barksdale, Watson, and Park (2007) suggest the following websites for locating pen pals.

Intercultural E-mail Classroom Connections, www.friends-partners.org/CCSI/penpals/iecc.htm

Classroom exchange for grades K–12, www.epals.com

Kidlink, www.kidlink.org

International Pen Friends, www.ipf.net.au/

Connecting with Authors — GRADES 1–8

Many authors of children's and young adult literature have websites that provide age-appropriate writing activities and/or word puzzles for their readers. Some authors sponsor writing contests, while others ask readers for feedback on their latest books. Some authors correspond with students through e-mail, while others encourage readers to subscribe to their electronic newsletters. Jan Brett's website offers electronic postcards that feature her art. Students can choose a postcard, write a message, and send it to anyone in the world. These authors frequently update their sites so they stay fresh and exciting for students to visit. Be sure to check them periodically to make sure the URLs still work and to share authors' new ideas with students. The following is a list of sites of popular children's authors:

Avi	www.avi-writer.com
Judy Blume	www.judyblume.com
Jan Brett	www.janbrett.com
Betsy Byars	www.betsybyars.com
Eric Carle	www.eric-carle.com
Tomie dePaola	www.tomie.com
Mem Fox	www.memfox.net
Jean Craighead George	www.jeancraigheadgeorge.com
Gail Gibbons	www.gailgibbons.com
Dan Gutman	www.dangutman.com
Virginia Hamilton	www.virginiahamilton.com
Katherine Paterson	www.terabithia.com
Gary Paulsen	www.garypaulsen.com
Patricia Polacco	www.patriciapolacco.com
J. K. Rowling	www.scholastic.com/harrypotter/index.htm
Louis Sachar	www.louissachar.com
Jon Scieszka	www.jsworldwide.com
Jerry Spinelli	www.jerryspinelli.com
Audrey Wood	www.audreywood.com

Websites often change or disappear. Most authors can also be located through a simple Google search.

Digital Storytelling — GRADES 3–8

As stated previously, digital storytelling may be one activity that motivates struggling writers to create dynamic stories because they get to combine traditional story writing with new literacies (Sylvester & Greenidge, 2009). Most students, even reluctant writers, know how to use computers, video games, digital music players, cell phones, digital cameras, and other electronic devices. Encourage students to use their technology skills to create digital stories using either Windows Movie Maker or Apple's iMovie. Using the writing process a student begins writing a story, which eventually becomes the project's narration. After the story is complete, the author decides how to divide it into scenes and which photographs or illustrations will go along with them. Then the student finds photographs or clip art or draws illustrations to complement each page of text and scans all illustrations to get them into digital form. Next, the student records the story, using expression that conveys the story's mood and action and that will captivate the listeners. When the story is recorded error-free, the student is ready to make the movie. Some students may want to enhance their movie by adding appropriate music and/or sound effects just like a real movie. The last step is for the student to add a title frame, transitions between frames, and rolling credits that cite all the sources for their clip art, photographs, and so on. Finally, the student publishes his work by inviting peers to watch his movie either online or on an interactive whiteboard. Figure 11.20 lists tools that are helpful to beginning digital storytellers.

figure 11.20 Tools to help create digital stories.

Either a Mac or PC computer

Flash drive to save story pieces

Headset/microphone for recording narrative

Digital camera if students want to include photographs

Windows Movie Maker or Apple's iMovie

Microsoft PowerPoint or Photo Story or Apple Keynote to create story slides

Audacity, an open source audio utility, for recording and editing

For beginners, one Microsoft website makes digital storytelling easy; it's a long URL, so simply Google "create-first-photo-story" (include the hyphens) to find the site

Source: Adapted from R. Sylvester & Wendy-lou Greenidge (2009). Digital storytelling: Extending the potential for struggling writers. *The Reading Teacher, 63*(4), p. 293.

Publishing on the Web — GRADES 2–8

A number of websites publish students' work. Those listed below invite students to submit their work for others to read. Publishing poetry or stories for the world to read is exciting for young writers.

Cyberkids, www.cyberkids.com/index.html
Scholastic, http://teacher.scholastic.com/writewit/index.htm

Webquest — GRADES 3–8

Plug the phrase "webquest writing" into a search engine and you will find a range of writing assignments for students. The website address typically explains what type of writing the students will be doing (e.g., persuasive writing, story writing, literary responses to novels, research reports about the Middle Ages or other topics, writing folktales, and so on). For example, Teacherweb (www.teacherweb.com) offers excellent resources for webquests. The websites walk students through the five steps of the writing process and give a number of questions for students to research regarding the topic. Students can publish their final composition on the Internet. This assignment makes good writing purposeful by providing an audience that reaches beyond the classroom. You may also visit www.webquest.org to find and create webquests.

WRITING AND TECHNOLOGY

As is clear from the number of writing activities included above, computers and authentic writing tasks can and do go hand in hand. Technological tools will help your students develop the skills needed to explore online publishing outlets.

To many students and adults, word processing programs are to writing as calculators are to math. These programs, with spell-checker, thesaurus, and grammar-checker capabilities, have helped many frustrated writers. However, these tools are not magical; students still need to decide on a topic or story idea, articulate those ideas, have a good understanding of the grammar and spelling of words and sentences, and be able to recognize the correct spelling from a given list.

It is imperative that young students first learn adequate keyboarding skills before they are taught how to use word processing software. The following is a list of software that is useful for writers.

DEVELOPING KEYBOARD SKILLS

- Kid Keys (DOS, Mac)
- Mario Teaches Typing (Mac, Windows)
- Mavis Beacon Teaches Typing (Mac, Windows)
- Ultra Key (Mac, Windows)

WORD PROCESSING PROGRAMS

- ClarisWorks (Mac, Windows)
- Apple Works (Mac, Windows)
- Microsoft Creative Writer (Mac, Windows)
- Microsoft Word (Mac, Windows)
- Storybook Weaver (DOS, Mac, Windows)
- Storybook Weaver Deluxe (Mac, Windows)
- The Amazing Writing Machine (Mac, Windows)
- Ultimate Writing and Creativity Center (Mac, Windows)
- Writer's Toolkit (Mac)

Most sophisticated word processing programs allow users to work in outline view. This enables students to create headings for main ideas with supporting information and to move the information around in order to achieve a satisfactory structure. The Amazing Writing Machine (Mac and Windows) is a program that permits students to create outlines and concept maps. Many struggling writers often omit the prewriting stage. Teaching students to use this feature will save them time during the writing and revising processes.

Word processing programs are especially useful to students in the revising stage when they know how to use the copy and paste feature. (This feature is preferable to cut and paste, because it eliminates the possibility the student will press the wrong key and accidently erase part of the composition.)

These programs give encouragement to students who have messy handwriting. They do not excuse students from practicing penmanship, but they allow students to focus on content, not handwriting, when they are composing. The two tasks should be approached separately. When teachers want students to practice penmanship, students should be permitted to copy favorite poems or environmental print in the classroom.

ReadWriteThink

The ReadWriteThink website (www.readwritethink.org), established as a partnership between the International Reading Association, the National Council of Teachers of English, and the Verizon Foundation, permits individuals to publish ideas, collaborate on projects, and/or carry on online conversations. The site includes a series of lessons that incorporate online activities for K–12 students. Example activities include an online tool that enables students to learn about and write acrostic poems, a book cover creator that allows users to design front and back book covers or full dust jackets using type and illustrations, and a story tool that enables students to create their own fractured fairy tales.

Teachers must be cautious when introducing sites that allow students to publish, collaborate, and converse online. Rely on reputable websites such as ReadWriteThink because they are created by respected organizations specifically for teachers and students.

Websites as Tools to Develop Writing Skills

Students may use the following websites to develop specific writing skills.

1. Write Express at www.rhymer.com offers a free online rhyming dictionary.
2. Bruce Lansky's site, www.gigglepoetry.com, invites students to fill in the blanks of his poems.
3. The Guide to Grammar and Writing website provides information on parts of speech at http://grammar.ccc.commnet.edu/grammar/.
4. Kate DiCamillo's website at www.katedicamillo.com introduces students to the notion that authors are real people.
5. Picture books at www.readwritethink.org/lessons/lesson_view.asp?id=101 will help students with developing characters in their stories.
6. The site www.readwritethink.org (search for "graphic organizer") provides students with graphic organizers to help them develop vivid characters. The graphic organizer is divided into a character's physical appearance, actions, and reactions.
7. Descriptive passages are the focus at http://teacher.scholastic.com/writewit/diary/index.htm.
8. Pick and choose graphics from a variety of artists and then create your own story to accompany the illustrations atwww.storybird.com. Stories can be printed as PowerPoint slide shows or posted on a class website or interactive whiteboard.
9. The five-step writing process is explained at www.funbrain.com. Students can also write their own Mad Lib stories.
10. Writing lessons for reluctant writers are provided at www.writingfix.com, sponsored by the Northern Nevada Writing Projects.

CONCLUDING THOUGHTS

Students must become fluent writers as well as fluent readers. As with reading, some students need special attention to develop the skills and confidence to express themselves. Teachers can better understand why particular students may not enjoy writing by administering writing attitude surveys and self-assessments.

Students learn to write by writing texts; many require mentoring in the five steps of the writing process to become proficient. When students understand this process, they know to gather information before they write. When they begin writing, they know to get their ideas down on paper before they work on revisions and mechanics. Developing writers need to feel good about their work by "publishing" their final copy and sharing it with an audience.

Reflective Learning — RELUCTANT WRITERS

Scenario. Ms. Bryant has been teaching fifth grade for 27 years. She loves children's literature and also knows the importance of students being able to write well. Her favorite author is Avi, and she uses many of his books for read-alouds throughout the year. She has multiple copies of all his books, and students are required to read at least one of them during the school year. Many students read more than one Avi book because they, too, enjoy how he tells a good story. One of Ms. Bryant's assignments at the end of the year is for students to select their favorite Avi book and focus on the book's main topic (e.g., What animal is featured in the story? In what country does the story take place? What is the major problem of the protagonist? In what period of history does the story take place?). Students must research that topic, write a report, and give an oral presentation on it. Topics taken from the books over the years have included the owls and field mice from *Poppy* (2005), the porcupines from *Ereth's Birthday* (2001), the Alaskan malamute from *The Good Dog* (2004), the beavers from *Poppy and Rye* (2005), and the era of the 1400s from *Midnight Magic* (1999).

This year when Ms. Bryant presents the assignment, D.D., a reluctant writer, asks, "Why do I have to write a report when I am going to tell the class what I learned?" Ms. Bryant knows there is some truth in what he says, but she wants him to write and give an oral presentation.

QUESTIONS:

1. What should Ms. Bryant do to make the writing assignment authentic?
2. What type of writing assignment would give D.D.'s report a different audience?
3. What technology might Ms. Bryant include to motivate students like D.D.?
4. How should Ms. Bryant implement the new writing assignment?

CHAPTER TWELVE

SPELLING

The road to success is often under construction.

JIM MILLER

scenario

Ms. Bird, a sixth-grade language arts teacher, loves to write and wants every one of her students to become fluent writers. In the first couple weeks of school, she provides many opportunities for students to do Quick Writes so she can observe and assess their needs. During the Quick Writes, she notices that Mindy hesitates to write and that her writing is very stilted. For example, when asked to share their favorite event of the summer, she writes: "I went to kamp. It was many miles away. It was in Colordo." That is her entire composition after forty minutes of writing. Many of her other writings have also been similarly brief. Ms. Bird checks Mindy's records and finds her reading level is at grade level.

One day Ms. Bird announces a five-minute free write. The students can write whatever they want, but their pens cannot stop. When she collects their papers, she sees that Mindy has written the same sentence over and over again: "I do not like to right." This is Ms. Bird's opportunity to talk with Mindy.

During conferencing time, Ms. Bird approaches Mindy with the paper in her hand. She says, "I understand you don't like to write. Everyone has different likes and dislikes, but I am wondering if you can tell me why you don't like to write, and maybe I can help you." Mindy does not respond, so Ms. Bird asks, "Do you not know what to write about, or is there another reason?" Mindy responds, "I'm a terrible speller, and I don't want my teachers to know. I have plenty of ideas in my head, but I don't know how to spell the words. I've always been a bad speller." "Well," Ms. Bird says, "I can see how that makes writing hard for you. But I tell you what, if you come to my room during study period, I'll help you. That's something we can fix. You do know that during study period you can go to any teacher for extra help, right? You come to me, and I will help you. Deal?" "A deal!" Mindy replies.

The next day Mindy comes to Ms. Bird during study period. Ms. Bird says they are going to play a game. She hands Mindy a CAFÉ sheet that has 60 boxes (see the Assessment section later in this chapter for more information). She explains that she will set the timer for ten minutes and Mindy has to fill in as many boxes as possible. Mindy can put any words in the boxes that she wants to, but she cannot use any names. She can use *mom, dad, sister,* and so on, but not their proper names. Figure 12.1 is Mindy's work.

guiding questions

As you are reading the chapter, consider the following questions:

1. Analyze Mindy's word list on the CAFÉ sheet and think about her spelling strengths and weaknesses. Do you see any pattern to her spelling?
2. What particular strategy or strategies would you use to help Mindy with her spelling needs?
3. How can Ms. Bird help the English learners in her class become proficient spellers?

figure **12.1** CAFÉ sheet with Mindy's words.

mum	dad	me	I	do
white	blak	gren	pink	yelo
purpel	red	blue	freind	class
lunch	carots	sanwish	grapes	milk
shool	hall	math	speling	reeding
teachure	sience	vacashun	wekends	slep
is	was	do	run	fun

INTRODUCTION

Although spelling is secondary to composing (Hughes & Searle, 2000), it is an important skill for effective writing (Turbill, 2000). As noted in previous chapters, effective readers may be poor spellers. Merely reading words does not ensure that students can spell them (Hughes & Searle, 2000; Turbill, 2000). Assigning a list of spelling words one day of the week and testing them a couple of days later does not ensure that students use, much less correctly spell, those words in their writing (Fresch, 2000; Gentry, 1987; Heald-Taylor, 1998; Hughes & Searle, 2000; Pinnell & Fountas, 1998). Assigning writing projects does not ensure good spelling either (Turbill, 2000). Hughes and Searle (2000) suggest that students begin to spell correctly when they "care about what they are writing and about how their ideas are received by readers" (p. 204). Good spellers see "the link between spelling and the role of the audience" (p. 205). Hughes and Searle argue that good spellers are skilled, avid readers and committed writers who have found their writing voice. Good spellers' writing is personal. They learn how to spell interesting words when they encounter them in reading and when they desire to use them in their writing.

SPELLING INSTRUCTION

Good spelling instruction is "teaching children how to spell, not what to spell" (Rosencrans, 1998). The traditional technique for teaching spelling is to assign a list of words on Monday and test the students on Friday. The students are expected to memorize the words by writing them a number of times. No thought is given to the individual needs of students; there is one list for everyone. Most often these lists are not connected to other subject areas. With this technique good spellers are not challenged because they already know the words, and poor spellers memorize the words only for the test (Fresch, 2000; Gentry, 2004, 2007; Hughes & Searle, 2000; Rymer & Williams, 2000). Such assigned lists fail to impact students' writing (Fresch, 2000; Gentry, 2004, 2007; Rymer & Williams, 2000). The worksheets that typically accompany such lists focus on parts of speech, definitions, using the word correctly in the sentence, or on mnemonic rules such as "when two vowels go walking, the first one does the talking." Because only 46 percent of English words are spelled phonetically (Heald-Taylor, 2001), it is not beneficial for students to memorize the rules and the few words that fit the rule. Instead, students need to be taught to look for patterns within words (Bear, Invernizzi, Templeton, & Johnston, 2008; Fresch, 2000; Rosencrans, 1998).

Abandoning commercial spelling lists does not mean teachers must take a laissez-faire attitude toward spelling. Rather, teachers should intervene and use direct, explicit spelling instruction when students need it (Sipe, 2001). Teachers should become an active participant in the "co-construction" process, based on Vygotsky's (1978) theory of the zone of proximal development. Teachers must assist students as they progress from what they know about spelling to what they do not know. This active teaching and active learning complement one another. To become an active participant a teacher must first develop background knowledge about (1) the developmental stages of spelling, (2) the orthographic patterns of words, and (3) the complexities of English spelling.

DEVELOPMENTAL STAGES OF SPELLING

Researchers disagree on the number and names for each stage of spelling development. Chapter 11 discussed Zecker's (1999) seven stages of emergent writers. Bear et al. (2008), Gentry and Gillet (1993), Rosencrans (1998), and Ferroli and Shanahan (1987) all identify five stages of spelling but differ regarding their contents. Fresch and Wheaton (1997) and Bear and Templeton (1998) identify six stages, while Sipe (2001) identifies seven. Figure 12.2 lists and explains many of these developmental stages. The various progressive stages may be similar and may overlap. Some researchers divide stages into smaller units than other researchers do. The variations are not intended to confuse you, but rather to provide all relevant information so you can use it to better understand your struggling spellers.

Instructional Practices for Each Spelling Stage

This section relies on the spelling stages in Bear et al. (2008), but given the similarities in how researchers define spelling stages it should be easy to adapt them.

Emergent spelling stage

Children in this stage make scribbles or letter-like shapes and understand that writing proceeds from left to right. They need ample opportunity to "write" and adults who respond by asking the child to "read" their story or poem.

In transitioning from the pre-phonetic to phonetic stage, children begin representing their thoughts with words, and often "they use the names of the letters as cues to the sound they want to represent" (Bear et al., 2008, p. 12). To facilitate this process you can label items around the classroom and point them out. Draw attention to name cards on students' desks and ask them to find other names or words that begin with the same letter, or to find the longest and shortest names in the class. Also demonstrate writing lessons by (1) writing short captions under student's pictures, (2) spelling out the letters of each word, (3) saying each word aloud, (4) reading the caption, and finally (5) asking the child to point to each word as he reads the caption. After sharing a big book with a group, play "I spy" by asking students to point to a particular letter or word on the page. Spellers in this stage need lots of practice examining letters and hearing letter sounds.

Alphabetic spelling stage

Students in this stage are aware of the initial sounds of words. At the early alphabetic stage students often think there are always as many letters in a word as there are syllables. Thus, they spell *baby* as *bb* and *horse* as *h*. Later in the alphabetic stage they begin to write the main sounds within a word. *Baby* becomes *babe*. Give students at this stage plenty of demonstrations and chances to listen to the sounds within words.

One strategy for this stage is interactive writing. During the Morning Message, the teacher can spell out the words aloud as he writes them. When he comes to a familiar word he asks a student who knows the beginning letter of that word to come and write it. If the teacher always begins the Morning Message with "Good Morning, boys and girls," he can invite students to write the familiar letters they know.

Within word pattern spelling stage

During this stage a teacher must help students discover patterns within words. You can begin with three-letter phonograms (word families) and write the rime of a phonogram on a flip chart and ask students to provide the onsets to create as many words as possible. You may copy poems that identify word families onto flip charts and ask students to name the word family. Also, ask students to find rhyming words (words that share the same sound but not the

figure 12.2 Developmental spelling stages.

BEAR, INVERNIZZI, TEMPLETON, AND JOHNSTON'S STAGES

1. Emergent: Scribbles or letter-like shapes; conventional left-to-right direction.
2. Alphabetic: Uses beginning and ending consonants and consonant blends; vowels in every word.
3. Within Word Pattern: Long vowels spelled correctly; confuse long vowel digraphs.
4. Syllables and Affixes: Uses inflectional endings correctly (double consonant with short vowel sounds); prefixes and suffixes spelled correctly.
5. Derivational Relations: Most polysyllabic words spelled correctly; unaccented vowels in derived words spelled correctly.

GENTRY AND GILLET'S STAGES

(see Figure 12.3 for sample work from the following stages)

1. Precommunicative: Random letters; scribbles; drawings; no knowledge of letter–sound relationships.
2. Semiphonetic: Realizes letters represent sounds in words; uses initial letter and ending letters of words; writes left to right; may or may not have spacing.
3. Phonetic: Hears most consonants in words.
4. Transitional: Includes vowels in each syllable; begins to use knowledge of affixes and inflectional endings.
5. Conventional: Most words spelled correctly.

FERROLI AND SHANAHAN'S STAGES

1. Preliterate: No letter–sound relationships.
2. Initial Consonant: Initial letter is correct.
3. Consonant Frame: Initial and ending consonant sounds are present.
4. Phonetic: Initial, medial, and final sounds are present.
5. Transitional: Words are spelled as they sound ("wuntz" for *once*)

ROSENCRANS'S STAGES

1. Pre-phonetic: Drawings of sticks and shapes; no letter–sound relationships.
2. Phonetic: Letter–name strategy (e.g., r = *are*); only initial and final sounds; similar sounds may be substituted (e.g., "sete" = *city*).
3. Graphophonic: Uses sound–symbol cues; uses phonic rules for letter sounds.
4. Ortho-phonic: Uses knowledge of sound–letter sequence (*qwd* is not a possible answer).
5. Morpho-phonic: Understands affixes, derivations, and structural units.

FRESCH AND WHEATON'S STAGES

1. Preliterate/Prephonetic: Scribble; aware that words are print.
2. Preliterate/Phonetic: Learns alphabet; strings letters together to spell words.
3. Letter Name: Uses environmental print as aid; learns some sight words; exchanges short vowel sounds for closest long vowel sounds; spells words as they sound (e.g., *r* for *are*).
4. Within Word: Develops sight words; use short vowels correctly; confuses long vowel digraphs (*boat* is "bote"); uses *d* for all past tense words; knows every word has vowel; internalizes rules (silent e); over-generalizes rules.
5. Syllable Juncture: Correctly doubles consonants before inflectional endings; struggles with schwa sound.
6. Derivational Constancy: Understands relationship of words, derivations, and multiple meanings.

SIPE'S STAGES

1. Scribbles: Scribble.
2. Letter-like Shapes: Mostly scribble with some letters and numbers randomly included.
3. Sequence of Letters: Understands words are more than one letter, but letters are random.
4. Encode Words with Initial Consonants: Initial consonant represents the entire word.
5. Encode Words with Initial and Ending Consonants: Both initial and ending consonants are present.
6. Encode Words with Medial Sounds: Adds the medial sound.
7. Conventional Forms: Most words are spelled correctly.

figure 12.3 Graphic examples of spelling stages.

Precommunicative:
"Grey is king on his birthday" (age 4).

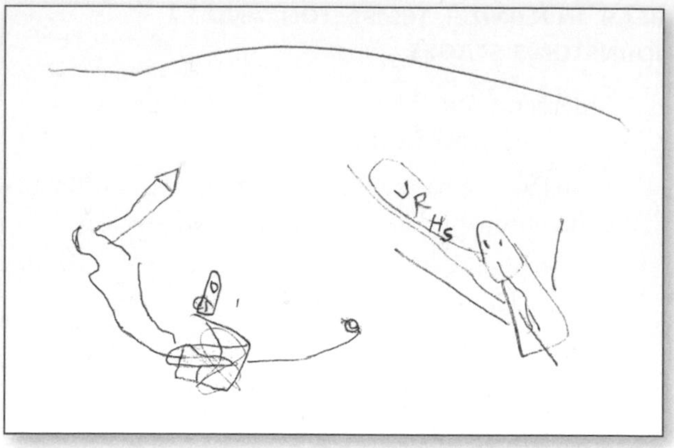

Semiphonetic:
"You are hurting us!" Grey's drawing (age 5).

Phonetic:
"Destroy" (Grey's man, age 5).

Transitional Stage: "God Loves You"
(Grey's feeling after Bible school, age 6).

Transitional:
"Half Man, Half Bat" (Grey's batman, age 6).

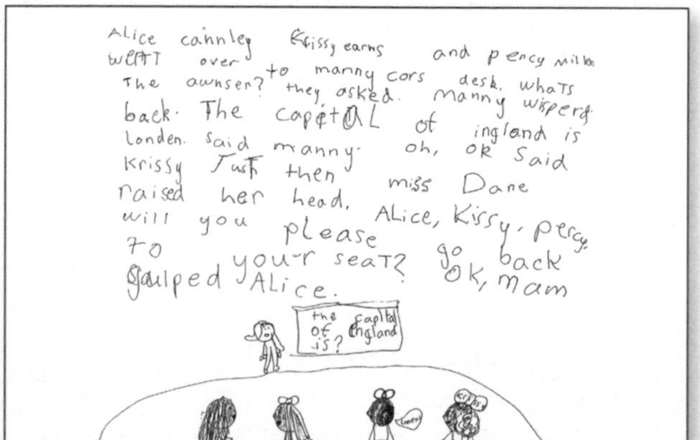

Conventional:
"India's Friend" (story, age 7).

same letters) and identify pairs of words that rhyme. The following passage from *Guess Who's Coming, Jesse Bear* (1998) by Nancy White Carlstrom allows the teacher to draw attention to the rhyme of *whale* and *tail* despite their different spellings.

> Saturday
> Sara swims like a shark,
> Or should I say a whale?
> She says she'll nibble on a fish
> And tries to grab my tail. (unpaged)

Encourage students to spell by having them write the letters they think might be in a word and then checking the sounds of the word. When they ask if a word is correct, direct them to a page in a book or have them use sound boxes (refer to Figure 4.6).

In the opening scenario Mindy has trouble with a couple of word patterns, one of which is vowel digraphs, as evident in her spelling of *reeding* for *reading* and *gren* for *green*. She will benefit from learning different ways to spell the long vowel sounds such as the long /*e*/ spelling of double *e* (ee), *ei* (*receive*), *ea* (*read*) and so on. She also needs direct instruction on doubling consonants, given her spelling of *yellow* and *carrot*. Learning a few spelling generalizations and using the spell-check feature on a word processor would help Mindy with her writing.

Syllable and affixes spelling stage

At this stage your goal is to help students recognize chunks within words, or prefixes, suffixes, and root words and help them spell them. Recognizing these groups of letters is far easier than listening for single letters in multisyllabic words.

Use big books to show how many words end in *ing* or *ed*. After reading a book together, play "I spy" and ask students to point to words that end with *ing* or *ed*. You may also call out a verb and ask students write down that verb in its *ing* and *ed* forms. Later, challenge students to find other prefixes and suffixes that go along with the word.

Teachers can design an exercise using one-inch cards with prefixes in green, root words in red, and suffixes in blue. Challenge students to match three cards together (one of each color) to make words. This exercise is especially helpful for tactile learners.

Derivational relations spelling stage

Students at this stage are now spelling most words correctly, so you might encourage them to check each other's papers for spelling errors. Students can apply simple spelling rules, such as when to double consonants before adding an *ing*. (See Appendix B.9 for a list of spelling generalizations.) The rules can be written on a chart posted in the classroom, and students should be encouraged to check the rules when they have spelling questions. During this stage students should learn how to use the spell-check feature on word processors. They should be able to recognize the word in question in a group of possible options.

Instructional Practices for English Learners' Stages of Spelling Development

English learners pass through stages of spelling development just as native English speakers do. Not all students develop at the same rate. Some may spend a long period of time in the first stage, but as their self-confidence increases they may pass through other stages quickly. The stages of development are (1) emergent stage, (2) letter name–alphabetic stage, (3) within word pattern stage, (4) syllable and affixes stage, and (5) derivational relations stage (Bear et al., 2008). Students develop certain skills in each stage, and teachers can facilitate this development by providing activities based on their needs.

Emergent stage

The strategies parents use with their English-speaking toddlers are also appropriate for English learners in the emergent stage. Read to the students while pointing to words and emphasizing their sounds. Stories with rhyming words are appropriate texts; talk about the rhyming words as you read. Sharing alphabet books helps students hear initial sounds and learn names for objects. Singing songs with rhyming words is also helpful. Ebooks that highlight the text as the student listens to the passage are good activities. In addition, you can have students learn the names of everyday foods, objects, clothing, or jobs using picture cards. Give students at this stage a pencil and paper so they can "write" stories. Most often their writing will be pictures.

Letter name–alphabetic stage

If the English learners are not literate in their native language during the letter name–alphabetic stage, teach the sounds of the alphabet as you would with English-speaking students. If the English learners are literate in their native language, explain explicitly how the English alphabet differs from their native alphabet and, if possible, point out common letters in the two languages. Some languages (e.g., German, Spanish, Italian, and French) share most letters of the English alphabet; other languages have a very different alphabet. Figure 12.4 shows the Spanish alphabet, and Figure 12.5 shows the Thai consonants and the Arabic alphabet. Notice how differently the letters are shaped.

The alphabetic stage is a good time to share alphabet books that show uppercase and lowercase letters along with one or two familiar objects. Using the picture sorts English learners can sort the pictures first to the initial sound, then the ending sound, and finally according to the long or short vowel sound. Dominoes and any of the other strategies found at the end of Chapter 5 are also good for English learners.

figure **12.4**

Spanish alphabet.

Aa, Bb, Cc, CHch, Dd, Ee, Ff, Gg, Hh, Ii, Jj, Kk, Ll, LLll, Mm, Nn, Ññ, Oo, Pp, Qq, Rr, Ss, Tt, Uu, Vv, Ww, Xx, Yy, Zz

Note: At the Tenth Congress of the Association of Spanish Language Academies, held in 1994, it was decided that for academic dictionaries, at the request of various international organizations, the *ch* and the *ll* would not be considered independent letters. The two letters come to be alphabetized in the places that correspond to them within the letter C (between -cg- and -ci-) and within the letter L (between -lk- and -lm-), respectively.

Within word pattern stage

As English learners reach the within word pattern stage, they learn about the English patterns of one-syllable words and eventually multisyllabic words. One of the easiest word patterns for both native English students and English learners is the CVC pattern, because it has consistent short vowel sounds. Many word families follow this pattern: *hat, man, pen, rug, sit, pot, top, cup,* and *bed.* Other word patterns include CVVC (*road, meet*) and CVCe (*cake, hope, cane*). Words in the CVVC pattern have only one vowel sound, and in the CVCe pattern the silent *e* makes the first vowel long. Word family flip books (as shown in the Intervention section of Chapter 5), word family word walls, and word family Concentration are activities that help students learn patterns within words and thus recognize more words.

Syllable and affixes stage

Simple rules to teach English learners about two-syllable words are (1) a closed syllable (one that ends in a consonant) has a short vowel sound: *cam-per, cab-in;* (2) words with double consonants in the middle of the word are divided between the two consonants, and the vowel in the first syllable is short: *but-ter, com-ment;* and (3) an open syllable (one that ends in a vowel) usually has a long sound (*o-pen, pro-vide*). Engaging students in many writing activities

figure **12.5** Sample alphabets with various scripts.

ARABIC ALPHABET

خ	ح	ج	ث	ت	ب	أ
XAA'	HA'AA'	JIIM	TH!AA'	TAA'	BAA'	'ALIF
ص	ش	س	ز	ر	ذ	د
SAAD	SHIIN	SIIN	ZAAY	RAA'	THAAL	DAAL
ق	ف	غ	ع	ظ	ط	ض
QAAF	FAA'			TH:AA'	TAA'	DAAD
ي	و	ه	ن	م	ل	ك
	WAAW		NUUN	MIIM	LAAM	

THAI CONSONANTS

ก ข ฃ ค ฅ ฆ ง จ ฉ
ช ซ ฌ ญ ฎ ฏ ฐ ฑ
ฒ ณ ด ต ถ ท ธ น บ
ป ผ ฝ พ ฟ ภ ม ย ร
ล ว ศ ษ ส ห ฬ อ ฮ

Source: Bear, Donald R.; Helman, Lori; Invernizzi, Marcia R.; Templeton, Shane; Johnston, Francine R., *Words Their Way with English Learners: Word Study for Spelling, Phonics, and Vocabulary Instruction,* 1st ed., © 2007, p. 35. Reprinted by permission of Pearson Education, Inc., Upper Saddle River, NJ.

helps them learn the spelling patterns. Other activities include teachers modeling how print works in shared reading (see Chapter 1), sharing the pen (see Chapter 11), and language experience approach (see Chapter 7) (Bear et al., 2008).

Derivational relations stage

In the derivational relations stage English learners become aware of root words, prefixes and suffixes, and the changes in words when they become different parts of speech. Among the first suffixes students learn are the inflectional endings of verbs (*singing, walking, walked, smiled*) in which the base word does not change. Next they learn inflectional endings in which the base word undergoes a slight spelling change (*hop* to *hopping, hope* to *hoping, marry* to *married*). Students also learn that prefixes have meaning. Some of the first prefixes they learn are *un, non, re,* and *pre.* They also learn how some base words change when they are used as different parts of speech (*music* becomes *musical* or *musician; nation* becomes *national; comedy* becomes *comical*). Your job is to help students understand the relationship between the spelling and the meaning of these different word forms. More strategies for this stage are discussed in the Intervention section of Chapter 5.

PATTERNS OF ENGLISH SPELLING

Orthographic Patterns of Words

Researchers suggest that good spellers understand orthography—letters and their sequence in words (Fresch, 2000; Hughes & Searle, 2000; Pinnell & Fountas, 2001; Rymer & Williams, 2000; Turbill, 2000). Therefore, the purpose of explicit spelling instruction is to expand students' "knowledge of the principles of English orthography and broaden the range of strategies they use to spell unknown words" (Rymer & Williams, 2000, p. 242).

Aim to make all students word solvers who call upon their knowledge of orthographic categories at will (Fountas & Pinnell, 2001). They know different spellings for the same sound and understand how words are organized. They easily identify patterns within words and make connections among words instead of memorizing whole words. Word solvers learn unknown words through:

- sound (phonemic strategy)
- vision (visual strategy)
- meaning (morphemic strategy)
- analogies (linking strategy)
- inquiry (dictionary usage) (Fountas & Pinnell, 2001; Heald-Taylor, 1998; Zecker, 1999)

Being a word solver "is not so much about learning individual words as it is about learning how written language is organized—how written language 'works'" (Fountas & Pinnell, 2001, p. 369).

Teaching English orthography requires that you understand some generalizations about word patterns. Appendix B.9 lists generalizations teachers must understand to help students learn to spell unknown words. These are not rules your students should memorize. Instead, they are generalizations you can point out as students solve specific spelling problems. Students need to learn to recognize word patterns, not memorize the rules!

As noted earlier, teaching students to see patterns in words or showing them how words are put together is more beneficial than having them memorize word lists. Understanding visual connections such as consonant blends, digraphs, and diphthongs aids young students as they learn word patterns. Making lists of words that follow certain patterns can be fun for students. They can keep the lists in a booklet and use them as a reference during independent writing. Appendix B.10 lists complex word patterns with a few examples. Encourage your students to see how many words they can add to each list.

Help students learn word patterns with consonant blends (e.g., *tr, gr, fl*), vowel digraphs (e.g., *oa, ie*), diphthongs (e.g., *oi* [*oil*], *au* [*taught*]), and controlled-r sounds. Those in the later writing stages need help with patterns based on meaning. Focusing on prefixes, suffixes, inflectional endings, and homonyms aids students in learning patterns in words as they spell. Direct instruction allows them to understand how words change when they become different parts of speech (e.g., *musical* to *musician*). Students can also have fun as they discover how accents change with different forms of words (e.g., MUS-ic, but not MUS-ic-ian).

Complex Patterns of English Spelling

Learning to spell is a complex developmental process (Heald-Taylor, 1998; Johnston, 2001a; Pinnell & Fountas, 2001; Rymer & Williams, 2000), and teachers need to understand these complexities to help their students master the process. The English playwright George Bernard Shaw demonstrated these complexities by spelling the word *fish* "phonetically" as *ghoti*. The *gh* came from the sound in *rough*, the *o* from its sound in *women*, and the *ti* from its sound in *nation* (cited in Johnston, 2001a). However, Johnston points out that (1) *gh* never calls for an /f/ sound at the beginning of a word, and (2) the *ti* for the /sh/ sound occurs only in the medial position of words. Appendix B.10 lists other complex patterns of English spelling. Understanding these patterns will help you effectively aid your students with their spelling. Remember that students do not need to memorize these patterns.

Comparisons Between English and Spanish Spelling Patterns

Native Spanish speakers are the fastest growing minority group in the United States and in U. S. classrooms as well, so it is to the teacher's advantage to understand the relationship between English and Spanish spelling patterns. Both English and Spanish have alphabetic foundations (phoneme–grapheme correspondence); however, the English spelling of words "does not mirror their pronunciations in a reliable fashion" (Perez-Canado, 2005). Spanish spelling is considered to have a stronger alphabetic foundation. Nevertheless, Perez-Canado (2005) believes there are similarities between the two languages, including the following:

1. One phoneme can be represented by more than one letter. For example, in Spanish the /x/ phoneme can be the letter *g* (e.g., *gente*), *j* (e.g., *joya*), or *x* (e.g., *Mexico*). (See Figure 12.6 for more examples.) In English the /k/ phoneme can be the letter *c* (e.g., *cake*) or *k* (e.g., *kite*).
2. One letter can have more than one sound. In Spanish the letter g can have the /g/ phoneme (e.g., *gato*) or the /x/ sound (e.g., *gente*). (See Figure 12.6 for more examples.) In English the letter g can be the /g/ phoneme (e.g., gate) or the /j/ sound (e.g., gym).

Knowing these similarities when working with Spanish-speaking students allows you to build on their background knowledge or give analogies when explaining how some letters make more than one sound (e.g., *c* can be /k/ or /s/) and some sounds can have a number of different spellings (e.g., long /a/ as *ei* in *eight*, *ey* in *they*, or *ay* in *day*).

GOOD VERSUS POOR SPELLERS

You will discover distinctive differences between good and poor spellers. When good spellers proofread their work, they recognize their spelling errors and correct them without seeking outside help (Hughes & Searle, 2000; Turbill, 2000). When they encounter a word they do not know how to spell, they "generate sensible written alternatives that can be compared in order to select the one that makes the most sense and 'looks right'" (Hughes & Searle, 2000, p. 205). Good spellers understand the writing process (Turbill, 2000) and know not to worry about spelling conventions during a first draft. The purpose of editing is to focus on mechanics, which includes spelling. As you work with struggling spellers, recognize what good spellers do naturally and help poor spellers do the same things. Figure 12.7 lists traits of good and poor spellers.

ASSESSMENT

Informal Assessment

As with all skills, teachers must learn what students already know about spelling and give them tasks that develop their ability and knowledge. Informal spelling instruments such as inventories and checklists are effective ways to determine students' spelling skills so you can plan appropriate instruction.

Spelling inventories

Bear, Invernizzi, Templeton, and Johnston (2008) have designed a developmental spelling task that assesses what children already know. The inventory contains lists that progress from easy words (with CVC and CVCe patterns) to more difficult (multisyllabic words) and that are intended as individual tests. Observe students as they spell the words if possible; often this will help you understand what students can and cannot do. The purpose of the inventory is to have students spell dictated words so you can analyze what they already know about spelling; it will also identify those who need individual help. Administer the inventory throughout the year to track your students' progress; the lists are included in Appendix C.54. To give the inventory, say a word from the list once or twice and use it in a sentence. Keep the student at ease by assuring her that she is not expected to know these words, but to write them how she thinks they are spelled. Most sets of words are presented in groups of five. When a student misses three out of five, stop the test. Remember that these tests are not intended to compare children's abilities; they are inventories to assess what a student knows about constructing words.

A student's spelling stage can be determined by how many words he spells correctly. For example, using the two inventories in Appendix C.54, the following criteria apply (Bear et al., 2006):

SPELLED CORRECTLY	STAGE OF DEVELOPMENT
0	Emergent
1–5	Alphabetic
5–10	Within word pattern
10–15	Syllables and affixes
15–25	Derivational relations

figure 12.6 Spanish phonemes represented by more than one letter and Spanish letters associated with more than one phoneme.

PHONEME	LETTER	SPANISH	ENGLISH
/i/	i	iglesia	church
	final y	hoy	today
/b/	b	bebé	baby
	v	vaca	cow
/s/	c before e or i	cesta	basket
		cigüeña	stork
	s	sapo	toad
	x as initial letter (usually)	xilófono	xylophone
	z	zorro	fox
/k/	c before a, o, u or consonant (other than c)	casa	house
		cola	tail
		cuchillo	knife
		clase	class
		democracia	democracy
	final c (rare)	bloc	pad (of paper)
	k	kilogramo	kilogram
	qu	queso	cheese
/g/	g before a, o, or u or consonant	gato	cat
		gota	drop
		gusano	worm
		guerra	war
		guía	guide
		gramo	gram
/x/ (When speaking Spanish, English speakers often substitute /h/.)	g before e or i	gente	people
		gitano	gypsy
	j	joya	jewel
		hijo	child, son
	x in certain words with indigenous origins	México	Mexico
	x as first letter in name	Xavier	Xavier
/j/	ll	llave	key
	y (except as final y)	yeso	plaster, chalk
/ks/	cc	lección	lesson
	x other than initial	examen	exam
		extra	extra
		fax	fax
/ʃ/	x in certain words with indigenous origins	Xela (name of city in Guatemala)	Xela

Created by F. Johnson (2007). Used with permission.

figure 12.7 Traits of good and poor spellers.

GOOD SPELLERS	POOR SPELLERS
1. Pay attention to internal details of words.	1. Attempt to learn whole spelling of each word.
2. Are excellent, avid readers.	2. May be good or poor readers.
3. Are committed writers who find their voice.	3. Do not have their own writing voice.
4. Learn to spell new words when they want them in their writing.	4. Use words they know.
5. Self-monitor.	5. Do not understand self-monitoring.
6. Correct their own errors.	6. Get someone else to correct errors.
7. Quickly recognize their own errors.	7. Do not recognize their own errors.
8. Self-edit.	8. Attempt to memorize words.
9. Learn orthographic patterns within words.	9. Do not see orthographic patterns in words.
10. Learn different spellings for the same sounds.	10. Do not know different spellings for same sound.
11. Slow down when a word looks wrong.	11. Believe spelling is arbitrary.
12. Use a wide range of strategies.	12. Know no strategies.
	13. Sample only parts of words when they read.

Sources: Hughes, M., & Searle, D. (2000). Spelling and "the second 'R.'" Language Arts, *77*(3), 201–208. Turbill, J. (2000). Developing a spelling conscience. *Language Arts, 77*(3), 209–217. Fresch, M. (2000). What we learned about Josh: Sorting out word sorting. *Language Arts, 77*(3), 232–240.

To assess students' spelling stages, use the following guidelines:

1. In the emergent stage, students will first write the initial sound, then add the ending sound.
2. In the alphabetic stage, students correctly spell short vowel sounds and later digraphs and blends.
3. In the within word pattern stage, students can spell long vowels (including the silent *e* when the word has the CVCe pattern) and vowels that are controlled by *r*.
4. In the syllable/affixes stage, students add inflectional endings, prefixes, and suffixes. They also know when to double the consonant if they add *ed* or *ing*.
5. In the derivational stage, students are able to spell unknown words by listening for the root words and adding the correct prefixes and suffixes.

Once you understand the spelling stages, you can develop your own inventories. You can also determine a student's spelling stage by recording and analyzing the spelling of words from his independent writing tasks. The template demonstrated in Figure 12.8 is for recording and analyzing these words. The first step is to record the words exactly as the student spells them. List the words in the column that corresponds to the appropriate spelling stage. (See Figure 12.2 for descriptions of how words might be spelled in each stage.) Then assess how the student spelled each word in a five-word set to determine his spelling stage. (Appendix C.55 has a blank form.) The developmental stages are based on Gentry and Gillet's (1993) classification.

CAFÉ, Word writing assessment

CAFÉ (Complexity, Accuracy, and Fluency Evaluation) is an assessment that evaluates students' word writing ability (Leal, 2005). It does not measure students' ability to compose; rather it measures their ability to write as many words correctly (accuracy) in a given amount of time (fluency). The teacher assesses how many one-syllable and multisyllable words (complexity) students have written. This assessment can be administered to an entire class and is appropriate for any grade. Students are given a page with boxes (refer back to Figure 12.1). The number of boxes on the page varies depending on grade level. First and second graders have only 30 boxes on a page, while grades 9–12 have 90. Boxes for young students are larger to accommodate their developing fine motor skills, while the boxes for older students are smaller.

After providing the students with the CAFÉ sheet, follow these steps:

figure 12.8 Samples of recording students' spelling.

STUDENT Jon GRADE K

Word	Precommunicative	Semiphonetic	Phonetic	Transitional	Conventional
1. lady	(scribble)				
2. once	abc				

STUDENT Krystal GRADE 1

Word	Precommunicative	Semiphonetic	Phonetic	Transitional	Conventional
1. lady		ld			
2. once		wn			

STUDENT Mary B. GRADE 2

Word	Precommunicative	Semiphonetic	Phonetic	Transitional	Conventional
1. lady			lade		
2. once			wunz		

STUDENT Kim GRADE 3

Word	Precommunicative	Semiphonetic	Phonetic	Transitional	Conventional
1. popping				poping	
2. caught				cought	

STUDENT Cooper GRADE 5

Word	Precommunicative	Semiphonetic	Phonetic	Transitional	Conventional
1. popping					popping
2. caught					caught

- Give students ten minutes to fill in the boxes with only one word per box.
- Instruct them to write a word only once, not to use people's names, or abbreviations, or numerals (unless they spell out the word).
- Instruct them to write any words they want—words that explain what they like to do or eat, or that describe what they can smell, feel, see, or touch, or words that describe places.
- When you administer CAFÉ, the room should be free from environmental print or the students' desks should be turned so they cannot see any words or other printed material.

Record how many words the students attempted, how many were correct, how many had one syllable, and how many had multiple syllables. This assessment will allow you to learn about the strengths and weakness of students' word-writing skills. As you carefully analyze the completed sheets, you will learn what students know about synonyms, antonyms, word families, compound words, plurals, homophones, and handwriting (Bromley, Vandenberg, & White, 2007). However, know that CAFÉ does not indicate students' composing abilities.

Checklists based on state standards

Many states (such as Texas) have added standards specific to students' spelling ability. A checklist is one way you can monitor which students need extra help. Group students with similar needs together and help them with specific problems. The partial checklist in Figure 12.9 indicates that at the end of the second quarter, Phil, Kim, Heather, and Marc need help with inflections, prefixes, and suffixes. Most students need to learn how to use resources such as dictionaries and spell-checkers on word processors. A blank checklist is available in Appendix C.56.

figure 12.9 Checklist for spelling standards.

TEACHER Mr. Green QUARTER 1 (2 circled) 3 4

STANDARD **STUDENTS** + = always x = sometimes o = seldom/never

ACCURATE SPELLING:	April	Colby	Candace	Phil	Cole	Sara	Juan	Kim	Mike	Heather	Jamie	Steven	Marc	Evette	Evonne	Jon	Cy	Alonzo
Closed, open syllables	+	+	X	X	+	+	+	+	X	+	+	X	X	+	+	X	X	+
Consonant before *le*	X	+	X	X	+	X	X	X	X	X	+	X	X	+	+	X	+	X
Qu patterns	+	+	X	+	+	+	+	+	+	+	+	+	+	+	+	+	+	+
N before *v*	+	+	X	X	+	+	X	+	X	X	+	X	X	+	+	X	+	X
M before *b*	+	+	X	X	+	+	X	X	X	O	+	X	X	+	X	X	X	X
M before *p*	+	+	X	X	+	+	X	X	X	O	+	X	X	+	X	X	+	X
Change *z* to *c* with *es*	+	+	X	X	X	+	+	X	X	X	+	X	X	+	X	X	X	+
Root words	+	+	+	+	+	+	+	+	+	X	+	X	X	+	+	X	X	+
Tense inflections	X	X	X	O	X	+	+	O	X	O	+	X	O	+	+	X	X	X
Number inflections	X	X	X	O	X	+	X	O	X	O	X	X	O	+	+	O	X	X
Suffixes *-able* & *-less*	X	+	O	O	X	X	O	X	O	O	+	O	O	X	+	O	X	O
Prefixes *re-* & *un-*	X	+	X	O	+	+	X	X	+	O	+	X	O	+	+	+	X	X
Use resources to find correct spelling	O	O	O	O	O	O	X	O	X	O	X	O	O	X	O	O	X	O
Accurate spelling in final draft																		

Formal Assessment

Standardized tests, such as the Iowa Test of Basic Skills, Comprehensive Test of Basic Skills, California Achievement Test, and Metropolitan Achievement Test have subtests for spelling. In some of these subtests, students must select the correctly spelled word from a list of four or five words. This type of testing assesses the students' ability to edit, not to spell words. However, because editing is an important step in the writing process, teachers understand that they must assess the process as well as the product. In other subtests, students must select the correct letter combination to fill in the blank in a word. This type of test assesses students' knowledge of word patterns.

Intervention STRATEGIES & ACTIVITIES

Before presenting specific classroom activities, here are some general strategies that are beneficial to all students—English speakers as well as English learners.

1. Use visualization. Teach students to visualize the word in their mind by writing the word in the air.
2. Divide monosyllable and multisyllable words into segments. With monosyllable words have students find the onset and rime or spelling patterns (CVC, CVCe, CVVC, and so on). With multisyllable words have them segment the word into the affixes and root or base word.

3. Focus on similarities and differences between words. For example, *hear* (action) has *ear* in the word (we need ears to hear), while *here* (location) is *there* (another location) without the letter *t*.

Keep these general strategies in mind as you use the activities in this section. The first activities focus on working with word patterns. These strategies are best taught in tutoring sessions so you can observe the student as she makes sense of patterns in words.

MAGNETIC LETTERS GRADES 1–5 ACTIVITY

Working with magnetic letters helps students who are tactile learners and those who do not like to erase because it is messy. For students who are really weak with spelling, preselect letters and put them in a pile. First work with word families (onset and rimes) that have the CVC pattern (e.g., *at, ap, am, an,* and *up* families).

1. Select magnetic letters to spell the word and then pronounce the word.
2. Have the student pronounce the word and then you both pronounce it slowly, drawing out the sounds.
3. Mix up the three letters and ask the student to spell the word again.
4. Return the original letters to the pile and tell the student another word from the same word family.
5. For the second word, ask the student to find all three letters from the pile; she should not merely change the first letter, because it is important that she sees four or five words with the same pattern.

Much time should be given to manipulating the letters to spell new words. Have the student copy all the magnetic letter words onto a personal word wall (a sheet of paper with the rime written at the top and words listed from the bottom). An example of the *at* family is given below.

"at" family

cat

bat

fat

sat

mat

gnat

flat

This same activity can be performed with word stamps. Students in grades 3–5 can complete this activity on small dry-erase boards. Many older students also need practice with listening to the sounds within words and seeing patterns. Older students can work with the *ight* (*light, sight*), the *ound* (*found, sound*), and *own* (*clown, frown*) families.

FOAM BOARD LETTERS GRADES 1–5 ACTIVITY

You can make letter tiles from foam-board sheets purchased in a school supply or art supply store. (See samples of tiles in Appendix D.14.) For this activity:

1. Cut the foam board into half-inch squares.
2. Using a permanent marker, write one letter on a square.
3. Have students spell word family words or unscramble the letters to make other words.

For example, after reading a book about the jungle, select animal names (*lion, tiger, elephant, kangaroo*), scramble the letters for each word and have the student put the letters in correct order. These same foam-board letters can be used to play Scrabble, a game most children already know. Students who perceive themselves to be poor spellers benefit from playing this game with the teacher; mistakes are usually less embarrassing than when playing with peers.

ACTIVITY

WORD SEARCHES

GRADES 1–5

The goal in a word search is to find as many words as possible by reading up, down, backward, and diagonally. Again, base word searches on stories the student has read or on words that trouble her. Figure 12.10 shows an example of a word search based on Mem Fox's *Possum Magic* (1983).

figure **12.10** Word search based on *Possum Magic*.

WORDS TO FIND IN *POSSUM MAGIC* WORD SEARCH

Australia	magic	Lamington	koala	scones
Grandma	tail	invisible	see	adventure
stop	poss	sea	dingoes	his
possums	ate	hush	Pavlova	

A	L	A	O	K	A	T	E	I	N
I	G	R	A	N	D	M	A	N	E
L	I	S	H	A	E	Z	G	V	A
A	T	T	U	E	M	C	I	I	V
R	P	O	S	S	U	M	S	S	O
T	E	P	H	I	S	X	S	I	L
S	E	O	G	N	I	D	O	B	V
U	S	E	N	O	C	S	P	L	A
A	D	V	E	N	T	U	R	E	P
A	N	O	T	G	N	I	M	A	L

ANAGRAMS

GRADES 2–4 ACTIVITY

Finding words in other words or rearranging letters from one word to form a new word is fun for most students, especially if performed in a risk-free environment with a teacher. After reading *Word Wizard* (1998) by Cathryn Falwell, write the student's first and last names and have him make as many words out of his name as possible.

VARIATION: ANAGRAMS WITH ALPHABET CEREAL

GRADES 1–3 ACTIVITY

Using anagrams made with alphabet cereal is a tasty way to play with words. You spell one word for the student, and by adding, deleting, or rearranging one letter at a time, the student creates new words. Manipulating and eating the letters can make spelling an enjoyable task!

WHEEL-OF-FORTUNE

GRADES 3–5 ACTIVITY

Following the model of the television game show "Wheel-of-Fortune," think of a phrase with which the student is familiar and that includes words that might give her trouble. Or, using Fred Gwynne's books *The King Who Rained* (1988), *A Chocolate Moose for Dinner* (1988), or *A Little Pigeon Toad* (1999), you can work with homonyms, stressing the correct spelling of the words in the "Wheel-of-Fortune" blanks. You write out the blanks, and the student must guess the letters. Figure 12.11 presents two examples from Gwynne's books.

***figure* 12.11** Wheel-of-Fortune based on Fred Gwynne's books.

_ _ _ _ _ _   _ _ _ _   _   _ _   _   _ _ _ _ _ _   _ _ _ _.

(Mother says I am a little dear.)

_ _ _   _ _ _ _   _ _ _   _ _ _ _ _ _ _.

(The king who reigned.)

MNEMONICS, MEMORY AIDS

GRADES 3–6 ACTIVITY

Mnemonic strategies are unique ways to remember difficult or unusual words. For example, the sentence "George Ellen's old grandfather rode a pig home yesterday" spells GEOGRAPHY. Also, it is easy to remember the difference between *dessert* and *desert* because children want two *desserts* (two *s*'s). The *c* and *s* are not confusing in *license* when one remembers that a *c*ar always needs to *s*top at a *s*top sign. (The *c* comes before the *s* in the sentence and in the word.) *Attendance* creates a command: "At ten dance!" And *capacity* is the command to "Cap a city!" Teach students how to create their own mnemonics and when to use them.

ACTIVITY SPELLING IN PARTS (SIP) GRADES 3–8

Some spelling problems for students are (1) alternative phonetic patterns (e.g., *education* sounds like *edukashun*), (2) spelling patterns that are less common (e.g., *ch* for the /sh/ as in *Michigan*), (3) double letters (e.g., *occur*), (4) the "schwa" sound that can be any vowel (e.g., *lemon, about*), and (5) commonly mispronounced words (e.g., *library*).

Powell and Aram (2008) suggest using the following SIP (Spelling In Parts) strategy to help struggling spellers. The goal of this strategy is to help students listen for and identify syllables within words. For example, if the student is struggling with September, write the word down on a piece of paper and follow these steps. Have the student:

1. Clap out the syllables so he knows how many parts there are in the word. Remember: every syllable has at least one vowel.
2. Say the first syllable and circle it (e.g., Sep).
3. Pronounce the next syllable and draw a line under it (e.g., tem).
4. Pronounce the last syllable and draw vertical line after it (e.g., ber/).
5. Pronounce the first syllable and write it down: *S-e-p*
6. Say the second syllable and write it down: *t-e-m*
7. Say the last syllable and write it down: *b-e-r*
8. Next, ask the student which syllable might cause a spelling problem and why. For example, the second syllable of *September* may sound like *tim,* instead of *tem.*
9. Discuss how the last syllable is found in three more months: *October, November,* and *December.*

Helping students listen for syllables and teaching them about troublesome syllables such as *tion* (e.g., *vacation, station, addition*) will help them with multiple words. Teach struggling spellers to be word-pattern detectives instead of having them memorize each word independently.

SPELLING AND TECHNOLOGY

Spell Checking

Word processors are a great tool for enabling students to check their manuscripts for spelling errors. Take the time to demonstrate how the spell-checker works on the word processing programs available to your students. Perhaps give a demonstration like the following.

- Type the following sentence: *The children put their unbellas in the stand.*
- Draw the students' attention to the incorrectly spelled *unbellas*, which has a red line under it.
- Put the cursor in front of the word *unbellas* and show how to correct the error.
- A screen appears with the suggested spelling. Demonstrate how to accept the suggested spelling and note how the word is changed automatically.
- Open a document with multiple misspellings. Indicate how the red lines highlight the misspellings, and show how to correct the errors again.
- Have students practice correcting the words while you watch so that you can be sure they are using the spell-checker correctly.

Once you have taught students to use the spell-checker, encourage them to type the final drafts of their work and require that all spelling be correct.

The Internet

A number of websites feature word searches, word puzzles, and other spelling activities. One good website that builds spelling skills is www.mindfun.com.

The following websites offer word searches and other word puzzles that focus on the spelling of words:

www.qualint.com/wsdownload.html ■ Allows teachers to create word searches.

www.eduplace.com/kids/games/wwf/ ■ Hosts weekly word find puzzles on a variety of subjects.

www.edHelper.com ■ Allows teachers and students to enter word lists and have the site build word puzzles based on them.

www.playkidsgames.com ■ Designed for grades K–3; includes many different spelling games.

www.kidsspell.com ■ For grades K–5; teachers can create their own spelling lists for different grades.

www.funbrain.com ■ Features spelling games for grades K–6; user-friendly with bright graphics.

CONCLUDING THOUGHTS

Spelling is a critical skill for students' writing. When working on spelling skills, teachers need to understand their students' developmental spelling stage and provide strategies that will help them reach the next stage. Strategies for each stage should focus on identifying patterns within words so students learn to spell groups of letters within words.

Reflective Learning IMPROVING SPELLING

Scenario. After the first week of school, Ms. O'Nelly realizes her eighth-grade students have a wide range of spelling abilities. She is surprised to find some good readers who struggle with spelling. Others will not write a word unless it is spelled correctly; in fact, one student spends significant time attempting to find the correct spelling of a word in the dictionary. Other students select only words they know how to spell; thus, their expression of ideas is very limited. A few students write the words as they as sound; for example, *once* is spelled *wunz*.

QUESTIONS

1. What instrument should Ms. O'Nelly use to assess her students' spelling?
2. What type of instruction—large group, small group, or individual—should she use?
3. What strategies should she teach the students who will not write a word unless it is spelled correctly?
4. What strategies should she teach the student who tries to find a word in the dictionary?
5. What strategies should she teach the students who use only the words they know?
6. What strategies should she teach the students who are writing words according to their sounds?

CHAPTER THIRTEEN

TUTORING

Education's purpose is to replace an empty mind with an open one.

MALCOLM FORBES

scenario

Dr. Read, a reading professor in the Education Department of a university located in a large urban area, was inundated with calls asking about tutors from parents whose children attend a school in which the principal is one of Dr. Read's former students. Dr. Read calls the principal, Ms. Wilson, to find out about the sudden need for tutors. Ms. Wilson explains that the school has established a three-tier plan for the RTI (Response to Intervention). The school has just released the scores of the first benchmark assessment, and many parents are concerned their child's score is below grade level. These parents want to get individual help for their children. The school has decided that students below grade level after the first benchmark would receive extra small group tutoring during the school day.

Dr. Read understands the parents' concerns about their children's success, and he wants to help them. He decides his preservice elementary majors can gain valuable experience by tutoring the struggling readers. He tells his three Reading Diagnosis classes about the situation and asks for volunteer tutors. Many of his students are interested. He schedules a Tuesday afternoon meeting with them to explain his expectations for the tutors he will recommend to parents. Under his supervision, all the preservice students are currently tutoring a struggling reader from the university lab school. He tells them he expects the same type of lesson plan for these new students and that he will be available during tutoring hours.

Dr. Read calls Ms. Wilson with the news that he has 16 education majors who would like to tutor the students with the low benchmark scores. He asks the parents to share the benchmark scores with the tutors so they can focus on the areas that will benefit the child.

A week later 16 students come to the university reading clinic for tutoring. At the end of the first semester, they take another test at school to determine their growth. The college students are thrilled to learn that every student they tutored tested at grade level. The parents are thrilled with their children's progress and, realizing the benefits of tutoring, ask if the college students will continue to tutor their children. They say their children like the individual attention and being able to read without other classmates listening in; they also think it is "cool" to attend the university.

guiding questions

As you read this chapter, consider the following questions:

1. What other options would Ms. Wilson have in terms of providing the students with tutoring?
2. What key elements were likely part of the lesson plans Dr. Read's students used with struggling readers?
3. What adaptations to the plan would they have made for English learners?
4. If Dr. Read's students encounter a reader who stops when he does not know a word, what responses would you suggest they use with that reader?

INTRODUCTION

Teachers recognize that many students need one-on-one or small group instruction in order to show adequate yearly progress on state-mandated and standardized tests. They know that tutoring lessons are based on the student's strengths and needs, and tutors can focus on particular ways to motivate that one student. As with any teaching, tutors need to remember to focus on motivating the student so she desires to read and write. This motivation may take the form of reading a fashion magazine or writing to a friend who moves away. Tutoring tailored to a reader's interests can be a great motivator for learning to develop literacy skills.

Administrators and teachers need to recognize that "tutoring is a complex task that requires understanding of the content, use of appropriate tutoring strategies (e.g., scaffolding), gauging the tutee's understanding and need, and adapting to each move that the tutee makes" (Meyer et al., 2010, p. 65).

This chapter focuses on (1) the benefits of tutoring, (2) types of tutors, and (3) planning and conducting a tutoring session.

BENEFITS OF TUTORING

Tutoring is one-on-one instruction. Struggling readers benefit from being tutored, and tutoring can be effective for second language learners (Otaiba & Pappamihiel, 2005). First, because instruction is based on the individual needs of the student, the reader receives instant feedback (Chambers, Abrami, McWhaw, & Therrien, 2001; Medcalf, Bessete, & Gibbs, 2009; Fitzgerald, 2001; Cartwright, Savage, Morgan, & Nichols, 2009; Clay, 1985; Meyer et al., 2010; Houge & Geier, 2009). Because it is tailored to the individual student, tutoring is one of the most effective forms of instruction for struggling elementary and middle school students (Houge, Peyton, Geier, & Petrie, 2007). Most tutoring programs target students in the primary grades, because research reveals that children who are not reading by the third grade have higher chances of dropping out before graduating from high school (Chambers, Abrami, McWhaw, & Therrien, 2001).

Research (Elbaum, Vaughn, Hughes, & Moody, 2000; Murrow & Woo, 2001; Otaiba & Pappamihiel, 2005) indicates that tutoring is effective in preventing reading failure when five conditions exist:

1. Tutoring is based on classroom instruction and assessment. In the case of children with special needs, it is also based on Individualized Education Plans (IEPs).
2. Tutors are well trained before they begin tutoring and receive continual training throughout the year.
3. Students are tutored at least three times a week.
4. Tutors develop a rapport with the tutees.
5. Programs are well implemented.

The downside to tutoring is that it is costly for school districts. One-on-one tutoring programs drain school districts' budgets, especially when they use certified teachers as tutors. A teacher who is a tutor works with one student at a time instead of 20 to 30. Even though certified teachers are more effective than uncertified tutors (Allington, 2006; Clay, 1985), many school districts seek volunteer tutors in order to save money. This often includes retired community members, college students, business leaders, and parents. All volunteers can be effective tutors, particularly if a certified teacher trains them (Johnston, Invernizzi, & Juel, 1998), but college students are most effective (Houge, Peyton, Geierk, & Petrie, 2007; Elbaum, Vaughn, Hughes, & Moody, 2000).

TYPES OF TUTORS

Tutors can be categorized into five different types: (1) reading specialists/literacy coaches, (2) certified teachers, (3) paraprofessionals, (4) computer-assisted, and (5) web-based.

Reading Specialists

The International Reading Association (IRA) defines the qualifications for reading specialists, who are the ones most responsible for tutoring struggling readers and for supervising other tutors. Reading positions in the schools have different titles: reading specialist, literacy coach, reading intervention teacher, and reading supervisor/coordinator. Because reading specialists are qualified to fulfill many duties, they are assigned various titles based on responsibilities.

Qualifications

According to the IRA a literacy coach, a reading intervention teacher, and a reading supervisor/coordinator all should be considered reading specialists; therefore, their qualifications should be the same. Reading specialists should have a master's degree with a concentration in reading. The master's degree must consist of at least 24 hours of graduate credit hours in reading and language arts and other related reading courses. Six of the 24 hours must be supervised reading practicum experiences. Reading specialists must have previous teaching experience and be able to relate to diverse populations.

The IRA (2004) outlines the minimum qualifications for reading specialists.

1. They are excellent classroom teachers themselves.
2. They have deep knowledge of reading processes, acquisition, assessment, and instruction.
3. They have experience working with teachers to improve their practice.
4. They are experienced presenters and familiar with presenting to teacher groups in schools and at professional conferences.
5. They have training that enables them to master the complexities of observing in classrooms and providing feedback to teachers.

Responsibilities

Some of the reading specialists' responsibilities may include (1) providing individualized reading and writing instruction, (2) providing assessment in cooperation with other professionals such as special education teachers and school psychologists, (3) diagnosing students' reading problems and recommending appropriate interventions, (4) serving as a resource for the school district, (5) providing professional development in reading at the local and state levels, (6) training paraprofessionals, and (7) providing leadership in student advocacy (International Reading Association, 2003).

As stated earlier, reading specialists are often given different titles based on their responsibilities. The IRA uses the following definitions, but you may find that your school district uses the terms in a somewhat different manner.

The **literacy coach's** main role is providing professional development for teachers. They constantly assess their school's literacy needs, research new literacy programs, and then develop and implement a program that meets the literacy needs of their school. A literacy coach must have good leadership skills.

A **reading intervention** teacher provides intensive instruction to English learners, students with learning disabilities, and other students who struggle with reading. Sometimes the reading intervention teacher works side-by-side with the struggling reader in the classroom, and sometimes he works in a separate room.

A **reading supervisor/coordinator** has many of the same responsibilities as a reading coach, but works more with systematic change at the district level. This person assumes the responsibility for implementing a good scope and sequence to the district's literacy program.

Certified Teachers

The **school or district reading specialist** usually trains certified teachers. Tutoring by certified teachers is best for the student, because teachers are able to diagnose reading problems, assess the learning style of readers, and match specific strategies to specific literacy problems (Allington, 2006; Clay, 1993c; Meyer et al., 2010; Houge & Geier, 2009). However, certified teachers are very expensive due to the teacher/student ratio of 1:1 instead of 1:25, and they often suffer tutoring fatigue due to the number of students they see each day. Working with struggling readers for long periods of time is taxing because tutors are constantly assessing what the student is doing as he makes sense of a passage. Many struggling readers do not enjoy reading, which means the tutor must maintain a positive tone and a fast pace. Good tutors also need to seize the "teachable moment" by selecting instructional strategies that hold the tutee's interest and that are tailored to his needs and learning style.

Paraprofessionals

Many school districts cannot afford a reading specialist, a teacher with a master's degree in reading. However, principals like Ms. Wilson understand the importance of providing support to the teachers as they work with struggling readers. Therefore, many schools hire paraprofessionals or use preservice education majors if the school is near a university. The IRA applauds districts that use paraprofessionals to provide literacy support to students; however, they are concerned about these individuals' qualifications. The IRA requires paraprofessionals to have completed two years of college "with an emphasis on human development and educational processes" (International Reading Association, 2006b). Twelve semester hours must be in literacy and language development. Because paraprofessionals have not had extensive training in assessing students' reading and in providing appropriate strategies based on the assessment, reading specialists are responsible for educating paraprofessionals. Good training includes information about how children learn to read and how to assess their reading problems, as well as how to help children decode words, learn sight words, and comprehend different types of text. The training also includes instruction on how to match specific reading strategies with specific reading problems.

After paraprofessionals complete the initial training, their tutoring sessions are supervised by the reading specialist who mentored them. The reading specialist assesses the students, develops the lesson plans, organizes instructional materials, and provides feedback to the tutors. When paraprofessionals have questions or problems, the reading specialist is on hand to assist them.

Paraprofessionals usually tutor a couple of times a week for no more than an hour or two at a time. This schedule keeps them from suffering fatigue. A successful tutoring session is usually 30 to 45 minutes long and includes the following four components:

1. *Rereading familiar texts.* This gives the tutee opportunities to improve fluency, automaticity, and comprehension while experiencing success and gaining confidence.

2. *Working with word analysis.* These activities help the student to focus on the orthographic structure of words. They recognize patterns within words, listen for all the sounds, and link sound sequences with letters. Activities may include spelling words with magnetic letters, word sort, and syllable segmentation.

3. *Writing activities in which the student composes a passage.* Most passages are only one or two sentences long. The tutor helps the student listen for letter–sound relationships and to recognize spelling patterns while she is writing.

4. *Reading new stories on the student's instructional level.* The tutor creates interest in the story by providing background information and/or by looking through the pictures. New vocabulary words are introduced and discussed while they read the passage. During this process the tutor teaches reading strategies.

To maintain a steady pace during a tutoring session, each activity is allotted a certain amount of time. The steady pace helps the tutor and the student stay on task. For paraprofessionals to impact student literacy during these sessions, they must follow certain guidelines (Wasik, 1997). Figure 13.1 lists the major guidelines for successful tutoring sessions.

figure **13.1**

Guidelines for paraprofessional tutors.

1. Tutors should be trained by certified reading specialists.
2. Tutors need ongoing training and feedback.
3. The child should work with the same tutor in each session.
4. Tutors must be reliable and punctual.
5. A certified specialist should be present during the tutoring sessions to answer questions and provide input.
6. Tutoring sessions need to be structured.
7. Tutors should use high-quality instructional materials.
8. The reading specialist needs to assess the tutee on a regular basis.
9. The instruction in the tutoring session must coordinate with classroom instruction.

Sources: Allington, R. (2006). *What Really Matters for Struggling Readers: Designing Research-Based Programs* (2nd ed.). Boston: Pearson/Allyn & Bacon. Invernizzi, M., Rosemary, C., Juel, C., & Richard, H. (1997). At-risk readers and community volunteers: A three-year perspective. *Scientific Studies of Reading, 1*(3), 277–300. Wasik, B. (1998). Using volunteers as reading tutors: Guidelines for successful practice. *The Reading Teacher, 51*(7), 562–571.

Computer-Assisted Tutoring

The computer can serve as a tutor in itself or it can be used as a tool in tutoring sessions. If the tutees use tutorial software programs themselves, teachers should first provide instruction. Students need to spend their computer time developing literacy skills and not figuring out how a program works. Reading specialists should also train tutors how to use these programs effectively with their students.

Effective computer programs meet the following criteria. They are (1) motivational, (2) self-monitoring, (3) skill reinforcing, and (4) self-pacing. They should be able to record and analyze students' progress. The best programs suggest reading strategies based on the student's performance. A wide variety of computer programs are designed to reinforce literacy skills. Some programs build fluency, comprehension, and/or word attack skills. Some focus on writing skills, while others connect reading and writing. Appendix A.11 contains a list of skills with software programs that help develop each. Many interactive ebooks allow students to listen to a story on the computer or read it on-screen to increase their fluency and build vocabulary. Appendix A.12 has a list of interactive books.

Reading CAT is a computer-assisted tutoring program that can be used by the classroom teacher, tutor, and tutee. The teacher shares with the tutor the materials the student is using in the classroom. For example, if the student is reading *Betty Doll* by Patricia Polacco, the tutor uses that book to record the tutee's miscues into the Reading CAT; the program then offers reading strategies relevant to the student, such as breaking longer words into single syllables. The tutee selects from various strategies to assist in building word identification skills. This program also models how to sound out words by blending phonemes. Students receive immediate feedback on whether they have decoded the word correctly.

Based on five years of research, the National Center for Supported eText (NCSET) designed a guide for teachers to use when selecting electronic texts (see Figure 13.2). Although specifically designed for evaluating electronic versions of classroom texts developed for students who are visually impaired or have learning disabilities, the guide is useful for evaluating any electronic text used in computer-assisted tutoring.

figure **13.2** NCSET guide for evaluating electronic texts.

RESOURCE	DESCRIPTION	EXAMPLES
Presentational	Enables the text and accompanying graphics to be presented in varying ways, hence customizable to meet the needs of individual readers	Font size and style, text and background color, line and page length, page layout and juxtaposition with other pages, graphics in relationship to text
Navigational	Provides tools that allow the reader to move within a document or between documents	Within-document links, across-document links, embedded menus, links from other resources such as Table of Contents, Glossary, Bibliography
Translational	Provides a one-to-one equivalent or simplified version that is more accessible or familiar to the reader; may focus on a word, phrase, paragraph, picture, or whole document; may be of same or different modality or media	Synonyms, definitions, digitized or synthesized text-to-speech, alternative language equivalents (Spanish), video of American Sign Language translation, simplified version at lower reading level, text descriptions for images, captions for video
Explanatory	Provides information that seeks to clarify the what, where, how, or why of some concept, object, process, or event	Clarifications, interpretations, or descriptions that point to causes, operations, components, mechanisms, parts, methods, procedures, context, or consequences; list of influencing factors
Illustrative	Provides a visual representation or example of something in the text; designed to support, supplement, or extend comprehension of the text through illustrations or examples	Drawings, photos, simulations, video, photos, reenactments, sounds, music, information that something is representative of its type (". . . is a typical example of . . .")
Summarizing	Provides a summarized or condensed way of viewing some feature of the document	Table of contents, concept map, list of key ideas, chronology, timeline, cast of characters, abstract
Enrichment	Provides supplementary information that is not strictly needed to comprehend the text, but adds to the readers' appreciation or understanding of its importance or historical context	Background information, publication history, biography of the author, footnotes, bibliography, influence on other writers
Instructional	Provides prompts, questions, strategies, or instruction designed to teach some aspect of the text or how to read and interpret the text	Tutorials, self-monitoring comprehension questions, annotations, instructions prompts, study guides, embedded study strategies, online mentoring, tips for effective reading
Notational	Provides tools for marking or taking notes on the text to enable later retrieval for purposes of studying or completing assignments	Electronic highlighting, bookmarking, margin notes, outlining, drawing; ways to gather and group these notes for postreading review
Collaborative	Provides tools for working or sharing with other readers, the author, or some other audience	Threaded discussion, online chat, e-mail links, podcasts, blogs
Evaluational	Provides materials, prompts, and assignments designed to assess student learning from the text	Questions, quizzes, tests surveys, online interviews, assignments leading to products

Source: Anderson-Inman, L., & Horney, M. A. (2007). Supported eText: assistive technology through text transformation. *Reading Research Quarterly, 42*(1), 153–160. Reprinted with permission from the International Reading Association via Copyright Clearance Center.

Web-Based Tutoring

Web-based tutoring frees up the classroom teacher just as peer tutoring and computer-assisted tutoring do. Often students in upper elementary and middle school have trouble understanding expository text found in their science and social studies textbooks because they do not recognize the book's organizational structure. Intelligent Tutoring for Structure Strategy (ITSS) is a research- and web-based tutoring program effective with fifth through seventh graders as they read expository texts. The program tutors students in social studies and science texts. These types of text are organized similarly, following a structure based on sequence, description, comparison, problem-and-solution, or cause-and-effect. Each of these structures provides signal words to help readers determine how the text is organized. For example, *first, next,* and *finally* are found in sequence passages, while *causes* and *problems* are found in cause/effect passages.

ITSS provides 12 passages for each type of text structure (e.g., 12 comparison, 12 cause-and-effect, and so on). "ITSS has a software agent, interactive flash activities, parsers, spell checking, synonym checks . . . lesson choices, informative feedback, and human voice to motivate and teach students how to use the structure strategy" (Meyer et al., 2010, p. 73). The computer screen looks like a double-page book. The first time a student uses a passage, the passage appears on the left side of the screen and the student's responses are typed on the right-hand side of the "book." When he uses a passage the second time, his responses appear on the left-hand side and his new responses to the more detailed questions appear on the right-hand side. The first time the organizational structure is taught, the computer tutor (the voice of an eighth grader) guides the student through a graphic organizer. The program reads all the texts during the first lesson on each passage, and after that the student reads the passage himself. However, if the student comes across an unfamiliar word he can cursor over it and the computer pronounces the word and gives the definition. When the student completes the reading, he needs to "(a) identify the overall TLS [top level structure] of expository text . . . (b) write the main idea using patterns for each of the different text structures . . . , and (c) organize reading comprehension and recall by using the structure and main ideas" (Meyer et al., 2010, p. 73). Students are required to write responses rather than answer multiple-choice questions for a more accurate comprehension assessment.

The results of a research study conducted with 56 students in fifth grade and 55 students in seventh grade who were reading below grade level and who used ITSS for 90 minutes each week for approximately 21 weeks "showed that ITSS with elaborated feedback substantially increased reading comprehension on a standardized test" (Meyer et al., 2010, p. 86).

Teachers can evaluate web-based tutoring software programs as they become available to see if they offer assistance in the areas their students need.

SUCCESSFUL TUTORING PROGRAMS

Teachers may choose from many successful tutoring programs. Howard Street Tutoring Program (Morris, 1999), developed in Chicago as an after-school program, was designed to help second- and third-grade readers. Success for All, developed by Slavin et al. (1996), is based on the premise that all students must succeed at reading in the early grades and on the principles of immediate and intensive intervention (Nunnery et al., 1999). The program is designed for first through third grades. Book Buddies, developed by Charlottesville City School, the University of Virginia, and the city of Charlottesville, Virginia, is a tutoring program for first- and second-grade struggling readers. Perhaps one of the most used tutoring programs found in schools across the United States is Reading Recovery, which was developed in New Zealand.

Reading Recovery

The Reading Recovery program is used in more than 6,000 schools in the United States (Wasik, 1998). It was developed in New Zealand as an early intervention and remediation program for first graders having extreme difficulty learning to read and write (Clay, 1985; Fountas & Pinnell, 2006b). The program uses certified teachers who tutor one child for 30 minutes each day. The goal is to help struggling readers read at grade level as soon as possible, usually within 15 to 22 weeks. The student then either tests out of the program because she has reached the reading level of her class, or she is referred to a long-term tutoring program, such as those supported by Title I. Reading Recovery uses certified teachers who are trained by certified Reading Recovery instructors. The program is effective (Pinnell, 1989; Wasik, 1997) but expensive due to the specialized training, the staff of certified teachers, and the use of leveled books. The recommended books are organized into fine gradients, labeled 1 through 20 for first graders. (See the discussion in Chapter 2.) Some publishers of Reading Recovery books include Sundance, Rigby, Newbridge, and AKG Educational Services. Figure 13.3 lists the addresses of these publishers.

figure **13.3**

Publishers of Reading Recovery books.

Sundance
Department 0502
P.O. Box 1326
Littleton, MA 01460
www.sundancepub.com

Newbridge
Department 0502
P.O. Box 1270
Littleton, MA 01460
www.newbridgeonline.com

AKG Educational Services, Inc.
5609-2A Fishers Lane
Rockville, MD 20852

Rigby
P.O. Box 797
Crystal Lake, IL 60039-0797
www.rigby.com

Reading Recovery tutorial sessions are scheduled every day for 30 minutes. Each session has the following structure:

1. The student rereads two or more familiar books on an easy reading level to experience success.
2. The student rereads a book on instructional level that was introduced in the previous session. The tutor keeps a running record of this reading to analyze and assess growth.
3. The tutor gives isolated word study instruction, often using plastic letters on a magnetic board.
4. The student writes a short story, focusing on writing for meaning and on listening for the sounds in words. Stories are only one or two sentences long. Tutor uses sound boxes to aid student in letter–sound recognition.
5. The tutor writes the story on a sentence strip and cuts the words apart. The tutee must arrange the words to construct the sentence. The tutor puts the pieces in a plastic bag and writes the sentence on the bag so the student can take it home and practice putting the pieces back together.
6. The tutor introduces a new book on the student's instructional level, and the student attempts to read the new book, which becomes the text used for the running record the following day.

PLANNING AND CONDUCTING THE TUTORING SESSION

Tutors need to plan each tutoring session just as effective teachers plan for every classroom lesson. This does not mean tutors should never deviate from the plan to seize teachable moments. Whenever possible, a reading specialist or other trained tutor should observe tutoring sessions to provide feedback for the tutor.

Lesson Plans for Tutoring Sessions

Each tutoring session should be based on a lesson plan to ensure that it is directed toward a particular goal and that the planned activities help the student meet that goal. Figure 13.4 presents a completed form for a sample tutoring session and Appendix D.29 includes a template. The lesson plan includes (1) written objectives for each area of the tutoring session, (2) the sequence of the lesson, (3) needed materials, and (4) reflection on each area of the lesson.

Written objectives. Tutors need to reflect on the tutee's past accomplishments, current progress, and future goals to define objectives for each area of the lesson. Like all objectives, these should state what the child is expected to do with a targeted degree of accuracy. Figure 13.5 provides sample objectives for each area of the lesson. At the beginning of the school year, the tutor may write simple objectives that reflect the level of accuracy that is intended for easy reading and instructional reading. A tutor may write, "Marie will read *I Paint* with 95 percent accuracy." As the year progresses and the tutor understands the unique needs of the tutee, he should set more specific and challenging goals. For example, if the tutee is an inexpressive reader, he may write, "Marie will raise her voice at the end of each question in *I Went Walking, What Did I See?*"

Sequence of the lesson. As stated previously, the Reading Recovery program follows a consistent format. The major components—reading easy material, rereading a book to keep a running record, word study, writing, and new reading—are all used in the sample lesson plan that is provided in this chapter.

Research shows that effective tutorial programs have a pace that keeps tutees engaged and motivated, motivated, motivated! Students who are interested in a task will stay with the task; students who are not interested are not engaged (Houge & Geier, 2009; Meyer et al., 2010). For this reason tutoring programs should include the following elements:

1. 30-minute sessions at least twice a week.
2. Consistent format in each session:
    a. Ten minutes for easy read.

figure **13.4** Lesson plan for tutoring.

LESSON PLAN

TUTOR: Terri DATE: 9-23

TUTEE: Marie GRADE: 2

Easy Reading Objective: Marie will read Bear's Cave with 95% accuracy.

Rereading of Last Session's Book Objective: When Marie rereads Wobbly Tooth, she will learn to pause when she comes to a period.

Word Study Objective: Marie will create a list of at least five words that have the /oo/ sound, as in tooth.

Writing Objective: Marie will compose two sentences about pulling a loose tooth, spelling all words correctly.

Reading of Instructional Material Objective: When reading Grandma's Bicycle, Marie will use picture clues to determine unknown words.

LESSON PLAN	PLANNED ACTIVITY	TIME	REFLECTION
Easy Reading	Book: Bear's Cave	8 min.	Marie read with 97% accuracy. She only struggled with "growled."
Rereading	Book: Wobbly Tooth	7 min.	She self-corrected 85% of errors. On the running record, she used visual cues more than reading for meaning.
Word Study	Materials: Dry-erase board, magnetic letters	10 min.	Her list: food, moon, broom, loose, noon. She also created a list of "oo" words that do not rhyme with loose tooth: book, look, cook. She liked the dry-erase board better than the magnetic letters.
Writing	Materials: Her tutoring journal	10 min.	Marie wrote 3 sen.: My dad pulls my tooth. It hurts (we used sound boxes for this word) when my dad pulls my tooth. I have six new tooths. (I explained that the plural form of tooth is teeth.)
New Reading	Book: Grandma's Bicycle	10 min.	She read with only 80% accuracy. She reads too fast. She needs to slow down. She told me fast reading is good reading. She liked the funny story. Her grandma rides a bicycle too.

figure **13.5**

Sample objectives.

EASY READING OBJECTIVES:

Sally will read *I Paint* with 95% accuracy.

When George reads *Grandma's Bicycle,* he will observe 95% of the periods with a pause.

When Juan reads *Do Whacky Do,* he will appropriately inflect his voice at the phrase, "Do Whacky Do."

REREADING OF LAST SESSION'S BOOK OBJECTIVES:

Lee will read *Bear's Cave* with 90% accuracy.

When Jon reads *Bear's Cave,* he will self-correct 80% of his errors.

WORD STUDY OBJECTIVES:

Roberto will identify 90% of the "an" family words when he plays Wordo.

Emily will correctly push and say, with 95% accuracy, the letters of these three-letter words: *hop, pup, dad, map.*

WRITING OBJECTIVES:

Heather will write the following sentence with 95% accuracy: "I like to jump rope and play ball." (Early in the semester, children can write anything about their personal lives; this is an example of such a sentence.)

Ben will compose a sentence of at least six words with 95% accuracy.

READING NEW MATERIAL OBJECTIVES:

When Virginia comes to an unknown word in *Sea Animals,* she will read to the end of the sentence to understand the context.

When reading *Making a Cake,* Marie will use picture clues to determine unknown words.

b. Five minutes to reread the material introduced in the previous session. (Tutor keeps a running record during this reading.)
c. Ten minutes for word study.
d. Five to 10 minutes for writing.
e. Ten to 15 minutes introducing and reading new material at the tutee's instructional level.

The purpose of the easy reading is to build the tutee's reading confidence, rate, fluency, and expression. Many struggling readers read word-for-word, with no expression, and at a slow rate, and need to hear themselves read fluently to make a story exciting. These first 10 minutes are a time for struggling readers to experience success! During the rereading of the previous session's material, the tutor should keep a running record in order to analyze the percentage of words read correctly and what cueing systems the reader uses with materials at the instructional level. Chapter 3 provides detailed instructions on running records. Appendix C.5 includes a blank form to use for a running record and Figure 3.14 provides a conversion table for quick analysis of the percentage of words read correctly. An easy text for students is one in which they make less than 1 error for every 20 words read. Students read with 99 percent accuracy if they make only 1 error for every 100 words read.

Appropriate materials. Because tutoring sessions are fast-paced, the tutor needs all necessary books and supplies at her fingertips. The lesson plan should include all the materials that will be needed, such as books, a computer, whiteboards, magnetic letters, letter stamps, salt or sand trays for writing, pencils, paper, and sentence strips. Before a session, tutors should make sure they have the materials on the list. This ensures no tutoring time is wasted searching for materials.

Reflection on the lesson. An essential part of teaching is reflecting on every lesson taught. The lesson-plan form (shown in Figure 13.4) allows the tutor to reflect on each aspect of the lesson. Effective tutors reflect on what the student did well, her improvement from previous lessons, and how her attitude changed. For example, the tutor should note if the goal was reached in the easy reading section and how the tutee responded to the story. If a specific skill was taught, such as reading to the end of the sentence to figure out an unknown word, this should be noted in the reflection. If a running record was kept during the repeated reading, the tutor should note the degree of accuracy and what cueing system the tutee used. If a goal in word study or writing was not met, the tutor should reflect on why the student failed to reach the goal. Sometimes, the tutee's fatigue may be the reason. These reflections should be honest and accurate so that the tutor can plan more effectively for the next session. When preservice teachers serve as tutors, the professor can observe the session and help the tutor understand the tutee's responses.

Getting Started

The first tutoring session is a time for the tutor and tutee to become acquainted.

Session one

During the first session establish a comfortable rapport and learn about each other's interests. Completing a personal interest survey such as the one in Figure 3.24 encourages such a discussion. First the tutor and tutee can complete the activity, discussing the tutee's interests, and then they can complete one for the tutor. Tutees who are at least emergent writers can "share the pen" with the tutor as they fill out the form. Tutees are encouraged to write what they can, while the tutor helps complete each thought. Sharing the pen gives the tutor an idea of the tutee's writing ability.

Making a collage of "favorites" is also a good icebreaker. Using old magazines, the tutee and tutor can cut out some of their favorite things and glue them on a piece of construction paper. They can exchange collages at the end of the session. Creating collages gives tutor and tutee time for informal discussion of their personal interests.

The tutor should have a number of books on hand to read to the tutee at the first session. This allows the tutee to choose the book he most wants the tutor to read. This gives the tutee a feeling of ownership in the reading process. Books with repetitive text permit the tutee to chime in on familiar phrases. For young children, books like *It Looked Like Spilt Milk* (Shaw, 1947) and *Brown Bear, Brown Bear, What Do You See?* (Martin, 1983) are easy enough for them to chime in on the repetitive lines. *Jump, Frog, Jump* (Kalan, 1981) and *"Not Now!" Said the Cow* (Oppenheim, 1989) are good for beginning readers, while *Shoes from Grandpa* (Fox, 1989) and *The Napping House* (Wood, 1964) are suitable for older struggling readers. Appendix A.7 has a list of books with repetitive text.

Session two

After the first session the tutor should have an idea of what books are an easy read for the tutee and select four or five from which the tutee can choose. It is important for the tutor to choose books easy enough for the tutee to experience success. During the second session, the tutor can administer one of the Reading Attitude and Writing Attitude Surveys found in Appendices C.14–18. Insight into the tutee's attitudes helps the tutor pinpoint aspects of reading and writing the tutee does or does not enjoy. Often a tutee enjoys being read to but does not enjoy reading in front of peers because she is embarrassed about being a "poor" reader. If this is the case, the tutor assures her they will be reading together where no one else can hear them. The Attitude Survey may also reveal that the tutee prefers expository text over stories. The tutee's Writing Attitude Survey may indicate she thinks writing is synonymous with composing long stories. The tutor can correct this misunderstanding by having the tutee compose short lists or sentences, thereby demonstrating that writing can also be about creating lists of favorite things to do or eat. This session ends with the tutor reading a book to the tutee. Again, the book should be a repetitive text so the tutee can join in. The tutor, of course, models fluent, expressive reading.

Session three

During this session the tutor begins to assess the tutee's reading and writing ability. If the student is an emergent reader, the tutor should assess his knowledge of letter names and sounds by using a chart such as the one in Appendix C.28. If the student is a beginning reader, the tutor should assess the child's knowledge of letter recognition, sight words, phonics, and word and passage comprehension by administering the Woodcock Tests (see Chapter 3). Conducting a miscue analysis gives the tutor an opportunity to analyze the type of miscues the beginning reader makes most frequently. Administering the Bear, Invernizzi, Templeton, and Johnston Qualitative Spelling Inventory (2007) will aid the tutor in assessing the tutee's current level of word knowledge. (See Chapter 12 and Appendix C.54 for further information.) Assessment is an ongoing process, but it must begin early so the tutor can plan appropriate lessons.

Tutoring Sessions for English Learners

All tutors who work with second language learners must not only possess the five characteristics shown later in Figure 14.7; they must also be culturally sensitive and understand second language acquisition. (See Chapter 1 for review of the Progressive Stages of English Language Development.) They must understand the difference between oral proficiency that most English learners acquire in two years and academic proficiency that usually takes five to seven years. Tutors must support English learners as they take active roles in the classroom, because successful social interaction leads to increased peer acceptance that aids academic growth (Vaughn, Elbaum, Schumm, & Hughes, 1998). Tutors build English learners' confidence by accepting and reaffirming them as individuals and taking an interest in their likes and dislikes. Allow ample time for discussion during the tutoring session so the English learner becomes confident in expressing herself. This will increase her confidence in speaking with peers so she feels comfortable interacting in class activities and discussions.

Tutoring sessions for English learners and tutoring sessions for English native speakers are similar in principle, but different in format. For both, the tutor assesses the tutee's literacy skills and creates lessons based on the tutee's interests, strengths, and needs. The tutor must consider the tutee's oral English language skills, age, and native language literacy skills. Tutors working with students who know very little English and are not literate in their native language will need to spend time on oral language development. If tutees are literate in their native language, tutors can use this knowledge to build their English skills.

Session one

Just like the native speaker's tutor, the English learner's tutor gets to know the tutee and make him feel comfortable during the first session. To determine the tutee's literacy skills in his native language, ask him to read concept books that are in his native language. If he cannot read the words you can assume he is not literate in his native language. Have magazines available and point to pictures such as a slice of pizza or a glass of milk. Say the object's name, point to yourself, nod, and say "I like pizza." Then point to the tutee and ask, "Do you like pizza?" Use lots of gestures to help him understand the flow of conversation.

Magazines are excellent resources for determining a tutee's vocabulary skills, because they have many pictures of everyday objects that are not usually found in children's literature; for example, toasters, hamburgers, peanuts, lettuce, coffee pots, and so on.

Session two

Strive to make the tutee feel safe and relaxed. During this session use the alphabet chart found in Appendix C.28 to see if the tutee knows the letter names and/or sounds. Spanish-speaking tutees may say the letters in Spanish and the sounds in Spanish. Use the picture cards found in Appendix D.4 and the Bingo cards in Appendix D.5 to informally assess the tutee's oral vocabulary, placing three cards in front of her, saying one of the pictures, and pointing to the correct picture. Then place three different cards in front of her, say one object, and ask her to point to the correct card. Again, you may need to make the directions clear by using hand gestures.

Sample format for subsequent sessions

After two or three sessions of making the tutee feel comfortable and safe, use the following format. You may modify the format to meet the needs of a particular tutee, but it is important for the sessions to have a format so the tutee begins to feel comfortable with the tasks he will be asked to do. Also, a set format keeps instruction systematic. The following format is for tutees who know some words in English and are ready to begin reading and writing.

1. *Review from previous lesson.* Review words from flash cards. The tutee says the word and points to something that refers to the definition. For example, if the word is *one* he can hold up one finger. If the word is *red* he can point to something in the room that is red. This activity helps you determine whether the tutee pronounces the word correctly and knows its meaning.

2. *Phonics.* Five to 10 minutes of work with letters and their sounds. Say the name with its common sound and give at least one word that begins with that letter sound. (To review the sounds unique in English refer to Chapters 5 and 6.) Keep a record of the letters and sounds the tutee has mastered and those he is still developing.

3. *Building vocabulary.* Using alphabet books, colors and shapes, and number books, read a page and discuss the picture(s). Some books are bilingual; English and Spanish bilingual books are the most common. (See Appendix A.8 for a short list of English–Spanish bilingual books.) Reread the page and have the tutee echo read. Next, read the page in unison. Then invite the tutee to read the page, assisting if necessary. Depending on the tutee's age, create flash cards with the words featured in the concept book. This helps him recognize words without picture clues.

4. *Sentences.* Write a short sentence featuring a vocabulary word on a sentence strip. Then (1) read the sentence to the tutee, (2) echo read with her, (3) read in unison, (4) have her read it by herself, and finally, (5) cut the sentence strip into words and have her put the pieces back in order as she reads it to you.

5. *Writing.* The tutee should write at every session. Emergent readers may write letters. When possible the tutee should dictate a sentence to the tutor. Share the pen and compose the sentence together by inviting her write the letters and/or words she knows.

6. *Reading to the tutee.* The tutee needs to hear fluent reading. Choose a short picture book on a topic that interests her; read the text and discuss the pictures. Books with repetitive text permit the tutee to join in on repetitive lines. Rebus books for young emergent readers are good because the tutees can read the pictures while they learn directionality and the concept of space between words.

Each session should be relaxed, with the tutees talking a lot so they become accustomed to hearing themselves say English words. The tutors should be encouraging and speak slower than normal so the tutee can hear the space between words. Remember, they are learning language just as an infant learns it. They need to be able to distinguish one word from the next; it is easier for them to process the words and the sounds when you speak slower than normal.

Sample lesson plan

Figure 13.6 has a sample lesson plan for a first-grade English learner whose native language is Spanish and is classified as a beginning reader. Appendix D.1 contains a template. The tutee in Figure 13.6 came to the United States in February and attended kindergarten from February through May. Notice the tutor states objectives for each part of the session.

figure **13.6** Sample lesson plan for a first-grade English learner.

LESSON PLAN

TUTOR: Sarah DATE: 9-15

TUTEE: Bonita GRADE: 1

Review from previous lesson: Bonita will be able to read the color flash cards with 95% accuracy.

Phonics: Bonita will identify the letters B, P, H, L, and M, say their sounds, give two words that begin with each of the sounds, and use each of the words correctly in a short sentence.

Vocabulary building: After echo reading I can!/¡Yo puedo!, Bonita will independently read the book with 90% accuracy.

Sentences: Bonita will identify three words from I can!/¡Yo puedo!, dictate three sentences, read the sentences each two times, and correctly put the sentences back together after they are cut apart.

Writing: Bonita will write a short sentence, using a word from her flash cards.

Listening to tutor: Bonita will listen to The Little Red Hen and chime in on the phrases "Not I said the______."

LESSON PLAN	PLANNED ACTIVITY	TIME	REFLECTION
Review:	Color flash cards	5 min.	Bonita has difficulty pronouncing yellow and black.
Phonics:	The B, P, H, L, M cards	8 min.	She correctly identified the letters; struggled with B and P sounds; struggled with putting words into sentences.
Vocabulary:	I can!/¡Yo puedo!	8 min.	Bonita enjoyed the book and echo read it with 95% accuracy.
Sentences:	Sentence strips	8 min.	She started each sentence with I can read/play, laugh.
Writing:	Penmanship paper	5 min.	She wrote: "I lk red" with help on hearing the sounds in like.
Listening:	The Little Red Hen	7 min.	She really studied the pictures to understand the story. She had much expression with "Not I said the ___."

Intervening with the Tutee During Reading

Tutors always scaffold struggling readers as they tackle materials with challenging new words. Simply giving the word to students does not teach them a strategy, and telling them to "sound it out" may not constitute a clear direction for struggling readers. Tutors can give a number of responses when readers come to unfamiliar words or when they give incorrect responses. Figure 13.7 lists appropriate responses for different circumstances.

Throughout this text I include instructional strategies to develop phonemic awareness, word identification, comprehension, vocabulary, and so on. Many of these activities are suitable for use in tutoring sessions. For example, the games found in the Intervention sections of the Phonemic Awareness and Word Identification chapters are intended to be played by a struggling reader paired with an adult.

It is also helpful for the tutor to log all the reading strategies a student learns and all the books read to and by him. If tutors log the strategies taught, they can refer to the log sheet and remind the tutee of each. This will help him understand that he should apply these strategies in new situations. You can also share these logs with classroom teachers so they understand the strategies the tutee has mastered. The classroom teacher then can remind the student of the strategy by asking, "What did you learn to do with your tutor when you come to an unknown word?" Many young children do not automatically transfer information from one setting to another. The log of learned strategies will help connect the tutoring session to the classroom.

Figures 13.8 and 13.9 contain completed log sheets. Blank forms are found in Appendices D.30 and D.31.

TUTORING AND TECHNOLOGY

It is "estimated that 70 percent of adolescents—students in grades 4–12—have difficulty reading in some manner and require direct, explicit instructional interventions to expand their word recognition, decoding, reading fluency and comprehension skills" (Houge & Geier, 2009, p. 154). Many of

figure **13.7** Helping tutees tackle challenging words.

When a reader gets stuck on a word, always wait five seconds before intervening!

When readers lose their place or skip words:

- Have them point to each word.

When readers stop because they do not know the word:

- Have them read to the end of the sentence and ask them what would make sense.
- Have them look at the picture for clues.
- Have them read the sentence with what they think the word is and ask if that word makes sense.
- Have them check their first response with the spelling of the written word and ask them if that looks like the written word.
- If their response is incorrect, provide the correct word and ask them to read the sentence with that word to see if it makes sense.
- If there is a part of the word they know (e.g., *am* in *ham*), cover with your finger the part they do not know and ask them to read the part they do. Then ask them to try again.

When readers read incorrect words:

- Read the sentence to the students as they have just read it and ask them if it makes sense.
- Ask them if their response matches the printed word.
- Help them find familiar elements in the printed word.
- Have them reread the sentence with the new word and ask them if that makes sense.

When readers self-correct:

- Ask them how they knew that the first response was incorrect.
- Ask them how they figured out the correct word.
- Compliment them on using the strategy!

When readers do not pause for periods:

- Read the passage back to the students and ask them if it sounds correct.
- Have them point to periods in the same manner as they point to words.

Source: Adapted from Johnston, F., Invernizzi, M., & Juel, C. (1998). *Book Buddies: Guidelines for Volunteer Tutors of Emergent and Early Readers.* New York: The Guilford Press.

figure 13.8 Log sheet for strategies.

STRATEGIES TAUGHT TO: Marie BY: Terri

DURING EASY READ

Read phrases instead of words.
Slow down.
Raise voice with questions.
Pause for periods.
Change voice with different speakers.

DURING WORD STUDY

Words that rhyme with cat.
Learn the first 20 words of Dolch list.
Words that rhyme with sound.
Words that rhyme with Sam.
Learn 21–40 words of Dolch list.
How to add "ing" to verbs.
How to separate the onset from the rime in word families (looking for small parts within words).
How to segment sounds when writing new words.
Worked with homonyms: hear/here, dear/deer, two/too/to, four/for.

DURING WRITING

Put spaces between words.
Stop for periods.
Begin sentences with capital letters.
Make sure all sentences are complete (they make sense).
Do not connect all ideas with "and."
Capitalize people's names.
Use question marks with questions.

DURING NEW BOOK

How to read to end of sentence when encountering new words.
How to find smaller parts within one-syllable words.
How to use picture clues when encountering unknown words.
How to look at pictures to predict what will happen next.
How to fill in a story map.
How to do a cluster of facts learned in book.

figure 13.9 Log sheet for books.

BOOKS READ DURING TUTORING

TUTOR: Chan TUTEE: Jackson

BOOKS READ BY TUTOR	DATE	BOOKS READ BY TUTEE	DATE
The Remarkable Farkle McBride (J. Lithgow)	12–1	Noses (E)	12–1
Too Much Noise (A. McGovern)	12–1	Koalas (E)	12–1
If You Take a Mouse to the Movies (L. Numeroff)	12–2	Nesta (E)	12–2
Shoes from Grandpa (M. Fox)	12–2	Dragonflies (E)	12–2
The Snow Tree (C. Repchuk)	12–3	What's Inside (F)	12–3
Too Much Noise (A. McGovern)	12–3	Bruno's Birthday (E)	12–3
The Napping House (A. Wood)	12–4	Mr. Wind (F)	12–4
Seven Candles for Kwanzaa (M. Pinkney)	12–4	Frog's Lunch (F)	12–4

these students do not live near a university with a research-based literacy tutoring program. However, most attend schools that have appropriate software programs and Internet access that allows face-to-face tutoring through videoconferencing. Many teacher education programs have videoconferencing capabilities. Houge and Geier (2009) completed a research study with sixty-one adolescents (grades 4–12) who were experiencing problems with word recognition, decoding, fluency, and comprehension. The purpose of the study was to determine if tutoring via videoconference resulted in higher reading scores. Students received 16 one-hour sessions of individual tutoring by a university student in a teacher education program. Each tutor received instruction in administrating and interpreting assessment instruments and strategies that focused on the main components of reading—word identification, vocabulary, comprehension, and fluency. The study indicated that tutoring via videoconference does improve students' comprehension and fluency as shown on the growth from the pre-test to the post-test (Houge & Geier, 2009).

This indicates that tutoring via videoconference is yet another way technology can be used to help struggling readers.

CONCLUDING THOUGHTS

For educators to meet the goals set by state and federal legislation, they must tap the resources of their communities by drawing on paraprofessionals, preservice teachers, and technology for tutoring. For these tutors to be effective they must be trained and supervised by reading specialists. They need to implement appropriately structured programs and use appropriate materials. Teachers must remember the goal of all of tutoring is to help struggling readers and writers to become literate. All tutoring sessions must be interesting and worthwhile for the tutee.

Reflective Learning — ENGLISH LEARNERS

Scenario. Miss Thomas is a first-year teacher in an urban school in the city where she attended college. During her four years at the university, she observed in this school and volunteered to read to the students. She is thrilled to get a second-grade position in the school because she wants to make a difference in children's lives. She knows her students' success in life will hinge on a good education and a love of learning. She has enough experience to understand that school and learning must be interesting and fun.

However, after two weeks she is overwhelmed by the needs of her students. Many are native Spanish speakers who have been in the United States less than two years. Through informal observation, she finds that many do not know the letter names or their sounds. The school has two reading specialists: one whose main job is to assess the students, and the other who is a reading intervention teacher providing small group instruction. Miss Thomas knows her students need more help than the small group instruction will offer.

QUESTIONS

1. Where should Miss Thomas go for help?
2. Should she approach the reading specialists about the problem?
3. Should she go to the reading specialists with an idea or a plan?
4. If the school has no funds to pay for outside help, where can she go?
5. If the school chooses to use tutors, should the reading specialists train the tutors?
6. What lesson format should the tutors follow?
7. Where should the students receive the extra help?
8. What materials will the school need to provide for the tutors?
9. When should the tutors work with the students? Should the students miss the literacy instruction in class? Should the tutors tutor while the class has reading?

CHAPTER FOURTEEN

TEACHERS, CAREGIVERS, AND THE COMMUNITY WORKING IN COLLABORATION

Act as if it were impossible to fail.

DOROTHEA BROUDE

scenario

It is the end of May and Mr. Blackhawk has just completed his first year of teaching kindergarten. He reflects on the year by compiling two lists—one of triumphs and one of trials. He lists his triumphs first and is pleased with his accomplishments. Then he begins his list of trials. At the top he writes: PARENTS. As an undergraduate he learned that teachers are responsible for working with parents and making them a part of their children's education. He never expected, however, the wide range of parents' personalities and their unpredictable reactions. In general, he has encountered six approaches from parents and caregivers: (1) those who are concerned and want to do everything to aid their child; (2) those who appear not to care in the least about their child's education and seem to not want to be "bothered" with school; (3) those who refuse to believe that their child has any problem with school; (4) those who cannot help their child because of a language barrier but do care about their child's progress; (5) those who are new to the United States and do not understand its educational system; and (6) those who blame him for everything—these parents are frequently at the school interrupting his class.

Mr. Blackhawk decides his top priority for the summer is to research professional journals and books on working with and understanding parents. As he thumbs through some of his back issues of *The Reading Teacher,* he finds many schools and teachers have made it their priority to involve parents by giving them a simple yet effective routine for reading with their child each evening. He particularly likes Kindervater's (2010) research on using Padak and Rasinski's (2008) idea of using kinesthetic motions while reading poetry, chants, and songs. Mr. Blackhawk likes how it actively engages children in a fun way and that the idea might be new to parents. He figures most parents are like anyone else—they like new ideas. He also likes that it will not take much time each evening.

He finds a wide array of short poems, chants, and songs at the local library. He decides to use humor as a central theme. He believes humorous poems are more fun for the family to read than serious poems. Using *Fast Star: Getting Ready to Read* (Padak & Rasinski, 2008), Mr. Blackhawk types up pages listing the focus sound for each poem, the directions to the motion, and the poem; he adds his own illustration to make the page more appealing. See Figure 14.1.

He decides to use this as an action research project. During the first weeks of school, he will obtain a benchmark of each student's letter, letter-sound, and word knowledge. He plans to use the same assessment at the end of the year to record growth. He also needs parents to record the time they spent each evening, so he makes

figure **14.1** Sample poem, "The Town Clock," with motions.

Parents: Every time you and your child hear the /t/ sound at the beginning of a word, quickly tap your index finger on your thumb. Your child has learned this motion in school so he/she may want to "teach" you the motion.

The Town Clock
Tick, tock, tick, tock sounds the old town clock
Telling tiny tots in town
It's time to take a nap.

a simple form (Figure 14.2) that parents can use to record the amount of time and their reaction to the poem. He will introduce the project to his parents during the first open house in the fall and share one or two poems and motions with them so they will become excited about the project.

figure **14.2** Weekly log of reading together.

DAY	AMOUNT OF TIME SPENT	COMMENTS
Monday		
Tuesday		
Wednesday		
Thursday		
Friday		

Parent Signature:

guiding questions

As you are reading the chapter, consider the following questions:

1. Describe the six different approaches/attitudes of parents toward their child's education that Mr. Blackhawk encountered.
2. How do you think Mr. Blackhawk should involve parents who exhibit each of these approaches/attitudes in their child's education?
3. What are some effective ways you would recommend that he communicate with parents?
4. What other guidance would you have to help him establish a home-school connection?

INTRODUCTION

Parental involvement is an important ingredient in children's education. Initiatives at the local and national levels have aimed to promote parental involvement. The Goals 2000: Educate America Act states: "Every school will promote partnerships that will increase parental involvement and participation in promoting social, emotional, and academic growth of children." The National PTA has developed national standards for parental involvement programs, which charge both the school and parents with specific responsibilities. The school is responsible for (1) scheduling regular communication between home and school, (2) supporting parenting skills, and (3) involving parents in major decisions. The parents are responsible for (1) assisting in their child's learning, (2) volunteering at school, and (3) collaborating with the community to provide resources to the schools. Many local districts have also initiated school literacy programs. These programs challenge students to read books at home and to have their caregivers document it. The purpose is not only to have children read at home, but also to make literacy a family affair.

Parental involvement encompasses two basic categories: involvement at school and involvement at home. The involvement at school includes activities such as attending scheduled family–teacher conferences, attending PTA or PTO meetings, holding positions on local school boards, being part of decision-making committees, chaperoning class field trips, and volunteering on a regular basis in the classroom, on the playground, or in the library. Involvement at home includes such activities as providing breakfast for one's children, monitoring their homework, reading and writing with them, and making sure they get the proper amount of rest. Studies have shown that parental involvement at home impacts students' learning more than parental engagement at school (Southwest Educational Development Laboratory, 2006; Michigan Department of Education, 2002). However, both affect students' grades, test scores, and attitudes (Sheldon, 2002).

This chapter focuses on (1) the importance of teachers understanding their students' home lives; (2) the benefits of parental involvement; (3) attributes of engaged parents; (4) how to communicate with parents; (5) initiating parental involvement that makes a difference; (6) working with difficult parents; (7) working with community volunteers; and (8) parental involvement and technology. Remember that not all students in your classroom live with their biological parents. Instead of using the word *parent* in communications, use *caregivers*. References to parents in this chapter also refer to caregivers.

THE IMPORTANCE OF TEACHERS UNDERSTANDING THEIR STUDENTS' HOME LIVES

It is imperative that teachers understand the homes from which their students come. Many teachers work in cultural environments that differ from their own backgrounds. Different cultures sometimes emphasize different value systems and ways of communicating.

Teachers must consider that:

- Some families value cooperation. These students may readily share answers with someone who does not know them.
- Some parents instruct children to lower their eyes when they are being reprimanded. These students may avoid eye contact when they are being reprimanded.
- Some parents will never ask a child a question if they already know the answer. These students may not respond to questions if they think the teacher knows the answer.
- In some cultures children bring disgrace to the family if they complete a task incorrectly. These students may not respond in class or hand in work unless they know the answers are correct.
- In some families men expect women to do as they are told. Students from these families may not accept instruction from a woman.

Be careful not to make assumptions about a student based on his neighborhood. Often teachers work in communities where the average socioeconomic status differs from their own. Here are some situations to consider:

- Not all poor students who live in urban areas come from homes affected by crime and drugs.
- Not all middle-class students who live in the suburbs come from homes that are free from crime and drugs.
- Some working parents are often on business trips and have little time to spend with their children.
- Some parents work two or three jobs to keep food on the table. They may have little energy to read and write with their child when they are home.
- Some students may live with two dads or two moms.
- Some impoverished families move frequently due to circumstances beyond their control. These students may attend two or three different schools a year.
- Some children live in ethnically blended families.
- Some children live with an aging grandparent, another relative, or in a foster home.
- Some children live in homes where domestic employees do everything for them. They may lack practical skills.
- Some children, regardless of their class or neighborhood, live with abusive parents.
- Some children are neglected for long periods of time while a parent engages in illicit behavior.
- Some parents overemphasize the importance of being popular or thin.
- Some parents who do not speak English strongly desire their children to succeed.
- Some parents will not recognize their child has difficulty learning.

Teachers must consider all of these situations and many others when thinking about parental involvement.

Because a positive home–school connection results in higher student performance, you may want to follow these effective principles (Risko & Walker-Dalhouse, 2009).

1. Learn as much as possible about the student, his family, and the community.
2. Warmly greet parents at open houses, parent-teacher conferences, or on the street.
3. Share a student's success with her parents.
4. Ask parents what they observe about their child's literacy skills.
5. If there is a language barrier try to find someone in the school or community to help during con-

ferences and to write notes home in the parents' native language.

6. Attend community events so parents see teachers as people interested in their community.
7. Invite parents to sessions that demonstrate how parents can help their child at home.
8. Work with community groups that offer free tutoring to students in the neighborhood. Teach the tutor some basic strategies, such as creating story maps or graphic organizers for informational text.
9. Research available health and social services in the community and link the agencies with the families who need them.
10. Provide parent networks to help new families who have moved into the school district.

BENEFITS OF PARENTAL INVOLVEMENT

Students benefit in a number of ways—academically, physically, socially, and emotionally—if their parents or caregivers are actively involved in their education. Studies indicate that students who are more successful academically have parents who are involved in their schooling (Berkowitz & Bier, 2005; SEDL, 2006; Porter Decusati, & Johnson, 2004; Rasinski & Padak, 2003; Sheldon, 2002). This is true of students from across the socioeconomic spectrum and from both majority and minority groups (SEDL, 2006; Ho, 2002). Their improved academic success is reflected in the daily grades and test scores. Students who have parents who value learning and monitor homework also have a more positive attitude toward learning. Students whose parents discuss school with them also earn higher grades (SEDL, 2006).

Students who have academically involved parents also enjoy better physical well-being (Finn, 1998). Involved parents make sure the child eats well-balanced meals; they discourage sugary snacks and provide regular meals. Involved parents who qualify for free or reduced-cost breakfast at school make sure the child is at school in time to eat it. Involved parents monitor their child's sleep habits and make sure the child gets plenty of rest. They also understand the importance of regular physical exercise; they play outside with their children and allow ample time for physical activity. Involved parents monitor the number of hours their child sits in front of the computer or the television. They are aware of the websites the child visits and the shows he watches. They often watch and discuss shows together.

Students who have involved parents are socially well-adjusted (SEDL, 2006). Parents model the importance of social interaction when they are involved with PTA or PTO, school-wide projects, or class field trips. Through their parents' involvement, students learn the importance of contributing to society by helping others.

Students also benefit emotionally from parental involvement in school (SEDL, 2006). When there is communication between the school and parent, the student knows that two sets of people who are significant in her life are caring for her. Parents and teachers who have common goals for a child prevent conflict between home and school expectations. Children benefit from that stability.

Parental involvement not only improves students' performance, but it also improves parents' perception of school effectiveness (Jensen, 2006; Ho, 2002) and gives them ownership in the school's process. Parents who become involved in a school project work hard toward its success and take pride in their work. However, if the project is not as successful as expected, they understand the factors that hindered their goal and are not as critical as uninvolved parents.

ENGAGED PARENTS

Parents become engaged when they believe that (1) they can affect their child's education, (2) they are important in their child's development, (3) their school wants their help, (4) they feel comfortable helping at school, and (5) they can be successful in helping with their child's learning (Jensen, 2006; Rasinski & Padak, 2008). Which parents are most involved in their children's school? Statistically, they are more likely to be white middle-class families (SEDL, 2006); other characteristics include parents with higher education and higher incomes, families with two parents, and parents who have ties with other parents from their child's school (Ho, 2002; Sheldon, 2002). However, demographics alone do not explain why parents become involved. Parents are inclined to become involved at school when they feel welcomed and needed by teachers and administrators (SEDL, 2002).

Who are the parents involved in children's education at home? Caucasian and non-Caucasian mothers have similar levels of parental involvement at home. Parents who have more ties with other adults—such as relatives or parents from other schools—are more involved than parents who are isolated. Urban parents have lower involvement at home than do rural or suburban parents (Sheldon, 2002). Sheldon found that when parents are connected to at least one or two parents from the same school, they become more involved in their children's education at school and at home. The social interactions give parents the opportunity to discuss mutual concerns and to offer advice. Teachers and administrators must work at forming connections between parents and understanding parents' needs.

WAYS TO COMMUNICATE WITH PARENTS

Teachers must communicate with parents so they feel connected to the school and understand their involvement greatly influences their children's learning (Morrow, Kuhn, & Schwanenflugel, 2006; Jensen, 2006; White & Kim, 2008; Kindervater, 2010; Rasinski & Padak, 2008). Teachers can communicate with parents a number of ways—introductory letters, newsletters, bulletin boards, parents' nooks, good news calls, happy grams, portfolios with personal notes, greeting parents in the morning or after school, and family–teacher conferences (Risko & Walker-Dalhouse, 2009; Jensen, 2006).

Introductory Letters

Introductory letters from new or first-year teachers are very important to parents whether they are mailed or e-mailed. Parents are often wary of a first-year teacher who is new to the community or building. Introductory letters give parents a brief description of a teacher's past experiences and hobbies. Sharing this information makes the teacher sound both professional and human. The letter should also include a brief description of the educational goals for the class, any school-wide initiatives for the year, a description of any new national or state standards, and a brief statement of their teaching philosophy. The letter can also include a list of materials that would be useful for the class throughout the year, such as empty plastic containers, old appliances for students to disassemble, materials for science experiences, or old magazines. The letter should also include important lists of materials the students are required to have for class, a telephone number and e-mail address with the best times to contact the teacher, and reminders about upcoming events. The letter should conclude with an invitation for parents to become involved at school and name some specific opportunities, such as reading and playing literacy games with the students or writing the classroom's newsletter. Figure 14.3 presents a sample letter of introduction from a fourth-grade teacher.

Introductory Parent–Teacher Conference

An informal introductory parent–teacher conference at the beginning of the school year is another way teachers can begin collaborating with their students' parents. The conference can be at school or at the student's home. If the meeting takes place at the home, arrange for another professional to accompany you. The purpose of this conference is for you to listen to the parents and student to begin building rapport; it is an opportunity to find out information about the student the parents want to share. During conferences later in the semester, such a discussion is often not possible due to the educational matters that need to be discussed. The initial conference builds a relationship between the teacher and the parents that centers on the child and not the curriculum; it allows you to communicate a genuine interest in the child. Later, the relationship solidifies as the teacher and parents discuss the child's academics, behavior, and social interactions in detail. If issues arise about the student later, the rapport established in the early conference may make them easier to resolve.

Newsletters

Communication with parents via newsletters is often a one-way communication made from school to home. Teachers share what topics are being studied in math, science, social studies, and health and what stories they are reading. They may describe strategies they are teaching in reading and writing and share information about an author study and/or information about any technology the students are learning to use.

Jensen (2006) suggests teachers create newsletters that invite parents to initiate some home activities with the child, such as looking up information on particular websites or viewing certain educational television programs. Or, when the class is learning how to create timelines use the newsletter to ask parents to assist their child in designing a timeline of the child's life from birth to the present day, highlighting main events. If the class is studying different jobs around in the community, use the newsletter to invite parents to talk about their job(s) with their child so he can tell the class about it.

When newsletters encourage their involvement, parents feel like they are a source of support for their child's learning. They feel connected to the school and are much more positive about it. Students are more successful and happier when they know that teachers and parents are communicating (SEDL, 2006).

Jensen (2006) suggests the following guidelines for creating newsletters:

1. The tone of the newsletter should be warm and inviting; avoid educational jargon.
2. Use a format that is simple in design and easy to read, including bold or italic print and color for headlines.

figure **14.3** Sample letter of introduction.

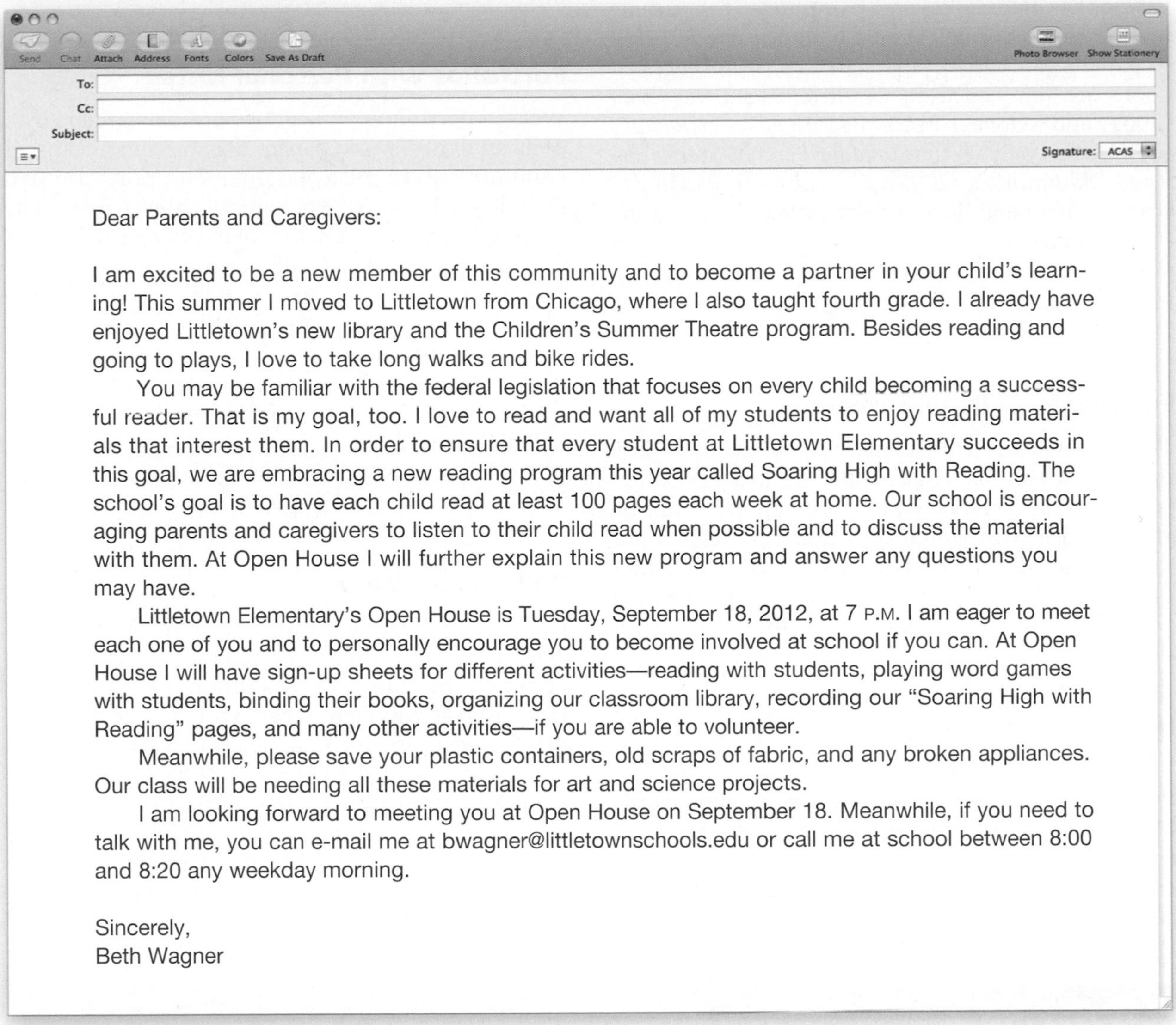

Dear Parents and Caregivers:

I am excited to be a new member of this community and to become a partner in your child's learning! This summer I moved to Littletown from Chicago, where I also taught fourth grade. I already have enjoyed Littletown's new library and the Children's Summer Theatre program. Besides reading and going to plays, I love to take long walks and bike rides.

You may be familiar with the federal legislation that focuses on every child becoming a successful reader. That is my goal, too. I love to read and want all of my students to enjoy reading materials that interest them. In order to ensure that every student at Littletown Elementary succeeds in this goal, we are embracing a new reading program this year called Soaring High with Reading. The school's goal is to have each child read at least 100 pages each week at home. Our school is encouraging parents and caregivers to listen to their child read when possible and to discuss the material with them. At Open House I will further explain this new program and answer any questions you may have.

Littletown Elementary's Open House is Tuesday, September 18, 2012, at 7 P.M. I am eager to meet each one of you and to personally encourage you to become involved at school if you can. At Open House I will have sign-up sheets for different activities—reading with students, playing word games with students, binding their books, organizing our classroom library, recording our "Soaring High with Reading" pages, and many other activities—if you are able to volunteer.

Meanwhile, please save your plastic containers, old scraps of fabric, and any broken appliances. Our class will be needing all these materials for art and science projects.

I am looking forward to meeting you at Open House on September 18. Meanwhile, if you need to talk with me, you can e-mail me at bwagner@littletownschools.edu or call me at school between 8:00 and 8:20 any weekday morning.

Sincerely,
Beth Wagner

3. Include students' work, with the permission of the parents or caregivers.
4. Always suggest websites, books, or projects that the parents can do with their child.
5. Include the topics being studied in each subject area and any new activity or project the students are doing.
6. Include a feedback section, in which parents tear off a section or link to an e-mail address to provide comments, ask questions, or express concerns.
7. Remember the parents whose first language is not English. Seek help translating some version of the newsletter if possible; students who speak the language may be able to assist you. Online translation websites may help, also, but beware: they tend to work best for single words or phrases.

Bulletin Boards

A bulletin board with notices of upcoming school events, field trips, fundraisers, assemblies, performances, meetings, and school pictures should be placed where parents see it when they enter the building. Important school policies, such as what happens during a tornado warning, a snowstorm, or a lockdown should also be posted on the board. Upcoming community events can also be posted. The bulletin board should be colorful and neat. Old notices should be removed and personal advertising prohibited.

Parents' Nook

A parents' nook is a special corner of the school that has books, magazines, and pamphlets that parents may borrow. The nook should include a checkout list so parents can sign out the materials. Two suggested books are Jim Trelease's *The Read-Aloud Handbook* (2001) and Margaret Read MacDonald's *The Parent's Guide to Storytelling: How to Make Up New Stories and Retell Old Favorites* (2001). The school librarian can post an annotated bibliography of new books in the school library or a recommended reading list for each grade level. The nook can also serve as the school's lost and found area and as a place for parents to exchange games, toys, or books.

Telephone Calls or E-mails

Teachers usually contact parents when there is a problem with their child. However, teachers often fail to contact parents with a good report. It may be about a task with which the student struggled but now has mastered, or about a kind deed the child did for another student. All parents enjoy hearing about the positive actions and accomplishments of their child.

Happy Grams

Try communicating good behavior to parents through happy grams. Happy grams include words of praise, comments about kind acts, and reports of accomplishments. Happy grams must be honest and genuine. Parents appreciate hearing good news, and students are sure to give these notes to parents. You can design your own happy gram or use the design in Figure 14.4. Happy grams can be photocopied on bright yellow card stock paper.

Portfolios with Personal Notes

Weekly portfolios with personal notes attached to each student's work papers are another means of communicating with parents. The portfolio can include graded work from all the subject areas. The notes can give tips on how parents can help children master a skill that still needs to be mastered or encourage parents to ask their children to explain a concept they have learned. These personal notes make parents a part of their children's education. It is important for teachers to include personal comments on every student's paper. Some teachers include a form that parents must sign, indicating that they have read the note. A sample of a return form is presented in Figure 14.5.

Daily Welcome

Parents appreciate seeing friendly faces at the school door when they drop their child off at school or pick her up in the afternoon. Just a brief, "How are you? Have a great day!" gives parents the assurance that their child is in caring hands. Many children ride the bus to school. Teachers should take turns greeting the children as they come off the bus. This greeting should be more than a duty; it should be a time to make children feel welcome. Parents appreciate knowing that their child is arriving in a friendly, caring atmosphere.

figure **14.4** Sample happy gram.

figure **14.5** Sample portfolio return form.

DATE: ______________________________

DEAR ______________________________

Thanks for reviewing and discussing the enclosed papers with your child. I am interested in your comments and questions. Please sign the form and give it to your child to return on Monday.

Thanks again for letting me share in your child's education!

Sincerely,

- -

I reviewed and discussed ______________ (child's name) work that you placed in the portfolio.

______ I have no comments or questions.

______ I have these comments, questions, or concerns:

SIGNATURE: ______________________________

Family–Teacher Conference

Family–teacher conferences are important opportunities for teachers, parents, and students to exchange information about the student's education. When preparing for the conference, consider the following:

1. Schedule a time that is good for parents. Many working parents cannot come during the school day. Ask them for times and days when they will be available. Parents who have a number of children in the same building appreciate scheduling siblings' conferences around the same time.

2. Find out if the parents are able to read and/or speak English. It is important that teachers communicate clearly with these parents about the time and place of the conference. You may need to schedule an interpreter for the conference.

3. Be aware of who is coming to the conference. Not all children live with their biological parents. Children may live in a foster home, with grandparents, or with another relative. Also, be sensitive if there has been a recent death in the family, a divorce, or another difficult event.

4. Be sensitive regarding parents who live in poverty. They may not have transportation to the school and may not have a working telephone. Do not pressure the caregivers so they feel guilty or hostile. Be creative in letting these caregivers know they are an important part of the student's education.

5. Prepare for the conference by gathering samples of children's reading, writing, and other work. It is a good practice for you to record a student's reading on a recording device. The parents can listen to the recording during the conference, and they can discuss the student's strengths and weaknesses.

6. Involve students. Have students help select the work they want their parents to view. Discussing concerns about children when they are present reassures them that both parents and the teacher care about their progress.

7. Arrange a clean, comfortable place for the conference. Do not sit behind your desk! The desk

becomes a wall between the parents and the teacher. Also remember that student desks are not comfortable for most adults. A round table with adult-size chairs is the best setting. The room should be clean with no extra clutter.

8. Use a timer if you have conferences that run back-to-back. For example, set your cell phone to vibrate five minutes before the conference ending time. It is impolite to keep the next set of parents waiting.

9. Begin on a positive note. All parents like to hear something positive about their child. This is also a time when you can help negative parents understand that their child can do things well.

10. Have goals. Know what you want to accomplish during each conference. A few written notes can keep the conversation on track.

11. Listen to parents' concerns and questions. Parents may also have goals for the conference. It is important that you understand how parents perceive their children.

12. Don't become defensive when parents question your instructional approach or classroom policies. Many parents think they know what should be done in the classroom and disagree with how a teacher conducts her class. Give the parents plenty of time to air their concerns. If appropriate, tell them that you will consider their criticisms and suggestions.

13. Never talk about another student. Often highly competitive parents want to compare their child to classmates. Avoid mentioning the other students. Some parents may also complain about other students. Listen to what they say and reassure them that you will give their child a safe and effective learning environment.

14. Do not use jargon. The purpose of the conference is to inform the parents about their child's progress, not impress them with your knowledge.

15. End the conference with specific goals. The goals should be attainable for the child and should be goals that the parents can help the child attain. Always thank parents for coming. It is important that parents go away with valuable information and a positive feeling about the child's classroom.

Communicating with parents is an important way to get and keep them interested and involved in their children's education.

PARENTAL INVOLVEMENT THAT MAKES A DIFFERENCE

When parents ask you what they can do at home to help their children, here are general suggestions and specific activities you may offer them.

General Suggestions to Share with Parents

First, effective parental home involvement includes having a distinct style of interacting with the child. Parents need to ask about their child's day: "What did you learn?" "What problems did you have in your subjects?" "What fun things did you do with your friends?" and "What problems did you have with classmates?" Parents need to listen attentively and provide encouragement. Second, parents should provide an emotionally supportive home environment. Children need to feel safe discussing anything without fear that their parents will become angry or stop listening. Third, parents need to provide reassurance when children encounter failure. When their children are having a difficult time with reading, writing, or spelling in school, parents should encourage them to practice, without resorting to pressure or ridicule. The parents' primary duty when it comes to education is helping their children understand that practice is necessary to become skillful in any task.

Boers (2002) collected a list of traits that teachers desire parents to have:

1. Parents who initiate communication about their child's learning style, personality, family arrangements, extracurricular activities, and perceived school problems.
2. Parents who monitor homework at home.
3. Parents who create a time and place for homework and work with their child's basic reading and writing skills.
4. Parents who value learning by allowing time for homework.
5. Parents who get involved by coming to family–teacher conferences, open houses, and other school activities.
6. Parents who discuss school matters with their child at home.
7. Parents who establish good student behavior by teaching respect, courtesy, patience, and clean language.
8. Parents who do not cover for their child.
9. Parents who respect teachers by encouraging them.
10. Parents who emphasize reading. They read with their child, to their child, and model reading for their child.
11. Parents who respond to notes promptly.
12. Parents who monitor their child's eating and sleeping habits and make sure the child comes to school clean.

Administrators can tactfully list such "Good Parenting Tips" in a newsletter that is sent home to all parents at the beginning of the year. Parents need to understand that when they perform these acts at home, they exert a positive impact on their child's education.

Suggestions for Establishing a Home–School Literacy Connection

Many parents appreciate specific advice on how to help their child become a successful reader. The following different strategies have proven to be successful based on completed studies by reading specialists, researchers, and teachers.

Reading together

Rasinski and Padak (2003, 2007) provide the following basic guidelines for teachers to help parents read with children at home or to have the children read to the parent.

1. Limit the time to 10–20 minutes; remember that parents are tired and very busy.
2. Give parents options, such as reading to the child, reading with the child, or listening to the child read.
3. Provide the texts or booklists.
4. Teach parents how to select books at the child's reading level. If a child comes across more than five words on one page that he/she cannot read, the text is too hard for independent reading.
5. Encourage all types of reading.
6. Send home audio versions of the books if parents are learning English.
7. Share one or two new strategies with parents so they stay motivated.

Recommend that parents do the following during a reading session:

1. First, the parent reads a passage to the child (or they both listen to an audio version) and then they discuss the story.
2. Parent and child read the passage in unison (or child reads along with the audio version).
3. Parent listens as the child reads the passage.
4. Parent and child choose words from the passage and write them on index cards.
5. They use these cards to play different word games such as concentration or word sorts. They can sort words according to syllables, word patterns, or by root words.
6. To help parents who have a limited number of books in the home and do not have access to the public library, send books home with students in a plastic or canvas bag. For parents who do not read English, you can include a portable CD/DVD player with audiobooks on disks.

It is important that parents and children read together at home; however, they do not need to limit themselves to stories (Rasinski & Padak, 2008). Here are suggestions for interacting with a variety of materials:

1. Read environmental print on billboards, specials in fast-food restaurants, labels on food items, and newspaper ads.
2. Read and write lists, such as recipes and birthday wish lists.
3. Read rhymes and poems and write their own version or a parody of one.
4. Sing songs and read the lyrics together. www.kids.niehs.nih.gov/music.htm includes many lyrics of children's songs.
5. Read parts of the newspaper together, such as the sports section, comics, the entertainment section, and ads from grocery stores. Play the word games found in newspapers.
6. Read mail together, including bills, so children learn how to read the amount due and the date that it is due.
7. Read from religious texts.
8. Read from song or hymnbooks.
9. Families with Internet access can visit word play sites.

Kindervater (2010) took Rasinski and Padak's suggestion about using poetry (see the chapter's opening scenario) and conducted a study to see if using poetry, chants, and songs would strengthen the home–school connection with kindergarten students. The home–school activity described in the study included the following steps:

1. Display a poem, song, or chant on a whiteboard or large poster so the class can read it a couple of times throughout the day.
2. Points to each word as you read it chorally with the class. This helps students learn directionality of reading and also learn to identify words.
3. Use kinesthetic motions that correspond to particular sounds of the consonants (Padak & Rasinski, 2008). For example, for the /t/ sound, the students put their index finger on their thumb as they would to indicate the OK gesture. When they hear the initial /t/ sound they quickly press their index finger to the thumb a couple of times and end with the index finger released from the thumb. Other consonant movements are explained in *Fast Start: Getting Ready to Read* (Padak & Rasinski, 2008).
4. After reading the poem using the kinesthetic motions, have each student take a copy of the

poem home and read it with her parents. The student gets to teach the parents the motions. Parents are encouraged to listen to their child read the poem, read the poem in unison, or do alternate readings in which the parent reads one line and the child reads the next.

Kindervater (2010) reported that 81 percent of the kindergarten students who did this activity with parents scored very well at the end of the year on their tests. Kindervater also reported that the parents really got involved and were excited to learn the new motions. Many reported that they would look for words in the environment and would say the word and do the motions; they found it a fun way to get their child excited about print.

Imperato (2009), a reading specialist, also used poetry to connect parents to the school. She suggested that teachers introduce a poem to the children on Monday, then send a copy home with students in an envelope with the general directions glued on the front and a parent-activity sheet glued on the back. On the activity sheet, parents record what activity they did with their child that evening and the amount of time they spent on the activity. The routine took about 10 to 15 minutes each evening. Imperato (2009) gave parents the following general directions:

1. Parent and child sit side by side so both can see the text.
2. Parent reads the poem two to four times as they point to each word.
3. Parent and child read the poem in unison two to four times, again pointing to the words.
4. The child reads the poem two to four times to the parent as the child points to each word.
5. Parent and child focus on a phonemic awareness or phonics activity. If the poem uses the rime /at/, the parent and child can find all the words in the poem that follow that pattern and then think of other words that come from that word family. If the poem has alliteration of the /s/, they can find all the /s/ words and then think of other words that begin with the /s/ sound.

Imperato (2009) found this activity brought good results in the first half year that the school implemented the routine. In January 66 percent of the students were nonreaders, while at the end of the year only 19 percent were nonreaders.

Summer reading programs

White and Kim (2008) were interested in connecting school to home by involving parents in their child's summer independent reading time. They believed that when students read for enjoyment, their reading skills, such as word recognition, fluency, vocabulary, world knowledge and comprehension, all improve. They also knew that maintaining students' motivation to read relied on providing them with books at their easy and independent reading levels. The summer program White and Kim (2008) started matched students with books at their reading level. Before the students left for summer break, they taught students some basic strategies to help them with comprehension as they read independently. They also taught parents how to listen and give positive feedback to their children regarding fluency. They were also prompted to ask their child to retell the story. At the end of the summer the students involved in the program had 1.3 additional months of school learning and their total reading scores on the Iowa Test of Basic Skills were higher than for students who were not involved in the program.

Students and parents were responsible for recording information about each book the student read on postcards. A copy of the postcard that White and Kim used is in Appendix D.32.

Traveling Tales

Another literacy activity for parents and children is Traveling Tales. Reutzel and Fawson (1990) designed Traveling Tales to promote writing at home. Teachers explain the process of Traveling Tales to the parents at Opening Night at the beginning of the year and give them a list of instructions. The teacher puts together a backpack or old briefcase of writing materials that travels from one student to the next. Each child receives the backpack for two nights. Figure 14.6 lists materials that should be included in the backpack.

In the Traveling Tales program parents are encouraged to write a story with their child using all of the steps of the writing process as follows:

1. The parent and child brainstorm ideas for a topic for a poem, skit, puppet play, recipe, or story.
2. They decide on the intended audience and begin to write the first draft. The draft focuses on content and not mechanics.
3. They read the passage and decide how to revise it. They are encouraged to add information, delete unnecessary material, to rearrange the material so it is easier for the reader to understand, and to look at word choice.
4. They read the second draft carefully to check for spelling and the other issues of writing mechanics. The final copy must be neat, clear, and accessible.
5. After the activity is completed, parents are invited to come to school and share the result with the class.

figure **14.6** Materials for Traveling Tales backpack.

Instructions and ideas	Stapler with staples	Unlined paper
Brass fasteners	Lined paper	Card stock paper
Various colors of construction paper	Hole punch	Drawing paper
Yarn	Poster paper	Wallpaper for book covers
Crayons	Glue sticks	Watercolors
Tape	Water-based markers	Ruler
Colored pencils	Letter stencils	Pencils
Paperclips	Felt-tip pens	Sticky notes
Plastic scissors	Examples of other books made by students	

Source: Reutzel, D. R., & Fawson, P. C. (1990). Traveling tales: Connecting parents and children through writing. *The Reading Teacher, 44,* 222–227. Reprinted with permission of the International Reading Association via Copyright Clearance Center.

Word study

Teachers can encourage word study by making word puzzles, sending them home and having the parents complete them with their children. Other game-like activities are listed in Chapter 4 (Phonemic Awareness), Chapter 6 (Word Identification), and Chapter 7 (Vocabulary Building). After you have introduced these activities to students, send examples home so they can play them with their parents. Children have the satisfaction of teaching their parents a new game! All of these activities reinforce literacy skills.

WORKING WITH DIFFICULT PARENTS

Teachers would be living in utopia if all parents were involved in their child's education and fully supported their schools. However, three types of parental approaches pose challenges for both seasoned and beginning teachers. They are (1) parents who do not seem to value education, (2) parents who seem highly critical of everything the teacher does, and (3) parents who seem not to accept that their child is struggling in reading or writing. The first group of parents appears to avoid responsibility for any aspect of their children's education. They may not seem to care if their child learns to read and write or if their child is in school at all. The parents in the second group may frequently be at school demanding the teacher's attention. They may often come at inappropriate times, such as in the middle of class instruction. In their eyes the teacher is almost always at fault, and they frequently blame the teacher for their child's poor progress. Parents in the third group are often highly educated and have high expectations for their child. They may not accept that their child has a difficult time with something as basic as reading and writing. All three groups of parents present different challenges.

Each of these parents is worthy of the teacher's respect. A teacher needs to remember the child when dealing with these parents. Every child deserves a fair education.

Parents Who Do Not Seem to Value Education

For students with this type of parent, provide as much extra help as possible in school because they are unlikely to receive any help at home. Pairing these students with an older, caring adult (either a retiree or a university student) or with a buddy from a middle school may help them see the importance of learning to read and write. Send home happy grams as often as possible so the parents come to see education in a more positive light. If the class presents puppet shows or readers theater for parents, encourage them to come see their child perform. Call these parents to schedule family–teacher conferences, encouraging them to come in and see the good work their child has completed. These parents need help changing their attitude about education; a positive teacher doing positive work can be just what they need.

Parents Who Seem Highly Critical

These parents present a totally different problem; they are negative and may attempt to control the teacher and the class. Giannetti and Sagarese (1998) present suggestions on how to transform these potential adversaries into educational partners:

1. Roll out the welcome mat when it is appropriate. When these parents come at inappropriate times, get out your calendar and ask them to schedule a time when you can give them your full attention.

2. Let them know you are an expert at what you do.
3. Show these parents a positive portrait of their children. Let them know that you too think their child has potential, but be honest!
4. Convey long-term goals you know you share with the parents. Plan with the parents some short-term goals that will help the child attain the long-term goals.
5. Reassure the parents that their child is in a physically and emotionally safe environment.
6. Be consistent.
7. Do not at any time make negative comments about other students. They will think you say negative things about their child to other parents.
8. Listen! Listen! Listen! They will eventually run out of steam!
9. Do not turn any conversation into a shouting match!
10. Ask the parents what they suggest you do with "the situation."

Parents Who Seem Not to Accept Their Child's Academic Difficulties

These parents frequently care a great deal for their child, involve him in many extracurricular activities, and set high goals for him. Use some of the same tactics here that you use with the aggressive parent:

1. Share with the parents the things that the child does well. Be positive about the child. Let them know that you too think their child has potential.
2. Be friendly, warm, consistent, and honest.
3. Never compare their child to another student in the class.
4. Never talk about another student.
5. Share honestly the concepts and skills with which their child struggles. Have examples of the child's work on hand to share with the parents. Your goal is to help them understand there are some skills that are difficult for their child. Convey that their goal is your goal: academic success for their child.
6. Let the parents know that with extra help from them and in class, the child will succeed.
7. With the parents, set long-term goals.
8. Also set short-term goals so that parents can see progress.
9. Send progress reports regularly to the parents.

Parents are right to expect that their child's teacher cares about their child and provides a safe learning environment in which every student can succeed.

COMMUNITY VOLUNTEERS

Teachers can involve other members of the community besides parents in the classroom. Many volunteers are retired persons who are interested in helping young children succeed or business leaders who understand the importance of reading for success in life. Successful volunteer tutors possess the fundamental characteristics presented in Figure 14.7 (Otaiba & Pappamihiel, 2005).

Volunteers who read to children should receive training from a reading specialist about effective reading techniques with students. First, they need to know how to model fluent, expressive reading so that the story comes alive for the listener. Reading specialists train volunteers by demonstrating expressive reading and "echo reading" (in which the tutee repeats the phrase or short sentence the volunteer has just read, using the same rate and intonation). Later the volunteers read to each other so they are comfortable reading with expression. Because students are introduced to new vocabulary words as they listen to stories, volunteers should learn how to prompt tutees to make guesses about the meaning of new words using picture and context clues. For example, when a tutee comes to an unknown word, he should be encouraged to read to the end of the sentence and ask, "Does the picture tell me what the word is? What word makes sense? Does that word sound right? Does it look right?"

Volunteers also need to be trained to encourage tutees to predict what will happen next in a story and how to discuss books without making the discussion seem like a quiz. For example, the following

figure **14.7**

Characteristics of effective volunteer tutors.

1. Meet state and district required background checks.
2. Have prior experience reading to children.
3. Be competent in the literacy skills they are to teach during tutoring (e.g., help children with graphophonic concepts and/or comprehension strategies) and be able to master skills taught during training.
4. Have positive attitudes about working with children of many cultures and backgrounds. (They must accept the child where he or she is.)
5. Be proficient in English if volunteers are second language learners.

Source: Otaiba, S., & Pappamihiel, N. E. (2005, July/August). Guidelines for using volunteer literacy tutors to support reading instruction for English language learners. *Teaching Exceptional Children, 37*(6), 6–11.

are two strategies that volunteers can use to help tutees make predictions. The first strategy involves discussing the cover illustration. The volunteer asks, "What do you think this book is about?" The tutee makes predictions based on the illustration. In the second strategy the volunteer and tutee preview the book by discussing all the pictures. While they discuss the pictures, the volunteer uses words that are found in the text. For example, while previewing the book *The Koalas,* from the Literacy 2000 Satellite series, the tutee may see a picture and predict that the koala is sleeping. While discussing how the koala is hanging in the tree, the volunteer uses the word *resting,* the word used in the text.

Discussions with tutees should evoke higher-level thinking. Volunteers need to be taught the difference between lower-level questions in which the answer is written on the page and higher-level questions that have no simple right or wrong answers. Volunteers need to understand the importance of having the student explain answers to higher-level questions, because sometimes the answers appear to be incorrect until they give their reasoning. Volunteers also need to encourage students to ask questions as they read stories and concept books. Volunteers do not diagnose reading problems nor do they provide instruction; however, they are important allies in students' literacy development. These volunteers' main goal is to provide enrichment experiences without emphasizing the diagnostic and intervention aspects of reading events. They accomplish this goal by supporting students as they read and by modeling good fluent reading. Research indicates that reading to students is positively related to children's reading success (Morrow, 2005; Kindervater, 2010; Padak & Rasinski, 2008; Imperato, 2009). As volunteers spend time listening to tutees read, they also teach them new words. They encourage tutees to work on expression, fluency, and rate by reading easy books. When a tutee reads a book that is at his or her instructional level, the volunteer and the tutee can read in unison so that the tutee does not struggle with unknown words. If possible, volunteers should record a tutee's reading and then listen to the recording with him or her, pointing out areas of improvement. This procedure permits students to evaluate their own reading. Volunteers provide encouragement and give struggling readers a chance to read without fear of being ridiculed by classmates.

Throughout this text, there are many game-like activities that build reading and writing skills. Volunteers can conduct these activities with tutees to make reading a more enjoyable experience for tutees. Reading specialists should explain how these activities build literacy skills so the volunteers understand their importance in helping a child learn to read.

CAREGIVER INVOLVEMENT AND TECHNOLOGY

Technology Nights

Many parents understand that computers are essential tools in the 21st century. Schools can share with parents what they are doing with computers. One event that can connect parents to the school is a technology night at the school (DuPont, 1998) in which parents come to see what their child can do on the computer. The children serve as teachers for the evening with the classroom teacher monitoring the activities. Present a sample of each student's writing and have the student demonstrate to his parents how he uses the word processor for revisions, adds clip art to his story, or creates PowerPoint presentations of his research. For parents who lack computer skills such a demonstration may be impressive. Parents who work on a computer daily will appreciate that their child is learning to use this important tool.

On a technology night, a younger child can demonstrate how she reads along with the computer. Using one of the many interactive books, the child can share how the computer helps her pronounce unknown words and how the computer gives her the definitions of words she does not know.

Technology Classes for Parents

Some schools are in neighborhoods where most parents do not have a computer at home. These schools can sponsor a technology class for parents on a Saturday morning or another time when most parents can attend. The instructor must know which computer programs are available to the parents in the public library so they can introduce those programs first. Then parents can go with their child to the library and use the computer together.

Technology in the Home

Teachers who work in neighborhoods where most households have computers may find it helpful to share educational websites with parents. Many authors of children's literature have websites featuring various types of activities that are age-appropriate for the author's readers. Many of these authors allow interested readers to subscribe to free e-mail newsletters through their websites. An activity in Chapter 11 includes a list of authors' websites.

Other educational websites are designed for home use. One such site is www.afterschool.gov. This site links to other enriching websites that reinforce skills and provide information about the world (Henkel, 2002).

Padak and Rasinski (2007) suggest teachers share the following websites with parents to assist them in choosing quality literature for their children.

American Library Association's site of notable children's books: www.ala.org/ala/mgrps/divs/alsc/awardsgrants/notalists/ncb/index.cfm.

Booklists by grade level: www.waterborolibrary.org

The IRA children's choice of books: www.reading.org/Resources/Booklists/ChildrensChoices.aspx

NEA teachers' top 100 books list: www.nea.org/grants/13154.htm

Carol Hurst's children's literature site: www.booksintheclassroom.com/allreviewed.php

The Horn Book's list of recommended books: www.hbook.com/resources/books/default.asp

The Children's Book Council book lists: www.cbcbooks.org/readinglists/

A comprehensive guide to English-language children's book awards: www.ucalgary.ca/~dkbrown/awards.html

Links to children's book lists compiled by public libraries nationwide: www.bookspot.com/readinglists/childrens.htm

The following sites focus on poetry. Some include poems to read, while others help children write poems.

www.gigglepoetry.com

www.poetry4kids.com

http://teacher.scholastic.com/writewit/poetry/index.htm

Encourage parents to explore these websites with their child. It gives them an opportunity to read, write, and learn together in an enjoyable setting. Parents are encouraged to share with the class appropriate websites they have found, but always check out these websites yourself before you pass them along to other teachers and parents. Be sure to publicly thank the parents who suggest the sites.

CONCLUDING THOUGHTS

Working with parents can be one of the most challenging pieces of the teaching puzzle. However, the benefits for children are great when parents become involved in their children's education at school and at home. Parents can be very helpful to teachers by offering ideas and resources. It is important to remember that parents and teachers share a common goal: they want the child to succeed in school and to remain a lifelong learner.

Reflective Learning PARENT VOLUNTEERS

Scenario. Ms. Green is a first-year, first-grade teacher who wants the parents of her students to be a part of their learning. At the open house during the second week of school, she encourages parents and caregivers to become involved with their children's learning at home and at school. She shares a list of things they can do with their children at home, such as provide a quiet space for reading and other homework, provide healthy snacks and meals, set a consistent bedtime, and talk to them about their school day.

Ms. Green also invites the parents to volunteer at school by organizing the classroom library, listening to children read, and copying learning materials. She is quite pleased when one mother comes up to her after the meeting and says she would love to volunteer in the classroom and would be there in the morning.

The first morning the mother helps out by organizing the bookshelves; by the afternoon she is talking to Ms. Green about her child's progress and what Ms. Green should do to help her son. Ms. Green wants to be friendly so she accepts the advice with a smile. But as the days progress the mother becomes more aggressive, insisting that Ms. Green treat her son differently by giving him extra help and not being as strict with him as she is with the others. Ms. Green does not know what to do, but she continues to take the advice with a smile and does give some extra help to the mother's son. Then one day Ms. Green discovers the mother in the teachers' lounge talking about Ms. Green's inadequacies. Of course, Ms. Green is crushed.

QUESTIONS:

1. What should Ms. Green do?
2. What could Ms. Green have done differently to avoid these complications?

APPENDIX A

RESOURCES

A.1 NCTE/IRA Standards for the Assessment of Reading and Writing 374

A.2 Commercial Informal Reading Inventories 377

A.3 Alphabet Books 377

A.4 Poetry Collections and Mother Goose Books 378

A.5 Wordless Books 379

A.6 Wordless (or Almost Wordless) Picture Books for Content Area Learning 379

A.7 Books with Rhyme, Phonograms, Alliteration, and Other Language Play 380

A.8 Suggested Bilingual English–Spanish Concept Books 381

A.9 Suggested Bilingual English–Spanish Narrative Picture Books 382

A.10 Suggested Multicultural Picture Books 382

A.11 Computer Programs for Developing Various Skills 383

A.12 E-Storybooks 384

A.13 Audio Chapter Books 385

A.14 Computer Programs That Promote Comprehension and Problem Solving 385

A.1 NCTE/IRA STANDARDS FOR THE ASSESSMENT OF READING AND WRITING

1. The interests of the student are paramount in assessment.

Assessment experiences at all levels, whether formative or summative, have consequences for students (see standard 7). Assessments may alter their educational opportunities, increase or decrease their motivation to learn, elicit positive or negative feelings about themselves and others, and influence their understanding of what it means to be literate, educated, or successful. It is not enough for assessment to serve the well-being of students "on average"; we must aim for assessment to serve, not harm, each and every student.

2. The teacher is the most important agent of assessment.

Most educational assessment takes place in the classroom, as teachers and students interact with one another. Teachers design, assign, observe, collaborate in, and interpret the work of students in their classrooms. They assign meaning to interactions and evaluate the information that they receive and create in these settings. In short, teachers are the primary agents, not passive consumers, of assessment information. It is their ongoing, formative assessments that primarily influence students' learning. This standard acknowledges the critical role of the teacher and the consequences and responsibilities that accompany this role.

3. The primary purpose of assessment is to improve teaching and learning.

Assessment is used in educational settings for a variety of purposes, such as keeping track of learning, diagnosing reading and writing difficulties, determining eligibility for programs, evaluating programs, evaluating teaching, and reporting to others. Underlying all these purposes is a basic concern for improving teaching and learning. In the United States it is common to use testing for accountability, but the ultimate goal remains the improvement of teaching and learning. Similarly, we use assessments to determine eligibility for special education services, but the goal is more appropriate teaching and better learning for particular students. In both cases, if improved teaching and learning do not result, the assessment practices are not valid (see standard 7).

4. Assessment must reflect and allow for critical inquiry into curriculum and instruction.

Sound educational practices start with a curriculum that values complex literacy, instructional practices that nurture it, and assessments that fully reflect it. In order for assessment to allow productive inquiry into curriculum and instruction, it must reflect the complexity of that curriculum as well as the instructional practices in schools. This is particularly important because assessment shapes teaching, learning, and policy. Assessment that reflects an impoverished view of literacy will result in a diminished curriculum and distorted instruction and will not enable productive problem solving or instructional improvement. Because assessment shapes instruction, the higher the stakes of the assessment, the more important it is that it reflect this full complexity.

5. Assessment must recognize and reflect the intellectually and socially complex nature of reading and writing and the important roles of school, home, and society in literacy development.

Literacy is complex, social, and constantly changing. The literacies of students graduating from high school today were barely imaginable when they began their schooling. Outside of school, students live and will go on to work in a media culture with practices unlike those currently occurring in school (even in the setting of the school media center). Students need to acquire competencies with word processors, blogs, wikis, Web browsers, instant messaging, listservs, bulletin boards, virtual worlds, video editors, presentation software, and many other literate tools and practices. Traditional, simple definitions of literacy will not help prepare students for the literate lives of the present—let alone the future. Consequently, reading and writing cannot usefully be assessed as a set of isolated, independent tasks or events. It is critical to gather specific information about materials, tasks, and media being used with students for both instructional and assessment purposes. In addition, we need to assess how practices are used to participate in the broader media culture as well as to examine how the broader culture assigns status to some practices over others (e.g., texting as contrasted to writing paragraph summaries in language arts class).

Whatever the medium, literacy is social and involves negotiations among authors and readers around meanings, purposes, and contexts. Literate practices are now rarely solitary cognitive acts. Furthermore, literate practices differ across social and cultural contexts and across different media. Students' behavior in one setting may not be at all representative of their behavior in another. This may be particularly true of English-language learners who may lack the fluency to express themselves fully inside the classroom but may be lively contributors in their families and communities.

6. Assessment must be fair and equitable.

We live in a multicultural society with laws that promise equal rights to all. Our school communities must work to ensure that all students, as different as they are in cultural, ethnic, religious, linguistic, and economic background, receive a fair and equitable education. Assessment plays an important part in ensuring fairness and equity, first, because it is intimately related to curriculum, instruction, and learning, and second, because assessment provides a seemingly impartial way of determining who should and who should not be given access to educational institutions and resources. To be fair, then, assessment must be as free as possible of biases based on ethnic group, gender, nationality, religion, socioeconomic condition, sexual orientation, or disability. Furthermore, assessment must help us to confront biases that exist in schooling.

7. The consequences of an assessment procedure are the first and most important consideration in establishing the validity of the assessment.

Tests, checklists, observation schedules, and other assessments cannot be evaluated out of the context of their use. If a perfectly reliable and comprehensive literacy test were designed but using it took three weeks away from children's learning and half the annual budget for instructional materials, we would have to weigh these consequences against any value gained from using the test. If its use resulted in teachers building a productive learning community around the data and making important changes in their instruction, we would also have to weigh these consequences. This standard essentially argues for "environmental impact" projections, along with careful, ongoing analyses of the consequences of assessment practices. Responsibility for this standard lies with the entire school community, to ensure that assessments are not used in ways that have negative consequences for schools and students. Any assessment procedure that does not contribute positively to teaching and learning should not be used.

8. The assessment process should involve multiple perspectives and sources of data.

Perfect assessments and perfect assessors do not exist. Every person involved in assessment is limited in his or her interpretation of the teaching and learning of reading and writing. Similarly, each text and each assessment procedure has its own limitations and biases. Although we cannot totally eliminate these biases and limitations from people or tests, we can try to ensure that they are held in balance and that all stakeholders are made aware of them. The more consequential the decision, the more important it is to seek diverse perspectives and independent sources of data. For example, decisions about placement in or eligibility for specialized programs have a profound influence on a student's life and learning. Such decisions are simply too important to make on the basis of a single measure, evaluation tool, or perspective.

9. Assessment must be based in the local school learning community, including active and essential participation of families and community members.

The teacher is the primary agent of assessment and the classroom is the location of the most important assessment practices, but the most effective assessment unit is the local school learning community. First, the collective experience and values of the community can offer a sounding board for innovation and multiple perspectives to provide depth of understanding and to counter individual and cultural biases. Second, the involvement of all parties in assessment encourages a cooperative, committed relationship among them rather than an adversarial one. Third, because language learning is not restricted to what occurs in school, assessment must go beyond the school curriculum.

The local school learning community is also a more appropriate foundation for assessment than larger units such as the school district, county, state, province, or country. These larger units do not offer the relational possibilities and commitments necessary for a learning community. The distance from the problems to be solved and among the participants reduces the probability of feelings of involvement and commitment and increases the possibility that assessment will become merely a means of placing blame.

10. All stakeholders in the educational community—students, families, teachers, administrators, policymakers, and the public—must have an equal voice in the development, interpretation, and reporting of assessment information.

Each of the constituents named in this standard has a stake in assessment. Students are concerned because their literacy learning, their concepts of themselves as literate people, and the quality of their subsequent lives and careers are at stake. Teachers have at stake their understandings of their students, their professional practice and knowledge, their perceptions of themselves as teachers, and the quality of their work life and standing in the community. Families clearly have an investment in their children's learning, well-being, and educational future. The public invests money in education, in part as an investment in the future, and has a stake in maintaining the quality of that investment. The stewardship of the investment involves administrators and policymakers. Assessment is always value laden, and the ongoing participation of all parties involved in it is necessary in a democratic society. When any one perspective is missing, silenced, or privileged above others, the assessment picture is distorted.

11. Families must be involved as active, essential participants in the assessment process.

In many schools, families stand on the periphery of the school community, some feeling hopeless, helpless, and unwanted. However, the more families understand their children's progress in school, the more they can contribute to that progress. If teachers are to understand how best to assist children from cultures that are different from their own, families are a particularly important resource. Families must become, and be helped to become, active participants in the assessment process.

A.2 COMMERCIAL INFORMAL READING INVENTORIES

Bader, L. A. (2009). *Bader Reading and Language Inventory and Graded Word List* (6th ed.). Upper Saddle River, NJ: Prentice Hall.

Burns, P. & Roe, B. (2007). *Informal Reading Inventory* (7th ed.). Boston: Houghton Mifflin.

Ekwall, H. & Shanker, J. (2010). *Ekwall–Shanker Reading Inventory* (5th ed.). Boston: Allyn & Bacon.

Flynt, E. & Cooter, R. (2004). *Flynt–Cooter Reading Inventory for the Classroom* (5th ed.). Upper Saddle River, NJ: Prentice Hall.

Johns, J. (2008). *Basic Reading Inventory: Pre-Primer Through Grade Twelve and Early Literacy Assessment* (10th ed.). Dubuque, IA: Kendall/Hunt.

Manzo, A., Manzo, U., & McKenna, M. (1999). *Informal Reading–Thinking Inventory*. New York: Harcourt Brace College Publishers.

Wheelock, W. & Silvaroli, N. (2008). *Classroom Reading Inventory* (11th ed.). New York: McGraw-Hill.

APPENDIX A

A.3 ALPHABET BOOKS

The following alphabet books are by Jerry Pallotta and Fred Stillwell. All are published by Charlesbridge Press.

The Airplane Book
Albertina and Arriba
The Bird Alphabet Book
The Boat Alphabet Book
The Butterfly Alphabet Book
Children from Australia to Zimbabwe
Crayon Count
The Desert Alphabet Book
The Dinosaur Alphabet Book
The Flower Alphabet Book
The Freshwater Alphabet Book
The Frog Alphabet Book
The Furry Animal Alphabet Book
Going Lobstering
The Icky Bug Alphabet Book
The Jet Alphabet Book
The Ocean Alphabet Book
The Spice Alphabet Book
The Underwater Alphabet Book
The Vegetable Alphabet Book
The Yucky Reptile Alphabet Book

The following is a partial list of the over 6,000 alphabet books found at www.amazon.com using the search term *alphabet books*.

A Is for Appalachia by L. Hager-Pack (2002). Louisville, KY: Harmony House.

A Mountain Alphabet by M. Ruurs and A. Kiss (1996). Toronto, Canada: Tundra Books.

A Swim Through the Sea by K. Pratt (1994). Dawn Publishing.

A Walk in the Rainforest by K. Pratt (1992). Nevada City, CA: Dawn.

ABC Book (Books of Wonder) by C. B. Falls and P. Glassman (2002). New York: Morrow Junior.

ABC I Like Me by N. Carlson (1999). New York: Puffin.

ABC3D by Marion Bataille (2010). New York: Roaring Brook Press.

ABCs of Wisconsin by D. Hillestad-Butler (2000). Black Earth, WI: Trails Books.

Alpha Bugs: A Pop-Up Book by D. Carter (1994). New York: Little Simon.

Alphabet Theme-A-Saurus: The Great Big Book of Letter Recognition by J. E. McKinnon and G. Bittinger (1991). Everett, WA: Warren Publishing House.

Animal ABC by P. Steward (1999). Mineola, New York: Dover.

Animalia by G. Base (1987). New York: Abrams Books for Young Readers.

Anno's Alphabet: An Adventure in Imagination by M. Anno (1987). New York: HarperCollins.

Barney's ABC, 123 and More by G. Davis and D. McKee (1999). Lyrick Publishers.

Birding Montana: A Falcon Guide by T. McEneaney (1993). Guildford, CT: Falcon.

Black and White Rabbit's ABC by A. Baker (1999). Boston: Larousse Kingfisher Chambers.

Chicka Chicka Boom Boom by J. Archambualt (2000). New York: Aladdin Library.

Dr. Seuss's ABC (I Can Read by Myself) by Dr. Seuss (1963). New York: Random House.

Journey Around Boston from A to Z by M. Zschock (2001). Beverly, MA: Commonwealth Editions.

Journey Around Cape Cod and the Islands from A to Z by M. Zschock (2001). Beverly, MA: Commonwealth Editions.

Journey Around New York from A to Z by M. Zschock (2002). Beverly, MA: Commonwealth Editions.

Mr. Paint Pig's ABC's by R. Scarry (2002). New York: Random House.

My Whole Food ABC's by D. Richard (1997). Bloomingdale, IL: Vital Health Publishing.

Navajo ABC: A Dine Alphabet Book by L. Tapahonso and E. Schick (1999). B+ Bound.

Parading with Piglets: An ABC Pop-Up by B. Akerberge-Hansen (1996). Peterborough, New York: National Geographic.

Q Is for Quark by David M. Schwartz (2009). New York: Tricycle Press.

Robert Crowther's Most Amazing Hide-And-Seek Alphabet Book by R. Crowther (1999). Cambridge, MA: Candlewick Press.

The Alphabet Book by P. Eastman (2000). New York: Random House.

The Alphabet Mouse Books by M. Felix (1994). Creative Editions.

The Alphabet Tree by L. Lionni (1990). New York: Knopf.

The Amazing Alphabet Maze Book by P. Baldus (2002). Los Angeles: Price Stern Sloan.

The Amazing I Spy ABC by K. Laidlaw (1996). New York: Dial Books for Young Readers.

The Graphic Alphabet by D. Pelletier (1996). New York: Orchard Books.

The Hidden Alphabet by Laura Vaccaro Seeger (2010). New York: Roaring Brook Press.

The Secret Code by D. Meachen-Rau (1998). San Francisco: Children's Press.

Z is for Zamboni: A Hockey Alphabet by M. Napier (2002). Chelsea, MI: Sleeping Bear Press.

A.4 POETRY COLLECTIONS AND MOTHER GOOSE BOOKS

A Hippopotamusn't by J. P. Lewis (1990). New York: Trumpet Club.

A Light in the Attic by S. Silverstein (1981). New York: HarperCollins.

A Pizza the Size of the Sun by J. Prelutsky (1994). New York: Greenwillow Books.

Falling Up by S. Silverstein (1996). New York: HarperCollins.

I Can Draw a Weeposaur and Other Dinosaurs by E. Greenfield (2001). New York: Greenwillow Books.

If Pigs Could Fly . . . and Other Deep Thoughts by B. Lansky (2000). New York: Meadowbrook.

Miles of Smiles: Kids Pick the Funniest Poems, Book #3 edited by B. Lansky (1998). New York: Meadowbrook.

My Tooth Ith Loothe: Funny Poems to Read Instead of Doing Your Homework by G. Ulrich (1995). New York: Bantam Doubleday Dell Books.

Noisy Poems collected by J. Bennett (1987). Oxford, New York: Oxford University Press.

Ready . . . Set . . . Read! Compiled by J. Cole and S. Calmenson (1990). New York: Doubleday.

Side by Side: Poems to Read Together collected by L. Bennett Hopkins (not dated). New York: Trumpet Club Special Edition.

Sing a Song of Popcorn selected by B. Schenk de Regniers, E. Moore, M. Michaels White, and J. Carr (1988). New York: Scholastic.

Something Big Has Been Here by J. Prelutsky (1990). New York: Greenwillow Books.

Spooky Riddles by Marc Brown (1983). New York: Random House.

Sylvia Longs' Mother Goose collected and illustrated by S. Long (1999). San Francisco, CA: Chronicle Books.

The Book of Pigericks by A. Lobel (1983). New York: Harper & Row.

The New Kid on the Block by J. Prelutsky (1984). New York: Greenwillow Books.

The Random House Book of Poetry for Children: A Treasury of 572 Poems for Today's Children selected by J. Prelutsky (1983). New York: Random House.

The Real Mother Goose collected and illustrated by B. Fisher Wright (1916). New York: Checkerboard Press.

The 20th Century Children's Poetry Treasury selected by J. Prelutsky (1999). New York: Alfred A. Knopf.

Tomie dePaola's Book of Poems collected by T. dePaola (1988). New York: Putnam's Sons.

Treasury of Poetry selected by A. Hedley (2000). Bath, UK: Parragon Publishing.

Where the Sidewalk Ends by S. Silverstein (1974). New York: HarperCollins.

Zoo Doings: Animal Poems by J. Prelutsky (1983). New York: Trumpet Club.

A.5 WORDLESS BOOKS

A Boy, A Dog, and A Frog by M. Mayer (1967). New York: Dial.

Ah-Choo! by M. Mayer (1976). New York: Dial.

Amanda and the Mysterious Carpet by F. Krahn (1985). New York: Clarion Books.

Ben's Dream by C. Van Allsburg (1982). Boston: Houghton Mifflin.

Carl's Afternoon in the Park by A. Day (1991). New York: Green Tiger.

Clown by Q. Blake (1996). New York: Holt.

Deep in the Forest by B. Turkle (1976). New York: Dutton.

Do You Want to Be My Friend? by E. Carle (1971). New York: Putnam.

The Flower Man by M. Ludy (2005). Windsor, CO: Green Pastures Pub.

Free Fall by D. Wiesner (1988). New York: Clarion.

Frog Goes to Dinner by M. Mayer (1974). New York: Dial.

Frog on His Own by M. Mayer (1973). New York: Dial.

Frog, Where Are You? by M. Mayer (1969). New York: Dial.

Good Dog, Carl by A. Day (1985). New York: Farrar, Straus & Giroux.

Junglewalk by N. Tafuri (1988). New York: William Morrow.

Mouse Around by P. Schories (1991). New York: Farrar, Straus & Giroux.

Noah's Ark by P. Spier (1977). New York: Doubleday.

Pancakes for Breakfast by T. dePaola (1978). New York: Harcourt Brace.

ReZoom by I. Banyai (1995).

Sector 7 by D. Wiesner (1997). New York: Clarion.

The Bear and the Fly by P. Winter (1976). New York: Crown.

The Grey Lady & the Strawberry Snatcher by M. Bang (1980). New York: Four Winds.

The Hunter and the Animals by T. dePaola (1981). New York: Holiday.

The Patchwork Farmer by C. Brown (1989). New York: Greenwillow.

The Snowman by R. Briggs (1978). New York: Random House.

The Swan by V. Mayo (1994). Haupauge, NY: Barron's Educational Series.

The Three Pigs by D. Wiesner (2001). New York: Clarion.

The Yellow Umbrella by H. Drescher (1987). New York: Atheneum.

Tuesday by D. Wiesner (1991). New York: Clarion.

Where's My Monkey? by D. Schubert (no date). New York: Dial.

Zoom by I. Banyai (1995). New York: Puffin.

A.6 WORDLESS (OR ALMOST WORDLESS) PICTURE BOOKS FOR CONTENT AREA LEARNING

Anno, M. (1978). *Anno's Journey*. Cleveland, OH: Collins-World.

Anno, M. (1980). *Anno's Italy*. New York: Harper-Collins.

Anno, M. (1983). *Anno's U.S.A.* New York: Philomel Books.

Anno, M. (2004). *Anno's Spain*. New York: Philomel Books.

Baker, J. (1991). *Window*. New York: Greenwillow Books.

Blake, Q. (2003). *Tell Me a Picture*. Brookfield, CT: Millbrook Press.

Collington, P. (1987). *The Angel and the Soldier Boy*. New York: Knopf.

dePaola, T. (1979). *Flicks*. San Diego, CA: Harcourt Brace.

Feelings, T. (1995). *The Middle Passage: White Ships/ Black Cargo*. New York: Dial Books.

Goodall, J. (1976). *An Edwardian Summer*. New York: Atheneum.

Goodall, J. (1986). *The Story of a Castle*. New York: M. K. McElderry Books.

Goodall, J. (1987). *The Story of a Main Street*. New York: Macmillan.

Goodall, J. (1990). *The Story of the Seashore*. New York: M. K. McElderry Books.

Gurney, J. (1998). *Dinotopia: A Land Apart from Time*. New York: HarperCollins.

Lehman, B. (2006). *Museum Trip*. Boston: Houghton Mifflin.

Oakley, G. (1980). *Graham Oakley's Magical Changes*. New York: Atheneum.

Raczka, B. (2006). *Unlikely Pairs: Fun with Famous Works of Art*. Minneapolis, MN: Millbrook Press.

Rockhill, D. (2005). *Ocean Whisper/Susurro del Oceano*. (E. de la Vega, Trans.). Green Bay, WI: Raven Tree Press.

Rohmann, E. (1995). *Time Flies*. New York: Scholastic.

Spier, P. (1977). *Noah's Ark*. Garden City, NY: Doubleday.

Van Allsburg, C. (1984). *The Mysteries of Harris Burdick*. Boston: Houghton Mifflin.

Vincent, G. (2000). *A Day, a Dog*. New York: Front Street.

Wiesner, D. (1988). *Free Fall*. New York: Lothrop, Lee & Shepard.

Wiesner, D. (1997). *Sector Seven*. New York: Clarion Books.

A.7 BOOKS WITH RHYME, PHONOGRAMS, ALLITERATION, AND OTHER LANGUAGE PLAY

A B C by Dr. Seuss (1963). New York: Beginner Books.

A Fly Went By (In *The Big Blue Book of Beginner Books*) by M. McClintock (1994). New York: Random House.

A Giraffe and a Half by S. Silverstein (1964). New York: HarperCollins.

A Hippopotamusn't by J. P. Lewis (1990). New York: Trumpet Club.

A Summery Saturday Morning by M. Mahy (1998). New York: Puffin.

Alphabears: An ABC Book by K. Hague (1984). New York: Henry Holt.

Bears in Pairs by N. Yektai (1987). New York: McClanahan.

Carrot/Parrot by J. Martin (1991). New York: Trumpet Club.

Daisy-Head Mayzie by Dr. Seuss (1994). New York: Beginner Books.

Four Famished Foxes and Fosdyke by P. D. Edwards (1995). New York: HarperCollins.

Fox in Socks by Dr. Seuss (1963). New York: Beginner Books.

Frog Went A-Courting by J. Langstaff (1966). San Diego, CA: Voyager Books.

Going to Sleep on the Farm by W. C. Lewison (1992). New York: Trumpet Club.

Good-Night Moon by M. W. Brown (1947). New York: Harper & Row.

Green Eggs and Ham by Dr. Seuss (1960). New York: Beginner Books.

Guess How Much I Love You by S. McBratney (1994). New York: Scholastic.

I Know an Old Lady Who Swallowed a Fly retold by N. Westcott (1980). Boston: Little Brown.

I Know an Old Woman Who Swallowed a Pie by A. Jackson (1997). New York: Scholastic.

I Read With My Eyes Shut by Dr. Seuss (1978). New York: Beginner Books.

If You Were My Bunny by K. McMullan (1996). New York: Scholastic.

In the Haunted House by E. Bunting (1990). New York: Trumpet Club.

Is Your Mama a Llama? by D. Guarino (1989). New York: Scholastic.

It's the Bear by J. Alborough (1994). New York: Scholastic.

Jamberry by B. Degen (1983). New York: HarperCollins.

Jesse Bear, What Will You Wear? by N. W. Carlstrom (1986). New York: Aladdin Paperbacks.

Miss Spider's New Car (Board Book) by D. Kirk (1999). New York: Scholastic.

Mitten/Kitten by J. Martin (1991). New York: Trumpet Club.

"Not Now" Said the Cow by J. Oppenheim (1989). New York: Bantam Little Rooster Books.

Oh, the Places You'll Go by Dr. Seuss (1990). New York: Beginner Books.

Oh, the Things You Can Count by Dr. Seuss (1995). New York: Scholastic.

Oh, the Thinks You Can Think by Dr. Seuss (1975). New York: Beginner Books.

One Fish Two Fish Red Fish Blue Fish by Dr. Seuss (1960). New York: Beginner Books.

One Green Frog by Y. Hooker (1981). New York: Grosset and Dunlap.

Pigs Aplenty, Pigs Galore! by D. McPhail (1993). New York: Scholastic.

Put Me in the Zoo by R. Lopshire (1960). New York: Random House.

Rachel Fister's Blister by A. MacDonald (1990). Boston: Houghton Mifflin.

Ready . . . Set . . . Read! compiled by J. Cole and S. Calmenson (1990). New York: Doubleday.

Sheep in a Jeep by N. Shaw (1986). New York: Houghton Mifflin.

Sheep Out to Eat by N. Shaw (1992). New York: Trumpet Club.

So Many Bunnies by R. Walton (1998). New York: Lothrop Lee & Shepard Books.

Some Smug Slug by P. D. Edwards (1996). New York: HarperCollins.

The Book of Pigericks by A. Lobel (1987). New York: HarperCollins.

The Brand New Kid by K. Couric (2000). New York: Doubleday.

The Cat in the Hat by Dr. Seuss (1957). New York: Beginner Books.

The Cat in the Hat Comes Back by Dr. Seuss (1958). New York: Beginner Books.

The Itsy Bitsy Spider retold by I. Trapani (1993). New York: Scholastic.

The Roly-Poly Spider by J. Sardegna (1994). New York: Scholastic.

There's a Bug in My Mug by K. Salisburg (1997). New York: McClanahan.

There's a Wocket in My Pocket by Dr. Seuss (1974). New York: Beginner Books.

This Old Man retold by P. Adams (1974). Singapore International Ltd: Child's Play.

Today I Feel Silly and Other Moods That Make My Day by J. L. Curtis (1998). New York: HarperCollins.

Twinkle, Twinkle, Little Star illustrated by S. Long (2001). New York: Scholastic.

When the Fly Flew In . . . by L. W. Peters. (1994). New York: Trumpet Club.

Who Is the Beast? by K. Baker (1993). New York: Trumpet Club.

Zin! Zin! Zin! A Violin by L. Moss (1995). New York: Scholastic.

APPENDIX A

A.8 SUGGESTED ENGLISH–SPANISH BILINGUAL CONCEPT BOOKS

The first 20 books listed are by Gladys Rosa-Mendoza, published by Me+Mi Publishing, since 2000.

The Alphabet/El alfabeto
Numbers 1 2 3/Los numeros 1 2 3
Colors and Shapes/Los colores y las figures
My Family and I/Mi familia y yo
Opposites/Opuestos
The Weather/El tiempo
What Time Is It?/Que hora es?
My Body/Mi cuerpo
Jobs Around My Neighborhood/Oficios en mi vecindario
Fruits and Vegtables/Frutas y vegetales
I can!/iYo puedo!
When I am/Cuando estoy
Cars, Truck and Planes/Carros, camions y aviones
My Clothes/Mi ropa
Lupe Lupita, Where Are You?/Lupe Pupita donde estas?
It's My Birthday!/Es mi cumpleanos!
My House/Mi casa
I Live Here! I Yo vivo aqui!
Lola
Animals at the Farm/Animales de la granja

Cisneros, S. (1997). *Hairs/Pelitos.* Dragonfly Books.

Flor Ada, A. (1997). *Gathering the Sun: An Alphabet in Spanish and English.* Rayo Publishing. (Using the Spanish alphabet, each letter is a poem about Mexican farmers and their families.)

Garza, L. (1990). *Family Pictures/Cuadros de Familia.* Children's Book Press.

Lomas Garza, C. (2000). *In My Family/En Mi Familia.* Children's Book Press.

A.9 SUGGESTED BILINGUAL SPANISH–ENGLISH NARRATIVE PICTURE BOOKS

Ehlert, L. (2000). *Cuckoo.* New York: Voyager. A tale with a moral: You can't tell much about a bird by looking at its feathers.

Ehlert, L. (1996). *Moon Rope.* New York: Voyager. A Peruvian tale of a fox and a mole trying to climb to the moon on a rope woven of grass.

Gonzalez, L. M. (1994). *The Bossy Gallito.* New York: Scholastic. A traditional Cuban folktale.

Herrera, J. F. (2000). *The Upside Down Boy.* San Francisco: Children Book Press. A young Hispanic boy adjusts to an Anglo school.

Mora, P. (2001). *Listen to the Desert.* New York: Clarion. A repetitive text in which all lines by a coyote, an owl, a dove, a toad, a snake, a fish, mice, and rain give their sound. The lines are repeated twice in English and twice in Spanish.

Moroney, (1998). *Baby Rattlesnake.* San Francisco: Children's Book Press. Baby rattlesnake who lives in the desert cries constantly because he does not have a rattle.

Perez, A. I. (2000). *My Very Own Room.* San Francisco: Children's Book Press. A young girl wants her own space in her home so she can read books.

Perez, A. I. (2002). *My Diary from Here to There.* San Francisco: Children's Book Press. Each entry is a little girl's true emotions about leaving her beloved Mexico. This is based on the author's life experience. The family finally gets the green cards so they can join the father.

Perez, K. (2002). *First Day in Grapes.* New York: Lee & Low. Chico is about to begin his first day in Grapes—his fourth school. He stands up to some bullies and succeeds in other ways that make him sure he will like his days in Grapes.

Rohmer, H. (1993). *Uncle Nacho's Hat.* San Francisco: Children's Book Press. A Jamaican folktale about Nacho, who wears a hat full of holes.

Soto, G. (1993). *Too Many Tamales.* New York: G. P. Putnam's Sons. As part of the story, it explains how tamales are made.

Zubizarreta, R. (1994). *The Woman Who Outshone The Sun.* San Francisco: Children's Books Press. A Mexican folktale.

A.10 SUGGESTED MULTICULTURAL PICTURE BOOKS

Bunting, E. (2001). *Jim Woo.* New York: Clarion Books. The first page lets readers see that the narrator is not happy like his parents are about the arrival of the new adopted baby from Korea.

Cheng, A. (2000). *Grandfather Counts.* New York: Lee & Low. On the title page readers see two sheets of paper, one with Helen spelled five times, the other with Helen written in Chinese. The beginning of the book has a glossary with Chinese words, the Chinese characters, the pronunciation, and the English word.

Demi. (1990). *The Empty Pot.* Boston: New York: Henry Holt. A folktale about a boy who has a magical touch with flowers and about how his honesty is rewarded.

Heo, Y. (1996). *The Green Frogs: A Korean Folktale.* Houghton Mifflin. Korean children will recognize this tale from their homeland.

Pak, S. (1999). *Dear Juno.* New York: Viking. The narrator receives a letter from his grandmother written in Korean; the boy doesn't speak Korean but finds a way to communicate with his grandmother, who doesn't speak English.

Park, L. S. (2005). *Bee-bim Bop!* New York: Clarion Books. Park introduces preschoolers to culinary culture of Korea.

Recorbits, H. (2003). *My Name Is Yoon.* New York: Frances Foster Books/Farrar, Straus & Giroux. A story about Yoon, who comes from Korea and longs to go back to Korea. She does not like how her name, which means Shining Wisdom, looks in English—in Korean "The symbols dance together."

Say, A. (1997). *Allison.* Boston: Houghton Mifflin. When Allison receives a Kimono from her grandmother and looks into the mirror with her parents in the background, she realizes that they are not her "real" parents.

Simond, N. (2002). *Moonbeams, Dumplings and Dragon Boats.* Fairbanks, AK: Gulliver Books. Explains Chinese holidays and includes Chinese tales.

Stickler, J. (2003). *Land of Morning Calm: The Korean Culture Then and Now.* Walnut Creek, CA: Shen's Books. A picture book written for grades 5–8 about the history and politics of Korea. Each chapter's title is written using the Korean alphabet.

Tan, A. (2001). *Sagwa, the Chinese Siamese Cat.* New York: Aladdin. A folktale of a mother cat telling a story of her Chinese ancestry.

Touba, J. (1998). *Lisa Lin's Painting "Making Mooncakes."* New York: Powerkids Press. This Taiwanese artist describes her paintings of her family making mooncakes.

Yang, B. (2004). *Hannah Is My Name.* Cambridge, MA: Candlewick Press. The book's art is Chinese-influenced. The narrator is concerned that her name in the United States, Hannah, doesn't sound at all like her Chinese name, Na-Li, which means *beautiful.* She describes her feeling as her family waits for green cards.

A.11 COMPUTER PROGRAMS FOR DEVELOPING VARIOUS SKILLS

IDENTIFYING UPPERCASE AND LOWERCASE LETTERS OF THE ALPHABET

1. *I Spy Junior* (riddle section)
2. *Kidspiration* (reading and writing section)

PHONEMIC AWARENESS

1. *Kidspiration* ("Initial Me" permits students to place first initial and last letter of name in two boxes and then identify symbols with those beginning sounds.)
2. *I Spy School Days* ("Wood Block City" and "Chalkboard" use riddles to promote listening to the sounds in rhyming words.)

PHONICS

1. *Kidspiration* ("Alphabet Examples" has activities to match beginning sounds with letters.)
2. *I Spy School Days* ("Code Breaker" has activities to match beginning and ending sounds with letters.)

WORD IDENTIFICATION

1. E-books (See Appendix A.12.)
2. *I Spy School Days* ("Wood Block City" helps students to develop visual discrimination of words and to increase visual memory.)
3. *Inspiration* ("Vocabulary Template" permits students to build words with root word, prefixes, and suffixes.)
4. *I Spy Spooky Mansion* ("Mystery Bins" promotes logical- and creative-thinking skills in developing strategies to identify words.)

VOCABULARY BUILDING

1. *Kidspiration* (Students can create personal dictionaries.)
2. *Stories and More: Animal Friends* ("Gunnywolf" and "Trek Map" focus on vocabulary building.)
3. *I Spy School Days* ("Code Breaker" and "Chalkboard" have activities to assist vocabulary building.)
4. *Inspiration* ("Vocabulary Template" has synonyms, antonyms, and homonyms; this template also gives students an opportunity to create personal dictionaries.)
5. *I Spy School Days* ("Make Your Own I Spy" gives students an opportunity to write riddles using synonyms, antonyms, and homonyms.)

WRITING

1. *Kidspiration* (Students can create graphic web for main topic and supporting details; "Duckling Journey" is a template for creating personal stories.)
2. *Stories and More: Animal Friends* ("My Thoughts" gives opportunity for student to retell story and write personal reflections.)
3. *Stories and More: Time and Place* ("Galimoto" is a pen pal activity.)

COMPREHENSION

1. E-books (See Appendix A.12.)
2. *Stories and More: Animal Friends* ("My Thoughts" permits students to retell the story and write personal connections.)
3. *I Spy Junior* ("Puppet Maker," "The Gunnywolf," and "Owl and the Moon" develop listening skills in sequencing.)
4. *Kidspiration* ("Duckling's Journey" permits students to write their own stories.)
5. *Stories and More: Time and Place* ("House on Maple Street" has sequencing activities. The "Thinking About" part of each story is an activity that focuses on reinforcing the content of the story. All stories in this program have activities for students to make predictions, based on clues.)

A.12 E-STORYBOOKS

LIVING BOOKS SERIES BY BRODERBUND

101 Dalmatians
An American Tail
Ariel's Story Studio
Arthur's Birthday
Arthur's Computer Adventure
Arthur's Teacher Trouble
Berenstein Bears Collection
Dr. Seuss' The Cat in the Hat
Dr. Seuss' Green Eggs and Ham
D. W.: The Picky Eater
Harry and the Haunted House
Imo and the King
Just Grandma and Me
Just Me and My Day
Just Me and My Grandpa
Just Me and My Mom
Lion King
Little Golden Books, Sailor Dog
Little Monster at School
Mike Mulligan and His Steam Shovel
Pocahontas
Ruff's Bone
Stellaluna
The New Kid on the Block
The Tortoise and the Hare
Winnie the Pooh
Winnie the Pooh and Tigger Too

DISCIS BOOKS

A Long Hard Day on the Ranch
A Promise Is a Promise
Aesop's Fables
Anansi
Cinderella
Heather Hits Her First Home Run
Johnny Appleseed
Moving Gives Me a Stomach Ache
Mud Puddle
Northern Lights: The Soccer Trails
Paul Bunyan
Pecos Bill
Scary Poems for Rotten Kids
Somebody Catch My Homework
The Paper Bag Princess
The Tale of Benjamin Bunny
The Tale of Peter Rabbit
Thomas' Snowsuit

ANTELOPE PUBLISHING

The Tale of Peter Rabbit
The Tale of Jemima Puddle Duck
The Tale of Benjamin Bunny
The Tale of Squirrel Nutkin
The Rooster, the Mouse and the Little Red Hen
Grass Is Always Sweeter
Betty Bunny's Ballet Class
Tuff
The Pickle and the Watermelon Man Visit Sam
The Turtle and the Paint Box
Don't Bug Me
Hickory
Chitter and Chatter
The Tale of Brownie Beaver
A Child's Garden of Verse
Chimes and Rhymes
Old Mother Hubbard Nursery Rhymes and Jingles
Old Time Fairytales
Old Time Nursery Rhymes

A.13 AUDIO CHAPTER BOOKS*

A Year Down Yonder by R. Peck
Bud, Not Buddy by C. P. Curtis
Out of the Dust by K. Hesse
From the Mixed-up Files of Mrs. Basil E. Frankweiler by E. L. Konigsburg
A Wrinkle in Time by M. L'Engle
The Giver by L. Lowry
Shiloh by P. R. Naylor
Island of the Blue Dolphins by S. O'Dell
Missing May by C. Rylant
Holes by L. Sachar
Brian's Return by G. Paulsen
Joey Pigza Loses Control by J. Gantos
Call It Courage by A. Sperry
Charlotte's Web by E. B. White
The Cricket in Times Square by G. Selden
Ella Enchanted by G. Carson Levine
The Fledgling by J. Langton
Hatchet by G. Paulsen
A Long Way from Chicago by R. Peck
Ramona Quimby, Age 8 by B. Cleary
The Sign of the Beaver by E. George Speare
The Watsons Go to Birmingham–1963 by C. P. Curtis
Bloomability by S. Creech
The Boxcar Children by G. C. Warner
Bunnicula: A Rabbit Tale of Mystery by D. Howe
The Amber Brown Collection I & II by P. Danziger

*Available from Bantam Books.

APPENDIX A

A.14 COMPUTER PROGRAMS THAT PROMOTE COMPREHENSION AND PROBLEM SOLVING

SCHOLASTIC PUBLISHING

Oregon Trail, 5th ed. (Upper Elementary)
Road Adventures USA (Upper Elementary)
Playhouse Disney's the Book of Pooh: A Story Without a Tail (Ages 3–6)
Scooby Doo! Showdown in Ghost Town (Ages 5–10)
Zobooma Foo: Animal Kids (Ages 3–8)
I Spy Junior (Ages 3–6)
Reader Rabbit First Grade: Capers on Cloud Nine
Reader Rabbit Second Grade: Mis-cheese-ious Dreamship Adventure
I Spy Spooky Mansions (Ages 6–10)
My First Amazing World Explorer/USA (Ages 6–10)
Carmen San Diego (Ages 8–10)
Castle Explorer (Age 10–Adult)
I Spy Treasure Hunt (Ages 6–10)
Jump Start Animal Adventure (Ages 6–10)

JOURNEYED.COM

Harbor Town Games Master Guru (Based on New York State's Learning Standards for language arts, math, science, and social studies)
Encyclopedia of Endangered Wildlife (Grades 4–6)
Riverdeep Oregon Trail, 5th ed. (Grades 4–6)
Spark Space Kidspart (Grades 1–4)
Sunburst Imagination Express Destination: Castles (Grades 4–6)
Sunburst Make a Map 3D (Grades 4–6)
Kidspiration (Grades K–3)
Inspiration (Grades 4 and Up)
Interactive Garfield Typing Pal Deluxe (Grades 1–3)

APPENDIX B

LISTS AND GUIDES

B.1 Most Common Word Families 388

B.2 Vowel Diphthongs, Digraphs, and Variants with Examples and Utility of Each 391

B.3 Consonant Pronunciation Guide 392

B.4 High-Frequency Word List 394

B.5 Dolch Word Lists 395

B.6 The Fry Phrase Lists 396

B.7 Frequently Used Suffixes and Prefixes 399

B.8 Greek and Latin Word Roots with Definitions and Examples 400

B.9 Generalizations About Word Spellings 409

B.10 Complex Patterns of English Spelling 410

B.1 MOST COMMON WORD FAMILIES

AT	AN	AM	ALL	AND	AD
bat	ban	dam	ball	band	bad
cat	can	ham	call	hand	dad
hat	Dan	jam	fall	land	had
mat	fan	ram	hall	sand	lad
pat	man	clam	mall	brand	mad
rat	pan	cram	tall	grand	sad
sat	ran	gram	wall	stand	fad
brat	tan	slam	small	strand	pad
chat	van	swam	stall		glad
flat	clan	yam			
that	plan	wham			
	scan				
	than				

AG	AP	AB	AR	ART
bag	cap	cab	bar	cart
rag	lap	dab	car	dart
sag	map	jab	far	mart
wag	nap	nab	jar	part
brag	rap	lab	star	tart
flag	tap	tab		start
drag	clap	crab		chart
shag	flap	stab		smart
snag	slap	grab		
tag	trap	slab		
	snap			
	wrap			
	strap			

ACK	ASH	ANK	ELL	ET	ED
back	bash	bank	bell	bet	bed
jack	cash	sank	cell	get	fed
lack	dash	tank	fell	jet	led
rack	gash	yank	sell	let	red
sack	hash	blank	tell	met	bled
tack	mash	crank	well	net	fled
black	rash	drank	shell	pet	shed
crack	sash	plank	smell	set	sled
quack	crash	prank	spell	vet	shred
shack	clash	spank	swell	wet	
snack	flash	thank	dwell	yet	
stack	smash				
track	slash				
	trash				

APPENDIX B

EN	EG	EST	ECK	IT	IG
Ben	beg	best	deck	bit	big
den	peg	nest	neck	fit	dig
hen	leg	pest	peck	hit	fig
men	keg	rest	check	kit	pig
pen		test	speck	lit	rig
then		vest	wreck	pit	wig
when		west		sit	
wren				quit	
				skit	
				spit	

IN	ILL	IP	ING	INK	ICK
bin	bill	dip	king	link	kick
fin	dill	hip	ping	mink	lick
pin	fill	lip	ring	pink	pick
tin	kill	nip	sing	rink	sick
win	mill	rip	wing	sink	tick
chin	pill	sip	bring	wink	brick
grin	will	tip	cling	blink	chick
thin	chill	zip	fling	clink	flick
twin	drill	chip	sling	drink	quick
shin	grill	clip	sting	stink	stick
skin	skill	drip	thing	think	thick
spin	spill	flip	wring	shrink	trick
	still	ship	spring		
		skip	string		
		slip			
		trip			
		whip			

OT	OP	OG	OB	OCK	ONG
cot	cop	bog	cob	dock	bong
dot	hop	dog	gob	lock	gong
got	mop	fog	job	rock	long
hot	pop	hog	mob	sock	song
jot	top	jog	rob	tock	strong
lot	drop	log	sob	block	throng
not	flop	clog	blob	flock	
pot	shop	frog	glob	frock	
blot	slop		snob	shock	
knot	stop			smock	
plot					
shot					
slot					
spot					

UT	UB	UG	UM	UN	UNG
but	cub	bug	bum	bun	hung
cut	hub	dub	gum	fun	lung
gut	rub	hug	hum	gun	rung
hut	tub	jug	chum	run	sung
nut	club	mug	drum	sun	slung
rut	grub	rug	plum	spun	strung
shut	stub	tug	scum	stun	sprung
		drug			wrung
		slug			
		snug			
		plug			

UCK	UMP	UP	UFF
buck	bump	cup	buff
duck	dump	pup	cuff
luck	hump		huff
suck	jump		muff
tuck	lump		puff
yuck	pump		fluff
cluck	plump		
pluck	stump		
stuck	thump		
truck			

B.2 VOWEL DIPHTHONGS, DIGRAPHS, AND VARIANTS WITH EXAMPLES AND UTILITY OF EACH

VOWELS	EXAMPLES	UTILITY
aw	law	100%
oy	boy	98%
oi	oil	98%
ay	day	96%
ew	dew	95%
au	haul	94%
oa	road	94%
ee	fleet	86%
ai	rain	74%
oo	moon	59%
oo	foot	36%
ey	key (long /e/)	58%
ey	they (long /a/)	20%
ea	leaf (long /e/)	51%
ea	bread (short /e/)	26%
ie	chief (long /e/)	51%
ie	lie (long /i/)	17%
ie	ancient (schwa)	15%
ow	know (long /o/)	50%
ow	now (/ou/)	48%
ei	eight (long /a/)	40%
ei	receive (long /e/)	26%
ei	foreign (short /i/)	13%
ei	seismic (long /i/)	11%

B.3 CONSONANT PRONUNCIATION GUIDE

LETTER	FORMATION	COUNTERPART	OTHER SPELLINGS	OTHER SOUNDS	VOICED	VOICELESS
B Bat Cab	Lips are lightly pressed together. A puff of breath opens the lips to create sound.	P	silent in final position *(comb, lamb)*		+	
C Soft as in Cent	Edge of tongue touches toward top of mouth near upper teeth. Hissing sound comes when breath strikes teeth.	Z		/K/	+	
C Hard as in Cut	Back part of tongue is raised. Breath erupts through mouth.	/g	k	/s/		+
D Dog Bed	Front of tongue is in back of upper front teeth. Jaws are slightly open.	T			+	
F Fun Leaf	Lower lip is under upper teeth. Breath moves out between teeth and lower lips to create sound.	V	gh *(laugh)* ph *(phone)* lf *(half)* ft *(often)*	/v/ of		+
G Gate Dog	Back part of tongue is raised and pressed against lower part of front teeth.	/K/	gh *(ghost)* gue *(plague)* x *(excite)*	/j/ *(gym)* silent *(gnat)* ng *(sing)* gh = f *(rough)*	+	
H Hat	It is made with a simple breath.		silent *(heir)* *(ghost) (rhyme)* *(exhaust)*			+
J Jeep	Lips are slightly rounded, stick out. Teeth are together with tongue pressed against them.	ch	d *(educate)* di *(soldier)* dg *(bridge)* de *(grandeur)*		+	
K Keep Book	Back part of tongue is raised. Breath erupts through the mouth.	/g/	ck *(sock)* c *(cat)* q *(queen)* k *(except)*	silent when followed by n *(know)*		+
L Leaf Bail	Front of the tongue is behind the upper front teeth while allowing vibrating breath to emerge.	None	None	None	+	
M Milk Drum	Lips are lightly pressed together. Lips vibrate when breath passes through sinuses.		mb *(lamb)* lm *(calm)* mn *(column)*		+	

LETTER	FORMATION	COUNTERPART	OTHER SPELLINGS	OTHER SOUNDS	VOICED	VOICELESS
N Nut Run	Tongue is pressed tightly against upper teeth. Breath passes through sinuses.		gn (*gnat*) kn (*knee*) pn (*pneumonia*) mn (*mnemonic*)		+	
P Pet Soup	Lips are closed and pressed together. Sound comes when breath quickly passes through lips.	B	ph (*diphtera*)	silent when followed by *n, s, t* *ph* = /f/		+
Q Queen Bouquet	Back part of tongue is raised. Breath erupts through mouth.	/g/	always followed by u, except in *Iraq*	/kw/ (quite) /k/ (bouquet)		+
R Run Four	Tip of tongue is raised toward the top of mouth with jaw slightly open.		wr (*wren*) rhy (*rhythm*) rps (*corps*)		+	
S Sun Bus	Edges of tongue touch the jaws near the sockets of upper teeth. Hissing sound comes when breath strikes teeth.		c (*city*) ps (*psychology*) z (*waltz*)	/z/ (*dogs*) /sh/ (*sugar*) /zh/ (*pleasure*)		+
T Ten Tent	Mouth is slightly open. Tongue is pressed against inside of upper palate.	D	th (*thyme*) bt (*debt*) ed (*talked*) ght (*light*) tw (*two*) pt (*receipt*)	silent after *f & s* (*often, listen*) silent with quet (*bouquet*) ch (*natural*) sh (*question*)		+
V Van Five	Lower lip is slightly under the upper teeth.	F	f (*of*) ph (*Stephen*) lv (*half*)		+	
W We	Lips closed, but not pressed together. Vibrating the vocal chords produces sound.	Wh	ju (*marijuana*) ou (*Ouija*)	silent in *wr*	+	
Y Yo-yo	With teeth separated, sides of tongue are pressed against upper teeth.		i (*onion*) e (*azalea*) j (*hallelujah*)	/i/ (*fly*) /e/ (*happy*) ay (*day*) /i/ (*lymph*)	+	
Z Zip Quiz	Edges of tongue touch the jaws near sockets of the teeth.	S	s (*does*) ss (*scissors*) x (*xylophone*) sc (*discern*) cz (*czar*) si (*business*) sp (*raspberry*)	/s/ (*pretzel*)	+	

APPENDIX B

B.4 HIGH-FREQUENCY WORD LIST

about	don't	it	phone	they're
after	down	it's	play	thing
all	drink	joke	presents	this
am	each	jump	pretty	those
an	eat	junk	question	time
and	family	kick	rain	to
animal	father	know	ride	too
are	favorite	like	right	trip
as	first	line	run	truck
at	fly	little	said	two
be	for	long	sale	up
because	friend	look	saw	us
been	from	made	school	use
best	fun	mail	see	very
big	get	make	she	want
black	girl	many	sister	was
boy	give	me	slow	way
brother	go	more	skate	we
bug	good	mother	small	went
but	green	my	snap	were
by	gym	name	so	what
call	had	new	some	when
can	has	nice	sports	where
can't	have	night	stop	which
car	he	no	street	who
caught	her	not	talk	why
children	here	now	teacher	will
city	him	of	tell	with
clock	his	off	than	won
coat	house	old	thank	won't
come	how	on	that	would
could	hurt	one	the	write
crash	I	or	their	you
day	if	other	them	your
did	in	out	then	zoo
didn't	into	over	there	
do	is	people	they	

Source: From Cunningham, Patricia M., *Phonics They Use: Words for Reading and Writing*, 3rd Ed. Copyright © 2000, pp. 63, 94. Reprinted by permission of Pearson Education, Inc., Upper Saddle River, NJ.

B.5 DOLCH WORD LISTS

EASIER 110			HARDER 110		
a	go	over	about	hurt	small
after	going	play	again	just	start
all	good	put	always	keep	take
am	green	ran	any	kind	tell
an	had	red	ask	laugh	thank
and	has	ride	ate	let	that
are	have	round	because	light	their
around	he	run	been	live	them
as	help	said	before	long	then
at	her	saw	best	many	there
away	here	see	better	much	these
be	him	she	both	must	they
big	his	so	bring	myself	think
black	I	some	buy	never	those
blue	if	soon	clean	new	today
brown	in	stop	could	now	together
but	into	ten	cut	off	try
by	is	the	does	once	upon
call	it	this	done	only	us
came	its	three	draw	open	use
can	jump	to	drink	or	very
carry	know	too	eight	our	walk
cold	like	two	every	own	want
come	little	under	fall	pick	warm
did	look	up	far	please	wash
do	made	was	five	pull	were
down	may	went	found	read	when
eat	me	what	four	right	where
fast	my	who	full	say	which
find	no	will	gave	seven	white
fly	not	with	goes	shall	why
for	of	yellow	got	show	wish
from	old	yes	grow	sing	work
funny	on	you	hold	sit	would
get	one	your	hot	six	write
give	out		how	sleep	

Source: Basic Sight Vocabulary, *Elementary School Journal, 36,* 456–560. Published by the University of Chicago Press,

APPENDIX B

B.6 PHRASES AND SHORT SENTENCES FOR REPEATED READING PRACTICE (THE FRY PHRASE LISTS)

These phrases contain the words from the Fry Instant Word List (1980), which represent some of the most common words students encounter in their reading. The complete list of 300 words contains approximately two-thirds of all the words students encounter in their reading. Repeated reading of a few phrases per week gives students practice reading high-frequency words and developing fluency and general proficiency. These phrases may be written on sentence strips, transparencies, or a chart for use in a literacy center or small group instructional setting.

FIRST 100 WORDS

The people
By the water
You and I
He called me.
What did they say?
No way
One or two
More than the other
How many words?
This is a good day.
Sit down.
But not me
Not now
From my room
Will you be good?
Then we will go.
An angry cat
Write your name.
That dog is big.
Two of us
The first word
I like him.
Out of the water
We were here.
Could you go?
We like to write.
Into the water

Look for some people.
So there you are.
A long time
Have you seen it?
One more time
All day long
It's about time.
Up in the air
Which way?
He has it.
If we were older
It's no use.
With his mom
As big as the first
When will we go?
From here to there
More people
Go down.
Did you like it?
When did they go?
She said to go.
Each of us
What are these?
There was an old man.
It may fall down.
See the water
But not for me

Write it down.
Who will make it?
What will they do?
We had their dog.
When would you go?
A number of people
How long are they?
Come and get it.
Part of the time
Can you see?
Now and then
Go find her.
At your house
It's been a long time.
Give them to me.
Now is the time.
May I go first?
This is my cat.
Get on the bus.
Did you see it?
How did they get it?
Number two
Look up.
All or some
A long way to go
For some of your people
The other people

APPENDIX B

SECOND 100 WORDS

Over the river
After the game
Take a little.
Just the same
It's only me.
Think before you act.
Live and play.
Try your best.
Any old time
Study and learn
Mother means it.
The good American
A little boy
Back off.
We want to go.
Turn the page.
A small house also
It's still here.
Set it up.
I study in school.
I don't feel well.
Point it out.
Read the sentence.
Big and small
Such a big house
Show and tell
They went here.
Good and plenty
Even the animals
I think so.

A good man
Another great sound
Our best things
Only a little
That's very good
Three years ago
Where are you?
I work too much.
We found it here.
Right now
Spell your name.
Tell the truth.
Play it again.
We came home.
Answer the phone.
Form two lines.
Read my letters.
Write one sentence.
We need more.
Where does it end?
Such a mess
It turned out well.
It's a small world.
Hand it over.
Around the clock
A different land
Tell the truth.
Because we should.
It turned out well.
Good things

My new place
Most of the animals
Give it back.
My last name
I know why.
Mother says to now.
I need help.
Move over.
Through the line
Kind of nice
Same time tomorrow
Change your clothes.
The following day
Give it away.
Show us around.
The air is warm.
Another old picture
Where in the world
Put it there.
I'm an American.
My home is large.
Right now
This must be it.
Home sweet home
The men asked for help.
You must be right.
Get to the point.
Help me out.
It's your place.
Read the book.

THIRD 100 WORDS

Near the car	Stay a while.	Between the lines
A few good men	My own father	Don't open the door.
In the country	You might be right.	Add it up.
It seemed too good.	Read every story.	Along the way
Below the water	Next time	Plants and flowers
It's hard to open.	Will it last?	Something good
Keep it up.	For example	Plant the trees.
In the beginning	Light the fire.	Those other people
The light in your eyes	A group of friends	In my head
We got together	Under the earth	We left it here.
We saw the food.	Both children	Close the door.
It's my life.	The big city	Always be kind.
We started the fire.	Read the paper.	It never happened.
Run for miles.	A good thought	Once upon a time.
Do it often.	Is it really true?	We walked four miles.
It's time to eat.	Until the end	Let me carry it.
A second later	Near the sea	Stop the music.
Talk to my father.	Read your book.	The young face
Sing your song.	The long list	State your case.
My family	I miss you.	I cut myself.
A very important person	Above the clouds	On my side
Watch the game.	I took the car.	The peaceful Indians
So far so good.	Without a care	The young girl
I like being on the team.	My feet hurt.	The tall mountains
The dark night	Next to me	A good idea
A few children	It began to grow.	A long life
Watch the river.	A group of Indians	White clouds
He started to cry.	Too soon	I hear the sea.
Leave it to me.	An important idea	I hear the waves.
The first day of school	Almost enough	Almost four miles

B.7 FREQUENTLY USED SUFFIXES AND PREFIXES

SUFFIXES	COMMON MEANING	EXAMPLE
s, es	plural	boys, churches
ed	past tense	walked
ing	verb form/present participle	smiling
ly	characteristic of	quickly
er, or	person connected with	printer, editor
ion, tion	act, process	transportation
ation, ition	process of, condition of, result of	action
ible, able	can be done	edible
al, ial	having characteristics of	denial
y	characterized by	discovery
ness	state of, condition of	happiness
ity, ty	state of	responsibility
ment	action or process	management
ic	having characteristics of	heroic
ous, eous	possessing the qualities of	courageous
ious	full of	glorious
en	made of	forgotten
er	comparative	happier
ive, ative, itive	adjective form of noun	expensive
ful	full of	playful
less	without	helpless
est	superlative	homliest

PREFIXES	COMMON MEANING	EXAMPLE
un	not, opposite	unhappy
re	again	redo
in, im, ir, ill	not	impossible
dis	not, opposite of	disagree
en, em	cause to	encourage
non	not	nonliving
in, im	in or into	invade
over	too much	overzealous
mis	wrongly	mislead
sub	under	submerge
pre	before	prelude
inter	between, among	interstate
fore	before	foreground
de	opposite of	decompose
trans	across	transport
super	above	supercede
semi	half	semicircle
anti	against	antisocial
mid	middle	midway
under	too little	underweight

APPENDIX B

B.8 GREEK AND LATIN WORD ROOTS WITH DEFINITIONS AND EXAMPLES

ROOT	MEANING	EXAMPLES
acer, acid, acri	bitter, sour, sharp	acerbic, acidity, acrid, acrimony
acu	sharp	acute, acupuncture, accurate
ag, agi, ig, act	do, move, go	agent, agenda, agitate, navigate, ambiguous, action
ali, allo, alter	other	alias, alibi, alien, alloy, alter, alter ego, altruism
alt(us)	high, deep	altimeter, altitude
am, amor	love, liking	amiable, amorous, enamoured
anni, annu, enni	year	anniversary, annually, centennial
anthrop	man	anthropology, misanthrope, philanthropy
anti(co)	old	antique, antiquated, antiquity
arch	chief, first, rule	archangel, architect, archaic, monarchy, matriarchy, patriarchy, Archeozoic era
aster, astr	star	aster, asterisk, asteroid, astronomy, astronaut
aud, aus	hear, listen	audiology, auditorium, audio, audition, ausculate
aug, auc	increase	augur, augment, auction
auto, aut	self	automobile, autograph, automatic
belli	war	rebellion, belligerent, casus belli, bellicose
bibl	book	Bible, bibliography, bibliomania
bio	life	biology, biometrics, biome, biosphere
brev	short	abbreviate, brief
cad, cas	to fall	cadaver, cadence, cascade
calor	heat	calorie, caloric, calorimeter
cap, cip, cept	take	capable, intercept, forceps, capture, except, reciprocate
capit, capt	head	decapitate, capital, captain, caption
carn	flesh	carnivorous, incarnate, reincarnation, carnal
caus, caut	burn, heat	caustic, cauldron, cauterize
cause, cuse, cus	cause, motive	because, excuse, accusation
ced, ceed, cede, cess	move, yield, go, surrender	procedure, proceed, cede, concede, recede, precede, accede, success
cenetri	center	concentric, centrifugal, centripetal, eccentric
chrom	color	chrome, chromosome, polychrome, chromatic
chron	time	chronology, chronometer, synchronize
cide, cise	cut down, kill	homicide, exorcise, germicide, incision, scissors

ROOT	MEANING	EXAMPLES
cit	call, start	incite, citation, cite
civ	citizen	civic, civil, civilian, civilization
clam, claim	cry out	exclamation, clamor, proclamation, reclamation, acclaim
clud, clus, claus	shut	include, conclude, recluse, claustrophobia, occlusion, occult
cognoac, gnosi	know	recognize, prognosis, cognoscenti, incognito, agnostic
cord, cor, cardi	heart	cordial, concord, discord, courage, encourage
corp	body	corporation, corporal punishment, corpse, corpulent, corpus luteum
cosm	universe, world	cosmos, microcosm, cosmopolitan, cosmonaut
crat, cracy	rule	autocrat, aristocrat, theocracy, technocracy
crea	create	creature, recreation, creation
cred	believe	creed, credo, credence, credit, credulous, incredulous, incredible
cresc, cret, crease, cru	rise, grow	crescendo, concrete, increase, decrease, accrue
crit	separate, choose	critical, criterion, hypocrite
cur, curs	run	current, concurrent, concur, incur, recur, occur, courier, precursor, cursive
cura	care	curator, curative, manicure
cycl, cyclo	wheel, circular	Cyclops, unicycle, bicycle, cyclone, cyclic
deca	ten	decade, decalogue, decathlon, decahedron
dem	people	democracy, demography, epidemic
dent, dont	tooth	dental, denture, orthodontist, periodontal
derm	skin	hypodermic, dermatology, epidermis, taxidermy
dict	say, speak	dictation, dictionary, dictate, dictator, Dictaphone, edict, predict, verdict, contradict, benediction
doc, dokein	teach	doctrine, indoctrinate, document, dogma, dogmatic
domin	master	dominate, dominion, predominant, domain
don	give	donate, condone
dorm	sleep	dormant, dormitory
dox	opinion, praise	orthodox, heterodox, paradox, doxology
drome	run, step	syndrome (run together), hippodrome (place where horses run)
duc, duct	lead	induce, seduce (lead aside), produce, reduce

ROOT	MEANING	EXAMPLES
dura	hard, lasting	durable, duration, endure
dynam	power	dynamo, dynamic, dynamite, hydrodynamics
endo	within	endorse, endocardial, endoskeletal, endoskeleton, endosperm
equi	equal	equinox, equilibrium, equipoise
erg	work	energy, erg, allergy, ergometer, ergograph, ergophobia
fac, fact, fic, fect	do, make	factory, fact, manufacture, amplification, confection
fall, fals	deceive	fallacy, falsify, fallacious
fer	bear, carry	ferry, coniferous, fertile, defer, infer, refer, transfer
fid, fide, feder(is)	faith, trust	confidante, fidelity, confident, infidelity, infidel, federal, confederacy, semper fi
fila, fili	thread	filigree, filament, filter, filet, filibuster
fin	end, ended, finished	final, finite, finish, confine, fine, refine, define, finale
fix	fix	fix, fixation, fixture, affix, prefix, suffix
flex, flect	bend	flex, reflex, flexible, flexor, inflexibility, reflect, deflect
flu, fluc, fluv	flowing	influence, fluid, flue, flush, fluently, fluctuate
form	form, shape	form, uniform, conform, formulary, perform, formal, formula
fort, forc	strong	fort, fortress, fortify, forte, fortitude
fract, frag	break	fracture, infraction, fragile, fraction, refract
gam	marriage	bigamy, monogamy, polygamy
gastr(o)	stomach	gastric, gastronomic, gastritis, gastropod
gen	birth, race, produce	genesis, genetics, eugenics, genealogy, generate, genetic, antigen, pathogen
geo	earth	geometry, geography, geocentric, geology
germ	vital part	germination, germ, germane
gest	carry, bear	congest, gestation
gloss, glot	tongue	glossary, polyglot, epiglottis
glu, glo	lump, bond, glue	glue, agglutinate, conglomerate
grad, gress	step, go	grade, gradual, graduate, progress, graduated, egress
graph, gram	write, written	graph, graphic, autograph, photography, graphite, telegram
grat	pleasing	congratulate, gratuity, grateful, ingrate
grav	heavy, weighty	grave, gravity, aggravate, gravitate
greg	herd	gregarious, congregation, segregate, gregarian

ROOT	MEANING	EXAMPLES
hypn	sleep	hypnosis, hypnotherapy
helio	sun	heliograph, heliotrope, heliocentric
hema, hemo	blood	hemorrhage, hemoglobin, hemophilia, hemostat
here, hes	stick	adhere, cohere, cohesion, inherent, hereditary
hetero	different	heterogeneous, heterosexual, heterodox
homo	same	homogeneous, homonym, homogenize
hum, human	earth, ground, man	humus, exhume, humane
hydr, hydra, hydro	water	dehydrate, hydrant, hydraulic, hydraulics, hydrogen, hydrophobia
ignis	fire	ignite, igneous, ignition
ject	throw	deject, inject, project, eject, interject
join, junct	join	adjoining, enjoin, juncture, conjunction, injunction, conjunction
juven	young	juvenile, rejuvenate
lau, lav, lot, lut	wash	launder, lavatory, lotion, ablution, dilute
leg	law	legal, legislate, legislature, legitimize
levi	light	alleviate, levitate, levity
liber, liver	free	liberty, liberal, liberalize, deliverance
liter	letters	literary, literature, literal, alliteration, obliterate
loc, loco	place	locality, allocate, locomotion
log, logo, ology	word, study, speech	catalog, prologue, dialogue, logogram (symbol representing a word), zoology
loqu, locut	talk, speak	eloquent, loquacious, colloquial, circumlocution
luc, lum, lus, lun	light	translucent, luminary, luster, luna (moon goddess)
macr, macer	lean	emaciated, meager
magn	great	magnify, magnificent, magnanimous, magnate, magnitude, magnum
man	hand	manual, manage, manufacture, manacle, manicure, manifest, maneuver, emancipate
mand	command	mandatory, remand, mandate
mania	madness	mania, maniac, kleptomania, pyromania
mar, mari, mer	sea, pool	marine, marsh, maritime, mermaid
matri	mother	matrimony, maternal, matriarchate, matron

ROOT	MEANING	EXAMPLES
medi	half, middle, between, halfway	mediate, medieval, Mediterranean, mediocre, medium
mega	great	megaphone, megalopolis, megacycle (a million cycles), megaton
mem	remember	memo, commemoration, memento, memoir, memorable
meter	measure	meter, voltammeter, barometer, thermometer
micro	small	microscope, microfilm, microcard, microwave, micrometer
migra	wander	migrate, emigrant, immigrate
mit, miss	send	emit, remit, submit, admit, commit, permit, transmit, omit, intermittent, mission, missile
mob, mot, mov	move	mobile, motionless, motor
mon	warn, remind	monument, admonition, monitor, premonition
mor, mort	mortal, death	mortal, immortal, mortality, mortician, mortuary
morph	form	amorphous, dimorphic, metamorphosis, morphology
multi	many, much	multifold, multilingual, multiped, multiply
nat, nasc	to be from, to spring forth	innate, natal, native, renaissance
neo	new	Neolithic, nuveau riche, neologism, neophyte, neonate
neur	nerve	neuritis, neuropathic, neurologist, neural, neurotic
nom	law, order	autonomy, astronomy, gastronomy, economy
nomen, nomin	name	nomenclature, nominate, ignominious
nov	new	novel, renovate, novice, nova, innovate
nox, noc	night	nocturnal, equinox, noctilucent
numer	number	numeral, numeration, enumerate, innumerable
numisma	coin	numismatics
oligo	few, little	Oligocene, oligosaccharide, oligotrophic, oligarchy
omni	all, every	omnipotent, omniscient, omnipresent, omnivorous
onym	name	anonymous, pseudonym, antonym, synonym
oper	work	operate, cooperate, opus
ortho	straight, correct	orthodox, orthodontist, orthopedic, unorthodox
pac	peace	pacifist, pacify, pacific ocean
paleo	old	Paleozoic, Paleolithic, paleomagnetism, paleopsychology

ROOT	MEANING	EXAMPLES
pan	all	Pan-American, pan-African, panacea, pandemonium (place of all the demons)
pater, patr	father	paternity, patriarch, patriot, patron, patronize
path, pathy	feeling, suffering	pathos, sympathy, antipathy, apathy, telepathy
ped, pod	foot	pedal, impede (get feet in a trap), pedestrian, centipede, tripod, podiatry, antipode
pedo	child	orthopedic, pedagogue, pediatrics
pel, puls	drive, urge	compel, dispel, expel, repel, propel, pulse, impulse, pulsate, compulsory, expulsion, repulsive
pend, pens, pond	hang, weigh	pendant, pendulum, suspend, appendage, pensive
phage	eat	macrophage, bacteriophage
phil	love	philosophy, philanthropy, philharmonic, bibliophile
phlegma	inflammation	phlegm, phlegmatic
phobia, phobos	fear	phobia, claustrophobia, acrophobia, aquaphobia, ergophobia, homophobia
phon	sound	phonograph, phonetic, symphony, homophone, euphonious
photo	light	photograph, photoelectric, photogenic, photosynthesis
plac, plais	please	placid, placebo, placate, complacent
plu, plur, plus	more	plural, pluralist, plus
pneuma, pneumon	breath	pneumatic, pneumonia
pod (see ped)		
poli	city	metropolis, police, politics, Indianapolis, megalopolis, acropolis
poly	many	polysaccharide, polyandrous, polytheistic
pon, pos, pound	place, put	postpone, component, opponent, proponent, expose, impose, deposit, posture, position, expound, impound
pop	people	population, populous, popular
port	carry	porter, portable, transport, report, export, import, support, transportation
portion	part, share	portion, proportion
pot	power	potential, potentate, impotent
prehendere	seize, grasp	apprehend, comprehend, comprehensive, prehensile
prim, prime	first	primacy, prima donna, primitive, primary, primal, primeval

ROOT	MEANING	EXAMPLES
proto	first	prototype, protocol, protagonist, protozoan, Proterozoic, protoindustrial
psych	mind, soul	psyche, psychiatry, psychology, psychosis
punct	point, dot	punctual, punctuation, puncture, acupuncture, punctuation
reg, recti	straighten	regiment, regular, rectify, correct, direct, rectangle
ri, ridi, risi	laughter	deride, ridicule, ridiculous, derision, risible
rog, roga	ask	prerogative, interrogation, derogatory
rupt	break	rupture, interrupt, abrupt, disrupt, ruptible
sacr, sanc, secr	sacred	sacred, sacrosanct, sanction, consecrate, desecrate
salv, salu	safe, healthy	salvation, salvage, salutation
sat, satis	enough	satient (giving pleasure, satisfying), saturate, satisfy
sci, scientia	know	science, conscious, omniscient, cognocienti
scope	see, watch	telescope, microscope, kaleidoscope, periscope, stethoscope
scrib, script	write	scribe, scribble, inscribe, describe, subscribe, prescribe, manuscript
sed, sess, sid	sit	sediment, session, obsession, possess, preside, president, reside, subside
sen	old	senior, senator, senile
senescere	to grow old	senescence, evanescent
sent, sens	feel	sentiment, consent, resent, dissent, sentimental, sense, sensation, sensitive, sensory, dissension
sequ, secu, sue	follow	sequence, consequence, sequel, subsequent, prosecute, consecutive, second, ensue, pursue
serv	save, serve	servant, service, subservient, servitude, preserve, conserve, reservation, deserve, conservation, observe
sign, signi	sign, mark, seal	signal, signature, design, insignia, significant
simil, simul	like, resembling	similar, assimilate, simulate, simulacrum, simultaneous
sist, sta, stit	stand	assist, persist, circumstance, stamina, status, state, static, stable, stationary, substitute
solus	alone	solo, soliloquy, solitaire, solitude
solv, solu	loosen	solvent, solve, absolve, resolve, soluble, solution, resolution, resolute, dissolute
somnus	sleep	insomnia, somnambulist
soph	wise	sophomore (wise fool), philosophy, sophisticated

ROOT	MEANING	EXAMPLES
spec, spect, spic	look	specimen, specific, spectator, spectacle, aspect, speculate, inspect, respect, prospect, retrospective, introspective, expect, conspicuous
sphere	ball, sphere	sphere, stratosphere, hemisphere, spheroid
spir	breath	spirit, conspire, inspire, aspire, expire, perspire, respiration
string, strict	draw tight	stringent, strict, restrict, constrict, boa constrictor
stru, struct	build	construe (build in the mind, interpret), structure, construct, instruct, obstruct, destruction, destroy
sume, sump	take, use, waste	consume, assume (to take, to use), sump, pump, presumption (to take or use before knowing all the facts)
tact, tang, tag, tig, ting	touch	tactile, contact, intact, intangible, tangible, contagious, contiguous
tele	far	telephone, telegraph, telegram, telescope, television, telephoto, telecast, telepathy
tempo	time	tempo, temporary, extemporaneously, contemporary, pro tem, temporal
ten, tin, tain	hold	tenacious, tenant, tenure, untenable, detention, retentive, content, pertinent, continent, obstinate, contain, abstain, pertain, detain
tend, tent, tens	stretch, strain	tendency, extend, intend, contend, pretend, superintend, tender, extent, tension, pretense
terra	earth	terrain, terrarium, territory, terrestrial
test	to bear witness	testament, detest, testimony, attest
the, theo	God, a god	monotheism, polytheism, atheism, theology
therm	heat	thermometer, theorem, thermal, thermos bottle, thermostat, hypothermia
thesis, thet	place, put	antithesis, hypothesis, synthesis, epithet
tom	cut	atom (not cuttable, smallest particle of matter), appendectomy, tonsillectomy, dichotomy, anatomy
tort, tors	twist	torture (twisting to inflict pain), retort, extort (twist out), distort, contort, torsion, tortuous, torturous
tox	poison	toxic, intoxicate, antitoxin
tract, tra	draw, pull	tractor, attract, traction, subtract, tractable, abstract (to draw away), subtrahend (the number to be drawn away from another)
trib	pay, bestow	tribute, contribute, attribute, retribution, tributary
turbo	disturb	turbulent, disturb, turbid, turmoil

ROOT	MEANING	EXAMPLES
typ	print	type, prototype, typical, typography, typewriter, typology, typify
ultima	last	ultimate, ultimatum
umber, umbraticum	shadow	umbra, penumbra, (take) umbrage, adumbrate
uni	one	unicorn, unify, university, unanimous, universal
vac	empty	vacate, vacuum, evacuate, vacation, vacant, vacuous
vale, vali, valu	strength, worth	equivalent, valiant, validity, evaluate, value, valor
ven, vent	come	convene, intervene, venue, convenient, avenue, circumvent, invent, convent, venture, event, advent, prevent
ver, veri	true	very, aver, verdict, verity, verify, verisimilitude
vert, vers	turn	avert, divert, invert, introvert, convertible, reverse, controversy, versatile
vic, vicis	change, substitute	vicarious, vicar, vicissitude
vict, vinc	conquer	victor, evict, convict, convince, invincible
vid, vis	see	video, evident, provide, providence, visible, revise, supervise, vista, visit, vision
viv, vita, vivi	alive, life	revive, survive, vivid, vivacious, vitality, vivisection
voc	call	vocation, avocation, convocation, invocation, evoke, provoke, revoke, advocate, provocative, vocal
vol	will	malevolent, benevolent, volunteer, volition
volcan	fire	volcano, vulcanize, Vulcan
volvo	turn about, roll	revolve, voluble (easily turned about or around or talkative), voluminous, convolution
vor	eat greedily	voracious, carnivorous, herbivorous, omnivorous, devour
zo	animal	zoo (short for zoological garden), zoology, zoomorphism (attributing animal form to god), zodiac (circle of animal constellations), protozoan

Source: www.msu.edu/~defores1/gre/roots/gre_rts_afx2.htm.

APPENDIX B

B.9 GENERALIZATIONS ABOUT WORD SPELLINGS

1. Every syllable has a vowel sound.
2. Blends and digraphs always stay together (e.g., *fa-ther,* not *fat-her*).
3. Syllables ending with a vowel have a long sound. Pattern = CV
4. Syllables ending with a consonant have short vowel sounds. Pattern = CVC
5. Inflectional endings are usually separate syllables (e.g., *play-ing*).
6. Prefixes are usually separate syllables (e.g., *re-turn*).
7. The consonant before a final *le* is part of the last syllable (e.g., *dou-ble, a-ble*).
8. When words end in silent *e*, the *e* is dropped before adding the ending (e.g., *giving, having, hoping*).
9. When words end in *y*, change *y* to *i* before adding the suffix, unless the ending is ing (e.g., *married, marrying*).
10. When words have a CVC pattern, double the final consonant before adding an ending that begins with a vowel (*sit, sitting; hop, hopping*).
11. The letter *q* is followed by *u* (exception: *Iraq*).
12. The final *e* remains on root word when suffix begins with a consonant (e.g., *lately*).
13. When singular noun has a consonant before y, the y is changed to i to form plural (e.g., *babies*).
14. When singular noun has a vowel before *y*, only the *s* is added to form plural (e.g., *boys*).
15. The letter *i* before *e* except after *c* or when digraph sounds like the long /a/ sound (e.g., *receive, eight*).
16. In one-syllable words with the pattern CVCe (*cape*), the vowel is long.
17. In one-syllable words with the pattern CVVC (*road*), one vowel is usually long.
18. In one-syllable words with the patterns CVC (*hop*) the vowel is short.
19. In two-syllable words with pattern CVC-CV (*rabbit*), the vowel is short in the first syllable.

Sources: Bear, D., Invernizzi, M., Templeton, F., & Johnston, F. (2006). *Words their way: Word study for phonics, vocabulary and spelling instruction* (4th ed.). Upper Saddle River, NJ: Merrill.

Fountas, I. & Pinnell, G. S. (2001). *Guided readers and writers: Grades 3–6: Teaching comprehension, genre and content literacy.* Portsmouth, NH: Heinemann.

Heald-Taylor, B. G. (1998). Three paradigms of spelling instruction in grades 3–6. *The Reading Teacher, 51*(5), 404–413.

B.10 COMPLEX PATTERNS OF ENGLISH SPELLING

1. "gh" in *sigh, light, night,* etc. serves as a marker for the long /i/ sound.
2. double consonants mark short vowels (*hill, pass, butter, silly*).
3. "ck" at end of word makes vowel short (*truck, clock*).
4. "tch" at end of word makes vowel short (*match, itch*).
5. "ch" at end of word makes vowel short when there is only one vowel (*rich, such*); when the word has a vowel digraph, the vowel is long (*teach, coach*).
6. "ge" at the end of a word makes the "soft" g sound (*orange, ledge, ridge, sponge*).
7. "ge" within a word makes the "soft" g sound (*dungeon, pigeon, angel*).
8. "ce" at the end of a word gives *c* the /s/ sound (*prince, dance*).
9. "c" at the end of word calls for the /k/ sound (*magic, picnic*).
10. "c" followed by *e, i, y* makes a "soft" *c* (*city, cent, cycle*).
11. "c" followed by *a, o, u* makes a /k/ sound (cat, cot, cut).
12. initial "g" followed by *a, o, u* makes a "hard" g (*gate, goat, gut*).
13. initial "g" followed by *y* makes a "soft" g (*gym*).
14. initial "g" followed by *i* or *e* is often inconsistent (*give, get, giant, gem*).
15. the "k" in "kn" at the beginning of words is silent (*know, knee*).
16. the "g" in "gn" at beginning of words is silent (*gnaw, gnat*).
17. When long /u/ sound is at end of a word, it is spelled "oo" (*zoo*), "ew" (*few*), or "ue" (*blue*). The one is exception is *you*.

Source: Johnston, F. R. (Dec 2000/Jan 2001). Spelling exceptions: Problems or possibilities? *The Reading Teacher, 54*(4), 372–378. Reprinted with permission of Francine R. Johnston and the International Reading Association.

APPENDIX B

APPENDIX C

ASSESSMENT DEVICES

C.1 Checklist for Assessing Students' Multiple Intelligences 412
C.2 Concepts of Print Checkist 415
C.3 Concepts of Writing Checklist 416
C.4 Miscue Analysis Grid 417
C.5 Running Record Form 418
C.6 Sample Literacy Checklist 419
C.7 Checklist for Observations of Progress Toward Standards 420
C.8 Observational Checklist of Literacy Habits: Early Emergent Literacy Stage 422
C.9 Observational Checklist of Literacy Habits: Emergent Literacy Stage 423
C.10 Observational Checklist of Literacy Habits: Beginning Reading and Writing Stage 424
C.11 Observational Checklist of Literacy Habits: Nearly Fluent Stage 425
C.12 Observational Checklist of Literacy Habits: Fluent Reading and Writing Stage 426
C.13 Personal Interest Survey 427
C.14 Reading Attitude Survey for Primary Students 428
C.15 Writing Attitude Survey for Primary Students 430
C.16 Scoring Sheet for Attitude Surveys 432
C.17 Reading Attitude Survey for Older Students 433
C.18 Writing Attitude Survey for Older Students 434
C.19 Reader Self-Perception Scale 435
C.20 Writer Self-Perception Scale 437
C.21 Reading Log for Primary Students 440
C.22 Reading Log for Intermediate Students 441
C.23 Reading Reflection Log 442
C.24 Quick Phonemic Awareness Assessment Device 443
C.25 Pre-Assessment for Phonemic Awareness 444
C.26 Post-Assessment for Phonemic Awareness 448
C.27 Checklist for Phonemic Awareness for Primary Grades 452
C.28 Checklist of Known Letter Names and Sounds 453
C.29 Checklist for Letter–Sound Relationships, First Grade 455
C.30 Phonics Mastery Survey 456
C.31 Decoding and Word Recognition Checklist 459
C.32 Scoring Sheet for Word or Phrase Lists 460
C.33 Vocabulary Growth Checklist 461
C.34 Rubric for Narrative Reading Comprehension 462
C.35 Narrative Reading Rubric 463
C.36 General Reading Rubric 464
C.37 Interest Inventory for Informational Texts 465
C.38 Observation Checklist of Student's Expository Reading 466
C.39 Expository Reading Rubric 467
C.40 Checklist of Basic Internet Skills 468
C.41 Fluency Checklist 469
C.42 Fluency Checklist for Narrative Text 470
C.43 Oral Reading Fluency Rubric 471
C.44 Fluency Questions for Self-Evaluation 472
C.45 6 + 1 Traits® Writing Assessment 473
C.46 Rubric for Assessing the Writing Process of Writers in Primary Grades 475
C.47 Rubric for Assessing the Writing Process of Third Graders 477
C.48 Rubric for Writing Stories 479
C.49 Rubric for Research Paper 480
C.50 Rubric for Story Writing 481
C.51 Research Report Rubric 482
C.52 Multimedia Group Project Rubric 483
C.53 Writing and Spelling Self-Assessment 484
C.54 Bear, Invernizzi, Templeton, & Johnston Qualitative Spelling Inventory 485
C.55 Recording and Analyzing Spelling 486
C.56 Checklist for Spelling, Fifth Grade 487

C.1 CHECKLIST FOR ASSESSING STUDENTS' MULTIPLE INTELLIGENCES (p. 32)

NAME OF STUDENT: ______________________

Check items that apply:

LINGUISTIC INTELLIGENCE

- ○ writes better than average for age
- ○ spins tall tales or tells jokes and stories
- ○ has a good memory for names, places, dates, or trivia
- ○ spells words accurately (or if preschool, does developmental spelling that is advanced for age)
- ○ enjoys word games
- ○ enjoys reading books
- ○ appreciates nonsense rhymes, puns, tongue twisters
- ○ enjoys listening to the spoken word (stories, commentary on the radio, talking books)
- ○ has a good vocabulary for age
- ○ communicates to others in a highly verbal way

OTHER LINGUISTIC ABILITIES:

LOGICAL–MATHEMATICAL INTELLIGENCE

- ○ asks a lot of questions about how things work
- ○ enjoys working or playing with numbers
- ○ enjoys math class (or if preschool, enjoys counting and doing other things with numbers)
- ○ finds math and computer games interesting (or if no exposure to computers, enjoys other math or science games)
- ○ enjoys playing chess, checkers, or other strategy games
- ○ enjoys working on logic puzzles or brainteasers (or if preschool, enjoys hearing logical nonsense)
- ○ enjoys putting things in categories, hierarchies, or other logical patterns
- ○ likes to do experiments in science class or in free play
- ○ shows interest in science-related subjects
- ○ does well on Piagetian-type assessments of logical thinking

OTHER LOGICAL-MATHEMATICAL ABILITIES:

SPATIAL INTELLIGENCE

- ○ reports clear visual images
- ○ reads maps, charts, and diagrams more easily than text (or if preschool, enjoys looking at more than text)
- ○ daydreams a lot
- ○ enjoys art activities
- ○ good at drawings

- ○ likes to view movies, slides, or other visual presentations
- ○ enjoys doing puzzles, mazes, or similar visual activities
- ○ builds interesting three-dimensional constructions (e.g., LEGO buildings)
- ○ gets more out of pictures than words while reading
- ○ doodles on workbooks, worksheets, or other materials

OTHER SPATIAL ABILITIES:

BODILY–KINESTHETIC INTELLIGENCE

- ○ excels in one or more sports (or if preschool, shows physical prowess advanced for age)
- ○ moves, twitches, taps, or fidgets while seated for a long time in one spot
- ○ cleverly mimics other people's gestures or mannerisms
- ○ loves to take things apart and put them back together again
- ○ puts his/her hands all over something he/she's just seen
- ○ enjoys running, jumping, wrestling, or similar activities (or if older, will show these interests in a more "restrained" way—e.g., running to class, jumping over a chair)
- ○ shows skill in a craft (e.g., woodworking, sewing, mechanics) or good fine-motor coordination in other ways
- ○ has a dramatic way of expressing herself/himself
- ○ reports different physical sensations while thinking or working
- ○ enjoys working with clay or other tactile experiences (e.g., fingerpainting)

OTHER BODILY-KINESTHETIC ABILITIES:

MUSICAL INTELLIGENCE

- ○ tells you when music sounds off-key or disturbing in some other way
- ○ remembers melodies of songs
- ○ has a good singing voice
- ○ plays a musical instrument or sings in a choir or other group (or if preschool, enjoys playing percussion instruments and/or singing in a group)
- ○ has a rhythmic way of speaking and/or moving
- ○ unconsciously hums to himself/herself
- ○ taps rhythmically on the table or desk as he/she works
- ○ sensitive to environmental noises (e.g., rain on the roof)
- ○ responds favorably when a piece of music is put on
- ○ sings songs that he/she has learned outside of the classroom

OTHER MUSICAL ABILITIES:

INTERPERSONAL INTELLIGENCE

- ○ enjoys socializing with peers
- ○ seems to be a natural leader
- ○ gives advice to friends who have problems
- ○ seems to be street-smart
- ○ belongs to clubs, committees, organizations, or informal peer groups

- ○ enjoys informally teaching other kids
- ○ likes to play games with other kids
- ○ has two or more close friends
- ○ has a good sense of empathy or concern for others
- ○ others seek out his/her company

OTHER INTERPERSONAL ABILITIES:

INTRAPERSONAL INTELLIGENCE

- ○ displays a sense of independence or a strong will
- ○ has a realistic sense of his/her abilities and weaknesses
- ○ does well when left alone to play or study
- ○ marches to the beat of a different drummer in his/her style of living and learning
- ○ has an interest or hobby that he/she doesn't talk much about
- ○ has a good sense of self-direction
- ○ prefers working alone to working with others
- ○ accurately expresses how he/she is feeling
- ○ is able to learn from his/her failures and successes in life
- ○ has good self-esteem

OTHER INTRAPERSONAL ABILITIES:

NATURALISTIC INTELLIGENCE

- ○ talks a lot about favorite pets, or preferred spots in nature, during class sharing
- ○ likes field trips in nature, to the zoo, or to a natural history museum
- ○ shows sensitivity to nature formations (e.g., while walking outside with the class, will notice mountains, clouds; or if in an urban environment, may show this ability in sensitivity to popular culture "formations" such as sneakers or automobile styles)
- ○ likes to water and tend to the plants in the classroom
- ○ likes to hang around the gerbil cage, the aquarium, or the terrarium in class
- ○ gets excited when studying about ecology, nature, plants, or animals
- ○ speaks out in class for the rights of animals, or the preservation of planet earth
- ○ enjoys doing nature projects, such as bird watching, butterfly or insect collections, tree study, or raising animals
- ○ brings to school bugs, flowers, leaves, or other natural things to share with classmates or teachers
- ○ does well in topics at school that involve living systems (e.g., biological topics in science, environmental issues in social studies)

OTHER NATURALISTIC ABILITIES:

Source: *Multiple Intelligences in the Classroom*, 2nd ed. (pp. 24–27), by Thomas Armstrong, Alexandria, VA: ASCD.

C.2 CONCEPTS OF PRINT CHECKLIST (p. 50)

STUDENT: ______________________ DATE: ______________

	YES	NO
1. Knows which is the front of the book.	○	○
2. Holds a book correctly.	○	○
3. Knows that the words, not the print, are what is read when asked, "Where do I start to read?"	○	○
4. Knows that one reads from the top of the page to the bottom.	○	○
5. Knows that one reads the left-hand page and then the right-hand page. Can point to where to go after completing the left-hand page.	○	○
6. Knows the return sweep concept (where to go when he/she reaches the end of a line).	○	○
7. Is able to point from word to word.	○	○
8. Knows the difference between		
a word	○	○
a letter	○	○
a sentence	○	○
9. Knows letter order is important and different in each word (recognizes the misspelled words).	○	○
10. Is able to identify the first and last letters in words.	○	○
11. Knows the purpose of		
a period	○	○
question mark	○	○
exclamation mark	○	○

Source: Los Angeles County Office of Education. (2000). *Kindergarten and Grade One Reading: Basic to Success.* Retrieved January 7, 2007, from http://teams.lacoe.edu/documentation/classrooms/patti/K-1/teacher/assessment/print/concepts.html.

C.3 CONCEPTS OF WRITING CHECKLIST (p. 51)

STUDENT: ______________________ DATE: ______________

	YES	NO
1. Understands that writing carries a message.	○	○
2. Understands that what is spoken can be written down.	○	○
3. Sees the unique differences between letters.	○	○
4. Has learned to embellish letters while retaining their identities.	○	○
5. Enjoys producing patterns in writing.	○	○
6. Combines or arranges elements of print in an inventive manner.	○	○
7. Writes from left to right and from top to bottom.	○	○
8. Can distinguish differences between the shapes, meanings, and sounds in letters and words.	○	○
9. Understands that a space is needed between words.	○	○
10. Understands that letters construct words.	○	○

Source: Adapted from Clay, M. (2006). *Principles and Concepts of Early Writing.* www.learningtowrite.ecsd.net/principles%20and%20concepts.htm.

C.4 MISCUE ANALYSIS GRID (p. 53)

TEXT	Substitution	Mispronun-ciation	Insertion	Omission	Repeats	Self-correction	Syntax acceptable	Meaning disrupted
TOTAL MISCUES:								

NOTES:

C.5 RUNNING RECORD FORM (p. 58)

STUDENT: ____________________ DATE: ____________________

TEACHER: ____________________ READING LEVEL: ____________________

STORY: ____________________

NUMBER OF ERRORS: ____________________ PERCENTAGE: ____________________

RUNNING WORDS: ____________________ LEVEL FOR STUDENT: EASY, INSTRUCTIONAL, FRUSTRATION

COMMENTS:

TEXT	ANALYSIS			
	Number		System Used	
	E	SC	E	SC
PAGE				

APPENDIX C

C.6 SAMPLE LITERACY CHECKLIST (p. 64)

TEACHER: DATE:

+ = always X = sometimes O = seldom/never

STANDARD	STUDENTS																	
1. Reads and comprehends fiction suitable for grade level.																		
2. Reads and comprehends nonfiction suitable for grade level.																		
3. Uses prereading strategies to preview and make predictions.																		
4. Uses picture clues and graphic organizers as prereading strategies.																		
5. Asks questions to aid comprehension of fiction and nonfiction.																		
6. Makes inferences about events, characters, and ideas in fiction.																		
7. Connects knowledge and experience to story.																		
8. Supports interpretations with examples from text.																		
9. Retells story in sequence.																		
10. Produces oral and written summaries of main ideas and supporting details.																		
11. Identifies cause/effect relationships.																		
12. Makes comparisons and draws conclusions based on reading.																		
13. Describes character traits, changes, and relationships.																		
14. Integrates the use of semantics, syntax, and graphophonics to grasp meaning.																		

Source: Oklahoma State Department of Education (revised 2002). *A Core Curriculum for Our Children's Future: Priority Academic Student Skills (PASS).* Oklahoma City: Oklahoma State DOE.

C.7 CHECKLIST FOR OBSERVATIONS OF PROGRESS TOWARD STANDARDS (p. 64)

NAME: GRADE: DATE:

STANDARDS	CONTEXT	DATE OBSERVED	CONTEXT	DATE OBSERVED	CONTEXT	DATE OBSERVED
1. Reads a wide range of print and nonprint texts						
2. Reads a wide range of literature (many time periods, many genres)						
3. Applies a wide range of strategies to comprehend, interpret, evaluate, and appreciate texts						
4. Adjusts use of spoken, written, and visual language to communicate effectively						
5. Employs a wide range of strategies for writing and different writing process elements to communicate effectively						
6. Applies knowledge of language structure, conventions, media techniques, figurative language, and genre to create, critique, and discuss print/nonprint texts						
7. Conducts research by generating ideas and questions, and by posing problems						
8. Uses a variety of technological and informational resources to gather/synthesize information and create/communicate knowledge						

STANDARDS	CONTEXT	DATE OBSERVED	CONTEXT	DATE OBSERVED	CONTEXT	DATE OBSERVED
9. Understands and respects diversity in language use, dialects, and cultures						
10. If ELL, makes use of native language to develop develop English competency						
11. Participates in a variety of literacy communities						
12. Uses spoken, written and visual language to accomplish own purposes						

*The standards used in this checklist are the NCTE/IRA Standards for the English Language Arts. Any state standards could be used and the checklist can be made grade-level specific as well.

Source: Cecil, N., & Gipe, J. (2009). *Literacy in Grades 4–8* (2nd ed.). Scottsdale, AZ: Holcomb Hathaway. Used with permission.

C.8 OBSERVATIONAL CHECKLIST OF LITERACY HABITS: EARLY EMERGENT LITERACY STAGE (p. 51)

STUDENT: ______________________ GRADE: __________

TEACHER: ______________________

− = BEHAVIOR NOT OBSERVED + = BEHAVIOR OBSERVED X = PROGRESSING

EARLY EMERGENT LITERACY STAGE:	DATES				
1. Shows pleasure in read-alouds.					
2. Can retell stories in sequence.					
3. Uses book language in retellings.					
4. Likes to make up stories.					
5. Holds books correctly.					
6. Recognizes environmental print (e.g., cereals, cookies).					
7. Pretends to read.					
8. Scribbles messages.					
9. Writes some letters correctly.					
10. Has phonemic awareness.					

C.9 OBSERVATIONAL CHECKLIST OF LITERACY HABITS: EMERGENT LITERACY STAGE (p. 51)

STUDENT: ______________________________ GRADE: __________

TEACHER: ______________________________

− = BEHAVIOR NOT OBSERVED + = BEHAVIOR OBSERVED X = PROGRESSING

	DATES				
EMERGENT LITERACY STAGE:					
1. "Reads" top to bottom of page.					
2. "Reads" front to back of book.					
3. "Reads" left to right.					
4. Recognizes nonstandard English.					
5. Enjoys jokes.					
6. Enjoys alliteration.					
7. Hears rhyming words.					
8. Knows difference between words and letters.					
9. Matches words with voice when reading.					
10. Knows, title, author, and illustrator of books.					
11. Recognizes letters in random order.					
12. Matches uppercase with lowercase letters.					
13. Recognizes name in print.					
14. Can write most letters.					
15. Uses phonemic awareness when writing.					
16. Can name initial and ending letter sounds of words.					
17. Shows interest in writing stories, notes, etc.					

APPENDIX C

C.10 OBSERVATIONAL CHECKLIST OF LITERACY HABITS: BEGINNING READING AND WRITING STAGE (p. 64)

STUDENT: GRADE:

TEACHER:

– = BEHAVIOR NOT OBSERVED + = BEHAVIOR OBSERVED X = PROGRESSING

	Dates				
BEGINNING READING AND WRITING STAGE:					
1. Self-corrects nonstandard English.					
2. Can paraphrase what others say.					
3. Can summarize a story.					
4. Participates in discussion.					
5. Enjoys nonsense and silly poems.					
6. Recognizes all letters in random order.					
7. Recognizes many sight words.					
8. Uses phonics to pronounce new words.					
9. Understands concepts of onset and rime.					
10. Reads own writing.					
11. Chooses to write independently.					
12. Word-by-word reading.					
13. Sounds out words instead of guessing.					
14. Lip-voicing movements in silent reading.					
15. Finger-points at every word.					
16. Uses spelling that reflects phonics knowledge.					
17. Uses word processing when writing.					
18. Uses all five steps of writing process.					
19. Adequate reading rate.					
20. Adequate vocabulary knowledge.					

APPENDIX C

C.11 OBSERVATIONAL CHECKLIST OF LITERACY HABITS: NEARLY FLUENT STAGE (p. 64)

STUDENT: ______________________ GRADE: __________

TEACHER: ______________________

− = BEHAVIOR NOT OBSERVED + = BEHAVIOR OBSERVED X = PROGRESSING

	DATES				
NEARLY FLUENT LITERACY STAGE:					
1. Uses oral standard English.					
2. Uses new vocabulary words correctly.					
3. Listens and questions speaker.					
4. Appreciates symbolic language.					
5. Uses structural analysis to determine unknown words.					
6. Uses context clues.					
7. Reads with 90% accuracy in grade-level materials.					
8. Self-corrects.					
9. Understands stories read to him/her that are above his/her grade level.					
10. Reads/comprehends a variety of genres.					
11. Prefers to read silently.					
12. Aware of own purpose for reading.					
13. Understands expository text structures.					
14. Beginning to synthesize information from a variety of sources.					
15. Can interpret simple graphs.					
16. Can locate information on a CD-ROM.					
17. Writes good stories.					
18. Writes good paragraphs.					
19. Uses word processing tools to revise and edit work.					
20. Uses five steps of writing process.					
21. Uses vivid language when writing.					

C.12 OBSERVATIONAL CHECKLIST OF LITERACY HABITS: FLUENT READING AND WRITING STAGE (p. 64)

STUDENT: ______________________________ GRADE: __________

TEACHER: ______________________________

− = BEHAVIOR NOT OBSERVED   + = BEHAVIOR OBSERVED   X = PROGRESSING

	DATES				
FLUENT READING AND WRITING STAGE:					
1. Enjoys readers theatre.					
2. Enjoys giving speeches in front of class.					
3. Understands the elements of stories.					
4. Understands differences in genres.					
5. Uses effective strategies when reading.					
6. Can self-correct when reading.					
7. Enjoys reading during free time.					
8. Knows where to locate information.					
9. Uses writing to persuade.					
10. Can edit classmates' work.					
11. Can edit own writing.					
12. Self-checks spelling and grammar.					
13. Revises own work when necessary.					
14. Recognizes authors' style and techniques in writing.					
15. Attempts to copy a writer's style.					

APPENDIX C

C.13 PERSONAL INTEREST SURVEY (p. 68)

NAME: ______________________ GRADE: ____________ DATE: ____________

Write more than one item for each category if more than one item interests you. Explain why for each response. For example, why do you enjoy football?

1. My favorite foods are
2. My favorite eating places are
3. My favorite snacks are
4. My favorite TV shows are
5. My favorite TV characters are
6. My favorite movies are
7. My favorite actors are
8. My favorite actresses are
9. The best book I ever read is
10. My favorite music group is
11. My favorite song is
12. My favorite sport is
13. My favorite school subject is
14. I know I am very good at
15. When I am alone, I like to
16. My favorite thing to do with my friends is
17. My least favorite thing to do is
18. My favorite thing to do on Saturday and Sunday is
19. The thing I fear most is
20. If I had a million dollars, I would

C.14 READING ATTITUDE SURVEY FOR PRIMARY STUDENTS (p. 69)

NAME: ______________________ GRADE: __________ DATE: __________

1. How I feel when the teacher reads to me.

2. How I feel when classmates read in class.

3. How I feel when asked to read aloud in class.

4. How I feel when asked to read aloud just for my teacher.

5. How I feel when I read stories to my family.

6. How I feel when I read to myself.

7. How I feel during “Drop Everything and Read.”

8. How I feel about reading mystery stories.

9. How I feel about listening to my teacher read mystery stories.

10. How I feel about reading funny stories.

11. How I feel about listening to my teacher read funny stories.

12. How I feel about reading scary stories.

13. How I feel about listening to my teacher read scary stories.

14. How I feel about reading poetry.

15. How I feel about listening to my teacher read poetry.

16. How I feel about reading informational books about sports.

17. How I feel about reading informational books about spiders, snakes, and other creatures.

18. How I feel about reading informational books on places to visit.

19. How I feel about reading stories on the computer.

20. How I feel about finding information on the computer.

See C.16, "Scoring Sheet for Attitude Surveys."

C.15 WRITING ATTITUDE SURVEY FOR PRIMARY STUDENTS (p. 69)

NAME: GRADE: DATE:

Pretest or Posttest (Circle one)

1. How I feel when asked to write a story.

2. How I feel when asked to write riddles.

3. How I feel when asked to write about my favorite sport or pet.

4. How I feel when asked to write to my favorite author.

5. How I feel when asked to write a poem.

6. How I feel when asked to write about myself.

7. How I feel when asked to write a thank-you note.

8. How I feel when asked to write in front of my classmates.

9. How I feel when I write on a dry-erase board.

10. How I feel when I write on the computer.

11. How I feel when I write *with* classmates.

12. How I feel when I write with my teacher.

13. How I feel about writing science reports.

14. How I feel when asked to check for mistakes in my writing.

15. How I feel about my spelling ability.

16. How I feel when asked to change something in my writing.

17. How I feel when my story or poem or article is posted for my classmates to read.

18. How I feel when my teacher reads my poem, story, or article to the class.

19. How I feel if I did not have to write in school.

20. How I feel if I had more time to write in school.

See C.16, "Scoring Sheet for Attitude Surveys."

C.16 SCORING SHEET FOR ATTITUDE SURVEYS (p. 69)

STUDENT: ______ GRADE: ______ PRETEST DATE: ______

TEACHER: ______ POSTTEST DATE: ______

SCORING GUIDE:

HAPPY CHARACTER = 4 POINTS

"SOMEWHAT" HAPPY CHARACTER = 3 POINTS

NEUTRAL CHARACTER = 2 POINTS

UNHAPPY CHARACTER = 1 POINT

ITEMS: PRETEST

1. ______ 2. ______ 3. ______ 4. ______ 5. ______

6. ______ 7. ______ 8. ______ 9. ______ 10. ______

11. ______ 12. ______ 13. ______ 14. ______ 15. ______

16. ______ 17. ______ 18. ______ 19. ______ 20. ______

TOTAL: ______

Comments:

ITEMS: POSTTEST

1. ______ 2. ______ 3. ______ 4. ______ 5. ______

6. ______ 7. ______ 8. ______ 9. ______ 10. ______

11. ______ 12. ______ 13. ______ 14. ______ 15. ______

16. ______ 17. ______ 18. ______ 19. ______ 20. ______

TOTAL: ______

Comments:

C.17 READING ATTITUDE SURVEY FOR OLDER STUDENTS (p. 69)

STUDENT: ______ GRADE: ______ DATE: ______

Pretest or Posttest (Circle one)

Respond to the statement by circling SL for Strongly Like, L for Like, O for Okay, DL for Dislike, and SD for Strongly Dislike.

1. Completing research on the Internet.	SL	L	O	DL	SD
2. Reading my science text.	SL	L	O	DL	SD
3. Reading my history text.	SL	L	O	DL	SD
4. Reading informational CD-ROMs.	SL	L	O	DL	SD
5. Reading informational books for a report.	SL	L	O	DL	SD
6. Reading realistic fiction.	SL	L	O	DL	SD
7. Reading historical fiction.	SL	L	O	DL	SD
8. Reading poetry.	SL	L	O	DL	SD
9. Reading a funny book.	SL	L	O	DL	SD
10. Reading the comics in a newspaper.	SL	L	O	DL	SD
11. Reading the sports section of a newspaper.	SL	L	O	DL	SD
12. Reading a sports magazine.	SL	L	O	DL	SD
13. Reading *People* magazine.	SL	L	O	DL	SD
14. Reading a fashion magazine.	SL	L	O	DL	SD
15. Reading *Newsweek* or *Time* magazine.	SL	L	O	DL	SD
16. Listening to classmates read.	SL	L	O	DL	SD
17. Listening to my teacher read.	SL	L	O	DL	SD
18. Reading in front of my peers.	SL	L	O	DL	SD
19. Reading on the weekend.	SL	L	O	DL	SD
20. Learning to become a better reader.	SL	L	O	DL	SD

Answer the following questions. Be honest in your responses.

1. Do you consider yourself a good reader? Explain.

______

2. Do you like to help other classmates with their reading problems? Explain.

______

3. What is the hardest thing for you to do in reading?

______

4. What do you do best as a reader?

______

C.18 WRITING ATTITUDE SURVEY FOR OLDER STUDENTS (p. 69)

STUDENT: ______________________ GRADE: __________ DATE: __________

Pretest or Posttest (Circle one)

Respond to the statement by circling SL for Strongly Like, L for Like, O for Okay, DL for Dislike, and SD for Strongly Dislike.

1. Writing a story for class.	SL	L	O	DL	SD
2. Writing about my science project.	SL	L	O	DL	SD
3. Writing a history or other report.	SL	L	O	DL	SD
4. Writing poetry.	SL	L	O	DL	SD
5. Writing lyrics for a song.	SL	L	O	DL	SD
6. Writing letters and notes to friends.	SL	L	O	DL	SD
7. Writing in a personal diary or journal.	SL	L	O	DL	SD
8. Writing in a dialogue journal with your teacher.	SL	L	O	DL	SD
9. Writing a script for a play or readers theater.	SL	L	O	DL	SD
10. Writing jokes or other funny material.	SL	L	O	DL	SD
11. Writing scary stories or mysteries.	SL	L	O	DL	SD
12. Prewriting in writing workshop.	SL	L	O	DL	SD
13. Writing my first draft in writing workshop.	SL	L	O	DL	SD
14. Revising and editing in writing workshop.	SL	L	O	DL	SD
15. Having other classmates read my story or report.	SL	L	O	DL	SD
16. Helping classmates edit their work.	SL	L	O	DL	SD
17. Having other classmates edit my work.	SL	L	O	DL	SD
18. Using a word processor for writing.	SL	L	O	DL	SD
19. Using paper and pen or pencil for writing.	SL	L	O	DL	SD
20. Writing in my spare time.	SL	L	O	DL	SD
21. Writing e-mails to friends.	SL	L	O	DL	SD
22. Writing information for web pages.	SL	L	O	DL	SD

Answer the following questions honestly.

1. I think I am a (good or not-so-good) writer because

____

2. I wish I could write like my favorite author because

____

3. The hardest thing for me to do in writing is

____

C.19 READER SELF-PERCEPTION SCALE (p. 69)

Listed below are statements about reading. Please read each statement carefully. Then circle the letters that show how much you agree or disagree with the statement. Use the following:

SA = Strongly Agree
A = Agree
U = Undecided
D = Disagree
SD = Strongly Disagree

Example: I think pizza with pepperoni is best.	SA	A	U	D	SD

If you are *really positive* that pepperoni pizza is best, circle SA (Strongly Agree).
If you *think* that it is good but maybe not great, circle A (Agree).
If you *can't decide* whether or not it is best, circle U (Undecided).
If you *think* that pepperoni pizza is not all that good, circle D (Disagree).
If you are *really positive* that pepperoni pizza is not very good, circle SD (Strongly Disagree).

[GPR]	1. I think I am a good reader.	SA	A	U	D	SD
[SF]	2. I can tell that my teacher likes to listen to me read.	SA	A	U	D	SD
[SF]	3. My teacher thinks that my reading is fine.	SA	A	U	D	SD
[OC]	4. I read faster than other kids.	SA	A	U	D	SD
[PS]	5. I like to real aloud.	SA	A	U	D	SD
[OC]	6. When I read, I can figure out words better than other kids.	SA	A	U	D	SD
[SF]	7. My classmates like to listen to me read.	SA	A	U	D	SD
[PS]	8. I feel good inside when I read.	SA	A	U	D	SD
[SF]	9. My classmates think that I read pretty well.	SA	A	U	D	SD
[PR]	10. When I read, I don't have to try as hard as I used to.	SA	A	U	D	SD
[OC]	11. I seem to know more words than other kids when I read.	SA	A	U	D	SD
[SF]	12. People in my family think I am a good reader.	SA	A	U	D	SD
[PR]	13. I am getting better at reading.	SA	A	U	D	SD
[OC]	14. I understand what I read as well as other kids do.	SA	A	U	D	SD
[PR]	15. When I read, I need less help than I used to.	SA	A	U	D	SD
[PS]	16. Reading makes me feel happy inside.	SA	A	U	D	SD
[SF]	17. My teacher thinks I am a good reader.	SA	A	U	D	SD
[PR]	18. Reading is easier for me than it used to be.	SA	A	U	D	SD
[PR]	19. I read faster than I could before.	SA	A	U	D	SD
[OC]	20. I read better than other kids in my class.	SA	A	U	D	SD
[PS]	21. I feel calm when I read.	SA	A	U	D	SD
[OC]	22. I read more than other kids.	SA	A	U	D	SD
[PR]	23. I understand what I read better than I could before.	SA	A	U	D	SD
[PR]	24. I can figure out words better than I could before.	SA	A	U	D	SD
[PS]	25. I feel comfortable when I read.	SA	A	U	D	SD

APPENDIX C

[PS]	26. I think reading is relaxing.	SA	A	U	D	SD
[PR]	27. I read better now than I could before.	SA	A	U	D	SD
[PR]	28. When I read, I recognize more words than I used to.	SA	A	U	D	SD
[PS]	29. Reading makes me feel good.	SA	A	U	D	SD
[SF]	30. Other kids think I'm a good reader.	SA	A	U	D	SD
[SF]	31. People in my family think I read pretty well.	SA	A	U	D	SD
[PS]	32. I enjoy reading.	SA	A	U	D	SD
[SF]	33. People in my family like to listen to me read.	SA	A	U	D	SD

The Reader Self-Perception Scale Scoring Sheet

Student name: ______________________________

Teacher: ______________ Grade: ______ Date: ______________

Scoring key:

5 = Strongly Agree (SA)
4 = Agree (A)
3 = Undecided (U)
2 = Disagree (D)
1 = Strongly Disagree (SD)

SCALES

General Perception (GPR)	Progress (PR)	Observational Comparison (OC)	Social Feedback (SF)	Physiological States (PS)
1. ____	10. ____	4. ____	2. ____	5. ____
	13. ____	6. ____	3. ____	8. ____
	15. ____	11. ____	7. ____	16. ____
	18. ____	14. ____	9. ____	21. ____
	19. ____	20. ____	12. ____	25. ____
	23. ____	22. ____	17. ____	26. ____
	24. ____		30. ____	29. ____
	27. ____		31. ____	32. ____
	28. ____		33. ____	
Raw score	____ of 45	____ of 30	____ of 45	____ of 40

Score interpretation	**PR**	**OC**	**SF**	**PS**
High	44+	26+	38+	37+
Average	39	21	33	31
Low	34	16	27	25

Source: Henk, W. A., & Melnick, S. A. (March 1995). The reader self-perception scale (RSPS): A new tool for measuring how children feel about themselves as readers. *The Reading Teacher,* 48(6), 470–482. Reprinted with permission of William A. Henk and the International Reading Association.

APPENDIX C

C.20 WRITER SELF-PERCEPTION SCALE (p. 69)

Listed below are statements about writing. Please read each statement carefully. Then circle the letters that show how much you agree or disagree with the statement. Use the following scale:

SA = Strongly Agree
A = Agree
U = Undecided
D = Disagree
SD = Strongly Disagree

	Example: I think Batman is the greatest super hero.	SA	A	U	D	SD

If you are *really positive* that Batman is the greatest, circle SA (Strongly Agree).
If you *think* that Batman is good but maybe not great, circle A (Agree).
If you *can't decide* whether or not Batman is the greatest, circle U (Undecided).
If you *think* that Batman is not all that great, circle D (Disagree).
If you are *really positive* that Batman is not the greatest, circle SD (Strongly Disagree).

[OC]	1. I write better than other kids in my class.	SA	A	U	D	SD
[PS]	2. I like how writing makes me feel inside.	SA	A	U	D	SD
[GPR]	3. Writing is easier for me than it used to be.	SA	A	U	D	SD
[OC]	4. When I write, my organization is better than the other kids in my class.	SA	A	U	D	SD
[SF]	5. People in my family think I am a good writer.	SA	A	U	D	SD
[GPR]	6. I am getting better at writing.	SA	A	U	D	SD
[PS]	7. When I write, I feel calm.	SA	A	U	D	SD
[OC]	8. My writing is more interesting than my classmates' writing.	SA	A	U	D	SD
[SF]	9. My teacher thinks my writing is fine.	SA	A	U	D	SD
[SF]	10. Other kids think I am a good writer.	SA	A	U	D	SD
[OC]	11. My sentences and paragraphs fit together as well as my classmates' sentences and paragraphs.	SA	A	U	D	SD
[GPR]	12. I need less help to write well than I used to.	SA	A	U	D	SD
[SF]	13. People in my family think I write pretty well.	SA	A	U	D	SD
[GPR]	14. I write better now than I could before.	SA	A	U	D	SD
[GPR]	15. I think I am a good writer.	SA	A	U	D	SD
[OC]	16. I put my sentences in a better order than the other kids.	SA	A	U	D	SD
[GPR]	17. My writing has improved.	SA	A	U	D	SD
[GPR]	18. My writing is better than before.	SA	A	U	D	SD
[GPR]	19. It's easier to write well now than it used to be.	SA	A	U	D	SD

[GPR]	20.	The organization of my writing has really improved.	SA	A	U	D	SD
[OC]	21.	The sentences I use in my writing stick to the topic more than the ones the other kids use.	SA	A	U	D	SD
[SPR]	22.	The words I use in my writing are better than the ones I used before.	SA	A	U	D	SD
[OC]	23.	I write more often than other kids.	SA	A	U	D	SD
[PS]	24.	I am relaxed when I write.	SA	A	U	D	SD
[SPR]	25.	My descriptions are more interesting than before.	SA	A	U	D	SD
[OC]	26.	The words I use in my writing are better than the ones other kids use.	SA	A	U	D	SD
[PS]	27.	I feel comfortable when I write.	SA	A	U	D	SD
[SF]	28.	My teacher thinks I am a good writer.	SA	A	U	D	SD
[SPR]	29.	My sentences stick to the topic better now.	SA	A	U	D	SD
[OC]	30.	My writing seems to be more clear than my classmates' writing.	SA	A	U	D	SD
[SPR]	31.	When I write, the sentences and paragraphs fit together better than they used to.	SA	A	U	D	SD
[PS]	32.	Writing makes me feel good.	SA	A	U	D	SD
[SF]	33.	I can tell that my teacher thinks my writing is fine.	SA	A	U	D	SD
[SPR]	34.	The order of my sentences makes better sense now.	SA	A	U	D	SD
[PS]	35.	I enjoy writing.	SA	A	U	D	SD
[SPR]	36.	My writing is more clear than it used to be.	SA	A	U	D	SD
[SF]	37.	My classmates would say I write well.	SA	A	U	D	SD
[SPR]	38.	I choose the words I use in my writing more carefully now.	SA	A	U	D	SD

Source: Bottomley, D. M., Henk, W. A., & Melnick, S. A. (Dec 1997/Jan 1998). Assessing children's views about themselves as writers using the Writer Self-Perception Scale. *The Reading Teacher, 51*(4), 286–291. Reprinted with permission of Diane M. Bottomley and the International Reading Association.

APPENDIX C

Writer Self-Perception Scale Scoring Sheet

Student name: ______________________________

Teacher: ______________ Grade: ______ Date: ______________

Scoring key:

5 = Strongly Agree (SA)
4 = Agree (A)
3 = Undecided (U)
2 = Disagree (D)
1 = Strongly Disagree (SD)

SCALES

General Progress (GPR)	Specific Progress (PR)	Observational Comparison (OC)	Social Feedback (SF)	Physiological States (PS)
3. ______	22. ______	1. ______	5. ______	2. ______
6. ______	25. ______	4. ______	9. ______	7. ______
12. ______	29. ______	8. ______	10. ______	24. ______
14. ______	31. ______	11. ______	13. ______	27. ______
15. ______	34. ______	16. ______	28. ______	32. ______
17. ______	36. ______	21. ______	33. ______	35. ______
18. ______	38. ______	23. ______	37. ______	
19. ______		26. ______		
20. ______		30. ______		

RAW SCORES

______ of 40	______ of 35	______ of 45	______ of 35	______ of 30

Score interpretation	**GPR**	**SPR**	**OC**	**SF**	**PS**
High	39+	34+	37+	32+	28+
Average	35	29	30	27	22
Low	30	24	23	22	16

Source: Bottomley, D. M., Henk, W. A., & Melnick, S. A. (Dec 1997/Jan 1998). Assessing children's views about themselves as writers using the Writer Self-Perception Scale. *The Reading Teacher, 51*(4), 286–291. Reprinted with permission of Diane M. Bottomley and the International Reading Association.

APPENDIX C

C.21 READING LOG FOR PRIMARY STUDENTS (p. 70)

Books I Have Read

Name: ____________________ Grade: ____________

Circle the face that best shows how you feel about the book.

BOOK	AUTHOR/ILLUSTRATOR	COMMENTS
		☺ 😐 ☹
		☺ 😐 ☹
		☺ 😐 ☹
		☺ 😐 ☹
		☺ 😐 ☹
		☺ 😐 ☹
		☺ 😐 ☹
		☺ 😐 ☹
		☺ 😐 ☹
		☺ 😐 ☹
		☺ 😐 ☹
		☺ 😐 ☹
		☺ 😐 ☹
		☺ 😐 ☹
		☺ 😐 ☹

C.22 READING LOG FOR INTERMEDIATE STUDENTS (p. 70)

Books I Have Read

Name: ______________ Grade: ______________ Quarter: 1 2 3 4

BOOK	AUTHOR	GENRE	DATE STARTED/ ENDED	COMMENTS

My favorite book I read this quarter was ______________

because ______________

C.23 READING REFLECTION LOG (p. 71)

My Thoughts About My Reading

Name: ______ Grade: ______ Quarter: 1 2 3 4

1. The informational books I read were about

______

______

______

2. The novels I read were mostly: realistic, historical, biographies, autobiographies, mysteries, science fiction, fantasy, folktales.

3. My favorite author is ______

______

4. The best book I read was ______

______

5. When I dislike a book, I ______

______

6. My favorite place to read is ______

______

7. My reading habits at home are ______

______

8. I do not enjoy reading books about ______

______

9. The book I recommended to my friends was ______

______

10. After I read a book, I like to ______

______

C.24 QUICK PHONEMIC AWARENESS ASSESSMENT DEVICE (p. 83)

A high correlation exists between the ability to recognize spoken words as a sequence of individual sounds and reading achievement. Explicit instruction can increase the phonemic awareness of children. To assist in determining the level of phonemic awareness of each child in your class, the following assessment items may be utilized. *Use as many samples as necessary to determine mastery.*

Assessment 1. Isolation of beginning sounds. Ask the child what the first sound of selected words is.

> "What is the first sound in *dog*?"

Assessment 2. Deletion of initial sound. Read a word and ask the child to say it without the first sound.

> "Say the word *cat.* Say *cat* without the /k/."

Assessment 3. Segmentation of phonemes. Ask the child to say the separate sounds of the word being read.

> "What are the two sounds in the word *go*?"

Assessment 4. Blending of phonemes. Slowly read the individual sounds of a word and ask the child to tell what the word is.

> "What word am I saying? /d/ /o/ /g/"

Assessment 5. Phoneme manipulation. Read a word and ask the child to replace the initial sound with another. Have the child say the new word.

> "In the word *fan,* the first sound is an /f/. If you replace the /f/ with an /m/, how would you say the new word?"

Source: Cecil, N. L. (2011). *Striking a Balance: A Comprehensive Approach to Early Literacy* (4th ed.). Scottsdale, AZ: Holcomb Hathaway. Used with permission.

C.25 PRE-ASSESSMENT FOR PHONEMIC AWARENESS (p. 83)

Name: _______________ Date: _______________

NOTE: The teacher will check "Yes" if the child can do the task, and "No" if the child cannot do the task. It is good to give one example to the child so they fully understand the task they are asked to perform. Examples are provided.

Syllabicating Words

Practice: "Words have different syllables. Some words have one syllable such as *hand* (clap once). *Mitten* has two syllables: mit- (clap once) tin (clap once). *Celebrate* has three syllables: cel- (clap once) e (clap once) brate (clap once). Clap and tell me how many syllables *table* has (   ). How about *shop* (   ) and *wandering* (   )."

	YES	NO
1. Clap each time you hear a syllable in the following word:		
Sally	○	○
Bob	○	○
Kimberly	○	○
Mary	○	○
John	○	○

TOTAL CORRECT _____

Distinguishing Initial Sounds

Practice: "Many words begin with the same sound. *Pig* and *penny* both begin with the /p/ sound. Tell me two words that begin with the same sound as *wind* (   ), *tent* (   ), and *jump* (   )."

2. Name two other words that begin with the same sound as the word:		
cat	○	○
Sally	○	○
bed	○	○
milk	○	○
fat	○	○

TOTAL CORRECT _____

APPENDIX C

Distinguishing Rime and Rhyme

Practice: "Rhyming words sound the same at the end. I can rhyme three words: *sad, bad, glad.* Tell me a word that rhymes with *pin* ( ), *round* ( ), and *cup* ( )."

	YES	NO
3. Tell me if the two words rhyme.		
sand – hand	○	○
big – pig	○	○
rule – milk	○	○
fair – farm	○	○
bat – hat	○	○

TOTAL CORRECT ______

Distinguishing Oddity

Practice: "Sometimes in a group of three words, two words will begin with the same sound, but the other word will begin with a different sound. For example, with the three words *fox, fur,* and *tree, tree* does not begin with the same sound as *fox* and *fur.* Tell me which word begins with a different sound: *juice, milk, mom* ( ), *wind, weather, sun* ( ), *big, funny, fat* ( )."

4. Tell me which word does not begin with the same sound as the other two words:		
hat – man – hot	○	○
leg – lips – nose	○	○
man – money – nose	○	○
dog – tag – time	○	○
big – pull – push	○	○

TOTAL CORRECT ______

Blending Onset with Rime

Practice: "Many one-syllable words have two parts that can be blended together. For example, I can put a /b/ sound in front of *ug* and get *bug.* I want you to put an /m/ sound in front of /at/ and say the new word ( ); now put /s/ in front of /and/ ( ); now put /m/ in front of /eat/ ( )."

5. I am going to give you two parts of a word. I want you to blend the two parts together to make a word:		
/s/ + *at*	○	○
/k/ + *ake*	○	○
/b/ + *ug*	○	○
/j/ + *ump*	○	○
/n/ + *ight*	○	○

TOTAL CORRECT ______

APPENDIX C

Blending Letter Sounds

Practice: "Words are made up of individual sounds. For example, if I put /m/ + /u/ + /g/ together, I get *mug*. I want you to put these three sounds together: /f/ + /u/ + /n/ ( ). Now add /b/ + /u/ + /g/ ( ). Now add /s/ + /i/ + /t/ ( )."

	YES	NO
6. I am going to give you three sounds. I want you to blend the sounds together and say the word:		
/c/ + /u/ + /t/	○	○
/f/ + /a/ + /n/	○	○
/b/ + /i/ + /g/	○	○
/h/ + /o/ + /t/	○	○
/l/ + /e/ + /g/	○	○

TOTAL CORRECT _____

Segmenting Sounds in Words

Practice: "I can hear sounds in words. For example, when I say *bit*, I hear /b/ + /i/ + /t/. Tell me what sounds do you hear in *cat* ( ), in *fan* ( ), and in *ham* ( )."

7. I want you to tell me what three sounds you hear in each word:		
sad (/s/ + /a/ + /d/)	○	○
pop	○	○
bun	○	○
him	○	○
hen	○	○

TOTAL CORRECT _____

Manipulating Initial Sounds in Words

Practice: "I can change a sound in a word to make a new word. For example, in the word *land*, I can change the /l/ to /s/ and get *sand*. Tell me what new word you get when you change one letter for another. In the word *round*, change the /r/ to /s/ ( ). In the word *light*, change the /l/ to /n/ ( ). In *frown*, change the /fr/ to /cl/ ( )."

8. I am going to say a word; then I will ask you to change one sound to make a new word:		
fan – change /f/ to /m/	○	○
hut – change /h/ to /c/	○	○
right – change /r/ to /n/	○	○
meat – change /m/ to /n/	○	○
fat – change /f/ to /b/	○	○

TOTAL CORRECT _____

Deleting Initial Sounds of Words

Practice: "With some words, I can take off the initial sound and get a new word. For example if I take /b/ off of *beat,* I get *eat.* Tell me what word you get when you take /m/ off of *man* ( ); /f/ off of *fit* ( )."

	YES	NO
9. I am going to say a word; then I will ask you to take off a sound and give me the new word:		
late – take off the /l/	○	○
sand – take off the /s/	○	○
ham – take off the /h/	○	○
fat – take off the /f/	○	○
land – take off the /l/	○	○

TOTAL CORRECT ______

GRAND TOTAL CORRECT ______

It is important to look at each section to determine strengths and weaknesses because each question is a different task. In each section, five correct responses indicate that the child has mastered the skill. Three or four correct responses indicate that the child is developing the skill and only one or two correct responses indicate that the child has difficulty with the task.

GENERAL COMMENTS:

C.26 POST-ASSESSMENT FOR PHONEMIC AWARENESS (p. 83)

Name: ______________________ Date: ______________________

NOTE: The teacher will check "Yes" if the child can do the task, and "No" if the child cannot do the task. It is good to give one example to the child so they fully understand the task they are asked to perform. Examples are provided.

Syllabicating Words

Practice: "Words have different syllables. Some words have one syllable such as *hand* (clap once). *Mitten* has two syllables: mit- (clap once) tin (clap once). *Celebrate* has three syllables: cel- (clap once) e (clap once) brate (clap once). Clap and tell me how many syllables *table* has ( ). How about *shop* ( ) and *wandering* ( )."

	YES	NO
1. Clap each time you hear a syllable in the following words:		
Peter	○	○
Jane	○	○
Nathaniel	○	○
Joe	○	○
Molly	○	○

TOTAL CORRECT ______

Distinguishing Initial Sounds

Practice: "Many words begin with the same sound. *Pig* and *penny* both begin with the /p/ sound. Tell me two words that begin with the same sound as *wind* ( ), *tent* ( ), and *jump* ( )."

	YES	NO
2. Name two other words that begin with the same sound as the word:		
coat	○	○
snake	○	○
banana	○	○
money	○	○
fish	○	○

TOTAL CORRECT ______

Distinguishing Rime and Rhyme

Practice: "Rhyming words sound the same at the end. I can rhyme three words: *sad, bad, glad.* Tell me a word that rhymes with *pin* ( ), *round* ( ), and *cup* ( )."

3. Tell me if the two words rhyme.

	YES	NO
clock – block	○	○
fan – man	○	○
drink – doughnut	○	○
zoo – child zoo – child	○	○
light – night	○	○

TOTAL CORRECT _____

Distinguishing Oddity

Practice: "Sometimes in a group of three words, two words will begin with the same sound, but the other word will begin with a different sound. For example, with the three words *fox, fur,* and *tree, tree* does not begin with the same sound as *fox* and *fur*. Tell me which word begins with a different sound: *juice, milk, mom* ( ), *wind, weather, sun* ( ), *big, funny, fat* ( )."

4. Tell me which word does not begin with the same sound as the other two words:

milk – man – nuts	○	○
lamp – hut – house	○	○
clock – meat – mouse	○	○
snake – goat – smile	○	○
sun – fun – friend	○	○

TOTAL CORRECT _____

Blending Onset with Rime

Practice: "Many one-syllable words have two parts that can be blended together. For example, I can put a /b/ sound in front of *ug* and get *bug*. I want you to put an /m/ sound in front of /at/ and say the new word ( ); now put /s/ in front of /and/ ( ); now put /m/ in front of /eat/ ( )."

5. I am going to give you two parts of a word. I want you to blend the two parts together to make a word:

/f/ + *un*	○	○
/l/ + *ight*	○	○
/r/ + *ug*	○	○
/s/ + *and*	○	○
/b/ + *ump*	○	○

TOTAL CORRECT _____

Blending Letter Sounds

Practice: "Words are made up of individual sounds. For example, if I put /m/ + /u/ + /g/ together, I get *mug*. I want you to put these three sounds together: /f/ + /u/ + /n/ ( ). Now add /b/ + /u/ + /g/ ( ). Now add /s/ + /i/ + /t/ ( )."

	YES	NO
6. I am going to give you three sounds. I want you to blend the sounds together and say the word:		
/f/ + /a/ + /t/	○	○
/r/ + /u/ + /g/	○	○
/p/ + /i/ + /g/	○	○
/p/ + /o/ + /t/	○	○
/m/ + /a/ + /n/	○	○

TOTAL CORRECT _____

Segmenting Sounds in Words

Practice: "I can hear sounds in words. For example, when I say *bit*, I hear /b/ + /i/ + /t/. Tell me what sounds do you hear in *cat* ( ), in *fan* ( ), and in *ham* ( )."

7. I want you to tell me what three sounds you hear in each word:		
pen = /p/ + /e/ + /n/	○	○
Dad	○	○
top	○	○
sun	○	○
fin	○	○

TOTAL CORRECT _____

Manipulating Initial Sounds in Words

Practice: "I can change a sound in a word to make a new word. For example, in the word *land*, I can change the /l/ to /s/ and get *sand*. Tell me what new word you get when you change one letter for another. In the word *round*, change the /r/ to /s/ ( ). In the word *light*, change the /l/ to /n/ ( ). In *frown*, change the /fr/ to /cl/ ( )."

8. I am going to say a word; then I will ask you to change one sound to make a new word:		
man – change /m/ to /f/	○	○
cut – change /c/ to /h/	○	○
might – change /m/ to /s/	○	○
cake – change /c/ to /b/	○	○
hat – change /h/ to /f/	○	○

TOTAL CORRECT _____

Deleting Initial Sounds of Words

Practice: "With some words, I can take off the initial sound and get a new word. For example if I take /b/ off of *beat*, I get *eat*. Tell me what word you get when you take /m/ off of *man* ( ); /f/ off of *fit* ( )."

	YES	NO
9. I am going to say a word; then I will ask you to take off a sound and give me the new word:		
fan – take off /f/	○	○
band – take off /b/	○	○
meat – take off /m/	○	○
Sam – take off /s/	○	○
rat – take off /r/	○	○

TOTAL CORRECT ______

GRAND TOTAL CORRECT ______

It is important to look at each section to determine strengths and weaknesses because each question is a different task. In each section, five correct responses indicate that the child has mastered the skill. Three or four correct responses indicate that the child is developing the skill and only one or two correct responses indicate that the child has difficulty with the task.

GENERAL COMMENTS:

C.27 CHECKLIST FOR PHONEMIC AWARENESS FOR PRIMARY GRADES (p. 84)

(Based on the Seven Dimensions)

Teacher: ______________________________ Date: ______________

+ = always X = sometimes O = seldom/never

DIMENSION	STUDENTS																	
1. Ability to hear syllables within words																		
2. Ability to hear initial sounds or recognize alliteration																		
3. Ability to hear rhyming words																		
4. Ability to distinguish oddity																		
5. Ability to blend words orally																		
6. Ability to segment words:																		
• Drop beginning sound																		
• Drop ending sound																		
7. Ability to manipulate sounds orally to create new words																		

C.28 CHECKLIST OF KNOWN LETTER NAMES AND SOUNDS (p. 111)

Student: ______________________ Date: __________

LETTER	UPPERCASE NAME	LOWERCASE NAME	SCRIPT NAME	SOUND	WORD WITH INITIAL SOUND	WORD WITH ENDING SOUND
K						
N						
E						
J						
A						
T						
B						
S						
I						
M						
O						
D						
C						
Y						
G						
V						
Z						
P						
F						

Photocopy this page, cut apart the cards, and enlarge each card (200% will double the size) for use with children.

Master Card of Letters

K	N	E	J	A	T
B	S	I	M	R	H
L	W	X	Q	O	D
C	Y	G	V	Z	P
U	F				

k	n	e	j	a	t
b	s	i	m	r	h
l	w	x	q	o	d
c	y	g	v	z	p
u	f				

Master Card of Script Letters

K	N	E	J	A	T
B	S	I	M	R	H
L	W	X	Q	O	D
C	Y	G	V	Z	P
U	F				

k	n	e	j	a	t
b	s	i	m	r	h
l	w	x	q	o	d
c	y	g	v	z	p
u	f				

C.29 CHECKLIST FOR LETTER–SOUND RELATIONSHIPS, FIRST GRADE (p. 112)

(p. 112)

TEACHER: PERIOD 1 2 3 4

+ = always X = sometimes O = seldom/never

SUBSTANDARD	STUDENTS																	
1. Names and identifies each letter																		
2. Understands that written words are composed of letters that represent sounds																		
3. Identifies letter–sound relationships for all consonants																		
4. Identifies letter–sound relationships for short vowels																		
5. Identifies letter–sound relationships for r-controlled vowels																		
6. Identifies letter–sound relationships for consonant blends																		
7. Identifies letter–sound relationships for consonant digraphs																		
8. Identifies letter–sound relationships for vowel digraphs																		
9. Identifies letter–sound relationships for vowel diphthongs																		
10. Blends onset with rime																		

Source: Adapted from the Texas Education Agency. (1997). *TEKS for English Language Arts and Reading.* Austin, TX: State Department of Education., pp. B-29–D-30.

C.30 PHONICS MASTERY SURVEY (p. 112)

Instructions: Before administering this survey, reproduce letters and words on 3- × 5-inch cards in large, lowercase letters, so the child can see them with ease. This survey should be administered to one child at a time. Use a separate sheet to document each child's progress. In the first section, stop if the child makes more than 10 errors. For every other section, stop when child makes five or more errors. When sounds are incorrect, write the sound the child makes above the word.

1. Consonant Sounds

Show the child one card at a time, featuring lowercase consonant letters. Ask the child to tell you what sound the letter makes. On the assessment sheet, circle the letter if an incorrect sound is given. Write the incorrect sound the child gives on top of the letter.

___	___	___	___	___	___	___	___	___	___	___	___	___	___	___	___	___	___	___
p	b	m	w	f	v	t	s	d	r	j	h	z	n	l	y	k	c	g

If the child is not able to identify at least 10 sounds, terminate this assessment.

2. Rhyming Words

Ask the child to read the following words and to say three words that rhyme with each of them. Nonsense words are acceptable.

1. be ______________________________
2. go ______________________________
3. say ______________________________
4. do ______________________________
5. make ______________________________
6. will ______________________________
7. get ______________________________
8. blink ______________________________
9. tan ______________________________
10. bug ______________________________

3. CVC Words

Ask the child to read the following short-vowel, CVC nonsense words. There are four examples of each short vowel sound. Indicate which vowel sounds were read correctly and which were not.

1. nid ____________
2. gat ____________
3. bul ____________
4. rup ____________
5. sen ____________
6. nat ____________
7. det ____________
8. rit ____________
9. nup ____________
10. nop ____________
11. wat ____________
12. vin ____________
13. lom ____________
14. hap ____________
15. yub ____________
16. pem ____________
17. dom ____________
18. kud ____________
19. wom ____________
20. zet ____________

4. Consonant Blends

Ask the child to read the following words and nonsense words that contain beginning or ending consonant blends (or both). Indicate any blends the child says incorrectly.

1. blithe ____________
2. clog ____________
3. plush ____________
4. flounce ____________
5. frisk ____________
6. dwelt ____________
7. skig ____________
8. crass ____________
9. trek ____________
10. swap ____________
11. trink ____________
12. brind ____________
13. scup ____________
14. stint ____________
15. smeat ____________
16. spole ____________
17. gluck ____________
18. brame ____________
19. dredge ____________
20. lasp ____________

5. Consonant Digraphs

Have the child read the following nonsense words containing consonant digraphs. Indicate any digraphs the child says incorrectly.

1. shan ____________
2. thort ____________
3. phrat ____________
4. chib ____________
5. phant ____________
6. yeth ____________
7. rosh ____________
8. lotch ____________
9. gresh ____________
10. chass ____________
11. scord ____________
12. squean ____________
13. sling ____________
14. sprill ____________
15. strug ____________
16. splom ____________
17. shred ____________
18. squim ____________
19. throbe ____________

APPENDIX C

6. Long Vowel Sounds

Have the child read the following nonsense words that contain long vowel sounds. There are four examples of each long vowel sound. Indicate which vowels are read correctly and which are not.

1. stope	______	11. ploan	______
2. kade	______	12. tayne	______
3. fede	______	13. sheed	______
4. gride	______	14. vied	______
5. blude	______	15. trewd	______
6. kroan	______	16. whade	______
7. jaike	______	17. strean	______
8. theade	______	18. blipe	______
9. smight	______	19. roke	______
10. dreud	______	20. krume	______

7. Other Vowel Sounds

Have the child read the following nonsense words that contain variant vowel sounds. Indicate vowel sounds the child reads incorrectly.

1. nook (oo)	______	8. gorn (or)	______
2. krouse (ou, ow)	______	9. chaw (aw, au)	______
3. sar (ar)	______	10. zout (ou)	______
4. moil (oi)	______	11. larm (ar)	______
5. noy (oy)	______	12. groil (oi)	______
6. thirl (ir, er, ur)	______	13. nirl (ir, er, ur)	______
7. floom (oo)	______		______

8. Number of Word Parts (Syllables)

Ask the child to read the following words and count the number of word parts or syllables in each word. (Correct answers are in parentheses.)

1. retention (3)	______	6. contaminate (4)	______
2. ride (1)	______	7. computer (3)	______
3. panic (2)	______	8. antagonist (4)	______
4. carnival (3)	______	9. guess (1)	______
5. monster (2)	______	10. consider (3)	______

Source: Cecil, N. L. (2011). *Striking a Balance: A Comprehensive Approach to Early Literacy* (4th ed.). Scottsdale, AZ: Holcomb Hathaway. Used with permission.

C.31 DECODING AND WORD RECOGNITION CHECKLIST (p. 133)

Based on California's Standard 1.10

TEACHER: ______________________________ DATE: ______________

+ = always X = sometimes O = seldom/never

STANDARD	STUDENTS																	
1. Recognizes consonant blends																		
2. Recognizes short vowel pattern: CVC																		
3. Recognizes long vowel patterns: CVCe and CV																		
4. Blends onsets with rime																		
5. Recognizes common irregular sight words																		
6. Uses knowledge of vowel digraphs to read words																		
7. Uses knowledge of r-controlled vowels to read words																		
8. Reads compound words																		
9. Reads contractions																		
10. Recognizes inflectional endings when reading words																		
11. Finds root words in order to recognize words																		
12. Reads common word families																		
13. Reads in manner that sounds like natural speech																		

Source: Based on California's State Standard: First Grade, Standard 1.10.

C.32 SCORING SHEET FOR WORD OR PHRASE LISTS (p. 134)

STUDENT: ______________________________ GRADE: __________

+ = YES − = NO

WORDS/PHRASES	BEGINNING OF YEAR	1ST QUARTER	2ND QUARTER	3RD QUARTER	4TH QUARTER

C.33 VOCABULARY GROWTH CHECKLIST (p. 162)

FOR FIRST GRADE, BASED ON FLORIDA'S STATE STANDARDS

TEACHER: ____________________ DATE: ____________________

\+ = always X = sometimes O = seldom/never

STANDARD	STUDENTS																	
1. Knows meaning of common words within basic categories																		
2. Uses knowledge of individual words in unknown compound words to predict their meanings																		
3. Uses reference resources to learn word meanings (e.g., beginning dictionaries and available technology)																		
4. Uses knowledge of suffixes (-er, -est, -ful) to determine meanings of words																		
5. Develops vocabulary by listening to and discussing both familiar and conceptually challenging selections read aloud																		

C.34 RUBRIC FOR NARRATIVE READING COMPREHENSION (p. 191)

(p. 191)

STUDENT: GRADE: GRADING PERIOD: 1 2 3 4

TRAIT	LEVEL OF MASTERY TARGET (5 POINTS)	 ACCEPTABLE (3 POINTS)	 UNACCEPTABLE (1 POINT)
1. C.1a Verify predictions	Can respond to questions that reflect higher-level thinking (e.g., analyze, synthesize, infer, and evaluate). ___	Sometimes responds to questions that reflect higher-level thinking (e.g., analyze, synthesize, infer, and evaluate). ___	Seldom responds to questions that reflect higher-level thinking (e.g., analyze, synthesize, infer, and evaluate). ___
	Generates questions that reflect higher-level thinking (e.g., analyze, synthesize, infer, and evaluate). ___	Sometimes generates questions that reflect higher-level thinking (e.g., analyze, synthesize, infer, and evaluate). ___	Seldom generates questions that reflect higher-level thinking (e.g., analyze, synthesize, infer, and evaluate). ___
	Uses evidence in text to support predictions and conclusions. ___	Sometimes uses evidence in text to support predictions and conclusions. ___	Seldom uses evidence in text to support predictions and conclusions. ___
1. C.1b Themes and topics	Makes interpretation of text with text-based support. ___	Sometimes makes interpretation of text with text-based support. ___	Seldom makes interpretation of text with text-based support. ___
	Identifies author's lesson, either stated or implied. ___	Sometimes identifies author's lesson, either stated or implied. ___	Seldom identifies author's lesson, either stated or implied. ___
1. C.1c Compares reading selections	Compares/contrasts themes, topics, and story elements. ___	Sometimes compares/contrasts themes, topics, and story elements. ___	Seldom compares/contrasts themes, topics, and story elements. ___
	Uses text information to make connections to other situations. ___	Sometimes uses text information to make connections to other situations. ___	Seldom uses text information to make connections to other situations. ___
1. C.1d Summarization	Retells in written form the main points of the story. ___	Sometimes can retell in written form the main points of the story. ___	Seldom can retell in written form the main points of the story. ___
	Retells orally the main points of the story. ___	Sometimes can retell orally the main points of the story. ___	Seldom can retell orally the main points of the story. ___

TOTAL SCORE: ______

Scoring:

28–45 pts = competent in narrative comprehension (end-of-year goal)

10–27 pts = becoming competent in narrative comprehension (midyear goal)

1–9 pts = unacceptable; needs intense instruction

Based on Illinois Early Elementary School English/Language Arts Standards 1.C.1a–1.C.1d, at www.isbe.state.il.us.

C.35 NARRATIVE READING RUBRIC (p. 191)

NAME: DATE:

3 POINTS	2 POINTS	1 POINT	0 POINTS	SCORE
Retells descriptive details of setting and all characters.	Retells main details of setting and only two main characters.	Retells some details of only main character.	Cannot recall details of setting or characters.	
Readily makes inferences about characters' actions, reactions, and motives.	With prompting, can make inferences about characters' actions, reactions, and motives.	Can make very few inferences about characters' actions, reactions, and motives.	Cannot make inferences about characters' actions, reactions, and motives.	
Vividly visualizes how setting looks, smells, and feels.	Visualizes how setting looks and smells.	Visualizes how setting looks.	Cannot visualize setting.	
Readily predicts plot and then affirms or changes prediction as he/she reads.	Predicts plot and affirms prediction as he/she reads.	Predicts plot, but cannot affirm or change predictions as he/she reads.	Cannot make predictions about plot.	
Retells sequence in exact order of plot.	Retells sequence of plot with only one event out of order.	Retells sequence of plot with only two events out of order.	Retells plot, but not in sequence.	
Self-monitors and slows down and rereads sentence or passage as necessary.	Self-monitors by slowing down and only rereads sentence.	Self-monitors by slowing down.	Does not self-monitor.	
Becomes engrossed with the story through laughter, tears, or facial expressions.	Becomes somewhat engrossed with the story through laughter or tears.	Becomes a little engrossed with the story.	Shows no emotion while reading the story.	
Uses at least three different strategies to decode unfamiliar words.	Uses at least two different strategies to decode unfamiliar words.	Uses only one strategy to decode unfamiliar words.	Uses no strategies to decode unfamiliar words.	
Understands new vocabulary through context clues, picture clues, or use of dictionary.	Understands new vocabulary through context clues or picture clues.	Understands new vocabulary through picture clues.	Does not use context clues, picture clues, or dictionary to under stand new vocabulary.	
Integrates relevant text information with background knowledge to comprehend story.	Integrates some background knowledge with text information to comprehend story.	Integrates little background knowledge with text information to comprehend story.	Cannot integrate background knowledge with text information.	
Understands idioms, metaphors, and figurative language and understands how author uses them for effect.	Understands idioms, metaphors, and figurative language.	Understands metaphors and some figurative language.	Does not understand figurative language.	
Develops valid interpretation of the theme that elucidates the author's purpose.	Somewhat develops valid interpretation of the theme that elucidates the author's purpose.	Develops a weak interpretation of the theme.	Does not develop an interpretation of the theme.	
Remembers content from previous reading sessions when reading longer texts such as chapter books.	Goes back to previous reading when reading longer texts such as chapter books.	Recalls vaguely content from previous readings.	Cannot recall content from previous readings.	
Readily draws conclusions about mood, style, and theme that demonstrates author's intent.	Draws conclusion about mood and theme that demonstrates author's intent.	With prompting from teacher, can draw conclusion about mood and theme that demonstrates author's intent.	Cannot draw conclusion about mood, theme, or style.	

Total ___ /42
(Acceptable score is 34 or 80%)

APPENDIX C

C.36 GENERAL READING RUBRIC (p. 191)

NAME: DATE:

3 POINTS	2 POINTS	1 POINT	0 POINTS	SCORE
Always establishes purpose for reading.	Usually establishes purpose for reading.	Seldom sets purpose for reading.	Never sets purpose for reading.	
Always previews book before reading (e.g., looks at pictures and charts).	Usually previews book before reading (e.g., looks at pictures and charts).	Seldom previews book before reading (e.g., looks at pictures and charts).	Never previews book before reading.	
Readily chooses books that are at appropriate reading level; recognizes if book is too difficult.	Usually chooses books that are at appropriate reading level; recognizes if book is too difficult.	Seldom chooses books that are at appropriate reading level; does not recognize if book is too difficult.	Cannot choose books that are at appropriate reading level.	
Readily abandons a book if it does not interest him/her.	After some time will abandon a book if it does not interest him/her.	Seldom abandons a book even if it does not interest him/her.	Never abandons a book that does not interest him/her.	
Uses at least four different strategies when comprehension breaks down.	Uses at least three different strategies when comprehension breaks down.	Uses at least two different strategies when comprehension breaks down.	Has no strategies to use when comprehension breaks down.	
Reads fluently; rate and intonation are better than average.	Reads fluently; rate and intonation are average.	Fluency is marginal; rate is 75% of average grade-level rate.	Fluency is weak; rate is less than 75% of average grade-level rate.	
Accurately retells all details.	Retells most details.	Retells only main points.	Can retell only a little bit of reading.	
Asks profound questions about passage; displays critical-thinking skills.	Asks some questions about passage; displays some critical-thinking skills.	Seldom asks questions about passage; does not display critical-thinking skills.	Never asks questions about passage.	
Integrates relevant text information with background knowledge to comprehend passage.	Integrates some background knowledge with text information to comprehend passage.	Integrates little background knowledge with text information to comprehend passage.	Cannot integrate background knowledge with text information to comprehend passage.	
Automatically recognizes a large bank of vocabulary; can readily break down unfamiliar words.	Automatically recognizes an average amount of words; has at least three strategies to break up unfamiliar words.	Automatically recognizes most familiar words; has at least two strategies to break up unfamiliar words.	Lacks automaticity of familiar words; has no strategy for identifying unfamiliar words.	
Effectively and efficiently uses graphophonics to decode unfamiliar words in a passage.	Effectively uses graphophonics to decode unfamiliar words in a passage.	Seldom uses graphophonics to decode unfamiliar words in a passage.	Struggles to use graphophonics to decode unfamiliar words in a passage.	
Effectively and efficiently uses the semantic cueing system to read unfamiliar words in a passage.	Often uses the semantic cueing system to read unfamiliar words in a passage.	Seldom uses the semantic cueing system to read unfamiliar words in a passage.	Struggles to use the semantic cueing system to read unfamiliar words in a passage.	
Effectively and efficiently uses the syntax cueing system to read unfamiliar words in passage.	Often uses the syntax cueing system to read unfamiliar words in a passage.	Seldom uses the syntax cueing system to read unfamiliar words in a passage.	Struggles to use the syntax cueing system to read unfamiliar words in a passage.	

TOTAL SCORE: ____ /39
(Acceptable score is 31 or 80%)

C.37 INTEREST INVENTORY FOR INFORMATIONAL TEXTS (p. 218)

THINGS THAT INTEREST ME

All of these questions are about your interests! You can list more than one thing for each question.

NAME: ______________________ DATE: ______________

1. What is your favorite subject in school?

____

2. What subject that is not offered in school do you wish you could study?

____

3. What is your favorite sport?

____

4. What is your favorite TV program?

____

5. Who is your favorite athlete?

____

6. Who is your favorite actor/actress?

____

7. On Saturday, what is your favorite thing to do?

____

8. What type of music do you like?

____

9. What do you want to be when you grow up?

____

10. What is your favorite book?

____

11. If you could hop on a magic carpet, where in the world would you like to go?

____

12. If you could live in "another time," what time would it be? In the future? In the past?

____

13. What subject would you like to read about when we are working together?

____

APPENDIX C

C.38 OBSERVATION CHECKLIST OF STUDENT'S EXPOSITORY READING (p. 236)

STUDENT: ______________________ GRADE: __________

BEHAVIOR	Most of the time	Sometimes	Seldom	Never
BEFORE READING				
1. Determines purpose for reading	○	○	○	○
2. Predicts by reading headings	○	○	○	○
3. Skims to get overview of passage	○	○	○	○
4. Checks how long the passage is	○	○	○	○
5. Relates prior knowledge to passage	○	○	○	○
DURING READING				
1. Does not omit unknown words	○	○	○	○
2. Attempts to pronounce new words	○	○	○	○
3. Decodes new words easily	○	○	○	○
4. Does not use finger or other object to keep place	○	○	○	○
5. Does not insert words	○	○	○	○
6. Reads punctuation correctly	○	○	○	○
7. Rereads if comprehension breaks down	○	○	○	○
8. Connects reading material to prior knowledge	○	○	○	○
9. Reads figures, pictures, etc.	○	○	○	○
10. Looks up unknown words in glossary	○	○	○	○
11. Does not mouth words when reading silently	○	○	○	○
12. Does not have difficult time staying on task during silent reading	○	○	○	○
AFTER READING				
1. Summarizes in logical order	○	○	○	○
2. Retells main points	○	○	○	○
3. Retells information not found in text	○	○	○	○
4. Relates information to prior knowledge	○	○	○	○
5. Interprets text correctly	○	○	○	○
6. Makes inferences	○	○	○	○
7. Shows signs of critical thinking	○	○	○	○
8. Asks questions about material	○	○	○	○
9. Desires to know more about topic	○	○	○	○

COMMENTS

C.39 EXPOSITORY READING RUBRIC (p. 236)
(p. 236)

NAME DATE

3 POINTS	2 POINTS	1 POINT	0 POINTS	SCORE
Always establishes purpose for reading.	Usually establishes purpose for reading.	Seldom sets purpose for reading.	Never sets purpose for reading.	
Analyzes large bank of technical terms with ease.	Analyzes most technical words with ease.	Analyzes a few technical terms.	Cannot analyze new technical terms.	
Integrates relevant text information with background knowledge to comprehend passage.	Integrates some background knowledge with text information to comprehend passage.	Integrates little background knowledge with text information to comprehend passage.	Cannot integrate background knowledge with text information.	
Readily makes accurate inferences about information in passage.	Most inferences are accurate about information in passage.	Makes a few accurate inferences about information in passage.	Cannot make accurate inferences about information in passage.	
Uses multiple fix-up strategies when comprehension breaks down.	Uses some fix-up strategies when comprehension breaks down.	Uses one or two different strategies when comprehension breaks down.	Uses no strategies when comprehension breaks down.	
Readily builds up relationships between larger units of text.	Builds up relationships between larger units of text.	Can build up some relationships between larger units of text.	Cannot build up relationships between larger units of text.	
Can readily create appropriate graphic organizer of text.	Can create appropriate graphic organizer of text.	With prompting from teacher, can create appropriate graphic organizer of text.	Cannot create an appropriate graphic organizer of text.	
Can synthesize information from at least four sources.	Can synthesize information from at least three sources.	Can synthesize information from at least two sources.	Cannot synthesize information from various sources.	
Easily chooses key terms for Internet use.	Can choose some key terms for Internet use.	With prompting from teacher, can choose key terms for Internet use.	Cannot choose key terms for Internet use.	
Can use search engines on the Internet and effectively choose helpful sites.	Can use search engines on the Internet when given enough time.	Can use search engines on the Internet when given large blocks of time.	Cannot use search engines effectively.	
Can readily identify author or organization of Internet material.	Can identify author or organization of Internet material when given enough time.	Can identify author or organization of Internet material when given large blocks of time.	Cannot identify author or organization of Internet material.	
Can readily determine if information on Internet sites is accurate by comparing it to background knowledge or other printed material.	Can determine if information on Internet sites is accurate by comparing it to background knowledge.	With prompting from teacher, he/she can determine if information on Internet site is accurate.	Cannot determine if Internet information is accurate.	
Can effectively and in a timely manner scan passages to find key dates, names, terms, and other information.	Can effectively scan passages to find key date, names, and terms.	Can scan passages to find key dates and names.	Cannot scan passages to find key dates, names, or terms.	
Can effectively skim text and pictures to gather main idea of passage to determine if he/she wants to read passage.	Can skim text and pictures to gather main idea of passage to determine if he/she wants to read passage.	Can skim pictures to gather main idea of passage.	Cannot skim text to gather main idea.	

TOTAL SCORE: ____ /42

(Acceptable score is 34 or 80%)

APPENDIX C

C.40 CHECKLIST OF BASIC INTERNET SKILLS (p. 255)

STUDENT: ______________________ DATE: ______________

	YES	NO
1. Has skills to locate materials.	○	○
2. Is able to identify important questions.	○	○
3. Knows how to use search engines and how to select words.	○	○
4. Knows how to refine search words so they are as specific as possible.	○	○
5. Knows how to read and evaluate the short descriptions found in search engine results.	○	○
6. Uses only the sites that address their topic.	○	○
7. Is able to evaluate the author's authority.	○	○
8. Understands the importance of the "back" button.	○	○
9. Is able to read and comprehend the text.	○	○
10. Takes notes from the sites.	○	○
11. Is able to synthesize material from the various sites.	○	○
12. Cites sources correctly.	○	○

Source: Adapted from Henry, L. (2006). Searching for an answer: The critical role of new literacies while reading on the Internet. *The Reading Teacher, 59*(7), 614–626.

C.41 FLUENCY CHECKLIST (p. 268)

NAME: ____________________ GRADE: ____________

EVALUATOR: ____________________

CHARACTERISTIC	DATE	DATE	DATE	DATE
STAGE 1				
Rate: Word-by-word reading with many pauses				
Prosody: No phrasing				
Prosody: Omits punctuation				
Automaticity: Sounds out letter by letter; ignores chunks in words				
Expression: Lacks expression				
STAGE 2				
Rate: Some two- or three-word phrases with many pauses				
Prosody: Aware of some end marks (periods, question marks)				
Automaticity: Begins to recognize chunks within monosyllabic words (onsets and rimes)				
Expression: Lacks expression				
STAGE 3				
Rate: Appropriate most of the time				
Prosody: Attentive to end marks and commas				
Automaticity: Recognizes chunks within words and inflectional endings				
Expression: Beginning to recognize dialogue				
STAGE 4				
Rate: Varies speed with difficulty of text				
Prosody: Attentive to all punctuation, good phrasing				
Automaticity: Recognizes syllables				
Expression: Appropriate for dialogue and mood				

C.42 FLUENCY CHECKLIST FOR NARRATIVE TEXT (p. 268)

NAME: ______________________ DATE: ______________

STORY: ______________________ NUMBER OF WORDS: ______________

TIME IT TOOK TO READ: ______________________ WPM: ______________

TRAIT	YES	NO
1. Stopped for periods	○	○
2. Raised voice for question marks	○	○
3. Read with excitement for exclamation marks	○	○
4. Made slight pause for commas	○	○
5. Read phrases correctly	○	○
6. Changed voice for different characters (watched quotation marks)	○	○
7. Changed volume for different moods	○	○
8. Changed rate for different moods	○	○
9. Paused for ellipses	○	○
10. Emphasized italicized words	○	○

C

C.43 ORAL READING FLUENCY RUBRIC (p. 268)

Rate the reader's fluency in each of the four categories below. Choose the appropriate score in each category and write the number of points on that line. Add all four scores for Total Score.

ORAL READING

___ (5 pts.) Reading is fluent, confident, and accurate.

___ (4 pts.) Reading is fluent and accurate for the most part, but reader occasionally falters or hesitates.

___ (3 pts.) Reader lacks confidence at times, and reading is characterized by frequent pauses, miscues, and hesitations.

___ (2 pts.) Reader consistently lacks confidence and occasionally lapses into word-by-word reading with frequent meaning-violating miscues.

___ (1 pt.) Reader demonstrates largely word-by-word reading with little or no inflection and numerous meaning-violating miscues, some of which may be nonwords.

INTONATION

___ (5 pts.) Intonation consistently supports meaning of the text.

___ (4 pts.) Intonations are largely meaningful but may include exaggerations or inflections inappropriate for the text.

___ (3 pts.) Intonation is characterized by some joining of words into meaningful phrases, but this element often breaks down when the reader encounters difficulties.

___ (2 pts.) Intonation is largely flat with lack of enthusiasm.

___ (1 pt.) Intonation is almost completely absent.

PUNCTUATION

___ (5 pts.) Reader demonstrates a natural use of and appreciation for punctuation.

___ (4 pts.) Reader demonstrates a solid use of punctuation as an aid to intonation.

___ (3 pts.) Reaction to punctuation marks results in pauses that are inappropriately long or short.

___ (2 pts.) Punctuation is occasionally ignored and meaning may be distorted.

___ (1 pt.) Reader demonstrates frequent ignoring of punctuation.

PACING

___ (5 pts.) Pacing is rapid but smooth and unexaggerated.

___ (4 pts.) Reading is well paced with only occasional weakness in response to difficulties with the text.

___ (3 pts.) Pacing relatively slow and markedly slower (or markedly faster) when reader encounters difficult text.

___ (2 pts.) Pacing is either very slow or inappropriately fast.

___ (1 pt.) Pacing is painfully slow and halting.

___ TOTAL SCORE

Source: Applegate, Mary D.; Quinn, Kathleen B.; Applegate, Anthony J., *Critical Reading Inventory, The: Assessing Student's Reading and Thinking,* 2nd ed., © 2008, p. 78. Adapted by permission of Pearson Education, Inc., Upper Saddle River, NJ.

C.44 FLUENCY QUESTIONS FOR SELF-EVALUATION (p. 268)

NAME: ______________________________ DATE: ______________

- ○ Did my reading sound like read speech, like people talking? Would someone listening understand what the author meant from my reading?
- ○ Did I have to work hard to pronounce the words correctly?
- ○ Did I make many mistakes in my reading? When I made a mistake that changed the meaning, did I go back and change it?
- ○ Did I read with good expression or in a monotone? Did I vary my volume when appropriate to express meaning?
- ○ Was I reading loudly enough?
- ○ Did I change speed when necessary, especially when I wanted to stress certain parts?
- ○ Did I read too slowly? Did I read too quickly?
- ○ Did I group the words correctly?
- ○ Did I pay attention to periods to make my voice go down? Did I pause for commas? Did my voice go up for question marks? Did I sound excited for exclamation marks?
- ○ Did I emphasize any words that needed it?
- ○ What is best about my reading? What should I work on to make my reading even better?

Source: Adapted from Rasinski (2003) and Cecil (2011).

C.45 6 + 1 TRAIT® WRITING ASSESSMENT (p. 299)

NAME: ______________________________ DATE: ______________

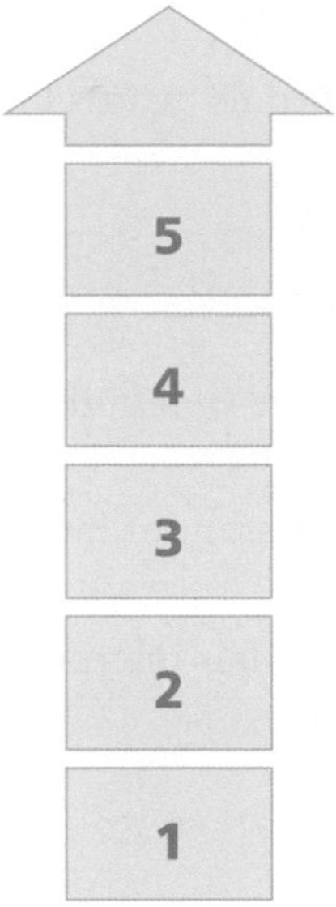

SCORING CONTINUUM

WOW! Exceeds expectations

5 *Strong* Shows control and skill in this trait; many strengths present

4 *Effective* On balance, the strengths outweigh the weaknesses; a small amount of revision is needed

3 *Developing* Strengths and need for revision are about equal; about half-way home

2 *Emerging* Need for revision outweighs strengths; isolated moments hint at what the writer has in mind

1 *Not Yet* A bare beginning; writer not yet showing any control

Circled number shows where you are on the continuum for each trait.

IDEAS

⑤ This paper is clear and focused. It holds the reader's attention. Relevant anecdotes and details enrich the central theme.

③ The writer is beginning to define the topic, even though development is still basic or general.

① As yet, the paper has no clear sense of purpose or central theme. To extract meaning from the text, the reader must make inferences based on sketchy or missing details. The writing reflects more than one of the problems.

ORGANIZATION

⑤ The organization enhances and showcases the central idea or theme. The order, structure, or presentation of information is compelling and moves the reader through the text.

③ The organizational structure is strong enough to move the reader through the text without too much confusion.

① The writing lacks a clear sense of direction. Ideas, details, or events seem strung together in a loose or random fashion; there is no identifiable internal structure. The writing reflects more than one of the problems.

VOICE

⑤ The writer speaks directly to the reader in a way that is individual, compelling, and engaging. The writer crafts the writing with an awareness and respect for the audience and the purpose for writing.

③ The writer seems sincere, but not fully engaged or involved. The writing has discernable purpose, but is not compelling.

① The writer seems indifferent to the topic and the content. The writing lacks purpose and audience engagement.

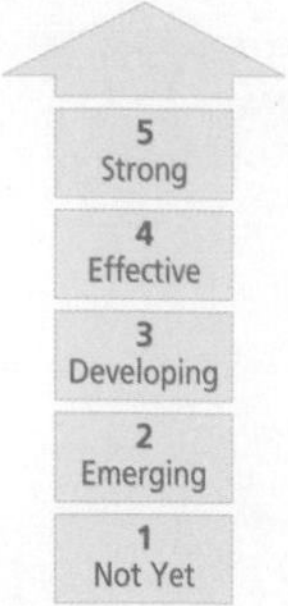

WORD CHOICE

⑤ Words convey the intended message in a precise, interesting, and natural way. The words are powerful and engaging.

③ The language is functional, even if it lacks much energy. It is easy to figure out the writer's meaning on a general level.

① The writer demonstrates a limited vocabulary or has not searched for words to convey specific meaning.

SENTENCE FLUENCY

⑤ The writing has an easy flow, rhythm, and cadence. Sentences are well built, with strong and varied structure that invites expressive oral reading.

③ The text hums along with a steady beat, but tends to be more pleasant or businesslike than musical, more mechanical than fluid.

① The reader has to practice quite a bit in order to give this paper a fair interpretive reading. The writing reflects more than one of the problems.

CONVENTIONS

⑤ The writer demonstrates a good grasp of standard writing conventions (e.g., spelling, punctuation, capitalization, grammar, usage, paragraphing) and uses conventions effectively to enhance readability. Errors tend to be so few that just minor touch-ups would get this piece ready to publish.

GRADES 7 AND UP ONLY: The writing is sufficiently complex to allow the writer to show skill in using a wide range of conventions. For writers at younger ages, the writing shows control over those conventions that are grade age appropriate.

③ The writer shows reasonable control over a limited range of standard writing conventions. Conventions are sometimes handled well and enhance readability; at other times, errors are distracting and impair readability.

① Errors in spelling, punctuation, capitalization, usage, and grammar and/or paragraphing repeatedly distract the reader and make the text difficult to read. The writing reflects more than one of the problems.

PRESENTATION (Optional)

⑤ The form and presentation of the text enhances the ability of the reader to understand and connect with the message. It is pleasing to the eye.

③ The writer's message is understandable in this format.

① The reader receives a garbled message due to problems relating to the presentation of the text.

C.46 RUBRIC FOR ASSESSING THE WRITING PROCESS OF WRITERS IN PRIMARY GRADES (p. 299)

NAME: GRADE:

SCORES: CONSISTENTLY PRESENT = 5, SOMETIMES PRESENT = 3, NOT PRESENT = 0

COMPETENCY	DATES/SCORES			
PREWRITING DATES:				
1. Generates own writing ideas.				
2. Reflects on idea before writing.				
3. Self-starter.				
4. Shares ideas with others.				
5. Draws before writing.				
DRAFTING				
1. Writes without worry about mechanics.				
2. Writes in various formats.				
3. Forms letters correctly.				
4. Uses invented spelling.				
5. Shows awareness of letter–sound relationships.				
6. Generates many ideas.				
7. Stories have beginning, middle, and end.				
8. Writes independently.				
9. Completes a passage.				
REVISING				
1. Rereads passage.				
2. Adds to passage.				
3. Deletes sections.				
4. Reads passage to peers.				
5. Reads ideas to others.				
6. Listens to others read.				

COMPETENCY	DATES/SCORES			
EDITING				
1. Looks at spelling patterns.				
2. Checks and corrects letter formation.				
3. Self-edits.				
4. Rewrites passage to make "clean" copy.				
5. Seeks help from teacher.				
6. Seeks help from peers.				
7. Helps peers with their editing.				
PUBLISHING				
1. Willing to share in author's chair.				
2. Willing to share written copy with others.				
3. Enjoys listening to others' stories.				
TOTAL:				

TEACHER'S COMMENTS:

APPENDIX C

C.47 RUBRIC FOR ASSESSING THE WRITING PROCESS OF THIRD GRADERS (p. 299)

STUDENT: ______________________________

TEACHER: ______________________________

SCORES: 0 = NEVER 1 = SELDOM 2 = SOMETIMES 3 = USUALLY 4 = ALWAYS

STRATEGY	DATES/SCORES			
PREWRITING DATES:				
1. Researches books, magazines, or ____________ (other).				
2. Brainstorms ideas on graphic organizers.				
3. Shares ideas with classmate(s).				
4. Makes notes.				
5. Plans for a particular audience.				
6. Makes good use of time.				
7. Has correct supplies.				
8. Records ideas through writing/drawing.				
9. Plans purpose.				
DRAFTING				
1. Uses plans and resources.				
2. Writes without deleting.				
3. Takes risk with new genre.				
4. Knows audience.				
5. Writes without worry about mechanics.				
6. Stays on task.				
REVISING				
1. Deletes material.				
2. Conducts more research.				
3. Reorganizes material.				
4. Seeks comments from peers.				
5. Seeks comments from teacher.				
6. Is willing to rewrite.				
7. Focuses on good word choice.				

STRATEGY	DATES/SCORES			
EDITING				
1. Self-checks spelling.				
2. Self-checks punctuation.				
3. Self-checks usage.				
4. Self-checks legibility.				
PUBLISHING				
1. Puts text in neat, final form.				
2. Shares with class.				
3. Shares with wider community.				
TOTAL:				

TEACHER'S COMMENTS:

APPENDIX C

C.48 RUBRIC FOR WRITING STORIES (p. 299)

NAME: DATE:

SCORES: EXCELLENT = 5 FAIR = 3 POOR = 0

COMPETENCY	EXCELLENT	FAIR	POOR
1. Setting description	○	○	○
2. Character description	○	○	○
3. Actions of characters	○	○	○
4. Dialogue of characters	○	○	○
5. Motives of characters	○	○	○
6. Story starter	○	○	○
7. Plot with roadblocks	○	○	○
8. Climax to plot	○	○	○
9. Resolution to plot	○	○	○
10. Choice of adjectives	○	○	○
11. Choice of verbs	○	○	○
12. Choice of nouns	○	○	○
13. Use of figurative speech	○	○	○
14. Quotation marks	○	○	○
15. Spelling	○	○	○
16. Punctuation	○	○	○
17. Paragraphing	○	○	○
18. Standard usage	○	○	○
19. Presentation	○	○	○

TEACHER'S COMMENTS:

APPENDIX C

C.49 RUBRIC FOR RESEARCH PAPER (p. 299)

NAME: ______________________ DATE: ______________________

SCORES: YES = 5 POINTS SOMEWHAT = 3 POINTS NO = 0 POINTS

COMPETENCY	YES	SOMEWHAT	NO
1. Used books to get information.	○	○	○
2. Used video to get information.	○	○	○
3. Used Internet to get information.	○	○	○
4. Interviewed others for information.	○	○	○
5. Wrote interesting introduction.	○	○	○
6. Developed ideas with explanations, details, or examples.	○	○	○
7. Organized information within paragraphs.	○	○	○
8. Good organization within report.	○	○	○
9. Used descriptive language, specific nouns.	○	○	○
10. Included new, interesting information.	○	○	○
11. Used writing conventions such as:			
Capitalization	○	○	○
Correct usage	○	○	○
Correct spelling	○	○	○
Indents paragraphs	○	○	○
Correct paragraphing	○	○	○
12. Wrote complete sentences.	○	○	○
13. Summarized ideas at end.	○	○	○
14. Included references in correct format.	○	○	○
15. Presented in neat format.	○	○	○

TOTAL ________

TEACHER'S COMMENTS:

APPENDIX C

C.50 RUBRIC FOR STORY WRITING (p. 299)

TITLE: ____________________

NAME: ____________________ DATE: ____________________

3 POINTS	2 POINTS	1 POINT	0 POINTS	SCORE
Title is creative, relates to action, and sparks interest in readers.	Title is related to action.	Title does not relate to action.	No title was given.	
Evidence of prewriting with descriptive setting and characters, with sequence of plot.	Evidence of some prewriting with names of characters and some events of plot.	Little evidence of prewriting with only names of characters.	No evidence of prewriting.	
Many vivid descriptive words to paint a picture of time and place.	Some descriptive words to explain time and place of action.	Few descriptive words to explain time and place of action.	No descriptive words to explain time and place of action.	
Many vivid, descriptive words to paint a picture of characters' physical appearance and actions.	Some descriptive words to explain characters' physical appearance and actions.	Characters are named, but reader knows little about their physical appearance.	Most characters do not have names; they are identified as "the boy" or "the girl."	
Characters come to life through appropriate amount of dialogue.	There is dialogue, but characters do not come to life.	There is very little dialogue and it is difficult to distinguish who is speaking.	There is no dialogue.	
The story comes to life through vivid action verbs (active voice). The story's action creates mood.	The story has active voice, but the verbs are not vivid.	The story shifts from active to passive voice.	The story is told in passive voice.	
The main character's problem is revealed at the beginning of the story with many roadblocks to make the plot exciting.	It is clear what the main character's problem is, but the plot lacks an appropriate number of roadblocks.	It is not clear what is the main character's problem, and there are only two roadblocks.	There is no clear problem because there are no roadblocks.	
The plot has a clear climax with an appropriate resolution.	The plot has a clear climax, but the resolution is too long.	The plot has somewhat of a clear climax, but there is no resolution.	There is no climax; thus no resolution.	
Original illustrations are detailed, colorful, attractive, and relate to the text on the page.	Original illustrations are somewhat detailed and colorful, but do not always relate to the text.	Original illustrations somewhat relate to the text. They lack color and details.	Illustrations are not present, or they are merely stick figures.	
All of the written requirements (number of pages, font size, font style, amount of text on pages) are present.	The required font size and style and the number of pages are present.	The required font size and font style are present.	The required font size is present.	
Title is creative, sparks interest, and is related to the story.	Title is related to the story.	Title is present, but does not relate to the story.	No title is present.	
The story contains many creative details, figures of speech, and other vivid words that contribute to the readers' enjoyment. Author's imagination is unique.	The story contains a few creative details and vivid words that contribute readers' enjoyment. Author has good imagination.	The details and word choice distract from the story.	There are no creative details or vivid word choice. The story lacks imagination.	
The story contains no spelling, punctuation, capitalization, or grammar errors.	The story contains no more than two of the following errors: spelling, punctuation, capitalization, or grammar.	The story contains no more than three of the following errors: spelling, punctuation, capitalization, or grammar.	The story contains four or more of the following errors: spelling, punctuation, capitalization, or grammar.	

TOTAL SCORE: ____ /39
(Acceptable score is 31 or 80%).

APPENDIX C

C.51 RESEARCH REPORT RUBRIC (p. 299)

TITLE:

NAME: DATE:

3 POINTS	2 POINTS	1 POINT	0 POINTS	SCORE
All sources (text and graphics) are accurately cited in the required format.	All sources are documented, but not in the required format.	At least one source is not documented, but others are in required format.	Two or more sources are not documented or some sources are not in required format.	
Notes are organized in a neat, orderly fashion.	Notes are recorded legibly and are somewhat organized.	Notes are recorded.	There are no notes.	
Graphic organizer or outline has been completed and shows clear, logical relationships between all topics and subtopics.	Graphic organizer or outline has been completed and shows all main topics with a few subtopics.	Graphic organizer or outline has been completed, showing only main topics.	Graphic organizer or outline has not been completed.	
At least three articles or books and at least three Internet sources were used.	At least two articles or books and at least three Internet sources were used.	At least two articles or books and at least two Internet sources were used.	Only one article or book and only one Internet source were used.	
Main topics and subtopics are addressed in report with at least one paragraph for each.	Main topics were addressed with at least one paragraph, but one subtopic was missing.	Main topics were addressed with at least one paragraph, but two subtopics were missing.	Not all topics or subtopics were addressed with at least one paragraph each.	
Student had three peers and teacher read report for content. Student accepted suggestions readily.	Student had two peers and teacher read report for content. Student accepted most suggestions.	Student had one peer and teacher read report for content. Student did not readily accept suggestions.	Student had no peer read report for content.	
Student had three peers edit the report. Student accepted suggestions readily.	Students had two peers edit the report. Student accepted only some of the suggestions.	Student had one peer edit the report. Student accepted few suggestions.	Student had no peer edit the report.	
Finished product was neatly prepared and shared and posted on the bulletin board or on the Web.	Finished product was neatly prepared and shared orally OR posted on the bulletin board or on the Web.	Finished product was somewhat neat. Student posted it on the bulletin board.	Student did not share his/her report in any manner.	
Finished product had title page, page numbers, table of contents, and reference page.	Finished product was missing one of the following: title page, page numbers, table of contents, or reference page.	Finished product was missing two of the following: title page, page numbers, table of contents, or reference page.	Finished product was missing three or more of the following: title page, page numbers, table of contents, or reference page.	
The report contained no spelling, punctuation, capitalization, or grammar errors.	The report contained no more than one of the following errors: punctuation, spelling, capitalization, or grammar.	The report contained no more than two of the following errors: spelling, punctuation, capitalization, or grammar.	The report contained more than three of the following errors: spelling, punctuation, capitalization, or grammar.	
The report was well organized with all paragraphs correctly constructed.	The report was well organized with only one paragraph not correctly constructed.	The report was organized with only two paragraphs not correctly constructed.	There was no clear organization to the report. It lacked well-constructed paragraphs.	
The topic was age appropriate and interesting.	The topic was age appropriate and somewhat interesting.	The topic was age appropriate with only a few new pieces of information.	The topic was age appropriate, but contained no new information.	

Total score: ______ /36
(Acceptable score is 29 or 80%)

APPENDIX C

C.52 MULTIMEDIA GROUP PROJECT RUBRIC (p. 301)

NAME: DATE:

CATEGORY	4	3	2	1
Sources POINTS ____	Source information collected for all graphics, facts and quotes. All documented in desired format.	Source information collected for all graphics, facts and quotes. Most documented in desired format.	Source information collected for graphics, facts and quotes, but not documented in desired format.	Very little or no source information was collected.
Permissions POINTS ____	All permissions to use graphics "borrowed" from web pages or scanned from books have been requested, received, printed and saved for future reference.	All permissions to use graphics "borrowed" from web pages or scanned from books have been requested and received.	Most permissions to use graphics "borrowed" from web pages or scanned from books have been requested and received.	Permissions were not requested for several graphics "borrowed" from web pages or scanned from books.
Attractiveness POINTS ____	Makes excellent use of font, color, graphics, effects, etc. to enhance the presentation.	Makes good use of font, color, graphics, effects, etc. to enhance to presentation.	Makes use of font, color, graphics, effects, etc. but occasionally these detract from the presentation content.	Use of font, color, graphics, effects etc. but these often distract from the presentaion content.
Rough Draft POINTS ____	Rough draft brought on due date. Student shares with peer and extensively edits based on peer feedback.	Rough draft brought on due date. Student shares with peer and peer makes edits.	Provides feedback and/or edits for peer, but own rough draft was not ready for editing.	Rough draft not ready for editing and did not participate in reviewing draft of peer.
Requirements POINTS ____	All requirements are met and exceeded.	All requirements are met.	One requirement was not completely met.	More than 1 requirement was not completely met.
Content POINTS ____	Covers topic in-depth with details and examples. Subject knowledge is excellent.	Includes essential knowledge about the topic. Subject knowledge appears to be good.	Includes essential information about the topic but there are 1 or 2 factual errors.	Content is minimal OR there are several factual errors.
Organization POINTS ____	Content is well organized using headings or bulleted lists to group related material.	Uses headings or bulleted lists to organize, but the overall organization of topics appears flawed.	Content is logically organized for the most part.	There was no clear or logical organizational structure, just lots of facts.
Originality POINTS ____	Product shows a large amount of original thought. Ideas are creative and inventive.	Product shows some original thought. Work shows new ideas and insights.	Uses other people's ideas (giving them credit), but there is little evidence of original thinking.	Uses other people's ideas, but does not give them credit.
Mechanics POINTS ____	No misspellings or grammatical errors.	Three or fewer misspellings and/or mechanical errors.	Four misspellings and/or grammatical errors.	More than 4 errors in spelling or grammar.
Workload TOTAL POINTS ____	The workload is divided and shared equally by all team members.	The workload is divided and shared fairly by all team members, though workloads may vary from person to person.	The workload was divided, but one person in the group is viewed as not doing his/her fair share of the work.	The workload was not divided OR several people in the group are viewed as not doing their fair share of the work.

Date Created: Dec 31, 2010 08:54 pm (UTC)

Source: Created using http://rubistar.4teachers.org.

C.53 WRITING AND SPELLING SELF-ASSESSMENT (p. 302)

NAME: ____________________

CIRCLE: FIRST QUARTER SECOND QUARTER THIRD QUARTER FOURTH QUARTER

1. I started ________ different writing projects this quarter.
2. I completed ________ writing projects this quarter.
3. I wrote the following genres (poem, mystery, adventure story, autobiography, informational composition, or any other genre).

 ____
 ____
 ____
 ____

4. My favorite writing was ____________________
 because ____________________
5. My most difficult piece to write was ____________________
 because ____________________
6. How did you share your writing with others? ____________________
 ____
7. What did you do when you did not know how to spell a word? ____________________
 ____
8. Do you think you are a good or poor writer? ____________________
 Why do you think that? ____________________
9. What did you learn as a writer this quarter? ____________________
 ____
10. What is the hardest part of writing? ____________________
 ____

TEACHER'S COMMENTS:

APPENDIX C

C.54 BEAR, INVERNIZZI, TEMPLETON, & JOHNSTON QUALITATIVE SPELLING INVENTORY (p. 113)

ONE

SET #1

1. bed 2. ship 3. when 4. lump 5. float

SET #2

1. train 2. place 3. drive 4. bright 5. shopping

SET #3

1. spoil 2. serving 3. chewed 4. carries 5. marched

SET #4

1. shower 2. cattle 3. favor 4. ripen 5. cellar

SET #5

1. pleasure 2. fortunate 3. confident 4. civilize 5. opposition

TWO

SET #1

1. net 2. trip 3. crime 4. dump 5. then

SET #2

1. chain 2. forest 3. trail 4. soap 5. reaches

SET #3

1. preparing 2. popping 3. cattle 4. caught 5. inspection

SET #4

1. comparing 2. topping 3. battle 4. fought 5. intention

SET #5

1. rupture 2. stellar 3. treasure 4. confident 5. tempest

Source: Bear, Donald R.; Helman, Lori; Invernizzi, Marcia R.; Templeton, Shane; Johnston, Francine R., *Words their way: Word study for phonics, vocabulary, and spelling instruction.* Top: 4th ed., © 2006, p. 35. Bottom: 2nd ed., © 2000, p. 294. Reprinted by permission of Pearson Education, Inc. Upper Saddle River, NJ.

C.55 RECORDING AND ANALYZING SPELLING (p. 332)

STUDENT: GRADE:

Word	Precommunicative	Semiphonetic	Phonetic	Transitional	Conventional
1.					
2.					
3.					
4.					
5.					
6.					
7.					
8.					
9.					
10.					

TEACHER'S COMMENTS:

C.56 CHECKLIST FOR SPELLING, FIFTH GRADE (p. 333)

TEACHER: PERIOD 1 2 3 4

+ = always X = sometimes O = seldom/never

STANDARD	STUDENTS																	
Accurate Spelling: Closed, open syllables																		
Consonant before *le*																		
qu patterns																		
n before *v*																		
m before *b*																		
m before *p*																		
Root words																		
Tense inflections																		
Number inflections																		
Suffixes -*able* and -*less*																		
Prefixes *re*- and *un*-																		
Uses resources to find correct spelling																		
Accurate spelling in final draft																		

APPENDIX D

INSTRUCTION MATERIALS

D.1 **Lesson Plan for English Learners** 490

D.2 **Directions for Creating Game Boards and Picture/Word Cards** 491

D.3 **How Many Syllables in the Zoo? Game Board and Picture Cards** *(Chapter 4)* 492

D.4 **Remember the Beginning Sound Picture Cards** *(Chapter 4)* 495

D.5 **Initial Sound Picture Bingo Cards** *(Chapter 4)* 508

D.6 **Toss the Cube Art** *(Chapter 4)* 518

D.7 **Go Fish Picture Cards** *(Chapter 4)* 527

D.8 **Humpty Dumpty Game Board and Picture Cards** *(Chapter 4)* 534

D.9 **Listen for the Initial Consonant Blend Sound Game Board and Picture Cards** *(Chapter 5)* 539

D.10 **Word Dominoes** *(Chapter 5)* 545

D.11 **Concentration Word Cards** *(Chapter 5)* 549

D.12 **Listen for the Vowel Sound Board and Game Pieces** *(Chapter 5)* 553

D.13 **Dolch List Bingo Word Cards** *(Chapter 6)* 559

D.14 **Onset and Rime Cards** *(Chapter 6)* 565

D.15 **Templates for Morphology Rummy Cards** *(Chapter 6)* 567

D.16 **Vocabulary Bookmark Template** *(Chapter 7)* 569

D.17 **Cognate Sort** *(Chapter 7)* 570

D.18 **Multiple Meaning Racetrack Board** *(Chapter 7)* 571

D.19 **Text Mapping Form** *(Chapter 8)* 572

D.20 **Narrative E-Book Evaluation Form** *(Chapter 8)* 573

D.21 **Informational E-Text Evaluation Form** *(Chapter 9)* 574

D.22 **Textbook and Trade Book Evaluation Checklist** *(Chapter 9)* 575

D.23 **Informational DVD/CD Evaluation Form** 577

D.24 **Record, Check, Chart** *(Chapter 10)* 578

D.25 **Record, Time, Chart** *(Chapter 10)* 579

D.26 **Fluency Log** *(Chapter 10)* 580

D.27 **Template for a Storyboard** *(Chapter 11)* 581

D.28 **Mt. Plot** *(Chapter 11)* 582

D.29 **Lesson Plan for Tutors** *(Chapter 13)* 583

D.30 **Log Sheet of Strategies** *(Chapter 13)* 584

D.31 **Log Sheet of Books Read** *(Chapter 13)* 585

D.32 **Postcard for Children Reading Books with Oral Reading and Comprehension Scaffolding** *(Chapter 14)* 586

D.1 LESSON PLAN FOR ENGLISH LEARNERS (p. 352)

TUTOR: ______________________ DATE: ______________

TUTEE: ______________________ GRADE: ______________

Review from previous lesson:

Phonics:

Vocabulary building:

Sentences:

Writing:

Listening to tutor:

LESSON PLAN	PLANNED ACTIVITY	TIME REFLECTION
Review:		
Phonics:		
Vocabulary:		
Sentences:		
Writing:		
Listening:		

APPENDIX D

D.2 DIRECTIONS FOR CREATING GAME BOARDS AND PICTURE/WORD CARDS

To assemble:

- Create a front title page.
- Glue the title on the front of a colored file folder.
- Copy the game board from appendix or create your own. Decorate and add color to game board. Glue the game board inside the file folder.
- Reproduce the pictures for the various activities on colorful stock card paper. Laminate and cut them out so that they can be stacked in a deck.
- Using the directions given in the chapter Intervention sections, copy or create a sheet of directions. Glue the directions and an envelope to store playing pieces on the back of the folder.

D.3 HOW MANY SYLLABLES IN THE ZOO? GAME BOARD AND PICTURE CARDS (pp. 90, 114)

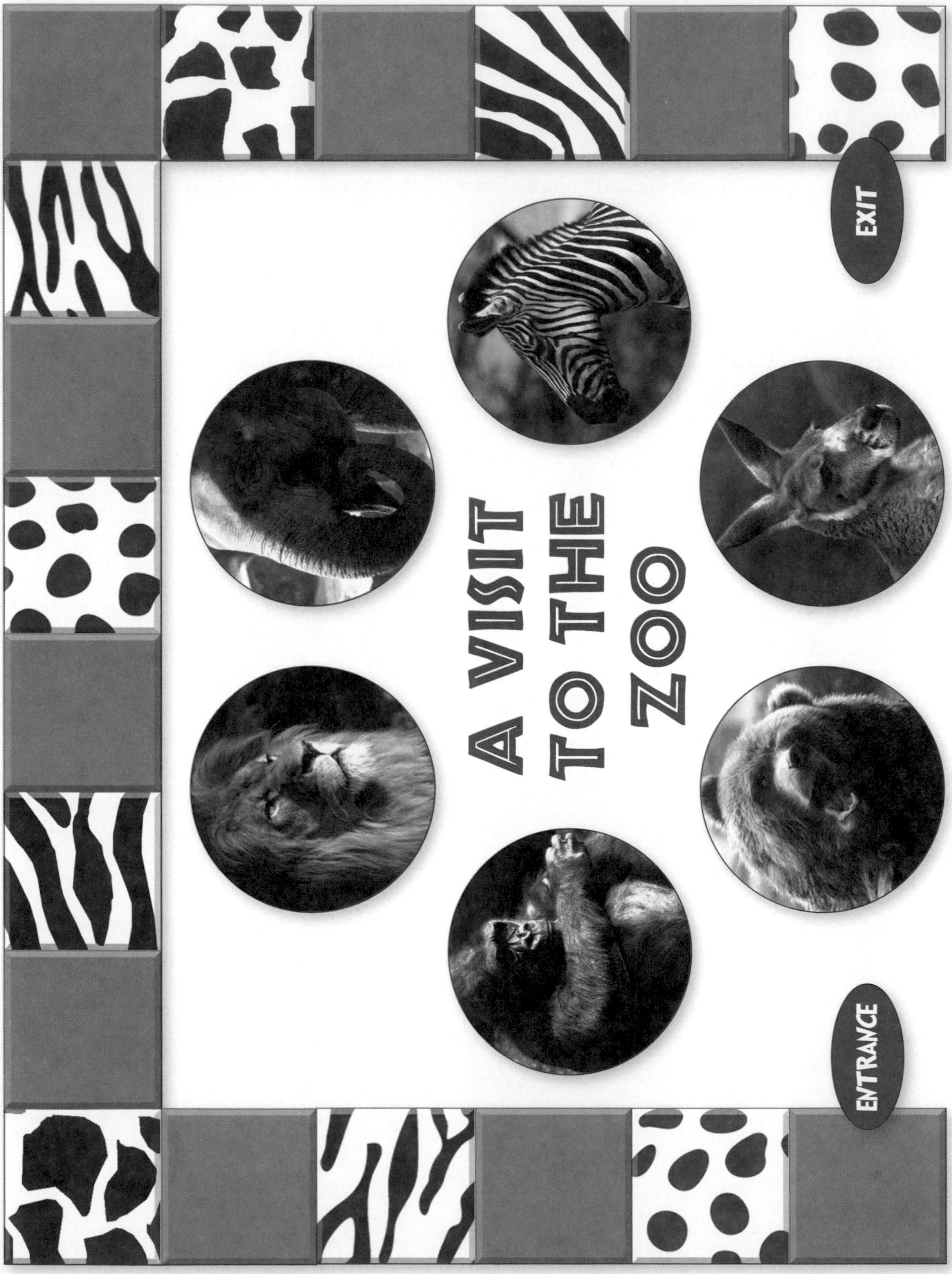

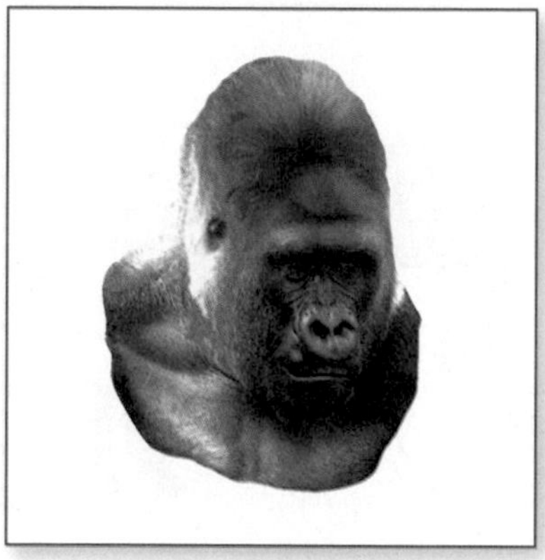

D.4 REMEMBER THE BEGINNING SOUND PICTURE CARDS (pp. 92, 113, 352)

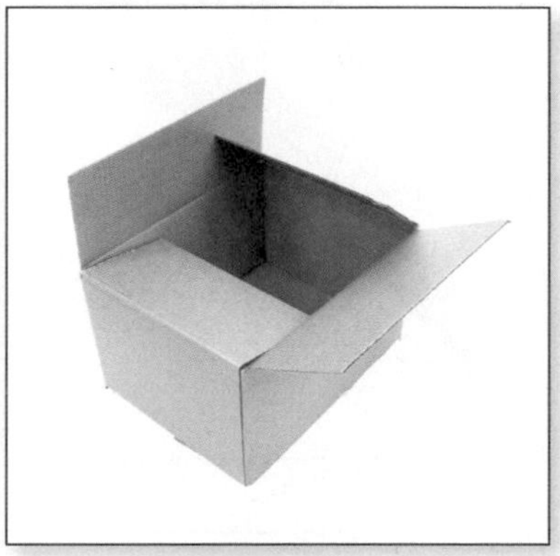

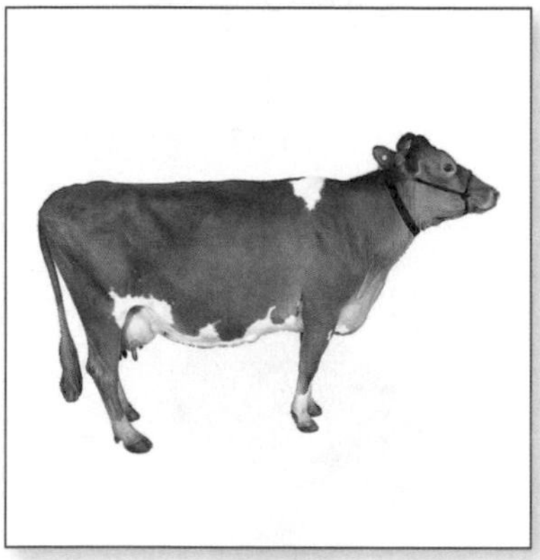

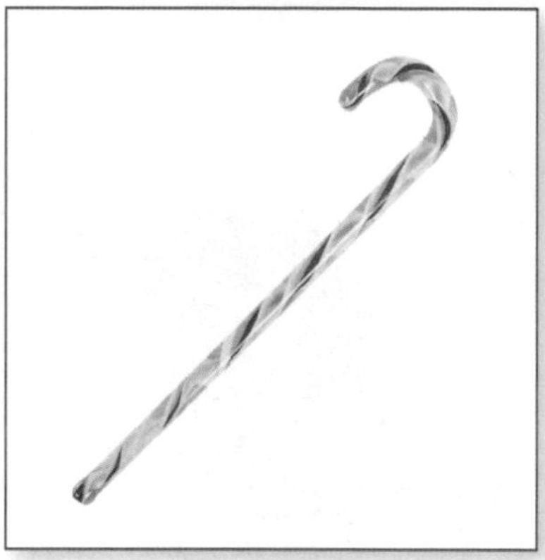

12
1
2
3
4
5
6
7
8
9
10
11

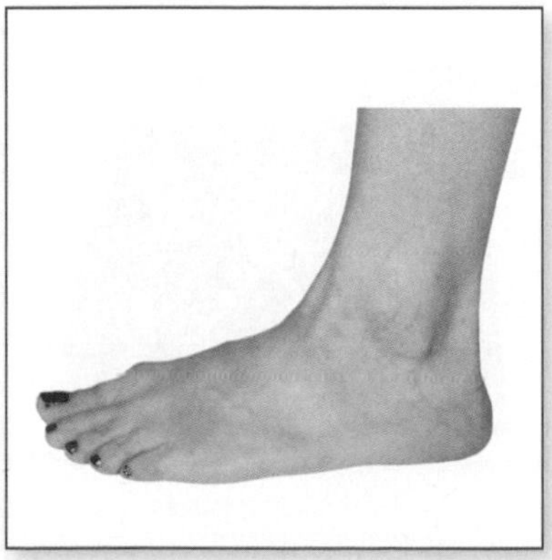

4

5

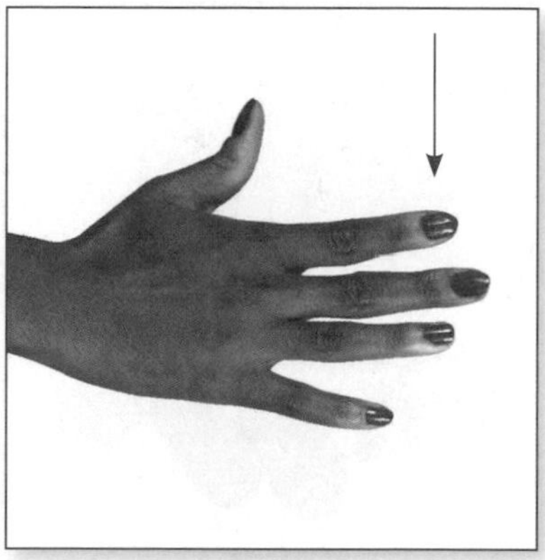

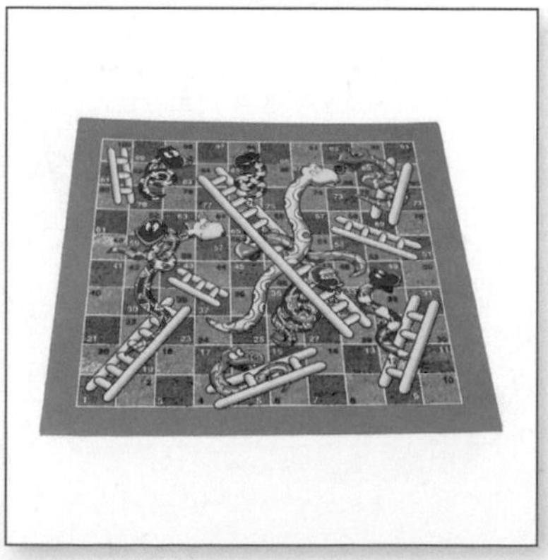

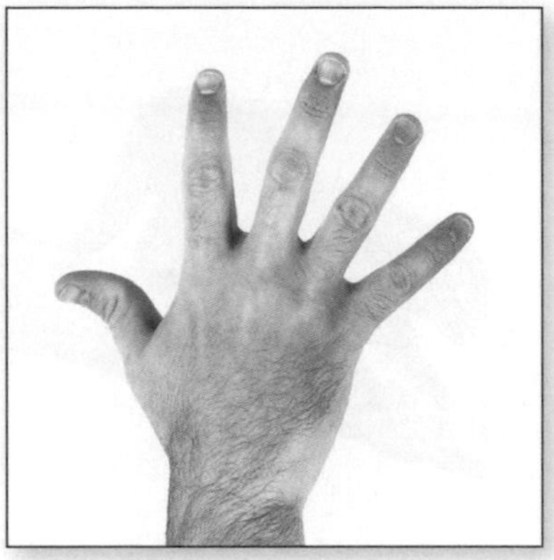

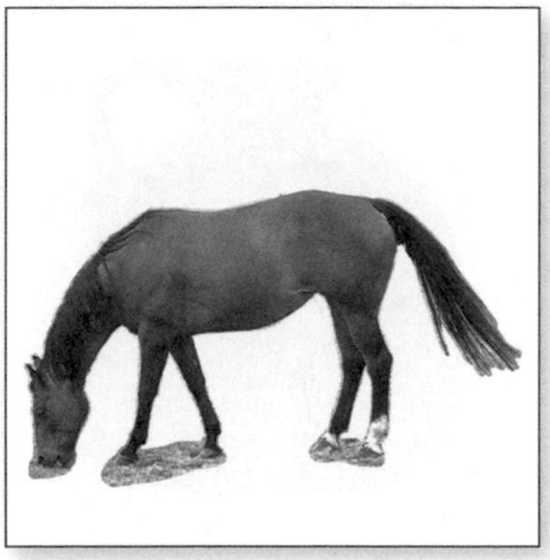

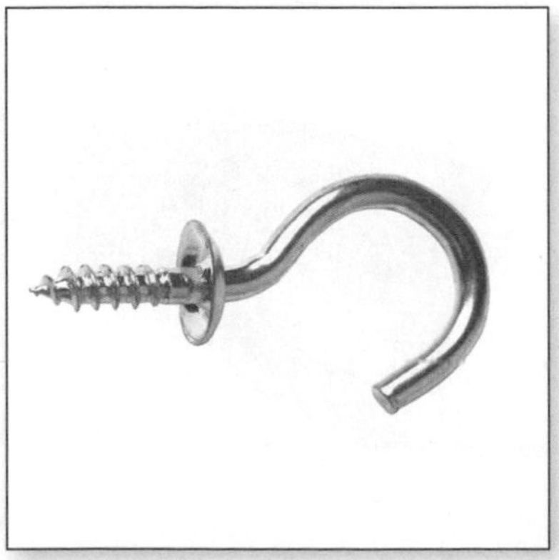

Milk

UNITED STATES OF AMERICA
FIVE CENTS

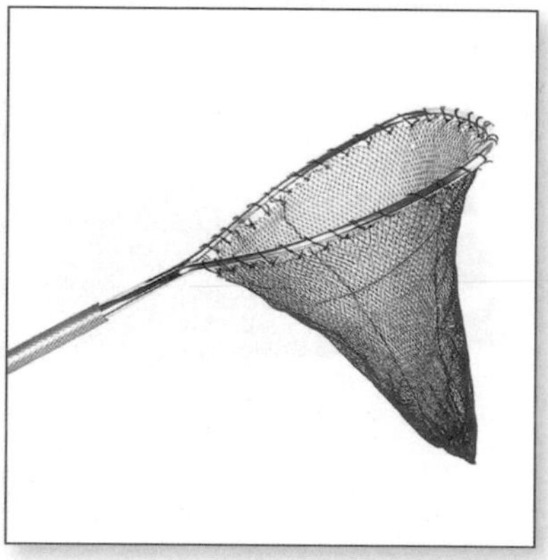

9

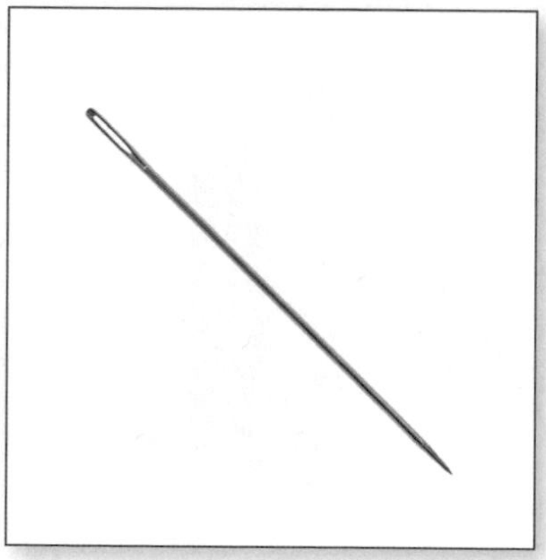

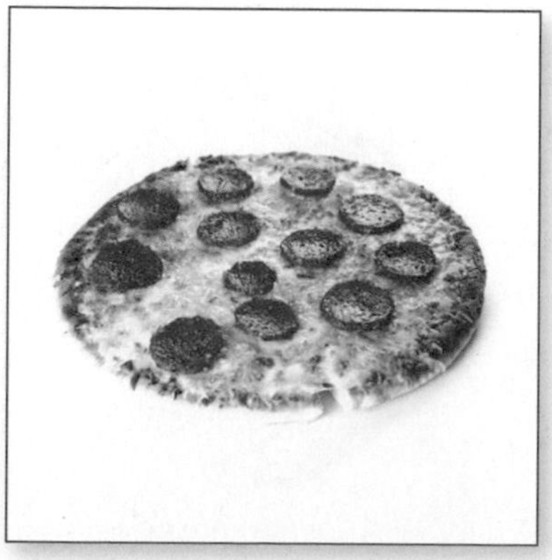

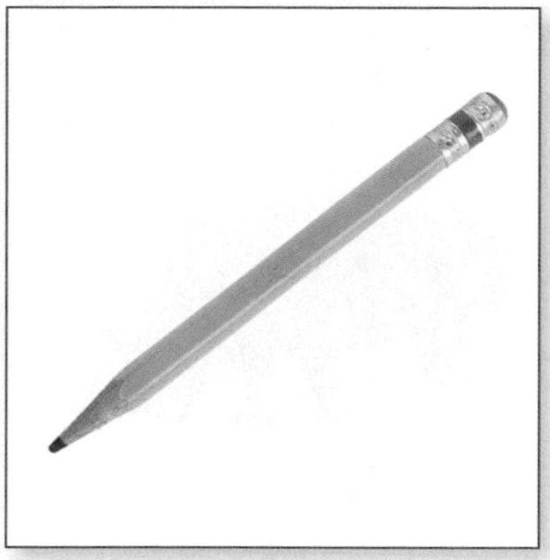

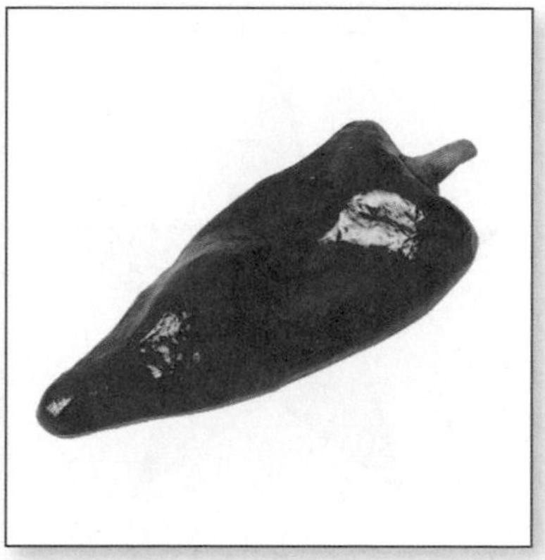

6

7

2

10

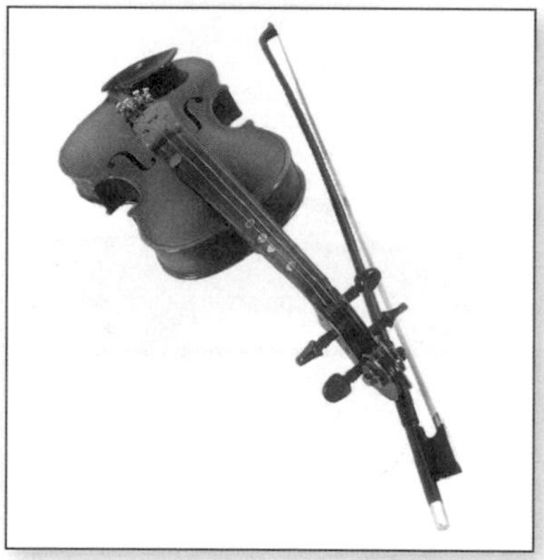

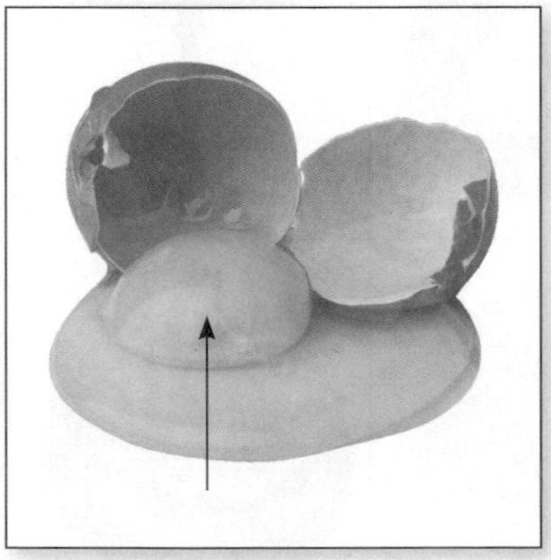

D.5 INITIAL SOUND PICTURE BINGO CARDS (pp. 92, 352)

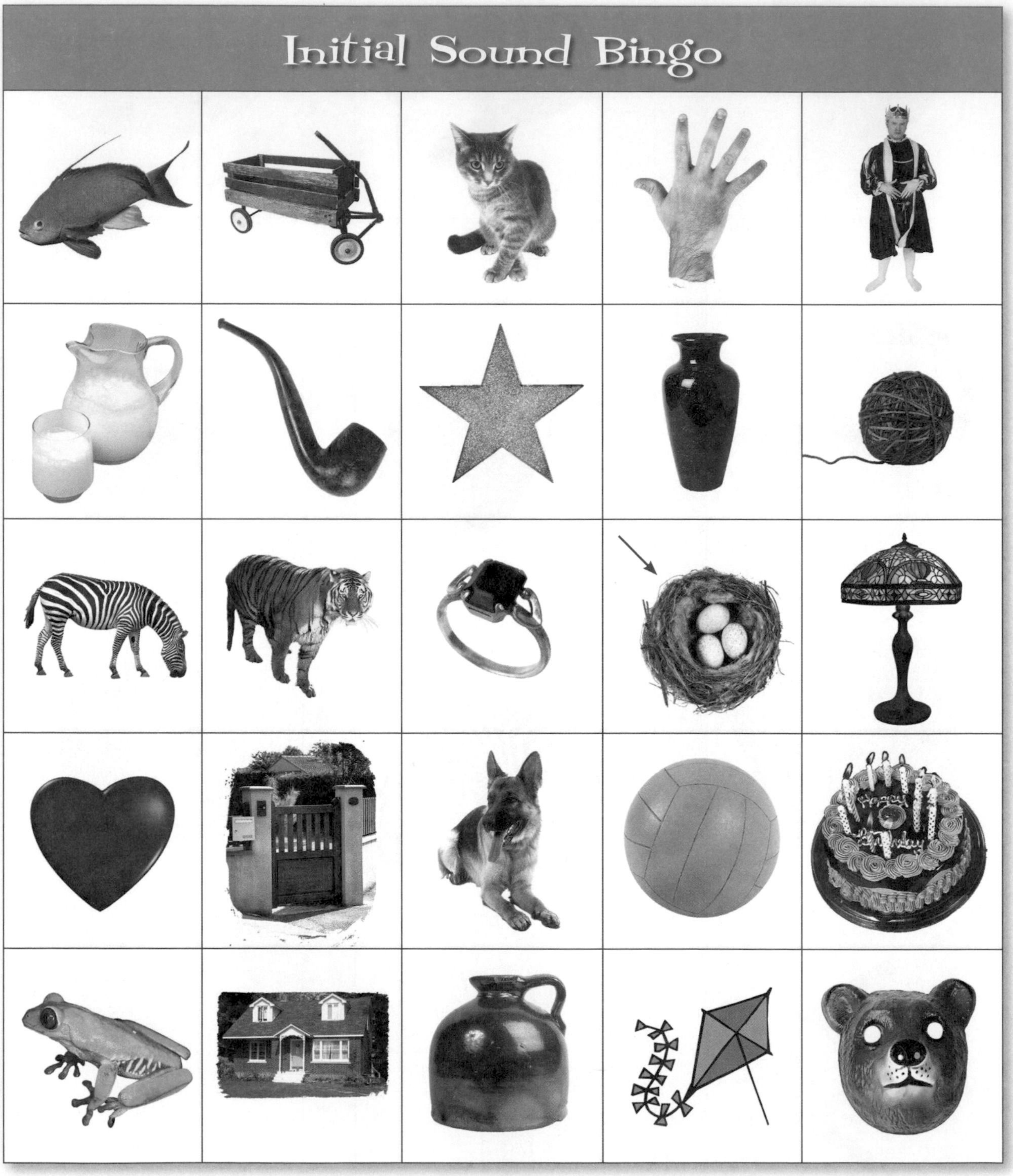

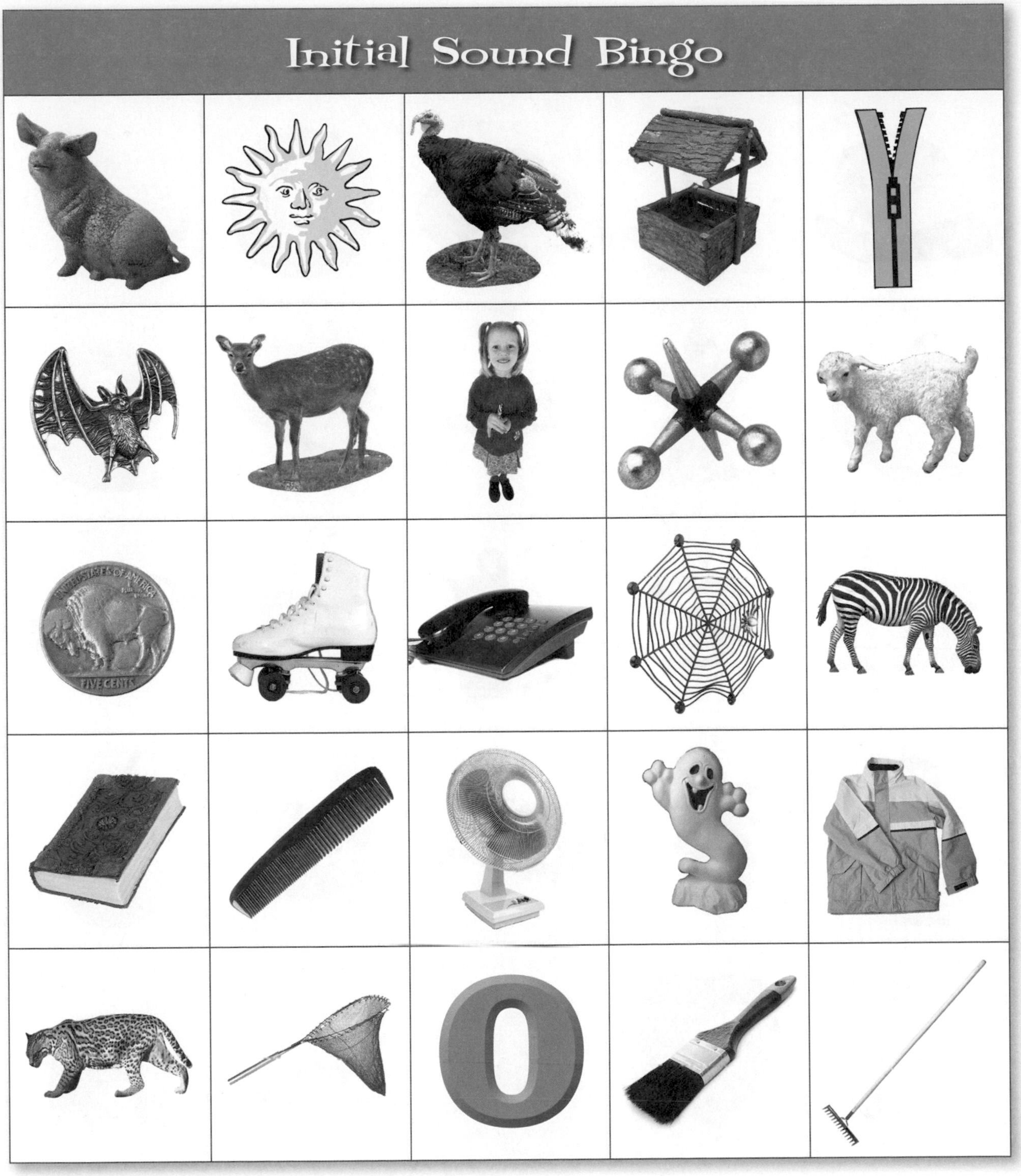
Initial Sound Bingo

Initial Sound Bingo

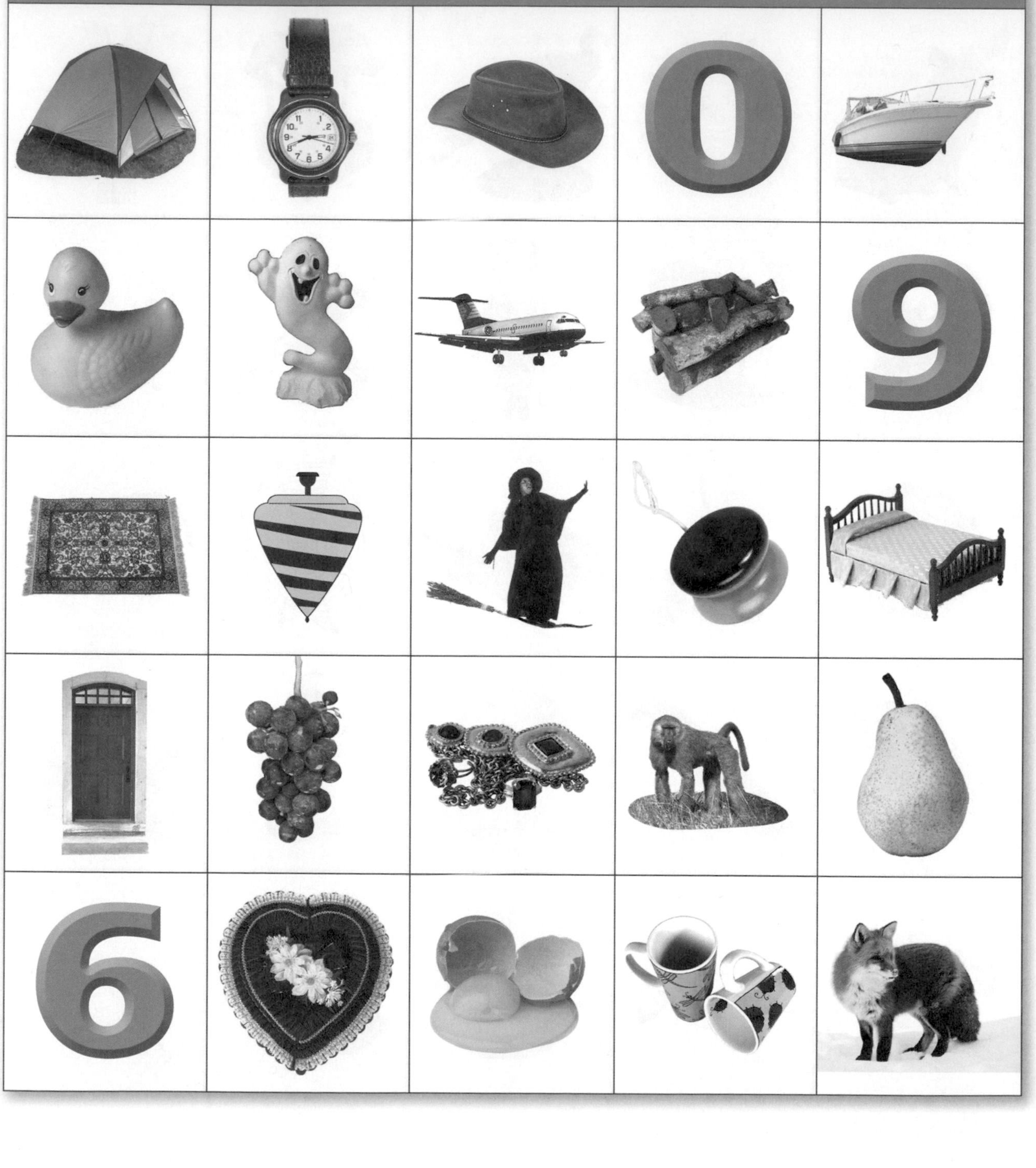

Initial Sound Bingo

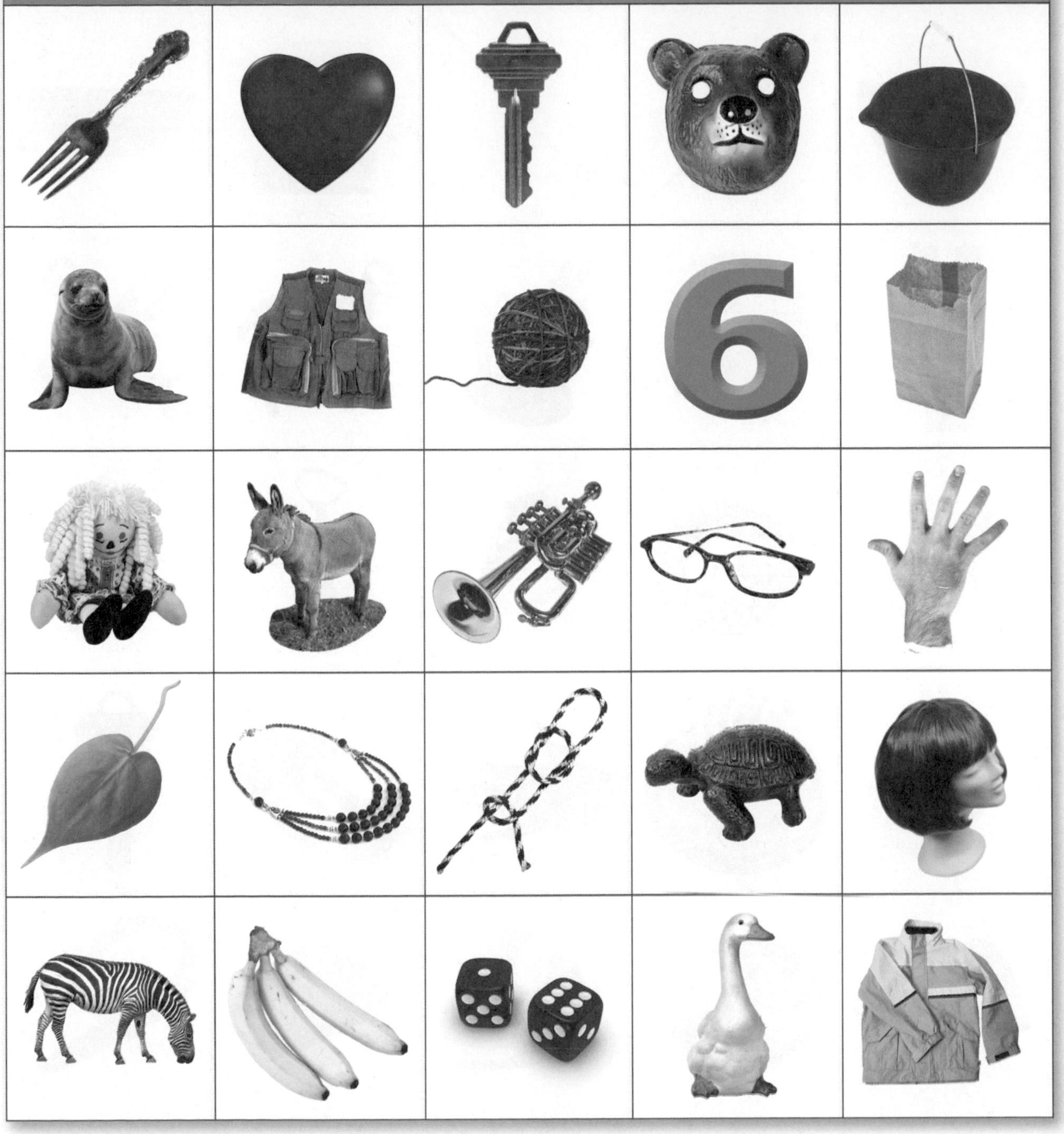

Initial Sound Bingo

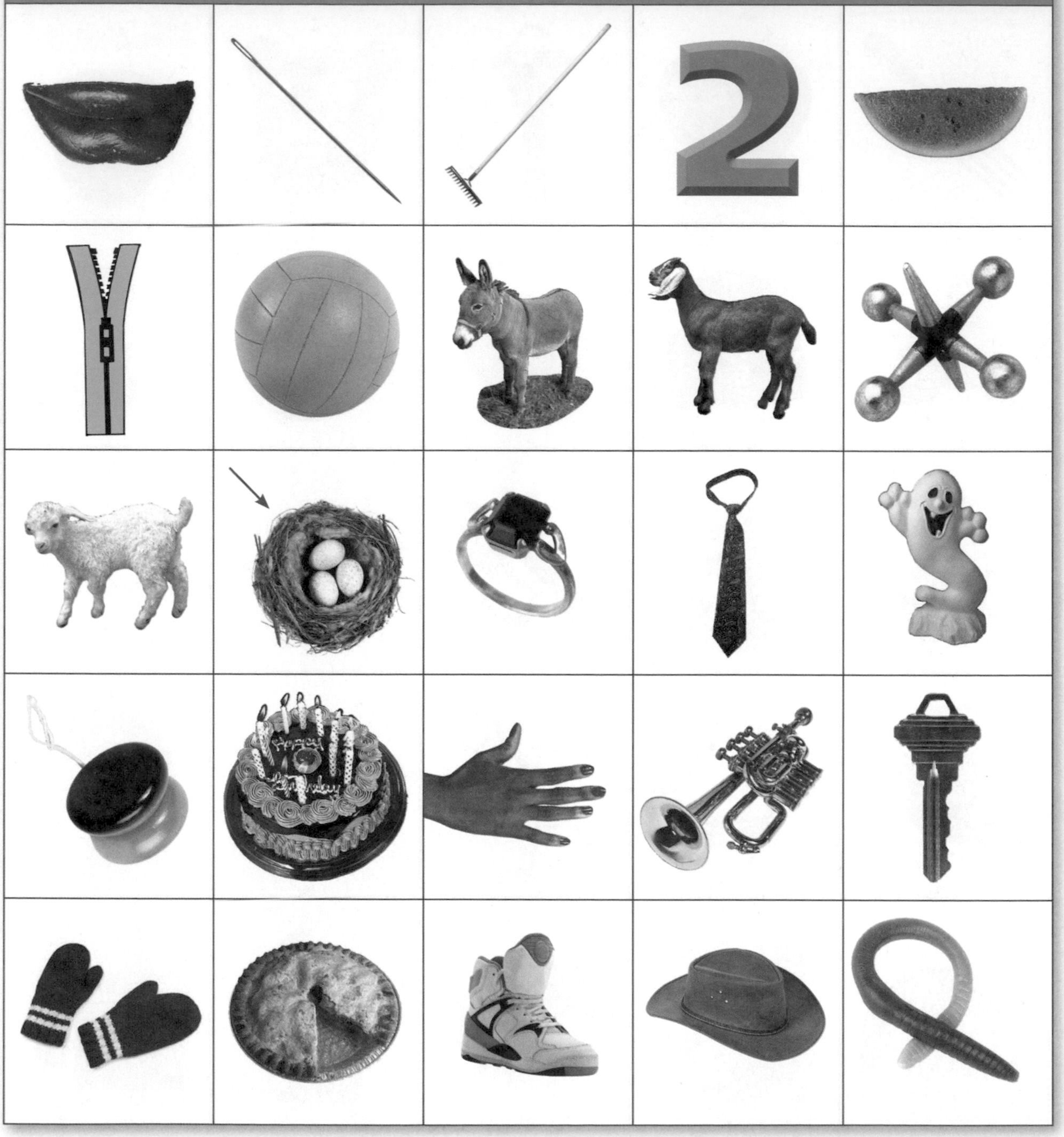

Initial Sound Bingo

Initial Sound Bingo

Initial Sound Bingo

Initial Sound Bingo

Initial Sound Bingo

D.6 TOSS THE CUBE ART (p. 92, 144, 174)

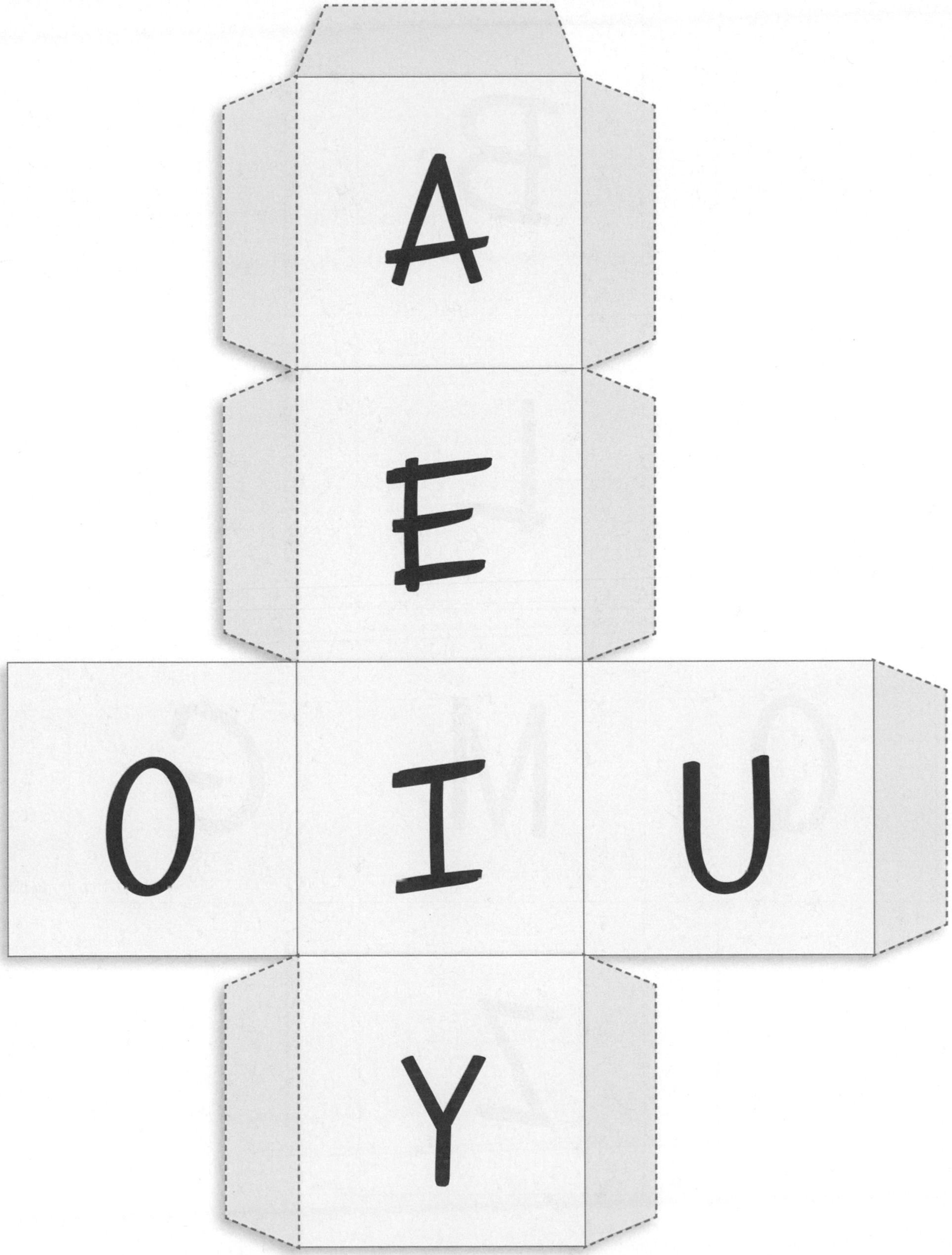
A
E
O
I
U
Y

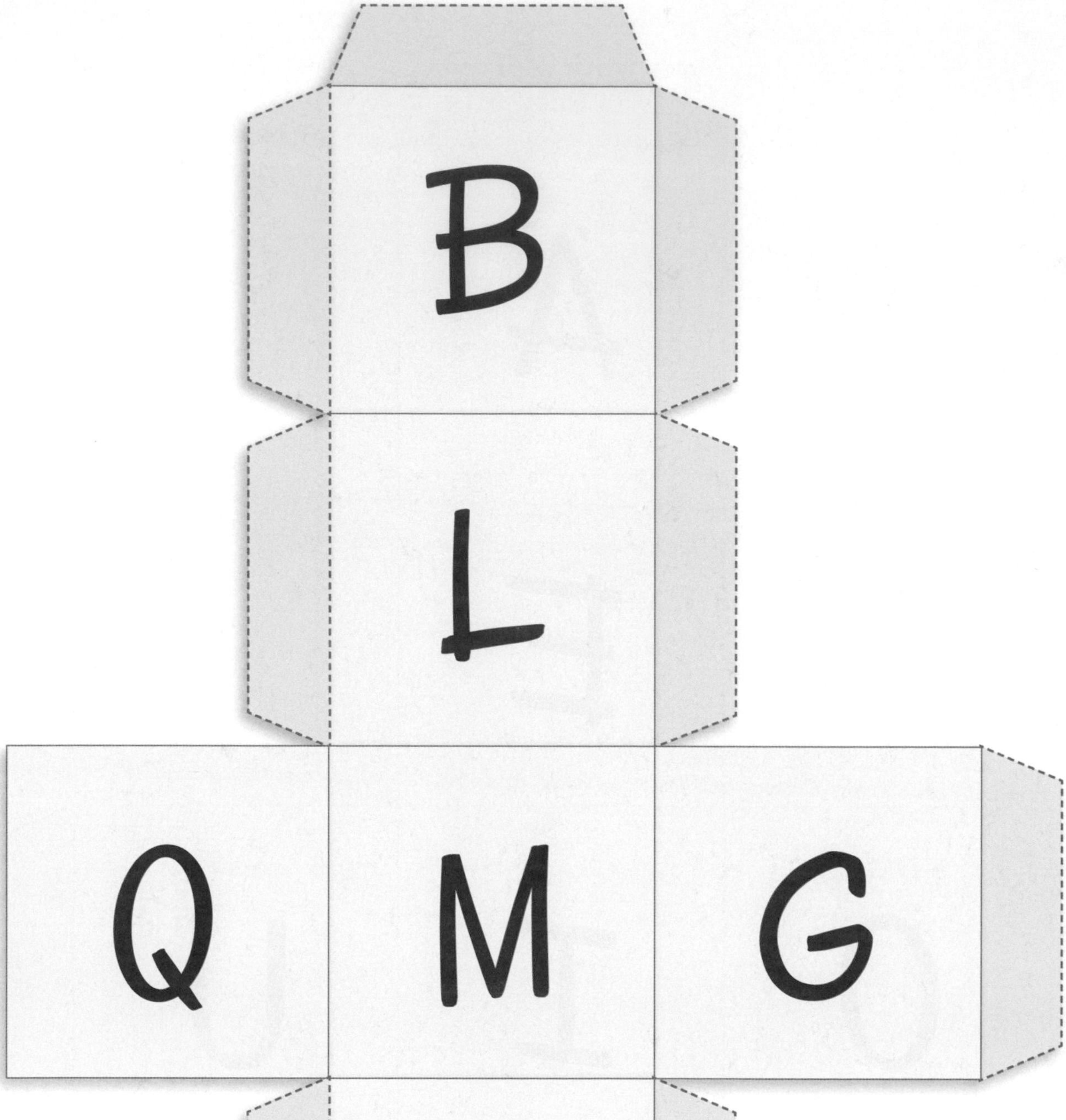
B
L
Q
M
G
Z

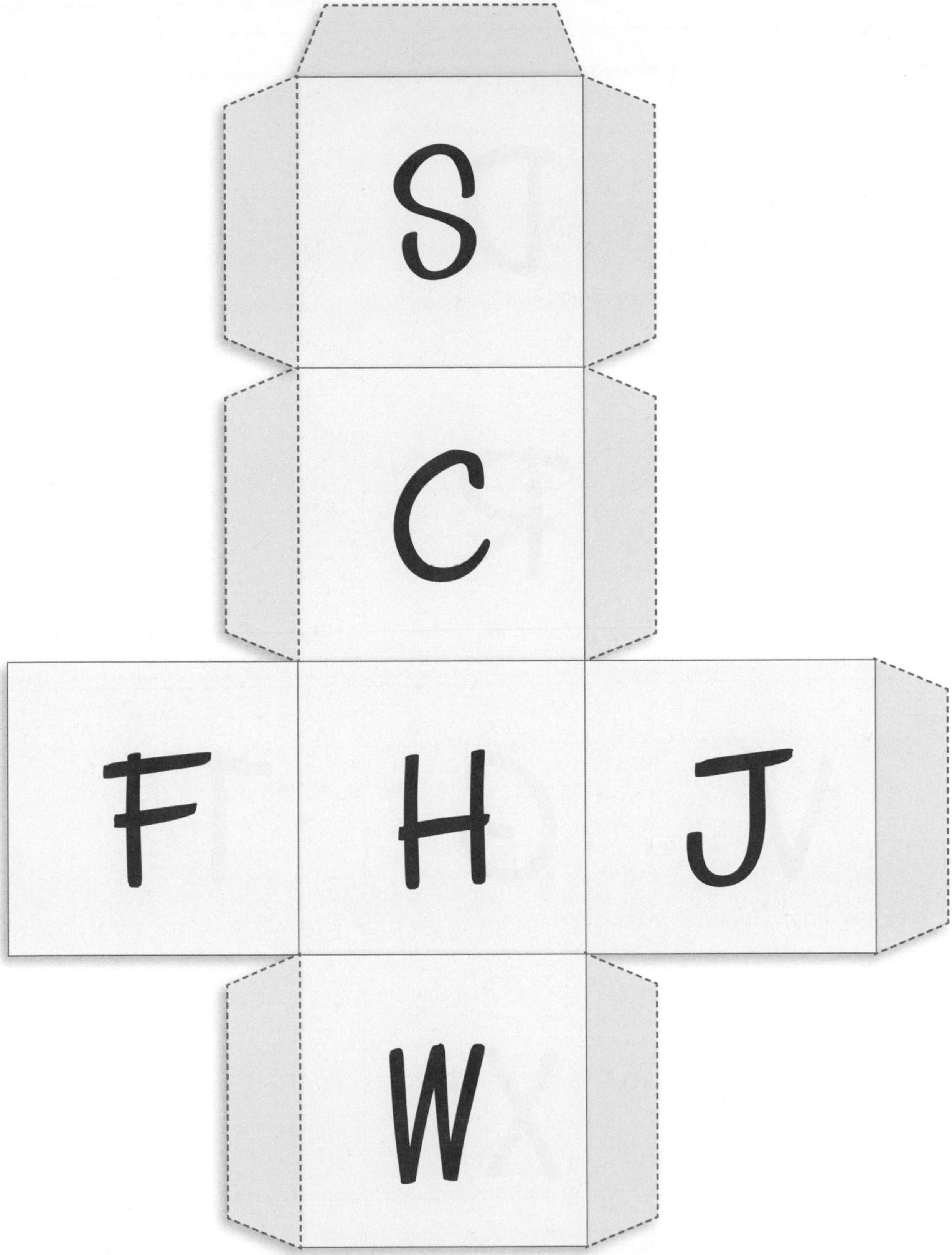
S
C
F
H
J
W

D
R
V
G
T
X

N
P
S
B
K
C

K
J
R
F
N
M

D
T
G
L
P
H

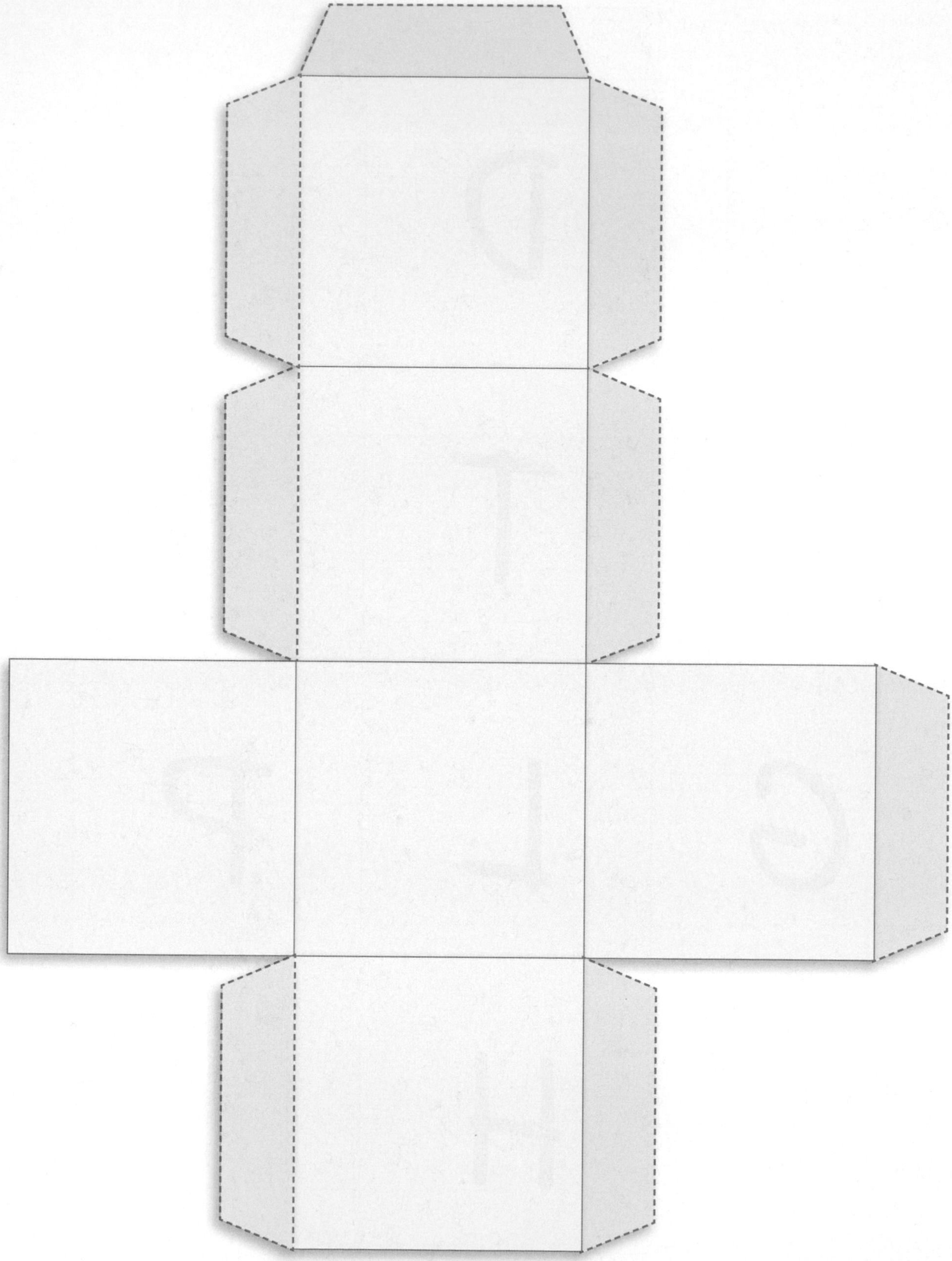

D.7 GO FISH PICTURE CARDS (p. 93)

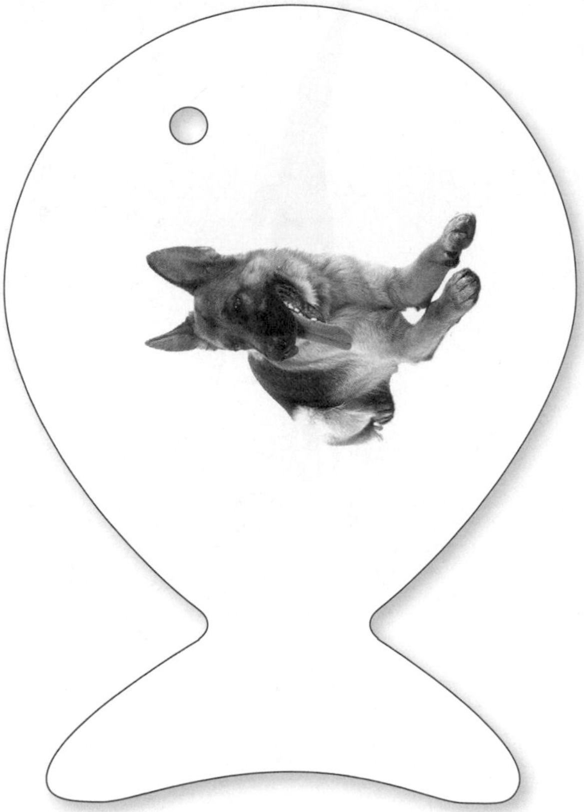

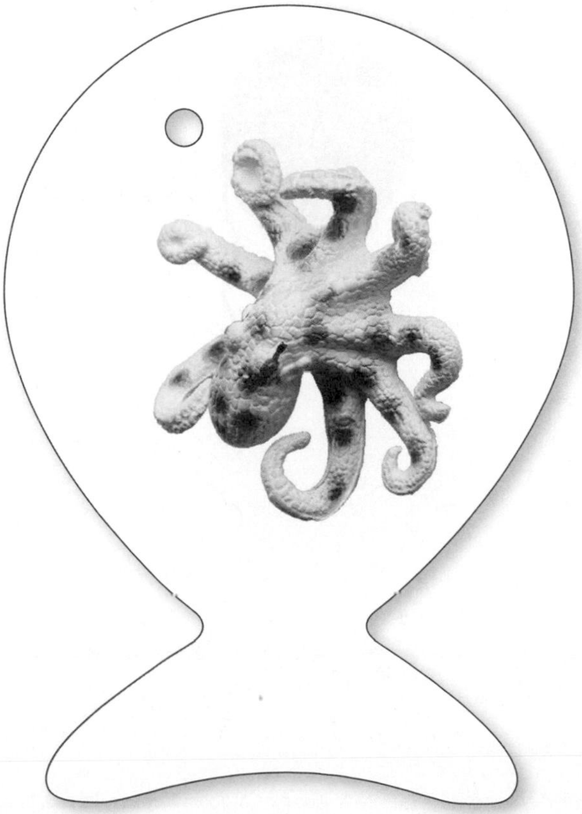

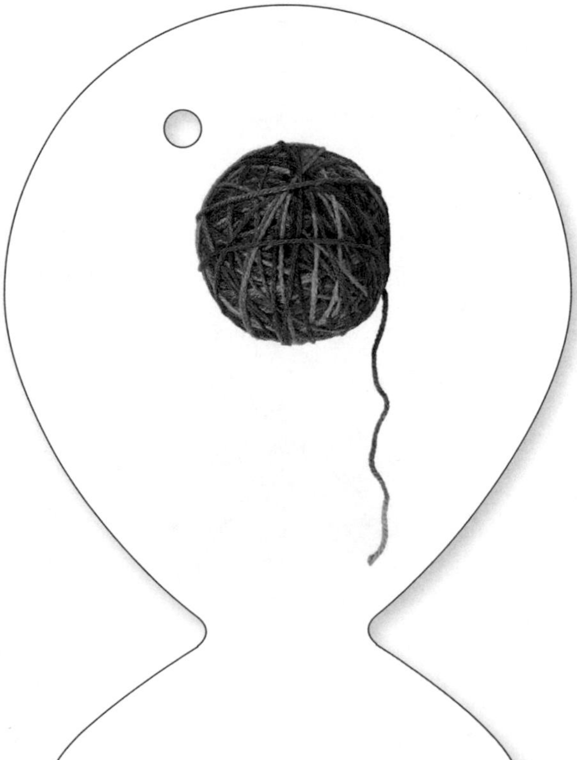

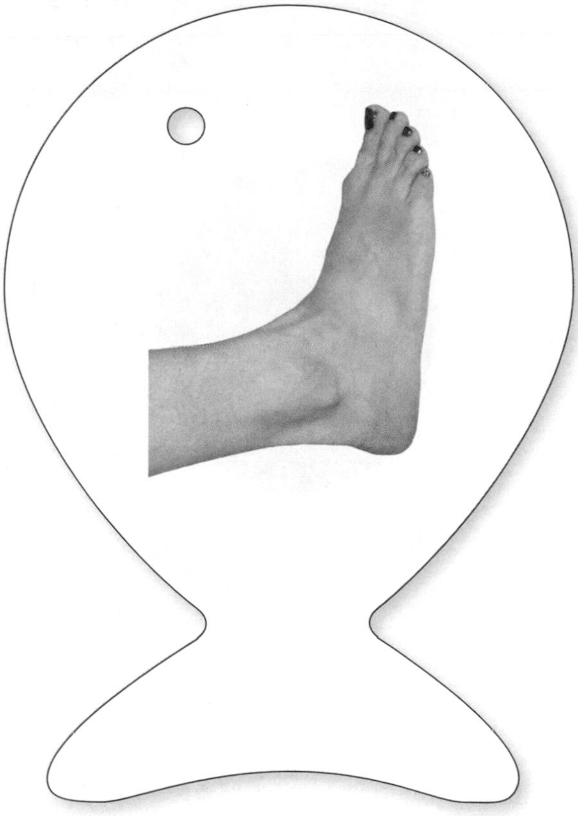

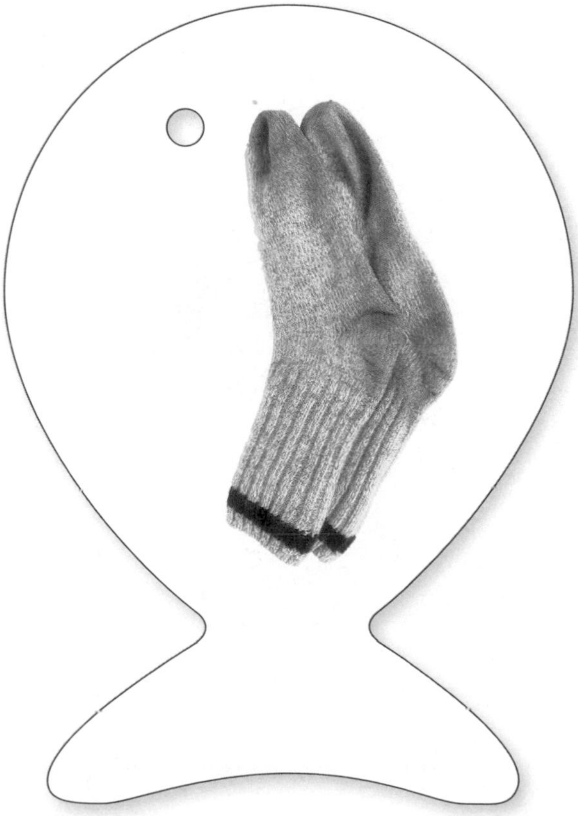

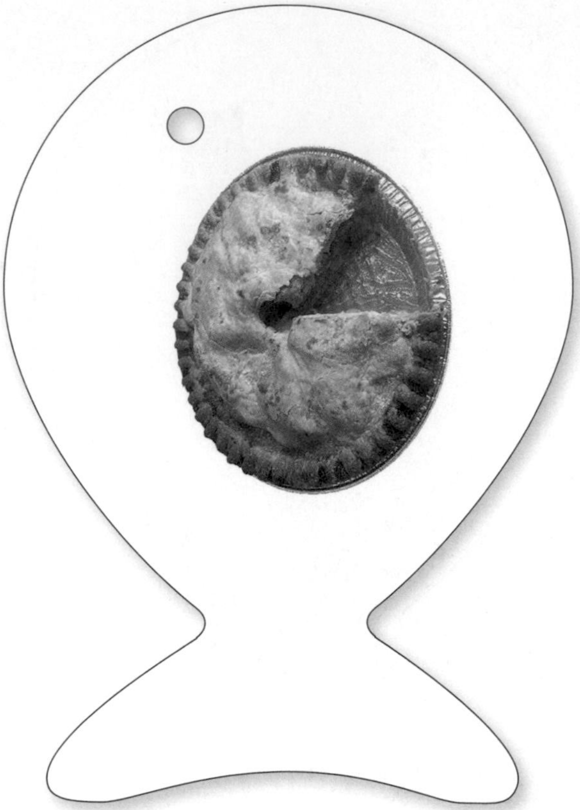

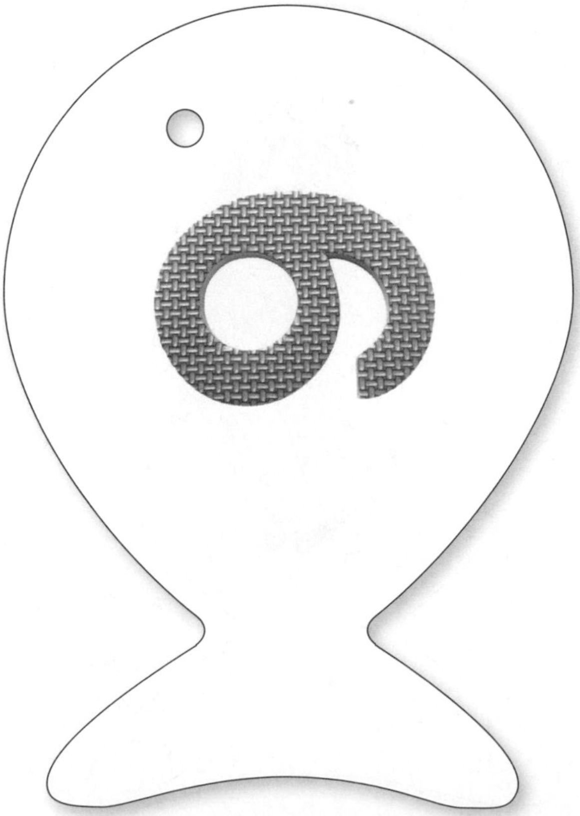

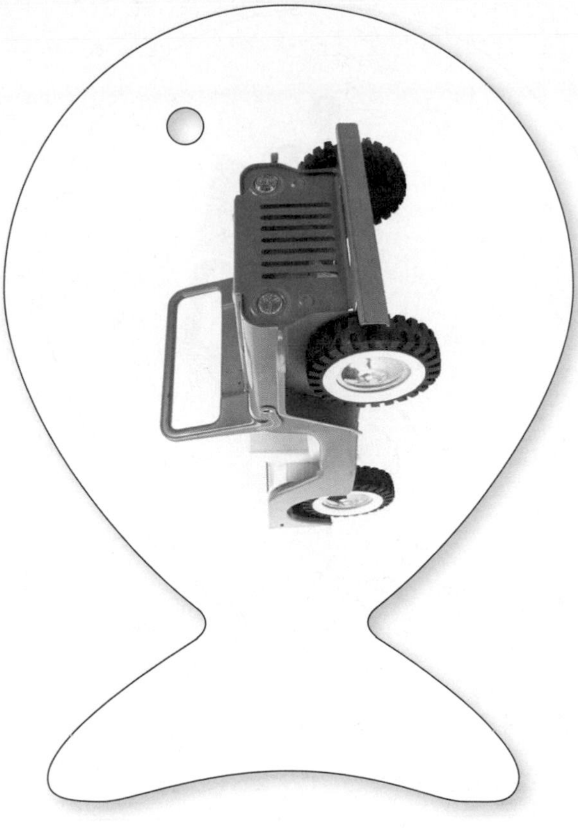

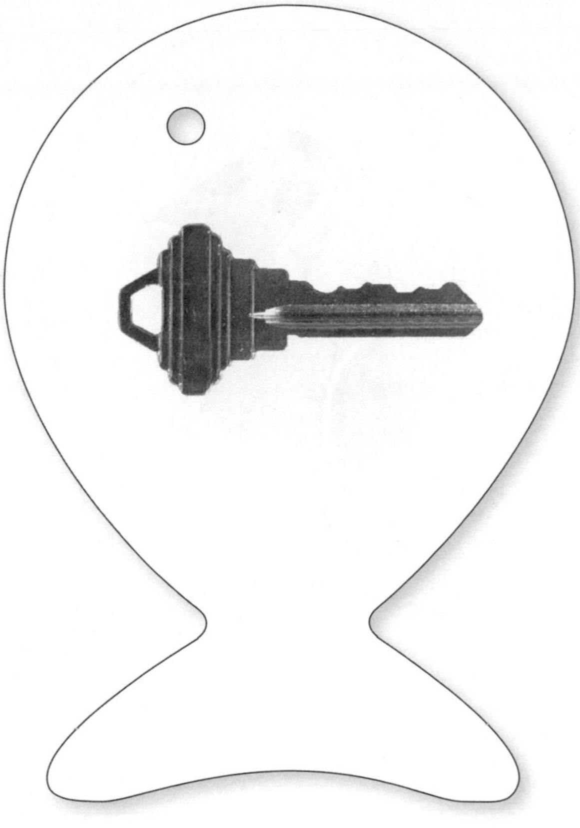

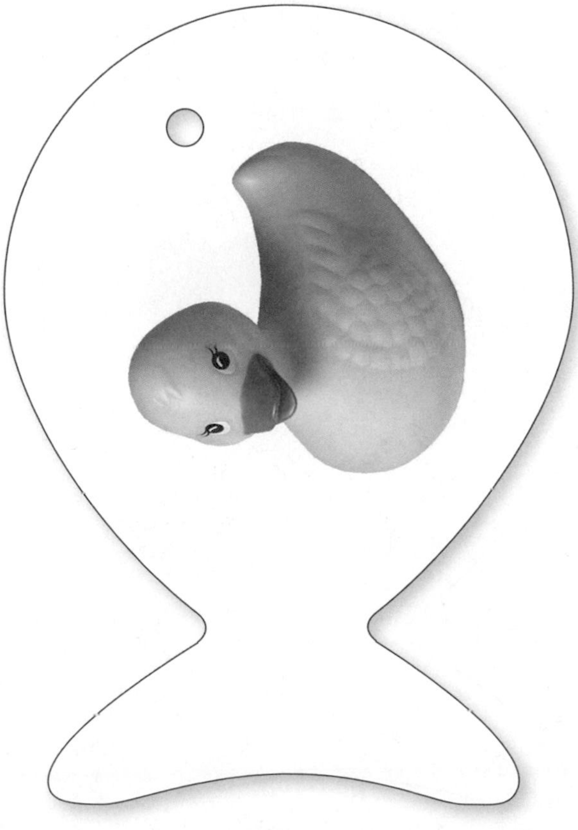

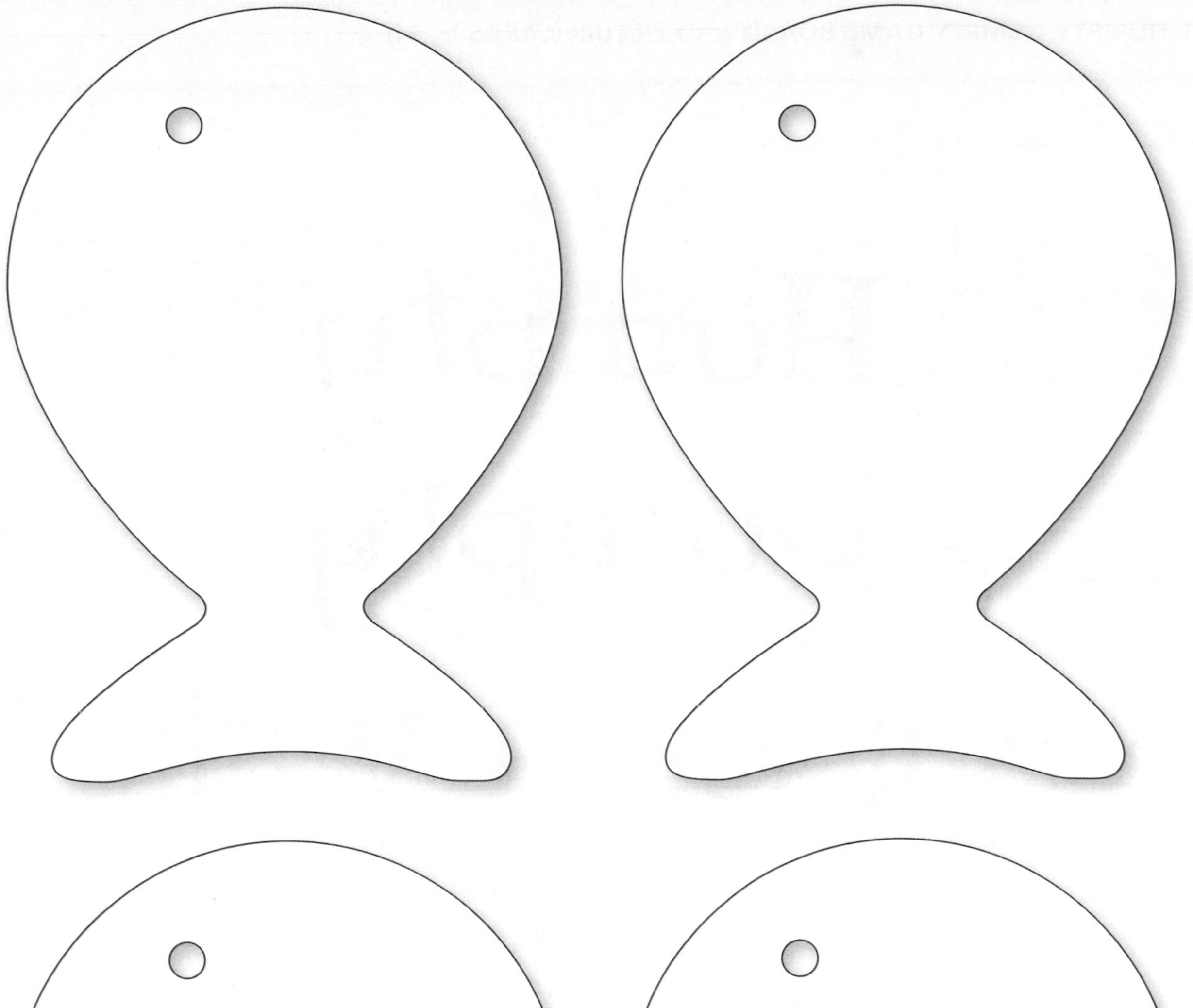

D.8 HUMPTY DUMPTY GAME BOARD AND PICTURE CARDS (p. 94)

Folder title (place on outside of folder)

Humpty Dumpty Sat on a Wall

Humpty Dumpty Had a Great Fall!

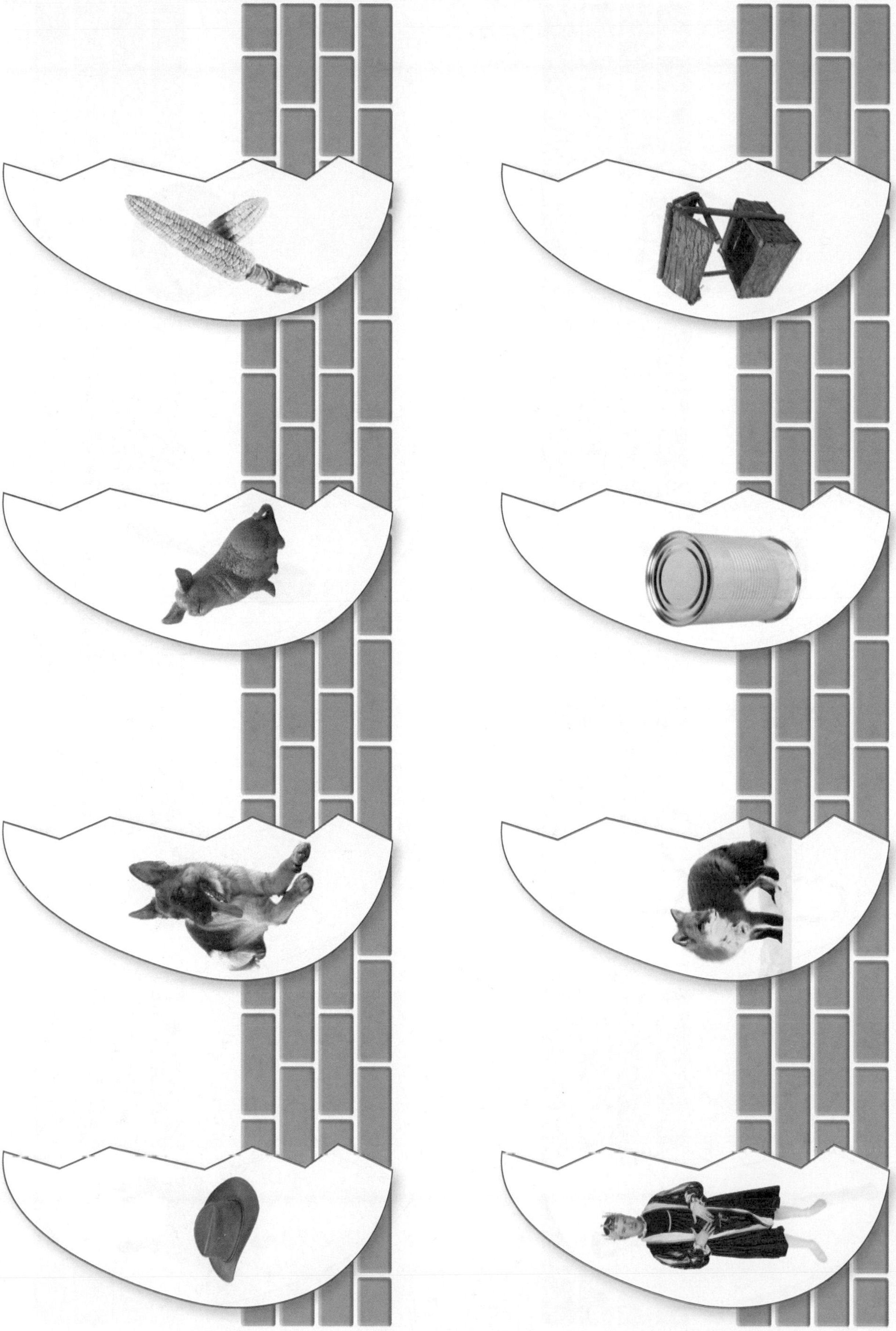

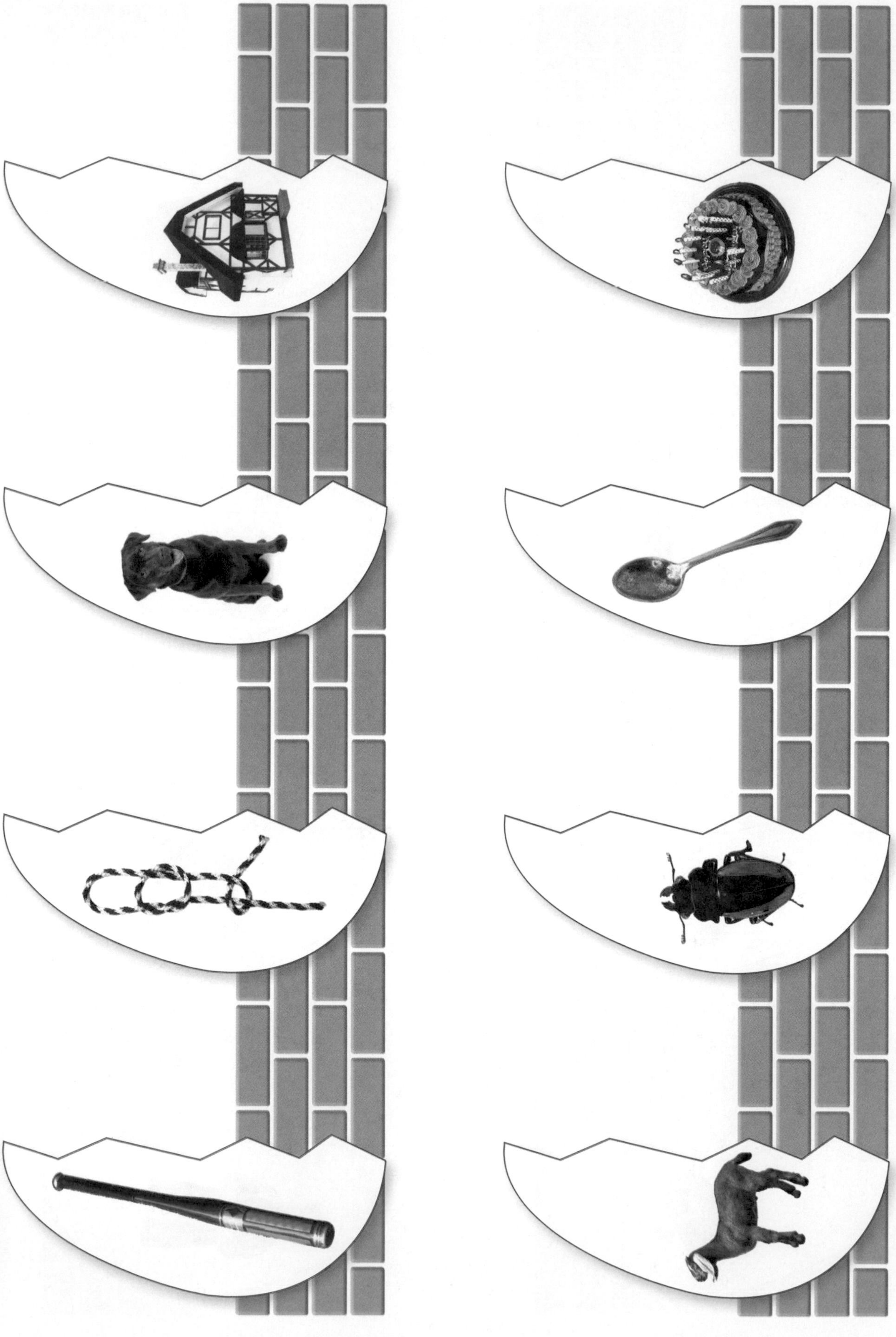

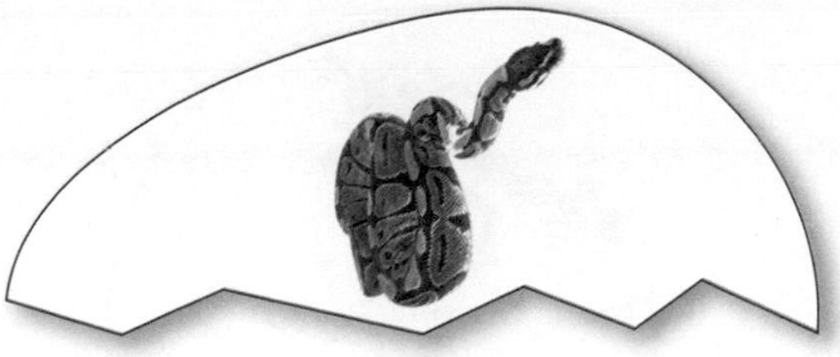

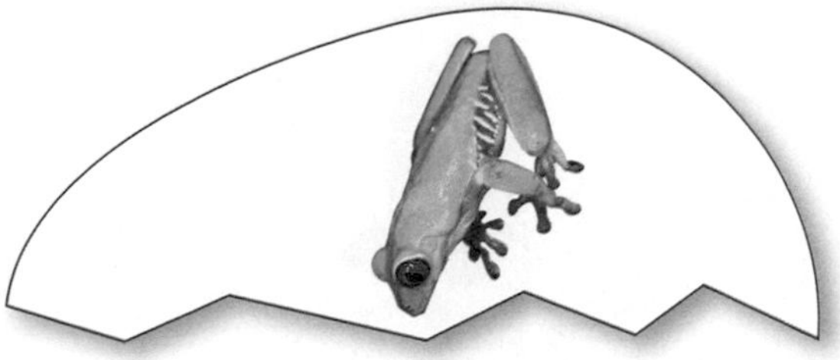

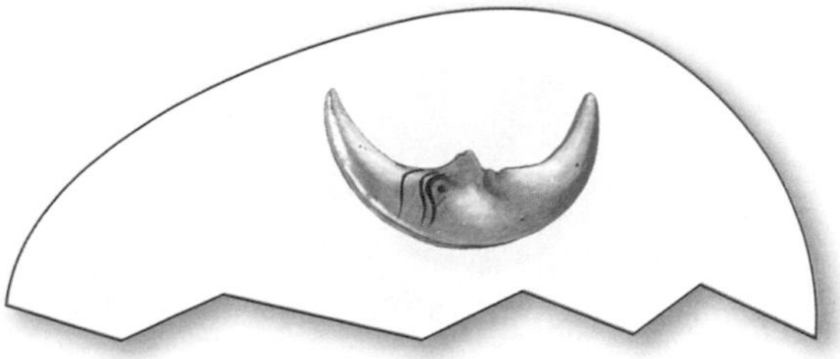

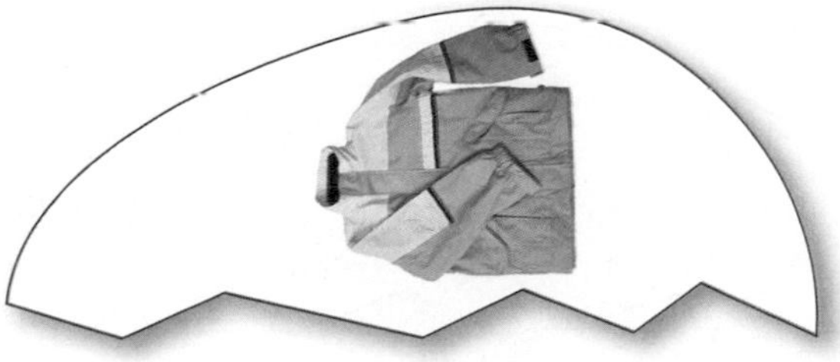

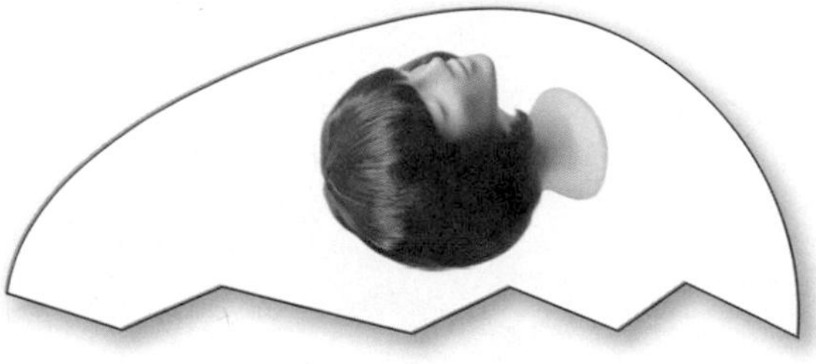

D.9 LISTEN FOR THE INITIAL CONSONANT BLEND SOUND GAME BOARD AND PICTURE CARDS (p. 114)

fr	br	gr	qu	tw
sk	sp	sw	st	sc
sm	dr	tr	pr	cr
fr	br	sc	sk	tr

cr	pr	tr	dr	sm
sc	st	sw	sp	sk
tw	qu	gr	br	fr
cr	sk	st	tr	sc

20
12
?
LIBERTY

$1.99

14.4V

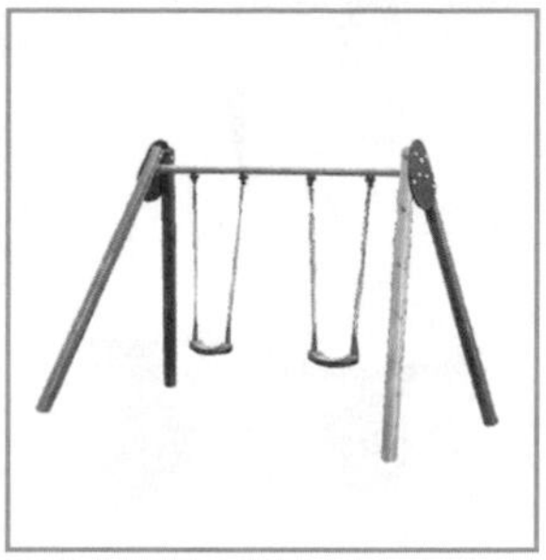

SCHOOL

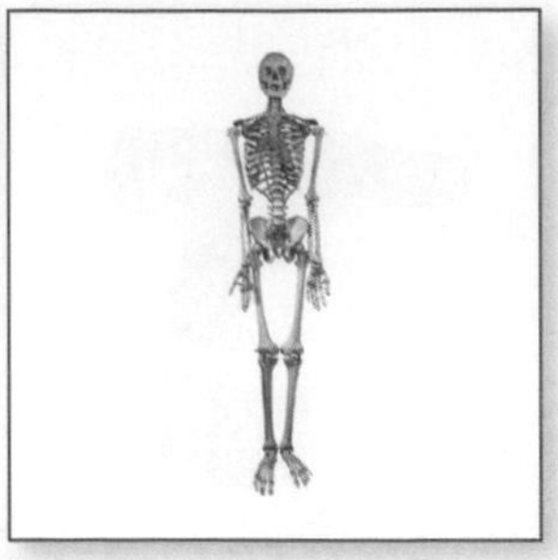

25¢

STOP

D.10 WORD DOMINOES (p. 116)

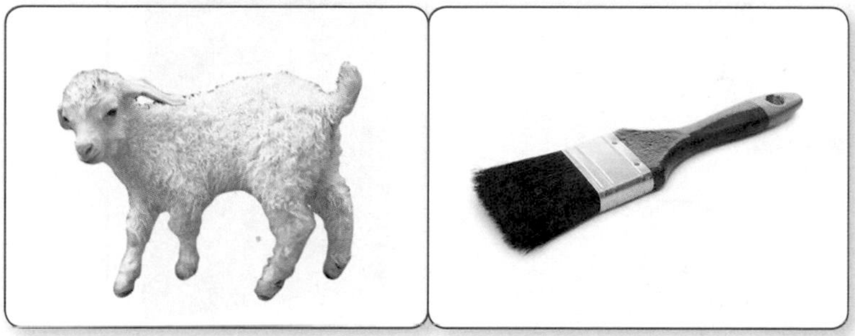

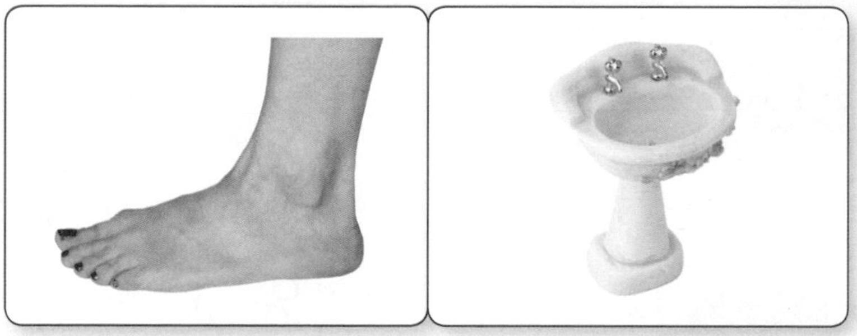

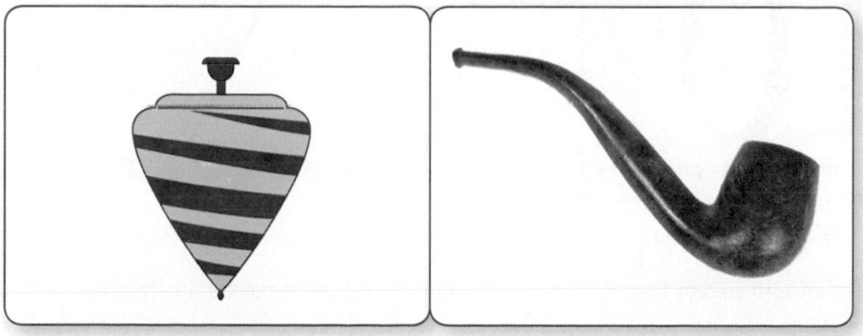

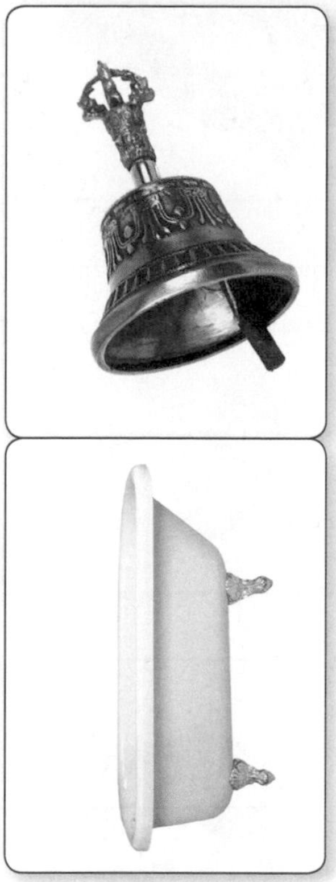

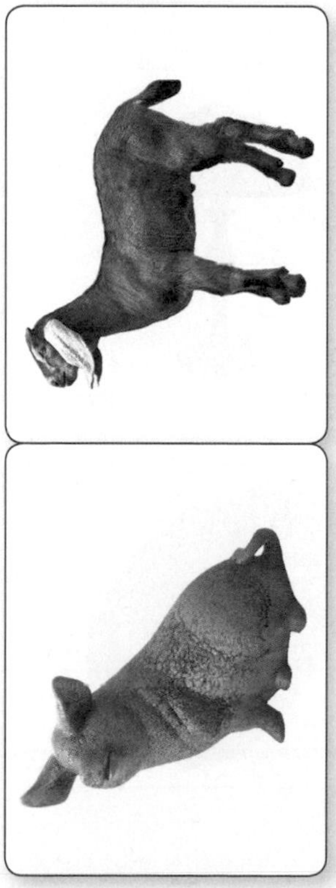

GUM
GUM

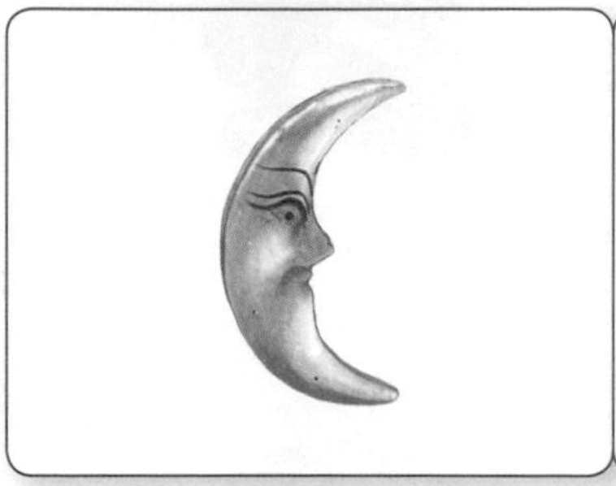

9

$199

10

NEWS

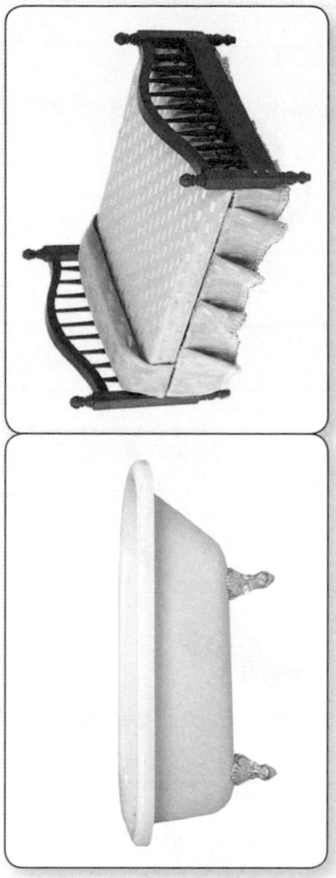

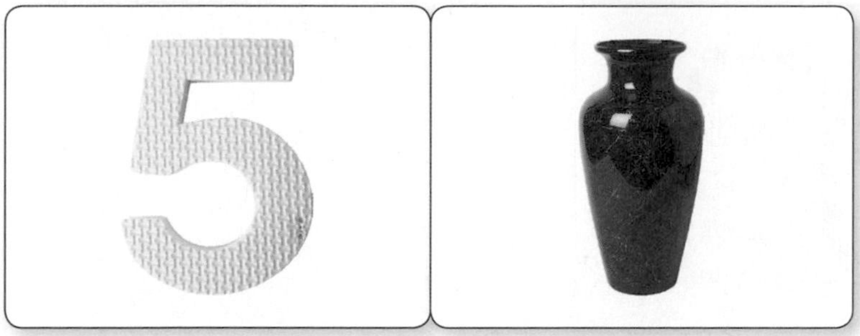

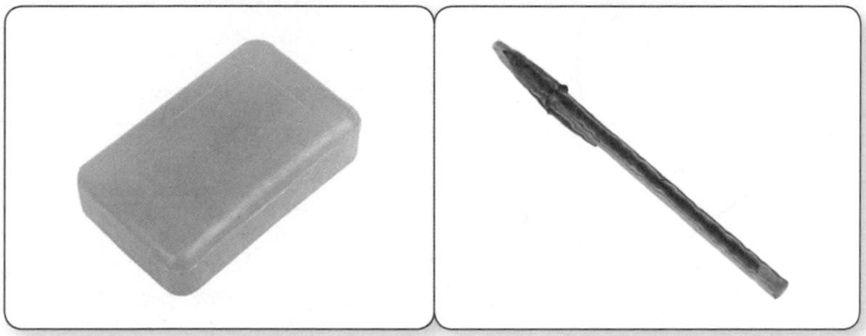

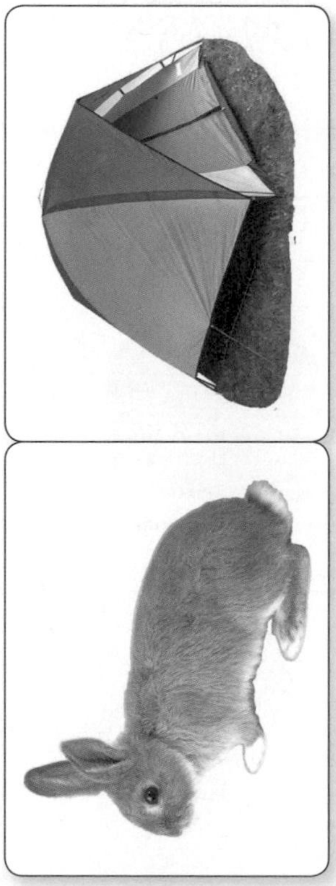

NEWS

REGULAR
UNLEADED
PREMIUM

D.11 CONCENTRATION WORD CARDS* (pp. 117, 121)

*Game pieces on this page are based on *Sheep Out to Eat* by Nancy Shaw (1992).

Eat	Seat	Sheep	Keep
Cake	Mistake	Smash	Crash
Slurp	Burp	Mop	Slop
Custard	Mustard	Bites	Appetites
Fill	Hill	Ear	Hear

Cat	Sat	Seen	Green
Arm	Farm	Hand	Sand
Ham	Sam	Goat	Coat
Where	There	Game	Shame
Let	Net	Feed	Seed

Llama	Mama	Dad	Glad
Pup	Up	Night	Might
Moon	Soon	Look	Book
Lock	Sock	Hog	Frog
Pack	Sack	Bake	Take

Sound	Found	Red	Bed
Fish	Wish	Box	Fox
Shut	Hut	Tall	Fall
Way	Day	Sing	Thing
Mess	Less	Stop	Top

D.12 LISTEN FOR THE VOWEL SOUND GAME BOARD AND GAME PIECES (p. 120)

i	ū	i	ā
ē	u	ō	a
e	ō	o	ē
ā	o	ū	e
a	ī	u	ī

ī	u	ī	a
e	ū	o	ā
ē	o	ō	e
a	ō	u	ē
ā	i	ū	i

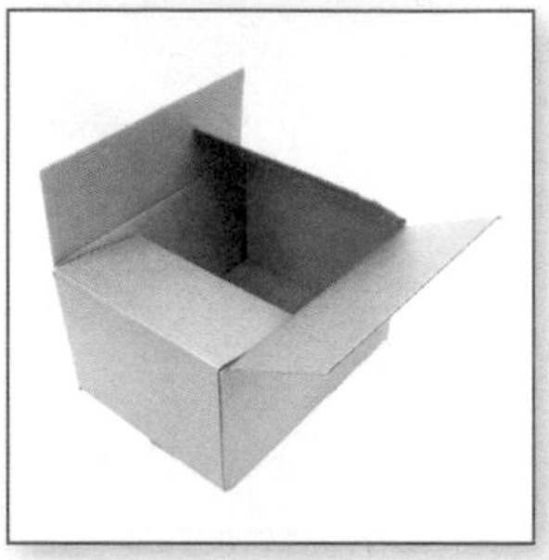

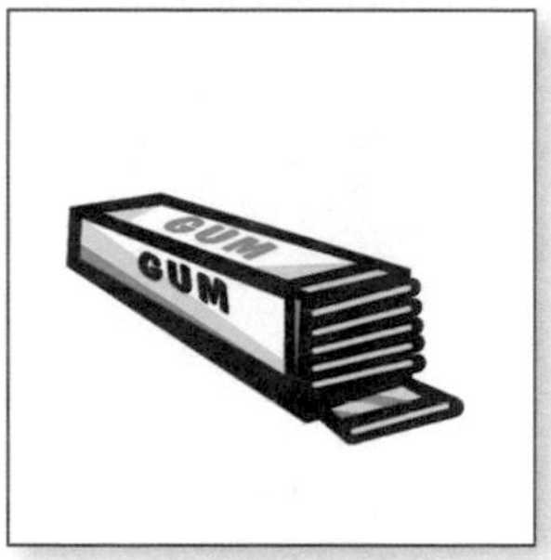
GUM
GUM

SCHOOL

From *Literacy Assessment and Intervention for Classroom Teachers* (3rd ed.), by Beverly DeVries. Copyright ©2011 by Holcomb Hathaway, Publishers, Scottsdale, AZ.

D.13 DOLCH LIST BINGO WORD CARDS (p. 141)

B	I	N	G	O
a	after	all	am	an
and	are	around	as	at
away	be	big	black	blue
brown	but	by	call	came
can	carry	cold	come	did

B	I	N	G	O
go	going	good	green	had
has	have	he	help	her
here	him	his	hurt	I
if	in	into	is	it
its	jump	know	like	little

B	I	N	G	O
look	over	play	put	ran
red	ride	round	run	said
saw	see	she	so	some
soon	stop	ten	the	this
three	to	too	two	under

B	I	N	G	O
up	about	again	any	ask
ate	because	been	before	best
better	both	bring	buy	clean
could	cut	does	done	draw
drink	eight	every	fall	far

B	I	N	G	O
hurt	just	keep	kind	laugh
let	light	live	long	many
much	must	myself	never	new
now	off	once	only	open
or	our	own	pick	please

B	I	N	G	O
small	start	take	tell	thank
that	their	them	then	there
these	they	think	those	today
together	try	upon	us	use
very	walk	want	warm	wish

D.14 ONSET AND RIME CARDS (p. 335)

C	B	F	H
M	P	S	at
B	C	D	F
M	N	P	R
V	an	B	H

S	St	L	and
Br	F	Fl	L
M	N	R	S
Fr	ight	B	F
H	M	P	R
S	ound		

D.15 TEMPLATES FOR MORPHOLOGY RUMMY CARDS (p. 146)

word
word
word
word
word
word
word
word
ROOT

PREFIX
word
word
word
word
word
word
word
word

word
word
word
word
word
word
word
word
SUFFIX

word
word
word
word
word
word
word
word
ROOT

PREFIX
word
word
word
word
word
word
word
word

word
word
word
word
word
word
word
word
SUFFIX

word
word
word
word
word
word
word
word
ROOT

PREFIX
word
word
word
word
word
word
word
word

word
word
word
word
word
word
word
word
SUFFIX

D.16 VOCABULARY BOOKMARK TEMPLATE (p. 163)

Name: Date:

VOCABULARY BOOKMARK

Title:

Author:

Word:

Definition:

Sentence:

Word:

Definition:

Sentence:

Name: Date:

VOCABULARY BOOKMARK

Title:

Author:

Word:

Definition:

Sentence:

Word:

Definition:

Sentence:

Name: Date:

VOCABULARY BOOKMARK

Title:

Author:

Word:

Definition:

Sentence:

Word:

Definition:

Sentence:

D.17 COGNATE SORT

bank 	music 	park 
train 	computer 	telephone 
parc	telefon	muziek
tren	banco	komputer
banque	musik	treno
computator	teléfono	musique
trem	parque	música
computador	musikk	

Bear, D. R., Helman, L., Templeton, S., Invernizzi, M., Johnston, F. (2007). *Words their way with English learners: Word study for phonics, vocabulary, and spelling instruction* (4th ed.). Upper Saddle River, NJ: Pearson.

D.18 MULTIPLE MEANING RACETRACK BOARD (p. 171)

D.19 TEXT MAPPING FORM (p. 202)

TITLE: ______________________________

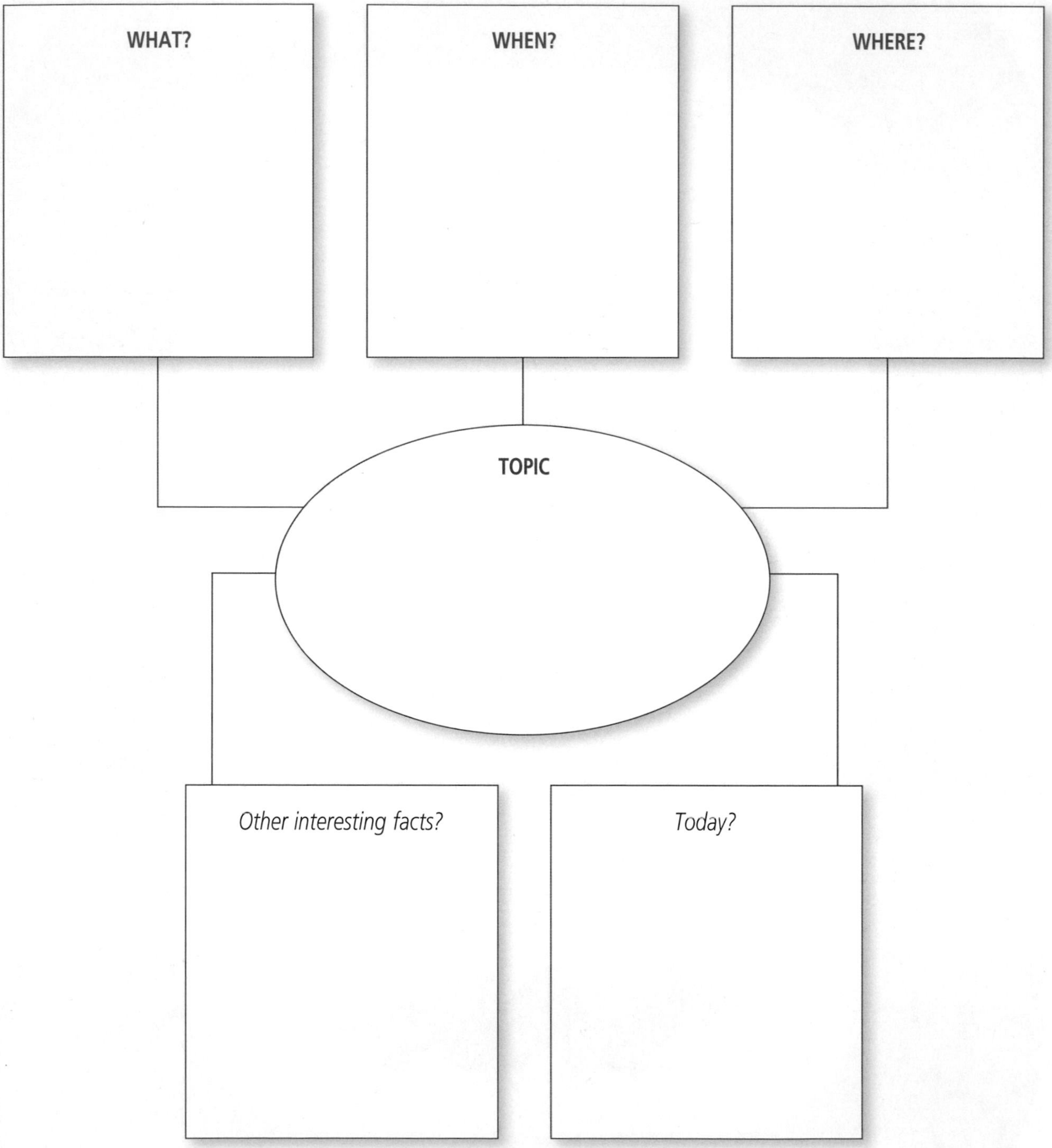

D.20 NARRATIVE E-BOOK EVALUATION FORM (p. 213)

BOOK TITLE ______ COPYRIGHT DATE ______

PUBLISHER ______ GRADE LEVELS ______

EVALUATOR ______ DATE ______

SCORES: 3 = SUPERIOR 2 = ADEQUATE 1 = POOR 0 = NOT INCLUDED

DESCRIPTOR	SCORE: 3	2	1	0
Written documentation with instructions.	○	○	○	○
Minimal download time.	○	○	○	○
Child-friendly installation.	○	○	○	○
Easy-to-follow instructions on screen.	○	○	○	○
Easy-to-comprehend verbal instructions.	○	○	○	○
Easy to quit at any point.	○	○	○	○
Verbal how-to-quit instructions.	○	○	○	○
Appropriate font size.	○	○	○	○
Appropriate amount of print on page.	○	○	○	○
Highlighted text correlates with computer voice.	○	○	○	○
Appropriate rate of computer's reading.	○	○	○	○
Appropriate fluency of computer's voice.	○	○	○	○
Easy-to-turn-off computer's voice.	○	○	○	○
User can click on words for pronunciation.	○	○	○	○
User can click on word for definition.	○	○	○	○
Music complements story.	○	○	○	○
Animations augment characters' actions.	○	○	○	○
Animations/music augment story's mood.	○	○	○	○
Hot spots are congruent story line.	○	○	○	○
Appropriate open-ended, exploratory features.	○	○	○	○

Total Score ____ /60

APPENDIX D

Source: Adapted from Shamir, A., & Korat, O. (2006). How to select CD-ROM storybooks for young children. *The Reading Teacher, 59*(6), 532–543.

D.21 INFORMATIONAL E-TEXT EVALUATION FORM (pp. 227, 255)

	YES	NO
AUTHOR CREDIBILITY		
• Who is the author/source or producer?	○	○
• What is the authority or expertise of the individual or group that created this site?	○	○
• Is there a way to contact the author or supply feedback?	○	○
ACCURACY AND RELIABILITY		
• Is the information accurate?	○	○
• How current is the information? Is a date of publication provided? How frequently is the resource updated?	○	○
• Is the information presented in an objective, balanced manner?	○	○
• Does the text follow basic rules of grammar, spelling, and composition?	○	○
• Are the sources of information stated? Can the information be verified?	○	○
• Does the information contradict something already known or learned from another source?	○	○
SCOPE		
• What is the primary purpose of the site (e.g., advertising, information)?	○	○
• Is the material covered adequately?	○	○
• Is it interactive enough to make students think?	○	○
• Is the information factual or opinion?	○	○
• Does the site contain original information or simply links?	○	○
FORMAT AND NAVIGATION		
• Can you find your way around and easily locate a particular page from any other page?	○	○
• How many links does it take to get to something useful?	○	○
• Is the arrangement of links uncluttered?	○	○
• If there are links to other sites, do they work?	○	○
• Do parts of it take too long to load?	○	○
• Can nonmembers still have access to part of the site?	○	○
• Do illustrations, video, or audio add value to the site?	○	○
• Do the multimedia, graphics, and art serve a function or are they decorative?	○	○
• What is the quality of the multimedia or graphic images? Do these images enhance the resource or distract from the content?	○	○
• Are the individual web pages concise, or does one have to scroll extensively?	○	○
• Is the site easily browsable or searchable?	○	○

Source: Adapted from Cecil, N. L., & Gipe, J. P. (2009). *Literacy in Grades 4–8: Best Practices for a Comprehensive Program* (2nd ed.). Scottsdale, AZ: Holcomb Hathaway.

D.22 TEXTBOOK AND TRADE BOOK EVALUATION CHECKLIST (pp. 229, 230)

Rate the statements below, using the following rating system:

5 = EXCELLENT
4 = GOOD
3 = ADEQUATE
2 = POOR
1 = UNACCEPTABLE
NA = NOT APPLICABLE

Further comments may be written in the space provided.

Book Title: ______________________

Publisher: ______________________

Copyright date: ______________________

FORMAT – EYE APPEAL

____ A. Photographs
____ B. Photographs that include different races and both sexes
____ C. Colorful charts and diagrams
____ D. White spaces on page
____ E. No two side-by-side pages of ALL text
____ F. Appropriate size of text for grade level
____ G. Appropriate text font for grade level

FORMAT – STRUCTURE

____ A. Detailed table of contents
____ B. Glossary
____ C. Index
____ D. Main headings in larger type
____ E. Subheadings in different font/size
____ F. New vocabulary in boldface or italics
____ G. Definitions of new vocabulary in margins
____ H. Appropriate captions under photographs and illustrations
____ I. Important facts repeated in illustrations and diagrams
____ J. Important facts highlighted in separate boxes
____ K. Pre-chapter questions—literal, inferential, and critical
____ L. Pre-chapter organizers
____ M. End-of-chapter questions—literal, inferential, and critical

TEXT

____ A. Readability appropriate for intended grade
____ B. New vocabulary explained adequately
____ C. Appropriate assumption of reader's vocabulary
____ D. Appropriate assumption of reader's background knowledge
____ E. Information logically presented
____ F. Important new information restated through visual aids
____ G. Clear explanation of new concepts
____ H. Text is not so oversimplified that relationships among ideas are not clear
____ I. Appropriate in-depth presentation of information
____ J. Information presented in a non-encyclopedic manner
____ K. Sentence structure grammatically correct
____ L. Appropriate use of conjunctions so relationships among ideas are clear
____ M. Good pronoun usage
____ N. Active voice

EXTENSION OF INFORMATION

____ A. Lists of books where students can get more information
____ B. Lists of websites where students can get more information
____ C. Suggestions for outside projects
____ D. In science texts, good description of appropriate step-by-step experiments

STRENGTHS OF BOOK:

____
____
____
____

WEAKNESSES OF BOOK:

____
____
____
____

Recommended for use by ______________________ (Child's name).

by ______________________ (Teacher's name).

D.23 INFORMATIONAL DVD/CD EVALUATION FORM (p. 255)

TITLE OF DVD/CD ______ COPYRIGHT DATE: ______

PUBLISHER ______ GRADE LEVELS ______

EVALUATOR ______ DATE ______

SCORES: 4 = SUPERIOR 3 = GOOD 2 = ADEQUATE 1 = POOR 0 = NOT INCLUDED

DESCRIPTOR	SCORE: 4	3	2	1	0
Written documentation with instructions.	○	○	○	○	○
Minimal loading time.	○	○	○	○	○
Child-friendly installation.	○	○	○	○	○
Easy-to-follow instructions on screen.	○	○	○	○	○
Easy-to-comprehend verbal instructions.	○	○	○	○	○
Easy to quit at any point.	○	○	○	○	○
Verbal how-to-quit instructions.	○	○	○	○	○
Appropriate font size.	○	○	○	○	○
Appropriate amount of print on page.	○	○	○	○	○
Appropriate diagrams or charts to explain concepts.	○	○	○	○	○
Vivid illustrations explain concept.	○	○	○	○	○
Cursor activates computer voice.	○	○	○	○	○
Appropriate rate of computer's reading.	○	○	○	○	○
Appropriate sound effects.	○	○	○	○	○
Videos describing concept.	○	○	○	○	○
Appropriate open-ended, exploratory features.	○	○	○	○	○

Total Score ____ /64

Source: Adapted from Shamir, A., & Korat, O. (2006). How to select CD-ROM storybooks for young children. *The Reading Teacher, 59*(6), 532–543.

D.24 RECORD, CHECK, CHART (pp. 39, 272)

NAME: GRADE:

STORY	1ST READING ERRORS	2ND READING ERRORS	3RD READING ERRORS	TEACHER COMMENTS
1.				
2.				
3.				
4.				
5.				
6.				
7.				
8.				
9.				
10.				

TEACHER'S GENERAL COMMENTS:

D.25 RECORD, TIME, CHART (p. 39)

NAME: GRADE:

STORY	1ST READING TIME	2ND READING TIME	3RD READING TIME	TEACHER COMMENTS
1.				
2.				
3.				
4.				
5.				
6.				
7.				
8.				
9.				
10.				

TEACHER'S GENERAL COMMENTS:

D.26 FLUENCY LOG (p. 273)

Books I Can Read

BY ______________________________

TITLE	AUTHOR	PARENTS' COMMENTS	DATE	NUMBER OF TIMES READ
1.				
2.				
3.				
4.				
5.				
6.				
7.				

APPENDIX D

D.27 TEMPLATE FOR A STORYBOARD (p. 292)

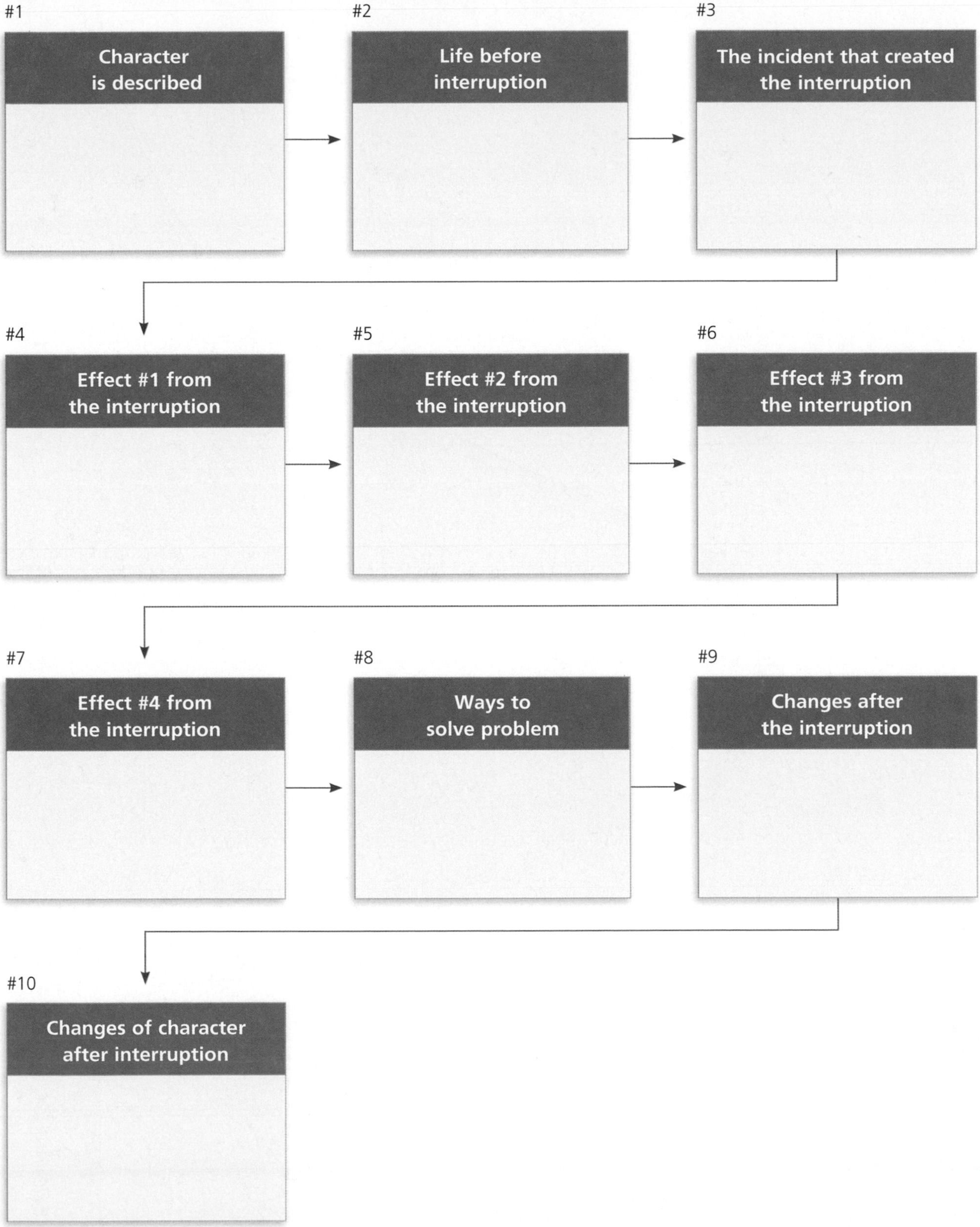

D.28 MT. PLOT (p. 307)

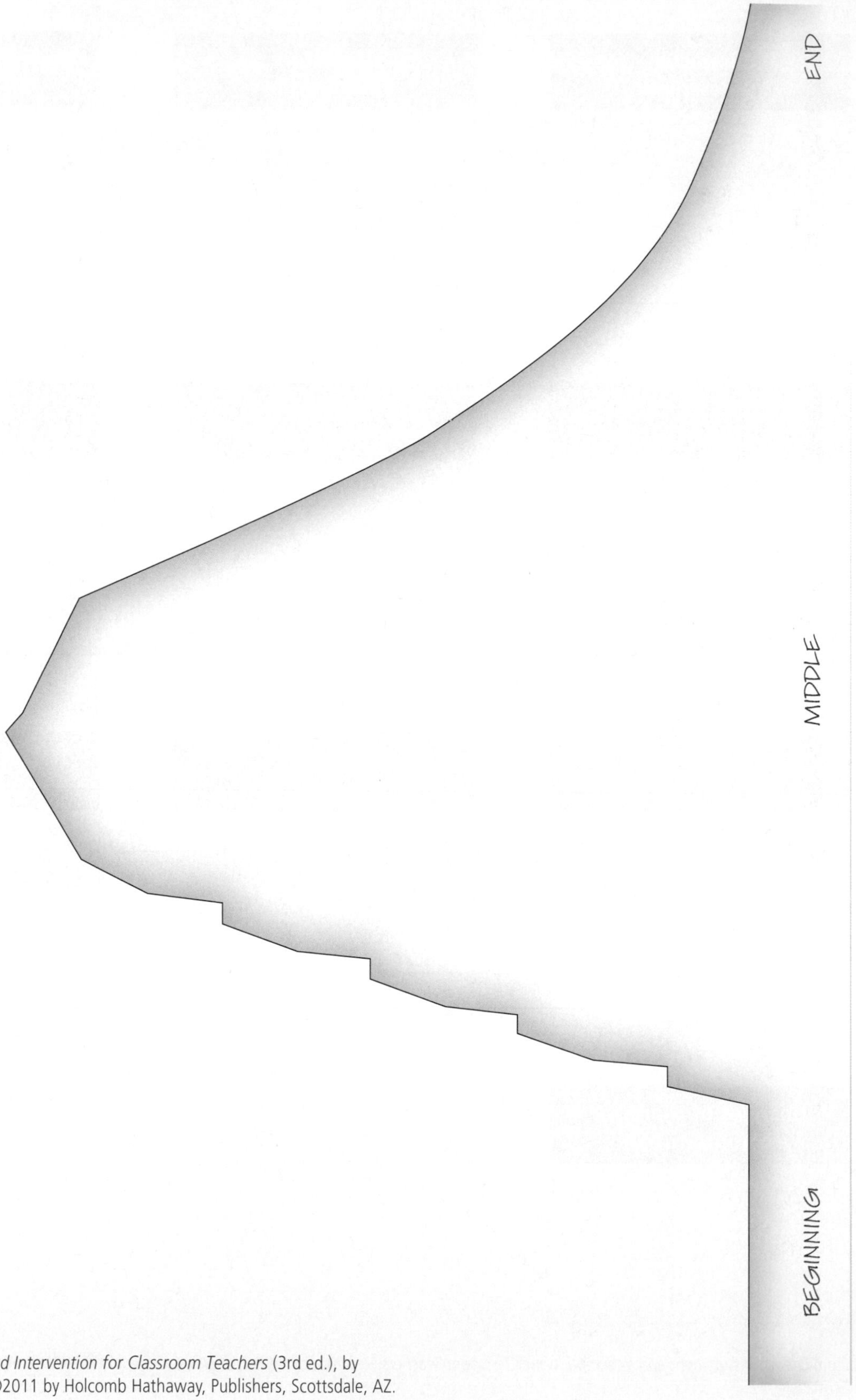

D.29 LESSON PLAN FOR TUTORS (p. 348)

TUTOR: ____________________ DATE: __________

TUTEE: ____________________ GRADE: __________

Easy Reading Objective:

Rereading of Last Session's Book Objective:

Word Study Objective:

Writing Objective:

Reading of Instructional Materials Objective:

LESSON PLAN	PLANNED ACTIVITY	TIME	REFLECTION

D.30 LOG SHEET OF STRATEGIES (p. 354)

STRATEGIES TAUGHT TO ______________________________ BY ______________________________

DURING EASY READ	DURING WRITING

DURING WORD STUDY	DURING NEW BOOK

D.31 LOG SHEET OF BOOKS READ (p. 354)

BOOKS READ DURING TUTORING

TUTOR: ______________________ TUTEE: ______________________

BOOKS READ BY TUTOR	DATE	BOOKS READ BY TUTEE	DATE

D.32 POSTCARD FOR CHILDREN READING BOOKS WITH ORAL READING AND COMPREHENSION SCAFFOLDING (p. 368)

1. What's the title of your book? ______________________
2. Did you finish reading this book? ○ Yes ○ No, I stopped on page _____.
3. How many times did you read this book? ○ Didn't finish ○ 1 time ○ 2 times ○ 3 times.
4. What did you do to better understand this book? (check all that apply)
   - ○ I reread parts of this book.
   - ○ I made predictions about this book.
   - ○ I asked questions about this book.
   - ○ I made connections (text-to-text, text-to-self).
   - ○ I summarized parts of the book.
5. After you read the book, tell someone in your family what the book was about. Pick a part of the book to read aloud two times. Ask him or her how you improved the second time you read the section and ask for his or her signature. (check all that apply)
   - ○ Did I read more smoothly?
   - ○ Did I know more words?
   - ○ Did I read with more expression?
6. Family member's signature: ______________________

Optional comment about this student's reading:

APPENDIX D

Source: T.G. White & J.S. Kim (2008). Teacher and parent scaffolding of voluntary summer reading. *The Reading Teacher 62*(2), p. 120.

REFERENCES

Acha, J. (2009). The effectiveness of multimedia programs in children's verbal learning. *British Journal of Educational Technology, 40*(1), 23–31.

Ada, A. F. (1998). *Yours truly, Goldilocks.* New York: Atheneum Books.

Adam-Just, M., & Carpenter, P. (2004). A theory of reading: From eye fixations to comprehension. In R. Ruddell & N. Unrau (Eds.), *Theoretical models and processes of reading* (5th ed.), pp. 1182–1218. Newark, DE: International Reading Association.

Adams, M. J. (1990). *Beginning to read: Thinking and learning about print.* Cambridge, MA: MIT Press.

Adler, D. (1990). *A picture book of Benjamin Franklin.* New York: A Trumpet Club Special Edition.

Afflerbach, P., & VanSledright, B. (2001). Hath! Doth! What? Middle graders reading innovative history text. *Journal of Adolescent & Adult Literacy, 44*(8), 696–708.

Ahlberg, J. (1986). *The jolly postman.* New York: Scholastic.

Alborough, J. (1994). *It's the bear.* New York. Scholastic.

Allinder, R. (2001). Improving fluency in at-risk readers and students with learning disabilities. *Remedial and Special Education, 22*(1), 48–56.

Allington, R. (1983). Fluency. The neglected goal. *The Reading Teacher, 36,* 556–561.

Allington, R. (2002). What I've learned about effective reading instruction: From a decade of studying exemplary elementary classroom teachers. *Phi Delta Kappan, 83*(10), 740–747.

Allington, R. (2006). *What really matters for struggling readers: Designing research-based programs* (2nd ed.). Boston: Pearson/Allyn & Bacon.

Allington, R. L. (2000). *What really matters for struggling readers: Designing research-based programs.* Boston: Longman.

Allington, R., & Cunningham, P. (2002). *Schools that work: Where all children read and write* (2nd ed.). Boston: Allyn & Bacon.

Allington, R., Johnston, P., & Day, J. (2002). Exemplary fourth-grade teachers. *Language Arts, 79*(6), 462–466.

Alyousef, H. S. (2005). Teaching reading comprehension to ESL/EFL learners. *The Reading Matrix, 5*(2), 142–153.

Ambruster, B. (1996). Considerate text. In D. Lapp, J. Flood, & N. Farnan (Eds.), *Content area reading and learning: Instructional strategies* (2nd ed.), pp. 47–58. Boston: Allyn & Bacon.

Anders, P., & Lloyd, C. (1996). The significance of prior knowledge in the learning of new content-specific ideas. In D. Lapp, J. Flood, & N. Farnan (Eds.), *Content area reading and learning: Instructional strategies* (2nd ed.), pp. 323–338. Boston: Allyn & Bacon.

Anderson, R. (1981). The missing ingredient: Fluent oral reading. *The Elementary School Journal, 81,* 173–177.

Anthony, H., & Raphael, T. (1996). Using questioning strategies to promote students' active comprehension of content area material. In D. Lapp, J Flood, & N. Farnan (Eds.), *Content area reading and learning: Instructional strategies* (2nd ed.), pp. 307–322. Boston: Allyn & Bacon.

Armstrong, T. (2000). *Multiple intelligences in the classroom* (2nd ed.). Alexandria, VA: Association for Supervision and Curriculum Development.

Armstrong, T. (2004). Making the words roar. *Educational Leadership, 61*(6), 78–81.

Asher, J. (1982). *Learning another language through actions.* Los Gatos, CA: Sky Oaks Productions.

Ashton-Warner, S. (1963). *Teacher.* New York: Simon & Schuster.

Associated Press (2010). Doubt cast on Afghan forces. *The Oklahoman.* July 22, 2010, p. 10A.

Atwell, N. (1987). *In the middle.* Portsmouth, NH: Heinemann.

August, D., Carlo, M., Dressler, C., & Snow, C. (2005). The critical role of vocabulary development for English language learners. *Learning Disabilities Research and Practice, 20*(1), 50–57.

August, D., & Shanahan, T. (2006). Developing literacy in second-language learners. Report of the National Panel on Language minority children and youth. Mahwah, NJ: Erlbaum.

Avi. (1999). *Midnight magic.* New York: Scholastic.

Avi. (2001). *Ereth's birthday.* New York: HarperTrophy.

Avi. (2004). *The good dog.* New York: Aladdin.

Avi. (2005) *Poppy* (New ed.). New York: Simon & Schuster.

Avi. (2005). *Poppy and Rye.* New York: HarperTrophy.

Avi. (2006). *Poppy's return.* New York: HarperTrophy.

Ayto, J. (1993). *Dictionary of word origins: Histories of more than 8,000 English-language words.* New York: Arcade.

Bagert, B. (1997). *The gooch machine: Poems for children to perform.* Honesdale, PA: Boyds Mills Press.

Bagert, B. (1999). *Rainbows, head lice and pea-green tile.* Gainesville, FL: Maupin House.

Bagert, B. (2006). *Hormone jungle: Coming of age.* Gainesville, FL: Maupin House.

Bailey-Beard, D. (1998). *The flimflam man.* New York: Farrar, Straus & Giroux.

Bailey-Beard, D. (1999). *Twister.* New York: Farrar, Straus & Giroux.

Banyai, I. (1995). *Zoom.* New York: Puffin.

Barksdale, M. A., Watson, C., & Park, E. S. (2007). Pen pal letter exchanges: Taking first steps toward developing cultural understandings. *The Reading Teacher, 61*(1), 58–68.

Barr, R., Blachowicz, C., Katz, C., & Kaufman, B. (2006). *Reading diagnosis for teachers: An instructional approach* (5th ed.). Boston: Allyn & Bacon.

Barrett, J. (1978). *Cloudy with a chance of meatballs.* Illus. by R. Barrett. New York: Aladdin Books.

Barry, A. (1998). The evolution of reading tests and other forms of educational assessment. *Clearing House, 71*(4), 231–236.

Baumann, J. F., Kame'enui, E. J., & Ash, G. E. (2003). Research on vocabulary instruction: Voltaire redux. In J. Flood, D. Lapp, J. R. Squire, & J. M. Jensen (Eds.), *Handbook on teaching the English language arts* (2nd ed.), pp. 752–785. Mahwah, NJ: Erlbaum.

Baumann, J. F., Ware, D., Carr-Edwards, E. (2007). "Bumping into spicy, tasty words that catch your tongue": A formative experiment on vocabulary instruction. *The Reading Teacher, 61*(2), 108–122.

Beall, P. C., & Nipp, S. H. (1979). *Wee sing: Children's songs and fingerplays.* New York: Price Stern Sloan.

Bean, T. W., & Pardi, R. (1979). A field test of a guided reading strategy. *Journal of Reading, 23,* 144–147.

Bear, D., Helman, L., Templeton, S., Invernizzi, M., & Johnston, F. (2007). *Words their way with English learners: Word study for phonics, vocabulary, and spelling instruction* (4th ed.). Upper Saddle River, NJ: Pearson.

Bear, D., Invernizzi, M., Templeton, S., & Johnston, F. (2007). *Words their way: Word study for phonics, vocabulary, and spelling instruction* (4th ed.). Upper Saddle River, NJ: Pearson, Merrill, Prentice Hall.

Bear, D., & Templeton, S. (1998). Exploration in developmental spelling: Foundations for learning and teaching phonics, spelling and vocabulary. *The Reading Teacher, 52*(3), 222–242.

Beauchat, K. A., Blamey, K., & Walpole, S. (2009). Building preschool children's language and literacy one storybook at a time. *The Reading Teacher, 63*(1), 26–39.

Beck, A. (2005). A place for critical literacy. *Journal of Adolescent and Adult Literacy, 48*(5), 392–400.

Beck, I., & McKeown, M. G. (1991). Developing questions that promote comprehension: The story map. *Language Arts, 58,* 913–918.

Beck, I., & McKeown, M. (2001). Text talk: Capturing the benefits of read-aloud experiences for younger children. *The Reading Teacher, 55*(1), 10–21.

Beck, I. L., McKeown, M. G., & Kucan, L. (2002). *Bringing words to life: Robust vocabulary instruction.* New York: Guilford.

Beckman-Anthony, A. (2008). Output strategies for English-language learners: Theory to practice. *The Reading Teacher, 61*(6), 472–482.

Behrman, E. H. (2006). Teaching about language, power and text: A review of classroom practices that support critical literacy. *Journal of Adolescent and Adult Literacy, 49*(6), 490–498.

Bemelmans, L. (1986). *Madeline and the gypsies.* New York: Viking.

Bennett, J. (Ed.). (1987). *Noisy poems.* Oxford, New York: Oxford University Press.

Bennett-Hopkins, L. (2009). *City I love.* Illus. by M. Hall. New York: Abrams Books for Young Readers.

Berger, M., & Berger, G. (2003). *Sharks.* New York: Scholastic.

Berkowitz, M. W., & Bier, M. C. (2005). Character education: Parents as partners. *Educational Leadership, 53*(1), 64–69.

Biancarosa, G., & Snow, C. E. (2004). Reading next—A vision for action and research in middle and high school literacy. A report to Carnegie Corporation of New York. Washington, D.C.: Alliance for Excellence in Education.

Bintz, W. (2010). Singing across the curriculum. *The Reading Teacher, 63*(8), 683–686.

Bintz, W. (2010). Fibbin with poems across the curriculum. *The Reading Teacher, 63*(6), 509–513.

Blachowicz, C., & Fisher, P. (2005a). *Teaching vocabulary in all classrooms* (3rd ed.). Upper Saddle River, NJ: Merrill.

Blachowicz, C., & Fisher, P. (2005b). Vocabulary lessons. *Educational Leadership, 61*(6), 66–69.

Blanton, W., Wood, K., & Taylor, D. (2007). Rethinking middle school reading instruction: A basic literacy activity. *Reading Psychology, 28,* 75–95.

Blevins, W. (1997). *Phonemic awareness activities for early reading success.* New York: Scholastic.

Blevins, W. (2001). *Teaching phonics and word study in the intermediate grades.* New York: Scholastic.

Blevins, W. (2006). *Phonics from A to Z: A practical guide* (2nd ed.). New York: Scholastic.

Bloodgood, J. W., & Pacifici, L. C. (2004). Bringing word study in intermediate classrooms. *The Reading Teacher, 58*(3), 250–263.

Bluestein, A. (2010). Unlocking text features for determining importance in expository text: A strategy for struggling readers. *The Reading Teacher, 63*(7), 597–600.

Blum, I., Koskinen, P., Bhartiya, P., & Hluboky, S. (2010). Thinking and talking about books: Using prompts to stimulate discussion. *The Reading Teacher, 62*(6), 495–499.

Boers, D. (2002). What teachers need of parents. *Education Digest, 67*(8), 37–41.

Bond, G., & Dykstra, R. (1967). The cooperative research program in first grade reading (Reprint). *Reading Research Quarterly, 32*(4), 345–427.

Bond, L. (1996). Norm- and criterion-referenced testing. *Practical Assessment, Research and Evaluation, 5*(2).

Booth, D. (1999). Language delights and word play: The foundation for literacy learning. In I. C. Fountas & G. S. Pinnell (Eds.), *Voices on word matters: Learning about phonics and spelling in the literacy classroom,* pp. 91–102. Portsmouth, NH: Heinemann.

Bos, C. S., & Vaughn, S. (1994). *Strategies for teaching students with learning and behavior problems.* Boston: Allyn & Bacon.

Bottner, B. (1996). *Nana Hannah's piano.* Boston: Houghton Mifflin.

Bottomley, D., Henk, W., & Melnick, S. (1998). Assessing children's views about themselves as writers using the Writer Self-Perception Scale. *The Reading Teacher, 51*(4), 286–296.

Bouchereau-Bauer, E., & Manyak, P. (2008). Creating language-rich instruction for English-language learners. *The Reading Teacher, 62*(2), 176–178.

Boyle, D. (1998). *Coral reef hideaway: The story of a clown anemonefish.* New York: Scholastic.

Branley, F. (1997). *Down comes the rain* (Illustrated ed.). New York: HarperTrophy.

Branley, F. (1999). *Flash, crash, rumble and roll* (Reprint ed.). New York: HarperTrophy.

Bray, M., Kehle, T., Spackman, V., & Hintze, J. (1998). An intervention program to increase reading fluency. *Special Services in the Schools, 14,* 105–125.

Brett, J. (1989). *The mitten.* New York: G. P. Putnam's Sons.

Brett, J. (1991). *Berlioz the bear.* New York: G. P. Putnam's Sons.

Brett, J. (1995). *Armadillo rodeo.* New York: G. P. Putnam's Sons.

Brett, J. (2002). *Daisy comes home.* New York: Putnam Juvenile.

Brewer, P. (2003). *You must be joking! Lots of cool jokes, plus 17 1/2 tips for remembering, telling, and making up your own jokes.* Battle Creek, MI: Cricket.

Bromley, K. (2008). Foreword. In T. Rasinski, N. Padak, R. M. Newton, & E. Newton, (Eds.), *Greek & Latin roots keys to building vocabulary,* pp. 7–8. Huntington Beach, CA: Shell Education.

Bromley, K., Vandenberg, A., & White, J. (2007). What can we learn from the word writing CAFÉ? *The Reading Teacher, 61*(4), 284–295.

Brophy, J., & Alleman, J. (1992/93). Elementary social studies textbooks. *Publishing Research Quarterly, 8*(4), 12–23.

Brown, K. (1999/2000). What kind of text— For whom and when? Textual scaffolding for beginning readers. *The Reading Teacher, 53*(4), 292–308.

Brozo, W. G. (2010). Response to intervention or responsive instruction? Challenges and possibilities of response to intervention for adolescents. *Journal of Adolescent and Adult Literacy, 53*(4), 277–281.

Brozo, W. G., & Flynt, S. E. (2007). Content literacy: Fundamental toolkit elements. *The Reading Teacher, 61*(2), 192–194.

Brozo, W. G., & Flynt, S. E. (2008). Motivating students to read in the content classroom: Six evidence-based principles. *The Reading Teacher, 62*(2), 172–174.

Bruner, J. (1960). *The process of education.* Cambridge, MA: Harvard University Press.

Bruner, J. (2003). *The process of education* (Rev. ed.) Boston: Harvard University Press.

Bulion, L. (2006). *Hey, there, stick bug!* Illus. by L. Evans. Watertown, MA: Charlesbridge.

Bunting, E. (1990). *In the haunted house.* New York: Trumpet Club Special Edition.

Buros Institute. (2002). *Reading.* Retrieved October 5, 2003, from www.unl.edu/buros/index13.html

Cadiero-Kaplan, K. (2002). Literacy ideologies: Critically engaging the language arts curriculum. *Language Arts, 79,* 372–381.

Calkins, L. (1983). *Lessons from a child on the teaching and learning of writing.* Portsmouth, NH: Heinemann.

Calkins, L., Montgomery, K., Santman, D., & Falk, B. (1998). *A teacher's guide to standardized reading tests.* Portsmouth, NH: Heinemann.

Calkins, L. M. (1994). *The art of teaching writing* (Rev. ed.). Portsmouth, NH: Heinemann.

Camilli, G., & Wolfe, P. (2004). Research on reading: A cautionary tale. *Educational Leadership, 61*(6), 26–29.

Canizares, S., & Reid, M. (1998). *Who lives in the rainforest?* New York: Scholastic.

Carbo, M. (1978). Teaching reading with talking books. *The Reading Teacher, 32,* 267–273.

Carbo, M. (1996a). Recorded books raise reading skills. *Education Digest, 61*(9), 59.

Carbo, M. (1996b). Selecting the "right" reading method. *Teaching PreK–8,* 27(1), 84.

Carbo, M. (1996c). Whole language or phonics? Use both! *Education Digest, 61*(6), 60–63.

Carbo, M. (1997). Four key questions to evaluate reading programs. *Education Digest, 62*(5), 64–68.

Carbo, M. (1998). *Reading styles: High rapid reading gains with diverse learners.* Syosset, NY: National Reading Styles Institute.

Carbo, M. (2007). *Becoming a great teacher of reading: Achieving high rapid reading gains with powerful, differentiated strategies.* New York: Corwin Press.

Carlo, M., August, D., McLaughlin, B., Snow, C., Dressler, C., Lippman, D., Lively, T., & White, C. (2004). Closing the gap: Addressing the vocabulary needs of English language learners in bilingual and mainstream classrooms. *Reading Research Quarterly, 39*(2), 188–215.

Carlstrom, N. (1986). *Jesse Bear, what will you wear?* New York: Aladdin Paperbacks.

Carlstrom, N. (1998). *Guess Who's Coming, Jesse Bear.* New York: Aladdin Paperbacks.

Carrell, P. (2010). Three components of background knowledge in reading comprehension. *Learning Language, 33*(2), 183–203.

Carrell, R. L. (1987). Content and formal schemata in ESL reading. *TESOL Quarterly, 21,* 461–481.

Cartwright, K., Savage, D., Morgan, K., & Nichols, B. (2009). Literacy partners programs: In-school tutoring in a school-university partnership. In J. C. Richards & C. A. Lassonde (Eds.), *Literacy tutoring that works,* pp. 56–89. Newark, DE: International Reading Association.

Cauley, L. B. (1992). *Clap your hands.* New York: Scholastic.

Cecil, N. L. (2007). *Striking a balance: Best practices for early literacy* (3rd ed.). Scottsdale, AZ: Holcomb Hathaway.

Cecil, N. L. (2011). *Striking a balance: A comprehensive programs for early literacy* (4th ed.). Scottsdale, AZ: Holcomb Hathaway.

Cecil, N., & Gipe, J. (2009). *Literacy in grades 4–8: Best practices* (2nd ed.). Scottsdale, AZ: Holcomb Hathaway.

Celenza, A. H. (2000). *The farewell symphony.* Watertown, WA: Charlesbridge Publishing.

Center for Public Education (2010a). How many English learners are in our schools? Retrieved June 25, 2010, from www.centerforpublic education.org

Center for Public Education (2010b). What is the racial and ethnic makeup of our school(s)? Retrieved June 25, 2010, from www.centerfor publiceducation.org

Cerullo, M. (1999). *Dolphins: What they can teach us.* New York: Scholastic.

Cervetti, G., Pardales, M. J., & Damico, J. S. (2001). A tale of differences: Comparing the traditions, perspectives, and educational goals of critical reading and critical literacy. *Reading Online, 4*(9). Retrieved March 12, 2011, from www.reading online.org/articles/cervetti/

Chall, J. S. (1983). *Learning to read: The great debate* (Rev. ed.). New York: McGraw-Hill.

Chall, J. S., & Jacobs, V. A. (2003). Poor children's fourth-grade slump. *American Educator, 27*(1), 14–15, 44.

Chambers, B., Abrami, P., McWhaw, K., & Therrien, M. (2001). Developing a computer-assisted tutoring program to help children at risk learn to read. *Educational Research and Evaluation, 7*(2–3), 223–239.

Chambers, B., Abrami, P., Tucker, B., Slavin, R., Madden, N., Cheung, A., & Gifford, R. (2005).

Computer-assisted tutoring in Success for All: Reading outcomes for first graders. Retrieved March 14, 2011, from www.successforall.net/images/edfs

Chandler-Olcott, K. (2009). Tale of two tasks: Editing in the era of digital literacies. *Journal of Adolescent & Adult Literacy, 53*(1), 71–74.

Ciardiello, A. (1998). Did you ask a good question today? Alternative cognitive and metacognitive strategies. *Journal of Adolescent & Adult Literacy, 42*(3), 210–220.

Ciardiello, A. V. (2004). Democracy's young heroes: An instructional model of critical literacy practices. *The Reading Teacher, 58*(2), 138–147.

Ciardiello, A. V. (2010). "Talking Walls": Presenting a case for social justice poetry in literacy education. *The Reading Teacher, 63*(6), 464–473.

Clarke, L., & Whitney, E. (2009).Walking in their shoes: Using multiple-perspective texts as a bridge to critical literacy. *The Reading Teacher, 62*(6), 530–535.

Clay, M. (1985). *The early detection of reading difficulties* (3rd ed.). Portsmouth, NH: Heinemann.

Clay, M. (1991). *Becoming literate: The construction of inner control.* Portsmouth, NH: Heinemann.

Clay, M. (1993a). *Sand.* Portsmouth, NH: Heinemann.

Clay, M. (1993b). *Stones.* Portsmouth, NH: Heinemann.

Clay, M. (1993c). *Reading Recovery: A guidebook for teachers in training.* Portsmouth, NH: Heinemann.

Clay, M. (2000a). *Follow me, moon.* Portsmouth, NH: Heinemann.

Clay, M. (2000b). *No shoes.* Portsmouth, NH: Heinemann.

Clay, M. (2000c). *Running records for classroom teachers.* Portsmouth, NH: Heinemann.

Clay, M. (2006). *Marie Clay's Principles and concepts of early writing.* Retrieved January 1, 2007, from www.learning towrite.ecsd.net/principles%20and%20concepts.htm

Coffey, H. (2010). Critical literacy. LEARN NC: University of North Carolina at Chapel Hill School of Education. Retrieved June 21, 2010, from www.learnc.org/lp/pages/4437

Coiro, J. (2009). Rethinking reading assessment in a digital age: How is reading comprehension different and where do we turn now. *Educational Leadership, 66,* 59–63.

Cole, J. (Ed.). (1989). *Anna Banana: 101 jump-rope rhymes.* New York: A Beech Tree Paperback Book.

Cole, J., & Calmenson, S. (Eds.). (1990). *Ready . . . set . . . read!* New York: Doubleday.

Cooper, J. D. (2006). *Literacy: Helping children construct meaning* (6th ed.). Boston: Houghton Mifflin.

Cooper, J. D., & Kiger, N. (2005). *Literacy assessment: Helping teachers plan instruction* (2nd ed.). Boston: Houghton Mifflin.

Cooper, J. D., & Kiger, N. (2006). *Instructor's resource manual and assessment guide* (6th ed.). Boston: Houghton Mifflin.

Cooter, R., Flynt, E. S., & Cooter, K. S. (2007). *Comprehensive reading inventory: Measuring reading development in regular and special education classrooms.* Upper Saddle River, NJ: Prentice Hall.

Couric, K. (2000). *The brand new kid.* New York: Doubleday.

Creech, S. (2001). *A fine, fine school.* New York: HarperTrophy.

Cudd, E. (1990). The paragraph frame: A bridge from narrative to expository text. In N. L. Cecil (Ed.), *Literacy in the 90s: Readings in the language arts.* Dubuque, IA: Kendall/Hunt.

Culham, R. (2005). *6 + 1 Traits of Writing.* New York: Scholastic.

Cummins, J. (1979). Cognitive/academic language proficiency, linguistic interdependence, the optimum age question, and some other matters. *Working Papers on Bilingualism, 19,* 121–129.

Cummins, J. (1981). Age on arrival and immigrant second language learning in Canada: A reassessment. *Applied Linguistics, 2,* 132–149.

Cunningham, A. (1990). Explicit versus implicit instruction in phonemic awareness. *Journal of Experimental Child Psychology, 50,* 429–444.

Cunningham, J. W. (2002). The National Reading Panel report [a review]. In R. Allington (Ed.), *Big Brother and the national reading curriculum: How ideology trumped evidence.* Portsmouth, NH: Heinemann.

Cunningham, J., Cunningham, P., Hoffman, J., & Yopp, H. (1998). *Phonemic awareness and the teaching of reading: A position statement from the Board of Directors of the International Reading Association.* Newark, DE: International Reading Association.

Cunningham, P. (2004). *Phonics they use: Words for reading and writing* (4th ed.). New York: Allyn & Bacon.

Cunningham, P., & Allington, R. (2006). *Classrooms that work: They can all read and write* (4th ed.). Boston: Allyn & Bacon.

Curtis, C. P. (1995). *The Watsons go to Birmingham 1963.* New York: Scholastic.

Curtis, C. P. (1999). *Bud, not Buddy.* New York: Scholastic.

Curtis, C. P. (2007). *Elijah of Buxton.* New York: Scholastic.

Dahl, K., & Scharer, P. (2000). Phonics teaching and learning in whole language classrooms: New evidence from research. *The Reading Teacher, 53*(7), 584–594.

Dale, E., O'Rourke, J., & Bamman, H. (1971). *Techniques of teaching vocabulary*. Palo Alto, CA: Field Educational Publication.

Danziger, P. (2001). *A is for Amber: It's Justin time, Amber Brown*. New York: G. P. Putnam's Sons.

Darling-Hammond, L. (2006). If they'd only do their work. *Educational Leadership, 63*(50), 8–13.

Davey, B. (1983). Think aloud: Modeling the cognitive processes of reading comprehension. *Journal of Reading, 27*, 44–47.

Day, A. (1991). *Carl's afternoon in the park*. New York: Farrar, Straus & Giroux.

Deeney, T. (2010). One-minute fluency measures: Mixed messages in assessment and instruction. *The Reading Teacher, 63*(6), 440–450.

DeFord, D. E. (1985). Validating the construct of theoretical orientation in reading instruction. *Reading Research Quarterly, 20*, 351–367.

DeKonty-Applegate, M., Applegate, A., & Modla, V. (2009). "She's my best reader; she just can't comprehend": Studying the relationship between fluency and comprehension. *The Reading Teacher, 62*(6), 512–521.

DeKonty-Applegate, M., Quinn, K. B., & Applegate, A. J. (2008). *The critical reading inventory: Assessing students' reading and thinking* (2nd ed.). Upper Saddle River, NJ: Pearson.

DeMauro, L. (1990). *Bats*. New York: Trumpet Club.

Demi. (1990). *The empty pot*. New York: Henry Holt.

dePaola, T. (1981a). *Fin M'Coul*. New York: Holiday House.

dePaola, T. (1981b). *Now one foot, now the other*. New York: Putnam Juvenile.

dePaola, T. (1984). *Clouds* (Reprint ed.). New York: Holiday House.

dePaola, T. (1997). *Strega Nona*. New York: G. P. Putnam's Sons.

dePaola, T. (1999). *26 Fairmount Avenue*. New York: G. P. Putnam's Sons.

Dix, S. (2006). I'll do it my way: Three writers and their revision practices. *The Reading Teacher, 59*(6), 566–573.

Dolch, E. W. (1948). *Problems in reading*. New York: The Garrard Press.

Doty, D., Popplewell, S., & Byers, G. (2001). Interactive CD-ROM storybooks and young readers' reading. *Journal of Research on Computing in Education, 33*(4), 374–385.

Dowhower, S. (1989). Effects of repeated reading on second-grade transitional readers' fluency and comprehension. *Reading Research Quarterly, 22*, 389–406.

Dowhower, S. (1999). Supporting a strategic stance in the classroom: A comprehension framework for helping teachers help students to be strategic. *The Reading Teacher, 52*(7), 672–688.

Drucker, M.J. (2003). What reading teachers should know about ESL learners. *The Reading Teacher, 57*(1), 22–29.

Duffy-Hester, A. (1999). Teaching struggling readers in elementary school classrooms: A review of classroom reading programs and principles for instruction. *The Reading Teacher, 52*(5), 480–495.

Duke, N. (2004). The case for informational text. *Educational Leadership, 61*(6), 40–44.

Duke, N. K. (2001). Building comprehension through explicit teaching of comprehension strategies. Presentation to the second annual MRA/CIERA Conference, September 22, 2001, East Lansing, MI.

Duke, N. K., Purcell-Gates, V., Hall, L., & Tower, C. (2006).Authentic literacy activities for developing comprehension and writing. *The Reading Teacher, 60*(4), 344–355.

Dunn, C. M., & Dunn, L. M. (1997). *Peabody picture vocabulary test* (3rd ed.). Circle Pines, MN: American Guidance Service.

Dunn, R., Denig, S., & Lovelace, M. K. (2001). Two sides of the same coin or different strokes for different folks? *Teacher Librarian, 28*(3), 9–16.

DuPont, A. (1998). Technology night. *Educational Leadership, 55*(8), 74–75.

Dworin, J. (2006). The family stories project: Using funds of knowledge for writing. *The Reading Teacher, 59*(6), 510–519.

Echevarria, J., & Short, D. (2007). The sheltered instruction observation protocol (SIOP). Retrieved February 2, 2007, from www.siopinstitute.net

Edmunds, K. M., & Bauserman, K. L. (2006). What teachers can learn about reading motivation through conversation with children. *The Reading Teacher, 59*(5), 414–424.

Edwards, P. D. (1996). *Some smug slug*. New York: HarperTrophy.

Ehri, L. C., Numes, S. R., Willows, D. M., Schuster, B. V., Yaghoub-zadeh, Z., & Shanahan, T. (2001). Phonemic awareness instruction helps children learn to read: Evidence from the National Reading Panel's meta-analysis. *Reading Research Quarterly, 36*(3), 250–287.

Ekwall, E., & Shanker, J. (1999). *Ekwall/Shanker reading inventory* (4th ed.). Boston: Allyn & Bacon.

Elbaum, B., Vaughn, S., Hughes, M. T., & Moody, S. M. (2000). How effective are one-on-one tutoring programs in reading for elementary students at risk for reading failure? A meta-analysis of the intervention research. *Journal of Educational Psychology, 92*(4), 605–619.

Elbow, P. (2004). Writing first! *Educational Leadership, 62*(2), 8–13.

Elkonin, D. B. (1973). U.S.S.R. In J. Downing (Ed.), *Comparative reading*, pp. 551–579. New York: Macmillan.

Ellery, V. (2005). *Creating strategic readers: Techniques for developing competency in phonemic awareness, phonics, fluency, vocabulary and comprehension.* Newark, DE: International Reading Association.

Ellis, D. (2002). *A company of fools.* Markham, ON: Fitzhenry & Whiteside.

Falwell, C. (1998). *Word wizard.* New York: Clarion Books.

Fargeon, E. (1987). Jazz-man. In J. Bennett (Ed.), *Noisy poems.* Oxford, New York: Oxford University Press.

Farndon, J. (2000). *All about planet earth.* New York: Anness Publishing.

Fawson, R., & Reutzel, D. R. (2000). But I only have a basal: Implementing guided reading in the early grades. *The Reading Teacher, 54*(1), 84–97.

Ferreiro, E. (2003). *Past and present verbs to read and to write: Essays on literacy.* Toronto, ON: Douglas & McIntyre.

Ferreiro, E., & Teberosky, A. (1982). *Literacy before schooling* (K. G. Castro, Trans.). Portsmouth, NH: Heinemann. (Original work published in 1979.)

Ferroli, L., & Shanahan, T. (1987). Kindergarten spelling: Explaining its relation to first grade reading. In J. E. Readence & R. S. Baldwin (Eds.), *Research in literacy: Merging perspectives* (36th yearbook of the National Reading Conference), pp. 93–99. Rochester, NY: National Reading Conference.

Fiderer, A. (1999). *40 rubrics and checklists to assess reading and writing.* New York: Scholastic.

Finn, J. (1998). Parental engagement that makes a difference. *Educational Leadership, 55*(8), 20–24.

Fisher, D. (2001). Cross-age tutoring: Alternatives to the reading resource room for struggling adolescent readers. *Journal of Instructional Psychology, 28*(4), 234–241.

Fisher, D., Frey, N., & Lapp, D. (2008). Shared readings: Modeling comprehension, vocabulary, text structure and text features for older readers. *The Reading Teacher, 61*(7), 548–556.

Fitzgerald, J. (2001). Can minimally trained college students volunteers help young at-risk children to read better? *Reading Research Quarterly, 36*(1), 28–46.

Fitzgerald, J., & Noblit, G. (1999). About hopes, aspirations, and uncertainty; First-grade English-language learners' emergent reading. *Journey of Literacy Research, 31,* 133–182.

Fleischman, P. (1985). *I am phoenix: Poems for two voices.* New York: HarperTrophy.

Fleischman, P. (1988). *Joyful noise: Poems for two voices.* New York: Harper & Row.

Fleischman, P. (2000). *Big talk: Poems for four voices.* Cambridge, MA: Candlewick Press.

Flood, J., Lapp, D., & Fisher, D. (2005). Neurological impress method plus. *Reading Psychology, 26*(2), 147–160.

Flynt, E., & Cooter, R. (2003) *Flynt–Cooter reading inventory for the classroom* (5th ed.). Upper Saddle River, NJ: Prentice Hall.

Flynt, E. S., & Brozo, W. (2008). Developing academic language: Got words? *The Reading Teacher, 61*(6), 500–502.

Flynt, E. S., & Cooter, R. B., Jr. (2005). Improving middle-grades reading in urban schools: The Memphis comprehension framework. *The Reading Teacher, 58*(8), 774–780.

Foorman, B., Novy, D., Francis, D., & Liberman, D. (1991). How letter–sound instruction mediates progress in first-grade reading and spelling. *Journal of Education Psychology, 83,* 456–469.

Fordham, N., Wellman, D., & Sandmann, A. (2002). Taming the text: Engaging and supporting students in social studies readings. *Social Studies, 93*(4), 149–159.

Fortenberry, C., & Fowler, T. (2006/2007). Mind magnets. *The Reading Teacher, 60*(4), 373–376.

Fountas, I. C., & Pinnell, G. S. (1999a). *Matching books to readers: Using leveled books in guided reading, K–3.* Portsmouth, NH: Heinemann.

Fountas, I. C., & Pinnell, G. S. (Eds.). (1999b). *Voices on word matters: Learning about phonics and spelling in the literacy classroom.* Portsmouth, NH: Heinemann.

Fountas, I. C., & Pinnell, G. S. (2001). *Guiding readers and writers: Teaching comprehension, genre & content literacy.* Portsmouth, NH: Heinemann.

Fountas, I. C., & Pinnell, G. S. (2006a). *Guiding readers and writers, grades 3–6: Teaching comprehension, genre, and content literacy.* Portsmouth, NH: Heinemann.

Fountas, I. C., & Pinnell, G. S. (2006b). *Guided reading: Good first teaching for all children.* Portsmouth, NH: Heinemann.

Fountas, I. C., & Pinnell, G. S. (2008). *When readers struggle: Teaching that works.* Portsmouth, NH: Heinemann.

Fountas, I. C., & Pinnell, G. S. (2009). *The Fountas and Pinnell leveled book list, K–8+: 2010–2012 edition.* Portsmouth, NH: Heinemann.

Fox, B., & Wright, M. (1997). Connecting school and home literacy experiences through cross-age reading. *The Reading Teacher, 50*(5), 396–403.

Fox, M. (1983). *Possum magic.* San Diego, CA: Gulliver Books.

Fox, M. (1987). *Hattie and the fox.* New York: Scholastic.

Fox, M. (1989). *Shoes for grandpa.* New York: Scholastic.

Freire, P. (1970). *Pedagogy of the oppressed.* New York: Continuum.

Fresch, M. J. (2000). What we learned from Josh: Sorting out word sorting. *Language Arts, 77*(3), 232–240.

Fresch, M. J., & Wheaton, A. (1997). Sort, search, and discover: Spelling in the child-centered classroom. *The Reading Teacher, 51*(1), 20–31.

Fried, M. (2006). Reciprocity: Promoting the flow of knowledge for learning to read and write. *The Journal of Reading Recovery, 5*(2), 5–14.

Fry, E. (1977). Fry's readability graph: Clarifications, validity, and extension to level 17. *Journal of Reading, 21,* 242–252.

Fry, E. (1987). Picture nouns for reading vocabulary improvement. *The Reading Teacher, 41*(2), 187.

Fry, E. (2002). Readability versus leveling. *The Reading Teacher, 56*(3), 286–291.

Fry, E. B., & Kress, J. E. (2006). *The reading teacher's book of lists* (5th ed.). San Francisco: Jossey-Bass.

Fry 1000 instant words. Retrieved March 12, 2011, from http://www.uniqueteachingresources.com/Fry-1000-Instant-Words.html

Frye, E., Trathen, W., & Schlagal, B. (2010). Extending acrostic poetry into content learning: A scaffolding framework. *The Reading Teacher, 63*(7), 591–596.

Fuchs, D., Fuchs, L., Mathes, R., & Simon, D. (1997). Peer-assisted learning strategies: Making classrooms more responsive to diversity. *American Educational Research Journal, 34*(1), 174–206.

Garan, E. M. (2002). Beyond the smoke and mirrors: A critique on the National Reading Panel report on phonics. In R. Allington (Ed.), *Big Brother and the national reading curriculum: How ideology trumped evidence,* pp. 90–91. Portsmouth, NH: Heinemann.

Gardner, H. (1983). *Frames of mind: The theory of multiple intelligences.* New York: Basic Books.

Gardner, H. (1993). *Multiple intelligences: The theory into practice.* New York: Basic Books.

Gauthier, L. (2001). Coop-Dis-Q: A reading comprehension strategy. *Intervention in School & Clinic, 36*(4), 217–221.

Gentry, J. R. (1982). An analysis of developmental spelling in GNYS at WRK. *The Reading Teacher, 36,* 192–200.

Gentry, J. R. (1987). *Spell . . . is a four-letter word.* Portsmouth, NH: Heinemann.

Gentry, J. R. (2004). *The science of spelling: The explicit specifics that make great readers and writers (and spellers!).* Portsmouth, NH: Heinemann.

Gentry, J. R. (2007). *Breakthrough in beginning reading and writing: The evidence-based approach to pinpointing students' needs and delivering targeted instruction.* New York: Scholastic.

Gentry, J. R., & Gillet, J. W. (1993). *Teaching kids to spell.* Portsmouth, NH: Heinemann.

George, W. (1989). *Box turtle at Long Pond.* New York: A Trumpet Club Special Edition.

Giannetti, C., & Sagarese, M. (1998). Turning parents from critics to allies. *Educational Leadership, 55*(8), 40–42.

Gibbons, G. (1992). *Weather words and what they mean.* New York: Holiday House.

Gibbons, G. (1993). *Weather forecasting* (Reprint ed.). New York: Aladdin.

Gill, S. (2000). Reading with Amy: Teaching and learning through reading conferences. *The Reading Teacher, 53*(6), 500–509.

Gill, S. R. (2009). What teachers need to know about the "new" nonfiction. *The Reading Teacher, 63*(4), 260–267.

Gillet, J. W., & Temple, C. (2004). *Understanding reading problems: Assessment and instruction* (6th ed.). New York: Allyn & Bacon.

Gipe, J. (1995). *Corrective reading techniques for classroom teachers* (3rd ed.). Scottsdale, AZ: Gorsuch Scarisbrick.

Glazer, T. (1973). *Eye Winker, Tom Tinker, Chin Chopper.* New York: Doubleday.

Goals 2000: Educate America Act. Retrieved March 9, 2011, from http://lamar.colostate.edu/~hillger/laws/goals-2000.html

Goldish, M. (1993). *Step inside the rain forest.* New York: MacMillan.

Goodman, K. (1969). Analysis of reading miscues: Applied psycholinguistics. *Reading Research Quarterly, 5*(1), 652–658.

Goodman, K. (1996). *Ken Goodman: On reading.* Portsmouth, NH: Heinemann.

Goodman, Y. (1972/1997). Reading diagnosis—qualitative or quantitative? *The Reading Teacher, 50*(7), 534–538.

Goodman, Y. (1996). *Notes from a kidwatcher: Selected writings of Yetta M. Goodman.* Portsmouth, NH: Heinemann.

Goodman, Y., & Burke, C. L. (1972). *Reading miscue inventory: Procedures for diagnosis and evaluation.* New York: MacMillan.

Goodman, Y., & Marek, A. (1996). *Retrospective miscue analysis: Revaluing readers and reading.* Katonah, NY: Richard C. Owen.

Goodman, Y., Watson, D., & Burke, C. (1996). *Reading strategies: Focus on comprehension* (2nd ed.). Katonah, NY: Richard C. Owen.

Goodman, Y., Watson, D., & Burke, C. (1987). *Reading miscue inventory: Alternative procedures* (2nd ed.). Katonah, NY: Richard C. Owen.

Graham, S., & Harris, K. (1997). It can be taught, but it does not develop naturally: Myths and realities in writing instruction. *School Psychology Review, 26*(3), 414–425.

Graves, D. (1983). *Writing: Teachers and children at work.* Portsmouth, NH: Heinemann.

Graves, D. (1990, July 27). The process-writing model. Paper presented at OKTAWL Conference, Norman, OK.

Graves, D. (1991). *Build a literate class.* Portsmouth, NH: Heinemann.

Graves, D. (1994). *A fresh look at writing.* Portsmouth, NH: Heinemann.

Graves, M. F., & Watts-Taffe, S. (2002). The place of word consciousness in a research-based vocabulary program. In A. Farstrup & S. Samuels (Eds.), *What research has to say about reading instruction* (3rd ed.), pp. 140–165. Newark, DE: International Reading Association.

Gregory, A., & Cahill, M. A. (2010). Kindergartners can do it, too! Comprehension strategies for young readers. *The Reading Teacher, 63*(6), 515–521.

Griffith, L. W., & Rasinski, T. (2004). A focus on fluency: How one teacher incorporated fluency with her reading curriculum. *The Reading Teacher, 58*(2), 126–137.

Grout, D. J. (1964). *A history of Western music.* New York: W. W. Norton.

Guarino, D. (1989). *Is your mama a llama?* New York: Scholastic.

Guerrero, A. M. (2003). *Visualization and reading comprehension.* San Marcos: Southwest Texas State University.

Gunning, T. (2001). *Building words: A resource manual for teaching word analysis and spelling strategies.* Boston: Allyn & Bacon.

Guthrie, J. T. (2003). Concept-oriented reading instruction. In A. P. Sweet & C. Snow (Eds.), *Rethinking reading comprehension,* pp. 30–50. New York: Guilford.

Guthrie, J. T., & Davis, M. H. (2003). Motivating struggling readers in middle school through an engagement model of classroom practice. *Reading & Writing Quarterly, 19,* 59–89.

Guthrie, J. T., & Humenick, N. M. (2004). Motivating students to read: Evidence for classroom practices that increase reading motivation. In P. McCardle & V. Chhabra (Eds.), *The voice of evidence in reading research,* pp. 329–354. Baltimore: Paul H. Brookes.

Gwynne, F. (1988a). *The king who rained.* New York: Aladdin.

Gwynne, F. (1988b). *A chocolate moose for dinner.* New York: Prentice Hall.

Gwynne, F. (1999). *A little pigeon toad.* New York: Aladdin.

Hadaway, N., Vardell, S., & Young, T. (2001). Scaffolding oral language development through poetry for students learning English. *The Reading Teacher, 54*(5), 796–806.

Hall, E. (2006). Learning styles—is there an evidence base from this popular idea? *Education Review, 19*(1), 49–56.

Hall, K. (1995). *A bad, bad day.* New York: Scholastic.

Hamilton, R., & Kucan, L. (1997). *Questioning the author: An approach for enhancing student engagement with text.* Newark, DE: International Reading Association.

Handsfield, L., Dean, T., & Cielocha, K. (2009). Becoming critical consumers and producers of text: Teaching literacy with Web 1.0 and Web 2.0. *The Reading Teacher, 63*(1), 40–50.

Hanf, M. B. (1971). Mapping: A technique for translating reading into thinking. *Journal of Reading, 14,* 225–230, 270.

Hansen, J. (1987). *When writers read.* Portsmouth, NH: Heinemann.

Harris, A. J., & Sipay, E. R. (1990). *How to increase reading ability* (8th ed.). New York: Longman.

Harris, T., & Hodges, R. (Eds.). (1995). *The literacy dictionary: The vocabulary of reading and writing.* Newark, DE: International Reading Association.

Harrison, D. (2008). *Pirates.* Illus. by D. Burr. Honesdale, PA: Wordsong.

Hart, B., & Risley, T. (1995). *Meaningful differences in the everyday experience of young American children.* Baltimore, MD: Brookes Publishing Co.

Hart, B., & Risley, T. R. (2003). The early catastrophe: The 30 million word gap. *American Education, 27*(1), 4–9.

Harvey, T. (1998). The curse of the foul-smelling armpit. In B. Lansky (Ed.), *Miles of smiles: Kids pick the funniest poems, Book #3*, pp. 66–67. New York: Meadowbrook Press.

Hasbrouck, J., & Tindal, G. (2006). Oral reading fluency norms: A valuable assessment tool for reading teachers. *The Reading Teacher, 59*(7), 636–644.

Hasbrouck, J. E., & Tindal, G. (1992). Curriculum-based oral reading fluency forms for students in grades 2 through 5. *Teaching Exceptional Children, 4* (Spring), 41–44.

Hassett, D., & Curwood, J. S. (2009). Theories and practices of multimodal education: The instructional dynamics of picture books and primary classrooms. *The Reading Teacher, 64*(4), 270–282.

Heald-Taylor, B. G. (1998). Three paradigms of spelling instruction in grades 3 to 6. *The Reading Teacher, 51*(5), 404–412.

Heath, S. B. (2004). The children of Trackton's children: Spoken and written language in social change. In R. B. Ruddell & N. J. Unrau (Eds.), *Theoretical models and processes of reading*, pp. 187–209. Newark, DE: International Reading Association.

Heilmann, J., Miller, J., & Dunaway, C. (2010). Properties of the narrative scoring scheme using narrative retells in young school-age children. *American Journal of Speech-Language Pathology, 19*, 154–166.

Heller, R. (1987). *A cache of jewels*. New York: Grosset & Dunlap.

Heller, R. (1989). *Many luscious lollipops*. New York: Grosset & Dunlap.

Helman, L., Bear, D., Invernizzi, S., & Templeton, S. (2008). *Words their way: Emergent sorts for Spanish-speaking English learners*. Upper Saddle River, NJ: Pearson/Prentice Hall.

Helman, L. A. (2004). Building on the sound system of Spanish: Insights from the alphabetic spellings of English-language learners. *The Reading Teacher, 57*(5), 452–460.

Helman L. A., & Burns, M. K. (2008). What does oral language have to do with it? Helping young English-language learners acquire a sight word vocabulary. *The Reading Teacher, 62*(1), 14–19.

Henk, W. A., & Melnick, S. A. (1995). The Reader Self-Perception Scale (RSPS): A new tool for measuring how children feel about themselves as readers. *The Reading Teacher, 48*, 470–482.

Henkel, J. (2002). Finding activities for kids after school. *FDA Consumer, 36*(3), 33.

Henkes, K. (1995). *Julius: The baby of the world*. New York: Greenwillow Books.

Henkes, K. (1996). *Lily's purple plastic purse*. New York: Greenwillow Books.

Henkes, K. (2006). *Lily's big day*. New York: Greenwillow Books.

Henry, L. (2006). Searching for an answer: The critical role of new literacies while reading on the Internet. *The Reading Teacher, 59*(7), 614–626.

Hesse, K. (1998). *Just juice*. New York: Scholastic.

Hesse, K. (1999). *Come on, rain!* New York: Scholastic.

Hessell, J. (1989). *Secret soup*. Crystal Lake, IL: Rigby.

Heubach, K. (December, 1995). Integrating literature into fourth-grade social studies curriculum: The effects on student learning and attitude. Paper presented at the meeting of National Reading Conference, New Orleans, LA.

Hiebert, E. (1999). Text matters in learning to read. *The Reading Teacher, 52*(6), 552–566.

Hindes, M. (2007). Readability and comprehension. Guidance Channel Online. Retrieved March 5, 2007, from www.csapmodelprograms.com/default.aspx?M=a&index-628&cat=29

Ho, B. (2002). Application of participatory action research to family school intervention. *School Psychology Review, 31*(1), 106–122.

Hoban, L. (1976). *Arthur's pen pal*. New York: HarperTrophy.

Holdaway, D. (1979). *The foundations of literacy*. Sydney, Australia: Ashton Scholastic.

Holdaway, D. (1986). The structure of natural language as a basis for literacy instruction. In M. L. Sampson (Ed.), *The pursuit of literacy: Early reading and writing*. Dubuque, IA: Kendall/Hunt.

Holt, K. W. (1998). *Mister and me*. New York: G. P. Putnam's Sons.

Houge, T., & Geier, C. (2009). Delivering one-to-one tutoring in literacy via videoconferencing. *Journal of Adolescent & Adult Literacy, 53*(2), 154–163.

Houge, T., Peyton, D., Geire, C., & Petrie, B. (2007). Adolescent literacy tutoring: Face-to-face and via webcam technology. *Reading Psychology, 28*(3), 283–300.

Hughes, M., & Searle, D. (2000). Spelling and "the second 'R.'" *Language Arts, 77*(3), 203–208.

Hurley, S. R., & Blake, S. (2000). Assessment in the content areas for students acquiring English. In S. R. Hurley & J. V. Tinajero (Eds.), *Literacy assessment of second language learners*, pp. 84–103. Boston: Allyn & Bacon.

Hurst, C. (2000). Guided reading can strengthen comprehension skills. *Teaching PreK–8, 31*(2), 70–72.

Illingworth, M. (1996). *Real-life math problem solving.* New York: Scholastic.

Imperato, F. (2009). Getting parents and children off to a strong start in reading. *The Reading Teacher, 63*(4), 342–344.

International Reading Association and The National Association for the Education of Young Children. (1998). Learning to read and write: Developmentally appropriate practices for young children. *Young Children, 53*(4), 30–46.

International Reading Association and The National Council of Teachers of English. (1996). *Standards for the English language arts.* Newark, DE: International Reading Association & Urbana, IL: National Council of Teachers of English.

International Reading Association. (1997). *The role of phonics in reading instruction.* Newark, DE: Author.

International Reading Association. (2000). All about assessment. *Reading Today, 18*(2), 34.

International Reading Association. (2001). *Second-language literacy instruction: A position statement of the International Reading Association.* Newark, DE: Author.

International Reading Association. (2002). Educators meet to discuss early childhood literacy issues. *Reading Today, 20*(1), 1.

International Reading Association. (2003a). International Reading Association's summary of the (U. S.) National Reading Panel Report. Retrieved October 5, 2003, from www.reading.org/advocacy/nrp/chapter2.html

International Reading Association. (2003b). *IRA's standards for reading professionals, revised 2003.* Retrieved June 12, 2006, from www.reading.org

International Reading Association. (2004). Meet ing spotlights ELL issues. *Reading Today, 21*(6). Retrieved May 31, 2006, from http://web10.epnet.com/citation.

International Reading Association. (2006). *IRA style guide: Standards for reading professionals.* Retrieved June 12, 2006, from www.reading.org/styleguide/standards_ reading_profs.html

International Reading Association (2009). IRA commission on RTI: Working draft of guiding principles. Retrieved March 10, 2007, from www.reading.org

International Reading Association (2010). Alphabiography. Retrieved February 27, 2011, from www.ReadWriteThink.org

Invernizzi, M., Rosemary, C., Juel, C., & Richard, H. (1997). At-risk readers and community volunteers: A three-year perspective. *Scientific Studies of Reading, 1*(3), 279–300.

Ivey, G., & Baker, M. (2004). Phonics instruction for older students? Just say, "No." *Educational Leadership, 61*(1), 35–39.

Ivey, G., & Broaddus, K. (2000). Tailoring the fit: Reading instruction and middle school readers. *The Reading Teacher, 54*(1), 68–78.

Ivey, G., & Fisher, D. (2005). Learning from what doesn't work. *Educational Leadership, 63*(2), 8–14.

Jackman, H. (1999). *Sing me a story! Tell me a song!* Thousand Oaks, CA: Corwin Press.

Jacobs, F. (1979). *Sam the sea cow.* New York: A Trumpet Club Special Edition.

Jacobson, J., Thrope, L., Fisher, D., Lapp, D., Frey, N., & Flood, J. (2001). Cross-age tutoring: A literacy improvement approach for struggling adolescent readers. *Journal of Adolescent & Adult Literacy, 44*(6), 528–537.

Janeczko, P. (2005). *A kick in the head: An everyday guide to poetic forms.* Illus. by C. Raschka. Cambridge, MA: Candlewick Press.

Jensen, D. (2006). Using newsletters to create home-school connections. *The Reading Teacher, 60*(2), 186–193.

Jitendra, A., Hoppes, M., & Xin, Y. P. (2000). Enhancing main idea comprehension for students with learning problems: The role of a summarization strategy and self-monitoring instruction. *Journal of Special Education, 34*(3), 127–140.

Johns, J. (2007). Monitoring progress in fluency: Possible unintended consequences. *Reading Today, 24*(6), 18.

Johnston, F. (2001a). Spelling exceptions: Problems or possibilities? *The Reading Teacher, 54*(4), 372–378.

Johnston, F. (2001b). The utility of phonics generalizations: Let's take another look at Clymer's conclusions. *The Reading Teacher, 55*(2), 132–143.

Johnston, F., Invernizzi, M., & Juel, C. (1998). *Book buddies: Guidelines for volunteer tutors of emergent readers.* New York: The Guilford Press.

Johnston, R. (2000/2001). Spelling exceptions: Problems or possibilities? *The Reading Teacher, 54*(4), 372–379.

Johnson-Higgins, J. (2002). Multicultural children's literature: Creating and applying an evaluation tool in response to the needs of urban educators. New Horizons of Learning. Retrieved June 19, 2010, from http://newhorizons.org/strategies/multicultural/higgins.htm

Jongsma, K. (1999/2000). Vocabulary and comprehension strategy development. *The Reading Teacher, 53*(4), 310–313.

Jongsma, K. (2000). Teaching—aids & devices—book review. *The Reading Teacher, 54*(1), 80–83.

Joosse, B. (1991). *Mama, do you love me?* New York: Scholastic.

Joyce, I. (1967). *Never talk to strangers.* New York: Scholastic.

Juel, C., & Deffes, R. (2004). Making words stick. *Educational Leadership, 61*(6), 30–34.

Kalan, R. (1981). *Jump, frog, jump!* New York: Greenwillow Books.

Kane, S. (1999). Teaching decoding strategies without destroying story. *The Reading Teacher, 52*(7), 770–772.

Kara-Soteriou, J., Zawilinski, L., & Henry, L. (2007). Children's books and technology in the classroom: A dynamic combo for supporting the writing workshop. *The Reading Teacher, 60*(7), 698–707.

Karchmer, R. (2001). The journey ahead: Thirteen teachers report how the Internet influences literacy and literacy instruction in the K–12 classrooms. *Reading Research Quarterly, 36*(4), 442–466.

Kaufman, M. (2002). Putting it all together: From one first-grade teacher to another. *The Reading Teacher, 55*(8), 722–726.

Keating, F. (2001). *Will Rogers.* Illus. by M. Wimmer. San Diego: CA: Silver Whistle/Harcourt, Inc.

Keehn, S. (2003).The effect of instruction and practice through Readers Theatre on young readers' oral reading fluency. *Reading Research and Instruction, 42*(4), 40–61.

Kelley, M., & Clausen-Grace, N. (2009). Facilitating engagement by differentiating independent reading. *The Reading Teacher, 63*(4), 313–318.

Kieffer, M. J., & Lesaux, N. (2007). Breaking down words to build meaning: Morphology, vocabulary, and reading comprehension in the urban classroom. *The Reading Teacher, 61*(2), 134–144.

Kindervater, T. (2010). Models of parent involvement. *The Reading Teacher, 63*(7), 610–612.

Kinniburgh, L., & Shaw, E. L. (2009). Using question-answer-relationships to build reading comprehension in science. *Science Activities, 45*(4), 19–26.

Kintsch, W. (2004). The construction-integration model of text comprehension and its implications for instruction. In R. Ruddell & N. Unrau (Eds.), *Theoretical models and processes of reading* (5th ed.), pp. 1270–1328. Newark, DE: International Reading Association.

Kirk, D. (1999). *Miss Spider's new car.* New York: Scholastic Press. (Board book)

Kletzien, S. B. (1991). Strategy used by good and poor comprehenders reading expository text of differing levels. *Reading Research Quarterly, 26,* 67–86.

Koskinen, P., Blum, I., Bisson, S., Phillips, S., Creamer, T., & Baker, T. (1999). Shared reading, books, and audiotapes: Supporting diverse students in school and at home. *The Reading Teacher, 52*(5), 430–444.

Krashen, S. (1981). *Second language acquisition and second language learning.* Oxford, England: Pergamon.

Krashen, S. (2004/2005). Skyrocketing scores: An urban legend. *Educational Leadership, 62*(4), 37–39.

Krashen, S., & Brown, C. L. (2005). The ameliorating effects of high socioeconomic status: A secondary analysis. *Bilingual Research Journal, 29*(1), 185–196.

Kuhlman, N. (2005). The language assessment conundrum: What tests claim to assess and what teachers need to know. *The ELL Outlook.* Retrieved June 28, 2010, from www.coursecrafters.com/ELLp Outlook/2005/mar_apr/ELLOutlook ITIArticle1.htm

Kuhn, M. (2000). *The effects of repeated readings and non-repeated readings on comprehension.* Unpublished doctoral dissertation. University of Georgia, Athens.

Lamoreaux, L., & Lee, D. M. (1943). *Learning to read through experiences.* New York: Appleton-Century-Crofts.

Lane, H. S., & Pullen, P. (2004). *Phonological awareness assessment and instruction: A sound beginning.* Boston: Allyn & Bacon.

Langeland, D. (1997). *Octopus' den.* New York: Scholastic.

Lansky, B. (Ed.). (1998). *Miles of smiles: Kids pick the funniest poems, book #3.* New York: Meadowbrook Press.

Lansky, B. (2000). *If pigs could fly . . . and other deep thoughts.* New York: Meadowbrook Press.

Lansky, B. (2009). *My dog ate my homework!* New York: Meadowbrook Press.

Lapp, D., Fisher, D., & Johnson, K. (2010). Text mapping plus: Improving comprehension through supported retellings. *Journal of Adolescent & Adult Literacy, 53*(5), 323–426.

Lapp, D., Flood, J., & Farnan, N. (1996). *Content area reading and learning: Instructional strategies* (2nd ed.). Boston: Allyn & Bacon.

Larkin, R. B. (2001). Can we act it out? *The Reading Teacher, 54*(5), 478–481.

Lauber, P. (1986). *Volcano: The eruption and healing of Mount St. Helens.* New York: Bradbury Press.

Leal, D. (2005). The word writing CAFÉ: Assessing student writing for complexity, accuracy, and fluency. *The Reading Teacher, 59*(4), 340–350.

Learning First Alliance. (2000). *Every child reading: A professional development guide*. Baltimore: Association for Supervision and Curriculum Development.

Lehr, F., Osborn, J., & Heibert, E. (2005). *A focus on vocabulary*. Pacific Resources for Education and Learning. Retrieved June 30, 2002, from www.tasaliteracy.com/rpe/instruction/vocab.html

Lenski, S. D., Ehlers-Zavala, F., Daniel, M. C., & Sun-Irminger, X. (2006). Assessing English-language learners in the mainstream classroom. *The Reading Teacher, 60*(1), 24–34.

Lepthien, E. (1997). *A true book: Sea turtles*. Illus. by E. Lepthien. New York: Children's Press.

Lewis, M. (1986). *Hooked on Caldecott Award winners! 60 crossword puzzles based on the Caldecott Gold Medal books*. New York: The Center for Applied research Education.

Lewis, P. (1990). *A hippopotamustn't*. New York: Dial Books for Young Readers.

Lewison, M., Flint, A. S., & Van Sluys, K. (2002). Taking on critical literacies: The journey of newcomers and novices. *Language Arts, 79,* 382–392.

Lloyd, C. (2003). Song lyrics as text to develop critical literacies. *Reading Online, 6*(10). Retrieved June 21, 2010, from www.readingonline.org/articles/lloyd

Lobel, A. (1983). *The book of pigericks*. New York: Harper & Row.

London, J. (1994). *Liplap's wish*. New York: Scholastic.

Los Angeles County Office of Education. (2000). *Kindergarten and grade one reading: Basic to success*. Retrieved Jan. 7, 2007, from http://teams.lacoe.edu/Documentation/classrooms/patti/k-1/teacher/assessment/print/concept

Los Angeles County Office of Education. (2001). *Yopp–Singer test of phonemic segmentation*. Retrieved October 5, 2003, from http://teams.lacoe.edu/reading/assessments/yopp.html

Low, A. (1993). *The popcorn shop*. Illus. by P. Hammel. New York: Scholastic.

MacDonald, M. (1995). *The old woman who lived in a vinegar bottle*. Little Rock, AR: August House.

MacDonald, M. R. (2001). *The parent's guide to storytelling: How to make up new stories and retell old favorites*. Little Rock, AR: August House.

MacLachlan, P. (1982). *Mama one, mama two*. New York: HarperCollins.

MacLulich, C. (1996). *Frogs*. New York: Scholastic.

Manning, M. (2001). Characterization. *Teaching PreK–8, 31*(8), 84–87.

Manning, M. L. (2002). Revisiting developmentally appropriate middle level schools. *Childhood Education, 78*(4), 225–227.

Manyak, P. C., & Bouchereau-Bauer, E. (2009). English vocabulary instruction for English learners. *The Reading Teacher, 63*(2), 174–176.

Marino-Weisman, D., & Hansen, L. (Sept./Oct. 2007). Strategies for teaching social studies to English-language learners at the elementary level. *Social Studies,* 180–184.

Markle, S. (1996). *Outside and inside sharks*. New York: Aladdin Paperbacks.

Marsalis, W. (2005). *Jazz ABZ*. Illus. by P. Rogers. Cambridge, MA: Candlewick.

Martens, P. (1998). Using retrospective miscue analysis to inquire: Learning from Michael. *The Reading Teacher, 52*(2), 176–180.

Martin, B., Jr. (1983). *Brown bear, brown bear, what do you see?* New York: Henry Holt.

Martin, B., Jr., & Archambault, J. (1987). *Knots on a counting rope*. New York: Trumpet Club.

Martin, B., Jr., & Archambault, J. (1998). *Here are my hands*. New York: Henry Holt.

Martin, J. (1991a). *Carrot/parrot*. New York: Trumpet Club Special Edition.

Martin, J. (1991b). *Mitten/kitten*. New York: Trumpet Club Special Edition.

Martinez, M., Roser, N., & Strecker, S. (1998/1999). "I never thought I could be a star": A readers theatre ticket to fluency. *The Reading Teacher, 52*(4), 326–334.

Maslow, A. (1987). *Motivation and personality* (3rd ed.). New York: Harper & Row.

Mason, J. A., Stahl, S. A., Au, K. H., & Herman, P. A. (2003). Reading: Children's developing knowledge of words. In J. Flood, D. Lapp, J. R. Squire, & J. M. Jensen (Eds.), *Handbook of research on reading of the English language arts* (2nd ed.), pp. 914–930. Mahwah, NJ: Erlbaum.

Mason, L., Benedek-Wood, E., & Valasa, L. (2010). Teaching low-achieving students to self-regulate: Persuasive quick writes responses. *Journal of Adolescent and Adult Literacy, 53*(4), 303–312.

Mass, W. (2005). *Twice upon a time: Rapunzel: The one with all the hair*. Illus. by W. Mass. New York: Scholastic.

Mastropieri, M., Leinart, A., & Scruggs, T. (1999). Strategies to increase reading fluency. *Intervention in School and Clinic, 34*(5), 278–285.

Matthew, K. (1997). A comparison of influence of interactive CD-ROM storybooks. *Journal of Research on Computing in Education, 29*(3), 262–276.

May, F. (2001). *Unraveling the seven myths of reading: Assessment and intervention practices for counteracting their effects.* Boston: Allyn & Bacon.

Mazzoni, S. A., Gambrell, L. B., & Korkeamaki, R. L. (1999). A cross-cultural perspective of early literacy motivation. *Reading Psychology, 20,* 237–253.

McBratney, S. (1994). *Guess how much I love you.* New York: Scholastic.

McCarrier, A., Pinnell, G. S., & Fountas, I. C. (2000). *Interactive writing: How language and literacy come together, K–2.* Portsmouth, NH: Heinemann.

McCarthy, P. (2008). Using sound boxes systematically to develop phonemic awareness. *The Reading Teacher, 62*(4), 346–349.

McCormick, S. (2006). *Instructing students who have literacy problems* (5th ed.). Upper Saddle River, NJ: Prentice Hall.

McGee, L., & Schickedanz, J. (2007). Repeated interactive read-alouds in preschool and kindergarten. *The Reading Teacher, 60*(8), 742–751.

McKenna, M., & Cournoyer-Picard, M. (2006). Revisiting the role of miscue analysis in effective teaching. *The Reading Teacher, 60*(4), 378–380.

McKenna M. C., & Kear, D. J. (1990). Measuring attitude toward reading: A new tool for teachers. *The Reading Teacher, 43,* 626–639.

McKeown, M., & Beck, I. (2004). Direct and rich vocabulary instruction. In J. F. Baumann, E. J. Kame'enui (Eds.), *Vocabulary instruction,* pp. 13–27. New York: Guilford.

McKeown, M., & Curtis, M. E. (Eds.). (1987). *The nature of vocabulary acquisition.* Hillsdale, NJ: Lawrence Erlbaum.

McLaughlin, M., & DeVoogd, G. (2004). Critical literacy as comprehension: Expanding reader response. *Journal of Adolescent & Adult Literacy, 48*(1), 52–62.

Medcalf, N., Bessette, K., & Gibbs, D. (2009). Everyone wins: A school–higher education partnership for reading improvement. In J. C. Richards & C. A. Lassonde (Eds.), *Literacy tutoring that works,* pp. 96–107. Newark, DE: International Reading Association.

Medearis, M., & Medearis, A. (2005). *Daisy and the Doll.* Illus. by L. Johnson. Lebanon, NH: University Press of New England.

Medema, K. (1997). "Storm the gate." *25 to life: For prisoners of hope everywhere.* Grandville, MI: Brier Patch Music.

Mesmer, E., & Mesmer, H. A. (2009). Response to intervention (RTI): What teachers of reading need to know. *The Reading Teacher, 62*(4), 280–290.

Meyer, B., Wijekumar, K., Middlemiss, W., Highly, K., et al. (2010). Web-based tutoring of the structure strategy with or without elaborated feedback or choice for fifth-and seventh-grade readers. *Reading Research Quarterly, 45*(1), 62–92.

Meyer, K. W. (2010). A collaborative approach to reading workshop in middle years. *The Reading Teacher, 63*(6), 501–507.

Michigan Department of Education (2002). What research says about parent involvement in children's education. Retrieved August 2, 2010, from www.michigan.gov/documents/final_parent_involvement_fact_sheet_14732_7.pdf

Micucci, C. (2003). *The life and times of the ant.* Boston: Houghton Mifflin.

Miller, M. (1996). *Quick and easy learning games: Math.* New York: Scholastic.

Miller, M. (2006). Where they are working with marginalized students. *Educational Leadership, 63*(5), 50–53.

Miller, W. (1988). *Reading teacher's complete diagnosis and correction manual.* New York: Center for Applied Research in Education.

Miller, W. (2000). *Strategies for developing emergent literacy.* Boston: McGraw Hill.

Mills, K. (2009). Floating on a sea of talk: Reading comprehension through speaking and listening. *The Reading Teacher, 63*(4), 325–329.

Moats, L. (1995). *Spelling, development, disability, and instruction.* Baltimore: York Press.

Molfese, V. J., Modglin, A., & Molfese, D. L. (2003). The role of environment in the development of reading skills. A longitudinal study of preschool and school-age measures. *Journal of Learning Disabilities, 36,* 59–67.

Montelong, J., Herter, R. J., Ansaldo, R., & Hatter, N. (2010). A lesson cycle for teaching expository reading and writing. *Journal of Adolescent and Adult Literacy, 53*(8), 656–666.

Moore, D., & Hinchman, K. (2006). *Teaching adolescents who struggle with reading: Practical strategies.* Boston: Pearson.

Moore, D. W., & Moore, S. A. (1986). Possible sentences. In E. K. Dishner, T. W. Bean, J. E. Readence, & D. W. Moore (Eds.), *Reading in the content areas,* pp. 174–178. Dubuque, IA: Kendall Hunt.

Moore, R., & Aspegren, C. (2001). Reflective conversations between two learners: Retrospective miscue analysis. *Journal of Adolescent & Adult Literacy, 44*(6), 492–504.

Moore-Hart, M. (2005). A writers' camp in action: A community of readers and writers. *The Reading Teacher, 59*(4), 326–338.

Morgan, H., & York, K. (2009). Examining multiple perspectives with creative think-alouds. *The Reading Teacher, 63*(4), 307–311.

Morris, D. (1999). *The Howard Street Tutoring manual: Teaching at-risk readers in the primary grades.* New York: Guildford Press.

Morris, D., & Nelson, L. (1992). Supported oral reading with low-achieving second graders. *Reading Research and Instruction, 31,* 49–63.

Morrow, L. M. (2005). *Literacy in the early years: Helping children read and write* (5th ed.). Boston: Allyn & Bacon.

Morrow, L. M., Kuhn, M., & Schwanenflugel, P. J. (2006). The family fluency program. *The Reading Teacher, 60*(4), 322–333.

Mortenson, G., & Relin, D. O. (2009). *Three cups of tea.* New York: Puffin.

Mosenthal, J. (1994). Text structure. In A. Purves, L. Papa, & J. Jordan (Eds.), *Encyclopedia of English studies and languages arts,* pp. 1201–1203. New York: Scholastic.

Moss, L. (1995). *Zin! Zin! Zin! A violin.* New York: Scholastic.

Moustafa, M., & Maldonado-Colon, E. (1999). Whole-to-parts phonics instruction: Building on what children know to help them know more. *The Reading Teacher, 52*(5), 448–456.

Mouza, C. (2005). Using technology to enhance early childhood learning: The 100 days of school project. *Educational Research & Evaluation, 11*(6), 513–528.

Murphy, S. (1995). Revisioning reading assessment: Remembering to learn from the legacy of reading tests. *Clearing House, 68*(4), 235–239.

Murrow, L. M., & Woo, D. G. (2001). *Tutoring programs for struggling readers.* New York: Guilford.

Music Little People. (1987). *Children's favorites.* Philadelphia, PA: Author.

Nagy, W. E., & Herman, P. A. (1987). Breadth and depth of vocabulary knowledge: Implications for acquisition and instruction. In M. G. McKeown & M. E. Curtis (Eds.), *The nature of vocabulary acquisition,* pp. 19–35. Hillsdale, NJ: Lawrence Erlbaum.

Nagy, W. E, & Scott, J. A. (2004). Vocabulary processes. In R. Ruddell & N. Unrau (Eds.), *Theoretical models and processes of reading* (5th ed.), pp. 574–593. Newark, DE: International Reading Association.

National Center for Education Statistics. (1996). *National assessment of educational progress facts: Listening to children read aloud: Oral fluency, 1 (1).* (Publication No. NCES 95–762).

National Center for Education Statistics. (2010). Fast facts. Retrieved from http://nces.ed.gov/fastfacts/

National Clearinghouse for English Language Acquisition. (2010). Standards and assessments. Retrieved from www.ncela.gwu.edu/assessment

National Council of Teachers of English. (1996). Standards for the English language arts. Retrieved March 3, 2011, from www.ncte.org/standards

National Council of Teachers of English. (2006). Taking a look at NAEP reading results. *The Council Chronicle, 15*(3), 1.

National Institute for Literacy. (2006). *What is scientifically based research?* Jessup, MD: U.S. GPO.

National Institute of Child Health and Human Development. (2000). *Report of the National Reading Panel: Teaching children to read.* Washington, DC: National Institute for Literacy.

National PTA. (1998). *1998 parent involvement policy.* Chicago, IL: Author.

National Reading Panel. (2000). *Report of the subgroups.* Washington, DC: National Institute of Child Health and Human Development. Retrieved September 30, 2001, from www.nationalreadingpanel.org/Publications/subgroups.htm

NGA & CCSSO (2010). Common Core State Standards for English Language Arts & Literacy in history/social studies, science, and technical subjects. *Common Core State Standards Initiative: Preparing America's Students for College & Career.* Online www.corestandards.org.

Ness, M. (2009). Laughing through rereadings: Using joke books to build fluency. *The Reading Teacher, 62*(8), 691–694.

Nicholson, T. (1998). The flashcard strikes back. *The Reading Teacher, 51*(2), 188–192.

Nieto, S. (1996). *Affirming diversity: The sociopolitical context for multicultural education* (2nd ed.). White Plains, NY: Longman.

Nilsen, A. P., & Nilsen, D. L. F. (2004). *Vocabulary Plus K–8.* New York: Pearson.

No Child Left Behind Act of 2001. Summary and overview. Retrieved March 8, 2004, from www.ed.gov/nclb/overview/Intro/Index.html

Northwest Regional Educational Laboratory (2001). *6 + 1 Trait(r) rubrics (aka scoring guides).* Retrieved from http://educationnorthwest.org/resource/464

Numeroff, L. (2005). *If you give a pig a party.* Illus. by F. Bond. New York: HarperCollins.

Numeroff, L. (2008). *If you give a cat a cupcake.* Illus. by F. Bond. New York: Laura Geringer Books.

Nunnery, J., Ross, S., Smith, L., Slavin, R., Hunter, P., & Stubbs, J. (1999). *An assessment of Success for All program component configuration effects on the reading achievement of at-risk first grade students.* Baltimore: Center for Research on the

Education of Students Placed at Risk, John Hopkins University.

O'Conner, J. (1986). *The teeny tiny woman.* New York: Random House for Young Readers.

O'Connor, R. E., White, A., & Swanson, H. (2007). Repeated reading versus continuous reading: Influences on reading fluency and comprehension. *Exceptional Children, 74*(1), 31–46.

O'Loughlin, J., & Haynes, J. (2004). Organizing and assessing in the content area classrooms. *Everything ESL.* Retrieved December 27, 2010, from www.everythingesl.net

Oakhill, J., & Patel, S. (1991). Can imagery training help children who have comprehension problems? *Journal of Research in Reading, 14,* 106–115.

Ogle, D., & Correa-Kovtun, A. (2010). Supporting English-language learners and struggling readers in content literacy with the "Partner Reading and Content, Too" routine. *The Reading Teacher, 63*(7), 532–543.

Ogle, D. M. (1986). K-W-L: A teaching model that develops active reading of expository text. *The Reading Teacher, 39*(7), 564–570.

Ohler, J. (2005/2006). The world of digital storytelling. *Educational Leadership, 63*(4), 44–49.

Oklahoma State Department of Education. (2002). *A core curriculum for our children's future: Priority academic student skills (PASS).* Oklahoma City: Author.

Oliver, K., Wilcox, B., & Eldredge, J. L. (2000). Effect of difficulty levels on second-grade delayed readers using dyad reading. *Journal of Education Research, 94*(2), 113–120.

Olson, K. M. (2001). *Chinese immigrants 1850–1900.* Bloomington, IN: Capstone Press.

Olson, M., & Gee, T. (1991). Content reading instruction in the primary grades: Perceptions and strategies. *The Reading Teacher, 45,* 298–307.

O'Neill, M. (1961). *Hailstones and halibut bones.* New York: John Walker.

Opie, I. (Ed.). (1996). *My very first Mother Goose.* Cambridge, MA: Candlewick Press.

Oppenheim, J. (1989). *"Not now!" said the cow.* New York: Byron Press Book.

Oster, L. (2001). Using the think-aloud for reading instruction. *The Reading Teacher, 55*(1), 64–70.

Otaiba, S., & Pappamihiel, N. E. (2005, July/August). Guidelines for using volunteer literacy tutors to support reading instruction for English language learners. *Teaching Exceptional Children, 37*(6), 6–11.

Padak, N., & Rasinski, T. (2008). *Fast start: Getting ready to read.* New York: Scholastic.

Padak, N., & Rasinski, T. (2007). Is being wild about Harry enough? Encouraging independent reading at home. *The Reading Teacher, 61*(4), 350–353.

Palmer, R., & Stewart, R. (1997). Nonfiction trade books in content area instruction: Realities and potential. *Journal of Adolescent & Adult Literacy, 40*(8), 630–642.

Palmer, R., & Stewart, R. (2005). Models for using nonfiction in the primary grades. *The Reading Teacher, 58*(5), 426–434.

Pappas, T. (1991). *Math talk: Mathematical ideas in poems for two voices.* San Carlos, CA: Wide World Publishing/Tetra.

Paquette, K. R., Fello, S., & Renck-Jalongo, M. (2007). The talking drawings strategy: Using primary children's illustrations and oral language to improve comprehension of the expository text. *Early Childhood Education Journal, 35*(1), 65–70.

Park, L. S. (2001). *A single shard.* New York: Clarion Books.

Parks, R. (1999). *I am Rosa Parks.* Illus. by J. Haskins & W. Clay. New York: Puffin.

Partin, K., & Hendricks, C. (2002). The relationship between positive adolescent attitudes toward reading and home literacy environment. *Reading Horizons, 43*(1), 61–84.

Paterson, K. (1991). *Lyddie.* New York: Lodestar Books.

Patrick, J. (2009). Home poem, or the sad dog song. In P. Janeczki, *A Foot in the mouth: Poems to speak, sing, and shout.* Somerville, MA: Candlewick.

Patterson, E., Schaller, M., & Clemens, J. (2008). A closer look at interactive writing. *The Reading Teacher, 61*(6), 496–497.

Pearson, P. D., & Fielding, L. (1991). Comprehension instruction. In R. Barr, M. Kamil, P. Mosenthal, & P. D. Pearson (Eds.), *Handbook of reading research* (Vol. 2), pp. 815–860. New York: Longman.

Peck, R. (1998). *A long way from Chicago.* New York: Puffin.

Peck, R. (2000). *A year down yonder.* New York: Dial Books for Young Readers.

Peebles, J. (2007). Incorporating movement with fluency instruction: A motivation for struggling readers. *The Reading Teacher, 60*(6), 578–581.

Perez-Canado, M. (2005). English and Spanish spelling: Are they really different? *The Reading Teacher, 58*(6), 522–530.

Piaget, J., & Inhelder, B. (1969). *The psychology of the child* (H. Weaver, Trans.). New York: Basic Books.

Pinnell, G. S. (1989). Reading Recovery: Helping at-risk children learn to read. *The Elementary School Journal, 90,* 161–183.

Pinnell, G. S. (1999). Word solving: Investigating the properties of words. In I. C. Fountas & G. S. Pinnell (Eds.), *Voices on word matters: Learning about phonics and spelling in the literacy classroom*, pp. 3–12. Portsmouth, NH: Heinemann.

Pinnell, G. S. (2006). Every child a reader: What one teacher can do. *The Reading Teacher, 60*(1), 78–83.

Pinnell, G. S., & Fountas, I. C. (1998). *Word matters: Teaching phonics and spelling in the reading/writing classroom.* Portsmouth, NH: Heinemann.

Pinnell, G. S., & Fountas, I. C. (2001). *Guiding readers and writers.* Portsmouth, NH: Heinemann.

Pinnell, G. S., & Fountas, I. C. (2007). *Continuum of literacy learning: Grades K–2.* Portsmouth, NH: Heinemann.

Piston, W. (1962). *Harmony* (3rd ed.). New York: W. W. Norton.

Polacco, P. (1987). *Meteor!* New York: Philomel Books.

Polacco, P. (1998). *Thank you, Mr. Falker.* New York: Philomel.

Polacco, P. (2001). *Betty doll.* New York: Philomel Books.

Porter DeCusati, C. L., & Johnson, J. E. (2004). Parents as classroom volunteers and kindergarten students' emergent reading skills. *Journal of Educational Research, 97*(5), 235–246.

Powell, D., & Aram, R. (2008). Spelling in parts: A strategy for spelling and decoding polysyllabic words. *The Reading Teacher, 61*(70), 567–570.

Powers, J. (1988). *Henny Penny.* New York: Checkerboard Press.

Prelutsky, J. (1983). *Zoo doings: Animal poems.* New York: Trumpet Club Special Edition

Prelutsky, J. (1984). *The new kid on the block.* New York: Greenwillow Books.

Prelutsky, J (1990a). *Beneath a blue umbrella.* New York: Greenwillow Books.

Prelutsky, J. (1990b). *Something big has been here.* New York: Greenwillow Books.

Prelutsky, J. (1994). *A pizza the size of the sun.* New York: Greenwillow Books.

Prelutsky, J. (Ed.). (1999). *20th century children's poetry treasury.* New York: Alfred A. Knopf.

Prelutsky, J. (2006). *Writing with writers: Poetry writing.* Retrieved from http://teachers.scholastic.com/writewit/poetry/jack_your_poem.htm

Puccelli, M., & Paez, M. (2007). Narrative and vocabulary development of bilingual children from kindergarten to first grade: Developmental changes and associations among English and Spanish skills. *Language, Speech and Hearing Services in Schools, 38,* 235–236.

RAND Reading Study Group (2002). *Reading for understanding: Toward an R & D program in reading comprehension.* Santa Monica, CA: RAND.

Rankin-Erickson, J., & Pressley, M. (2000). A survey of instructional practices of special education teachers nominated as effective teachers of literacy. *Learning Disabilities Research & Practice, 15*(4), 206–225.

Ransom, K., Santa, C. M., Williams, C., & Farstrup, A. (1999). *Using multiple methods of beginning reading instruction: A position statement of the International Reading Association.* Newark, DE: International Reading Association.

Raphael, T. E., & Au, K. H. (2005). QAR: Enhancing comprehension and test taking across grades and content areas. *The Reading Teacher, 59*(3), 206–221.

Rashotte, C., & Torgeson, J. (1985). Repeated readings and reading fluency in learning disabled children. *Reading Research Quarterly, 20*(2), 180–202.

Rasinski, T. V. (2000). Speed does matter in reading. *The Reading Teacher, 54*(2), 146–151.

Rasinski, T. V. (2003). *The fluent reader.* New York: Scholastic.

Rasinski, T. V. (2004). Creating fluent readers. *Educational Leadership, 61*(6), 46–51.

Rasinski, T. V. (2005a). *Word ladders.* New York: Scholastic.

Rasinski, T. V. (2005b). *Daily word ladders.* New York: Teaching Resources.

Rasinski, T. V., & Lenhart, L. (2007). Explorations of fluent readers. *Reading Today, 25*(3), 18.

Rasinski, T. V., & Padak, N. (2003). *Effective reading strategies: Teaching children who find reading difficult* (3rd ed.). Upper Saddle River, NJ: Prentice Hall.

Rasinski, T. V., & Padak, N. (2004). Beyond consensus—beyond balance: Toward a comprehensive literacy curriculum. *Reading and Writing Quarterly, 20,* 91–102.

Rasinski, T. V., & Padak, N. D. (2005). Fluency beyond the primary grades: Helping adolescent readers. *Voices from the Middle, 13,* 34–41.

Rasinski, T. V., & Padak, N. D. (2007). *Evidence-based instruction in reading: A professional development guide to comprehension.* Boston: Allyn & Bacon.

Rasinski, T. V., & Padak, N. D. (2008). Beyond stories. *The Reading Teacher, 61*(70), 582–584.

Rasinski, T. V., & Padak, N., Linek, W., & Sturtevant, E. (1994). Effects of fluency development on urban second-grade readers. *Journal of Educational Research, 87*(3), 158–165.

Rasinski, T. V., Padak, N. D., Newton, R. M., & Newton, E. (2008). *Greek & Latin roots: Keys to building vocabulary*. Huntington Beach, CA: Shell Education.

Read, S. (2005). First and second graders writing informational text. *The Reading Teacher, 59*(1), 36–44.

Reutzel, D. R., & Cooter, R. (2003). *Strategies for reading assessment and instruction: Helping every child succeed* (2nd ed.). Upper Saddle River, NJ: Merrill.

Reutzel, D. R., & Fawson, P. C. (1990). Traveling tales: Connecting parents and children through writing. *The Reading Teacher, 44*, 545–554.

Reutzel, D. R., & Hollingsworth, P. (1993). Effects of fluency training on second graders' reading comprehension. *Journal of Educational Research, 86*, 325–331.

Reutzel, D. R., Hollingsworth, P., & Eldredge, J. (1994). Oral reading instruction: The impact on student reading development. *Reading Research Quarterly, 29*, 40–62.

Rey, H. A. (1985). *Curious George visits the zoo*. Boston: Houghton Mifflin.

Rhodes, C. (2002). Mindful reading: Strategy training that facilitates transfer. *Journal of Adolescent and Adult Literacy, 45*(6), 498–513.

Richards, J. (2006). Question, connect, transform (QCT): A strategy to help middle school students engage critically with historical fiction. *Reading & Writing Quarterly, 22*, 193–198.

Richards, M. (2000). Be a good detective: Solve the case of oral reading fluency. *The Reading Teacher, 53*(7), 534–539.

Richardson, J., & Morgan, R. (2005). *Reading to learn in the content areas* (6th ed.). Belmont, CA: Wadsworth.

Richardson, W. (2005). Educator's guide to the read/write web. *Educational Leadership, 63*(4), 24–27.

Richek, M. A. (2005). Words are wonderful: Interactive, time-efficient strategies to teach meaning vocabulary. *The Reading Teacher, 58*(5), 414–423.

Richek, M. A., Caldwell, J. S., Jennings, J. H., & Lerner, J. W. (2006). *Reading problems: Assessment and teaching strategies* (5th ed.). Boston: Allyn & Bacon.

Riehle, M. A. M. (2002). *B is for bluegrass: A Kentucky alphabet book*. Chelsea, MI: Sleeping Bear Press.

Rinsky, L. A. (1993). *Teaching word recognition skills*. Scottsdale, AZ: Gorsuch Scarisbrick.

Risko, V., & Walker-Dalhouse, D. (2009). Parents and teachers: Talking with or past one another—or not talking at all? *The Reading Teacher, 62*(5), 442–444.

Risko, V. J., & Walker-Dalhouse, D. (2010). Making the most of assessments to inform instruction. *The Reading Teacher, 63*(5), 420–422.

Riverdeep.net. (2000). Welcome to the ????s. Retrieved March 12, 2010, from www.riverdeep.net/current/2000/01/front.100100.decade1.jhtml

Roessel, D., & Rampersad, A. (1994). *Poetry for young people: Langston Hughes*. New York: Scholastic.

Rose, D., Parks, M., Androes, K., & McMahon, S. (2000). Imagery-based learning: Improving elementary students' reading comprehension with drama techniques. *Journal of Educational Research, 94*(1), 55–64.

Rosenbloom, J., & Artell, M. (1999). *The little giant book of tongue twisters*. New York: Sterling.

Rosencrans, G. (1998). *The spelling book: Teaching children how to spell, not what to spell*. Newark, DE: International Reading Association.

Rossell, C. (2004/2005). Teaching English through English. *Educational Leadership, 62*(4), 32–36.

Rottman, S. L. (1997). *Hero*. Atlanta: Peachtree.

Rottman, S. L. (1997). *Rough waters*. Atlanta: Peachtree.

Rottman, S. L. (1999). *Head above water*. Atlanta: Peachtree.

Routman, R. (2002). *Reading essential: The specifics you need to teach reading well*. Portsmouth, NH: Heinemann.

Rubin, R., & Carlan, V. G. (2005). Using writing to understand bilingual children's literacy development. *The Reading Teacher, 58*(8), 728–732.

Ruddell, R. (1964). *A study of cloze comprehension technique in relation to structurally controlled reading material*. Proceedings of the International Reading Association, 9, 298–303.

Rumelhart, D. (2004). Toward an interactive model of reading. In R. Ruddell & N. Unrau (Eds.), *Theoretical models and processes of reading* (5th ed.), pp. 1149–1179. Newark, DE: International Reading Association.

Rylant, C. (1987). *Henry and Mudge in the green time*. New York: Trumpet Club.

Rymer, R., & Williams, C. (2000). "Wasn't that a spelling word?": Spelling instruction and young children's writing. *Language Arts, 77*(3), 241–249.

Saddler, B. (2005). Sentence combining: A sentence level writing intervention. *The Reading Teacher, 58*(5), 468–471.

Sadoski, M., & Paivio, A. (2001). *Imagery and text: A dual coding theory of reading and writing*. Mahwah, NJ: Erlbaum.

Samuels, S. J. (1979/1997). The method of repeated readings. *The Reading Teacher, 50*(5), 376–381.

Santoro, L. E., Chard, D., Howard, L., & Baker, S. (2008). Making the very most of classroom read-alouds to promote comprehension and vocabulary. *The Reading Teacher, 61*(5), 396–408.

Sardegna, J. (1994). *The roly-poly spider.* New York: Scholastic.

Savage, H. (2001). *Sound it out: Phonics in a balanced reading program.* Boston: McGraw Hill.

Schmidt, R., Rozendal, M., & Greenman, G. (2002). Reading instruction in the inclusion classroom. *Remedial and Special Education, 23*(3), 130–140.

Schneider, R. (1993). *That's not all!* Grand Haven, MI: School Zone.

Schreiber, P. (1991). Understanding prosody's role in reading acquisition. *Theory into Practice, 20,* 158–164.

Schulman, M., & Carleen, P. (2007). *Guided reading.* New York: Scholastic Teaching Resources.

Schulman, M. B., & Payne, C. D. (2000). *Guided reading: Making it work.* New York: Scholastic.

Scieszka, J. (1995). *The true story of the three little pigs.* New York: Dutton.

Scieszka, J. (1996). *The true story of the three little pigs.* Illus. by L. Smith. New York: Puffin.

SEDL (Southwest Educational Development Laboratory). (2006). Importance of family and community involvement continues to grow. *SEDL Letter, 28*(3). Retrieved March 12, 2011, from http://www.sedl.org/pubs/sedl-letter/v18n03/index.html

Seuss, Dr. (1957). *The cat in the hat.* New York: Random House.

Seuss, Dr. (1960). *Green eggs and ham.* New York: Random House.

Seuss, Dr. (1975). *Oh, the thinks you can think.* New York: Random House Books for Young Readers.

Seuss, Dr. (1978). *I can read with my eyes shut.* New York: Random House Books for Young Readers.

Shamir, A., & Korat, O. (2006) How to select CD-ROM storybooks for young children: The teacher's role. *The Reading Teacher, 59*(6), 532–543.

Shanahan, T., & Shanahan, S. (1997). Character perspective charting: Helping children to develop a more complete conception of story. *The Reading Teacher, 50*(8), 668–677.

Shanker, J. L., & Ekwall, E. E. (2002). *Locating and correcting reading difficulties* (8th ed.). Upper Saddle River, NJ: Prentice Hall.

Shaughnessy, M. (2010). An interview with Dan Willingham: Reading comprehension. *EducationNews.org.* Retrieved June 26, 2010, from www.ednews.org/articles/an-interview-with-dan-willingham-reading-comprehension.html

Shaw, C. (1947). *It looked like spilt milk.* New York: Harper Festival.

Shaw, N. (1992). *Sheep out to eat.* New York: A Trumpet Club Special Edition.

Sheldon, S. (2002). Parents' social networks and beliefs as predictors of parent involvement. *The Elementary School Journal, 102*(4), 301–316.

Short, D., & Echevarria, J. (2004/2005). Teacher skills to support English language learners. *Educational Leadership, 62*(4), 8–13.

Shoulders, M. (2003). *M is for magnolia: A Mississippi alphabet book.* Chelsea, MI: Sleeping Bear Press.

Showers, P. (1961). *The listening walk.* New York: HarperTrophy.

Sibenaller, K. (2001). Reading assessment tools and tangible improvement. *Median and Methods, 37*(5), 6–8.

Sidman, J. (2009). *Red sings from treetops: A year in colors.* Illus. by P. Zagarenski. Boston: Houghton Mifflin Books for Children.

Silverstein, S. (1974). *Where the sidewalk ends.* New York: HarperCollins.

Silverstein, S. (1981). *A light in my attic.* New York: HarperCollins.

Silverstein, S. (1996). *Falling up.* New York: HarperCollins.

Simon, S. (1989). *Whales.* New York: Scholastic.

Simon, S. (1992). *Storms* (Reprint ed.). New York: HarperTrophy.

Simon, S. (2001). *Tornadoes.* New York: HarperTrophy.

Simon, S. (2002). *Hurricanes.* New York: HarperTrophy.

Sindelar, P., Monda, L., & O'Shea, L. (1990). Effects of repeated readings on instructional and mastery-level readers. *Journal of Educational Research, 83,* 220–226.

Sipe, L. (2001). Invention, convention, and intervention: Invented spelling and the teacher's role. *The Reading Teacher, 55*(3), 264–273.

Sippola, A. (1997). Language master redux. *The Reading Teacher, 51*(3), 271–272.

Slavin, R. E., Madden, N. A., Dolan, L. J., Wasik, B. A., Rose, S. M., Smith, L. J., et al. (1996). Success for All: A summary of research. *Journal of Education for Students Placed at Risk, 1*(1), 41–76.

Smith, F. (1978). *Reading without nonsense.* New York: Teachers College Press.

Smith, F. (1992). Learning to read: The never-ending debate. *Phi Delta Kappan, 73,* 432–441.

Smith, F. (1999). Why systematic phonics and phonemic awareness instruction constitutes an education hazard. *Language Arts, 77*(2), 150–155.

Smith, F. (2005). *Reading without nonsense* (4th ed.). New York: Teachers College Press.

Smith, J., & Elley, W. (1997). *How children learn to write.* Katonah, NY: Richard C. Owen.

Smith, J. K., & Warwick, B. E. (1997). *How children learn to write.* United Kingdom: Paul Chapman Educational Publishing/Sage.

Smith, L. A. (2006). Think-aloud mysteries: Using structured, sentence-by-sentence text passages to teach comprehension strategies. *The Reading Teacher, 59*(8), 764–773.

Smith, M., Walker, B., & Yellin, D. (2004). From phonological awareness to fluency in each lesson. *The Reading Teacher, 58*(3), 302–307.

Smith, N. B. (1965). *American reading instruction.* Newark, DE: International Reading Association.

Snow, C., Burns, M., & Griffin, P. (Eds.). (1998). *Preventing reading difficulties in young children.* Washington, DC: National Academy Press.

Soalt, J. (2005). Bringing together fictional and informational texts to improve comprehension. *The Reading Teacher, 58*(7), 680–683.

Soares, L. B., & Wood, K. (2010). A critical literacy perspective for teaching and learning social studies. *The Reading Teacher, 63*(6), 486–494.

Sox, A., & Rubinstein-Avila, E. (2009, September). WebQuests for English-language learners: Essential elements for design. *Journal of Adolescent & Adult Literacy, 53*(1), 38–48.

Spence, L. (2010). Generous reading: Seeing students through their writing. *The Reading Teacher, 63*(8), 634–642.

Staal, L. (2000). The story face: An adaptation of story mapping that incorporates visualization and discovery learning to enhance reading and writing. *The Reading Teacher, 54*(1), 26–31.

Stahl, S. (1998). Saying the "P" word: Nine guidelines for exemplary phonics instruction. In R. Allington (Ed.), *Teaching struggling readers* (pp. 208–216). Newark, DE: International Reading Association.

Stahl, S., & Kuhn, M. (1995). Does whole language or instruction matched to learning styles help children learn to read? *School Psychology Review, 24*(3), 393–404.

Stahl, S., & Kuhn, M. (2002). Center for improvement of early reading achievement. *The Reading Teacher, 55*(6), 582–584.

Stahl, S., Heubach, K., & Cramond, B. (1997). *Fluency-oriented reading instruction* (Research Report No. 79). Athens, GA: National Reading Research Center.

Stanley, J. (1992). *Children of the Dust Bowl: The true story of the school at Weedpatch Camp.* New York: A Trumpet Club Special Edition.

Stanovich, K. E. (1991). Word recognition: Changing perspectives. In R. Barr, M. L. Kamil, P. Mosenthal, & P. D. Pearson (Eds.), *Handbook of reading research, Vol. 2,* pp. 418–452. Hillsdale, NJ: Erlbaum.

Staudt, D. H. (2009). Intensive word study and repeated reading improves reading skills for two students with learning disabilities. *The Reading Teacher, 63*(2), 142–151.

Steele, P. (1994). *I wonder why castles had moats and other questions about long ago.* New York: Kingfisher Books.

Stephens, K. (2008). A quick guide to selecting great informational books for young children. *The Reading Teacher, 61*(6), 488–490.

Sterling-Honig, A. (2007). Oral language development. *Early Child Development and Care, 177*(6 & 7), 581–613.

Strickland, D., Bodino, A., Buchan, K., Jones, K., Nelson, A., & Rosen, M. (2001). Teaching writing in a time of reform. *Elementary School Journal, 101,* 385–398.

Sturges, P. (1999). *The Little Red Hen makes a pizza.* New York: Puffin Books.

Swanson, P., & De La Paz, S. (1998). Teaching effective comprehension strategies to students. *Intervention in School & Clinic, 33*(4), 209–219.

Sylvester, R., & Greenidge, W. (2009). Digital storytelling: Extending the potential for struggling writers. *The Reading Teacher, 63*(4), 284–295.

Symons, S., & Pressley, M. (1993). Prior knowledge affects text search success and extraction of information. *Reading Research Quarterly, 28*(3), 250–259.

Taberski, S. (2000). *On solid ground: Strategies for teaching reading, K–3.* Portsmouth, NH: Heinemann.

Taylor, B., Hanson, B., Justice-Swanson, K., & Watts, S. (1997). Helping struggling readers: Linking small-group intervention with cross-age tutoring. *The Reading Teacher, 51*(3), 196–209.

Taylor, B., Pressley, M., & Pearson, D. (2000). *Research-supported characteristics of teachers and schools that promote reading achievement.* Ann Arbor, MI: Center for the Improvement of Early Reading Achievement (CIERA).

Teachers of English to Speakers of Other Languages. (2006). TESOL revises pre-K–12 English language proficiency standards. Retrieved June 28, 2010, from www.tesol.org/s_tesol/sec_document.asp?CID=1186 & DID=5349

TEAMS Educational Resources. (2006). *Assessing the student's concepts about print.* Retrieved June 10, 2010, from http://teams.lacoe.edu/documentation/classrooms/patti/k-1/teacher/assessment

Templeton, S., & Bear, D. R. (2005). *Spelling and vocabulary.* Upper Saddle River, NJ: Pearson/Prentice Hall.

Tempo, F. (1993). *Origami magic.* New York: Scholastic.

Terban, M. (1988). *Guppies in tuxedos.* New York: Clarion Books.

Terban, M. (2007). *Eight ate: A feast of homonym riddles.* New York: Scholastic.

Texas Education Agency. (1997). *TEKS for English Language Arts and Reading.* Austin, TX: Texas State Education Department.

Theroux, P. (2004). *Enhance learning.* Retrieved January 7, 2007, from http://members.shaw.ca/priscillatheroux/differentiating.html

Tierney, R. J., & Shanahan, T. (1991). Research on reading–writing relationships: Interaction, transactions and outcomes. In R. Barr, M. Kamil, P. Mosenthal, & P. D. Pearson (Eds.), *Handbook of reading research,* pp. 246–280. New York: Longman.

Tomlinson, C. A., & Jarvis, J. (2006). Teaching beyond the book. *Educational Leadership, 64*(1), 16–21.

Tompkins, G. (2002). *Language arts: Content and teaching strategies.* Upper Saddle River, NJ: Merrill.

Topping, K., & Ehly, S. (1998). *Peer assisted learning.* Mahwah, NJ: Lawrence Erlbaum.

Townsend, D. (2009). Building academic vocabulary in after-school settings: Games for growth with middle school English-language learners. *Journal of Adolescent and Adult Literacy, 53*(3), 242–251.

Trelease, J. (1996). Have your read to your kids today? *Instructor* (May–June), 56–60.

Trelease, J. (2001). *The read-aloud handbook.* New York: Penguin Books.

Tresselt, A. (1964). *The mitten.* Illus. by Yaroslava. New York: Lothrop, Lee & Shepard.

Truss, L. (2006). *Eats, shoots and leaves: Why, commas really do make a difference!* Illus. by B. Timmons. New York: Putnam.

Turbill, J. (2000). Developing a spelling conscience. *Language Arts, 77*(3), 209–217.

Turbill, J., Bean, W., & Fox, M. (2006). *Writing instruction K–6: Understanding process, purpose, audience.* New York: Richard C. Owen.

Turkle, B. (1976). *Deep in the forest.* New York: Dutton.

Ulrich, G. (1995). *My tooth ith loothe: Funny poems to read instead of doing your homework.* South Holland, IL: A Yearling Book.

U.S. Census Bureau. (2007). Language use in the United States: 2007. Retrieved March 2, 2011, from www.census.gov/prod/2010pubs/acs-12.pdf

U.S. Department of Education, National Center for Education Statistics. (2010). Reading achievement gaps. Retrieved March 12, 2011, from http://nces.ed.gov/programs/coe/2010/section2/table-rgp-1.asp

U.S. Office of Education. (1977). *Assistance to states for education for handicapped children: Procedures for evaluating specific learning disabilities.* Federal Register, 42, G1082–G1085.

Valencia, S., Smith, A., Reece, A., Li, M., et al. (2010). Oral reading fluency assessment: Issues of construct, criterion, and consequential validity. *Reading Research Quarterly, 45*(3), 270–291.

Van Allen, R. (1976). *Language experiences in education.* Boston: Houghton Mifflin.

Van Allsburg, C. (1988). *Two bad ants.* Boston: Houghton Mifflin.

Van Cleave, J. (1993). *200 gooey, slippery, slimy, weird and fun experiments.* New York: John Wiley.

Vardell, S. M., Hadaway, N. L., & Young, T. A. (2006). Matching books and readers: Selecting literature for English learners. *The Reading Teacher, 59*(8), 734–741.

Vaughn, S., Elbaum, J. S., & Hughes, M. T. (1998). Social outcomes for students with and without disabilities in inclusive classrooms. *Journal of Disabilities, 31*(5), 428–436.

Vaughn, S., et al. (2000). Fluency and comprehension interventions for third-grade students. *Remedial and Special Education, 21*(6), 325–335.

Vaughn, S., Mathes, P. G., Linan-Thompson, S., & Francis, D. (2005). Teaching English language learners at risk for reading disabilities to read: Putting research into practice. *Learning Disabilities Research & Practice, 20*(1), 58–67.

Vellutino, R. (1991). Introduction to three studies on reading acquisition: Convergent findings on theoretical foundations of code-oriented versus whole-language approaches to reading instruction. *Journal of Educational Psychology, 83*(4), 437–444.

Vygotsky, L. (1962). *Thought and language* (E. Hanfmann & G. Vaka, Eds. & Trans.). Cambridge, MA: MIT Press.

Vygotsky, L. (1978). *Mind in society: The development of higher psychological processes.* Cambridge, MA: Harvard University Press.

Wagner, R., & Torgesen, J. (1987). The nature of phonological processing and its causal role in the acquisition of reading skills. *Psychological Bulletin, 101,* 192.

Wagstaff, J. (1997/1998). Building practical knowledge of letter–sound correspondences: A beginner's word wall and beyond. *The Reading Teacher, 51*(4), 298–304.

Walker, B. (2004). *Diagnostic teaching of reading: Techniques for instruction and assessment* (5th ed.). Upper Saddle River, NJ: Prentice Hall.

Wall, H. (2008). Interactive writing beyond the primary grades. *The Reading Teacher, 62*(2), 149–152.

Wallace, B. (1988). *Beauty*. New York: A Minstrel Book.

Wang, J. H., & Guthrie, J. T. (2004). Modeling the effects for intrinsic motivation, extrinsic motivation, amount of reading and past reading achievement on text comprehension between U. S. and Chinese students. *Reading Research Quarterly, 39,* 162–186.

Wasik, B. (1997). Volunteer tutoring programs. *Phi Delta Kappan, 79*(4), 282–288.

Wasik, B. (1998). Using volunteers as reading tutors: Guidelines for successful practices. *The Reading Teacher, 51*(7), 562–571.

Wasik, B. A. (2006). Building vocabulary one word at a time. *Young Children, 61,* 70–78.

Watt, F. (1993). *Earthquakes and volcanoes*. New York: Scholastic.

Weaver, C. (1994). *Phonics in whole language classrooms*. ERIC Digest.

Weaver, C. (1996). *Teaching grammar in context*. Portsmouth, NH: Heinemann.

Weaver, C. (2002). *Reading process and practice* (3rd ed.). Portsmouth, NH: Heinemann.

Weber, R. (1991). Linguistic diversity: Reading in American society. In R. Barr, M. L. Kamil, P. B. Mosenthal, & P. D. Pearson (Eds.), *Handbook of reading research (Vol. 2),* pp. 97–110. White Plains, NY: Longman.

Weitzman, I. (2006). *Jokelopedia: The biggest, best, silliest, dumbest joke book ever*. New York: Workman.

Wells, J., & Lewis, L. (2006). *Internet access in the U.S. public schools and classrooms: 1994–2005.* National Center for Education Statistics, U.S. Department of Education. Retrieved March 11, 2011, from http://nces.ed.gov/pubsearch/pubsinfo.asp?pubid=2007020

White, A. L., & Swanson, A. H. L. (2007). Intensive word study and repeated reading improves reading skills for two students with learning disabilities. *The Reading Teacher, 63*(2), 141–151.

White, T. G, & Kim, J. S. (2008). Teacher and parent scaffolding of voluntary summer reading. *The Reading Teacher, 62*(2), 116–125.

Wiesner, D. (1988). *Freefall*. New York: Clarion Books.

Wiesner, D. (1991). *Tuesday*. New York: Clarion Books.

Wiesner, D. (1997). *Sector 7*. New York: Clarion Books.

Wiesner, D. (2001). *The three pigs*. New York: Clarion Books.

Wiesner, D. (2006). *Flotsam*. New York: Clarion Books.

Wigfield, A., & Guthrie, J. T. (1997). Relation of children's motivation for reading to the amount and breadth of their reading. *Journal of Educational Psychology, 89,* 420–432.

Wilfong, L. (2009). Textmasters: Bringing literature circles to textbook reading across the curriculum. *Journal of Adolescent and Adult Literacy, 53*(2), 164–171.

Wilkinson, T. (1994). *Bison for kids*. Minnetonka, MN: NorthWord.

Williams, K. T. (1997). *Expressive vocabulary test*. Circle Pines, MN: American Guidance Service.

Williams, L. (1986). *The little old lady who was not afraid of anything*. New York: HarperTrophy.

Williams, L. (1996). *I went walking*. New York: Red Wagon Books.

Wilson, R. M., & Cleland, C. J. (1989). *Diagnostic and remedial reading for classroom and clinic*. Columbus, OH: Merrill.

Winn, P., Graham, L., & Prock, L. (1993). A model of poor readers' text-based inferencing: Effects of explanatory feedback. *Reading Research Quarterly, 28*(1), 52–64.

Winter, P. (1976). *The bear and the fly*. New York: Crown.

Wolf, M., Miller, L., & Donnelly, K. (2000). Retrieval automaticity, vocabulary elaboration, orthography (RAVE-O): A comprehensive, fluency-based reading intervention program. *Journal of Learning Disabilities, 33*(4), 375–387.

Wolf, M. K., Crossen, A. C., & Resnick, L. B. (2004). Classroom talk for rigorous reading comprehension and instruction. *Reading Psychology, 26*(1), 27–53.

Wolf, S., & Wolf, K. (2002). Teaching true to the test in writing. *Language Arts, 79*(3), 229–240.

Wood, A. (1964). *The napping house*. San Diego, CA: Harcourt Brace Jovanovich.

Wood, J. (1990). *Caves: Facts and stories and activities*. New York: Scholastic.

Wood-Ray, K. (2006). *Study driven: A framework for planning units of study in the writing workshop*. Portsmouth, NH: Heinemann.

Woodruff, E. (1991). *Show and tell*. New York: A Trumpet Club Special Edition.

Wray, D., Medwell, J., Fox, R., & Poulson, L. (2000). The teaching of practices of effective teachers of literacy. *Educational Review, 52*(1), 75–85.

Yaden, D. B., Tam, A., Madrigal, P., Grassell, D., Massa, J., Altamirano, L. S., et al. (2000). Early literacy for inner-city children: The effects of reading and writing interventions in English and Spanish during the preschool years. *Reading Teacher, 54*(2), 186–190.

Yellin, D., Blake, M., & DeVries, B. (2004). *Integrating the language arts* (3rd ed.). Scottsdale, AZ: Holcomb Hathaway.

Yin. (2001). *Coolies*. New York: Penguin Books for Young Readers.

Yolen, J. (1992). *Encounter*. Illus. by D. Shannon. Orlando, FL: Voyager Books/Harcourt.

Yopp, H. K. (2005). A test for assessing phonemic awareness in young children. In S. J. Barrentine & S. M. Stokes (Eds.), *Reading assessment*, pp. 262–271. Newark, DE: International Reading Association.

Yopp, H. K., & Yopp, R. H. (2000). Supporting phonemic awareness development in the classroom. *The Reading Teacher, 54*(2), 130–143.

Yopp, R. H., & Yopp, H. K. (2007). Ten important words plus: A strategy for building word knowledge. *The Reading Teacher, 61*(2), 157–160.

Young, A., Bowers, E., & MacKinnon, G. (1996). Effects of prosodic modeling and repeated reading on poor readers' fluency and comprehension. *Applied Psycholinguistics, 17*, 59–84.

Young, C., & Rasinski, T. (2009). Implementing readers theatre as an approach to classroom fluency instruction. *The Reading Teacher, 63*(1), 4–13.

Zawilinski, L. (2009). HOT blogging: A framework for blogging to promote higher order thinking. *The Reading Teacher, 62*(8), 650–661.

Zecker, L. B. (1999). Different texts, different emergent writing forms. *Language Arts, 76*(6), 483–490.

Zipke, M. (2008). Teaching metalinguistic awareness and reading comprehension with riddles. *The Reading Teacher, 62*(2), 128–137.

AUTHOR INDEX

Acha, J., 174
Ada, A., 313
Adams, M., 6
Adams-Just, M., 283
Adler, D., 35, 221, 242
Afflerbach., P., 217
Ahlberg, J., 145
Alborough, J., 88
Alcott, L. M., 59
Allinder, R., 190, 194, 267
Allington, R., 8, 15, 16, 24, 27, 30, 33, 35, 38, 50, 258, 259, 260, 262, 266, 267, 272, 275, 343, 344, 345
Alyousef, H. S., 12
Ambruster, B., 229
Anders, P., 219
Anderson, R., 267
Anderson-Inman, L., 346
Anthony, H., 248, 250
Archambault, J., 118
Armstrong, T., 31, 32, 153
Asher, J., 165
Ashton-Warner, S., 164
Aspegren, C., 190
Atwell, N., 290, 297
August, D., 130, 153, 160, 217
Avi, 317, 320
Ayto, J., 153

Bagert, B., 93, 140, 141, 276
Bailey-Beard, D., 52, 186, 314
Banyi, I., 139
Barksdale, M. A., 316
Barr, R., 16, 295
Barrett, J., 205
Barry, A., 45
Baumann, J., 153, 163
Beall, P., 84, 90
Bean, T., 247
Bear, D., 79, 80, 90, 91, 105, 106, 107, 108, 109, 111, 112, 122, 131, 132, 137, 160, 170, 283, 285, 324, 325, 328, 329, 330, 351
Beauchat, K. A., 155
Beck, I., 4, 5, 154, 156, 179, 181, 184, 187, 194, 195, 206
Beckman-Anthony, A., 193
Behrman, E. H., 4
Bemelman, L., 105
Bennett, J., 85, 156, 159, 276
Bennett-Hopkins, L., 306
Berkowitz, M. W., 361
Berger, G., 230
Biancarosa, G., 131
Bintz, W., 231-232, 312
Blachowicz, C., 153, 154, 158, 161
Blevins, W., 77, 78, 79, 81, 106, 107, 108, 131, 137
Bloodgood, J. W., 137, 146
Bluestein, A., 249
Blum, I., 209
Blume, J., 317
Boers, D., 366
Booth, D., 84
Bos, C., 219, 221
Bottner, B., 310
Bottomley, D., 69, 301
Bouchereau-Bauer, E., 10, 193
Boyle, D., 36
Branley, F., 232
Bray, M., 267
Brett, J., 53-54, 88, 139, 140, 212, 264, 265, 316-317
Brewer, P., 275
Bridwell, N., 291
Bromley, K., 333
Brown, K., 180, 182, 207
Browning, C. R., 197
Brozo, W. G., 18, 26, 27, 38, 216, 217
Bruner, J., 3
Bulion, L., 306
Bunting, E., 88
Burns, P., 134
Byars, B., 317

Cadiero-Kaplein, K., 5
Calkins, L., 48, 283, 290, 307
Calmenson, S., 87
Camilli, G., 102
Canizares, S., 222
Carbo, M., 8, 31, 33, 205, 267, 272
Carle, E., 317
Carlo, M., 156, 160
Carlstrom, N., 58, 270, 327
Carrell, R. L., 29
Cartwright, K., 343
Cauley, L., 7
Cecil, N., 81, 83, 112, 227, 268, 308, 309
Celenza, A., 211
Center for Public Education, 10, 160
Cerullo, M., 222, 228, 229, 244
Cervetti, G., 4, 5
Chall, J., 6, 131
Chambers, B., 343
Chandler-Olcott, K., 20
Churchill, R., 239
Ciardiello, A., 188, 194
Clarke, L., 207
Clay, M., 30, 33, 50, 51, 55, 127, 190, 285, 288, 343, 344, 347
Cleary, B., 159
Clifford, P., 186
Coffey, H., 4, 5
Cole, J., 86, 87
Cooper, D., 209
Cooper, J., 62, 153, 183, 190
Couric, K., 183
Creech, S., 273
Cudd, E., 308
Cummins, J., 10, 283
Cunningham, A., 81
Cunningham, J., 15, 77, 82, 84, 87
Cunningham, P., 7, 102, 105, 108, 109, 110, 111, 121, 129, 130, 285
Curtis, C. P., 163, 164, 178

D'Agostino, J. V., 16
Dahl, K., 105, 109
Dale, E., 236
Danziger, P., 60, 187
Darling-Hammond, L., 24
Davey, B., 250

Day, A., 293
Deeney, T., 258
DeFord, D., 14
DeKonty-Applegate, M., 180, 188, 258, 259, 265
Demi, 164, 194, 310
dePaola, T., 68, 70, 155, 167, 186, 200, 205, 232, 317
Dix, S., 293
Dodds, B., 263
Dolch, E., 129
Doty, D., 181, 191, 213
Dowhower, S., 181, 191, 195, 267
Drucker, M. J., 12
Duke, N., 314
Duffy-Hester, A., 181, 267
Dunn, R., 162
DuPont, A., 371
Dworin, J., 283, 290, 295

Echevarria, J., 12
Edmunds, K. M., 26, 27
Edwards, P. D., 155, 159
Ehri, L., 82
Elbaum, B., 343
Elbow, P., 283
Elkonin, D., 90
Ellery, V., 180

Falwell, C., 159, 337
Farjeon, E., 86, 156
Farndon, J., 251
Fawson, P., 267
Ferreiro, E., 283, 289
Ferroli, L., 324, 325
Fiderer, A., 64
Finn, J., 361
Fisher, D., 228, 237
Fitzgerald, J., 10, 343
Fleischman, P., 278
Flood, J., 180, 265
Florian, D., 86
Florida Department of Education, 162
Flynt, E., 156, 183, 194, 196, 237
Foorman, B., 84
Fordham, N., 312
Foresman, S., 35, 225, 226
Fortenberry, C., 179
Fountas, I., 30, 33, 34, 35, 39, 50, 102, 108, 110, 138, 139, 184, 185, 191, 195, 259, 264, 267, 283, 285, 296, 302, 306, 329, 347
Fox, B., 267
Fox, M., 110, 121, 203, 317, 336, 351, 355
Franco, B., 277
Freire, P., 4
Fresch, M., 285, 323, 324, 325, 329, 332
Fried, M., 283
Fritz, J., 35
Fry, E., 35, 37, 130
Fry Readability Formula, 36-37
Frye, E., 288, 310
Fuchs, D. , 267
Fuchs, L., 267

Garan, E. M., 15
Gardner, H., 31
Gauthier, L., 194
Gentry, J., 122, 289, 323, 324, 325, 332
George, J., 317
George, W., 242, 243
Giannetti, C., 369
Gibbons, G., 232, 317
Gill, S., 224, 267, 275
Gillet, J., 59, 191, 193
Gipe, J., 136, 219
Glazer, T., 84
Glick, S., 197
Goldish, M., 138
Goodman, K., 7, 52, 190, 267
Goodman, Y., 7, 13, 50, 52, 55, 190
Graham, S., 291
Graves, M., 154, 283, 291
Greenfield, E., 35
Gregory, A., 184, 185, 208
Griffith, L. W., 180, 258, 265
Grout, D. J., 152
Gross, E. B., 197
Guarino, D., 78
Guerrero, A. M., 179, 184
Gunning, T., 129
Guthrie, J. T., 16, 27, 28, 179
Gutman, D., 317
Gwynne, F., 159, 337

Hadaway, N., 267
Hall, E., 31
Hall, K., 119
Hamilton, R., 195
Hamilton, V., 317
Handsfield, L., 295, 296
Hanf, M., 242
Hansen, J., 290, 297
Harris, A., 267
Harris, K., 291
Harris, T., 43, 55
Harrison, D., 306
Hart, B., 153
Harvey, T., 155
Hasbrouck, J. E., 261
Hassett, D., 19
Heald-Taylor, B., 323, 324, 329
Heath, S. B., 130
Heilmann, J., 153
Heller, R., 155, 159
Helman, L.A., 48, 79, 80, 108, 109, 130
Henk, W., 69
Henkel, J., 371
Henkes, K., 181
Henry, L., 255
Hesse, K., 264, 265, 270
Hessell, J., 272
Heubach, K., 242
Hiebert, E., 105, 109, 110
Hindes, M., 224
Ho, B., 361
Holdaway, D., 7, 164
Holt, K., 263
Houge, T., 343, 344, 348, 354, 356
Hughes, M., 283, 285, 291, 293, 323, 329, 330, 332
Hurley, S. R., 66
Hurst, C., 181, 189

Illingworth, M., 239
Imperato, F., 368, 371
Invernizzi, M., 345
IRA, 10, 16, 17, 18, 23, 24, 43, 77, 102, 109, 115, 129, 130, 344
IRA/NAEYC, 81, 82, 89
Ivey, G., 102, 180, 267

Jackman, H., 84
Jacobs, F., 228
Jacobson, J., 189
Janeczko, P., 172, 306
Jensen, D., 361, 362
Jitendra, A., 189, 191, 194
Johns, J., 258, 259
Johnson, F., 331
Johnson-Higgins, J., 193
Johnston, F., 105, 109, 283, 285, 329, 343, 351
Jongsma, K., 84, 189, 191
Joosse, B., 278
Joyce, I., 88
Juel, C., 153, 154

Kalan, R., 351
Kane, S., 105, 109, 110, 267
Kara-Soteriou, J., 288, 306
Karchmer, R., 227, 255
Kaufman, M., 6
Keating, F., 258
Keehn, S., 180
Kelley, M., 27
Kerr, J., 197
Kieffer, M. J., 128, 131, 132, 154
Kindervater, T., 358, 362, 367, 368, 371
King-Smith, D., 35
Kinniburgh, L., 249
Kintsch, W., 283
Kirk, D., 88
Kletzien, S., 219
Knapp, Z., 239

Koskinen, P., 267, 272
Krashen, S., 10, 12, 160
Krinitz, E. N., 1947
Ksypka, H., 86
Kuhlman, N., 66
Kuhn, M., 267

Lamoreaux, L., 164
Lane, H. S., 77, 82
Langeland, D., 252
Lansky, B., 86, 90, 93, 102, 118, 263, 276
Lapp, D., 187, 194, 202, 229
Larkin, R. B., 267, 276
Lauber, P., 223, 229
Leal, D., 332
Learning First Alliance, 283
Lehr, F., 156
Leinart, A.,
Lenski, S. D., 66, 67
Lepthien, E., 195
Lewis, M., 168
Lewis, P., 276
Lewison, M., 4
Lithgow, J., 355
Lloyd, C., 5, 178
Lobel, A., 276
Los Angeles County Office of Education, 50
Low, A., 205
Lynch, T., 70

MacDonald, M., 181, 210, 265, 364
MacLachlan, P., 186, 203
MacLulich, C., 222
Maestro, G., 159
Manning, M., 10
Manyak, P. C., 156, 160
Marino-Weisman, D., 231
Markle, S., 222
Marsalis, W., 306
Martens, P., 190
Martin, B., 118, 310
Martin, J., 351
Maslow, A., 4
Mason, L., 153, 155, 282, 288, 303
Mass, W., 187
Mastropieri, M., 267
Matthew, K., 267
May, F., 183
Mazzoni, S. A., 28
McBratney, S., 145
McCardle, P., 16
McCarrier, A., 283
McCarthy, P., 91
McCormick, S., 3, 235
McGee, L., 199
McGovern, A., 355
McKenna, M., 69, 128
McKeown, M., 179
McLaughlin, M., 178, 188
Medcalf, N., 343
Medearis, M., 195
Medema, K., 178
Mesmer, E., 17
Meyer, B., 254, 343, 344, 347, 348
Michigan Department of Education, 360
Micucci, C., 195
Miller, M., (1996, 2006) 239
Miller, W., (1988, 2000) 45
Mills, K., 179, 187, 231
Moats, L., 104
Molfese, V. J., 128
Montelong, J., 246
Moore, D., 258, 267, 275, 276
Moore, R., 190, 267
Moore, S., 167
Moore-Hart, M., 293, 312
Morgan, R., 5
Morris, D., 275, 347
Morrow, L., 362, 371
Mosenthal, J., 242
Moss, L., 88, 278
Moustafa, M., 105, 109
Mouza, C., 19
Murphy, S., 48
Murrow, L. M., 343

Nagy, W., 154, 155
National Association for the Education of Young Children, 77
National Center for Education Statistics, 15, 28
National Clearinghouse for English Language Acquisition, 47
National Council of Teachers of English, 43, 44
National Institute for Literacy, 15
National Reading Panel, 258, 267
NEA Today, 181
Nesbitt, K., 86
Ness, M., 274
Neufield, P., 221
Nicholson, T., 273
Nieto, S., 188
Nilsen, A. P., 130
Nipp, S., 84, 90
Northwest Regional Education Library, 297, 298
Novick, M., 159
Numeroff, L., 185, 355
Nunnery, J., 347

O'Connor, J., 16, 110, 180, 265
O'Loughlin, J., 47
O'Neill, M., 276
Oakhill, J., 219
Ogle, D., 231, 246
Ohler, J., 284, 292
Oklahoma State Department of Education, 63
Oliver, K., 267, 275
Olson, M., 195, 229
Opie, I., 85, 89
Oppenheim, J., 351
Oster, L., 181, 189, 203
Otaiba, S., 10, 11, 343, 370

Pacquette, K. R., 235
Padak, N., 267, 358, 367, 371, 372
Palmer, R., 220, 227, 229
Pappas, T., 278
Parish, P., 159
Park, L., 187
Parks, R., 195
Partin, K., 27
Paterson, K., 179, 211, 317
Patterson, E., 27
Paulsen, G., 317
Pearson, P., 207
Peck, R., 163, 385
Peebles, J., 279
Perez-Canado, M., 108, 290, 330
Piaget, J., 3, 109
Pinkney, M., 355
Pinnell, G., 127, 137, 284, 323, 329, 347
Piston, W., 152
Polacco, P., 197, 202, 203, 209, 317
Porter Decusati, C. L., 361
Powell, D., 338
Powers, J., 88
Prelutsky, J., 85, 86, 155, 276, 295
Puccelli, M., 153, 160

RAND Reading Study Group, 179, 216
Rankin-Erickson, J., 25, 30
Ransom, K., 79
Raphael, T., 249, 254
Rashotte, C., 270
Rasinski, T., 7, 8, 121, 128, 129, 130, 133, 134, 137, 155, 156, 168, 180, 258, 259, 260, 266, 267, 268, 273, 274, 361, 362, 367
Read, S., 284
Repchuk, C., 355
Reutzel, D., 6, 267, 271, 368, 369
Rey, H. A., 142
Rhodes, C., 180
Richards, M., 188, 211, 254, 264, 267
Richardson, J., 217, 218, 219, 228, 229, 284, 295
Richek, M., 153, 172, 180, 190, 217
Riehle, M. A. M., 314
Rinsky, L. A., 110
Risko, V. J., 43, 50, 360, 362
Riverdeep.net, 153
Roessel, D., 276
Root, B., 70

Rose, D., 179, 181, 191
Rosenbloom, J., 115
Rosencrans, G., 323, 324, 325
Rossell, C., 10
Rottman, S. L., 182
Routman, R., 6, 7
Rowling, J. K., 317
Rubin, R., 283, 289, 290
Rubin, S. G., 197
Ruddell, R., 59
Rumelhart, D., 283
Rylant, C., 274
Rymer, R., 283, 323, 324, 329

Sachar, L., 318
Saddler, M., 315
Sadoski, M., 179, 184
Salley, C., 185
Samuels, S. J., 260, 267, 275
Santoro, L. E., 181, 183, 184, 195
Sardegna, J., 88
Savage, H., 6, 7, 111
Schmidt, R., 25, 30, 38
Schneider, R., 119
Schreiber, P., 267
Schulman, M., 35, 57
Scieszka, J., 187, 310, 318
Seuss, Dr., 7, 51, 87, 117, 263
Shamir, A., 213
Shanahan, T., 211
Shanker, J., 52, 129, 134
Shaughnessy, M., 29
Shaw, C., 309, 351
Shaw, N., 117
Sheldon, S., 360, 361
Short, D., 10
Shoulders, M., 314
Showers, P., 165
Sibenaller, K., 213
Sidman, J., 306
Silvaroli, N., 134
Silverstein, S., 118, 276
Simon, S., 221, 222, 228, 232
Sindelar, P., 267
Sipe, L., 324, 325
Sippola, A., 267
Slavin, R., 347
Smith, A., 239
Smith, F., 79, 82, 84, 126, 127
Smith, L. A., 204
Smith, M., 102, 118
Snow, C., 154
Soalt, J., 179, 195
Soares, L. B., 188, 232
Southwest Educational Development Laboratory, 360, 361, 362
Sox, A., 19
Spence, L., 19, 285, 290
Spinelli, J., 197, 318
Staal, L., 185, 186, 209
Stahl, S., 30, 31, 102, 264, 267
Standards for the English Language Arts, 195
Stanley, J., 223, 242, 245
Stanovich, K., 6
Staudt, D. H., 156
Steele, P., 218, 228
Stephens, K., 224
Sterling-Honig, A., 157
Sturges, P., 70
Swanson, P., 194, 219
Sylvester, R., 19, 295, 317, 318
Symons, S., 219

Taberski, S., 127, 130, 137
Taylor, B., 16, 82, 84, 89, 267
Teachers of English to Speakers of Other Languages, 47
Templeton, S., 102
Tempo, F., 239
Terban, M., 159, 168, 275
Texas Education Agency, 112
Theroux, P., 24, 26
Tierney, R., 16
Tolkien, J. R. R., 35
Tomlinson, C.A., 24
Tompkins, G., 224
Topping, K., 267, 271
Townsend, D., 153, 156, 160, 173, 174
Trelease, J., 364
Tresselt, A., 212
Truss, L., 306
Turbill, J., 283, 291, 293, 323, 329, 330, 332
Turkle, B., 164

Ulrich, G., 85
Urton, A., 239
U.S. Census Bureau, 80
U.S. Department of Education, 15, 17

Valencia, S., 258, 259, 266
Van Allen, R., 164
Van Allsburg, C., 195
Van Cleave, J., 239
Vardell, S., 193, 232
Vaughn, S., 12, 89, 96, 160, 180, 181, 190, 194, 230, 267, 276, 351
Vellutino, R., 6
Vygotsky, L., 3, 19, 20, 159, 254, 285, 324

Weber, R., 10
Wagner, R., 109
Wagstaff, J., 109
Walker, B., 29, 30
Wall, H., 285
Wallace, B., 155
Wang, M., 28
Wasik, B., 128, 130, 345, 347
Watt, F., 228, 239, 242, 245
Weaver, C., 6, 7, 30, 53, 106, 228, 283, 285
Weitzman, I., 275
Wells, J., 295
White, A. L., (2007) 180
White, T. G., (2008) 362, 368
Wiese, J., 239
Wiesner, D., 164, 168, 206
Wigfield, A., 28
Wilfong, L., 238
Wilkinson, T., 223, 228
Williams, K. T., 195
Williams, L., 162, 210, 264
Williams, S., 309
Wilson, R., 161
Winn, P., 219
Winter, P., 164
Wolf, M., 231, 259
Wolf, S., 284
Wood, A., 318, 351, 355
Wood, J., 223, 228, 247, 251
Wood-Ray, K., 283, 293
Woodruff, E., 205, 310
Wray, D., 25

Yaden, D. B., 10
Yellin, D., 9
Yin, 195
Yolen, J., 207
Yopp, H., 77, 81, 83, 154, 155
Yopp, R., 77, 78
Young, A., 267, 276

Zawilinski, L., 315
Zecker, L., 284, 285, 324, 329
Zipke, M., 157, 172

SUBJECT INDEX

Accelerated Reader program, 33, 191
Accent, definition of, 103
Accomplishment and goal-setting logs, 71–72
Accuracy, of oral reading, 259, 260–262, 266, 269, 280
Achievement tests, 45–48, 73, 236–237 (*see also* Standardized tests)
Acronyms, 158
Acrostic Poems activity, 310
Action Jeopardy activity, 174
Active learning:
  examples, 22–23
  and spelling, 324
  vignettes, 240
Activities:
  fluency, 270–279
  phonics, 114–122
  informational text, 237–256
  narrative text, 195–213
  phonemic awareness, 89–98
  phonics, 114–122
  reading, before, during, and after, 195–212, 238–255
  science, 164–165, 239, 249
  spelling, 98, 272, 334–338
  vocabulary, 139–140, 163, 163–174
  word identification, 137–148
  writing, 239, 285, 288, 302–319
Adequate yearly progress (AYP), 2, 15, 39, 73, 343
Advantage Learning Systems, 34
Affixes, 103, 130, 156, 238
activities, 145–146, 334
sequence for teaching to English learners, 132
African-American learners, 10, 15, 29, 132, 178, 214
AIMS Standard Reading Assessment (RAPs)
A is for Amber (Danziger), 60
All About Planet Earth (Farndon) activity, 251
Allington, Richard, alternative view of reading instruction, 16
Alliteration, 77, 78, 84–88, 115, 155–156, 310
  books with, 380–381
Allophones, 106
Alphabet:
  Arabic, 328
  books, 328, 377–378
  Spanish, 328
Alphabet Booklet activity, 91–92
Alphabetic spelling stage, 105, 324, 325, 332
Alphabets other than English, 327–328
Alphabiography activity, 115
Alternate Writing activity, 201
Amazing Writing Machine software, 319
American Library Association website, 372
America Reads Challenge Act, 15
Anagram activities, 337
Analogies, 105, 109, 329
  activity, 167–168
Analytical learning style, 31
Analytic phonics, 103, 109
Anecdotal records, 50, 60–62, 66, 268
Antelope books, 384
Antonyms, 156, 157, 158
Arabic alphabet, 328
Assessment (*see also* Diagnostic tests; Formal assessment; Informal assessment):
  authentic, 50, 66–68
  classroom-based, 50
  comprehension, reading, 51, 132, 180, 190–194, 234–237, 255, 256
  critical literacy, 237
  defining, 43
  devices, listing of, 411
  emergent reading and writing, 50–52
  fluency, 258, 266, 268–269
  formative, 43
  hierarchy of types, 44
  of informational/expository text, 234–237
  multiple intelligences, 412–414
  personal philosophy of, forming, 13
  phonemic awareness, 82–84, 99, 443-451
  phonics, 109, 111–113
  of print concepts for emergent writers, 50, 415
  of reading rate, 269
  rubrics for, 73, 191, 269, 299–301, 302
  self- (student), 69–72
  spelling, 330–334
  summative, 43
  technology and, 73
  validity and reliability, 4–5, 44, 48, 301
  vocabulary, 133–136, 161–162
  word identification, 132–136
  writing, 297–302, 475–482
Assonance, 84, 85, 88, 310
Attitude:
  positive, 218, 370
  surveys, 69, 301, 320, 428–436
Audiobooks, 12–13, 38, 39, 147–148, 159, 272, 385
  activity, 205–206
Auditory learners, 31
Authentic:
  assessment, 50, 66–68, 67
  children's literature, 110
  communication, 12
  fluency instruction, 274
  language activities, 17
  learning experiences/texts, 3, 7, 9
  literacy tasks, authentic, 38–39
  reading and writing, 25, 214, 295
  writing tasks, 315–318

Authors, websites for children's books, 316–317
Automaticity, 126–127, 128, 259, 260–262, 269, 273, 280
Avi books for read-alouds, 320

Babe the Gallant Pig (King-Smith), 35
Background knowledge of reader, 185–187, 188, 222, 228–229 (*see also* Prior knowledge)
  assessing, 235–236
Base / root word, 103, 329, 334
Bear, Invernizzi, Templeton, and Johnston:
  spelling inventory, 485
  spelling stages, 324–325
Bear and Templeton spelling stages, 324
BEARS (Basic Early Assessment of Reading Scope and Sequence), 18, 49, 113
Beginning sounds activities, 92, 95, 495–507
Benchmarks, 237 (*see also* Standards)
  establishing, 18, 137
BICS (basic interpersonal communicative skills), 10
"Big Mary" poem (Dodds), 263
Bilingual (*see also* English learners):
  books, 381–382
  programs, 10
  publishing on Internet, 295
  writing stages of Spanish-English writers, 289–290
Bingo activities, 508–517, 559–564
Biopoems, 312
Blend(s):
  consonant, 104, 180, 234, 329, 457
  definition of, 103
Blending, 78–79, 262
  activities, 95–96, 144–147
  assessment of, 136, 446, 450, 457, 445–446, 450, 457
  strategies, 137
  in word analysis, 129, 130, 131, 133
Blogging and blogs, 296, 315, 316
Bob series, 7
Bodily–kinesthetic intelligence, 31, 32, 413
Book(s) (*see also* Audiobooks; Ebooks; Texts; Trade books):
  alphabet, 91–92, 115, 328, 377–378
  art, 239
  big/large, 25, 140, 324
  children's 372
  for choral reading, 278
  as comprehension aids, 224–227
  for English learners, 230
  English–Spanish, 381–382
  e-story, 384
  fiction and nonfiction, pairing activity, 195–197
  flip, and flip charts, 117, 324
  Fountas & Pinnell guided reading, 34, 35, 139
  interactive, 147–148, 371
  with language concepts, 159
  leveled, 33–35
  logs, 69–70, 440–441
  Mandarin example, 194
  math, 239
  Mother Goose, 85, 86, 378–379
  multicultural, 193, 382–383
  picture, 182, 193
  poetry, suggested books, 306
  Reading Recovery, 348
  with rhyme, phonograms, alliteration, and language play, 380–381
  science, 239
  student-created, 22, 115, 294–296
  and websites for grade levels, 33, 34
  wordless, 139, 140, 164, 206, 293, 314, 379–380
Book Buddies tutoring program, 347
Bookmarking, online references, 296
Brain's role in reading, 127
Brochures, creating, 314–315
Brown Bear, Brown Bear, What Do You See? (Martin) activity, 310
Buddy reading, 9, 23, 27, 39, 76–77, 275
Building blocks of words activity, 145
Bulletin boards, 363–364
Bush, George W., 15

Cache of Jewels, A, (Heller), 155
CAFÉ word writing assessment, 322, 323, 332–333
California Achievement Tests, 46, 162, 302, 334
California Critical Thinking Test, 237
California Standard 1.10 checklist, 133, 459
California Test of Mental Maturity, 45
CALP (cognitive academic language proficiency), 10
Capitalization, 293, 294
Carbo Recorded-Book Method, 272
Card games, for phonemic awareness, 96, 97
Card stacking, 242, 246
Caregivers, *see* Parent/caregiver
Categorization activities, 158, 166
Cause/effect graphic organizer, 245
Caves (Wood) activity, 247, 251
Center for Public Education, 160
Change Hen to Fox activity, 121
Character Perspective Chart activity, 211–212
Character Sketch activity, 213
Checklists:
  for assessment, 61–64
  California standard 1.10, 133
  for *Caves* activity, 251
  decoding and word recognition, 459
  for expository reading, 466
  for fluency, 268, 425–426, 469–472
  for informal assessment, 61–64, 73
  for informational text, 246
  for Internet skills, 468
  IRA, 64
  letter–sound relationships, 453–455
  literacy, sample, 419
  Literacy Habits, 64, 422–426
  multiple intelligence assessment, 412–414
  for narrative text, 470
  NCTE/IRA Standards for the English Language Arts, 420–421
  for phonemic awareness, 83–84, 452, 453
  for phonics assessment, 111–112
  for print concepts, 415
  for proofreading, 294
  for sounds, 453
  for spelling, 330, 333, 487
  strategy for reading, 251
  text and trade book evaluation, 575–576
  vocabulary assessment, 133, 161–162, 461
  word identification, 133, 459
  writing concepts, 416
Checklist of Known Letter Names and Sounds, 111
Children of the Dust Bowl-based organizer, 245
Children's literature and authors, 87–89, 110, 129, 317, 372
Choral reading, 12, 26–27, 270, 275, 277–279
Chunks, *see* Syllables
Cinquain poems, 305, 311
Clapping syllables activities, 89–90
Class groupings, 38
Classification
  environment for writing, 297
  graphic organizer, 243
  in organizational structure, 222
Classroom:
  -based assessment, 50
  blog, 315
  community, 297
  context / climate, 38

critical literacy, 4–5
environment, 4, 220, 297
"family," 4
library, 8, 28, 295
poetry book, 294
strategies in comprehensive approach, 9
traditional, 4
Classroom Alphabet Books activity, 314
Clay's assessment of early writing, 50–51
Clinton, President Bill, 15
Clown activity, 94
Cloze tests / procedures, 50, 58–60, 135, 161, 191, 235
activity, 144
Cluster, *see* Blend(s)
Cognates, 10, 170, 238
Cognate Picture Cards, 170–171, 570
Cognitive:
learning domain, 8
processes, 283
strategy, morphology as, 131
Collaboration/collaborative:
activities, 173, 241, 254, 279, 302
by child's peers, 3
by classroom teachers, 17, 18
conversations, 193
learning, 10, 153
for motivation, 27
websites, 296
Collage, creating, activity, 351
Colorado reading standard for reading comprehension, 234
Common Core State Standards, 43
Communication:
by English learners, 11, 12
home–school, 359, 361
multimodal, 19
paralinguistic, 12
teachers' fostering, 24
writing as key component of, 3
Community:
environment affecting comprehension, 219–220
volunteers, 270–371
Comparison/contrast:
graphic organizers, 244
text, 222
Compound words, 103, 122, 131, 132, 145, 162
activity, 144–145
Comprehension, 49, 180, 195, 272, 283 (*see also* Informational Text; Narrative text; Reading comprehension)
assessing, 51, 180, 190–193
computer programs promoting, 385
and critical literacy, 188
factors affecting, 217–220
fluency and, 259, 260, 265–266, 280
strategies and activities, 179, 180, 181, 183–188, 194–213, 237–238
technology and, 213, 255–256, 345
text, 47, 126, 179
vocabulary, 152, 153
Comprehension Test of Phonological Processing (CTOPP), 49
Comprehensive approach to reading, 6, 7–8, 9
Comprehensive Tests of Basic Skills, 46, 113, 162, 193, 237, 302, 334
Computer (*see also* Internet; Software; Technology):
assessment, 73
-based assessment, 73
-assisted tutoring, 345–347
programs promoting comprehension and problem solving, 383–385
student use of, 283
for writing tasks, 284, 315–318
Computer Curriculum Corporation, 191
Concentration activity and word cards, 169–170, 549–552
Concepts of Comprehension Assessment (COCA) website, 256
Conferences:
family–teacher, 365–366, 369
in reading and writing workshops, 9
Connecting with Authors activity, 316
Consonant(s), 78, 103–106
activities emphasizing, 114–116
blends, 104, 180, 234, 329, 457, 539–544
cluster, 103, 105, 106
digraphs, 104, 107, 131, 180, 457
fricative, 104
generalizations, 106
initial, 113, 114–116, 114
nasal, 104
plosive, 104
pronunciation guide, 392–393
sounds, 108, 456
in visual analysis, 131
Consonant-vowel-consonant pattern, *see* CVC
Constructivist theory, 3
Context:
meaningful, 111
phonics in, 109
reading, 38, 39
for word identification, 128
Context clues, 31, 59, 109, 129, 130, 133, 137, 149, 157, 238
activity, 144
assessing, 135
explicit instruction in, 157–158
Cornell Critical Thinking Test, 237
Couplets, in poems, 86, 87–88
Critical literacy, 2, 180, 217, 232–233, 256
activities / resources, 22, 178–179
assessments, 237
classrooms and lessons, 4–5
comprehension and, 188
QCT strategy for, 211
themes and topics, 188
theory, 4–5, 188
Critical stance, 188, 189
Critical thinking and tests for, 237, 316
Criterion-referenced tests, 46–48, 73, 191, 236–237
state-designed, for English learners, 47–48
Crossword Puzzle activity, 168–169
Cueing systems, 30, 55, 57–58, 113, 127–128, 235
Cultures, differences in value systems, 360
CVC pattern/words, 79, 90–91, 105, 118–119, 131, 328, 330, 334, 225, 456–457
CVCe pattern, 105, 119, 328, 330, 334
CVVC pattern, 105, 131, 328, 334

Daisy Comes Home (Brett) example, 264, 265
DEAR (Drop Everything and Read) time, 8, 9
Decoding, 11, 98, 103, 105, 180, 181, 216, 234, 259, 260, 284
and word recognition checklist, 459
Definitions, as feature of texts, 225, 236
DeFord Theoretical Orientation to Reading Profile (TORP), 13, 14
Deleting:
activities emphasizing, 97–98
assessment, 447, 451
Derivational relations spelling stage, 325, 327, 332, 329
Description or enumeration, graphic organizer, 243
Diagnostic Reading Scales, 48, 113, 269
Diagnostic tests, 180
individual and group, 48–50, 73, 162
for fluency, 269
for reading, 48–50
for sight words, 136
Diamante poems, 305, 311

Diary Entries activity, 207–208
DIBELS (Dynamic Indicators of Basic Early Literacy Skills), 18, 19, 73–74, 83, 100, 113
Dick and Jane reading series, 7
Dictionary:
personal/personalized 146, 297, 305, 399, 400–408
students' using, 157, 305, 333
Differentiating instruction, 24, 26
Digital:
storytelling, 295, 296, 317–318
text, writing, 283
Digraphs, 104, 107, 131, 180, 234, 327, 329, 391, 457
Diphthongs, 104, 105, 106, 107, 131, 132, 180, 234, 329, 391
Directed Reading–Thinking activity (DR–TA), 202
Directed Listening–Thinking activity (DL–TA), 201
Direct instruction, 8, 195, 266, 271, 290, 327, 329 (*see also* Explicit instruction):
Discrepancy method, IQ-achievement, 17
Discis series, 147, 174, 279, 384
Disfluency and disfluent readers, 259–260, 262, 264, 266, 268, 272: (*see also* Fluency)
Dolch word lists, 8, 19, 129, 133, 395
Bingo activity, 141, 559–564
Dolphins-based graphic organizers, 244
Dominoes activity, 116, 545
Drafting stage of writing, 293, 475, 477
Drawing stage of writing, 285, 286
Dr. Seuss books, 7, 87, 117, 263
Durrell Analysis of Reading Difficulties, 48, 113, 162, 269
Dyad reading activity, 275
Dynamic Indicators of Basic Early Literacy Skills, *see* DIBELS

Early literacy stage, *see* Emergent
Ebooks, 9, 12, 39, 157, 159, 174, 213, 226, 255–256
narrative, evaluation form, 573
Echo reading, 263, 264, 265, 270–271, 370
Editing in writing process, 293, 334, 476, 482
Education for All Handicapped Children Act, 17
Education Northwest 6 + 1 writing assessment, 297
Ekwall/Shanker Reading Inventory, 52
E-Pals, 9
Electronic (*see also* software):
books, *see* Ebooks
portfolios, 66
postcards, 316–317
texts, 226–227, 346
Elementary and Secondary Education Act (ESEA), 15
Ellipses, 265
Emergent:
literacy stage, observational checklist, 422–423
reading assessment, 50–52
literacy stage, checklist, 422-423
spelling stage, 324, 325, 327, 332
writing, 50–51, 284, 285–287, 324
Emerson, Ralph Waldo, 125
Empty Pot, The (Demi), 194
Encoding, 104, 105, 122, 284
English:
alphabet, 103, 327
language development and stages, 10, 11
phonemes, and in other languages, 79–81, 108
sentence structure, 127
sounds, 89
and Spanish spelling comparison, 330 (*see also* Bilingual)
spelling and spelling patterns, 105–108, 329–330, 410
as symbolic, 284
words added every year, 153
English language proficiency (ELP) standards, 47
English learners, 10, 12–13, 29, 160
activities suited for, 114, 173–174, 195, 241, 270–271, 277, 302
audiobooks with, 205
and BICS (basic interpersonal communicative skills), 10
books for, 230
and CALPS, 110
and expository text, 230–232
fluency of and fluency instruction for, 11, 268
graphophonic system of, 108, 109, 122
informal assessments for, 66–68
lesson plan for, 490
motivating, 153
and narrative texts, 193–194
1 + 1 theory for, 12
and phonemic awareness, 79–81, 89
phonics instruction of, 102, 106
picture sorts for, 328
poetry for, 102
read aloud strategy with, 195
reading intervention teacher for, 344
sight vocabularies of, 130, 149
SI (sheltered instruction) model for, 12, 231
singing to facilitate, 231–232
small groups for, 12, 230
socioeconomic status of, 160
spelling stages and instruction for, 327–329
state criterion-referenced tests for, 47–48
strategies for, 160, 163, 180, 195, 334–335
syntactic system/syntax of, 128
teacher-designed tests for, 47
technology for, 213
text selection for, 145, 193, 231
tutoring, 10, 11, 12, 351–352
vocabulary of, 130, 149, 160–161, 174–175
websites for, 67, 255
word study sequence for, 132
workshop, 283
writing instruction and activities for, 283, 284, 285, 290, 302
English–Spanish concept books, 381–382
Environment:
classroom, for writing, 297
community, 219–220, 370–371
enriched, 26, 159
home, affecting comprehension, 218
influence on literacy, 153–154 (*see also* Experiences)
risk-free/supportive/safe, 12, 160, 283, 297, 370
school, 220
Enumeration, 222, 243
ESA word list, 135
ESL (English as a second language) learners, *see* English learners
E-story books, 384
E-texts and websites, 213, 224, 574
Euphemisms, 158
Existential intelligence, 31
Experience(s):
affecting comprehension, 128, 217–218
language, 129, 158, 160
life, 154, 156, 175, 185, 186–187, 217
vicarious, 154–156, 175
Explicit instruction, 156, 195, 266, 271, 290, 327
in context clues, 157–158
NRP report and, 15
in spelling, 329
in word hierarchies, 158
in writing workshop, 290–291
Expository:
frames, 292, 308–309
writing, 291, 279, 298

Expository text, 38, 126, 130, 218, 256, 466 (*see also* Informational text):
activities for, 246, 254
assessing students' growth in, 236, 256
collaborative approach to, 254
English learners and, 230–232, 241, 290
frames, 292, 308–309
graphic organizers, 220, 224, 231, 242–246, 291–292
observation checklist, 466
organizational structure of, 220–224
rubrics for, 234, 284, 467
sequence for teaching, 234
in social studies, 232–233
strategies, 237–238
technical vocabulary in, 228
technology and websites for, 255–256
Expressive reading, 264–265
Expressive vocabulary, 128–129, 137, 139, 140
Expressive Vocabulary Test (Williams), 162
Eye appeal, evaluating, 575 (*see also* Visual appeal)

Family involvement, *see* Parent/caregiver
Family–teacher conferences, 365–366, 369
Ferroli and Shanahan's spelling stages, 324, 325
Fibbin Poems activity, 312–313
Figurative speech activity, 163–164
Finger play and songs, 84
Flash cards, 7, 8, 19, 126
activities, 141, 273
The Flimflam Man example (Bailey-Beard), 186
Flip books /charts, 117, 324
Florida state standards, 161–162, 461
Fluency, 180, 280
activities, 270–279
assessment of, 258, 266, 268–269
automaticity/accuracy component of, 260–262
checklists, 268, 425–426, 469–472
choral reading activities, 277–279
components, 259–266, 269, 280
and comprehension, 258, 265–266
defined, 258, 259
and disfluency, 259, 260, 266
echo reading activity for, 270–271
of English learners, 11, 68, 268, 270
flash cards, 273
instruction, 266–268, 274
as literacy skill, 8, 20, 47, 49
logs, 274, 580
NAEP definition and fluency scale, 259
and oral reading, 261, 471
Oral Recitation Lesson (ORL) strategy for, 271
phrasing/prosody component of, 262–265, 274
poetry as means to develop, 263, 276
PPPP strategy for, 271
punctuation and, 264–265
Record, Check, Chart activity, 272–273, 578
research related to, 266, 267
rubrics, 269, 270, 471
self-evaluation, 472
sentence, 298
strategies, 7, 9, 258, 270–279, 280, 371
and technology, 279, 345
tutoring for, 270–273
and WCM (words correct per minute), 258, 266, 268
Fluency Checklist for Narrative Text, 269
Fluency Development Lesson (FDL), 273–274
Foam Board letters activity, 335–336
Follow Me, Moon (Clay), 50
Formal assessment, 43, 44–49, 73, 193 (*see also* Standardized tests)
of fluency, 269
of phonemic awareness, 83
of phonics, 113
of reading comprehension, 226–237
of spelling, 334
of vocabulary, 162
of word identification, 136
of writing, 302
Fourth-grade and fourth grade slump, 23, 216, 258
Frames, expository, 292, 308–309
French language system, 152
Fresch and Wheaton's spelling stages, 324, 325
Friendly Letters strategy, 304, 313–314
Frontline Phonics, 73
Fry.
phrase list (Instant Word List), 129, 133, 134, 148, 396–398
readability formula, 35, 36–37, 126, 229

Games, 89 (*see also* Activities)
collaborative, 160
and creating game boards, 144, 491
phonics, 111
with blending emphasis, 95–96
for phonetic awareness, 76, 82
vocabulary building, 174, 175
Gardner's theory of multiple intelligences, 31–32
Gates-MacGinitie Reading Tests, 46, 162
Gates-McKillop-Horowitz Tests, 48, 113, 162
Generalizations:
phonics, 102, 106, 107, 108, 109
spelling, 327, 329
to aid visual analysis, 131
Gentry and Gillet's spelling stages, 324, 325, 326
German words, 127
Gilmore Oral Reading Test, 48, 269
Global learning style, 31
Glossary in books, 225, 249
Goal-setting logs, 71–72
Goals 2000: Educate America Act, 359
Go Fish activity, 93, 527–533
Goodman's *Taxonomy of Reading Miscues*, 52
Grade leveling of books, 33
Gradient leveled books, 34
Grapheme, 103, 104, 108
Graphic and graphophonic components of writing, 284–285
Graphic organizers, 11, 19
activities, 197–199, 209–210, 238, 241–246, 249
in assessment, 67
for expository text, 220, 224, 231, 242–246, 291–292
for narrative text, 209–210
in writing, 293
Graphophonic system, 30, 55, 57, 103, 122, 127, 128, 190
assessment of, 268
in reading and writing, 283, 284–285
and English learners, 108
Grammar, study of, 30
Gray Oral Reading Test, 48, 269
Greek words and roots, 132, 400–408
Group(s) (*see also* Small groups):
diagnostic tests for, 48
and grouping strategies, 24
homogenous and heterogeneous, 38, 109
at middle school level, 28
multicultural, 33
multimedia project rubric, 483
Guess Who's Coming, Jesse Bear (Carlstrom) activity/example, 270–271, 327
Guided instruction and practice, 9, 11

Guided reading , 42, 137, 144, 159, 267
activity, 138–139
Fountas and Pinnell publications, 34, 35, 139
Guided Reading Strategy (GRS), 247–248
Guided writing, 9
-activity, 306–307
Gwnne, Fred, activities based on books by, 337

Happy grams, 364, 369
Harry Potter series, 184
Hearing impaired students, 24
Henny Penny story web, 210
Hierarchy:
of human needs (Maslow), 4
in organizational structure, 222
Higher-level thinking, 24, 25, 38, 160, 187, 189, 197, 203, 214, 220, 222, 371
Hink Pinks activity, 171–172
Hispanic, reading gap for students, 15, 29 (*see also* Spanish speakers)
Home–school connection, 360–361, 367–369 (*see also* Parent/caregiver)
Homonyms, 128, 159
Homophones and homographs, 132, 158
Howard Street Tutoring Program, 347
Humpty Dumpty Board Game, 94, 534–538

Idioms, books with, 159
Illinois rubric for reading comprehension, 191, 192, 269
Independent practice/reading, 3, 8, 28, 33, 38, 163, 180, 194, 231, 236, 368
Individualized Education Plans (IEPs), 343
Individualized instruction, grouping strategies, 24
Individuals with Disabilities Education Act (IDEA), 16, 258, 266
Individuals with Disabilities Education Improvement Act (IDEA 2004), 17
Inference(s) / inferential:
questions, 226, 249
reading activity, 206
strategies, 183–184
training activity, 248
Informal assessment, 43, 214 (*see also* Anecdotal records; Checklists; Cloze tests; Miscue analysis; Running records)
expository text, 234–236
fluency, 268–269
for phonemic awareness, 83
phonics, 111–113
for English learners, 66–68
informal reading inventories (IRIs) and, 51–52, 113, 190, 234–236
instruments, 49–50
of prior knowledge, 235
websites, 256
spelling, 330, 332–334
vocabulary 133–136, 161–162
writing, 299–302
Informational DVD/CD evaluation form, 577
Informational literacy, 19
Informational text, 195, 216, 217 (*see also* Expository text)
activities, 90–93, 114–116, 238–255
assessment of, 234–237
chronology or sequence in, 221
comprehension, factors affecting, 217–220
for English learners, 230–232
features of, 223–227
graphic organizers, 231, 242–246
and guided reading activity, 590
and inference training, 238
interest inventory for, 465
on Internet, 255
and K-W-L method, 240, 246–247
learning logs activity, 252–253
organizational structure of, 220–224, 242
PReP (pre-reading plan), 250
QCT activity, 211, 254
and Re-Quest strategy, 252
rubrics for, 234, 465
scanning activity, 252
and science activities, 239
selecting, 232
strategies, 237–254
teaching sequence, 224
technology and websites, 255–256
texts, analysis of, 224–230
think-aloud for, 250–251
Initial sounds, 105, 113, 114–116, 324, 327
activities emphasizing, 90–93
assessment, 444, 446–447, 448, 450–451
Bingo cards 508–517
Insertions (miscue), 52, 53, 55
Instruction (*see also* Explicit instruction):
differentiating, 24, 26
for gifted students, 24
guided, 11
indirect, 271
individualized grouping strategies for, 24
laws affecting, 15, 17
meaningful contexts in, 111
self-evaluation of writing by teacher, 295, 297
whole group vs. small-group, 8
Instructional reading level, 8, 33
Intelligence:
determining one's own, 31
and multiple intelligences (Gardner) 31, 32, 412–415
tests, 45, 75
Intelligences, multiple, *see* Multiple intelligences
Intelligent Tutoring for Structure Strategy (ITSS), 256, 347
Interactive Read-Aloud activity, 199
Interactive writing, 9, 12, 109, 285, 290, 293, 302, 324
activities, 302
Interest surveys/inventory, 235, 465
International Pen Pals activity, 316
International Reading Association (IRA), 16, 23–24
Alphabiography activity, 115
checklist, 64
commission on RTI, 17–18
comprehension strategies, 195
definition of phonemic awareness, 77
and NCTE Standards for Assessment of Reading and Writing, 44, 374–377, 420
qualifications for paraprofessionals, 344–345
reading level chart, 55
and phonics instruction 102
Reading Online articles, 178
and reading specialists, qualifications for, 343–344
ReadWriteThink website, 122, 213, 319
Internet, 73, 255 (*see also* Computer; Technology)
basic skills for using, 255
book selection and resources, 217, 220
checklist for skills, 468
credible research sources, 301
as critical literacy source, 188
to introduce vocabulary, 156, 159
publishing on, 295
skills checklist, 468
spelling websites, 338
expository text websites, 256
writing instruction using, 283
Interpersonal and intrapersonal intelligence, 31, 413–414

Interventions, *see* Activities; Strategies
Intonation, 274
Inventories:
Bear et al. spelling, 485
commercial informal, 377
interest, for informational texts, 465
Scholastic Reading Inventory (SRI), 34, 191
spelling, 330, 332
Iowa Silent Reading Test, 48, 162
Iowa Test of Basic Skills, 46, 113, 162, 175, 193, 302, 334
IQ-achievement discrepancy method, 17
IRA commission on RTI guiding principles, 17–18 (*see also* International Reading Association)
checklist for NCTE/IRA standards, 420–421
It Looked Like Spilt Milk (Shaw) activity, 309
I Went Walking (Williams) activity, 309

James Madison Test of Critical Thinking, 237
Jokes:
as language play, 84
telling, activity, 274–275
Journal writing / journaling, 9, 188
Jump-rope jingles, 82, 84, 86–876
Just Juice (Hesse), 264, 265
running record, 58

Keyboarding skills, 284, 318–319
Key words associated with text structure 220–221, 224
Kinesthetic:
activities, 95, 98, 279, 358–359, 367–368
intelligence, 31, 32, 413
learners, 111
Knowledge (*see also* Prior knowledge):
literary, 29–30
morphological, 131–132
rhetorical, 130
world, 185–186
K-W-L method/chart, 240, 246–247

Language:
components of, 20
figurative, 188
receptive and expressive, 284
rhythms, 84
systems, 30–31, 284
Language Assessment Scales–Oral (LAS–O), 47–48, 66
Language Assessment Scales–Reading Writing (LAS–R/W), 47–48, 66
Language experience approach (LEA), 9, 11, 12, 67
activities, 164–166
Language play, 82, 84, 88, 89, 380–381
books with 380–381
LAS–O, 47–48, 66
LAS–R/W, 47–48, 66
Latin word roots, 400–408
Lau v. Nichols, 47
Launch Pad, 191
LEA, *see* Language experience approach
LeapTrack by Leapfrog Schoolhouse, 191
Learning:
active, 22–23, 240, 324
content area books, 379–380
disabilities, 17
environment, 12, 23, 38, 39
essential components of, 23
experience, meaningful, 23
logs activity, 252–253
styles, 26, 31
theories, 3, 20
LearningableKids, 73
Learning Advantage, 191
Learning disabilities, students with, 16–17, 24
oral and written, 129
Learning domains, 8 (*see also* Affective learning domain; Cognitive learning domain)
Learning logs activity, 252–253
Lesson Cycle activity, 246
Letters (alphabet) (*see also* Letter–sound relationships):
foam-board activity, 335–336, 454–455
magnetic, activity, 335, 345
cards, 454
ending, 105
formation of, 284
names and sounds, checklist, 453, 454
silent, 104
Spanish, 331
Letter name alphabetic spelling stage for English learners, 327–328
Letter–sound relationships, 30, 102, 105, 108, 109, 111, 180, 260, 284 (*see also* Phonics)
activities, 114, 302, 345
assessing, 234, 450
blending, 450
checklists, 112, 453–455
and middle school students, 112
strategies to learn, 113
Leveled books and publishers, 33–35
Lexical and Structure Riddles activity, 172
Lexile leveling of books, 34
Library:
community, 219
school, 27, 28, 364
Life experiences, 154, 156, 175, 185, 186–187, 217
Lindamood-Bell Auditory Conceptualization Test, 83
Linguistic(s), 104
approach to reading, 6–7
intelligence, 32, 412
Listen for the Initial Consonant Blend sound game board and picture cards, 539–545
Listen to the Vowel Sound game board and pieces, 553–558
Listening and listening skills, 188, 235
Listening Walk activity, 165
Listing, as organizational structure, 222
Literacy (*see also* Critical literacy):
activities, 22, 82
assessment, 50, 69–73
checklist, sample, 419
coach, 344
club, 9
computer programs for, 345
context/learning environment for, 38
essential components, 23
knowledge, 29–30
importance of, 2–3
laws affecting instruction, 15, 17
media, 19
multimodal, 19–20
philosophy, personal, 2–3, 6, 8, 11, 13, 19, 20
self-perception, 69
skills, 4, 11, 17, 20
social aspects of, 38
tasks, authentic, 38–39
teachers, effective, 23, 25
technological, 19
theories, 3–5
Literacy Habits checklists, 64, 422–426
Literacy 2000 Satellite series, 371
Literary knowledge, 185
Literature circles, 238
Little Men (Alcott) sample cloze test, 59
Living Books series, 147, 174, 279, 384
Logical analysis, 4

Logical–mathematical intelligence, 31, 32, 412
Logs:
 accomplishment and goal-setting, 71–72, 73
 book, 69–70, 440–441
 of books read by tutor and tutee, 585
 fluency, 274, 580
 learning, activity, 252–253
 reading, 64, 359, 440–442
 reflection, 71, 72
 for science, 239, 253
 skill, 71
 strategies, 584
 by students, 71–72, 111
 by tutors, 354–355, 584, 585
 for writing conventions, sample, 307

Magical E! cards, 119
Magnetic letters activity, 335, 345
Mama, Do You Love Me? (Joosse), in activity, 278
Manipulating sounds, 79, 98, 99
Mapping and webbing, and websites, 242, 296
Maslow's hierarchy of human needs, 4
Matching Game, 173
Mathematical intelligence, *see* Logical–mathematical intelligence
Math games and books, 239
Maze tests, 50, 60, 161, 191, 235
Meaning(s), 181
 construction of, 3, 29, 179
 processing, 260
 word, 153, 157, 162, 262, 329
Media literacy, 19
Memphis Comprehension Framework, 196–197
Metacognition and metacognitive strategies, 25, 29–30
Metaphors, 298, 310
Metropolitan Achievement Tests, 46, 113, 162, 193, 302, 334
Middle school students, 18, 10–20, 112, 115, 118
 activities for, 139, 140, 141, 144, 146–147, 238
 assessment of, 18
 critical literacy focus for, 233, 237
 language play for, 172
 reading strategies for, 182–183
 motivation for learning, 26, 28, 153
 phonics survey for, 112
 QCT activity for, 211
 and semantics, 157
 textbooks for, 231
 tutoring with, 343
 WebQuest and Wikipedia examples, 19–20
Mime, 222
Minilessons, 9, 297, 306
Miscues and miscue analysis, 42, 50, 52–55, 56, 66, 113, 235, 236, 268 (*see also* Retrospective miscue analysis)
 grid, 417
Mispronunciations, 52, 53, 268, 279
Mitten, The, 53, 54, 212
Mnemonic strategies, 337
Modeling (*see also* Teacher modeling):
 for English learners, 11
 fluency activities, 280
 by parents, 154
 parent, 361
 peer, 3
 of language sounds, 84–85
 by tutors, 371
Morning Message, 324
Morphemic structure and strategy, 129, 329
Morphology, teaching, 131–132, 137, 157, 267
Morphology Rummy game, 146–147, 567–568
Mother Goose books, 85, 86, 378–379
Motivation(al), 26–28, 39, 153, 179, 343, 368
 activities, 22–23, 279, 316
 recommendations for reading, 26–28
 through text selection, 217
 by tutors, 348
Moving the Tiles activity, 98–99
MSV (Meaning, Structure, Visual), 57
Mt. Plot activity, 307, 582
Multicultural groups and books, 33, 188, 193, 382–383
Multimedia group project rubric, 483
Multimodal literacy, 2, 19–20
Multiple intelligences and checklist for assessment, 31–32, 412–414
Multiple meanings, 128, 157, 160, 207, 262
Multiple Meaning Racetrack activity, 171, 571
Music activities, 90, 152, 173, 178
Musical intelligence, 31, 32, 413

Nana Hannah's Piano (Bottner) activity, 310
Narrative text, 153, 156, 179, 180 (*see also* Comprehension; Reading)
 activities/strategies, 181–187, 195–213
 checklist, 470
 dialogue in, 298
 evaluation form for e-books and e-texts, 573, 574
 graphic organizers for, 209–210
 instruction, 194
 proficient readers and poor readers of, 189, 190
 rubrics, 191–192, 462–463, 463–465
 for English learners, 193–194
 Spanish–English, 382
 technology and, 213
 Venn diagram activity, 212
National Association for the Education of Young Children, definition of phonemic awareness, 77
National Center for Education Statistics (NCES) reading scores, 15, 28–29
National Center for Supported eText (NCSET) guide for evaluating electronic texts, 346
National Council of Teachers of English (NCTE), 195
 ReadWriteThink website, 122, 213, 319
 Standards for Assessment of Reading and Writing, 43, 44, 64, 374–377, 420–421
National Institute of Child Health and Human Development, 15
National Institute for Literacy, 15–16
National Reading Panel Report, 15, 258
 quantitative meta-analysis, 82
National Standards for the English Language Arts, 64
Naturalistic intelligence, 31, 32, 414
NCTE/IRA checklist for observations of progress, 420–421
Nelson-Denny Reading Test, 48, 162
Neologisms, 158
No Child Left Behind Act (NCLB), 2, 15, 237, 266
Norm-referenced tests, 45–46, 237 (*see also* Achievement tests; Assessment)
Noun Stories (from *Twister* by Bailey-Beard), 314
Nursery rhymes, 77, 82, 84–85, 86

Observation:
 for assessment, 67, 236, 268
 of expository reading, 466
 of progress toward NTE/IRA standards, 420–421
 of literacy habits, 422–426
Odd-Card Out! activity, 95
Oddity:
 activity emphasizing, 95

assessment, 445, 449
Oklahoma:
Core Curriculum Guide (PASS), 62–64, 65
Land Run topic, 233
standards for conducting and writing a research report, 301–302
Omissions (miscue), 52, 53, 55
1 + 1 Theory, 12
Online (*see also* Software; Technology):
activities, 319
journals, 315
publishing outlets, 318
reading comprehension assessments (ORCAs), 255
social networking, 296
writing references, 296
Onomatopoeia, 77, 82, 84–88, 158
Onset, 6–7, 102, 104, 105, 149, 262
assessment, 445, 449
games and activities, 96, 116–117, 118, 565–566
in instruction, 109, 113, 156, 324
words with, 135
Oral language, 20
development, 48
fluency rubric, 471
instruction, 82, 84, 111
testing, 67
undeveloped, 161
Oral reading and oral reading rate, 55, 190, 259, 260–262, 266, 269, 471
Oral Recitation Lesson (ORL), 271
Oral vocabulary development:
assessing, 132
of English learners, 230
at home and daycare, 128
strategies, 164
of struggling readers, 129
ORCAs, 255
Organizational structure of expository text, 220–224
Origin of Words activity, 168
Orthography:
English and French 108
word patterns, 329, 345
OWL–LD, 129
Oxford Reading Tree series, 30
Oxymoron, 158

Pairing Nonfiction and Fiction Texts activity, 195
Painting Mental Pictures activity, 208
PALS (Phonological Awareness Literacy Screening), 18
Paragraphing, 293, 294
Paralinguistic communication, 12
Paraphrasing, 12
Paraprofessionals, 344–345, 356
Parent/caregiver, 8, 17, 19, 44, 218–210, 280, 358, 359–360
communicating with, 362–365
demographics, 361
difficult, working with, 369–370
e-mails and telephone calls to, 364
Happy grams to, 364, 369
introductory letters and newsletters to, 362–363
nook, 364
suggestions for involving, 366–369
technology and websites for, 371–372
Parodies, 309–310
Partner Reading and Content Too (PRC2), 241
Part-to-whole reading model, 6–7
PASS (Oklahoma), 62–65
Patterns, spelling, 105–108, 329–330, 345
PBSKids website for games, 122
Peabody Picture Vocabulary Test, 45, 162
Peer interaction/involvement, 3, 5, 9, 12, 19, 24, 160, 175, 280, 290, 293
Personal interest surveys, 68–69, 427
Persuasion:
graphic organizer, 246
as organizational structure in texts, 223
Phonemes, 129
definition, 103, 104
in English and other languages, 79–81, 108
most common, 78
Spanish, 331
Phonemic awareness, 15, 18, 20, 47, 49, 81, 87, 99
activities, 89–99
assessment, 82–84, 99, 443–451
checklists, 83–84, 452–453
commercial assessments, 83
definition, 77, 99, 104
dimensions, 77–79, 81, 83–84, 83–84, 89
elements of, 82
and English learners, 79–81
game format for, 76
instruction, 81 82
kindergarten testing of, 99–100
poems for, 82, 84, 85, 89
songs / singing for, 82, 84, 89, 232
strategies, 89–99, 329
technology and websites, 99
what teachers should know, 81–82
Yopp's dimensions of, 77–78
Phonetics, definition of, 104
Phonetic spelling stages, 324
Phonics:
activities/games, 111, 113–122
analytic, 103, 109
approach to / component of reading, 6, 7, 15, 18, 20, 49
assessment, 111–113
checklists, 111–112
in context, 109, 111
definitions, 103, 104
formal assessment, 113
generalizations, 102, 106, 107, 108, 109
glossary, 103–104
how students learn, 105
informal assessment, 111–113
instruction, 102–103, 109–111, 113, 122
interactive website (IRA), 122
logs by students, 111
modeling by teacher, 105
programs, 31, 109
sequence, 109, 110
singing to facilitate, 232
strategies, 113–122
student growth in, 102
surveys, 112, 456–458
synthetic, 109
systemic, 47
teacher modeling, 105
technology and websites, 122
texts for, 109–110
-through-spelling, 109
Phonics Criterion Test, 113
Phonics Mastery Survey, 112, 456–457
Phonograms, 7, 104, 110, 119, 324
books with, 380–381
Phonological skill, 259
Photo Booth computer application, 42
Phrases:
parsing, 263
lists for practice (Fry) 396–398
scoring sheet for, 460
Phrases and Short Sentences for Repeated Reading Practice list (Rasinski), 129, 396
Phrasing component of fluency, 262–265, 274
Physical learners, *see* Kinesthethic; Tactile learners
Pictionades activity, 174
Picture cards activities, 491–517
Picture clues, 130
Picture Books activity, 139–140
Portmanteaus, 158
Poetry / poems, 77, 126, 378–379 (*see also* Rhyme)
acrostic, 310, 319

activities using, 93, 118, 140, 141, 270–271, 276, 278, 305, 306, 310–313, 318, 358
biopoems, 312
books, suggested, 306
for choral reading, 278
cinquain, 305, 311
classroom book, 294
diamante, 305, 311
for English learners, 102
for fluency, 263, 276
at home, 367–368
for linguistic awareness, 82, 84, 85, 89
with natural phrasing, 263
reading, 28, 39
for sight-word learning, 129–130
in spelling instruction, 324
story-, 222
student-written, 295
teaching literacy through, 25
vocabulary and, 155–156
websites, 278, 372
Poetry Party activity, 275
Pop Off the Beads! activity, 97
Portfolios:
best work, electronic, growth, and working, 64, 66
for parent communication, 364, 365
for reading assessment, 50, 64, 66
for writing assessment, 299
Possible Sentences activity, 167
Possum Magic (Fox) word search activity, 336
Postcard for reading and scaffolding, 586
POW writing strategy, 282, 303
Pragmatic system, 30, 127, 128, 283, 284
Pre-Assessment for Phonemic Awareness, 89, 90, 97, 98
Predicting, 181–183, 218, 238, 239, 249, 271, 283
Predict-o-Gram activity, 163
Prefixes, 129, 131, 132, 136, 144–146, 149, 262, 327, 329, 399
Pre-Language Assessment Scales-2000, 47–48
Pre-literacy scales, 47–48
Pre-Reading Plan (PReP), 250
Prescriptive Reading Performance Test, 113
Preview-Pause-Prompt-Praise (PPPP) strategy, 271
Prewriting stage, 291–292, 319, 475
Print concepts:
checklist, 415
for emergent writers, 50, 415
Priority Academic Student Skills (PASS), 62–64, 65
Prior knowledge, 29, 127, 128, 179, 185, 217–218, 235, 238, 240, 249, 250
Problem/solution organizational structure and graphic organizer, 223, 245
Proficiency standards, Teachers of English to Speakers of Other Languages (TESOL), 47
Pronunciation, 106, 155, 392–393
Proofreading checklist, 293, 294
Propaganda as a persuasive technique, 223–224
Prosody, 259, 262–265, 266, 269, 271, 274, 280
PTA:
national standards for parental involvement programs, 359
parent involvement in, 361
Publishing:
stage of writing, 293–295, 320, 476, 478
on the web, 318, 320
Punctuation, 260, 264–265, 268, 269, 274, 284, 293–294
Puns, 158, 158, 159
Puppet activity / shows, 9, 95–96, 111, 210
Puzzles, *see* Crossword Puzzles activity

Qualitative analysis:
of miscue and running records, 55, 57–58
by National Reading Panel, 82
Qualitative Spelling Inventories (BEAR), 113
Quantitative scoring (miscue), 54, 56, 57
Question-answer-relationship (QAR), 249, 254
Question Connect Transform (QCT), 211, 254
Questioning activities, 203, 250
Questions:
higher-level, 371
inferential, 226, 249
literal, 249
open-ended, 183, 193, 196
pre-reading, 250
self-evaluation of fluency, 472
types of, 203
Quick Phonemic Awareness Assessment Device, 83
Quick Write strategy, 282, 303, 322

Readability levels:
determining, 32–33
and tests / software, 35, 36
of texts, 32, 229–230
Read-along Radio Dramas, 279
Read-alouds, 195, 199, 240–241, 262, 320
Readers (*see also* Reading; Students):
background knowledge, 228–229
beginning and emergent, 50–51, 64, 102, 105, 114, 127, 161, 222
characteristics of skilled and unskilled, 219
disengaged, 27
disfluent, 259–260, 262, 264, 266
experiences, differing, 128
environment, 218–220
fluent / proficient, 23, 38, 127, 153, 185–187, 190, 221, 259–266
growth, assessing, 236
listening to, 268
self-perception scale, 435–436
skilled versus unskilled, good versus poor, 188–190, 194, 218–219
Reader Self-Perception Scale (RSPS), 69
Readers theater, 9, 27, 39, 265, 270, 275, 276
Reading (*see also* Fluency; Guided reading; Reading comprehension; Reading rate):
activities, 237–255, 275
assessment, 43–44, 48–50, 191
attitude surveys, 428–429, 433
before, during, and after, activities and strategies, 195–213, 238–255
brain's role in, 127
buddy, 9, 23, 27, 39, 76–77. 275
coach, 24, 344
choral, 12, 26–27, 275, 277–279
components, 15, 16, 49
comprehensive approach to, 6, 7–8, 9
context, 38–39
echo, 263, 264, 265, 270, 271, 370
emergent, assessing, 50–52
expressive, 370, 264
Fry Instant Word List for practice, 396–398
independent, 8, 38–39, 163, 194, 368
informational text, 220 (*see also* Informational text)
inventories, 377
logs, 64, 359, 440–442
materials, 8, 16, 33, 236 (*see also* Texts)
models, 5–8, 20

motivation for, 26–28
narrative text, *see* Narrative text
paired, 38, 39, 275
parentheses in, 265
with parents, at home, 367–368
pauses in, 53, 55, 265, 274
portfolios for assessment, 50, 64, 66
practice (Fry Instant Word List), 396–398
programs, summer, 368
purpose of, 126, 188
reforms, history of, 13, 15–16
repeated, 7, 207, 267, 272, 275, 278, 396
rubrics, 462–464
self-consciousness about, 26–27
shared/dyad, 7, 9, 12, 109–110, 159, 163, 237
silent, 38, 51, 190, 260, 262, 266
skills, 180–181, 217, 230
stages, observational checklist for, 424
summer programs, 368
texts, 109–110
tutoring, 354
unison, 264, 265, 267, 275
vocabulary development through, 155
websites for grade levels, 33, 34
word-by-word, 262
workshop, 9, 254
Reading and writing:
attitude surveys, 69, 301–302, 320, 351, 428–434
integrated/connected, 8, 137, 201, 231, 252, 283–284, 289, 320, 345
self-perception scales, 69
Reading Assistant Expanded Edition (Scientific Learning), 279
Reading CAT for tutors, 345–346
Reading comprehension, 11, 13, 15, 18, 20, 29–30, 49, 149, 152, 175, 179, 180, 217 (*see also* Comprehension; Narrative text)
assessment, 190–193, 214, 255 (*see also* Assessment)
rubrics, 462 (*see also* Rubrics)
self-monitoring, 184
strategies, 180, 181–187, 194, 195
Reading Fluency Monitor/Read Naturally, 269
Reading instruction (*see also* Instruction):
essential components/ characteristics of, 15, 24
national laws affecting, 15
philosophy of, 13
Reading intervention teacher, 344
Reading levels, 3, 48, 49, 52, 54, 55, 180
software to assess, 191
of trade books, 232
Reading rate, 258, 259, 260–261, 266, 269, 280, 371
Reading Recovery method/program/ books, 34, 35, 288, 347–348
Reading specialists, 17, 18, 19, 42, 271, 280, 343–344, 345, 356, 368, 370, 371
Reading strategies, before, during, and after, 29–30, 181–187, 195–196, 238–255
Reading supervisor/coordinator, 344
Reading–writing interaction/ relationship, 16, 283, 345
ReadWriteThink website (IRA), 122, 213, 319, 461
Receptive vocabulary, 128–129, 130, 133, 137, 139, 162, 461
Reciprocal Questioning activity, 203
Reciprocal theory, 265
Record, Check, Chart activity, 272–273, 578
Record, Time, Chart, 579
Reflection logs, 71, 72, 442
Regionalisms, 158
Reliability (test), 4–5, 44, 48, 301
Remember the Beginning Sound picture cards, 95, 495–507
Renaissance Learning, 33, 191
Repeated reading, 7, 207, 267, 272, 396 (*see also* Fry)
activity, 275, 278
Repetitions (miscue), 52, 53
ReQuest strategy, 252
Research:
on assisted reading, 272
rubrics for assessment of students' writing, 480, 482
scientifically based, 15–16, 17
Retelling, 53, 180, 184, 187, 190–191, 196–197, 368
with puppets activity, 210
Retrospective miscue analysis (RMA), 55, 190, 268–269
Revising stage of writing, 293, 319, 475, 477
Rhetorical knowledge, 130
Rhyme(s) / rhyming words, 77, 78, 84–88, 102, 104, 105, 110, 324, 327
activities, 89–90, 93–94, 117–118, 172
assessment, 445, 449, 456
books with, 380–381
survey, 456
Rhythm, 77, 84–86
Rhythm Walks activity, 279
Riddles, 84, 89, 111, 172
Rime(s), 6–7, 78, 102, 105, 149, 262
assessment, 445, 449
card game and activities, 96, 97, 116–117, 565–567
definition, 104
in phonics instruction, 109, 113
in spelling instruction, 324
words with, 135
Risk-free learning environment, 12
Role model, teacher as, 29 (*see also* Teacher modeling)
Root words, 103, 130, 131, 132, 146, 149, 156, 262, 329, 334
Greek and Latin, 400–408
Rosencrans's spelling stages, 324, 325
RTI (Response to Intervention) method, 2, 16–17, 342
Rubrics, 47, 50
for assessment, 73, 191, 269, 299–301, 302
for expository/informational text, 234, 284, 465, 467
for fluency, 269
for multimedia group project, 483
for narrative reading, 462–463
for reading comprehension, 64–66, 192, 234
for research report writing, 480, 482
for student growth, 112
for writing, 475–482
Ruby Bridges example of logical analysis, 5
Running records, 50, 55–58, 66, 113, 190, 235, 268, 350
form, 418

Sad story face story mapping, 186
Safety needs:
emotional, 24
at school, 4
Sand (Clay) assessment, 50
Scaffolding, 3, 188
activities, 203, 308
for English learners and struggling students, 11, 12, 180, 213, 230
postcard for, 586
by tutors, 354
visual, 12
Scanning activity, 252
Scholastic Phonemic Awareness Assessment, 83
Scholastic Publishers books, magazines, and strategies, 148, 241, 385
Scholastic Reading Counts, 34
Scholastic Reading Inventory (SRI), 34, 191
School:

environment, 4, 24, 220
-family relationships, 19 (*see also* Parent/caregiver)
library and librarian, 27, 28, 364
psychologists / counselors, 17, 45, 216, 344
Schoolyard Safari activity, 165
Schwa vowels / sounds, 103, 104, 120, 131, 132
Science activities and logs, 164–165, 239, 249, 253, 314–315
Scientifically based research, 15–16
Secretary of Education's Reading Leadership Academy, 283
Secret words activity, 122
Segmenting, 137
activities, 96–97
assessment, 446, 450
words, 79, 345
Self-assessment, student, 69–72
writing and spelling, 302, 320, 484
Self-correction, 53, 58
Self-evaluation, fluency questions for, 472
Self-monitoring, 67, 179, 184, 188, 266, 267
Self-perception scales, reader and writer, 69, 435–439
Self-questioning and critical literacy, 188, 217
Semantic(s):
assessment, 268
complexities of English, 157
cognitive systems, 283
cueing system/cues, 57, 127, 128, 267
definition of, 30
as fluency skill, 259
system/component, 128, 190, 284
Sentence Combining activity, 315
Sentence fluency, 298
Sequence, graphic organizer, 243
Sequencing, 210, 308
Sequels activity, 310
SES, 160
Shared reading/shared book experience, 7, 109–110
Sharing the Pen activity, 302
Share time, 9
Shaw, George Bernard, 329
Sheltered Instruction (SI) model, 12, 231
Sight vocabulary, 113, 128, 129, 130, 132, 134, 137, 149
activities emphasizing, 141–142
Sight word(s), 127, 129, 149, 217, 261 (*see also* Dolch word lists; Fry)
activities, 140–141, 273
assessing, 133–134, 136
Cunningham's list, 129, 394
and phonemic awareness, 81
reading approach to, 7
Shanker and Ekwall phases, 129
in systematic phonics instruction, 109
technology for, 148
and word identification, 126, 129–130
Silent letters, 104
Silent reading, 38, 51, 190, 260, 262, 266
SI (sheltered instruction) model, 12, 231
Singing, *see* Songs
Sipe's spelling stages, 324, 325
Sipay Word Analysis Test, 48, 113
6 + 1 Trait Writing Assessment and Instruction Framework, 282, 297–299, 303–305, 473–474
Skills (*see also* Phonics; Reading; Writing):
approach to reading / skills-based instruction, 6, 7
definition of, 29
Skill logs, 71
Slosson Intelligence Test (SIT), 45
Small groups, 4, 343
activities/games for, 95, 96, 97, 98, 137–139, 141, 144, 173, 195, 278
with English learners, 12
fluency activities with, 270, 273–279, 280
for phonemic awareness, 82, 89
for guided writing activity, 306–307
for informational / expository text learning, 230–231. 236
radio plays for reading in, 279
reading and vocabulary instruction in, 16, 38–39, 161, 179
strategies with small groups, 273–279, 280
writing in, 285, 297, 302
Social:
critical theorists / social injustice, 4
learning, 19, 238, 254
networking, online, 296
Socioeconomic status (SES) of English learners, 160
Socio-psycholinguistic approach, 6
Software (*see also* Computer; Electronic; Technology):
educational and informational, 148, 220
Portfolio Assessment Kit, 66
Portfolio Builder for PowerPoint, 66
readability, 35
for reading level assessment, 191
Scholastic Electronic Portfolio, 66
Super School, 66
tutorial programs, 345
word processing, 315–319, 338, 371
Songs / singing:
activities, 84, 89–90, 367
for English learners, 231–232
to develop critical literacies, 178
and language, 77, 82, 84, 89
Sound boxes, 90–91, 288
Sounds:
activities, 84, 90–93, 96, 98–99, 120–122, 345
automaticity and, 261–262
beginning, activities for, 92, 95, 495–507
blending, assessment, 450
checklist, 453
consonant, 456
deleting, activities emphasizing, 97–98
ending, 105
English, 89
initial, 105, 113, 114–116, 324, 327, 508–517
manipulating, 79, 98, 99
medial, 105
segmenting, 96–97, 446
substituting, 79
vowel, 103, 106, 107, 108, 109, 120, 262, 327, 458
Sounds within words activities, 120–122, 345
Spanish, and Spanish speakers, 10 (*see also* Hispanic):
alphabet, 328
and graphophonic system, 108, 123
language ability, 153, 160
phonemes and letters, 80, 331
technology for, 279
teaching morphology to, 132
Spanish/English Concept Books, 92, 382
Spanish and English spelling patterns compared, 330
Spatial intelligence, 31, 32, 412–413
Special education teachers and tutors, 17, 19, 24, 343, 344
Speech:
figurative, activity, 163–164
parts of, 84, 155, 329
pathologists, 17
reading activity, 274
Spell check word-processing feature, 327, 333, 338
Spellers, good versus poor, 330, 332
Spelling:
activities, 98, 272, 334–338

assessment, 330–334
alphabetic stage, 324, 332
Bear et al. stages of, 324–325, 485
checklists, 293, 294, 330, 333–334, 487
commercial lists, 324
conventional stage of, 285, 287, 288
derivational stage of, 325, 327, 329, 332
developmental stages, 324–329
emergent stage of, 324, 325, 327, 332
English learners and, 284
English patterns, 105–108, 329–330, 410
English and Spanish comparison, 330
Ferroli & Shanahan's stages of, 324, 325
Fresch & Wheaton's stages of, 324, 325
generalizations about, 409
Gentry and Gillet's stages of, 325–326
high-frequency patterns, 108
instruction, 323–327, 329
invented stage of, 285, 287
inventories, 330, 332
as literacy skill, 20
of long vowels and diphthongs, 107
patterns, 105, 108, 329–330, 345, 409, 410
phonetic, 324, 325, 326
poetry in instruction, 324
recording and analyzing students', 332, 333, 486
Rosencrans's stages of, 324, 325
self-assessment, 302, 320, 484
Sipe's stages of, 324, 325
strategies, 329, 334–337, 339
and technology/websites, 338
tutoring, 335
and vowel sounds activities, 120–121
within word pattern stage, 332
in Zecker's stages of emergent writing, 285, 287
Spelling in Parts (SIP) activity, 338
Spelling–meaning relationships, 137
Spin the Discussion activity, 209
Standardized tests, 44–49, 302, 343
achievement, 45–46, 162, 193, 236–237
criterion-referenced, 236, 237
diagnostic, individual and group, 48–49
with phonics sub-tests, 113
scores, types of, 46
for spelling, 334
Standards:
California 1.10, 133, 459
Colorado, for reading comprehension, 234
Common Core State, 43
Florida, for vocabulary assessment, 161–162, 461
Illinois, for reading comprehension, 191, 192, 269
for fluency and rate, 269
IRA / NCTE Standards for Assessment of Reading and Writing, 43, 44, 374–377, 420–421
National Standards for the English Language Arts, 64
Oklahoma, for conducting and writing a research report, 301–302
PASS, 62–64, 65
for spelling, 333
TESOL English language proficiency (ELP) standards, 47
Stanford Achievement Tests, 46, 113, 162, 162, 193
Stanford-Binet Intelligence Scale, 45
Stanford Diagnostic Reading Test, 48, 113, 269
State:
criterion-referenced tests, 47–48, 178, 216 , 237
English Language Proficiency (ELP) standards, 47
literacy standards, 133
-mandated tests, 5, 43, 231, 282, 303, 343
standards, *see* Standards
Stories:
digital, 295, 296, 317–318
rubric for writing, 479
as teaching tool, 82, 84, 89, 111, 155
Story:
grammar, 130, 180
maps/mapping, 186, 188, 209, 211–212
-poems, 222
publishing on Internet, 319
rubric for writing, 481
time, 23
web, 210
Storyboards, 292, 293, 581
Story Lines activity, 200
Storytelling, digital, 295, 296, 317–318
Strategies (*see also* Activities; Instruction):
comprehension, 179, 180, 181–195, 194, 237–238
of effective readers, 188–189
fluency, 270–279, 280
grouping, 24
inferential, 183–184
informational text, 237–254
log sheet, 584
mnemonic, 337
narrative text, 185–213
oral language, 164
phonemic awareness, 89–99
phonics, 113–122
for reading, before, during, and after, 181–187, 195–202, 249–254
with small groups, 273–279, 280
spelling, 329, 334–338
vocabulary, 139–142, 152, 163–174
word identification, 137–148
writing, 282, 302–319
Structural analysis, 129, 131
activities, 144–148
assessing, 136
strategies, 137
Student-centered lessons, 5
Students:
attitude, 218
computer use by, 283
with disabilities, 29
experiences upon entering school, 29
goal setting by, 71–72
home life, 360–361
individual needs of, 8
interests, reading, 218
in RTI process, 18–19
self-assessment, 69–72
self-efficacy, 27
thank you notes by, 293, 294
uniqueness of, 28–29, 31, 39
with vocabulary limitations, 161
Substituting sounds, 79
Substitutions, 52, 53, 268
Success for All tutoring program, 347
SuccessMaker, 191
Suffixes, 129, 131, 132, 136, 144, 146, 149, 162, 262, 327, 329, 399
Super School Software, 66
Supported-reading strategy, 275
Surveys, 73
attitude, 69, 301, 320, 428–436
for informational text, 465
interest and attitude, 50, 68–69, 320
personal interest, 68 69
phonics, 112, 456–458
reading and writing attitude, 69, 301–302, 320, 428–434
rhyming, 456
of text features, 249–250
Sustained Silent Reading (SSR), 9
Syllables, 77, 99, 131, 458
assessment, 444, 448

automaticity and, 262
activities emphasizing, 89–90
closed and open, 103, 104
decoding, 234
definition, 104
recognizing, 126
teaching, 132, 156
Syllables and affixes spelling stage, 325, 327, 332
for English learners, 328–329
Synonyms, 156, 157, 158, 161
activity, 169–170
Syntactic:
clues, 30–31, 57, 268
cognitive systems for reading and writing, 283, 284
cueing system, 127, 267
language system, 127–128, 284
Syntax, 30, 128, 190
Synthetic phonics, 104, 109

Table of contents as book feature, 224
Tactile learners, 327 (*see also* Kinesthetic)
Talking Drawings informal assessment, 235–236
Teachers (*see also* Home–school connection):
assessment / tests by, 3, 45, 50, 51–53, 57, 67, 192
audiobooks made by, 205
of English learners, 10–13
IRA qualities for, 18, 23–24
middle school, 18
modeling by, 8, 9, 11–12, 25, 85–86, 87, 105, 184, 220, 224, 263, 264, 297
philosophies, developing, 6, 8, 13, 19, 20
phonics-oriented, 6
professional growth of, 297
and RTI principles, 17
selection of reading materials/ texts/books, 8, 10, 23, 32
tutoring by certified, 344
in activities, 203–204, 209, 237–238, 242, 250–251, 315
Teachers, successful/effective, 5, 8, 10, 20, 23, 24, 25, 29, 30, 38
of comprehension, 194
of informational text, 220, 237
of phonics, 105, 109
of reading, 237
of writing, 283, 297
Teachers of English to Speakers of Other Languages (TESOL) proficiency standards, 47
Teaching (*see also* Instruction; Teachers):
eight ways of, 32
6 + 1 traits, 299
Technical terms / vocabulary, 155, 218, 228, 230 (*see also* Vocabulary)
activity, 142–143, 241
Technological literacy, 19
Technology (*see also* Computer; Software):
and assessment, 73
comprehension of expository text and, 255–256
comprehension of narrative text and, 213, 255–256
to create crossword puzzles, 168
fluency and, 279
multimodal literacy and, 19, 20
with parents and at home, 371–372
phonemic awareness and, 99
phonics and, 122
spelling and, 338
tutoring and, 345, 354, 356
vocabulary building and, 174–175
word identification and, 147–148
writing and, 315–316
Tests (*see also* Assessment; Diagnostic tests; Standardized texts):
achievement, 45–48
benchmark, 18, 137
commercial, for reading, 190
criterion-referenced, 46–48, 73, 191, 236–237
multiple-choice, 44–45, 162, 180, 236
norm-referenced, 45–46, 237
teacher-designed/created, 47, 67
Test 4 Free, 73
Testing of Reading Fluency (TORF), 269
Test of Phonological Awareness (TOPA), 83
Text (*see also* Expository text; Informational text; Narrative text):
comprehension, 126, 179, 188
connecting prior knowledge to, 185–187
predictable, 110, 111, 118
repetitive, 351
self-selected, 39
sequence for teaching, 224
student-written, 39
Text Mapping activity, 202, 572
Textmasters activity, 238
Texts/textbooks:
abstract vocabulary in, 231
activity, 195
analysis of informational, 224–230
appropriate/interesting, 26, 27, 28
award-winning nonfiction, 224
cause/effect in, 223
chronological, 221
classification or hierarchy, 222
comparison/contrast, 222
considerate and inconsiderate styles, 229
decodable, 110
defining words within, 157
electronic, 226–227, 346
expository/informational, 220, 232
eye appeal, 38, 224
evaluation checklist, 575–576
features of, 224–227, 249
glossary, sample entry, 225
nonfiction and fiction, pairing, 195
organizational structure of, 220–230
persuasion, 223
for phonics, 109–110
problem/solution, 223
questions, end-of chapter, 226
readability and tests for, 35, 36, 229–230
for reading acquisition, 109–110
scientific, 222
selecting, 32–38, 145, 216, 232
table of contents, sample, 225
technical vocabulary in, 228–229
writing style, 227–228
zip, 161
Text talks, 187, 206
Thai alphabet, 328
Thesaurus, 293, 297
Think-alouds, 9, 30, 185–186, 191
activities, 203–205, 250–251
"Through a Dragon's Eyes" (Garath Half-Elven), 295
Tiers and three-tier plan, 17, 154, 342
Timeline, example of graphic organizer, 242
Title I schools / funding, 15, 47
Tongue twisters, 84, 87, 89
activities, 93, 115
TORP (Theoretical Orientation to Reading Profile), 13, 14
Toss the Cube activity, 92, 144, 518–526
Total physical response (TPR), 2, 11, 12
activity, 165–166
Touchstone Applied Science, 34
TPR, *see* Total Physical Response
Trade books, 28, 156, 191, 217, 220, 224, 232, 236, 252
evaluation checklist, 575–576
Travel Tales activity, 368–369
TREE strategy, 282, 303
"Tunnel vision," 127
Tutoring / tutors, 16, 17, 19
active learning vignettes, 240
in activities, 113, 114, 116. 117, 169, 195, 239–240

assessment by, 351
benefits of, 343
by community groups, 361
computer-assisted, 345–346
cross-age, 267
of English learners, 10, 11, 12, 351–352
fluency activities with, 270–273
for comprehension, 195
lesson objectives and plan, 349, 350, 583
logs by, 354–355, 584, 585
of middle school students, 343
modeling by, 371
paraprofessionals, and guidelines for, 344–345, 356
planning and conducting sessions, 348–351
programs, 347–348
reading, 354
Reading Recovery program for, 347
sample lesson plan, 352–353
for sight vocabulary, 141–142
for spelling activities, 335
for students' growth, 236
Success for All program, 347
and technology, 345, 354, 356
types of, 343–347
videoconferencing for, 356
volunteer, 342, 343, 370
web-based, 347–348
for word identification skills, 144–147
Twister (Bailey-Beard) activity, 314
Two Cube game, 174

Unscramble the Sentence activity, 141
Unscramble the Word activity, 142
U.S. Secretary of Education on NRP, 15

Validity (test), 4–5, 44, 48, 301
Venn diagrams, 6, 67, 212
Verizon Foundation website, 319
Vicarious experiences, 154–156, 175
Videoconferencing, 356
Video sharing websites, 296
Visual:
aids, 12, 67
blending assessment, 136
clues, 31, 58, 235
cuing system, 57
learners activity, 95
literacy, 19
scaffolding, 12
strategies, 329
Visual analysis:
activity, 144
assessing, 135–136, 190
generalizations to aid, 131
of monosyllabic and polysyllabic words, 129, 130–131, 133
Visual appeal:
of informational texts and websites, 224
of writing and writing products, 298, 299
Visualizing/visualization, 184–185, 221–222, 238, 334
Vocabulary, 149, 152, 175, 180, 216
academic, 230
activities, 163–174
assessment, 133–136, 161, 236
background knowledge and, 228–229
benchmarks, establishing, 18
bookmark template, 569
books emphasizing, 159
checklists to assess, 133, 161–162, 461
and comprehension, 152, 153, 179
of English learners, meeting needs of, 160–161, 230–231
explicit, 156–158
expressive, 128–129, 137, 139, 140, 162
instruction, 154–160
as literacy area, 47
listening, 181
poetry and, 155–156
as reading component, 15, 20, 49, 175
receptive, 128–129, 130, 133, 137, 139, 162, 461
sight, 113, 128, 129, 130, 132, 134, 137, 141–142, 149
strategies, 102, 139–142, 163–174, 238
technical, 228, 228, 241
and technology/websites, 174–175
ways to increase, 154–158
words in textbooks, 224, 231
Vocabulary Bookmarks activity and template, 163, 569
Vocabulary Test website, 73
Voice, writer's, 298
Volunteers, 152, 342
community, 370–371
parents as, 359–360
Vowel(s), 103, 104, 106
activities, 119, 120–133
articulation of, 107
digraphs, 104, 107, 131, 180, 327, 391
diphthongs, 106, 391
long, 106, 107, 120, 131, 458
r-controlled, 104, 120
schwa, 103, 104, 120
short, 104, 106, 119, 120
spellings for, 107
variant, 107, 391
Vowel sounds, 103, 106, 107, 108, 109, 120, 262, 327, 458
gameboard and pieces, 553–558
Vygotsky's zone of proximal development and social learning theory, 3, 159, 254, 285, 324

Web:
-based tutoring, 347
publishing on, 318
WCPM (words correct per minute), 258, 259–261, 266, 268
Web organizer activity, 143
WebQuest, 19–20, 318
Websites (*see also* Internet; Software; Technology):
for blogs, 315
for children's authors, 317
definitions of words, 157
developing, 19–20
educational, 371–372
for grade level designations, 33, 34
for informational, texts, 224, 227
for international pen pals, 317
for parents, 372
for pen pals, 316
phonetic, 99
for phonics, 122
with poetry focus, 278
for publishing students' work, 318
reputable, 255
for publishing students' work, 318
video sharing, 296
word identification, 148
for spelling, 338
for writing, 295, 296, 315–319
Wechsler Intelligence Scale for Children, 45
Wheel-of-Fortune activity, 337
Whole-part-whole approach to reading, 6, 7, 129
Whole word approach, 104
Wikis/Wikipedia, 316
Within word pattern spelling stage, 324, 325, 327, 328, 332
Wobbly Tooth as reading example, 30
Woodcock Language Proficiency Battery, 153
Woodcock Reading Mastery Test, 48, 113, 162, 269
Word (*see also* Words):
analysis skills, 127, 129, 130–132, 259, 268, 269, 345
bank(s), 234 (*see also* Sight words)
bubbles (Willem), 298
cards, activities, 491, 559–564
choice, importance of, 298
games, 111
hierarchies, 158

knowing a, 154, 160, 236
knowledge, 128–130
ladders activity, 121–122
lists for assessment, 51, 135, 395, 460
patterns, 329
play, 154, 159
puzzles, 369
recognition checklist, 459
solvers, 329
sorts, 112–113, 121, 345
unscrambling activity, 142
web, sample, 143
Word cards for Concentration activity, 549–552
Word Dominoes activity, 116, 545–549
Word Expert Cards, 172–173
Word families 7, 78, 105, 118, 137, 144, 238, 324, 328
activities, 115, 116–117, 335
most common, 388–390
Word identification, 6, 126, 149, 259, 272: (*see also* Reading)
activities, 137–149
assessment, 132–136
components, 128–132
and cueing systems, 127–128
elements of, 127
skills, 127, 137
strategies, 137–147
technology for, 147–148
Wordless books, 139, 140, 164, 206, 293, 314, 379–380
Word lists, *see* Dolch word lists
Word part, *see* Syllables
Word-part dictionaries activity, 146
Word patterns, 7, 105, 113, 149, 284–284, 324, 328, 329, 334
activities, 118–119, 335
Word processing programs/software, 318–319, 338, 371
Words (*see also* Monosyllabic words; Root words; Sight words):
base/root, 103, 131, 329, 334
compound, 103, 122, 131, 132, 145, 162
high-frequency, 129, 130, 160, 394
monosyllabic, 130–131, 136, 137, 144, 334
multisyllabic, 122, 130–131. 285, 334
nonsense, 84, 112, 113
polysyllabic, 126, 129, 131, 132, 135, 137
with prefixes and suffixes, list of, 136
rhyming, 7, 102, 105, 110, 111, 456
slang, 164
sounding-out, 53
teaching new, 156
unknown, 130, 137, 147, 157, 180, 181, 217, 259, 262, 371
within words activity, 122
Words correct per minute (WCPM), 258, 259–261, 266, 268
Word search activity based on *Possum Magic* (Fox), 336
Word sorting with pictures activities, 114
Word walls, 130, 288, 297, 328
activities, 115–116, 142, 163, 305
Working portfolios, 64, 66
World-English, 73
World knowledge, 185–186
Writer Self-Perception Scale (WSPS), 69, 301
Writers:
fluent, 298
self-perception scale, 437–439
skilled versus unskilled, 290–291
workshop, *see* Writing, workshop
Zecker's stages of emergent, 324
Writing:
activities, 239, 285, 288–289, 302–318, 345
assessment and checklists, 297–302, 416, 424, 475, 482
attitude surveys, 301–302, 320, 430–432, 434
bilingual stages of, 289–290
to an audience, 293
components of, 284–285
computers used for, 318
concepts checklist, 416
emergent/beginning, 50–51, 284, 285–287, 324, 424
expository, 298
formal assessment of, 302
graphic and graphophonic components, 284–285
graphic organizers in, 293
guided, 9, 306–307
informal assessment, 299–302
instruction, 284–289, 295, 297
journal writing, 9
as key communication component, 3
letter-like forms stage of, 285, 286
letter strings stage, 285, 286
as literacy skill, 20
presentation, 305
process, 6, 290–295, 319, 320
and reading connection, 201, 283–284, 289
rubrics for assessing, 299, 301, 475–481, 475–482
schedule, 297
shared, 285
and 6 + 1 traits, 299
and spelling self-assessment, 484
stages, 283, 285–287
stages of bilingual Spanish-English writers, 289–290
strategies, 127, 282, 302–319
teacher as role model for, 297
tests, state mandated, 303
and text style, 227–228
and technology, 318–319
tutoring, 345
web publishing, 295
workshop, 9, 283, 290–295, 303, 306

Yankee Doodle poetry activity, 118
Yopp's phonemic awareness assessments, 77–78, 83

Zecker's stages of emergent writing, 285, 324
Zin! Zin! Zin! A Violin (Moss) activity, 278
Zip tests and texts, 161
Zone of proximal development, 3, 159, 254, 285, 324
Zoo game board and picture cards, 492–494